Reinventing Canada

Politics of the 21st Century

Edited by

Janine Brodie
University of Alberta

Linda Trimble
University of Alberta

Toronto

National Library of Canada Cataloguing in Publication

Reinventing Canada : politics of the 21st century / [edited by]
Janine Brodie, Linda Trimble.

Includes index.
ISBN 0-13-082634-0

1. Canada—Politics and government—1993– I. Brodie, M.
Janine, 1952– II. Trimble, Linda, 1959–

FC635.R45 2003 320.971'09'0511 C2002-904883-4
F1034.2.R45 2003

0-13-082634-0

Vice-President, Editorial Director: Michael J. Young
Acquisitions Editor: Lori Will
Marketing Manager: Christine Cozens
Developmental Editor: Adrienne Shiffman
Production Editor: Cheryl Jackson
Copy Editor: Imogen Brian
Senior Production Coordinator: Peggy Brown
Page Layout: Christine Velakis
Art Director: Julia Hall
Cover Design: Julia Hall
Cover Image: PhotoDisc

2 3 4 5 06 05 04

Printed and bound in Canada.

Contents

Preface

This collection was inspired by the University of Alberta's Political Science Department's 1998–99 Speakers' Series, *Making Sense of the Millennium.* Millennium angst and anxiety spurred our speakers to reflect upon the rapid evolution of politics at the end of the 20th century. These scholars made it clear that fundamental aspects of political life were in transition, prompting us to observe that almost every element of Canadian politics was changing, too, in response to both global and internal forces. The assumptions that informed Canadian politics for the second half of the 20th century—from identity, to institutions, to relationships with the outside world—were under pressure, shifting in original meaning and intent.

We decided to invite a number of scholars working in these areas to explain the changes and speculate about how they will shape the politics of the 21st century in Canada. Their chapters invite students to think about how Canadian governments, political actors, citizens and institutions are challenged in this new century. As well, several of the authors offer insights into aspects of Canadian political life generally overlooked by standard textbooks, including race, sexual orientation, and disability politics. The chapters in this book are designed to provoke debate, prod readers out of any complacency about the allegedly boring and staid nature of Canadian political life and, perhaps most importantly, prompt reflections on the future.

A number of people were instrumental to this project. The authors responded to our rather amorphous request for "something innovative and forward-looking" with thoughtful, creative chapters. Brandy Cox, Ph.D. student in Political Science, along with our wonderful department support staff, Sharon Moroschan and Cindy Anderson, helped compile the manuscript. We owe a special thank-you to Cindy for having the patience to sort out the formatting. Finally, we are grateful to the editorial staff at Pearson for enduring our missed deadlines with good humour, and thank Imogen Brian for her diligent editing.

introduction

Reinventing Canada

An Overview

Janine Brodie

Linda Trimble

INTRODUCTION

Thousands of anti-globalization activists who gathered in protest of the Summit of the Americas in Quebec City in the summer of 2001 were kept out of the meeting area by a chain fence and liberal doses of tear gas. Less than a year later, thousands of Canadians rallied in cities across Canada to draw attention to the G-8 economic summit in Kananaskis, Alberta, and to the social and economic costs of the trade policies fostered and implemented by the G-8 nations. Evidence of such costs is abundant. With no apparent resolution to the U.S.–Canada softwood lumber dispute in sight, the Canadian lumber industry is anticipating the application of substantial import tariffs, despite previous rulings in Canada's favour by the World Trade Organization (WTO). This may be but one reason why, despite their government's enthusiasm for the extension of a free-trade agreement across the Americas, Canadians are pessimistic about this country's prospects for economic prosperity (Gallup, 2002). And, in the aftermath of the horrific events of September 11, 2001, followed by the U.S.-led "war on terror" and heightened conflict in the Middle East, it is not surprising that a majority of Canadians expect even more international conflict in the future (Gallup, 2002). Pessimism and uncertainty are coupled with growing cynicism about politics and governance. Confidence in elected politicians and parliamentary institutions continues to plummet while support for the courts and Charter rights are at an all-time high in public opinion polls (Leger, 2002; CRIC, 2002).

These recent events, which on the surface have little in common, in fact reflect several underlying and interconnected forces. For the past quarter century, Canadians have been mired in a complex process of fundamental change which has challenged long-held assumptions about the nature of the Canadian community, the relevant actors in politics, the role of governments, and relationships with political forces located outside the country's formal territorial boundaries. These changes, which have been linked both to globalization and to the ascendancy of neoliberalism, represent a significant departure from the familiar political, economic, and social landscapes which characterized Canada for much of the past century. Throughout the advanced capitalist world, many of the organizing signposts of the twentieth century either have disappeared or have lost much of their initial intent—among them, national sovereignty; liberal–democratic, and especially, social citizenship rights; and collective political identities and alliances. The latter are said to have become "decentred, dislocated, and fragmented" (Hall, 1996, 596). This tectonic shift in the epicentres of Canadian politics, moreover, was not accomplished through constitutional change or, for the most part, through the creation of new institutions of government.

As the early twenty-first century unfolds, there is a growing sense of rupture and uncertainty. As one federal policy agency concluded in the late 1990s, "civil society [in Canada] is becoming less civil, and uncertainty about the future, the danger of economic polarization and declining confidence in government is causing widespread anxiety among Canadians" (Canada, Policy Research Initiative, 1998, iv). A poll conducted in April 2002 found that more than two thirds of Canadians (69%) think the Canadian political system is somewhat or highly corrupt, and most blame politicians for widespread abuse of patronage and the resulting degradation of democracy (Leger, 2002, 2). Fully one quarter of Canadians regard the national political system as undemocratic (ibid, 2). Canadians have been challenged to reorient their daily lives to mesh with a paradigmatic shift in the dominant philosophy of governance.

All governments are necessarily grounded in a particular way of thinking about governance and, although these philosophies tend to have long shelf lives, dramatic shifts have occurred previously in Canadian history. Indeed, Confederation itself represented a particular strategic response to transformations in the political environment of the mid-nineteenth century. The chapters in this book flesh out the ways in which government is currently being reinvented in Canada. They explore how Canadians have been invited to rethink the fundamental aspects of community, to recast themselves and others into a new model of citizenship, to reinvent the formative institutions of government to mesh with new ways of thinking about governance, and finally to redraw the metaphoric boundaries between Canada and a dramatically altered global environment.

THE MAKING OF THE WELFARE STATE

The experience of the past quarter century in Canada very much resembles the period, more than sixty years ago, leading up to the formation of the postwar welfare state. These years witnessed a breakdown in the logic of governance that had prevailed in Canada since Confederation, various attempts to "reinvent" government, and finally, the emergence of a broad-based consensus about a new way of organizing our common affairs.

At the height of the Depression, over a third of the non-agricultural workforce was unemployed. Provincial governments were constitutionally responsible for providing some sort of relief for these unfortunates but, as the Depression years drew on, it became increasingly obvious that the provinces did not have the fiscal capacity to cope with the enormity of the problem. By the mid-1930s, it was apparent to all that the federal government would have to find some way to intervene, if only to contain mounting social unrest. The 1935 Speech from the Throne explained the government's shift in thinking in terms that have rarely been heard in Canadian political debate. "In the anxious years through which you have passed," the Governor General told Canadians, "you have been the witnesses of grave defects and abuses in the capitalist system. Unemployment and want are the proof of these. Great changes are taking place about us. New conditions prevail. These require modifications in the capitalist system to enable that system more effectively to serve the people" (Canada, 1935, 3).

Throughout the Depression and during the Second World War, Canadians were offered a menu of different visions of a new governing order by a broad spectrum of ideology peddlers, including a revived Canadian Communist Party and two new political parties, the Co-operative Commonwealth Federation (CCF) which embraced a uniquely Canadian version of socialism and the Social Credit (SC) with its particular formula for right-wing populism. Eventually a broad-based consensus was formed around a new blueprint of governance which prescribed a radical realignment of the commonly accepted boundaries between the state, the market, civil society, and the home as well as between the federal and provincial governments. This new way of thinking about government, variously termed the "postwar compromise," "Keynesianism," and "the welfare state," shaped Canada's political geography for more than thirty years, and indeed, continues to inform some influential streams of contemporary political thinking. The public consensus surrounding this new approach in the immediate postwar years was so deeply held and broad-based that it was rarely considered as only one formula among many possible ways of governing a modern society. The welfare state was considered the mark of a civilized society and a necessary precondition for maintaining political stability and social cohesion in a class-based society. The welfare state, its proponents were convinced, represented the end of divisive ideological battles and the democratic resolution of class struggle.

The postwar compromise departed from the pre-Depression years by insisting that economic activity be collectively regulated by government in order to provide economic security for all citizens as a right of citizenship. Moreover, the federal government would underwrite the costs of social citizenship rights even though these protections were the formal constitutional responsibility of the provinces. To distribute the benefits of the welfare state in a calculable and impersonal manner, policies were designed and delivered by an increasingly professionalized bureaucracy intent on improving program delivery through better planning. Citizens became bearers of social rights which, in turn, were linked to broader commitments to progress, democracy, social planning, and equality (Brodie, 1997). The welfare state, in theory, promised a better and more secure future for all Canadians regardless of their background or where they lived.

In the immediate postwar years, the federal and provincial governments began, on a piecemeal basis, to construct Canada's social safety net. Although the provinces retained their constitutional responsibility for welfare, health and education, the federal government used its spending power to establish national social programs. The federal government built the foundations of the postwar welfare state by promising to match, dollar for dollar, provincial spending on social programs. This form of inter-governmentalism has been termed "co-operative federalism" even though these programs were designed by a burgeoning federal bureaucracy with little or no consultation with the provinces. Not all provinces, however, had the same financial capacity to buy into these shared-cost programs, thus threatening the postwar goal of implementing a pan-Canadian social citizenship rights regime. The federal government's solution to this impediment was to introduce equalization payments in 1957. These payments transferred income from "have" to "have not" provinces, allowing the latter to afford their half of the costs of the postwar welfare state.

Although a national unemployment plan was created with a constitutional amendment during the Second World War, the Canadian social safety net was largely fashioned by the federal government with the provinces in tow during the 1950s and 1960s. Per capita grants were given to the provinces to build universities and to enhance opportunities for all Canadians to obtain a degree or enter a profession. The old age security benefit, a social program that predated the Second World War, was improved with tax revenues. Later, in the 1960s, three critical threads were woven into the welfare state. The first, the Medical Care Act, provided universal health care to all Canadians regardless of income or province of residence. The second was the creation of the Canada Pension Plan (CPP), which promised upon retirement a basic income for all contributing workers. Finally, the Canada Assistance Plan (CAP) was implemented to provide better welfare benefits and services.

Paradoxically, the Canadian welfare state reached its apex about the same time that the federal state began to lose its capacity to effectively regulate the national economy through Keynesian demand management techniques. The oil shocks of the 1970s brought externally generated stagflation (simultaneously high levels of unemployment and inflation) which were seemingly impervious to federal policy interventions. In the 1980s, the globalization of industry, corporate restructuring, rapid technological innovations and free trade with the United States brought persistently high levels of unemployment, indeed, the highest levels since the Great Depression; a slowing of economic growth; increases in part-time employment; and growing inequalities or a "polarization" among working people. All of these factors began to feed mounting government deficits and increased pressures on the federal and provincial governments from international lenders to reduce their debt and "put their financial houses in order."

In these years, the federal government found its policy options increasingly constrained by mounting interest payments that it had itself intensified by its unapologetic embrace of monetarism in the late 1970s. At the same time, the business community and conservative think-tanks, taking their cue from the ascendancy of neoliberalism in the United States and Britain, began to draw a link between social welfare spending and the mounting federal debt. These neoliberals argued that unwarranted government intervention in the economy in the postwar years had distorted the market and caused the sluggish growth, weak productivity, stagflation, and rising deficits. The only solution to the growing economic malaise, they suggested, was to slash government spending, eliminate the growing deficits of both the federal and provincial governments, deregulate businesses so that they could better compete in the global market and return government assets to the market where they "naturally" belonged.

Neoliberal elites used a variety of rhetorical devices to promote their project in the media and among the general public. For example, the language of crisis served to evoke a sense of radical fatalism, which sent the clear message that Canadians had no political choices left to them about how to shape their collective future other than to follow a market-driven approach to governance (Brodie, 1997, 234). The MacDonald Commission, appointed in the early 1980s to recommend strategic alternatives to the postwar formula of governance, suggested that Canadians should take a "leap of faith" and join with the United States in a free trade agreement. Another rhetorical device, the language of universality, depicted the rational individual/taxpayer/market player as the ideal Canadian and as a universal social actor whose interests were paramount in the policymaking process. Indeed his interests (for in the gendered social and economic order, market players are predominately male) were represented as being tantamount to the common good. Others, who made demands on the state, particularly demands arising from social and economic inequality, were accused of acting selfishly, impeding economic recovery, and insisting on special rights that were not available to other hard working and deserving Canadians. Finally, the language of choice was used to equate democratic choice with economic choice, especially the freedom to choose from a wide variety of products and services. Public services were represented as constraints on consumer freedom and choice.

GLOBALIZATION AND THE NEOLIBERAL TURN

Since the early 1980s, then, the postwar formula has been progressively eroded by neoliberalism—a new set of assumptions about governance which, it is argued, is a necessary response to the ever-intensifying impacts of globalization. Globalization is fast becoming an umbrella term that informs the way we make sense of our everyday lives, domestic public policy, and international affairs. Yet the meaning and implications of globalization remain elusive and contested. For many, globalization primarily consists of changes in the reorganization of the international economy, which in turn have consequences both for national governments and individual citizens. Hart, for example, defines globalization as the "rapid and pervasive diffusion around the globe of goods, services, technology, and capital" (1993, 4). From this perspective, globalization includes, among other things, the rapid growth in international financial transactions, the emergence of a global market, the creation of new markets, the expanded volume of trade by and between transnational corporations, the simultaneous transmission of ideas and transactions through new technologies, and the appearance of new global actors and institutions such as international financial institutions and binding trade agreements (UNDP, 1999, 1).

In addition to the economic globalization that relates to capital, markets, production, and technology, contemporary societies are also characterized by the globalization of lifestyles and consumption patterns; of regulations, especially with respect to trade and investment; and of the perception of the world as a single space and of people as planetary citizens (Yeates 2001, 5-7). These ongoing and multidimensional processes stretch social, political, and economic activities across political frontiers and the formal boundaries of national states, intensify our dependence on one another, accelerate social interaction and exchange, and blur the boundaries between domestic matters and global affairs (Held and McGrew, 1999, 484). As such, globalization affects almost everything that national states do in the realm of public policy (Johnson and Stritch, 1997, 9).

More significantly, many argue that globalization has fundamentally transformed the national state itself by progressively disrupting the hard-won correspondence in liberal democratic polities among national territory, state sovereignty, public space, and political community (Held and McGrew, 1999, 495). The geography of power, it is argued, has shifted: 1) *upward* to the international, transnational, and global through international financial institutions (IFI's), to regionally binding institutions and agreements such as the European Union (EU) and the North American Free Trade Agreement (NAFTA) and to transnational corporations; 2) *downward* to subnational and local and informal political structures through devolution and decentralization and; 3) *outward* to the market and civil society through privatization, government downsizing, and the new public management. Combined, these factors create another kind of erosion of the power of the national state, notably a growing *inward* push on the legitimacy of the state (Brodie, 2002). This crisis is manifest in the de-linking of the citizen from the state, the trumping of national electorates and interests by binding regional and international regulatory regimes, the growing gap between the rich and the poor, the marginalization of specific social groups, the shrinkage of public space, the embrace of market logics within critical state institutions, a growing alienation from politics, and the diminishing capacity of states to maintain, let alone, enhance social and political rights. This condition, moreover, is potentially more acute in Canada, which, having survived under the imposing shadow of the United States, has surrendered control over key policy fields to NAFTA and to its unelected trade dispute panels.

It is tempting to ascribe all of the changes in contemporary Canadian politics to the seemingly inevitable and unstoppable forces of globalization. This gesture, however, confuses the different impacts and implications of the two distinct forces, *globality* and *globalism*, that make up contemporary globalization. G*lobality* refers to transformative changes in our daily lives that result from unprecedented levels of global connectedness wherein effectively all countries in the world, if not all parts of their territory and all segments of their society, are now functionally part of global systems. People travel to every corner of the globe, communicate in an instant over the World Wide Web, and share a stake in global processes and events whether through the air we breathe, the work we do, the things we buy, or the causes we champion. The concept of globality suggests that closed national spaces no longer capture the essence of social or political life because the local is now infused with transnational and transcultural networks. These flows above, below, and through national boundaries are effectively reshaping societies, countries, and the international order (Held, et al, 1999, 7). The so-called "hard" globalization thesis goes further arguing that globalization has "penetrated the walls of sovereign states," thus spelling "the end of national politics as a domestic activity capable of deciding a society's future" (Perez Baltodano, 1999, 40).

The second component of contemporary globalization, *globalism*, in contrast, refers to the worldwide embrace of a common world-view or ideology such as neoliberalism. The politics of the contemporary era, in many ways, can be characterized as a struggle between interests which have made considerable progress in implementing a neoliberal version of globalism and the so-called anti-globalization movement, an array of organizations struggling to arrest and reverse the imprint of market logics across the globe. Neoliberalism, as discussed in more detail below, seeks to create markets where none existed before and to construct an unfettered global capitalist market, a globally integrated production process that transcends national boundaries and regulatory capacities, and the uninhibited and spontaneous flow of capital everywhere.

Neoliberal globalism, however, is neither an obvious nor an inevitable effect of globalization, for which, as Dame Margaret Thatcher once pronounced, "there is no alternative." To the contrary, neoliberal globalism is a profoundly political project that relies on national states to accept and to respect international regulatory regimes and to shape national social geographies to attract and to retain transnational investment. In the process, it is argued, all countries, representing diverse political histories, social and political antagonisms, and institutional frameworks, are growing more alike with respect to governing structures, policies, and processes (Drezner, 2001, 53). Specifically, neoliberal globalism encourages convergence at the national level around an amalgam of policy postures including decentralization, privatization, individualization and, above all else, the elevation of the market and market principles over the public sector and democratic politics.

Decentralization transfers power, responsibility, and accountability from a single centre to smaller administrative units. This governing strategy is generally applauded on the grounds that it enhances democratic accountability and corrects the worst excesses of an overly centralized and bureaucratized welfare state. Decentralization holds out the promise of more local control in the design and delivery of social programs but its democratic potential can be quickly diminished by fiscal restraints. In Canada, as some of the chapters in this text underline, decentralization, first and foremost, has involved the financial off-loading of the cost of social programs onto the provinces.

The second pillar of neoliberal governance, privatization (and deregulation, its ideological handmaiden) makes the claim that services and assets initially created or regulated in and through the public service are better delivered and maintained through market mechanisms and the price system. In the process, both the purview of the state and the idea of the social and collective provision are progressively undermined. Privatization, as experience demonstrates, can take a variety of forms, both direct and indirect. An obvious example of the former is the sell-off of public assets to the private sector, but privatization is also enhanced when governments withdraw or cut-back on public services, leaving it to private sector, families, or individuals to fill in the gap. Privatization has been deeply embedded in governmental calculations and actions through the widespread embrace of the principles of the *new public management*. This approach to public administration rests on the belief that the public sector should take responsibility only for those things that other social actors and institutions cannot. At the very least, governments should act in partnership with the private sector and civil society organizations. Moreover, governmental and corporate performance should be measured in much the same way—in terms of cost-effectiveness, short-term outcomes, and organizational parsimony.

At the heart of the new governing philosophy is a fundamental shift in thinking away from the postwar commitment to collective values and shared fate to those of family and individual responsibility, in other words, away from social rights and entitlements and towards personal obligation. Individualization insists that it is up to individuals to take personal responsibility for the risks involved in living in contemporary societies, whether that means adjusting to the changing demands of labour markets or providing for old age, and that it is the responsibility of families to look after their own. Government policies, in turn, are refashioned to ensure these outcomes. In a sense, the affirmation of family and individual responsibility is simply another manifestation of privatization, to the home rather than to the market.

In summary, then, policy convergence around a neoliberal model of governance has significantly changed the contours of Canadian politics. Whether or not one accepts the hard globalization thesis that national states are increasingly deemed irrelevant in the contemporary era, it is clear that the combined forces of globality and neoliberal globalism have dramatically altered the policy terrain for all national governments, challenging policy makers and citizens alike to find solutions to an array of problems, many of which would have been unimaginable only decades ago. The very idea of a national society has been complicated by an array of forces, identities, issues, and movements that draw citizens into "overlapping communities of fate" (Held et al, 199, 442). Global interactions run through the national social fabric while localities are often more directly linked to distant forces and actors than to the national state. The state's capacity to shield society, moreover, is diminished by the growing saliency in the daily lives of citizens of global policy issues that are largely immune from the policy interventions of any single state. As Held and McGrew put it, "drug smugglers, capital flows, acid rain, pedophiles, terrorists and illegal immigrants do not recognize borders" (1999, 489). The events of September 11, 2001, illustrate this point even more forcefully.

AN OVERVIEW

The chapters in this volume explore in detail the Canadian experience with many of the themes that have been touched upon in this introduction. Our focus is on change, as the headings for each part of the book suggest, and on the emerging contours of governance, broadly defined, in Canada in the twenty-first century.

Part I: Rethinking Community

There has been no shortage of debate and soul-searching about the meaning of community in Canada. Competing nationalisms are an enduring element of Canadian political discourse, pre-dating Confederation, and brought to the foreground by the Oka crisis of 1990 and the narrow victory of the "no" forces in the 1995 Quebec referendum on sovereignty. But the concept of national unity begs the question: What does it mean to be Canadian? In Chapter 1, Janine Brodie points out that the essence of "Canadianness" has always been contested, reflecting multiple visions of the Canadian national identity. She argues that since governments are active participants in the project of self-definition and national myth-making, official state rhetoric provides a window on the evolution of Canadian narratives about identity. Brodie sees federal Speeches from the Throne from 1867 to the present as historical transcripts that provide a record of shifting definitions of Canada, Canadians, and "Canadiannness." Speeches from the Throne illustrate the transition from the welfare state conception of the "caring-sharing Canadian" to the neoliberal-era "entrepreneurial Canadian," awash in the sea of the global economy without the protection of the nation-state. Janine Brodie wonders if Canadian identity in the twenty-first century has been reduced to the type of brand loyalty used to market beer and t-shirts.

The idea of complex and competing narratives about identity is taken up by Claude Couture and Nathalie Kermoal in their exploration of Quebec nationalism (Chapter 2). They reject various simplistic formulations of the Québécois identify as historically inaccurate, and in particular challenge the formulation of Quebec nationalism as essentially "ethnic," "racist," and perpetually preoccupied with the ghosts of the *Ancien Régime*. For instance, Couture and Kermoal point out that early Quebec nationalism defined "les Canadiens" as those who rejected the British monarchy and stood for democracy. Contemporary narratives illustrate not only the overlapping Quebec and Canadian identities but also multiple identity-based affiliations and the lingering consequences of colonialism.

The contradictory assumptions and practices of colonialism are further revealed by Kiera Ladner's discussion of aboriginal governance in Chapter 3. Like Couture and

Kermoal, Ladner argues that any understanding of the present is incomplete without an investigation of the past. Because contemporary Aboriginal paths to self-determination are grounded in pre-colonial political traditions and histories, re-thinking our shared history of colonialism is a crucial step toward decolonization. Ladner traces key political ideas, institutions, and practices to pre-contact Indigenous governments, and shows how Indigenous peoples were recognized as autonomous and self-governing by international law and judicial decisions. Original agreements between the settlers and the Aboriginal nations were made on a nation-to-nation basis, a practice Ladner calls treaty constitutionalism. The imposition of colonial practices, including cultural genocide and the Indian-Act reserve system, eroded the traditional political systems of Aboriginal nations. Ladner argues that dismantling the colonial regime requires a return to treaty constitutionalism.

The re-emergence or revitalization of ethnic, linguistic, and sub-national loyalties are often attributed to the forces of globalization, and can be argued to fragment the nation-state. As the discussion of the first three chapters indicates, these forces have shaped the Canadian political community since before Confederation and are not, therefore, the product of globalization. Nor are they necessarily destructive. Multiple and overlapping identities, and movements for self-determination invoke collectivist language and offer shared visions for social and political change, thus often serve as catalysts for identity construction and community-building. Movements for self-determination amongst First Nations and Québécois challenge the neoliberal mantra of performativity, "marketization," and one-size-fits-all economic policy by championing goals such as linguistic and cultural self-preservation, social responsibility, solidarity, justice, and human dignity. They clearly demonstrate that economic goals and market forces cannot, in and of themselves, sustain communities of the mind. On the other hand, the neoliberal mantra of individual responsibility, coupled with the individualizing assumptions underlying populist appeals for direct democracy, is reshaping democratic ideas and practices. Governments and political parties have "delegitimized the representative role of organized interests and made it more difficult to engage in advocacy" (Jenson and Phillips, 1996, 120). Groups articulating community or collective interests are pejoratively labelled "special interests" and cast as selfish players in the governance game.

In Chapter 4, Daniel Cohn investigates the relationships between sovereignty movements, democracy, and neoliberalism. His chapter traces the political and economic forces which prompted neoliberal thinking and shows how neoliberalism has altered the definition of the public interest. Neoliberalism tends to exclude or marginalize ordinary Canadians from decisions about what's in their best interests, and to assert one aspect of individual liberty—economic freedom in the marketplace—as the linchpin of a productive society. Cohn argues that strategies of external and internal separatism, including Quebec's sovereignty movement, represent a backlash against neoliberalism.

David Whitson further explores the impact of neoliberal globalism on changing notions of the public interest. Chapter 5 looks at the increasing pressure on Canada's cities to advance economic prosperity through the development (and public funding) of "world class" sports, leisure, and cultural facilities. Such development prompts intense competition between cities for sports franchises, media events, investors and tourists, leading cities to sell themselves as commodities to increasingly mobile investors and consumers. Market-oriented conceptions of the public interest are evidenced by the erosion of distinctive civic cultures, standardization of urban landscapes and social polarization. Ordinary people are cast as spoilsports when they challenge the vision and goals of the "world class" city.

The privileging of market principles over democracy is the topic of Steve Patten's Chapter 6. Patten argues that the quality of Canadian democracy is threatened by neoliberal governance. Layered on top of existing undemocratic institutions and practices, such as Canada's single-member plurality electoral system and concentration of power in the Prime Minister's office, neoliberal governance further shrinks the arena of democratic political participation. While neoliberalism accepts a minimalist version of democracy, called electoral democracy. Patten thinks it precludes the development of extensive democracy, or meaningful and egalitarian politics. Moreover, it promotes an atomistic, individualized version of society, thereby delegitimizing political claims based on group identities and collective visions of community. Steve Patten introduces a phenomenon called the "marketization of citizenship," whereby citizens are transformed into clients and consumers whose claims are depoliticized (ruled outside the boundaries of political discourse and/or state action).

Part II: Recasting Identities and Citizenship

Political identities, rather than partisan or ideological loyalties, are increasingly important ways in which Canadians engage in politics and make claims on the state as well as distinguish themselves from others. Canadians have marked themselves off from one another in terms of identification with First Nations or settlers, bi-culturalism, and, in recent years, multiculturalism. Each set of identifications, as Malinda Smith argues, conceals as much as it reveals. In Chapter 7, Smith demonstrates that Canadian history does not support the country's contemporary self-understanding as a tolerant, multi-ethnic, and even colour-blind society. The experiences of Blacks and the Chinese show that race has mattered throughout Canadian history even if Canadian manners discourage confronting the subject of racism head on. Smith suggests that the politics of intensifying globalization, and particularly South–North migration and cultural hybridism, demand that Canadians both recognize that threads of racialization weave through the Canadian social fabric and act upon social constructions of race that privilege some citizens and hinder others.

In Chapter 8, Linda Trimble examines the political forces that have shaped women's experiences of citizenship since Confederation, when women were denied most basic citizenship rights. While rights associated with liberty, equality, and solidarity have now been extended to women, contemporary debates about citizenship threaten these hard-earned victories. Welfare liberalism, neoliberalism, and neo-conservatism are the competing ideologies shaping Canadian citizenship debates in the twenty-first century, and they offer radically divergent ideas about the proper role of women. Trimble argues that neoliberalism is dominant but not unchallenged, thus allowing for political opportunities to reveal and contest the gendered assumptions that structure the neoliberal "good enough" citizen as a male citizen. Trimble's chapter, and others in this section, discuss the impact of the now 20-year-old Canadian Charter of Rights and Freedoms on identity and citizenship. Canadians have embraced the Charter and its norms of inclusive citizenship and Charter decisions have, in turn, tended to advance the citizenship claims of previously marginalized groups. Women, people with disabilities, and ethno-cultural and sexual minorities, groups whose claims were often sidelined by electoral and legislative institutions, have been presented with a means of confronting the state about structural discrimination and of demanding equal treatment under the law.

In Chapter 9, Laura Bonnett discusses the importance of the Charter to the citizenship claims of persons with disabilities, though she argues that formal legal rights are insufficient for substantive citizenship. Mobility, security, and independence are key goals of people with disabilities and their advocacy organizations, and Bonnett argues that state responsibility for assuring an equitable standard of living must be maintained if these goals are to be realized. She outlines a variety of social policies, including income support and replacement, accommodation, job training and healthcare that are threatened by the policy consequences of neoliberalism. Privatization, spending cuts, decentralization and downsizing seriously compromise the quest by people with disabilities for independent and meaningful citizenship.

A sense of belonging, on their own terms, is an important citizenship goal of people with disabilities. Similarly, sexual minorities have sought solidarity and social acceptance, but have been met with intense resistance to their inclusion into the mainstream of Canadian society. Chapter 10, by Gloria Filax and Debra Shogan, argues that, due to the Charter's equality rights guarantees, sexual minorities have achieved unprecedented legal rights and status in the last decade, thus opening up new possibilities for inclusive citizenship. However, legal and political gains reflect heterosexual norms, norms that continue to define sexual minorities as outside the ranks of the "normal" Canadian community. The importance of discourse, be it represented in legal decisions or popular culture, is noted by Filax and Shogan, and illustrated by the fluid and disruptive nature of queer politics.

In Chapter 11, Lois Harder examines how the identity of all Canadians as social citizens in the postwar years has been transformed by neoliberalism into a much more individualized conception of citizenship. Social rights were a key feature of the welfare state, and citizens expected the state to consider their social well-being when designing policy. The idea of a social safety net permeates Canadian notions of citizenship and national identity. However, as Harder shows, the market and not the state is the new arena for the delivery of social services in a neoliberal era. Social services are no longer universal, adequately funded, or effective in achieving their original goals. Moreover, responsibility for social well-being has been individualized and, at least in part, privatized. However, Lois Harder ends on an optimistic note, reflecting renewed opportunities for discussions about the future of social citizenship.

In the final chapter in this section on shifting identities, Xiaobei Chen further develops this theme with an analysis of the changing citizenship status of children. As Chapter 12 explains, liberal citizenship has been constituted as the rights, privileges, and duties of adults, thus the birth of the child-citizen signals a shift in the meaning and practices of citizenship. Neoliberal globalism, she argues, has transformed the child from a "future citizen" to an individualized, rights-bearing, innocent "citizen-victim." Chen points out that while this version of the child-citizen implies an expansion of citizenship entitlements, in actual fact the only children empowered by these newfound rights are those who meet the criteria of innocence and victimization. And at the same time, the child victim enables the state to employ its coercive powers in the protection of individual children, scrutinizing, regulating, and sometimes criminalizing the parents. Ignored in all of this is state responsibility for the forces that put children at risk, namely poverty, homelessness, unemployment, and housing shortages. The child victim serves as the neoliberal poster child, conveying the impression of a caring, sharing state while papering over the severe restrictions on the entitlements offered to citizens.

Part III: Reinventing Governance

All of Canada's key political institutions are currently under pressure to adapt to the assumptions of neoliberal governance, globalization and new international trading regimes, the emergence of new identity groups and social forces, and an ongoing demand to enhance democratic values and processes. For example, while the particular design of the Canadian welfare state assigned a central and strategic role to the federal government, neoliberalism prescribes the decentralization of power and responsibility to the provinces or the devolution of power outside the public sector to the market and the family. These years of transformation have also seen calls to "reinvent government," especially the complex and professionalized bureaucracies that were built up in tandem with the welfare state in the postwar years. Governments, according to the new logic, are best equipped "to steer rather than to row"—in other words, to point society toward particular policy goals without intervening in the market or civil society to realize these goals. At the same time, governments are expected to adapt to new demands for self-determination by groups that were previously marginalized. In Part III, we examine a series of pressure points which invite the adaptation, if not rejuvenation, of key institutions and government functions in the contemporary era.

Federalism remains a defining element of Canadian political reality. In Chapter 13, Garth Stevenson explains that while the formal constitutional framework of Canadian federalism has changed very little since Confederation, its practices have been fundamentally transformed. Three forces have shaped Canadian federalism and will continue to reconfigure the division of powers and relationships between federal and provincial governments into the twenty-first century: Quebec nationalism, economic integration with the United States, and the ascendance of neoliberalism. The latter, Stevenson argues, has led both levels of government to promise tax reductions, inevitably forcing service reductions and program cuts and prompting competition between governments over costs and responsibilities. The need for cooperation between governments on environmental policy is discussed by Kathryn Harrison in Chapter 14. Harrison examines four key trends in environmental governance, one of which is the changing relationship between federal and provincial governments. In this policy area, at least, confrontations have given way to harmony, with the federal government willing to meet key provincial demands. Both levels of government have recognized the importance of non-governmental actors to environmental policy, and increasingly favour partnerships with such actors to implement voluntary initiatives over regulatory programs. The privatizing impulse of neoliberalism can be seen in the shift toward industry self-regulation and the environmental movement's direct actions against private corporations. Deregulation and decentralization of environmental policy are trends Harrison argues will continue, despite pressures for centralization and harmonization of standards, emanating from the international environmental agenda. These competing pressures reveal the contradictions within neoliberal globalism.

Contradictions and controversies are illustrated as well by the application of business principles and practices to the bureaucracy. This new public management trend is often classed as the ideological handmaiden of neoliberalism, a gesture rejected by Allan Tupper (Chapter 15). While the new public management does indeed reflect market principles, such as alternative service delivery, partnerships with the private sector, performance indicators, and the conceptualization of citizens as clients or consumers of government services, Tupper argues that it may also offer progressive strategies for addressing the chronic inefficiencies of bureaucracy. Yet there is as yet no proof that this new style of government management resolves age-old problems with traditional methods of public administration. Citizens want more cost-effective and responsive government services, but not at the expense of public safety and accessibility of essential services.

In Chapter 16, David Schneiderman argues that the "new constitutionalism" confronting Canadian political realities stems not from the adoption and application of the Charter of Rights and Freedoms, but rather from the legal regime structuring national and international trade and investment. To make this case, Schneiderman first dismisses the popular argument that "special interests" have captured the national political agenda by commandeering the Charter's rights guarantees and forcing identity-based policy claims on the state through litigation. Such action is neither new nor revolutionary, and David Schneiderman maintains that the social change inspired by Charter "victories" is modest at best. Much more profound change is being fashioned by the successful economic rights claims of corporate interests and the movement to strengthen economic and consumer citizenship in the Canadian constitutional order. Constitutionalism now features agreements on free trade of goods, services, and persons within and outside Canada's boundaries, agreements that limit the capacity of the state to act, thereby restricting democratic decision making within national boundaries.

Chapter 17 turns the focus from the binding rules of constitutions, both new and old, to the more fluid and unpredictable world of partisan politics. David Stewart and Miriam Koene's analysis of the changing federal party system demonstrates both continuity and change. The dominance of the federal Liberal party throughout the twentieth century and into the twenty-first shows no signs of being disrupted, and regionalism still shapes the nature of party competition. Yet new parties continue to erupt on the federal scene and new technology has changed the relationships between parties, voters, and mass media. As mentioned earlier in this introduction, public distrust of parties and politicians has never been more acute, yet parties continue to shape public opinion, select leaders, and structure Parliament. Political parties could play a crucial role in addressing the democratic deficit discussed by Steve Patten (Chapter 6), but Stewart and Koene argue that federal parties show little inclination to abandon their pragmatic appeals in favour of the kind of ideologically distinct and principled stances essential to democratic revitalization.

Chapter 18, the final chapter in this section, reflects on one of the most important arenas of institutional change in Canada—the North. There, in response to the development of the territories and to land and governance claims of Aboriginal peoples the federal government has slowly reshaped the nature of governance. Gurston Dacks details the resulting institutional changes and their implications for the future of the territories. Dacks argues that the three territories are in the process of reinventing governance with a distinctly Northern twist, one that reflects both liberal-democratic principles and the cultural and political aspirations of Aboriginal peoples. The new territory of Nunavut, born in 1999, is a good example of this evolutionary approach as it integrates liberal democratic institutions with Aboriginal values, meshing public government with a contingent, or delegated, form of Aboriginal self-government. While these arrangements do not meet the criteria of treaty constitutionalism discussed by Kiera Ladner in Chapter 3, Dacks believes they will continue to evolve to meet the aspirations of Canada's northern Indigenous peoples.

Part IV: Redrawing Boundaries

The multiple processes of globalization have unleashed a number of forces that both transcend and run through the traditional borders of national states. States no longer have the power to keep many external influences from influencing national politics while many political issues now transcend the formal boundaries of states. Canada, as a major trading nation and as the host of immigrants from virtually every region of the world, has never been firmly enclosed by national borders. However, as this section explains, traditional ideas about national space are being challenged by a number of new forces, among them, terrorism and new security concerns, North American integration, international financial institutions, growing humanitarian issues, and the continuing threat of nuclear global catastrophe.

In Chapter 19, Yasmeen Abu-Laban and Christina Gabriel examine issues of security and immigration in a post-September 11 environment. They find a great deal of consistency in Canadian immigration policy in previous episodes when immigrants were scapegoated as the bearers of international instability. Since the tragic events of September 11, however, security concerns have increasingly been expressed as grounds for establishing a continental perimeter, one which would facilitate the free flow of goods in North America but not the free flow of people. Abu-Laban and Gabriel conclude that, contrary to the predictions of the hard globalization thesis, national states continue to exercise a great deal of power with respect to the policing of borders and of people in the contemporary era.

Terry Kading looks at the future of Canada's involvement in the Summit of the Americas process, including the Free Trade Agreement of the Americas (FTAA). Chapter 20 questions the federal government's enthusiasm for the FTAA, which, with 34 nations involved, would constitute the largest free trade region in the world. Canada is actively promoting hemispheric free trade on the grounds that it will solve the social and political problems of the Americas, but Kading argues that the FTAA will hamper rather than advance the possibilities for a more democratic and prosperous region and preclude the effective implementation of a wide range of environmental, anti-poverty, and democracy initiatives generated by the Summit of the Americas process. Moreover, he maintains that the new free trade regime is a covert strategy for establishing a preferential trading bloc for Canada and the United States and positioning these two countries more powerfully with respect to the World Trade Organization (WTO).

In Chapter 21, Elizabeth Smythe lays out the implications of old and new global trade and investment rules for Canadian sovereignty. As David Schneiderman does in Chapter 17, Smythe raises alarm bells about the impact of globalization on state sovereignty and democracy. The growing gulf between rich and poor, declining social cohesion, and rising economic uncertainty raise the policy stakes for national governments while free trade agreements and investment rules lower their capacity to respond to these problems. Yet there is still room for political contestation. As Smythe argues, the failure of the Multilateral Agreement on Investments (MAI) due to a concerted and well-organized global campaign of opposition shows that the same forces promoting economic integration and free trade—new information and communication technology allowing rapid and low cost diffusion of information and ideas around the world—allow for mobilization of opposition to its structures and consequences. With new trade agreements under negotiation, these new networks of opposition provide a check on the government of Canada's enthusiasm for further trade and investment liberalization.

The effect of neoliberal globalism on Canadian foreign policy is discussed by Paul Gecelovsky and Tom Keating in Chapter 22. These authors explore tensions between the humanitarian and economic aspects of Canada's foreign policy. On the one hand, the government pursues human security goals, yet at the same time it argues that many of these goals will be realized as a by-product of achieving economic goals through trade liberalization. While humanitarian and economic strategies may seem contradictory, both feature diminished concern for state sovereignty and territorial integrity. Free markets and rules-based international organizations supercede geopolitical boundaries and state-centred policymaking. Gecelovsky and Keating question the ability of liberalized trade and new multilateral governance structures to address the key factors that contribute to human insecurity.

In Chapter 23, Senator Douglas Roche takes this argument one step further in his analysis of Canada's reaction to the terrorist attacks on September 11, 2001. He argues that Canada's role as an international citizen has long reflected a balance between principles and pragmatism, but its commitment to ethical stances on matters concerning peace, human security, and world order seems to be waning. Canada's support of the U.S.-led Gulf War and the new "war on terrorism" signals the triumph of pragmatism (concern about Canada's trade relationship with the United States) over principle (Canada's tradition of humanitarianism and peacekeeping). A globalized world internationalizes risk as security concerns are heightened by the permeability of borders, massive scale migration, a growing gap between rich and poor nations, the amplification of new and old conflicts, and the global reach of drug cartels, mafias, and terrorists. In such a context, ethically based multilateral approaches designed to improve social justice and calmly restore order offer the best prospects for security. Canada's willingness to acquiesce to the United States and embrace militaristic strategies, most recently in Afghanistan, is evidence of the kind of "ethical ambiguity" Senator Roche sees as destructive to a truly secure global society.

REFERENCES

Brodie, Janine. 1997. "Meso-Discourses, State Forms and the Gendering of Liberal-Democratic Citizenship" *Citizenship Studies 1, 2.*

Brodie, Janine. 2002. "The Great U-Turn: Women and Social Policy in Canada." In Catherine Kingfisher (ed.), *Women's Poverty in an Era of Globalization*. Philadelphia: University of Pennsylvania Press.

Canada. Speech From the Throne. 1935.

———. Policy Research Initiative. 1998. *Rekindling Hope and Investing in the Future*. Ottawa: Policy Research Secretariat.

Centre for Research and Information on Canada (CRIC). 2002. *The Charter: Dividing or Uniting Canadians?* Montreal: CRIC.

Commission on Global Governance. 1995. *Our Global Neighbourhood.* New York: Oxford University Press.

Drezner, Daniel. 2001. "Globalization and Policy Convergence." *International Studies Review 3* Spring, 1.

Gallup. 2002, January 8. *The Gallup Poll,* 62: 02 Toronto: Gallup Canada.

Hall, Stuart. 1995. "The Question of Cultural Identity" In Stuart Hall, David Held, Don Hubert, and Kenneth Thompson (eds.), *Modernity: An Introduction to Modern Societies.* London: Blackwell.

Hart, Michael. 1993, January-February. "A Brave New World: Trade Policy and Globalization." *Policy Options 4.*

Held, David, Anthony McGrew, David Goldblatte, and Jonathan Perraton. 1999. *Global Transformations: Politics, Economics and Culture.* Stanford, CA: Stanford University Press.

Held, David and Anthony McGrew. 1999. "Globalization," *Global Governance 5* October, 4.

Johnson, Andrew and Andrew Stritch. 1997. "Introduction: Political Parties, Globalization, and Public Policy." In Johnson and Stritch (eds.), *Canadian Public Policy: Globalization and Political Parties.* Toronto: Copp Clark.

Leger. 2002. *Canadians and Government Corruption.* Montreal: Leger Marketing.

United Nations Development Program. UNDP. 1997. T*he Shrinking State: Governance and Sustainable Human Development.* New York: UNDP.

———. 1999. *Human Development Report.* New York: Oxford University Press.

Yeates, Nicola. 2001. *Globalization and Social Policy.* London: Sage.

part one

Rethinking Community

chapter one

On Being Canadian

Janine Brodie

INTRODUCTION

From campus pubs to sports events, almost anywhere in Canada, it is common to find someone wearing a hat or a T-shirt displaying a red maple leaf or inscribed with a phrase such as "I am Canadian" or "Canada Kicks Butt." These and other symbols of Canadian nationalism are especially apparent when Canadians make their mark internationally such as, in the winter of 2002, when the Canadian men's and women's hockey teams brought home Olympic Gold. Canadians emptied into the streets in a flag-waving frenzy to celebrate a victory that seemed especially sweet because it involved our neighbours to the South. Appeals to Canadian nationalism also grease many political wheels. The first Speech from the Throne (SFT) in this new millennium, for example, described the federal government's recent policy initiatives as the "Canadian Way" and asked every Canadian "to make a contribution to building our country" (30 January 2001, 5).

Canadian governments, however, have not always been able to rely on appeals to nationalism to rally popular support for themselves or for their policies. In fact, the very meaning of "Canadianness" has been contested since Confederation. For Canada, unlike other new countries, the proclamation of statehood did not mark the affirmation of a pre-existing cultural or ethnic entity or the creation of a singular vision of a new national identity. At the time of Confederation, in 1867, the territorial boundaries of the new state were still to be determined and sovereignty continued to be shared with Imperial

Britain. Moreover, the idea that the identity of the inhabitants of the new country could be forged around an inclusive definition of "Canadianness" was confounded by the fact that the new political community contained, minimally, three distinct ethnocultural groups—Indigenous, English, and French—each with different and often antagonistic visions of self and nation. Defining a national identity has become progressively more complex as Canada's population has grown ever more diverse, as a proliferation of competing identity groups make claims for recognition on the state, and as globalization increasingly disrupts the time-worn linkages among state sovereignty, national territory, and political community.

This chapter traces the evolution of various formulations of Canadian national identity from Confederation to the contemporary era of intensifying globalization. The chapter first examines the social and political processes through which nationalism grew to be one of the most potent political forces in the twentieth century. It then explains how Canadian governments have historically been active participants in defining *nation* and *national identity*, linking alleged characteristics of Canada and Canadians to their public policy agendas. Finally, the chapter assesses the future of Canadian nationalism in the contemporary era of neoliberal governance and intensifying globalization.

NATION STATES AND NATIONALITY

Citizenship, national identity, and nationalism are related political concepts that accompanied the rise of the modern state system. Citizenship, understood simply as legal inclusion within a bordered, territorially and internationally recognized state, was deeply implicated in the process of identity formation and the rise of nationalism. As citizens of a nation state, individuals were required to relinquish or subsume previous forms of allegiance, so-called deep identities, based on religion, ethnicity, and regional affiliations, in favour of the universal status of citizen. These deep identities were seen as being products of the traditional societies of the pre-modern era. The birth of the modern nation state saw the creation of national cultures as the principal source of individual identification and the emergence of nationalism as a good in its own right, indeed for some the supreme good. The ability to transcend particularisms in order to advance the collective good of the nation as a shared community of fate was the defining mark of the ideal citizen. As Gellner describes it, "The idea of a man without a nation seems to impose a great strain on the modern imagination. A man must have a nationality as he must have a nose and two ears" (1983, 6).

Citizenship spelled out the legal relationship between individuals and the state, particularly in relation to the creation and elaboration of civil, political, and, eventually, social rights. And nationalism was the primary mechanism which adhered the citizen to the state, contributing to its popular legitimacy. The manner in which national identities have been created and reproduced is far from obvious. Although various strains of nationalism promote the idea of a national character as being natural and enduring across history, influential students of modern nationalism insist that national identities are cultural and political creations. National identities arise out of historically shifting sets of symbols, representations, and discourses and profoundly influence both our actions and our concepts of self and others (Hall, 1995, 613). Anderson defined the nation as an "imagined community" and nationalism, not as the awakening of a nation to self-consciousness, but, instead, as the invention of a nation. To quote Anderson, "communities are to be distinguished, not by their falsity/genuineness, but by the style in which they are imagined" (1983, 6).

Hall suggests that nationalism can be studied as a narrative which contains a number of key elements, including a set of stories, images, or landscapes that stand for the nation; the idea that the national character remains unchanged throughout time; and a foundational myth that locates the origins of a nation, often in war or revolution. Most important, all nationalist discourses are replete with descriptions of the ideal member of the political community (Hall, 1995, 613–14). These descriptions set out who belongs to a nation and who does not, establish a hierarchy of the most to least desirable members of the nation state, and help to discipline citizens to aspire to appropriate behaviours and characteristics. As the history of the twentieth century underscores, nationalism has the power to inspire unquestioning loyalty, to turn one neighbour against another, and to motivate young men to venture their lives in the defence of abstract principles. States are thus deeply invested in these depictions insomuch as they contribute to state authority and to social solidarity. The very survival of the state depends on achieving and maintaining some level of popular legitimacy and social stability as well as the capacity to mobilize populations behind common projects. Nationalism, rightly or wrongly, has often provided the glue that holds diverse and unequal communities together, especially during periods of political crisis, economic hard times, and international conflict. From the perspective of the state and of governance, the promotion of a coherent national narrative provides what Castells calls a "legitimizing identity" which serves both to hold patterns of domination and exploitation in place and to maintain allegiance and social control (1997, 7).

Although the history of citizenship and nationalism are closely interwoven, the two concepts are not completely interchangeable, as the Canadian case clearly attests. From its conception, this national territory has housed different nationalist visions, grounded in different languages, cultures, and histories. These Aboriginal, francophone, and anglophone roots are what John Ralston Saul calls the "triangular foundations" of Canada. As Saul explains, "No matter how much each may deny the others at various times, each of their existences is dependent on the other two" (1997, 30). The Canadian story always has been more complicated than this, as significant differences exist within these three groups. More important, successive waves of immigration have placed an increasing proportion of Canadians completely outside Saul's triangle. In addition, recent decades have seen the rise in expression of new identities tied to, for example, gender, sexuality, and race, that cross-cut and transcend ethnic or national allegiances. All of these factors have complicated the construction of an inclusive and enduring national identity and the development of Canadian nationalism. Canadian citizenship has not coincided with a singular vision of nation, although our history is replete with attempts to evoke such a vision.

Perhaps it is part of the very condition of being Canadian that the narratives of other countries often figure more prominently in our popular culture than does our own. There is, for example, the ubiquitous American myth of being born out of a revolution fought for democracy and individual freedom. There is Britain's story of monarchy, continuity, civility, and tradition, and modern France's republican claim of liberty, equality, and fraternity. Canada, of course, has its own national myths but they are less pronounced and less widely held. One reason for this, as already discussed, is that Canada's national narrative was and continues to be an amalgam of many different and conflicting stories. Canada's uniqueness lies in this complex of identities rather than in any forced consensus about sameness. Second, and relatedly, the Canadian state has played an inordinate role in shaping Canadian identity in order to accommodate ethnic, religious, and regional antagonisms as well as to build support for its many nation-building projects. Lacking consensus about a foundational myth, a story that locates the origins of a nation, people, and national character, successive Canadian governments have tried to create one. Canadian journalist Richard Gwyn, in fact, has invented the term "state nation" (as opposed to nation state) to convey the idea that the Canadian path to statehood was unique in that it was not the result of nationalist claims for self-government (1995). The state came first and it has actively and variously attempted to shape a pan-Canadian vision of nation and national identity ever since. Moreover, this process of state-orchestrated identity construction has intensified rather than diminished in recent decades. Cairns describes the Canadian national identity as a moving target that has been caught up in governmental attempts to "refashion collectivities in light of state purposes." "The transformation in political identity and conceptions of community since the Second World War," he explains, "have already been immense, but the end is not yet in sight" (quoted in Policy Research Initiative, 1998, 5).

The rest of this chapter revisits some of the competing conceptions of Canadian national identity that have arisen since Confederation and links them to the prevailing governmental practices and policy priorities of the time. This ongoing process of identity formation is traced through an examination of federal Speeches from the Throne from 1867 to present. These historical transcripts, written by the government of the day and read by the Governor General at the opening of each new session of Parliament, convey the sitting government's perception of the "state of the nation" and outline its future legislative agenda. But, as soon will become apparent, these speeches also provide a historical record of how different ideas about Canada and "Canadianness" are evoked in order to rally support for governing practices and public policies. This exploration of the many faces of the Canadian identity begins with the immediate post-Confederation period.

NATIONAL IDENTITIES AND GOVERNING STRATEGIES

The Imperial Subject

In Canada's first half-century, the overriding focus of successive federal governments was, quite literally, nation building—laying a transcontinental railway and erecting all kinds of public infrastructures, as well as recruiting a population to exploit the untouched resources of Canada's vast and expanding territory. The Speeches from the Throne during these years very much focus on these concerns, while notions of nation and of national identity barely appear as topics of concern. The absence of appeals to nationalism in these early years is perhaps not surprising considering that Canada had no citizenship act of its own and was still very much tied to the orbits of Imperial Britain. "The people of Canada" and "the Canadian people," as they are invariably referred to in the speeches, are largely defined in reference to the monarch and to Great Britain instead of to their own country. Inhabitants of Canada were thought of as imperial subjects who were variously described as possessing "good intelligence" (SFT, 14 June 1872, 1144), "enterprise, contentment and loyalty" (SFT, 4 February 1875, 2), "loyalty and good will," "loyalty and affection . . . for her Majesty the Queen . . . and the unity of the British Empire" (SFT, 2 January 1896, 3), and "happy and contented people, whose character and prosperity . . . add strength to the great empire" (SFT, 25 March 1897, 4).

The ideal Canadian, in other words, was a contented and, above all, loyal subject of the British Empire. This description might come as a surprise, given the francophone fact in

Canada and the resentment that French Canadians displayed against Imperial Britain during these years. Amazingly, there is not a single mention of French Canadians in these early Speeches. References to the bilingual and bicultural origins of the settler society do not appear until the 1960s. During the early years, provincial muscle flexing over education had the effect of either assimilating francophones outside of Quebec or pushing them back into the province of Quebec. There *les Canadiens* were largely excluded from business and the professions, administered to by the Roman Catholic Church, regulated by a separate legal code, and governed by an inward-looking elite who dominated communication with the outside, and, especially, the federal government. The early political bargain in Canada involved a coalition of anglophone and francophone elites but ordinary French Canadians rarely fell directly into the governing spaces of the post-Confederation government.

"Indians," who also emerged in these early speeches as governable identities, provide an instructive example of how state discourses can construct minority groups into second-class or, indeed, non-citizens. During the 1870s and 1880s, when the federal government was rapidly negotiating treaties with Native populations and expanding the territorial sovereignty of the Canadian state, the "Indian" and "Indian Tribes" are recurring characters in the Speeches from the Throne. Moreover, these actors are represented as autonomous and competent political actors. In 1875, for example, the speech refers to "amicable relations with the Indian tribes [the Cree and Santeux of the North-West]" and in the following year reference is made to "the interest taken by the people of Canada in the welfare of their Indian fellow-countrymen" (SFT, 4 February 1875, 2). Again, in 1878, the speech refers to the "peaceful negotiation with the native tribes, who place implicit faith in the honour and justice of the British crown" (8 February 1878, 14).

However, as the terrain of the Canadian state expanded, and with the implementation of the *Indian Act* (1876), the identity of the First Nations was rapidly transformed from subjects to objects, from independent actors to faceless recipients of administration. In the early 1880s, for example, the government lamented mounting evidence that tribes, which had been moved to reservations, were starving. In a paternalistic tone, the Speech argued it was necessary to "induce [bands recently settled on reserves] to betake themselves to the cultivation of the soil" and to "induce them to betake themselves to the raising of cattle" (12 February 1880, 3). "We can only expect," the government contended, "by a long continuance of patient firmness to induce these *children of the Prairie and the Forest* to abandon their nomadic habits, become self-supporting, and ultimately add to the industrial wealth of the country" (emphasis added, SFT, 9 February 1882, 2). By the turn of the century, the speeches no longer mention Natives or their social plight. Instead, there are recurrent references to the government's intent to amend the *Indian Act*. Indeed, Natives only re-emerge in these historical transcripts in the 1960s, this time as "indigenous people" in need.

It was not until the First World War, almost 50 years after Confederation, that the speeches started to reflect an erosion of Canada's colonial ties with Britain and the growth of a nascent Canadian nationalism. In the early years of the war, the speeches praised the Canadian people and, especially, Canadian soldiers for their bravery in the defence of the British Empire. By the war's end, however, the Governor General announced that "From the terrible struggle in which our country has borne so notable a part, Canada . . . has taken a high place among the world's nations . . . Endowed with a vast heritage, we face the future with just confidence, firm in our determination to upbuild [sic] within our borders a great and prosperous nation" (Canada, Debates, 1919, 2). Ties to imperial Britain and, thus, the relevance of the imperial subject further unravelled during the 1920s, but the federal government appeared to be concerned with little more than public administration during this decade. The 1930s and early 1940s were accompanied by new depictions of the ideal citizen—one challenged by economic collapse and, then, by the atrocities of European fascism. Not surprisingly, the good Canadian in the 1930s was someone who could withstand the hardships of the Depression with "patience and fortitude" and with a "spirit of cooperation and mutual understanding." "These attributes of Canadianism," the 1931 Throne Speech read, "are national assets of real value" and "the surest bulwark of the nation's welfare and happiness" (12 March 1931, 1, 3). The onset of World War II predictably called on the duty of the Canadian people to meet their responsibilities and to show determination in the defence of freedom and "civilization confronted with savagery" (SFT, 22 January 1942, 1). The ideal citizens, of course, were "the fighting men of Canada" who, "at sea, on land and in the air . . . have displayed the highest courage, endurance and skill" (SFT, 27 January 1944, 2).

The Caring-Sharing Canadian

Near the end of the Second World War, the federal government embraced a new rationale for nation building based on the provision of social programs and a new sense of Canadian nationalism. The idea of social citizenship rights and of the caring-sharing Canadian was first advanced in the 1943 Speech from the Throne, which declared that it was "in the general interest that freedom from fear and from want should be the assured possession of all" (28 January 1943, 12). In the next two decades the federal government announced, in rapid succession, a flurry of social legislation for families, the sick, the blind and disabled, the unemployed, veterans, mothers, students, the elderly, and the poor. The new mark of Canadianness was the state-based assurance of security and well-being which, in turn, provided Canadians with a new sense of collective identity. The new ideal Canadian was an individual bearer of rights and other state-based assurances of universal equality of opportunity. The state would provide "a national minimum of social security and human welfare" for all Canadians (SFT, 6 September 1945, 4); "full equality of rights for all Canadian citizens"; and "all Canadians [would] retire in security and with dignity"; "all Canadians [would] feel equally served by Confederation" (SFT 16 May 1963, 7); "all Canadians [would] obtain needed health services, irrespective of their ability to pay" (SFT, 5 April 1965, 2); and "each Canadian [would have] the enjoyment of the maximum possible liberty, happiness and material well-being" (SFT, 18 January 1966, 9). Social policies gathered Canadians from all ethnic, religious, and regional backgrounds under the umbrella of a universal "we"—a single community of fate.

This new pan-Canadianism was reinforced with initiatives to build up the cultural and symbolic infrastructures of nationalism. During the same period, the federal government passed Canada's first *Citizenship Act;* selected an official Canadian anthem (*O Canada*) and flag; formed the Canada Council to support arts, letters, and social sciences; financed the Canadian Broadcasting Corporation (CBC); protected Canadian historic sites and built national museums; and, finally, established a *Canadian Bill of Rights*. National identity no longer rested on metaphors about founding peoples, a railway from sea to sea, a people in struggle with nature, a peaceable kingdom, and so on. Instead, a more elaborate national identity was created through the fusion of nationalism with social policy. This was especially the case after the introduction of universal healthcare (Medicare) in 1966, which, more than any other federal policy, completed the myth of the caring-sharing

Canadian. Medicare, moreover, provided many Canadians with what they considered to be a demonstrable measure of the moral and political superiority of Canada over its big brother to the South, the United States. One of anglophone Canada's nationalist icons, Pierre Berton, describes this period and, in particular, Canada's centennial year, as "the last good year." "We were all high in 1967," he recalls. "In those days we felt secure as Canadians, confident enough to push for a better, freer life." For Burton, Canada's centennial year seemed revolutionary because Canadians realized that they "had created a world-class, forward-looking nation" (1997, 365).

Social programs embodied the idea of shared vulnerability and responsibility and also informed governmental attempts to ensure national unity from the early years of the Quiet Revolution in Quebec to the election of the Parti Québécois. In 1963, Canada's bilingual foundations were finally acknowledged in a Speech from the Throne. "The character and strength of our nation," it read, "are drawn from the diverse cultures of people who came from many lands . . . . The greater Canada that is in our power to make will be built not on uniformity but on continuing diversity, and particularly on the basic partnership of English speaking and French speaking people" (16 May 1963, 6). During these years, nationalism and national unity were tied to the idea of social protection and progress. For successive governments, the challenge of national unity, whether related to Quebec nationalism, regionalism, or Aboriginal communities, could be met through the fulfillment of the promise of social programs. Indeed, in 1973, the government assured Parliament that it remained "fully committed to two preeminent goals, national unity and equality of opportunity for all Canadians" (SFT, 4 January 1973, 3).

The embellishment of Canada as a state nation continued, although not at such a frenzied pace, until the early 1980s. The ultimate statement of state-directed pan-Canadian nationalism came in 1982 with the patriation of the *British North America Act*, the proclamation of the *Constitution Act*, and the entrenchment of the *Canadian Charter of Rights and Freedoms.* At last, Canadians were free from the ties of British colonialism and the masters de jure of their own house. At the same time, nationalist policy initiatives such as Petro-Canada and the Canada Development Corporation were designed to keep at bay the threat to Canadian sovereignty of creeping American control of the economy and of key resources. But, as with all the earlier nationalist myths, this version of the caring-sharing and independent nation was selective, usually representing the aspirations of anglophone Canada. This narrative spoke little of the continuing marginalization, poverty, and assimilation of Aboriginal peoples and it could not comprehend the intensification of Quebec nationalism and the separatist movement. From the 1970s onward, the nationalist projects of Quebec and of the rest of Canada came into increasing conflict as evinced by the elections of the Parti Québécois, Quebec's refusal to endorse the new constitution and *Charter*, and the failed Meech Lake and Charlottetown accords. Although actively pursuing a nationalist project at the federal level, political elites watched with alarm the growing proportion of Canadians identifying themselves first as Québécois and second (if at all) as Canadians.

Yet, even though there were obvious and growing cracks in the postwar construction of pan-Canadianism, federal social policies continued to inform any remaining consensus between Quebec and the rest of Canada about national identity. In April 1996, for example, the Environics polling firm asked a representative sample of Canadians to indicate which among 15 national symbols were "very important" to them as markers of Canadian identity. The results show a stark difference between Québécois and other Canadians with respect to their assessment of the symbols commonly associated with Canada and with national identity. Canadians outside Quebec were much more likely to identify with the symbols and much more likely than Québécois to associate the RCMP, the Canadian flag, the national anthem, and bilingualism with being Canadian. Healthcare, however, was by far the most important symbol of national identity among all Canadians (70 percent of Québécois, 86 percent of other Canadians) (Canada, 1996, 9). This federal social policy, in other words, succeeds in bridging the two solitudes.

ENTER THE ENTREPRENEURIAL CANADIAN

Paradoxically, the postwar construction of pan-Canadianism, grounded in social policy, reached its apex at the same time as the federal government began to lose its capacity to nation-build through social programs and economic nationalism. The oil shocks of the 1970s brought externally generated stagflation—simultaneously high levels of unemployment and inflation—which proved impervious to federal policy interventions and fuelled government debt, which continued to push upward until the mid-1990s. These negative trends were accompanied by the beginning of a long-term restructuring of the international political economy that continues today. The globalization of production and finance, corporate downsizing and concentration, rapid technological innovations, and free trade brought, in the early 1980s, the highest levels of unemployment since the Great Depression of the 1930s, a slowing of economic growth, more part-time jobs, and an increasing income polarization between the rich and the poor. All of these factors put unsustainable pressures on the federal state's capacity to respond. Most obviously, the restructured economy put pressure on government budgets and revenue-raising capacity. By the early 1990s, for example, some 11 percent of Canadians were on some form of social assistance, and in just over a decade (from 1981 to 1994), federal expenditures on social welfare increased threefold to $8.2 billion (Rice and Prince, 2000, 124).

During these same years, the federal government called upon the ideal Canadian to ask less of government and to begin to think about social programs not as a mark of Canadian identity but, instead, as selective protection available only to those in obvious need. Signals that the social security regime would shift from a universal to a residual model were flagged in the mid-1970s when social security was designated first and foremost for those who could not work. By 1977, Canadians were told that it was "essential to the unity of the country" to show a "greater willingness to sacrifice . . . to take less so that others may have enough" (SFT, 18 October 1977, 3). In the 1980s, Canadians were informed that these actions were part and parcel of the national character. The 1980 Speech from the Throne, for example, noted that "Canada's tradition is one of sharing . . . a country whose people share their wealth first with those who need it most." "Canadians will accept sacrifice," the speech continued, and should understand that "the state cannot meet every demand or satisfy every group" (14 April 1980, 5). In 1986, the speech represented Canada as "a modern, tolerant, and caring nation," adding that Canadians "want their governments to give the highest priority in social policy to those who are in greatest need" (1 October 1986, 13). The idea of the universal vulnerability to insecurity as a foundation for Canadian identity gradually slid off the policy agenda.

During the 1980s, the assumptions motivating the welfare state were gradually replaced with those of neoliberalism, specifically its uncompromising confidence in the superiority of the market and market mechanisms, privatization, decentralization, and individualization. At its heart, neoliberalism prioritizes the market and market mechanisms both *over* the state and public sector and increasingly *inside* them. Rather than build national solidarities through public policy initiatives, the neoliberal state is expected to fashion itself as a market creator and facilitator (Brodie, 1997). This transition from the welfare to neoliberal state has also been accompanied by the birth of the entrepreneurial citizen, whose persona can be traced back to the mid-1980s when the newly elected Mulroney government embraced neoliberal governing practices. More recent celebrations of the entrepreneurial citizen, however, are motivated both by the federal state's abandonment of universal social security in the mid-1990s and by the challenges of global competition in an era of intensifying globalization.

Since the late 1980s, the Speeches from the Throne have stressed that Canadians are living through fundamental changes that deem the assumptions of the past invalid. The government noted that "Canada is inescapably part of the global economy" (SFT, 3 May 1991, 3) and Canadians are "citizens in a global economy" (SFT, 23 September 1997, 10). These statements represented a stark departure from the strains of economic nationalism voiced only a decade before. By the early 1990s, Canada's ability to compete, the government contended, as well as national unity itself, required a strong and innovative economy. In contrast to the postwar period when the state was central to realizing both national identity and national unity, these critical outcomes were now entrusted to the market. In 2001, the government portrayed an innovative economy rather than the broader political community as essential to creating opportunity for Canadians and for distributing wealth among citizens and across regions. Moreover, consistent with neoliberalism's core premise, the state was not identified as taking a leadership role in the creation of the new economy. Instead, future success would depend on "people with advanced skills and entrepreneurial spirit" (SFT, 30 January 2001, 4). And, in the same way we once relied on depictions of the loyal imperial subject and the caring Canadian, the future of the country had become dependent on the vitality of the entrepreneurial citizen. As the government explained in the 1991 speech, "there is much more to Canadian unity than amending the constitution. Our unity is strengthened by a strong economy" (3 May 1991, 2).

Fortunately, Canadians are well placed to succeed in the global market. In fact, the requisite qualities of the entrepreneurial citizen are argued to be embedded in our national tradition and value structure. The 1991 speech, for example, attempted to rewrite the national narrative by asserting that "Canada's history is the history of builders and achievers" (3 May 1991, 2). Later in the decade, the national character was elaborated with respect to the perceived demands of global competition. The speeches underlined that "our citizens have the qualities that are needed to succeed in the twenty-first century." Canadians "welcome innovation and new ideas" (SFT, 23 September 1997, 6) and "have the self-confidence to act, and to act successfully " (SFT, 30 January 2001, 1). These speeches also outline the alleged enduring characteristics of the ideal Canadian, which equip her or him for the new century and a competitive global economy. "Change does not frighten us—we have always harnessed it to our advantage." Moreover, "Canada is proud, optimistic and strong . . . and [can] face the challenges" (SFT, 30 January 2001, 3, 5). Together, this inherited inventory of national values helps define what the government now terms "our Canadian Way."

Such revelations about Canadian history and the Canadian character are the stuff of nationalist myth making—the invention of a tradition and a foundational story where none existed before. And, like all national myths, ours serves to contain dissent and to mobilize citizens around new governing practices and policy agendas. In the present era, the ideal Canadian, indeed all Canadians, already brimming with an entrepreneurial national character, have been asked to play their part. "Canada's ability to prosper," according to the government's analysis, will be determined by "our attitudes to work and to change" (SFT, 3 May 1991, 4). To meet the challenges, the speeches recommend that we work together, collaborate, partner, and volunteer—in effect, put our collective shoulder to the wheel. "Every citizen can contribute to building our nation," we are told; indeed, "every Canadian is called upon to make a contribution to build our country" (SFT, 30 January 2001, 5).

CANADIAN IDENTITY IN THE TWENTY-FIRST CENTURY

Although the past decade has been marked by governmental initiatives to recast the image that Canadians have of themselves, their country, and their governments to better mesh with neoliberal governing practices, the new face of Canadian nationalism has yet to lodge itself in the national psyche. There are a number of reasons for this. First, unlike during the postwar period, political and business elites, either seduced by the promises of neoclassical economics or squeezed by the fiscal realities of the new economy, implemented a neoliberal policy agenda without first building a broad-based public consensus for what was in effect a fundamental shift in popular understandings of self and nation. As Saul puts it, "our future was debated and decided as if we had no past" (1997, 11). Second, the pillars of neoliberal governance, in many ways, are incompatible with the very idea of a national narrative. The tidal shift in values away from collective pan-Canadian identity towards the celebration of the individual entrepreneur is antagonistic to the idea of a shared community of fate—the idea that we are all in this together. This idea of the individual entrepreneur is divisive because it orders the population into material and financial winners and losers, and completely devalues contributions to community, such as caring work or volunteerism, that do not entail market transactions or profit margins. These factors as well as the ongoing erosion of social programs, their devolution to the provinces, and increasing economic insecurity have meant that the Canadian social fabric is fraying, especially at the edges. "The citizenry seems to be withdrawing into a state of sullen non-cooperation," not the least because, as Saul explains, "they are repeatedly told that the mythologies, and indeed the realities, by which they built their country can no longer function" (1997, 227).

Federal government researchers also point to trends that suggest that social solidarity is under stress. Among other things, they point out that the attachment to Canada appears to be waning among youth, especially francophone youth; a cleavage is growing between haves and have nots "with possibly negative implications for a continuing sense of Canada as a sharing and caring community"; a gap is widening between elites and the public about the value and future of social programs; and there is a rapid and widespread loss of trust and respect for political leaders, public institutions, and the political process (Policy Research Initiative, 1998, 30). Reporting on another poll, the government researchers conclude that "with core societal values inextricably connected to the federal state, these findings suggest that the impact of federal retrenchment may be affecting not only programs but also Canadians' perception of their national identity and character" (Policy Research Initiative, 1999, 32).

In 1996, the federal government once again embraced its historical task of binding Canadians together with a new understanding of themselves and their country. The so-called social cohesion agenda, launched only a year after Quebec separatists came within a whisker of winning a sovereignty referendum, seeks to facilitate "the ongoing process of developing a community of shared values, shared challenges, and equal opportunity within Canada, based on trust, hope, and reciprocity among all Canadians" (Policy Research

Initiative, 1998, 5). Defined in this way, the concept of social cohesion looks very much like a proxy for national solidarity or identity. It is far from obvious, however, how the federal government can promote social solidarity during the contemporary era. Neoliberal governing practices have all but eliminated the postwar platform for a pan-Canadian identity grounded in shared vulnerability and social policy guarantees. Moreover, decentralization, a key neoliberal governing strategy, has pushed responsibility for both the design and the cost of social programs onto the provinces, many of which have neither the desire nor the finances to maintain a robust social safety net. Whatever sense of shared fate Canadians found in the postwar social policy regime is rapidly fading as provinces now compete among themselves to create the lowest tax regimes to attract international investment. If there is a central programmatic thread running through the provinces, it is that social policy is a low priority, residual, and indeed often an obstacle to establishing a competitive continental investment environment. The growing trend towards public–private partnerships and the privatization of government services and public goods has been embraced by some provincial governments precisely as a way to unload the costs of social policies onto individuals, to build new markets, and to capture new private-sector, often American, investment. Although Canadians still identify strongly with social programs such as Medicare, these programs are no longer capable of acting as a glue holding together a diverse social fabric. Their very future is currently on the negotiating table.

At the same time, many now argue that the multiple forces of globalization are detaching citizens from their allegiances to country and from their national cultures and identity. In particular, the idea of globality suggests that the current era is uniquely marked by the emergence of the planet as a distinct political, economic, and social space that transcends the groundedness of community, state, and territory. According to this argument, the world is fast becoming a coherent economic, cultural, and political unit supported by the prevalence of global markets, global brands and cultural industries, global governmental and non-governmental organizations, transnational corporations, global crime networks, global demands for human rights, global environmental concerns—the list goes on (Beck, 2000, 22–26). Globality challenges the idea that there is any longer such a thing as a national governable entity contained within territorial borders.

Globalization suggests that the notion of closed national spaces no longer captures the real dimensions of daily life because the local and the national are now infused with the transnational. They have become entwined in a complex of forces, identities, issues, and movements that draw individual members of national polities differently and at different levels of social organization into what Held and McGrew call "overlapping communities of fate" (1999, 442). Strings of transaction as well as non-territorial and pre- and post-national allegiances run up, down, and through the national social fabric, disarticulating national politics on both horizontal and vertical axes. Localities are often more directly linked to distant forces and actors than to the national state. The state's capacity to shield society, moreover, is diminished by the growing saliency in our lives of global policy issues that are largely immune from the policy interventions of any single state. As such, it is increasingly difficult for governments to speak on behalf of a distinct Canadian community of interest or to enact policies that are immune from outside forces. Gwyn's idea of state nation is all the more illusory.

CONCLUSION

At the dawn of the twenty-first century, being Canadian is both complex and paradoxical. As noted at the beginning of this chapter, symbols of the Canadian national identity abound in popular culture, especially outside Quebec. In fact, in the late 1990s, a Canadian beer commercial struck a deep chord with the public with the declaration "I am Canadian." In the commercial, called "The Rant," a typical Canadian, called "Joe," confronts a number of Canadian stereotypes such as being lumberjacks and living in igloos and reinforces others such as Canada's protection of diversity and the respect our flag meets around the world. The Rant has an Internet site (www.iam.ca) and an active chatroom. A recent poll shows that, while the majority of Canadians think that we have become more like the United States since the implementation of free trade, fully 81 percent of Canadians oppose the idea of a political union with the United States. This figure contrasts with 62 percent in 1964 (CRIC, 2001, 14–15). Moreover, more Canadians feel that Canadian culture benefits from free trade agreements (48 percent) as opposed to being harmed (22 percent) or being unaffected by them (CRIC, 2001, 15). Canadians, it would seem, are confident about the future of their autonomy and culture in the contemporary era.

Canadians do share a collective history and common values, especially with respect to an active state and to the collective provision of social benefits. Threads of the narrative of the caring and sharing Canadian continue to run through the national social fabric. At the same time, neoliberal governing practices have decreased state presence with respect to promoting social values and culture; downloaded responsibilities for most risks onto individuals, families, and communities; and increased state presence with respect to enforcing market relations in almost every dimension of daily life. This approach to governance, as well as the celebration of market icons such as the entrepreneurial citizen, atrophies the idea of a shared community and shared responsibility, closes political spaces, and further marginalizes the already marginalized. As Bauman rightly reminds us, "the foundational act of the market is to dissolve the bonds of sociality and reciprocity"—two necessary ingredients for building and maintaining the very ideas of a national public and of social solidarity (1999, 30). It is difficult to imagine how the market and civil society, without the intervention of governments, can construct a national narrative that could sustain social solidarity in a globalizing era. Canadian identity may survive in the contemporary era of neoliberal globalism, not as a foundation for collective responsibility and provision, but, instead, as a symbol on a T-Shirt and as a highly marketable commodity.

REFERENCES

Anderson, Benedict. 1983. *Imagined Communities.* London: Verso Books.

Bauman, Zygmunt. 1999. *In Search of Politics.* Stanford, CA: Stanford University Press.

Beck, Ulrich. 2000. *What is Globalization?* London: Polity Press.

Brodie, Janine. 1997. "Meso-Discourses, State forms, and the Gendering of Liberal-Democratic Citizenship" *Citizenship Studies, 1,* 2.

Berton, Pierre. 1997. *1967: The Last Good Year.* Toronto: Doubleday.

Canada. Speech from the Throne, 1867–2001.

_____. House of Commons, Debates, 1919.

Castells, Manuel. 1997. *The Information Age: Economy, Society and Culture,* Vol. II, *The Power of Identity.* London: Blackwell.

CRIC, Centre for Research and Information on Canada. 2001. *Trade, Globalization and Canadian Values.* Montreal.

Gellner, Earnest. 1983. *Nations and Nationalism.* Oxford: Basil Blackwell.

Gwyn, Richard. 1995. *Nationalism Without Walls: The Unbearable Lightness of Being Canadian.* Toronto: McClelland & Stewart.

Hall, Stuart. 1995. "The Question of Cultural Identity." In Stuart Hall, David Held, Don Hubert and Kenneth Thompson (eds.) *Modernity: An Introduction to Modern Societies.* London: Blackwell.

Held, David and Anthony McGrew. 1999. "Globalization" *Global Governance, 4,* 4.

Policy Research Committee. 1996. *Canadian Identity, Culture and Values: Building a Cohesive Society.* Ottawa: Privy Council Office.

Policy Research Initiative, Social Cohesion Network. 1998. "Rekindling Hope and Investing in the Future." Ottawa: Privy Council Office.

Policy Research Initiative. 1999. *Sustaining Growth, Human Development, and Social Cohesion in a Global World.* Ottawa: Privy Council Office.

Rice, James and Michael Prince. 2000. *Changing Politics of Canadian Social Policy.* Toronto: University of Toronto Press.

Saul, John Ralston. 1997. *Reflections of a Siamese Twin: Canada at the End of the Twentieth Century.* Toronto: Viking.

WEBLINKS

Joe Canadian Rant
http://canada4life.ca/joe.html

ProudCanadians.com
www.proudcanadians.com/>

About Canada
canada.gc.ca/canadiana/cdaind_e.html>

chapter two

The Multiple Affiliations of Quebec

Claude Couture
Nathalie Kermoal

INTRODUCTION

This chapter explores the place of Quebec in contemporary Canada by explaining several important narratives in Québécois social science, which purport to reveal both the origins of Quebec nationalism and the likely path of its future evolution. The chapter begins by contesting the ethnic-based narrative about Quebec, which is all too frequently encountered in political science textbooks and other analyses of Quebec written primarily in English for a francophone audience. Such a textbook narrative represents Quebec nationalism as ethnically based and a throwback to earlier times. However, as the chapter explains, independantist writers reject this narrative by providing three very different interpretations of Quebec's past and future. This chapter examines three models in detail—the Dumont Model, the Bouchard Model, and the "Revisionist Model." This discussion demonstrates that the Quebec narrative continues to hold a complex and contradictory place in any narrative about the contemporary Canadian community.

In most of the textbooks on Canadian politics, Quebec nationalism (that is, the nationalism of French Canadians living in Quebec) is described as "ethnic" (Dickerson, 1994; Jackson, 1994; Landes, 1995) or essentially racially based, comparable, for example, to the Afrikaner nationalism in South Africa, as described in the *Concise Oxford Dictionary of Politics* (McLean, 1996). This conclusion is generally based on a particular narrative comprising the following components. It begins with a depiction of Quebec as a seventeenth-century white settler colony, one grounded in an *ancien régime* of rural and religious values. The Conquest of 1760, it is argued, stigmatized those values in what became a very religious and rural French Canada in the nineteenth century, while the British—secular and urban—embraced the project of modernity. Finally, it is asserted that Quebec is still haunted by the ghosts of its past, and thus remained a pre-modern society until the Quiet Revolution of the 1960s. Consequently, its nationalism remains, in the twenty-first century, essentially "ethnic" and "racial."

This view of Quebec, apart from a few nuances, is basically reproduced everywhere in the literature, whether the authors claim to write from the "neutral" perspective of liberalism (Beiner and Norman, 2001), a comparative perspective (Modood and Werbner, 1997), "gender" and "race" perspectives (Yuval-Davis and Stasiulis, 1995), or "ex cathedra" (Habermas in Taylor, 1994; Habermas, 1998). The same narrative about Quebec, particularly before 1960, is also present in Taylor (1992, 1994). Kymlicka too has his "cut and paste" paragraph on traditional Quebec before the 1960s (1989, 1995). Michael Ignatieff reaped a fortune from his simplistic representation of "petty" nationalisms, including Quebec's, while francophone "experts" have also made a lucrative career out of these "miserabilist" visions (Gagnon, 1990; Maclure and Gagnon, 2001; Thériault, 1995; Sarra-Bournet, 2000). The list is endless.

But to what extent does this almost universally accepted narrative of Quebec's past reflect the complexity of the debates among francophone political writers and the historiography of the last 30 years? Since the 1960s, numerous schools of thought have emerged in Quebec about the definition of nation and the content of nationalism. Francophone Québécois have been divided in three different political camps: the Trudeauistes, the "soft federalists," and the independantists (McRoberts, 1997). Among the latter group, the independantists, there are at least three schools of thought. The first is represented by the work of sociologist Fernand Dumont. The second and third, the Gérard Bouchard paradigm and the "revisionist" view, are essentially reactions to the Dumont paradigm. Feminism, the First Nations issue, and multiculturalism have challenged each of the three models.

In order to avoid a simplistic reading of Quebec, "*à la* Ignatieff" for example, one should at least try to go beyond the usual narrative and consider the complexity of the discourses involved even among the strict advocates of an independent Quebec. The political ramifications are important because common understandings of nation guide both political opinion and action. Gérard Bouchard's argument, for example, advances the notion that Quebec will reach its full potential as a society of the New World only when it cuts its ties with the old colonialists, the British monarchy. Bouchard's project of an independent Quebec is thus shifting, using the "ethnic" nationalism stigmata as a tool to portray Canada as a society of the Old World, colonial and racist. Quebec thus could only reach its full progressive potential notably through a wider inclusion of diversity, which would only be possible by cutting its ties with a monarchist Canada. Even if today the support for sovereignty is shrinking, it does not necessarily mean that the sovereigntist project is dead. One has only to recall that in 1976, a few weeks before the election of the Parti Québécois, Prime Minister Trudeau declared the death of the separatist movement in Quebec. But the paradigm had shifted in 1976, from a nostalgic right-wing agenda to a social democratic one. Now, at the beginning of this new millennium, the paradigm is shifting again, from a vague, social-democratic project to a multicultural one, with French defined as the public language of a diverse society.

THE FERNAND DUMONT MODEL

The late Fernand Dumont was, in Quebec, the most important sociologist of his generation. Dumont thought that Quebec was not a nation, as indicated by the title of his *magnum opus—Genèse de la Société Québécoise*. He thought, to the contrary, that there was a "French" North American nation, mostly concentrated in the province of Quebec, but present in other regions of Canada as well as in the United States. In his *Genèse de la Société Québécoise* (1993), he advanced a narrative based on the idea of the "French" as a francophone nation or "people."

Dumont reminded his readers that the French North American empire before 1763 was a vast territory including the St Lawrence River valley, the Great Lakes region, and territories around the Missouri and Mississippi rivers from the Ohio River valley to the Gulf of Mexico. The James Bay region and the northern part of Quebec were officially British territories after the Treaty of Utrecht in 1713, half a century before the Conquest of 1760. It is important to note that the word *Canada* (meaning "village" in Iroquois), not *Québec*, was used by the French to refer to the territory of New France that lay along the St Lawrence River (Morin, 1997). There was a strong sense among the French population of belonging to North America (Couture and Cardin, 1996). The inclusion of the vast interior of the continent, reinforced by the fur trade and French exploration, has never completely disappeared from the complex sense of identity of francophone Québécois, or "Canadiens" as they have referred to themselves since the eighteenth century (Choquette, 1997). For example, in 1995, at the peak of the referendum in Quebec on sovereignty, still an important number of francophone Québécois kept some element of a Canadian identity. Asked about their identity, 20 percent of the people interviewed said they were Québécois only, another 20 percent said they were Québécois and Canadians, a third 20 percent answered that they were Canadians and Québécois, and only 6 percent said they were Canadians only. The Canadian identity of the old New France never vanished, thus confirming Dumont's emphasis on the French-Canadian identity (McRoberts, 1997).

Dumont, who was a religious man, also insisted on the religious factor as a founding element of New France (1993). At the end of the seventeenth century, religious minorities in Europe sought to emigrate in order to build societies according to their religious beliefs. France's minorities, such as the Huguenots, mainly moved to Central Europe, while religious minorities in Britain emigrated to North America. The refusal of the Church to allow religious minorities to move to New France, and the fertile soil and temperate climate of the Atlantic seaboard, led to a great disparity in the populations of New France and New England. Between 1608 and 1713, despite the success of its expansion on the continent, New France's population had grown from several hundred to only 15 000 inhabitants (1993). In comparison, New England had a population of 400 000 in 1715 and more than 2 million in 1763. Between 1715 and 1763 the population of New France grew from 15 000 to almost 70 000 inhabitants. But it was too late. Oddly, it was under the English regime after 1763 that the remaining French-speaking population grew substantially. From less than 70 000 the French population increased to some 100 000 in 1784, over 400 000 in 1825, and almost a million in 1860. By 1911, the French-speaking population in Quebec was about 2 million people, 4 million in 1951, and almost 6 million in 1960. Between 1840 and 1930, 1 million French-Canadians, most of them seeking jobs in the manufacturing sector in New England, left Quebec for the United States. Today, according to some authors (Balthazar and Hero, 1999), the Franco-American population could approximate 10 million people.

In 1791, with the *Constitutional Act*, the frontiers of the colony were reduced to what is essentially southern Quebec today (Couture and Cardin, 1996). The colony was also granted an elected assembly. But the territory, like any other British colony, was directly and undemocratically governed from the metropolis through a governor named by London and a body of councils also composed of non-elected members. The assembly, moreover, had limited powers.

The Canadiens developed a distinct identity by the end of the eighteenth century, and the initial struggle for democracy became, according to Dumont, synonymous with nationalism (1993). It is worth noting, according to Dumont, that the Patriots were defined as *Canadiens*, and included all of those who were against the British monarchy and in favour of democracy. Consequently, the idea of the "multi" was a key element of the political project of the *Canadiens*. After failed rebellions and amalgamation with Upper Canada (Ontario) in 1841, Quebec became part of a legislative union as a result of Lord Durham's recommendations. Quebec became a province of the Canadian federation in 1867.

According to Dumont (1993), the failure of the 1837–38 Rebellion, which meant the - failure of the "civic humanist" ideal, or the Republican project, provoked a realignment in the "French" nation and the emergence of a new project and a new national content called "survivance." Instead of creating a multinational republic, the elite of French-Canadian society, among them a new powerful Church after 1840, shifted their focus from politics to culture. They accepted the *BNA Act* of 1867 but for them Confederation was based on the principle of a federation of nations, namely the British and the French (both the French and the British of the era excluded the First Nations in their equation). But that interpretation of Confederation was never shared by the majority of English-speaking Canadians. British Canada tended to see Canada as a homogeneous nation composed of different regions represented by the provinces (Dumont, 1993; Bouchard, 2000; Létourneau, 2000). This unresolved debate about the nature of the federation has been at the core of every political and constitutional crisis in Canada and the province of Quebec since 1867. For Dumont, the Métis Rebellions of 1870 and 1885, the hanging of Louis Riel, the illegal and unconstitutional abolition of the use of the French language in Manitoba in 1890, the conscription crises in 1917 and 1942, the constant marginalization of the French language at the federal level until the Official Languages legislation of 1969—all these events contributed to a negative perception of the Canadian federation, and saw the rise, of a siege mentality that focused on Quebec.

Also, for Dumont, the project of sovereignty for Quebec was crucial to reinstating the Republican project of the Patriots. A sovereign Quebec, he argued, should create institutions based on the recognition of the numerous nations comprising Quebec, among them, as a majority, the "French" Canadian nation. Thus, Quebec, comprising, was not a nation, according to Dumont, but an eventual multinational state where the French as a majority were better positioned to help or even attract the other French Canadians of the continent. Dumont's detractors pointed out that his project of transforming a cultural nation into a political majority was ethically suspect in terms of avoiding the traps of ethnic nationalism, even if Dumont insisted on forming a federation of nations inside Quebec.

This federation would have included the First Nations as "founding people" (Morin, 1997; Dupuis, 1997, 2001), a major difference compared to the situation prevailing in the nineteenth century. For several leaders of the First Nations in Quebec, the concept of "founding people" was not necessarily perceived as colonialist (Bernard Cleary in Seymour, 1999). The recognition of the First Nations as "founding people" would mean their political acceptance in Canada and, consequently, would lead to "nation to nation" pacts. In fact, in February 2002, the Cree Nation in the James Bay area signed a treaty called "la paix des Braves" with the province of Quebec based on the principle of a "nation to nation" negotiation. Dumont would have recognized his project in this "paix des Braves" (*Le Soleil*, March 25, 2002).

However, if Dumont's notion of a federation of nations was inclusive when it came to the First Nations, his paradigm was not as clear about the inclusion of groups commonly associated with contemporary multiculturalism. Dumont's work did not provide a clear solution for the recognition of other cultural/ethnic groups—nor of [women]. In fact, his paradigm was particularly hostile to feminism (Lamoureux, 1995; Lamoureux, Maillé, and de Seve, 1999), a fact that is consistent with Dumont's strong Catholicism. Some of Dumont's current followers (Cantin, 1997) also seem to be indifferent, if not hostile, to feminism (Létourneau, 2000). Overall, although Dumont paradigm is still stigmatised as "cultural" nationalism, the content of its vision is more complex than the simple reproduction of an "ethnic" form of nationalism. Dumont, like many Catholics, was morally tormented by questions of ethics and did not seem to find a satisfying solution, in moral terms, to the problem of Quebec nationalism. More recent writers believe they have.

THE GÉRARD BOUCHARD MODEL

A student of Fernand Dumont in the 1960s, Gérard Bouchard completed his doctoral thesis in social history in Paris in 1971, and like Dumont, he has had a very prolific career (Mathieu, 2001). Gérard Bouchard's intellectual project can be divided into two periods. The first period, from 1971 to 1996, was devoted to a thorough study of the Saguenay population. This study concluded that there was a discrepancy between the representation, by the elite, of the popular classes in Quebec and what seemed to be the more complex reality of the popular classes. Following from that, Bouchard embarked on a comparative history project that led to his book *Genèse des Nations et Cultures du Nouveau Monde*, in which he compares the evolution of national identities in Quebec, Canada, the United States, Latin America, New Zealand, and Australia. He, too, seemed to be fascinated by the origins of identity formation.

Despite the first incursions of the French in 1534, the real beginning of French colonization in the St Lawrence Valley was in 1608, when Samuel de Champlain established a fort at Cap Diamant, today the site of Quebec City. The French North American empire expanded considerably during the seventeenth century (Choquette, 1997). In 1672 and 1673, Jolliet and Marquette explored the Mississippi River and, in 1682, Robert Cavelier de LaSalle reached the Gulf of Mexico by following the Mississippi River. Many institutions were established—hospitals such as the Hôtel-Dieu de Québec in 1639 and the Hôtel-Dieu de Montréal in 1657. In 1664, the Coutume de Paris became the law in the colony; in 1663, Bishop Laval opened the first seminary, the Grand Séminaire de Québec, while the Séminaire de Saint-Sulpice opened in Montreal in 1677 (Greer, 1997; Choquette, 1997). In 1713, the Treaty of Utrecht, following France's defeat by a coalition of European countries in the War of the Spanish Succession, demanded that France surrender Acadia (in Nova Scotia, excluding that area which is today Cape Breton Island), Newfoundland, and the lands around Hudson's Bay. Several thousand Acadians thus became part of the British Empire in North America. Following the Seven Years' War, Quebec City and Montreal were claimed by the British. It was the end of the French empire in North America (Couture and Cardin, 1996).

According to Bouchard's narrative (2000), a few years after the Conquest, the remaining French population of the new British colony benefited from tension between the Thirteen Colonies and Britain with the *Quebec Act* of 1774. The *Quebec Act* enlarged the frontiers of the Province of Quebec, recognized freedom of religion for Catholics, and established the legality of the seigneurial system and the French civil code. After the American Civil War, the *Constitutional Act of 1791* reduced the frontiers of the province for the purpose of establishing a new colony, Upper Canada (eventually Ontario), and guaranteed a legislative assembly, although with limited powers, in each colony (Upper and Lower Canada).

French Canadians were, during the years between 1791 and 1867, extremely active both politically and in every aspect of economic life. Local markets were extraordinarily complex and diversified. Some French Canadians, like Augustin Cuvillier and Joseph Masson, were also involved in international commerce and banking. Both men were administrators of the Bank of Montreal while other French Canadians opened French-Canadian banks such as the Banque du peuple in 1835 (Couture, 1998).

As for Dumont, for Bouchard the key period of the nineteenth century was 1837–38. The rebellions in Upper and Lower Canada over the principle of self-government resulted in military repression and the Durham Report of 1839. Lord Durham recommended the application of the principle of self-government but suggested that the only solution to the French Canadian problem was the union of the two colonies. The aim was to assimilate the French Canadians. That plan was implemented in 1841 through the *Union Act*, passed in London in 1840. Section 41 of the *Union Act* stipulated that English was the only language of the new colony (McRoberts, 1997). But, when Britain abolished the mercantilist system between 1846 and 1848, the principle of self-government was granted to the colonies as compensation for the loss of protected access to the British market. Following that decision, a coalition of reformists lead by Robert Baldwin and Louis Hippolyte Lafontaine formed the first democratic government of United Canada (the colony formed by the union of Lower and Upper Canada) in 1848 (McRoberts, 1997). The right of the French language was recognized by the reformists. By 1864, during negotiations for a new federation of British North American colonies, it was clear that there was a growing recognition of the French reality in the proposed federation. However, Bouchard argues that from the 1840s until the 1950s, Quebec elites were obsessed by a cultural approach defined as "la survivance." It was in "la survivance," the struggle to ensure the survival of French language and culture in an English continent, that one could find the root of the discrepancy between the "learned culture" and the "popular culture" (2000).

For Bouchard, French-Canadian cultural roots can be traced to the beginning of the nineteenth century in literature, painting, and sculpture. Debate about the significance of the arts in the francophone community has been passionate since the nineteenth century. In literature, Father Henri-Raymond Casgrain in the nineteenth century and Bishop Camille Roy in the twentieth century both sought to create a literature that would reflect what they defined as the essence of French-Canadian society. After the Quiet Revolution, many writers were, like Casgrain and Roy, exploring the identity of the French-speaking society now referred to as Quebec society. There was a constant search for identity and self-confidence (Lamonde, 2000).

A century later, the cultural infrastructure in Quebec is impressive by any standard (Andrew, 1999). There are 150 theatre companies; a dynamic music scene with over 100 musical organizations, including two that started their activities in the nineteenth century.

The Orchestre Symphonique de Montréal is ranked among the top orchestras in the world, while a large number of music schools, in universities and conservatories, provide musical training. In dance, Quebec enjoys an international reputation with companies like les Grands ballets canadiens and La La La Human Steps. Montreal has around 230 commercial cinemas and is the host of the prestigious Montreal Film Festival (Andrew, 1998). No wonder that even Mordecai Richler, the prominent English-language novelist well known for his mockery of Quebec nationalism, once described francophone Québécois as the most cultivated people in Canada (Bouchard, 2000). Also, there are 29 television stations in Quebec and a high proportion of the television watched by francophone Québécois is French-language programming produced in Quebec. Quebec has 58 AM and 77 FM radio stations and more than 150 rebroadcasting radio stations. The province has 10 French-language and 2 English-language daily newspapers, more than 200 weeklies, more than 300 periodicals, and over 30 publications in languages other than French and English (Andrew, 1998).

Thus, according to Bouchard and contrary to his mentor Dumont, this massive cultural infrastructure indicates that Quebec is a nation capable of including everyone who lives within its territory and is willing to use a public language, in this case French, the same way that English is the public language in the United States (2000). But like all the colonies of the New World that became independent and progressive new nations, at least in Bouchard's mind, Quebec has to cut its ties with the British monarchy or the symbolism of the old colonialism (the British colonialism) (2000). Consequently, according to Bouchard, since Canada has not fundamentally cut its ties with the old colonialism, despite its claim of embracing "civic" nationalism, Quebec must achieve independence in order to fully embrace the project of a nation of the "new world" (2000). This point of view has been shared recently by several commentators, one of them being Michel Seymour.

A philosophy professor at the Université de Montréal, Michel Seymour has authored or co-authored nearly a dozen books on nationalism since 1995. The starting point of Seymour's analysis is his refutation of the Dumont paradigm and the notion of "survivance," or cultural nationalism. According to this philosopher, Quebec was indeed a priest-ridden and ethnic society before the Quiet Revolution. Since the 1960s, however, modern Quebec has rejected the "survivance" model and embraced a more social-democratic and inclusive project. Thus Quebec is a nation composed of all the people living within its territory. But, as Canada has a socio-political majority with British roots, Quebec also has a socio-political majority, which is French. While more than 80 percent of Canadians outside Quebec speak English at home, more than 80 percent of Québécois speak French at home (Seymour, 1999). Thus, the public language in Canada is clearly English while the public language in Quebec is French.

Quebec constitutes a nation with a clear capacity to integrate its minorities with all due respect to their origins. Both Bouchard and Seymour dedicate a great deal of their writing to the question of the integration of the non–French Canadians in a "civic" form of nationalism, while they seem to assume that the question of feminism has been dealt with successfully since the 1960s by the inclusion of the most powerful feminist lobby in Canada in Quebec's institutions. This view is not shared, however, by many prominent feminists in Quebec (Lamoureux, Maillé and de Seve, 1999). Although these feminists were extremely critical of the condescension towards Québécois displayed by Canadian feminists during both the Meech Lake and Charlottetown crises, they do not engage easily in the new discourse about the justification of independence and remain conscious of the struggle of women in Quebec despite the gains of the last decades (Lamoureux, Maillé and de Seve 1999; Strong-Boag et al., 1998).

THE "REVISIONIST" MODEL

The word "revisionist" is used by the Quebec historian Ronald Rudin to refer to the work of certain historians who mainly wrote from the end of the 1970s to today (Rudin, 1997). This work is said to be revisionist because it challenges the notion of a traditional and monolithic society before the Quiet Revolution. These historians argue that there was no discrepancy between the popular classes and the elites in Quebec before 1960. On the contrary, support for liberalism was widespread and a French-Canadian bourgeoisie was influential in Canada. Thus, in the eyes of some of the revisionists, the idea of a separate Quebec would be a predictable conclusion for a normal evolution. The revisionists claim that many of the changes that occurred in Quebec were typical of political and social forces operating in all modern societies at the time.

For example, the revisionists point to the ample evidence of urbanization and migration in Quebec in the 1800s. During the nineteenth century, large numbers of French-Canadians moved to urban centres throughout North America. Despite the official but sometimes ambiguous opposition of the Church on the subject of migration, Québécois left their rural homes as early as 1840 and moved to urban centres in New England or to cities in the province of Quebec. From 1850 to 1930, the province's urban population grew steadily. In 1871, only 15 percent of Québ´cois lived in cities. Two decades later, the number had doubled, and by 1921, 52 percent of the people were urban. This figure was above the Canadian average and comparable to that of Ontario. By 2001, Quebec's urban population was 80 percent, the second highest proportion in Canada, just behind Ontario with 83 percent (Linteau et al., 1979; Roy, 1988; Couture and Cardin, 1996).

According to the revisionists, Quebec also housed considerable diversity. At the end of the eighteenth century, people of British origin made up 12.5 percent of the total population. Several thousand of these people were Loyalists who had come to Canada after the American Revolution. During the nineteenth century, the primary source of immigration was Britain, particularly Scotland and Ireland. In this period, 17 million people left Britain, 9 percent of whom came to Canada. These included over 200 000 Irish between 1825 and 1834, and approximately 200 000 more during the Great Famine of 1845–49. About 20 percent of the Irish immigrants settled in Quebec. By the end of the nineteenth century, the predominantly Irish immigration was replaced by East European Jews and Italians. The Jewish population in Quebec grew from 1.5 percent of the total population in 1901 to 5.7 percent in 1941. The Italian population was only 0.5 percent in 1901 and 2.3 percent in 1941. In 1996, the number of people claiming Italian origins totalled 4.2 percent of the Quebec population, while 2.6 percent claimed Jewish origins. According to the 1996 census, the other important groups, each of them making up between 0.5 and 1 percent of the population, were Greek, Portuguese, Chinese, Haitian, Lebanese, and Southeast Asian. Since the Irish immigration of the 1830s and 1840s, Quebec society has been demographically and culturally diverse (Linteau et al., 1979; Bouchard, 2000).

At another level, the history of political parties in Quebec reflects both the evolution of the identity of Québécois and, as in all societies, contradictions within that identity. From 1867 to 1897 the Conservative Party dominated provincial politics, ruling for all but five of those years. The power of the Conservative Party symbolized the alliance between the Church and business, and a commitment to a socially conservative society led by private enterprise. Wilfrid Laurier's victory at the federal level in 1896 propelled the provincial Liberals to power in 1897. They remained in power for half a century, except between 1936 and 1939, until 1944. The Liberals maintained the alliance between the Church and private enterprise. The Church was given a free hand in social affairs and education while the political and economical spheres were left to politicians and business people (Couture and Cardin, 1996).

The domination by the Liberals was interrupted in 1936 when Maurice Duplessis and the Union Nationale party took power. That party resulted from the 1935 merger of the provincial Conservative Party and a group of young Liberal dissidents active during the Depression. The name of the group was l'Action Libérale Nationale and among its aims was nationalization of the private hydroelectricity companies. Once in power, however, Maurice Duplessis, leader of the Union Nationale coalition, did not implement any of the reforms proposed by l'Action Libérale Nationale, and instead ruled the same way the Liberals had.

It was the new leader of the provincial Liberal Party, Adélard Godbout, re-elected in 1939, who enacted the Union Nationale's promised reforms. The Godbout government was perhaps the most socially progressive provincial government of the twentieth century in Quebec. Among its reforms were the right to vote for women at the provincial level, the formation of Hydro-Québec, and reforms in education. But World War II overshadowed its accomplishments when the federal government used its special wartime powers to intervene in provincial affairs. In 1944, the domination of the Liberal Party since 1897 came to an end when, with only 35 percent of the popular vote, Maurice Duplessis was elected and governed until 1959 (Couture and Cardin, 1996).

The Duplessis government was characteristic of the Cold War, being both right-wing and vehemently anti-communist. Opposition to Duplessis' extremely conservative style of government in the 1950s prepared the field for the reforms of the 1960s. When a group of young liberals led by Jean Lesage took power in 1960 it was the beginning of a new era and the period of reforms known as the Quiet Revolution. The Church was replaced by the provincial state in social affairs and the state intervened in the economy to promote French business interests. The emphasis on the provincial state corresponded with a change in the self-identification of many French Canadians in Quebec. Historians still debate the nature and effects of the Quiet Revolution. For some experts, the Quiet Revolution was a period of immense change that at last brought Quebec into the modern world (Bouchard, 2000). For others, the alliance of the Church and business, beginning from at least the second half of the nineteenth century, was a typical contradiction of modernity (Couture, 1998). To these observers, the changes of the 1960s, despite their magnitude, were simply a realignment of political and social forces in an already modern society, which is essentially what the "revisionists" argued.

POST-REVISIONISM

Most of the "revisionist" historiography was written when the Parti Québécois was a dominant force in Quebec politics. Formed in 1968, the Parti Québécois was elected less than a decade later on a clear social-democratic platform. Indeed, between 1976 and 1980, the government of the Parti Québécois initiated many controversial reforms, among them the reform of the automobile insurance system and the enactment of the famous Bill 101 on the regulation of the French language in the province. In 1980, as promised by René Lévesque, the Parti Québécois organized a referendum on the mandate to negotiate a new partnership with Canada referred to as "sovereignty-association" (Taucar, 2000). Many commentators have argued that this new partnership was in fact a proposal for a new confederation, a system where the central state could have very limited powers (Seymour, 1999). Others believe it would have represented a form of secession (Taucar, 2000).

Despite the fact that the question asked at the referendum seemed moderate, the federalist No side won convincingly—60 percent "no" to 40 percent "yes." However, in 1981, the Parti Québécois was re-elected, mainly because the Quebec voters were satisfied with its performance as a responsible government.

In 1983, the Parti Québécois appeared to turn to the right ideologically, coming into conflict with public sector unions and abandoning some of its social-democratic practices. This shift in policy posture played a crucial role in the Parti Québécois, defeat in 1985. Robert Bourassa, who had patiently rebuilt his control over the provincial Liberal Party after his astonishing defeat in 1976, became once again the premier of Quebec in 1985. Caught in the debate and eventual failure of the Meech Lake Accord between 1987 and 1990, and in the controversy of Bill 178 on language regulation in Quebec allowing French and other languages on signs inside stores or public buildings but French only on signs outside buildings, Bourassa managed his way to victory again in 1989 (Couture and Cardin, 1996). But this second mandate was also very controversial, marked by the Oka crisis in the summer of 1990, just after the failure of the Meech Lake Accord, and the no less catastrophic failure of the Charlottetown Accord in 1992. Bourassa was replaced by Daniel Johnson, and in 1994 the Liberal Party was defeated by the Parti Québécois, lead by Jacques Parizeau. One year after this victory, the Parti Québécois, in a second referendum on sovereignty, lost narrowly when the Yes side finished with a surprising 49 percent of votes (Taucar, 2000).

CONCLUSION

Since 1995, Quebec has continued its juggling act between its Quebec identity and its Canadian one. On the question of identity, the American author David Hollinger (1995), referring to the three major political identities of America, proposed the term *affiliation* instead of *identity*. It seems that Quebec also could be referred to as a society with several affiliations. These affiliations are complex, and this chapter only dealt with three affiliations used by several intellectuals to justify the project of an independent Quebec. However, it is clear that such a simplistic representation of Quebec does not do justice to all the contradictions of a society derived from European colonialism and still dealing with the consequences of that colonialism. It would be extremely naive to think that larger nations or societies, like Canada or the United States, do not have to deal with the same fundamental problems (Satzewich, 1992; Yuval-Davis and Stasiulis, 1995). It seems however that, in Quebec, the debates about the content of nationalism are broader and more public. Somehow, the international and national literature in English on Quebec should better reflect these debates.

REFERENCES

Andrew, Caroline (dir.). 1999. *Dislocation et permanence: l'intervention du Canada au Quotidien*. Ottawa: Les Presses de l'Université d'Ottawa.

Balthazar, Louis and Alfred O. Hero Jr. 1999. *Le Québec dans l'espace américain*. Montréal: Québec-Amérique.

Beiner, Ronald and Wayne Norman. 2001. *Canadian Political Philosophy*. Don Mills: Oxford University Press.

Blais, François, Guy Laforest et Diane Lamoureux (dir.). 1995. *Libéralismes et nationalismes: philosophie et politique*. Ste-Foy: Les Presses de l'Université Laval.

Bouchard, Gérard. 2000. *Genèse des nations et cultures du Nouveau Monde. Essai d'histoire comparée*. Montréal: Boréal.

Cantin, Serge. 1997. *Ce pays comme un enfant*. Montréal: L'Hexagone.

Choquette, Leslie. 1997. *De Français à paysans. Modernité et tradition dans le peuplement du Canada français*. Sillery: Septentrion.

Couture, Claude. 1998. *Paddling with the Current*. Edmonton: University of Alberta Press.

Couture, Claude and Jean-François Cardin. 1996. *Espace et differences*. Ste-Foy: Presses de l'Université Laval.

Dickerson, M.O. 1994. *Introduction to Government and Politics*. Scarborough: Nelson Canada.

Dumont, Fernand. 1993. *Genèse de la société québécoise*. Montréal: Boréal.

Dupuis, Renée. 1997. *Tribus, Peuples et Nations: les nouveaux enjeux des revendications autochtones au Canada*. Montréal: Boréal.

———. 2001. *Quel Canada pour les Autochtones: la fin de l'exclusion*. Montréal: Boréal.

Gagnon, Alain. 1990. *Quebec: Beyond the Quiet Revolution*. Scarborough: Nelson Canada.

Greer, Allan. 1997. *The People of New France*. Toronto: University of Toronto Press.

Habermas, Jürgen. 1998. *Après l'État-nation: une nouvelle constellation politique*. Paris: Fayerd.

Hollinger, David A. 1995. *Postethnic America*. New York: Basic Books.

Ignatieff, Michael. 1993. *Blood and Belonging: Journeys into the New Nationalism*. Toronto: Penguin Books.

Jackson, Robert J. 1994. *Politics in Canada*. Scarborough: Prentice-Hall Canada Inc.

Kymlicka, Will. 1989. *Liberalism, Community and Culture*. Don Mills: Oxford University Press.

———. 1995. *Multicultural Citizenship*. Toronto: Oxford University Press.

Laforest, Guy. 1992. *Trudeau et la fin du rêve canadien*. Québec: Septentrion.

Lamonde, Yvan. 2000. *Histoire sociale des idées au Québec (1760-1896)*. Montréal: Fides.

Lamoureux, Diane. 1995. Le patriotisme constitutionnel et les Etats multinationaux. In Blais, François, Guy Laforest, and Diane Lamoureux (dir.). *Libéralismes et nationalismes: philosophie et politique*. Ste-Foy: Les Presses de l'Université Laval.

Lamoureux, Diane, Chantal Maillé, and Micheline de Sève (dir.). 1999. *Malaises identitaires: échanges féministes autour d'un Québec incertain*. Montréal: Les éditions du remue-ménage.

Landes, Ronald. 1995. *The Canadian Polity*. Scarborough: Prentice-Hall.

Le Soleil. Les Cris à l'heure de la Paix des braves (Special dossier on La Paix des braves). (2002, March 25).

Létourneau, Jocelyn. 2000. *Passer à l'avenir, histoire, mémoire, identité dans le Québec d'aujourd'hui*. Montréal: Boréal.

Linteau, Paul-André, et al. 1979. *Histoire du Québec contemporain*. Montréal: Boréal.

Maclure, Jocelyn and Alain Gagnon. 2001. *Repères en mutation. Identité et citoyenneté dans le Québec contemporain*. Montréal: Québec Amérique.

Mathieu, Geneviève. 2001. *Qui est Québécois? Synthèse du débat sur la redéfinition de la nation*. Montreal: VLB Éditeur.

McLean, Iain (ed.). 1996. *The Concise Oxford Dictionary of Politics*. Oxford/New York: Oxford University Press.

McRoberts, Kenneth. 1997. *Misconceiving Canada: The Struggle for National Unity*. Don Mills: Oxford University Press.

Modood, Taria and Pnina Werbner. 1997. *The Politics of Multiculturalism in the New Europe*. London/New York: Zed Books.

Morin, Michel. 1997. *L'usurpation de la souveraineté autochtone*. Montreal: Boréal.

Roy, Fernande. 1988. *Progrès, Harmonie, Liberté. Le libéralisme des milieux d'affaires francophones à Montréal au tournant du siècle*. Montréal: Boréal.

Rudin, Ronald. 1997. *Making History in 20th Century Québec*. Montreal/Kingston: McGill-Queen's University Press.

Sarra-Bournet, Michel (dir.) avec la collaboration de Jocelyn Saint-Pierre 2000. *Les nationalismes au Québec du XIXe au XXe siècle.* Ste-Foy: Les Presses de l'Université Laval.

Satzewich, Vic (ed.). 1992. *Deconstructing a Nation: Immigration, Multiculturalism and Racism in '90s Canada*. Halifax/Saskatoon: Fernwood Publishing/University of Saskatchewan.

Seymour, Michel (dir.). 1999. *Nationalité, citoyenneté et solidarité*. Montréal: Liber.

———. 1999. *La nation en question*. Montreal: Éditions de l'Hexagone.

Strong-Boag, Veronica, Sherrill Grace, Avigail Eisenberg and Joan Anderson (Eds.). 1998. *Painting the Maple: Essays on Race, Gender, and the Construction of Canada.* Vancouver: UBC Press.

Taucar, Christopher Edward. 2000. *Canadian Federalism and Quebec Sovereignty*. New York: Peter Lang Publishing.

Taylor, Charles. 1992. *Rapprocher les solitudes.* Québec: Presses de l'Université Laval.

———. 1994. *Multiculturalism.* Princeton: Princeton University Press.

———. 1994. *Multiculturalisme*. Paris: Aubier.

Thériault, J. Yvon. 1995. *L'identité à l'épreuve de la modernité: écrits politiques sur l'Acadie et les francophonies canadiennes minoritaires*. Moncton: Les Éditions d'Acadie.

Yuval-Davis, Nira and Daiva Stasiulis. 1995. *Unsettling Settler Societies: Articulations of Gender, Race Ethnicity and Class*. London: Sage.

WEBLINKS

Excerpts from Lord Durham's Report, 1838
www.uni.ca/durhamreport.html

History of Quebec Nationalism
www.uni.ca/history.html

Quebec Premier Maurice Duplessis
www.wednesday-night.com/Duplessis.asp

chapter three

Rethinking Aboriginal Governance

Kiera Ladner

INTRODUCTION

Most Canadians know very little about Aboriginal peoples, and even less about Indigenous political traditions or contemporary political agendas. Most Canadians have never given much thought to the topic of colonization and how Europeans legally justified their occupation of Aboriginal lands. Similarly, most have never contemplated the meaning of Aboriginal governance prior to colonization and how it is that European explorers and theorists "invented" democracy, individual rights, liberty, freedom, and federalism in the Americas. Likewise, most have never thought about how Aboriginal peoples dealt with colonization and attempted to integrate the invading nations into their own constitutional orders using treaty federalism. That said, the majority of Canadians would likely be aware that there is political unrest in "Indian country" and that Aboriginal peoples are demanding self-government; however, many would be unable to explain why this is so.

With the patriation of the Canadian Constitution in 1982, the idea of Aboriginal governance emerged as an issue of debate among Canadians, particularly among students of Canadian politics. There was very little discussion of this topic in academic and political circles prior to 1982. Since this time, however, the number of studies of self-government has grown astronomically, as has the number of public policy initiatives. That said, while they have studied issues such as self-government, most scholars have not really studied "Indigenous" politics and governance. Instead they have begun mainly to study the interplay between Indigenous people and the settler-state, from the colonial perspective. For example, when Aboriginal politics is addressed in the field's main introductory texts, Aboriginal people are typically portrayed as representing an "ethno-linguistic cleavage." And self-government is typically depicted as a claim against the state resulting from historical governmental policies (Whittington and Williams, 1995); contemporary constitutional and policy debates (Brock, 1995); demographic changes within Aboriginal communities with respect to education, urbanization, and acculturation; and the perceived immorality and injustice of colonization which has resulted in abnormally high rates of substance abuse, suicide, incarceration, and unemployment (Dyck, 1996).

In depicting Aboriginal politics as the interaction of Aboriginal people and the state, the existence of Indigenous political traditions and the entire pre-colonial histories of Indigenous people are ignored. Heeding the age-old adage that it is impossible to move forward without understanding where we have been, this chapter attempts to rectify problems associated with existing scholarship by providing the reader with a new understanding of history. Simply stated, this chapter is a rethinking of our shared history of colonialism in Canada. It attempts to shed light on the past, present, and future of colonialism as it pertains to Aboriginal governance, explores the possibility of de-colonizing Aboriginal nations and the Canadian nation(s), and examines the relationship that exists between them.

RETHINKING COLONIZATION

In 1492 Columbus sailed the ocean blue and discovered America. In reality, the Indigenous inhabitants of Turtle Island discovered in 1492 a very lost and starving Christoble Colone searching for a new route to India. Since the time of this "great discovery," when people found Colone (a.k.a. Columbus) at the shores of their territory, this land and its peoples, wrongly referred to as Indians, have inhabited the imaginations of the world. Initially, the land and its bountiful wealth set astir the minds of European nobility and mercantilists who envisioned capitalizing on the riches of the new world to sustain the old world. In time, the land and its bountiful riches (renewable and non-renewable resources—including humans) were captured in the "American Dream." This "dream" still inspires people from around the globe to migrate to and/or "explore" the New World with the same hope of capitalizing upon its wealth and beauty. The Indigenous people's "discovery" of Colone at the shores of the Americas led to European knowledge of these lands and roused the minds of those seeking new wealth. Knowledge of the Americas and the peoples who lived there also captured the minds and imaginations of some of Europe's greatest political philosophers: More, Hobbes, Locke, Rousseau, Marx, Spencer, and Engels, to name but a few (Brandon, 1986). These "great" philosophers spent much time contemplating the life of the pre-colonial "savage," who they assumed lived the way Europeans had in some pre-historical time.

There exists a growing body of literature examining the relationship between the Indigenous peoples of the Americas and the Enlightenment (Gillespie, 1920). That is to say, there is evidence to suggest that the "Indian" influenced Western-Eurocentric political philosophy, and that in some cases, this influence constituted an implicit recognition of Indigenous political traditions and Indigenous political systems. For example, some argue that John Locke recognized the existence of government in the Americas and borrowed extensively from Indigenous political traditions. This view is supported by the fact that Locke had in his library 195 titles regarding voyages and travel "most of which described trips to the Americas by European explorers" (Arneil, 1993, 1).

Still, there are some who reject the idea that Enlightenment thinkers such as Locke recognized that Indigenous peoples in the Americas had separate and distinct political traditions worthy of study and emulation by European societies. Notwithstanding, a growing body of literature shows that Indigenous ideas and practices contributed to how concepts such as rights, liberty, happiness, equality, democracy, and federalism were understood by American founding fathers. Not only did Indigenous political traditions influence the ideas of the American forefathers, but there is much evidence to suggest that these leaders emulated the Haudenosaunee political system of he Iroquois confederacy. (Johansen, 1998). In so doing, they institutionalized Indigenous ideas and practices in the uniquely American federal and congressional system they created.

From the outset of the invasion of America, many Western-Eurocentric political theorists recognized Indigenous peoples as having separate and distinct political traditions worthy of both study and emulation. Similarly, many legal scholars were captivated by questions pertaining to the nature of Aboriginal rights, the existence of Aboriginal governments, and the relationship between these peoples, European nations, and the Papacy (the source of law at this time). In answering such questions, one scholar—Francisco de Vitoria—is credited with being one of the fathers of both international law and the European theory of Aboriginal rights (Davies, 1991, 21). It was as a "discoverer" of the Doctrine of Discovery, and a primary advisor to the Papacy, that Vitoria determined that both Indigenous peoples and their nations have rights. According to Vitoria, international law was not to be limited to the dealings between Christian monarchs, as certain laws were applicable to all nations, be they Christian or infidel. All nations held dominion over their lands and could not be unlawfully deprived of their possessions or sovereignty. While the right to discover the New World was granted by the Pope, the rights of discovery merely protected a nation's discoveries from the encroachment of other Europeans and allowed them the right to trade with the Indian and convert them to Christianity (de Vitoria, 1991, 277–92). Unless the land was determined to be unoccupied or *terra nullius* (as Australia and parts of British Columbia were erroneously deemed), the only means that European nations had of acquiring sovereignty over the territories discovered were "just war" or treaty (Churchill, 1998). Thus, the Indigenous peoples of the Americas were not only recognized by leading European scholars as having separate and distinct political systems, but they were recognized as constituting sovereign nations within both international law and European theories of Aboriginal rights.

Rethinking the Colonization of Canada

The Pope "gave" European nations dominion over the Americas, thus allowing Europeans to carve up and divide the "new" world amongst themselves. International law, meanwhile, established the terms of this dominion and the relationship between the colonizer and the colonized. As a domestication of principles of international law, King George III's Royal Proclamation of 1763 set forth the British doctrine pertaining to the rights of Aboriginal peoples and the colonization of the Americas. Referring to Aboriginal peoples as "nations," the proclamation established in British law the recognition of Aboriginal nationhood. As nations, Indigenous peoples could not be deprived of their territory without first granting consent through the negotiation of treaties between these distinct political systems and the Crown or its agent. It should be noted, however, that while First Nations were considered nations under international law, they were not accorded all of the rights of nations by the invaders, for to have done so would have precluded colonization. As Sharon Venne notes: "international law requires that a sovereign enters into formal agreements with another people's sovereign prior to entering lands occupied by those people." Treaties did not ensure for Indigenous peoples a place within the family of nations (Venne, 1998, 9).

Still, as most contemporary versions of history attest, despite their clear imperial ambitions, in practice, colonizing European powers recognized that Aboriginal nations were autonomous political units and capable of governing their own affairs (RCAP, Vol. 1, 1996, 130). This recognition of Aboriginal nationhood and the necessity of nation-to-nation relationships is further exemplified by the structure of the British Imperial Indian Department. This department "was a foreign office in every sense [as] department agents could not command; they could only employ the ordinary tools of the diplomat: cajolery, coercion, bribery, or, put more politely, persuasion" in dealing with Indigenous nations (Milloy, 1983, 56).

The idea that the Royal Proclamation and other British policies and practices recognized and affirmed the existence of Aboriginal nationhood and the continuing sovereignty of these nations is also supported by the courts. According to James (Sákéj) Youngblood Henderson, since 1705 the courts have recognized and affirmed the status of Aboriginal peoples as nations and the existence of nation-to-nation relationships. In 1705, a Royal Commission (supported by a decision of the Judicial Committee of the Privy Council) found the Mohegan nation to be a "sovereign nation [which] was not subservient to the colony" (Henderson, 1996, 6). Sovereign and not subservient, despite the fact that it had signed a treaty in 1659 and that Connecticut claimed jurisdiction (through a royal charter) over the Mohegans and their lands. During the early 1800s, the United States Supreme Court issued several decisions, based upon the 1763 Royal Proclamation and international law, in which Chief Justice Marshall recognized that "native nations within North America were 'nations like any other' in the sense that they possessed both territories they were capable of ceding, and recognizable governmental bodies empowered to cede these areas through treaties" (Churchill, 1993, 43–44).

Similarly, in *Connolly* v. *Woolrich* (1867), the Superior Court of Quebec recognized "Aboriginal peoples as autonomous nations living under the protection of the Crown, retaining their territorial rights, political organizations and common laws" (RCAP, Vol. 2, 1996, 188). The Royal Commission on Aboriginal Peoples (RCAP) not only accepts this case as justifying the inherent right to self-government, it argues that this case has, in fact, recognized Aboriginal rights and Treaty rights as a source of constitutional law right from the beginning. According to RCAP, this means that "the sources of law and authority in Canada are more diverse than is sometimes assumed. They include the common law and political systems of Aboriginal nations in addition to the standard range of Euro-Canadian sources" (1993, 7). This also means that "the courts have periodically upheld the original relationship between newcomers and Aboriginal peoples and enforced the rights it embraced. Among these was the right of Aboriginal peoples to conduct their affairs under their own laws, within a larger constitutional framework linking them with the Crown" (RCAP, 1993, 8).

During the early contact period, in accordance with principles of international law, constitutional law, and common law, colonial nations (France, Britain, and Canada) respected Aboriginal structures of governance and did not attempt to interfere with such internal matters. Further, it should be noted that, by law, colonial nations were forbidden to destroy or dismantle a nation's independence and structure of governance; the courts recognized the sovereignty (albeit limited) of Indigenous nations and the necessity of non-interference with said matters of sovereignty, jurisdiction, and autonomy. European nations did of course also use the law for their own purposes, often to justify colonization, genocide, and dispossession.

It is often argued that Europeans did not consider treaties as a means of establishing a relationship between two sovereign nations. Many scholars argue that treaties represent the prelude to the subjugation of Aboriginal peoples by Europeans at the time of first contact (Sprague, 1996, 341). This vision of treaty relationships has been a dominant position throughout Canadian history. Nonetheless, it is inconsistent with reality. During the period in which most treaties were signed, incoming Europeans (at least initially) were dependent upon Aboriginal peoples economically and politically and as such they recognized Indigenous polities as constituting nations and dealt with them as such. According to James Tully, the negotiators were quite aware that the Aboriginal peoples did not have European-style states and governing institutions, but this did not "cause them to situate the Aboriginal peoples in a lower stage of development" (Tully, 1995, 121).

This interpretation of the spirit and intent of the treaties between First Nations and the colonizing nations is commonly referred to as treaty federalism or treaty constitutionalism. In 1996, treaty federalism was accepted as both a valid understanding of the past and an acceptable vision of the future by the Royal Commission on Aboriginal Peoples. As RCAP concludes "the terms of the Canadian federation are found not only in formal constitutional documents governing relations between the federal and provincial governments but also in treaties and other instruments establishing the basic links between Aboriginal peoples and the Crown" (1996, RCAP, Vol. 2, 193–4).

COLONIAL PARADIGM SHIFTS: FROM ALLIES TO THE "INDIAN PROBLEM"

Treaties typically established a relationship of non-interference between coequals, allowing each nation to govern within its own area of jurisdiction in accordance with its political traditions (Henderson, 1994, 241–332). As soon as circumstances allowed, however, the colonizing nations legislated an authoritative regime of colonialism and genocide. To this end, at the same time as the Canadian government was negotiating treaty federalism, it was fine-tuning its genocidal goals of protection, civilization and assimilation (Tobias, 1991, 127–44). Following the War of 1812, colonial authorities began interfering directly with the internal autonomy and sovereignty of several Indigenous nations. They did so by destroying traditional structures of governance and institutionalizing their own "puppet" regimes which were supposed to aid in the goal of "civilizing" the Indian, politically, economically, socially, and religiously.

How and why was colonialism transformed from nation-to-nation relationships to a relationship characterized by oppression and domination? There are several explanations, all of which are historically accurate. According to RCAP, in the early 1800s changes occurred in the relationship between Aboriginal and non-Aboriginal peoples. Irrespective of the law or the status quo, new policies and practices were enacted by the colonizers (initially in eastern Canada and subsequently throughout the country) that led to the establishment and institutionalization of a new relationship based upon principles of inequality and subjugation. These changes were precipitated by socio-political (population, economic, and military) shifts in the colonies, which dramatically altered the balance of power in favour of the colonial nations. Also, as Darwin's and Spencer's theories of scientific racism and of the "dying race" gained credibility and importance, the relationship between the colonizer and the colonized became racialized. And, "the transition in the relationship was also pushed by the Western belief in 'progress' and in the evolutionary development in human beings from lesser to greater states of civilization" (RCAP, Vol. 1, 1996, 142). Early settlers saw themselves as more advanced than Aboriginal peoples, and as both culturally and morally superior (Schouls, 2002, 15).

The various interpretations of the disjuncture in the relationship between Aboriginal and non-Aboriginal people are complementary and create a fairly complete understanding of this complex topic. Aboriginal and non-Aboriginal people viewed the treaty process and the terms of the treaties quite differently. Aboriginal leaders tended to view the process and the resulting agreement as "sacred" and as establishing a constitutional order. European leaders seem to have viewed treaties as a means of securing peaceful relations, allies, trading partners, and territory to settle. The treaty order was abandoned as the realities of colonialism changed. Europeans no longer needed Aboriginal people as military and economic allies to survive, and consequently, colonizing nations abandoned the confines of international law for the more liberating ideas of social Darwinism, dominion (the idea that the Christian God had given Europeans dominion over the earth), and European superiority. Thus, while the colonial nations agreed to respect the sovereignty of Aboriginal nations and to establish a treaty order under international law, as soon as circumstances allowed they abandoned international law and institutionalized a new regime based on domestic law.

THE *INDIAN ACT* AND POLITICAL GENOCIDE

In 1876 the new colonial regime was institutionalized in the form of the *Indian Act,* which mandated policies and procedures that amounted to political genocide. The Canadian government had as its goal the "civilization" of Indigenous politics, a goal that amounted to the total destruction of all that was "Indigenous." Indigenous political systems, as well as Indigenous sovereignty and systems of government, were forcefully replaced with colonial structures and so-called civilized governance.

The federal government's policy of creating "civilized governments" in effect meant replacing inclusive, consensual, and democratic Indigenous political systems with the undemocratic and unrepresentative system of the colonizers. Arguably, the practice of "civilizing government" had the opposite effect of getting rid of the truly "civilized" form of government. Many Indigenous nations, such as the Haudenosaunee and the Blackfoot Confederacy, had developed complex democratic political systems. Most of these political systems were consensual and were predicated on the belief that everyone (including women) were to be represented in the decision-making process and in the decision itself. Colonial governments and their European counterparts, on the other hand, were at the time fairly unrepresentative and undemocratic. These so-called democracies excluded those who were not considered "persons" (women and people of colour) and those who were deemed "unworthy" (the landless, working class majority). It is also interesting to note that it was an Indigenous political system—the federal system of the Haudenosaunee, or Iroquois Confederacy—that inspired and influenced those who created the American political system (Johansen, 1998).

With the *Indian Act*, the Canadian government committed an act of genocide—political and otherwise—by ignoring international law and the domestication of that law, thereby denouncing Indian sovereignty and nationhood. Instead, they "legalized" and institutionalized practices aimed at the total destruction of Indigenous peoples, their political systems, and their ability to exercise sovereignty—or for that matter, even exist—within their own territory. For example, as was typical across "Indian country," the Mohawks of Akwesasne opposed the *Indian Act* and its band council form of government, a political system that functioned as little more than the puppet of the Canadian government. They maintained their traditional structures of governance until they were forced to comply in 1899 when colonial authorities (the RCMP) invaded their territory, murdered Chief Jake Fire, and imprisoned other chiefs (Mitchell, 1989, 118). What this amounted to was government-sanctioned murder of the political leader of a sovereign nation. Murder and the destruction of a political system were thus justified in the name of advancing "civilization" and imposing the "authority" of the Crown and the *Indian Act* system.

The *Indian Act* called for the destruction of Indigenous governments and the forced adoption of a new political system. It also ignored the sovereignty of the Indigenous peoples by limiting the powers of *Indian Act* band councils and subjecting them to the authority of the colonial administration. To this day, *Indian Act* chiefs and councils are only permitted to govern in areas of insignificance by passing bylaws concerning such issues as the use of buildings, noxious weeds, beekeeping, and poultry raising (*Indian Act*, 1985, s. 81). It must be emphasized that, while band councils are allowed to govern in these insignificant areas, even this is limited by and completely dependent on the colonial administration, which retains all powers of disallowance. Until the 1960s, the inferiority and dependency of *Indian Act* band councils was accentuated by the fact that all power on reserves was wielded by Indian Agents—delegates of the Minister of Indian Affairs. Further, most band councils did not even have a copy of the act and none had the means to hire lawyers or consultants to assist them in governing. Even today, the colonial government exercises vast power over inferior and dependent *Indian Act* band councils. For example, the Minister of Indian Affairs controls the electoral process, retains the power to depose and replace a chief and council, defines and controls financial accountability, and reserves the power to disallow all activities of the band council (and for that matter, every band member). Through the *Indian Act,* Canada tells band governments and their citizens what they can and cannot do with respect to everything from birth (by determining band membership) to death (by validating wills).

Indian Act band councils are an imposed system of governance that institutionalized a political system of inferiority and dependency and violated many pre- and post-Confederation treaties. Not surprisingly, most First Nations rejected the *Indian Act* from the outset, and many have been calling for its abolition ever since. The Nehiyaw (Plains Cree), for example, opposed the imposition of the colonial regime following the disappearance of the buffalo in the early 1880s. Visionaries like Big Bear refused to sign Treaty Number Six for reasons pertaining to the immanent imposition of the federal government's genocidal policies and practices of "civilization" and "assimilation." According to Big Bear, he was a free man and the Cree were a free and sovereign people, so no one had the right to confine them in their own territory or tell them how they were to live. They were not to be haltered and led like domesticated animals. Big Bear lobbied the government continuously for a better treaty and for the recognition of Cree sovereignty, to no avail. In the end, in the midst of overwhelming conditions of starvation and disease, Plains Cree warriors under the leadership of War Chiefs Wandering Spirit and Wild Child (Imasees) took matters into their own hands and led what was to become Canada's second "civil war" (the first being the Red River Rebellion), the North West Rebellion of 1885 (Dempsey, 1984).

The Mohawks of Akwesasne also opposed the oppressive colonial regime from the start. In defiance, they held steadfast to the terms of the relationship (nation-to-nation) that they had established between themselves and the colonizer at the outset of the occupation. In so doing, they maintained their traditional structures of governance until 1899 when Canada's military forced their compliance. This, however, did not stop the Mohawks of Akwesasne from continuing their battle against the imposed colonial regime, and they continued to assert their sovereignty and nation-to-nation relationships within Akwesasne, within Canada, and internationally. As part of the Mohawk nation and the Haudenosaunee Confederacy, the people of Akwesasne have pressured the governments of Canada, the United States, and other nation states to recognize the sovereignty of the Confederacy and its constituent nations. In 1927, Deskahth, a Cayuga Confederacy chief, sought entry to League of Nations for the Haudenosaunee. More recently, under the leadership of Mike Mitchell, the *Indian Act* band council of Akwesasne has continued its tradition of challenging the supremacy of the Canadian state, by taking the government of Canada to court over its violation of treaty and Aboriginal rights (*R.* v. *Mitchell*), Aboriginal people have kept their agenda for political change before Canadian governments since Confederation, but most actively in the post–World War II era.

The Canadian government has made many changes to the *Indian Act* over the years. In fact, in an effort to realize its long-standing policy objectives of "civilizing" and "assimilating" the Indian, [white paper] the Canadian government even proposed to eliminate the *Indian Act*. The white paper titled *Statement of the Government of Canada on Indian Policy 1969* set forth the federal government's plan for eliminating the "Indian problem" by means of assimilation. This federal policy paper proposed to dissolve reserves, eliminate "Indian" as a legal category, eliminate the federal responsibility for Indians, and to dismantle the *Indian Act* band. For all intents and purposes, this was the federal government's attempt to bring to fruition its genocidal aims. By eliminating the *Indian* and the *Indian Act* band—thereby destroying all vestiges of nationhood and assimilating Indians as individuals into the Canadian state—the federal government was attempting to make political genocide a final reality. There would be no chance to lay claim to sovereignty and nation-to-nation relationships for there would be no Indians, no Indian governments, no recognized Indian nations, and no Indian territories. Simply stated, there would only be Canadians.

Not surprisingly, Indians condemned the white paper and its vision of modernization, calling instead for an abandonment of the existing colonial regime and a return to nation-to-nation relationships. Aboriginal peoples engaged in mass mobilization and protest—in the streets, in the universities, on reserves, and in Ottawa—by forging new national Aboriginal political organizations (such as the National Indian Brotherhood). Aboriginal peoples were thereby able to force the government to abandon the white paper and the *Indian Act*'s goals of civilization and assimilation. Arguably, however, the federal government has not totally abandoned these goals.

Increasingly since the 1970s, the federal government has responded to the Aboriginal agenda by dealing with Aboriginal demands for self-government and self-determination. Initially, the government responded by engaging in a process of devolution, whereby *Indian Act* band councils were allowed to negotiate the transfer of the administrative responsibility for federal programs pertaining to Indian education, social services, and economic development. Aboriginal people were not satisfied with being granted the ability to simply *administer* federal programs in their communities—sovereign nations and as such should be allowed to do more than administer federal programs. Responding to such assertions and calls for greater control over federal programs, the federal government began negotiating Alternative Funding Agreements (AFAs) with band councils during the 1980s. Similar to federal-provincial equalization payments, AFAs were block-funding agreements which were intended to allow band councils to manage federal programs by distributing financial resources in accordance with community needs and priorities and federal standards. By and large, communities have viewed AFAs as perpetuating the existing colonial regime rather than enabling communities to re-establish self-determination.

THE DAWN OF A NEW ERA? CONSTITUTIONAL REFORM

When the constitutional debate arose in the 1980s, Aboriginal people jumped at the opportunity to become involved and assert their Aboriginal and treaty rights in a new forum. They did so en masse for a variety of reasons, including the fact that the federal government had yet to openly engage in discussions of de-colonizing the authoritative regime of colonialism and political genocide. They also did so because constitutional reform offered both a promise and a threat to Indigenous peoples—the promise of change and the threat to the status quo. That is to say, it offered the promise of realizing the Aboriginal agenda (if only in part) or destroying all hope of positive future change by affirming the constitutionality of the colonial regime. By and large, Aboriginal people pursued constitutional reform in great earnest. Venne highlights this struggle, stating that Aboriginal peoples "sought to participate in the renewal of the constitution on the same footing as the federal government, contending that if Indigenous peoples were to come under the mantle of the Canadian state, it must be as real partners, sharing equitably in determining the political and other powers of the state" (Venne, 1989, 107). After an arduous battle, they emerged victorious—at least on paper, and in the constitution of the settler society.

The revised Canadian Constitution (1982) contains several sections pertaining to the rights of Aboriginal peoples. These sections read as follows:

> 25. The guarantee in this Charter of certain rights and freedoms shall not be construed so as to abrogate or derogate from any aboriginal, treaty or other rights or freedoms that pertain to the Aboriginal peoples of Canada including:
>
> (a) any rights or freedoms that have been recognized by the Royal Proclamation of October 7, 1763; and
>
> (b) any rights or freedoms that now exist by way of land claim agreement or may so be acquired.
>
> 35. (1) The existing aboriginal and treaty rights of aboriginal peoples are hereby recognized and affirmed.
>
> (2) In this Act, "aboriginal peoples of Canada" includes the Indian, Inuit and Metis peoples of Canada.
>
> (3) For greater certainty, in subsection (1) "treaty rights" includes rights that now exist by way of land claims agreements or may so be acquired.
>
> (4) Notwithstanding any other provision of this Act, the aboriginal and treaty rights referred to in subsection (1) are guaranteed equally to male and female persons (Canada, 1989).

If success was indeed obtained, on paper, it was achieved because section 35 recognizes and affirms existing Aboriginal and treaty rights. Treaty rights refer to the obligations that were incurred as a result of the signing of peace, friendship, and land treaties throughout this country between the Crown and First Nations. The exact content of Aboriginal rights are, however, a matter of debate. Michael Asch, for example, argues that Aboriginal rights flow from the fact "that Aboriginal peoples were in sovereign occupation of Canada at the time of contact" and encompass a broad range of economic, social, cultural, and political guarantees (1984, 30). The *Constitution Act, 1982* thus began a new era for Aboriginal politics in Canada. As Noel Lyon explains, "Section 35 renounces the old rules of the game under which the Crown established the courts of law and denied those courts the authority to question sovereign claims made by the Crown" (1988, 100).

This new constitutional order affirms both treaty and Aboriginal rights, as a separate and distinct part of the supreme law of Canada. While the meaning of this as it pertains to issues of Aboriginal governance has been readily debated politically, legally, and scholarly since the 1980s, there is still no agreement. Some Eurocentric thinkers such as Tom Flanagan (2000) argue that little has changed, except that Aboriginal peoples now have the same rights as other Canadians and we can therefore abandon the *Indian Act* and allow Aboriginal peoples to govern themselves as Canadians do—using municipal, provincial, and federal governments. Others, such as Robert Cassidy and Frank Bish (1989), see the Constitution as recognizing a right to Aboriginal self-government. Such a right should allow *Indian Act* band councils to negotiate a municipality-plus style of government (similar to the *Sechelt Indian Band Self-Government Act, 1985)* with the federal government and the respective provincial governments. Meanwhile, many Aboriginal scholars (and other de-colonized thinkers) suggest that the constitutional amendments have restored the treaty order as a constitutional order, thus providing it both recognition and protection. As such, self-government is typically cast as a matter of severing Aboriginal nations from the Canadian state, which requires restoring the nation-to-nation and jurisdictional relationship established in the treaties. Where no treaty is in place, Aboriginal sovereignty and dominion continue to exist and thus it is necessary to negotiate the settler society's rights of occupancy and self-governance. For Aboriginal scholars such as Leroy Little Bear, Patricia Monture-Angus, Mary-Ellen Turpel, Taiaiake Alfred, and James (Sákéj) Youngblood Henderson, the new constitutional order enables Aboriginal peoples to reclaim and reassert their nationhood, sovereignty, and independence. Putting the Aboriginal order on an equal constitutional footing with the colonial order and making self-government a constitutionally protected right would allow Aboriginal people to stop "begging" the federal government for more control over their lives (Henderson, 2000, 161–171).

The *Constitution Act, 1982* inspired Aboriginal peoples to think that change was possible and that a post-colonial future was attainable. Not surprisingly, then, there emerged a reinvigorated demand for self-determination, a de-colonized relationship with the settler state, and a new regime of de-colonization.

Negotiated Inferiority

With the advent of constitutionally recognized Aboriginal and treaty rights it became much easier for Aboriginal peoples to get the government to talk about self-government and dismantling the colonial regime. In 1988, the federal government responded to the persistent Aboriginal agenda by announcing its *Indian Self-Government Community Negotiations* policy (Canada, 1995). Community-based negotiations were to have secured a limited form of self-government (read: self-administration) through the devolution of the government's legal and political responsibilities and its fiscal accountability. As a non-constitutional approach to self-government, community-based negotiations were intended to achieve nothing more than increased self-administration abilities using the processes, standards, and programs established in federal legislation. With this policy the government intended to engage in the negotiation of up to 15 reserve-based self-government agreements at a time.

While no agreements have yet been ratified, these agreements were to have replaced the *Indian Act* and provided *Indian Act* band councils with a very limited form of self-administration by delegating to them the authority to manage "essential" areas. Interestingly enough, many of the "essential" programs and policy areas which were open for negotiation—such as education and social services—were already being devolved to First Nations. From the outset, this policy failed to deliver on the decades-old Aboriginal agenda. It also failed to adequately reflect the new constitutional order, or to even pay lip service to Aboriginal and treaty rights. Moreover, this pilot project involved only 15 of the over 600 *Indian Act* band councils.

In 1995, the federal government adopted the *Federal Policy Guide to Aboriginal Self-Government: The Government of Canada's Approach to Implementation of the Inherent Right and the Negotiation of Self-Government* (Canada, 1995). The Inherent Right Policy recognized that self-government is an inherent Aboriginal right and thus an existing right under section 35 of the *Constitution Act, 1982*. The Inherent Right Policy suggests that Aboriginal people have an inherent right to self-government. Given the treaties and the nation-to-nation relationship that characterized Canada's early history, one may conclude that Aboriginal peoples have an inherent right to exercise authority over their land, constitute a government, and decide on the appropriate structure of said government. Nevertheless, while the Canadian government has recognized that Aboriginal peoples have an inherent right to govern themselves, the operationalization of this right is dependent on negotiations. These negotiations are limited to the jurisdictions, or the list of "essentials", that the federal government is willing to negotiate; for example, governing structures, electoral processes (subject to the *Charter*), Aboriginal languages and cultures, property rights including succession and estates, and on-reserve hunting, fishing, and trapping.

The federal government is "willing" to negotiate the devolution of "essential" program and policy areas, thereby granting Aboriginal peoples the delegated and negotiated ability to administer and/or govern in certain areas. Further to this, the policy also states that the government may also be willing to negotiate other power-sharing arrangements with respect to areas such as divorce, fisheries co-management, and environmental protection. The federal government is willing to negotiate the sharing of law-making authority whereby primary law-making authority would remain with the federal and/or provincial government. Essentially, self-government in non-essential areas means that Aboriginal people can negotiate their inferiority or their ability to "govern" (administer) for a superior in an area insofar as they comply with the policies and programs of the responsible government. As such, one must ask whether self-government is actually self-government and not "self-administration" or "negotiated inferiority" and whether the federal government's policy respects Indigenous visions of self-determination, Aboriginal governance, and sovereignty.

"Permitting" *Indian Act* band councils to administer and/or share law-making authority in certain areas, and enabling these councils to negotiate their ability to "govern" in essential areas is a step up from the *Indian Act*. Still, federal policy directives have completely failed to provide for the negotiation of a renewed relationship—a nation-to-nation relationship based upon principles of de-colonization and treaty federalism. Instead, the federal government perpetuates a vision of a relationship between *unequal* partners in Confederation. It holds a vision unacceptable to many Aboriginal peoples because it contradicts international law, treaties, the new constitutional order, the inherent right of self-determination, Aboriginal nationhood, the Aboriginal agenda, de-colonization, sovereignty, and the meaning of true partnerships. Regardless of what the treaties say, the federal vision assumes that Aboriginal peoples are not true nations and it fundamentally rejects the idea of sharing jurisdictions (power). Aboriginal peoples are expected to negotiate their inferiority by accepting the responsibility for jurisdictions over which the federal and provincial governments maintain sovereignty.

It is reasonable to ask why a nation would engage in negotiations when federal policies neither enable Aboriginal peoples to govern themselves in accordance with their own political systems nor recognize and affirm the nation-to-nation relationship. First Nations have not waited for scholars, lawyers, judges, and politicians to answer this question or for Canada to abandon colonization. Instead, they have taken the opportunity that these policies have created and have engaged the colonial administration in discussions pertaining to self-government. Often these discussions have been futile, as government goals and objectives hinder (if not oppose) the realization of the Aboriginal agenda. This has been the case even when that agenda has been compromised and dovetailed by the Aboriginal peoples themselves or limited to a demand for increased administrative and managerial responsibilities with respect to Aboriginal peoples and their land. Still, while no agreements have ever been finalized using the community-based negotiations policy, many agreements have been negotiated (for example, Sechelt, Nisga'a, and Nunavut) using the Inherent Right Policy, land-claim negotiations, and other negotiation strategies. Moreover, there are numerous communities that are engaged in negotiations or that have ratified agreements pertaining to sectoral devolution using the Inherent Right Policy or the *First Nations Land Management Act, 1999*. For example, using the devolution policy stipulated in the *Land Management Act*, several First Nations have been allowed to take on managerial responsibilities over issues pertaining to lands (such as the removal of septic tanks).

In negotiating these agreements (be they funding arrangements, land-claim agreements, or self-government agreements) the Canadian government deals with *Indian Act* band councils. Thus, one may argue that the *Indian Act*—an instrument of oppression and domination used to "protect," "civilize," and "assimilate" the Indian—could become the foundation for a new relationship. This is because *Indian Act* band councils have become the vehicle by which self-government is implemented and government-to-government relationships realized. That being said, it can be argued that this possibility perpetuates colonialism. It denies the existence of Indigenous political systems and continues to further the goal of civilizing and assimilating the Indian politically. Further, it denies Aboriginal peoples the opportunity to decide how they wish to govern themselves and quite possibly, how they wish to rebuild and re-establish Indigenous law and governance as the primary authority. Using the *Indian Act* as the foundation upon which to build a new relationship is surely not going to result in a true partnership. Rather, it will remain a paternalistic relationship among unequal and politically dependent governments. This is demonstrated by Nisga'a self-government. Nisga'a Elder Rod Robinson states that "according to Nisga'a legend the Creator grouped the Nisga'a into four tribes (the eagle, wolf, raven and the killer whale) and placed them on the Nass/Lisims River—The Creator also gave us laws to guide and regulate our lives " (2002, 187). While representatives of these four tribes negotiated a land-claim and self-government agreement with the federal government in accordance with the Creator's laws (as well as those made using this traditional political system), the self-government agreement is in many ways a culmination of the federal government's policies of civilization and assimilation because it institutionalized the *Indian Act* band council as Nisga'a government. Thus, the agreement transforms ("civilizes") and assimilates Nisga'a government and Nisga'a nationhood into the Canadian state as an inferior government with delegated responsibilities.

CHARTING A COURSE FORWARD

To summarize, the federal government envisions a renewed relationship based on an *unequal* partnership in Confederation or a superficial partnership between unequal and artificially created orders of government such as *Indian Act* band councils. This ignores the past (i.e., treaties) in order to create a renewed relationship of political genocide, colonial oppression, Western superiority, and negotiated inferiority. Thus, the federal government has fallen short of proposing an acceptable alternative to the colonial paradigm. Colonialism is still colonialism, no matter how it is disguised. For Canada to survive as a nation and for Aboriginal peoples to survive as nations, we must step beyond the colonial paradigm and begin the process of creating a post-colonial existence through de-colonization.

Aboriginal peoples have been arguing for the creation of a post-colonial state since the occupation began. They were not willing to allow Europeans to assert their authority over the people and their land, no matter what the law or the European theory of Aboriginal rights said. Moreover, they had achieved some success. Aboriginal peoples had their own laws, their own governments, and their own ways of dealing with the occupier. The treaties and the nation-to-nation relationship precluded the colonization of nations and attempted to establish a new "constitutional" order of treaty federalism, which specified the rights of all nations within the occupied territories.

What Indigenous peoples have been arguing for is an arrangement that ends their colonization and reaffirms their Aboriginal and treaty rights. Since colonialism began, Aboriginal peoples have been fighting for the right to govern themselves, in accordance with their own political and legal traditions (if they so choose) and in accordance with tenets of post-colonialism. Unfortunately there is no one vision of what post-colonialism and de-colonization mean. For some, de-colonization or post-colonialism means working towards the end of colonialism and thus, separating each nation and their respective traditions. For others, it means putting an end to genocide (all forms) and colonialism and renewing and rebuilding a non-hierarchical relationship of peace, respect, multinational sovereignty, sharing, non-coercion, and equality. For RCAP it means establishing a renewed relationship based on four principles: mutual recognition, mutual respect, sharing, and mutual responsibility. Mutual recognition, would mean that "Aboriginal and non-Aboriginal people acknowledge and relate to one another as equals, co-existing side by side and governing themselves according to their own laws and institutions" (RCAP, Vol. 1, 1996, 678). This renewed relationship would also be characterized by mutual respect, a (more equitable) sharing in the benefits derived from the lands upon which Aboriginal and non-Aboriginal people co-exist, and mutual responsibility whereby the colonial relationship would be transformed into a true partnership in which each partner has "a duty to act responsibly both toward one another and also to the land they share" (RCAP, Vol. 1, 1996, 689).

De-colonization means all of this. In terms of Aboriginal governance and the relationship between the colonizer and the colonized, de-colonization and post-colonialism mean allowing each nation to chart its own course forward and to decide how it is to govern itself and relate to other nations. Many Indigenous and Eurocentric thinkers alike thought these demands to be answered with the *Constitution Act, 1982*. But while the new constitutional order articulates a post-colonial vision based on treaty and Aboriginal rights, it has yet to be realized and mass de-colonization—of both Indigenous nations and settler society—has yet to occur.

De-colonization remains the only acceptable and viable path forward. The process of de-colonization is complex and multifaceted, for which there is no one path, and possibly no one unifying goal. Some see the goal as "recapturing an almost lost tradition," (Bedford and Pobihushchy, 1994, 28) while others strive to "replace the sameness of universality with the concepts of diversity, complimentarity, flexibility and equity or fundamental fairness" (Henderson, 2000, 268). A third view holds that de-colonization represents the process by which we attempt to address our present state of existence, brought about by over 500 years of occupation. De-colonization means attempting to end the paradigm paralysis which Canada is currently experiencing by putting a stop to the colonization of Indigenous peoples and their collectivities and deconstructing and then reconstructing Canadian society and Canadian institutions to reflect and embrace the new constitutional order built upon those original treaty agreements and relationships.

Canada has yet to attain the status of a post-colonial state because Aboriginal collectivities continue to be oppressed and dominated and are unable to interact with and within Canadian institutions (and even Canadian society) in a manner reflective of their status and history as nations. Several scholars have attempted to overcome this paradigm paralysis by theorizing new ways to conceptualize self-government. The problem with many of these visions, however, is that they abandon the past and theorize a new future. As RCAP has argued, the past cannot be ignored. Rather it should serve as the foundation upon which to build a renewed relationship and a more equitable and prosperous future. According to the commissioners: "it would be false and unjust to suggest that we start entirely anew, false and unjust to attempt to wipe the slate clean, ignoring both the wrongs of the past and the rights flowing from our previous relationships and interactions" (RCAP, Vol. 1, 1996, 676–677).

De-colonization involves a renewed relationship for *both* Canadians and First Nations. De-colonizing Canada necessitates, among other paradigmatic shifts, a re-education of society as to the true history of colonization. De-colonization also requires Canadian society to decide how it sees itself, how it wants to govern in a post-colonial order, and how it wants to define and realize that post-colonial order. Further, de-colonization means creating the necessary pre-conditions for negotiating a renewed relationship and thus ending the perpetuation of the colonial paradigm which sustains the oppression and domination of the Indigenous peoples and their occupied territories. A de-colonized Canada would no longer seek to control, dominate, and oppress Aboriginal nations, peoples and lands. De-colonization would mean that Canada would honour its obligations, rights, and responsibilities vis-à-vis Aboriginal and treaty rights. Finally, de-colonization would entail renewing the nation-to-nation relationship and principles of treaty federalism—meaning that Canada would have to come to the realization that it is just one of many nations with which power and resources must be shared.

Aboriginal communities also need de-colonization. In *Journeying Forward* (1999), Monture-Angus argues that de-colonization is more a matter of Aboriginal peoples asserting and attaining independence than it is about self-government and sovereignty. To deal with the "Indian problem" communities need to overcome their dependencies (i.e., emotional, physical, economic, political, substance) and renew their communities from the ground up. Grassroots leaders (women) need to engage in collective healing beginning with themselves and their families and work towards the assertion of political, economic, and legal independence from the Canadian state and the re-establishment of Indigenous ways of living. Meanwhile, in *Peace, Power, Righteousness* (1999). Alfred asserts that de-colonization can be achieved through the retraditionalization of leadership and political processes (Taiaiake, 1999). If leadership were "traditional" in thinking and action and if leaders governed according to the principles of the *Haudenosaunee* Great Law of Peace (peace, power, and righteousness) then they would engage in the transformation and re-traditionalization of the community.

Whether one focuses attention on the grassroots (Monture-Angus) or the leadership (Taiaike), both authors agree that Aboriginal communities are in need of de-colonization. In accordance with the new constitutional order, which recognizes and affirms the "Indigenous" as a parallel constitutional order, Aboriginal peoples need to engage in a process of personal and collective de-colonization (mental, physical, spiritual, and emotional). Further, they need to rebuild their communities, rebuild their languages, traditions, histories, economies, and political and legal systems (among other social phenomena) and assert independence as both individuals and nations. Finally, they need to construct a de-colonized vision of themselves and set forth a plan for the realization of a post-colonial community. What this would mean and how this could be achieved is dependent on the community (both grassroots and leaders) and will vary between communities.

At the same time that Indigenous nations and the settler society (or societies) are de-colonizing themselves and in accordance with the new constitutional order, the relationship between these nations has to be de-colonized. According to many scholars the most viable means of de-colonizing this relationship is to establish treaty federalism. Briefly, treaty federalism (or Tully's treaty constitutionalism) is premised on the idea that the treaties between the various Indigenous and colonial nations established (in law) federal relationships between these nations. In so doing, the treaties created the "treaty order" or "treaty federalism" as a constitutional order of asymmetrical federalism (asymmetrical because each treaty and each treaty relationship is different). This constitutional order is separate and distinct from the federal relationships established by the "Canadian order" or "provincial federalism" in the Constitution to govern the relationships between the immigrant societies. Treaty federalism, as distinct from contemporary federalism, refers to the federal (nation-to-nation) relationships established in the treaties and the division of powers that emerged from these agreements. While the specificities of jurisdiction varied from treaty to treaty, generally speaking the treaties "are written agreements that embody a consensual balance between reserved Aboriginal rights and certain delegated rights [to the Crown;] those Aboriginal rights not delegated remain in the customary law of Aboriginal nations. Together they define a new constitutional order of self-determination for Aboriginal peoples" (Henderson, 1994, 244).

CONCLUSION

There is a sense of uncertainty among Aboriginal people as to why RCAP and scholars such as Tully (1995), LaSelva (1996), and Barsh favour treaty federalism as a means of de-colonizing "Canada" and the relationships among the "nations in Canada." Likewise, there is uncertainty as to what treaty federalism would look like today. Still, it is a viable and mutually beneficial vision of a de-colonized future with de-colonized relationships, wherein we must reclaim our collective past by reaffirming those constitutional agreements (treaties) that established the way we could all live here as separate and self-governing nations. This is as necessary as the de-colonization of the nations. Without a de-colonized relationship or a renewal of treaty federalism, jurisdictions and resources will never be distributed for the mutual benefit of all, and the colonial paradigm of political genocide and negotiated inferiority will be perpetuated.

It is difficult to say what a post-colonial "Canada" will look like, and equally challenging to say exactly how de-colonization should proceed or how the new constitutional order of post-colonialism could be achieved. No one has a clear impression of what treaty federalism would look like today. It is clear, however, that the future of "Canada" is dependent on our ability to dream our way forward both collectively and as individual nations. We all share this responsibility.

REFERENCES

Arneil, Barbara. 1993. "All the World was America: John Locke and the Defense of Colonialism." Paper presented at the Canadian Political Science Association Annual Conference. Carleton University.

Asch, Michael. 1984. *Home and Native Land: Aboriginal Rights and the Canadian Constitution*. Toronto: Methuen Publications.

Bedford, David and Sidney Pobihushchy. 1994. "Aboriginal Voter Participation." Paper presented at the Canadian Political Science Annual Meeting. University of Calgary.

Brandon, William. 1986. *New Worlds for Old: Reports from the New World and Their Effect on the Development on Social Thought in Europe: 1500–1800*. Athens: Ohio University Press.

Brock, Kathy L. 1995. "Native Peoples on the Road to Self-Government." In Robert M. Krause and R.H. Wagenberg, (Eds.) *Introductory Readings in Canadian Government and Politics, 2nd edition*. Toronto: Copp Clark.

Canada. 1985. *Indian Act*. Ottawa: Public Works and Government Services Canada.

Canada. 1989. *The Constitution Acts 1867 to 1982*. Ottawa: Department of Justice.

Canada. 1995. *Federal Policy Guide Aboriginal Self-Government: The Government of Canada's Approach to Implementation of the Inherent Right and the Negotiations of Self-Government*. Ottawa: Public Works and Government Services Canada.

Cassidy, Frank and Robert L. Bish. 1989. *Indian Government: Its Meaning in Practice*. Lantzville, BC: Oolichan Books.

Churchill, Ward A. 1993. *Struggle for the Land: Indigenous Resistance to Genocide, Ecocide and Expropriation in Contemporary North America*. Monroe, Maine: Common Courage Press.

Churchill, Ward A. 1998. *Little Matter of Genocide: Holocaust and Denial in the Americas 1492 to the Present*. Winnipeg: Arbeiter Ring Publishing.

Davies, Maureen. 1991. "Aspects of Aboriginal Rights in International Law." In Bradford W. Morse (ed.) *Aboriginal People and the Law: Indian, Metis and Inuit Rights in Canada*. Ottawa: Carleton University Press.

de Vitoria, Francisco. 1991. In Anthony Pagden and Jeremy Lawrance (Eds.) *Political Writings*. Cambridge: Cambridge University Press.

Dempsey, Hugh A. 1984. *Big Bear: The End of Freedom*. Vancouver: Douglas and McIntyre.

Dyck, Rand. 1996. *Canadian Politics: Critical Approaches*, 2nd ed. Scarborough: Nelson.

Erasmus, Georges and Joe Sanders. 2002. "Canadian History: An Aboriginal Perspective." In John Bird, Lorraine Land and Murray MacAdam (Eds.) *Nation to Nation: Aboriginal Sovereignty and the Future of Canada*. Toronto: Irwin Publishing.

Flanagan, Thomas. 2000. *First Nations, Second Thoughts*. Montreal/Kingston: McGill-Queens University Press.

Gillispie, James E. 1920. *The Influence of Overseas Expansion on England to 1700*. New York: Columbia University Press.

Henderson, James (Sákéj) Youngblood. 1994. "Empowering Treaty Federalism." *Saskatchewan Law Review*, 58.

———. 1996. "First Nations Legal Inheritances in Canada: The Mikmaq Model." *Manitoba Law Journal 23*, (January).

———. 2000. "Post-Colonial Ledger Drawing." In Marie Battiste (ed.), *Reclaiming Indigenous Voice and Vision*. Vancouver: University of British Columbia Press.

———. 2000. "Ayukpach: Empowering Aboriginal Thought." In Marie Battiste (ed.), *Reclaiming Indigenous Voice and Vision*. Vancouver: University of British Columbia Press.

Johansen, Bruce E. 1998. *Debating Democracy: Native American Legacy of Freedom*. Santa Fe, New Mexico: Clear Light Publishers.

LaSelva, S.V. 1996. *The Moral Foundations of Canadian Federalism: Paradoxes, Achievements and Tragedies of Nationhood*. Montreal: McGill-Queens University Press.

Lyon, Noel. 1988. "An Essay on Constitutional Interpretation." *Osgoode Hall Law Journal 26,* 95.

Milloy, John S. 1983. "The Early Indian Acts: Developmental Strategy and Constitutional Change." In Ian A.L. Getty and Antoine S. Lussier, (eds.) *As Long as the Sun Shines and Water Flows*. Vancouver: University of British Columbia Press.

Mitchell, Michael. 1989. "An Unbroken Assertion of Sovereignty." In Boyce Richardson, (ed.) *Drumbeat: Anger and Renewal in Indian Country*. Toronto: Summerhill Press.

Monture-Angus, Patricia. 1999. *Journeying Forward: Dreaming First Nations Independence*. Halifax: Fernwood Publishing.

Robinson, Rod. 2002. "Nisga'a Patience: Negotiating Our Way into Canada." In John Bird, Lorraine Land and Murray MacAdam (eds.), *Nation to Nation: Aboriginal Sovereignty and the Future of Canada*. Toronto: Irwin Publishing.

Royal Commission on Aboriginal Peoples (RCAP). 1993. *Partners in Confederation: Aboriginal Peoples, Self-Government and the Constitution*. Ottawa: Canada Communications Group.

———. 1996. *Report of the Royal Commission on Aboriginal Peoples*, Vol. 1. Ottawa: Canada Communications Group.

———. 1996. *Report of the Royal Commission on Aboriginal Peoples*, Vol. 2. Ottawa: Canada Communications Group.

Schouls, Tim. 2002. "The Basic Dilemma: Sovereignty or Assimilation." In John Bird, Lorraine Land and Murray MacAdam (Eds.), *Nation to Nation: Aboriginal Sovereignty and the Future of Canada*. Toronto: Irwin Publishing.

Sprague, D.N. 1996, January. "Canada's Treaties with Aboriginal Peoples." *Manitoba Law Journal 23.*

Taiaiake, Alfred. 1999. *Peace, Power and Righteousness: An Indigenous Manifesto*. Don Mills: Oxford Unviersity Press.

Tobias, John L. 1991. "Protection, Civilization, Assimilation: An Outline History of Canada's Indian Policy." In *Sweet Promises: A Reader on Indian-White Relations in Canada*. Toronto: University of Toronto Press.

Tully, James. 1995. *Strange Multiplicity: Constitutionalism in an Age of Diversity*. Cambridge: Cambridge University Press.

Venne, Sharon Helen. 1989. "Treaties and the Constitution in Canada." In Ward Churchill, (ed.) *Critical Issues in Native North America*. Copenhagen: International Working Group for Indigenous Affairs.

Venne, Sharon Helen. 1998. *Our Elders Understand our Rights: Evolving International Law Regarding Indigenous Rights*. Penticton: Theytus Books.

Whittington, Michael S. and Glen Williams. 1995. *Canadian Politics in the 1990s*. Scarborough: Nelson.

WEBLINKS

Assembly of First Nations

www.afn.ca
Indian and Northern Affairs Canada

www.inac.gc.ca
Repeal Indian Act

www.members.shaw.ca/repeal-indian-act

chapter four

Changing Conceptions of the Public Interest

Daniel Cohn

INTRODUCTION

This chapter looks first at one recent effort to demonstrate that all Canadians would be better off if the freedom granted to business executives were expanded and their voice more prominently heard in the corridors of government. The chapter argues that although Canada began the transition to an economic policy based on neoliberalism in the early 1980s, this new policy paradigm did not become completely entrenched until the 1997 federal election. As with other adherents to the liberal ideology, neoliberals believe that we are all inherently rational and should be left, for the most part, to determine what is in our own best interests. What differentiates neoliberals from other modern liberals is their belief that in order to realize this freedom, it is essential to enlarge the role that the capitalist market plays in determining the living standard enjoyed by each individual, as well as to reduce state activities to the absolute minimum (Gamble, 1994, 46). Neoliberals believe that it is while acting in the market as autonomous individuals, that human freedom reaches its maximum potential (Forstmann and Crane, 1996, 13). Neoliberal ideas have been advocated and funded by a broad coalition of business executives representing almost all sectors of the economy (Kelley, 1997, 57–80). This undoubtedly helped neoliberals both to gain access to state officials and to win elected office, as well as to marginalize the voices of their critics.

The next section explores the relationship between capitalism and liberal democracy, the original liberal understanding of the role that the state should play in the economic life of society, as well as how it came to be transformed into a model sometimes called the postwar consensus or the Keynesian compromise. The third section discusses how the Keynesian compromise came to unravel, opening the way for the emergence of the neoliberal model. According to liberal thought, the state is only justified in restricting the autonomy of individuals or in showing them favour to the degree that these actions provide a universal benefit to all other individuals in society—what the seventeenth-century English philosopher John Locke referred to as the "publick [*sic*] good" (1965, 398–9). The chapter argues that the adoption of the Keynesian compromise and its contemporary replacement by neoliberalism cannot be understood without considering this liberal notion of the public interest. The final section looks at the backlash that neoliberal economic policy has created.

CLASSICAL LIBERALISM THROUGH TO THE KEYNESIAN COMPROMISE

Canada is a liberal democracy. Liberals believe that adult human beings are rational and therefore capable of determining for themselves what is in their own best interest. Given this, liberals argue that individual adult human beings should, for the most part, be left at liberty to decide how best to live their lives. Liberal assumptions underpin both our capitalist economy and our democratic political process.

In a capitalist economy the vast majority of the productive property is controlled by a small group of individuals who invest large sums of money in its creation or by those who supervise and control such investments on behalf of many smaller investors. For simplicity's sake we can refer to these people as business executives. Relying on our liberal ideology these people claim the freedom to determine what happens to the property that they control and the profits that are generated, and the right to make these decisions based on what they believe is their own best interests. In other words, most people have very little say in how the profits generated by capitalism are employed. Nevertheless, these profits go a long way towards determining the resources available to the state and the living standard enjoyed by each of us. Consequently, when business executives approach government for action on some issue, or to advocate for a specific direction in overall economic policy, they often get a more receptive hearing than other groups. Therefore, Lindblom refers to business executives as quasi-public officials and the relationship that they enjoy with government as "the privileged position of business" in a liberal society (1977, 172–8).

However, in a liberal democracy, all citizens are seen as being equal in the only way that really counts—our inherent rationality and our ability to determine what is in our own interest. Every citizen's opinion is assumed to be of equal value to the community. This is both symbolically and practically demonstrated at election time when each citizen has the right to the same single vote. But democracy is about more than voting. Descriptions of democracy also usually mention that public policy and those who carry it out must respect our rights, and that the public should have a fair chance at making representations to the state so as to participate in policymaking (Pocklington, 2000, 14–18). The privileged position of business can diminish the democratic equality of individuals to the narrow act of voting. Successfully combining capitalism and liberal democracy necessitates the creation of political structures and forms of behaviour that ensure that business gets heard but not at the expense of all other voices. Finding that balance has been a topic of debate for as long as capitalism and democracy have coexisted.

Canada was a liberal society long before it was a democratic one. Capitalism can only exist with difficulty in a society where the liberal philosophy is not well developed and the rights associated with it are not well protected. The liberal notion that we are all inherently and equally rational forms the foundation for capitalist markets. Capitalism requires that we be free, more or less, to buy and sell our labour and the products produced by property under our control to whomever we like, for whatever price we feel is appropriate. The liberal idea of equality of individuals also has important repercussions as it leads to the view that everyone should have equal rights before the law. If this is not the case it is difficult to ensure that once bargains are entered into, they will be honoured (Dahrendorf, 1988, 38–39). Recently some Canadians who invested in Russia have discovered this reality to their regret, for while Russia is no longer a communist country, it has yet to become a liberal one. Neither the principle that those who invest in productive property have a right to control over it (as an extension of their personal liberty) nor the principle of equality before the law are firmly established in today's Russia. Capitalism's need for liberalism and the rights which it bestows holds the potential to create a keyhole through which a broader freedom can emerge (Przeworski, 1985, 21).

Once liberal understandings of the right to enjoy, buy, and sell property and the right to equality before the law become established, it is increasingly difficult to explain how it is that people can be sufficiently rational to enter into contracts, yet not rational enough to enjoy full participation in politics, especially the right to vote. Those demanding such rights in non-democratic liberal capitalist societies are in a very strong position because they are not trying to undermine the dominant ideas of their societies but asking their rulers to live up to them. While hypocritical in a liberal society, the exclusion of some adults from the franchise and full participation in politics tends to grant a meaningful advantage in life to those who hold such rights. It takes very little effort to look back in Canada's history to find examples of how the state granted advantages to those with the right to participate fully in political life at the expense of those who did not, such as women, and Canadians of Aboriginal and Asiatic descent. Consequently, each extension of democracy tends to require significant struggle on the part of those demanding to be included and few societies have accepted such claims unless faced with crisis. Until the second half of the twentieth century most liberal countries still excluded large numbers of their residents from the franchise (Therborn, 1977). For example, Canadian women were not granted widespread access to the federal vote until 1917 and did not achieve the right to participate in politics on the same terms as men in all the provinces until 1940. Meanwhile, Canadian law continued to deny the vote to some people on racial grounds until 1960. The United States also removed the last racial barriers to full political citizenship from its laws during the 1960s.

Even after the majority of adults won full political citizenship, the freedom of business executives to control their property was still protected by the liberal idea of the public interest. This is the belief that we are all equal, and therefore the state should not undertake actions that favour some over others except to the degree that such actions provide a universal benefit to society. Business executives staked their claim to represent the public interest of society on their role as the organizers of production, given the freedom that liberalism theoretically granted them to determine the uses to be made of the productive property and profits under their control. Thus when business executives asked for assistance from the state, they were asking on behalf of society's wider interest, because it is through capitalist efforts to organize production that the new wealth needed to improve society is created (Przeworski, 1985, 139). When others asked for assistance they were, according to this logic, asking to consume resources that should be devoted to the creation of wealth for society as a whole.

This helps to explain much of Canada's economic policy prior to the Second World War. Even though the federal and provincial states were very hesitant to intervene in the economy to protect the interests of ordinary Canadians, they aggressively intervened to promote the welfare of business executives and the enterprises that they controlled. The best known of these interventions was the National Policy, developed by the Conservative government of Canada's first prime minister, Sir John A. Macdonald. This policy involved three separate initiatives—state subsidies to create a transcontinental railway system, a similarly state-sponsored settlement policy to introduce Europeans onto the prairies and to swell the already developing population of British Columbia (which would provide a market for the railway), and a high tariff policy to ensure that the population of the growing country would buy the products of Canadian manufacturers (carried to them on the railway) rather than imported American ones (Eden and Molot, 1993, 234–5). Not surprisingly, once well established, the populations of Western Canada resented the role assigned to them by the National Policy.

Even after receiving the franchise, the workers in Canadian industry saw their concerns marginalized so that those of business executives could be met. For example, between 1880 and 1886, three government bills and four private bills were introduced into Parliament to regulate working conditions, and all died on the order paper. Even if they had passed, it is likely that the courts of the time would have invalidated them (Waite, 1971, 180). That the entire province of Ontario had only three factory inspectors perhaps shows the degree of interest government had in enforcing what minimal labour law existed in the late 1800s (Morton and Copp, 1980, 84). More overtly, strikes were frequently put down by armed force. The most graphic example occurred in the days immediately after the First World War.

The overarching public policy that business executives are said to have wanted from the time of Confederation until the early part of the twentieth century has been described as "laissez-faire." Loosely translated as "leave be," this is the idea that the government should take no overt action that inhibits business. As seen above, policy in Canada deviated from laissez-faire in a number of important ways. However, they were primarily to the advantage of Canadian business executives and could therefore be justified in that—according to the understandings of the time—they promoted the public interest. In fact, Canada was not unique. The United States and every European country that successfully industrialized prior to the Second World War used similar interventionist policies to build their internal economies until their businesses were strong enough to compete internationally.

One particular aspect of laissez-faire that business executives, regardless of country, expressed a particularly strong consensus on during this era was the so-called gold standard. Countries practising the gold standard promised to buy back their currency at a fixed rate for precious metal. The goal was to prevent currency depreciation and inflation so that lenders and investors could be relatively certain that their money was safe from currency risk. This was particularly important for Canada at this time as much of the money needed to implement the National Policy had to be borrowed abroad and the gold standard gave Canada's lenders in Europe a degree of comfort (Verdier, 1998, 8–11). The problem was that governments could not spend more than their immediate income and their reserves of precious metals could support, nor create money beyond their capability to redeem it, even temporarily. This meant that in the event of an economic downturn all government spending had to be cut, which further complicated long-term development and planning. Although Canada would leave the gold standard in 1914 in order to finance the First World War, and would only briefly return to it from 1926 to 1931, the goal of the gold standard, to maintain the value of the currency against inflation and depreciation at almost any cost, was preserved, even after it was agreed that this policy no longer served Canada's interests (Green, 2000, 218–20).

In the late 1920s the United States fell into an economic downturn that soon spread to Canada and Europe, causing both widespread unemployment and financial losses to both small investors and business executives. The crisis, which lasted for a decade, eventually became known as the Great Depression. The Liberal government of W.L. MacKenzie King took no overt action to counteract the crisis. The Conservative government of R.B. Bennett, which replaced the Liberals in 1930, initially tried a series of palliative steps but soon gave up on the effort. In 1932 the government, following the dictates of the generally accepted economic theories of the time, dramatically cut spending to reflect the loss of tax income created by the depression. The hope was that the economy would recover once the price of goods and labour fell enough to restart demand. However, in 1933 unemployment went even higher, reaching an estimated 26.6 percent of the non-agricultural labour force (Thompson and Seager, 1985, 193–221, 350). Meanwhile, other countries began to grope for new solutions. Some countries broke with economic orthodoxy and tried to use government spending to re-ignite their stagnant economies, rather than just waiting for a recovery. Governments trying this new approach initially described their efforts as emergency measures, rather than the harbinger of a more permanent policy of active economic management. And it was indeed an emergency. Not just an economic emergency either, but an emergency for the entire world built on liberalism. States based on rival ideologies (communism in Russia and fascism in Germany and Italy) had emerged and appeared to have a much easier time in dealing with the global economic crisis. Given the depth of the crisis being experienced throughout the liberal world it is not at all surprising that many people became actively interested in these alternative ideologies. In Canada this was especially the case with communism and the Communist Party, which often appeared to be the only organization fighting to improve conditions for ordinary people. The heavy-handed tactics employed against the communists by the Bennett government only increased their popularity (Thompson and Seager, 1985, 222–30, 269–72).

Government efforts to promote economic recovery would have had little if any lasting impact on public policy if not for the work of the British economist John Maynard Keynes. In *The General Theory of Employment, Interest and Money* (1936), Keynes showed his readers that the active efforts being pragmatically employed to end the Great Depression were theoretically sound after all. The *General Theory* was a theoretical exercise which contained no detailed public policy program for ending the economic downturn or for preventing future reoccurrences. Yet Keynes is often said to have been the architect of just such a program and also to have been the parent of the welfare state, in which the government is committed to providing its citizens with a minimum level of economic security. To understand this irony, we have to look at what Keynes's work purported to show. Keynes theoretically demonstrated how the long-assumed ability of markets to self-correct can fail. A modern economy requires both producers and purchasers who are in fact the same people, workers and their families. At a certain point so many people become unemployed and cannot afford to purchase goods and services that a crippling downward spiral results which cannot be broken until some external force intervenes. Therefore, Keynes proposed that government should play the role of this external force, adding money to the economy so as to break the link between unemployment and further economic decline. He reassured those afraid of inflation (when too much money chases too few goods, prices inflate and the value of money declines) that the risks were low in such circumstances.

In essence, Keynes stood the gold standard on its head, arguing that the government should adjust the amount of money available to the needs of the economy, not adjust the needs of the economy to the amount of money available. Whether Keynes's ideas were right or wrong is somewhat irrelevant. In the short run, what was relevant was that he provided policymakers with a theoretical argument to justify what they already wanted to do. In the long run, Keynes showed that the public interest of society could be furthered by addressing the needs of workers and the middle classes for living wages and protection from market fluctuations (Przeworski, 1985, 36–37). Once it was accepted that addressing the economic security of ordinary people advanced the public interest, including that of business executives, the door was opened for the creation of the modern welfare state and the deeper participation of groups representing ordinary people in the policy deliberations of the state.

The adoption of this new outlook was furthered by the rise to prominence of industries that made their profits by selling mass-produced consumer goods (such as automobiles) to the workers of their own country. Unlike essential goods (such as food), people can often forego the purchase of consumer goods when they feel economically insecure. Furthermore, it might be many years between when an investment in new mass production is made and the products created by it come to market. If conditions change too dramatically in the interim, the venture may never pay off. Therefore, executives in these new industries saw how state efforts to stabilize the economy served their interests. As they grew in power so to did the likelihood of government listening. Ferguson (1995, 79–98, 113–72) shows that American business executives associated with these new industries played a leading role, alongside labour groups, in supporting President Franklin D. Roosevelt's "New Deal" to fight the Great Depression in the United States.

Similar support for government intervention was expressed in Canada by business executives representing these new industries and their financial backers (Finkle, 1977, 356–7). However, mass production of consumer goods, for domestic consumption, did not gain a strong enough position in the Canadian economy until after World War II. Therefore, business need for such a policy regime was less urgent (Banting, 1987, 59). This made it easier for business executives from more traditional sectors—who only saw additional costs and inflation potential in the proposed policies—to counter the arguments made by business executives from the new industries. In 1935, the last year of his government's life, Bennett tried to create a Canadian version of the policies adopted in the United States. However, he ran out of time. When the Liberals under MacKenzie King were returned to office, they proved receptive to the concerns expressed by the business executives opposing the plan. The new Liberal government sent the whole Bennett plan to the courts for judicial review. The Canadian Supreme Court ruled most of it legal. However, this decision was appealed to London where the Judicial Committee of the Privy Council, Canada's final court of appeal until 1949, struck it down almost in its entirety (Thompson and Seager, 1985, 278–82).

The courts placed a further complicating factor in the way of Canada creating an active program of economic management—the constitutional division of authorities between federal and provincial governments. Monetary policy and the broad taxation powers necessary to adjust the economy and build a modern welfare state were within the powers of the federal government. However, the constitutional responsibility for implementing the necessary social and labour market policies were mainly within the jurisdiction of the provinces (Banting, 1987, 48). This dilemma, and the federal–provincial tensions it provoked, led MacKenzie King to create a Royal Commission to study Dominion–provincial relations. Meanwhile, it would be a mistake to believe that the provinces were pleased with all of the jurisdiction given them by the courts. In 1940 they agreed to a constitutional amendment transferring responsibility for unemployment insurance to Ottawa. The constitutional and financial problems related to modern public policy were overcome gradually following World War II and a coherent program of state involvement in economic life began to take shape over the 25 years spanning 1945 to 1970. In fact, the story of Canadian federalism in these years is very much the story of how federal and provincial leaders dealt with this dilemma of constitutionally mismatched powers and resources. On the labour relations front, the federal government overrode provincial jurisdiction and introduced reforms along the line of the American *Wagner Act* through the emergency powers it granted itself during the Second World War. Most of the provinces followed suit by passing the reforms into provincial law, ensuring that they would survive the emergency (Morton and Copp, 1990, 184–6).

The stage was therefore set for a new policy regime, what became known as the postwar consensus or the Keynesian compromise. Liberal capitalism remained the economic doctrine of society, and the value placed on our work by the labour market continued to be the prime determinant of each family's standard of living. However, the state, operating under an increasingly participatory form of liberal democratic political oversight, intervened somewhat to ensure that most families enjoyed a reasonable standard of living through social programs that provided services and income security, and by ensuring that the wildest swings in the business cycle were moderated.

Most benefited from this new policy regime but many others were left out. Those least likely to benefit from the Keynesian compromise were visible minorities and women living in families without a male breadwinner. Women within so-called traditional families also saw little autonomy, given their economic dependence on male spouses. Some researchers argue that this was deliberate. Having a large population outside the protection of the Keynesian compromise provided business executives with a "reserve army" of workers who could be employed when times were good and discarded easily as business conditions worsened. Such a reserve army is said to help business executives and the state to reduce workers' demands for pay and benefits (Fudge, 1996, 66–67).

THE RISE OF NEOLIBERALISM

By the 1970s a macro-crisis developed in liberal democracies such as Canada and called into question every aspect of postwar public policy. During this decade changes in trade patterns and financial technology made it increasingly difficult for states to control their economies and to extract revenue from them. Meanwhile, the price of oil increased dramatically and economic growth rates slowed appreciably. These factors placed new, more complex demands on government (Cox, 1987, 273–84). As the decade progressed, things went from bad to worse and a new term came into use, "stagflation." Stagflation was a combination of conditions rarely seen before—stagnant economic growth, which produced unemployment, and rising prices, which produced inflation (Tobin, 1982, 518). For policy-makers trained in the Keynesian tradition, this posed a dilemma, forcing them to choose between stimulating employment, risking more inflation, or fighting inflation, and risking more unemployment (Boothe and Purvis, 1997, 210).

At the same time researchers began asking why shocks to the economy (such as the rise in oil prices) had such long-lasting consequences rather than simply passing into history, and more generally, why the economies of the liberal capitalist nations seemed so incapable of adjusting to new circumstances. As things failed to improve, as was the case during the Great Depression, countries began to adopt ad hoc policies in the hopes of turning their economies around, such as aggressively fighting inflation, which ultimately made the economic downturns even worse (Garrett, 1998, 107–9). Following the lead of its American counterparts, the Bank of Canada responded so severely to inflationary pressures in the early 1980s that it drove the Canadian economy into a deep recession with unemployment levels closing in on 13 percent (Boothe and Purvis, 1997, 215–18). Just as was the case 40 years before, a new theory was needed to turn the ad hoc into a policy revolution. This new theory was provided by Robert E. Lucas, Thomas J. Sargent, and other "rational expectations" economists (Svensson, 1996).

Lucas and Sargent (1979) argued that financial investors are forward-looking and base a substantial part of their predictions about the economy on what government does and says today. Take for example banks and other lenders. Their expectations about the rate of inflation over the life of a loan (which will reduce the value of the money that they have lent) help to determine the interest rate they charge. If lenders expect government to allow the inflation rate to increase in the future by stimulating employment today, they will demand a higher interest rate. This will make it more expensive to borrow, dampen demand, and cancel out the unemployment-fighting impact of the stimulus, unless the government surprises lenders and stimulates the economy more than expected. Recognizing their mistake, lenders will build a greater inflation risk premium into future loans. As a result, each time the government tries to stimulate the economy it must spend more money to get the same boost in employment, risking greater and greater government debts and inflation. Consequently, rational expectations economists argued that governments could not permanently reduce unemployment, or achieve any other long-term economic goals, because people, in pursuing their own self-interests, would behave in ways that subvert any policy and thus restore equilibrium (Thurow, 1983, 143–4, 155–9). If there is no public benefit, why risk rapidly increasing inflation and potential budget deficits by trying to stabilize the economy?

The rational expectations economists resolved the dilemma facing policy-makers as to whether they should fight inflation or unemployment by saying that there was nothing that could be done to fight unemployment (or provide any other short-term economic security for ordinary people) and that if governments would only stop trying to fight unemployment, inflation might correct itself. As with Keynes's work, in the short term, it mattered little whether the rational expectations economists were correct or not. What mattered was that they gave policy makers a theoretical argument to support what they already wanted to do. As with Keynes's work, there is also a larger, longer-term impact as well, but first we must consider one further theoretical insight. Looking at the question of why Western liberal-capitalist democracies had such difficulty adjusting to new circumstances from another angle, some political scientists argued that persistent stagflation was a symptom of governmental overload in many countries. Government was involved in ever-increasing areas of human activity. Meanwhile so many actors both looked to government and demanded a voice in determining its actions that it was no longer possible for the states in many liberal capitalist democracies to take swift action in a crisis. The government overload theorists argued that it would be difficult to improve policy unless something was done to narrow both the responsibilities of the state and access to its decision-making circles (Crozier, Huntington, and Watanuki, 1975).

The new orthodoxy in economics held that, although Keynes might have been correct in some previous time, his work was no longer a guide. There was no public benefit to be derived from ensuring that everyone had equal access to the material benefits of society and the increased capacity to enjoy our individual freedom that the welfare state brought. Meanwhile, the government overload political theorists proposed that there was too much democracy, a view that only a decade earlier would have seemed heretical. It was not only the benefits flowing from the Keynesian compromise that had to be curtailed, but also participation in liberal democracy. Taken together, the works of rational expectations economists and government overload political theorists form the basis of neoliberalism. In the early 1980s the neoliberal message represented a powerful missive stating that the postwar consensus had developed in such a way and to such a degree that business was no longer in a privileged position. The state had to tune out the voices of ordinary people, to some degree, if business was to be restored to its legitimate place and gain the freedom necessary to rebuild the economy.

Business executives have not been passive observers in this process. While government efforts to mitigate swings in the business cycle had obvious value, the events of the 1970s appeared to show them that these efforts could fail spectacularly. An alternative avenue for ensuring profitability was to be as flexible as possible, adapting rapidly to the market rather than expecting government action to adapt the market to the dictates of mass production industry (Piore and Sabel, 1984, 205–20). This raised the thorny question of who was to pay the price of achieving this flexibility, ordinary people or business executives? Costs to business executives could be direct, through having to offer more generous benefits and wages that reflected the new insecurity of work. They might also be indirect, through rising taxes that would be required to fund the greater use likely to be made of welfare state programs as work became less secure. Avoiding these costs would require a change in government attitudes and a sharp curtailment of the capacity of workers and other popular groups to organize and represent the interests of their members both in the labour market and in the corridors of power. This change would assist business executives in achieving the necessary managerial freedom, make it easier to reduce the cost of welfare state programs, and also help ensure that workers were compelled to lower their salary expectations when market forces so dictated by stripping out policies that helped to protect the incomes and working conditions of most citizens (Gordon, Weisskopf, and Bowles, 1994, 243–8). Therefore, business executives worked hard to propagate both the works of rational expectations economists and government overload political theorists, to persuade state officials to listen to such arguments, and to finance politicians willing to restore the privileged position that business executives felt they had lost and now wanted more than ever (Ferguson, 1995, 244–7; Kelley, 1997, 58–62). It should come as little surprise that in 1976 Canada's top business executives created the Business Council on National Issues (BCNI) whose aims were quite simply to change the way that Canada's political leaders thought about the world and to restore the influence that its members believed business executives had lost.

Like other countries, Canada had adopted ad hoc policies in an attempt to deal with the macro-crisis of the 1970s. However, serious pursuit of the neoliberal policy regime began with the Trudeau government's appointment of the Macdonald Commission to study Canada's economic union and development prospects in 1982. The creation of the commission was a tacit acknowledgement by the government that its state-led development efforts and day-to-day attempts to employ Keynesian economic management were failing. The commission, which published its main report in 1985, broadly endorsed the adoption of the neoliberal economic policy regime (Bradford, 1998, 115). The commission's central recommendation was to pursue trade and investment liberalization agreements with our economic partners, especially the United States. This would force Canadian business to become more flexible, so as to compete, and help give some urgency to the complicated task of making the transition to a neoliberal policy regime (Macdonald, 1985, 50–72).

As with the implementation of the Keynesian compromise, implementing neoliberalism was difficult in Canada. Establishing political structures that defuse power over social and labour market policies means at least 11 and now sometimes 14 policy regimes. Meanwhile, regional tensions, which inhibit swift federal action, have only increased since the early 1970s. The neoliberal policy regime can only be said to have been truly entrenched at the federal level with the re-election of the Liberals in the 1997 general election. Having run as opponents of neoliberalism in 1993, Prime Minister Chretien's Liberals did an about-turn once in office, restructuring most of the federal government and pressuring the provinces, which had held out, to follow suit by dramatically cutting the subsidies Ottawa gives them. Since their conversion to neoliberalism, the only opponents with even a remote chance of unseating the federal Liberals have also been advocates of this policy regime. Consequently, the 1997 and 2000 general elections were about how to continue further implementing neoliberalism, not whether or not it is beneficial.

Many of the groups that became involved in policy discussions as representatives of ordinary Canadians during the era of the Keynesian compromise increasingly have found themselves excluded from the state's decision-making process (just as the state overload theorists recommended they should be) once the state set its sights on the implementation of a neoliberal economic policy regime. Those that once received public support in order to carry out representational functions for the more marginalized members of society have also seen their support seriously curtailed (Jenson and Phillips, 1996). The most recent example of this narrower access to the decision-making process is the British Columbia "Progress Board." Established by the neoliberal government of Premier Gordon Campbell soon after taking power, the board's mandate is to set benchmarks for government performance in terms of taxes and regulatory and fiscal reform, across the whole range of government activities. Although Premier Campbell says that his aim is to "create highly paid jobs and new opportunities for all British Columbians," and "to receive advice from a broad cross-section of participants in the British Columbia economy," the guidelines establishing the board say that membership should be restricted to "12 to 16 senior business executives representing successful British Columbia small, medium and large businesses." And in fact, every single member of the board, save one (University of British Columbia President Martha Piper) is indeed a business executive (Government of British Columbia, 2001).

The pursuit of the neoliberal policy regime amounted to a frontal assault on the Keynesian consensus, as well as on countless social and economic relationships, based on new understandings of the role of government. Most important among these understandings was the notion that the state would ensure stability in our economic lives and a reasonable standard of living for most people. This would provide most people some capacity to act on their preferences so as to make the hypothesized liberal freedom of the individual meaningful. However, neoliberalism is also a positive program focused on substantially increasing one aspect of liberal freedom above all—the freedom to engage in market exchange (Gamble, 1994, 46). We can look at housing policy as an example. Many Canadian cities have a significant number of homeless residents. The problem affects Toronto and Grande Prairie alike. In the vast majority of cases, the cost of the homes made available by the market is simply beyond the means of these people. Neoliberals oppose any government action to relieve this problem by regulating the types of housing that can be built, imposing price limits, or creating public housing. They argue such actions will violate the right to market exchange and enjoyment of property that belongs to both those who develop real estate and those looking for homes. Therefore, it should come as little surprise that government spending on housing has been one of the public policy areas most deeply affected by the adoption of neoliberalism, with the federal and provincial governments virtually withdrawing from the field during the 1980s and 1990s (Layton, 2000, xxi-xxii, 152–3).

The net impact of neoliberalism for most Canadians is clearly observed in the determinants of their family's welfare. Increasing emphasis on determining each family's living standard is being placed on the value assigned to the labour of its working members by business executives operating in a quickly changing and highly volatile economy. This does not mean that all social contributions to living standards have been eliminated. However, these cannot be taken for granted when neoliberalism comes to dominate public life. One example of this is low-income intensity among families with children. Even as Canada recovered from the recession of the early 1990s poor families actually got poorer. The social policy cuts implemented by neoliberal governments across Canada were a significant contributor to this problem as they eroded any advances these families made in market income (Myles and Picot, 2000). Given this emphasis on using markets to determine living standards, it also should not be a surprise that the gap between rich and poor, which largely remained stable in Canada prior to the entrenchment of neoliberalism, began to increase in the late 1990s (Statistics Canada, 2000). Neoliberalism aims to guarantee individuals the maximum potential freedom—not the capacity to enjoy it, which the Keynesian compromise attempted to ensure to some degree. Under neoliberalism, a family's economic resources derived from market activity are the only guarantee of security. Forgetting about the larger role that the state once tried to play in stabilizing the economy, when a neoliberal policy regime is in place even such rudimentary tasks as ensuring safe drinking water appear to be occasionally beyond the capacity of the state as was demonstrated by the Walkerton tainted water tragedy in Ontario (Stanford, 2000, 17).

THE BACKLASH AGAINST NEOLIBERALISM

Neoliberals believe that freedom is maximized when we have the greatest potential to make choices in our lives, whether or not we have the capacity to act on these choices or not, and that markets which are as free of regulation and safeguards as is possible are the form of social interaction that can best realize this ideal. They believe that it is while acting in the market as an autonomous individual that human freedom reaches its maximum potential (Forstmann and Crane, 1996, 13). This presents both greater opportunities to achieve prosperity and more substantial risks for individual families. While people always like greater opportunities, most of us are even more afraid of greater risks. Therefore, it should come as little surprise that some people are engaging in strategies to restore the feeling of security that neoliberalism has robbed them of by making their life chances more fully dependent on the value that capitalist markets place on their labour. This concluding section examines two such strategies that are emerging in Canada. These are external and internal separatism.

External separatism is clearly present in Quebec. One third of Quebec's voters now consistently express preferences for political parties that want to transform the province into a sovereign country. Sometimes up to one half of the Quebec electorate support this view (Canadian Press, 2001). The neoliberal turn taken in Canada, symbolized by the 1995 federal budget, apparently helped to boost the sovereigntist vote in the referendum of that year. The federal argument, that sovereignty would produce economic dislocation, just did not resonate when Ottawa was implementing a neoliberal agenda and claiming it could no longer directly protect the living standards of its citizens. The sovereigntist leaders understood this, and exploited the opportunity (McCarthy, 1995). Gagnon and Lachapelle (1996, 182–5) argue that the 1995 federal budget marked a clear dividing line between Quebec and Canada. While the federal government and other provinces had fully embraced neoliberalism, Québécois still had their doubts and wished to see a continued strong role for the state in both the overall economy and in protecting the life chances of individual families.

Internal separatism as a strategy to cope with neoliberalism is only now emerging in Canada, but has had dramatic repercussions in the United States. The most obvious examples of internal separatism in the United States are gated communities, some of which are the size of cities and have formally separated from their parent municipalities (thereby eliminating their obligation to pay local taxes). Here we have the ultimate statement of the belief that one's standard of living is solely determined by the value placed on your labour by the market and your accumulated wealth. By the mid 1990s, roughly 3 million American families had retreated to limited, user-pay communities, seeking the quality of life and protection from risks that they believe citizenship in a liberal capitalist democracy can no longer guarantee (Blakely and Snyder, 1997). In gated communities neoliberalism is taken to its logical extreme in that membership in the democratic community is solely determined by the ability to pay and the free choice to enter into a contract with the community. No one is required to join the community and all those incapable of making the payments to the community are excluded (Bickford, 2000, 358–62). Thus, in contrast to external separatism, which recommends the severence of Quebec from Canada, internal separatism occurs within communities and promotes the isolation of the rich from the rest.

It was developments such as gated communities, which are the most overt example of the increasing economic, physical, and social gap between the prosperous and the ordinary citizens, that led the historian and philosopher Christopher Lasch (1995) to question whether the United States could survive as a liberal democracy. He saw little prospect when the only connection that the business executive and other prosperous citizens have to ordinary society is to drive through it on the way to the airport or a downtown office tower. When those speaking from the privileged position of business have no relation whatsoever to ordinary life and are the overwhelmingly loudest voice heard, liberal democracy becomes reduced to a simple formality, eventually losing its legitimacy and opening the door to other less-attractive forms of political organization.

Internal separatism is less advanced in Canada than in the United States. However, as neoliberalism takes firmer hold on our society, the conditions that promote it, along with all its damaging consequences, will grow. In the eyes of some of Canada's most important business executives neoliberal governing practices must be intensified and accelerated.

Canadian Pacific CEO David P. O'Brien and other leaders of the Business Council on National Issues not only made this request in a manifesto (2000) reprinted in Canada's leading newspapers, but also backed it up with a blunt threat: Give us what we want—greater freedom to manage our affairs any way we want and reduce our obligations to society—otherwise we will leave and take all the resources that we control with us. Neither of the choices put before us by our business executives are particularly appealing. Whichever way you look at it, neoliberalism appears to have placed Canada in a very vulnerable position, adding one more argument to the sovereigntist arsenal and creating a potential new threat of internal separatism. Unless we can forge a new understanding of how the public interests of society are served by addressing the needs and concerns of all citizens, it is very unlikely that this threat to Canada will recede.

REFERENCES

Banting, Keith G. 1987. *The Welfare State and Canadian Federalism, 2nd ed.* Montreal: McGill-Queen's University Press.

Bickford, Susan. 2000. "Constructing Inequality: City Spaces and the Architecture of Citizenship." *Political Theory 28* (June), 355–76.

Blakely, Edward J. and Mary Gail Snyder. 1997. *Fortress America: Gated Communities in the United States.* Washington, DC: The Brookings Institute.

Boothe, Paul and Douglas Purvis. 1997. "Macroeconomic Policy in Canada and the United States: Independence, Transmission, and Effectiveness." In Keith Banting, George Hoberg and Richard Simeon (eds.) *Degrees of Freedom: Canada and the United States in a Changing World.* Montreal: McGill-Queen's University Press.

Bradford, Neil. 1998. *Commissioning Ideas: Canadian National Policy Innovation in Comparative Perspective.* Toronto: Oxford University Press.

Canadian Press. 2001, August 11. "Landry Ready for First Real Test This Fall." *Toronto Star*, H2.

Cox, Robert W. 1987. *Production, Power and World Order: Social Forces in the Making of History,* New York: Columbia University Press.

Crozier, Michel J., Samuel P. Huntington, and Joji Watanuki. 1975. *The Crisis of Democracy: Report on the Governability of Democracies to the Trilateral Commission.* New York: New York University Press.

Dahrendorf, Ralf. 1988. *The Modern Social Conflict.* New York: Weidenfeld and Nicolson.

Eden, Lorraine and Maureen Appel Molot. 1993. "Canada's National Policies: Reflections on 125 Years." *Canadian Public Policy 19* (3): 232–251.

Ferguson, Thomas. 1995. *Golden Rule: The Investment Theory of Party Competition and the Logic of Money Driven Political Systems.* Chicago: Chicago University Press.

Finkel, Alvin. 1977. "Origins of the Welfare State in Canada." In Leo Panitch (ed.), *The Canadian State: Political Economy and Political Power.* Toronto: University of Toronto Press.

Forstmann, Theodore and Edward H. Crane. 1996. *Business and the Fight for a Free Society: Cato Letter 11.* Washington, DC: The Cato Institute.

Fudge, Judy. 1996. "Fragmentation and Feminization: The Challenge of Equity for Labour-Relations Policy." In Janine Brodie (ed.), *Women and Canadian Public Policy.* Toronto: Harcourt Brace.

Gagnon, Alain G. and Guy Lachapelle. 1996. "Quebec Confronts Canada: Two Competing Societal Projects Searching for Legitimacy." *The Journal of Federalism 26* (Summer): 177–191.

Gamble, Andrew. 1994. *The Free Economy and the Strong State: The Politics of Thatcherism, 2nd ed.* London: Macmillan.

Garrett, Geoffrey. 1998. *Partisan Politics in the Global Economy.* Cambridge: Cambridge University Press.

Gordon, David M., Thomas E. Weisskopf, and Samuel Bowles. 1994. "Right-wing Economics in the 1980s: the Anatomy of Failure." In Michael A. Bernstein and David E. Adler (eds.), *Understanding American Economic Decline.* Cambridge: Cambridge University Press.

Government of British Columbia. 2001. "Progress Board Will Set Benchmarks For Performance." *Government of British Columbia News Releases* Retrieved July 18, 2001 from http://os8150.pb.gov.bc.ca/4dcgi/nritem?4806

Green, Alan G. 2000. "Twentieth-Century Canadian Economic History." In Stanley L. Engerman and Robert E. Gallman, (eds.) *The Cambridge Economic History of the United States: Volume 3, The Twentieth Century.* Cambridge: Cambridge University Press.

Jenson, Jane and Susan D. Phillips. 1996. "Regime Shift: New Citizenship Practices in Canada." *International Journal of Canadian Studies, 14* (Fall): 111–135.

Kelley, John L. 1997. *Bringing the Market Back In: The Political Revitalization of Market Liberalism.* New York: New York University Press.

Keynes, John Maynard. 1936. *The General Theory of Employment, Interest and Money.* London: Macmillan.

Lasch, Christopher. 1994. *The Revolt of the Elites and the Betrayal of Democracy.* New York: Norton.

Layton, Jack. 2000. *Homelessness: The Making and Unmaking of a Crisis.* Toronto: Penguin.

Lindblom, Charles E. 1977. *Politics and Markets: The World's Political-Economic Systems.* New York: Basic Books.

Locke, John. 1965 [1698]. *Two Treatises of Government: A Critical Edition with an Introduction and Apparatus Criticus by Peter Laslett.* New York: Mentor Books.

Lucas, Robert E. Jr. and Thomas J. Sargent. 1979. "After Keynesian Macroeconometrics." *Federal Reserve Bank of Minneapolis Quarterly Review 3*; 1–6. Reprinted in Robert E. Lucas Jr. and Thomas J. Sargent (eds.), 1981. *Rational Expectations and Econometric Practice*. Minneapolis: University of Minnesota Press.

Macdonald, Donald S. (Chair). 1985. *Report of the Royal Commission on the Economic Union and Development Prospects for Canada: Volume One.* Ottawa: Minister of Supply and Services.

McBride, Stephen and John Shields. 1993. *Dismantling a Nation: Canada and the New World Order.* Halifax: Fernwood.

McCarthy, Shawn. 1995, November 6. "Will Vote Scuttle Deficit Battle?" *Toronto Star*, C1.

Morton, Desmond and Terry Copp. 1980. *Working People: An Illustrated History of the Canadian Labour Movement.* Ottawa: Deneau.

Myles, John and Garnett Picot. 2000. Social Transfers, Earnings and Low-Income Intensity Among Canadian Children, 1981–96: Highlighting Recent Developments in Low-Income Measurement. *Statistics Canada Analytic Studies 144*. Ottawa: Statistics Canada.

Piore, Michael J. and Charles F. Sabel. 1984. *The Second Industrial Divide: Possibilities for Prosperity.* New York: Basic Books.

Pocklington, Tom. 2000. "Thinking About Democracy, Rights, and Well-Being." In Don Carmichael, Tom Pocklington, and Greg Pyrcz (eds.), *Democracy, Rights, and Well-Being in Canada,* 2nd ed. Toronto: Harcourt Brace and Company.

Przeworski, Adam. 1985. *Capitalism and Social Democracy.* Cambridge: Cambridge University Press.

Stanford, Jim. 2000 June 1. "Taxes: Death by a Thousand Cuts." *Globe and Mail*, A17.

Statistics Canada, 2000. *The Daily: Family Income.* (June 12), Ottawa: Statistics Canada.

Svensson, Lars E.O. 1996. "The Scientific Contributions of Robert E. Lucas Jr." *Scandinavian Journal of Economics, 98* (1): 1–10.

Therborn, Göran. 1977. "The Rule of Capital and the Rise of Democracy." *New Left Review 103*, 3–41.

Thompson, John Herd with Allen Seager. 1985. *Canada 1922–1939: Decades of Discord.* Toronto: McClelland & Stewart.

Thurow, Lester C. 1983. *Dangerous Currents: The State of Economics.* New York: Random House.

Tobin, James. 1982. "Inflation." In Douglas Greenwald (ed.). *Encyclopedia of Economics.* New York: McGraw-Hill.

Verdier, Daniel. 1998. "Domestic Responses to Capital Market Internationalization." *International Organization, 52* (Winter). 87–120.

Waite, P.B. 1971. *Canada 1874–1896: Arduous Destiny.* Toronto: McClelland & Stewart.

WEBLINKS

The LockeSmith Institute
www.belmont.edu/lockesmith

The National Policy
www.nlc-bnc.ca/2/18/h18-2987-e.html

Public Interest Advocacy Centre
www.piac.ca

chapter five

Globalization, Culture, and the Canadian City

David Whitson

INTRODUCTION

As the twenty-first century begins, many Canadians are concerned about the challenges facing our cities. It is widely agreed, in language that echoes Jane Jacobs, that cities are more than ever before the engines of economic growth and prosperity (Bocking, 2001, 5–7). Canadians are moving in ever-greater numbers to our five or six most populous cities in search of economic opportunity, while those same cities are overwhelmingly the places where immigrants choose to settle and to build new lives. It is also increasingly acknowledged that, despite a reputation for liveability in the 1970s and 1980s and for being more successful than many of their U.S. counterparts, Canadian cities are now cracking under the strains of burgeoning populations, racial tensions, expanded service responsibilities, and revenues inadequate to meet these challenges. Roads, schools, and other public facilities built more than half a century ago are approaching the end of their useful lives; but our cities have neither the money to replace them nor the political power to raise it. As Winnipeg Mayor Glen Murray has recently argued, "Canadian cities face huge financial burdens while being challenged by U.S. cities in the post-NAFTA economy. . . . Our national and provincial governments—which receive [most] of the taxes generated by the economies of large cities—are hesitant to ensure our cities retain a sufficient proportion of the wealth they generate to maintain basic infrastructure . . .

[let alone] the cultural, sports, and social institutions vital to our quality of life" (Murray, 2002, A11).

In Murray's argument, there is explicit recognition that successful cities depend upon an intricate interaction between commerce and culture, jobs and leisure opportunities, and physical and social infrastructure, and that urban growth requires attention to all of these. There is also recognition that urban prosperity is now a more competitive issue than ever before. As writers like U.S. urbanist Saskia Sassen (1998) have observed, globalization appears to be producing a hierarchy of cities in which wealth and power will be concentrated in a handful of centres, while other cities will lose importance, both economically and culturally. This makes it all the more urgent, in Murray's view, that Canadian cities have access to revenues that enable them to renew infrastructure and invest in workforce development. Cities also need new resources, he suggests, in order to deal with social problems that concentrate in urban populations. This last point is underlined by Ottawa political scientist Caroline Andrew, who argues that Canada's major cities not only need new sources of revenues; they need new structures of governance, with powers sufficient to address the challenges facing them. These include stimulating economic renewal and providing new infrastructure, often on a regional basis, while also maintaining public services with the capacity to respond effectively to poverty and social polarization, and to increasing ethnic and racial tensions (Andrew, 2000).

In sum, the challenge that Canadian cities face amounts to substantially remaking themselves, indeed sometimes finding new economic raisons d'être, in a world economy that is very different from the one they grew up in. Throughout most of Canadian history, Montreal and Toronto have been the primary centres of manufacturing and finance capital for the whole of Canada, as well as the principal ports (along with Vancouver) through which our raw materials were exported to the rest of the world. Winnipeg, Vancouver, and Halifax (and later Calgary and Edmonton) have been important centres of regional commerce. However, their prosperity has typically reflected cycles in the resource economies of their regional hinterlands (agriculture, oil, forestry, and fishing), and prior to the 1980s none of them were serious rivals to the old metropolitan centres of Canadian capitalism. By the beginning of the new millennium, several of these cities (and Ottawa, too) have substantially reinvented themselves as thriving centres of "new economy" activities. However, today Canadian cities must not only compete with their traditional Canadian rivals, they must also seek to establish themselves as North American if not world cities. As this chapter explains, culture and especially sports are widely seen as crucial to the "corporate-civic project" of putting ambitious regional cities "on the map" (Betke, 1983).

It is in the context of just this project that Canada's most ambitious cities have hosted, or sought to host, Olympic Games and other international sports events—events that local leaders have hoped would showcase their cities as "world class." It is also in this context that Toronto, Montreal, and Vancouver (and other smaller Canadian cities, too) have actively pursued professional sports franchises in the U.S.-based major leagues. It has been argued elsewhere that the pursuit of major league sports franchises and "world class" events is best understood as part of a larger project in which corporate and civic elites struggle to establish and maintain their cities' status in a transnational economic and cultural hierarchy of cities (Whitson and Macintosh, 1993). It is also part of this story that in pursuit of this objective, Canadian cities (sometimes with assistance from other levels of government) have built state-of-the-art sports facilities, often at very considerable public expense. The Olympic Stadium in Montreal, the Saddledome in Calgary, and SkyDome in Toronto all illustrate this kind of civic ambition. The SkyDome ran up such big debts that it was sold to the private sector at an enormous loss to the Ontario treasury (Kidd, 1995).

Although events like the Olympics and spectacular facilities like the SkyDome are initially the projects of local business and political elites, they are usually genuinely popular, initially at least, with a wider spectrum of citizens who enjoy them as consumers. Civic and corporate leaders in Canada have generally succeeded in promoting these projects as initiatives that will benefit the city as a whole, and have been able to generate widespread popular support (Kidd, 1992). This chapter reviews the economic and cultural contexts in which major leisure and entertainment developments have become a popular strategy for downtown revitalization. Next it argues that the prices of "world class" sports and music are beyond the means of low- and even middle-income earners, and that when public money is allocated to such events or facilities, this is almost always followed by cutbacks to public services that hit hardest at vulnerable social groups. The chapter also examines different visions of what it means to be a "world class" city, and concludes by proposing that, for Canadian cities, the most pressing item on the agenda is not the downtown entertainment district. It is, rather, building (or, in some cases, rebuilding) the public institutions in which social and cultural diversity can flourish.

THE NEW DOWNTOWN ECONOMY: SPORTS, CULTURE, SPECTACLE, CONSUMPTION

Urban scholars have for several decades debated the effects of globalization and economic restructuring for North American cities. New communications and management technologies have combined with free trade agreements to produce an unprecedented mobility of investment capital and this, in turn, has led to the movement of many industries (and jobs) from their historical locations in North America to lower-wage, lower-cost jurisdictions. In less than two decades, industrial restructuring has destroyed the traditional economic base of many older industrial cities, and forced them to compete for new economic functions, especially in the emerging "knowledge economy" where most growth is now concentrated. Indeed, the values now placed on specialized kinds of intellectual expertise—scientific and technical expertise, creative expertise (e.g., in design or advertising), and especially financial and management expertise—are such that the profit potential of providing "soft goods" (such as software) and intellectual services (e.g., data management services, or many kinds of "consulting") in any of these knowledge-dependent fields is much greater than that in most traditional industries (Barber, 1996, ch. 4). Even in the manufacturing industries, when knowledge can be built into technologically advanced products—from fibre optics to pharmaceuticals—this "adds value" to those products, and creates better jobs (high-paying jobs requiring advanced education) than the employment associated with textiles, for example, or even automobiles.

It is also important to understand that tourism, entertainment, and consumption have together become a major engine of growth in the new urban economy. At one level, this is manifested in the construction or refitting of hotels and in the building of major new convention centres, sports venues, and concert halls. To this familiar list, Toronto sociologist John Hannigan (1998) suggests that one should now add theme parks, spectacular shopping complexes, and in some jurisdictions, casinos, while also noting that the lines between some of these categories are becoming increasingly blurred. All of these are major projects that can inject hundreds of millions of dollars into the local construction and real estate industries. There also is the further expectation (more realistic in some cities than others, perhaps) that such "fantasy city" venues, as Hannigan terms them, will attract substantial numbers of tourists, generating new business for a city's hospitality industry (hotels and restaurants), its other entertainment industries, and its downtown retailers. Construction of major new leisure facilities is projected as a likely catalyst to further, smaller-scale development in the surrounding area, often involving the spread of boutique restaurants and the sorts of shops in which urban tourists can spend money. When a critical mass of such development takes place, it is plausible to claim that entertainment and consumption have contributed in a major way to the revitalization of a city's downtown (Fainstein and Stokes, 1998).

Like urban renewal strategies, some combination of world class entertainment, shopping, and tourist attraction is also believed to attract "footloose companies and, in particular, their managerial and professional staffs" (Lash and Urry, 1994, 215). This is because the burgeoning of intellectual services alluded to above has seen the rapid growth of a class of highly mobile executives, specialized professionals, and consultants—"symbolic analysts" as former U.S. secretary of Labour, Robert Reich, calls them—who want access to their own cultural interests wherever they work and live, and are able and willing to pay for them (1991). This chapter will later consider whether this points to a highly problematic definition of world class culture. For now, the point is simply that many cities believe that attracting the economic prosperity associated with the knowledge industries and with tourism requires that they promote their lifestyle attractions, and re-image themselves as dynamic and cosmopolitan places, full of interest and enjoyment.

Indeed, what becomes clear, in looking at the sheer numbers and variety of "fantasy city" developments is that entertainment and popular culture have become important avenues of capital accumulation in the new global economy, and that the entertainment industries have become increasingly significant players in the transnational capitalism of the late twentieth century. Not surprisingly then, entertainment and popular culture have become increasingly important in the economies of our major cities, and they are seen as important in competitions between cities to attract and retain investment. This has helped to drive the expansion of major league sports in North America, as well as the construction of many new facilities for sports and culture in these cities, typically at public expense. It has also led to increasingly spectacular shopping developments, as both old and new cities now compete to attract the high value-added business associated with world famous entertainment and shopping. Indeed, sport, culture, and shopping have now become necessary conditions for any city that aspires to a place on the contemporary circuits of urban tourism, including the lucrative convention and conference trade.

Summarizing the argument thus far, civic competition has been transformed in the closing years of the twentieth century by the unprecedented mobility of capital, by the new economic importance of knowledge-based services, and by the increasing globalization of shared information and entertainment systems. Together, these dynamics are producing what Sassen describes as a new geography of centrality and marginality in which many cities feel themselves "propelled into a race to attract increasingly mobile investors (multinational corporations), consumers (tourists), and spectacles (sports and media events)" (Robbins, 1991). This leads to concern in regional cities, especially, about any loss of cultural attractions, and has left cities like Minneapolis and Ottawa vulnerable to pressures by team owners and by the "major league" monopolies. Indeed, civic and regional governments in both countries have repeatedly found themselves pitted against one another, by owners who have threatened to move their franchises elsewhere if their demands are not satisfied. Owners have demanded that arenas be renovated to include luxury boxes (for example, in Edmonton or Calgary), or that entire new facilities be built at public expense (in Winnipeg and Minneapolis). They also demand the rights to revenues from concessions and parking, from advertising space, and from the rental of the facility on other dates. They seek rent-free status if the facility remains under public ownership, or tax-free status and choice downtown land (and often rights to develop adjacent real estate) when private money is used to finance an arena or stadium (Whitson, Harvey, and Lavoie, 2000).

Against this background, civic leaders in U.S. and Canadian cities have given professional sports franchises most of what they wanted. Indeed, only in Quebec have civic and provincial leaders countered owners' demands with proposals in which public and private partners would have shared both revenues and risks. The Quebec Nordiques consequently moved to Denver in the mid-1990s, while with public funding refused for a downtown baseball stadium in Montreal, it now appears inevitable that the Expos will leave, and very soon. Does this matter? Has the loss of NHL franchises mattered to Winnipeg or Quebec? The sports industry argues that subsidies to sports franchises are an "investment," and teams regularly produce commissioned studies that purport to show that pro sports generate many millions of dollars of business in the civic economy. However, most independent research suggests that the economic impact of pro sports, as estimated in industry-commissioned studies, is widely overstated (Whitson, Harvey, and Lavoie, 2000). Meanwhile, both Winnipeg and Quebec, in 2002, appear to be thriving, by normal economic indicators.

Given the sums involved in hosting international events, there is a remarkable dearth of post-event analysis of how much economic growth actually materializes, whether increased levels of tourism are sustained in the years after the event, and whether growth is diffused beyond the tourism and hospitality industries themselves. In order to properly assess the economic impact of events like the Olympics, it is necessary to look beyond the money spent on mega-projects (typically the focus of most studies) and examine whether growth is registered and sustained according to more standard measures of regional economic health, such as business start-ups (and failures), consumer spending, employment, and income distribution. It is also important to examine the extent to which small- and medium-sized employers, who are generally local rather than transnational, participate in this growth. Measuring these things and connecting effects to causes present complex challenges, but evidence that special-event tourism is an answer to the challenges of economic restructuring is mixed at best (Whitson, 1999). Perhaps the most that can be said is that international events give a city a chance to put its attractions—its human and financial resources, as well as its cultural and social infrastructure—on display for global visitors and audiences, and that for provincial cities in particular, this can be a useful exercise. In Australia, for example, the Americas Cup and Expo '88 provided Perth and Brisbane respectively opportunities to "put the local on show for the global," in places that international tourists and investors had rarely visited (Hartley, 1988). Similarly, in Canada, the 1988 Olympics and Expo '86 enabled leaders in Calgary and Vancouver to re-image their cities as sophisticated international destinations, "come of age through recent economic development" (Hiller, 1989).

The importance of civic re-imaging is widely believed to be heightened, moreover, in what Lash and Urry call global economies of signs and space (1994). Cities themselves have become imaged commodities whose "sign value" is crucial to the values that can be realized from property, and from a wide variety of cultural products. As global media make the world a smaller place, and cities are forced to compete for increasingly mobile investors and consumers (whether citizens, tourists, or both), the attraction of outside money is believed to depend more and more upon the symbolic commodification of place. This is fairly easy to see in the case of tourism, where tourist promotion seeks to "sell" places "in order to generate sales of the multitude of services and material paraphernalia that are part of a tourist holiday" (Britton, 1991). Indeed, adding value to all manner of tourist goods and services—from tours to hotel rooms, and from arts and crafts to food and T-shirts—depends directly upon the numbers and spending power of the tourists who can be attracted, and on the values they attach to being there and taking home souvenirs of their visit. Symbolic values are thus translated into commercial values, and any significant erosion in the image of a tourist destination usually produces direct declines in the value of visitor spending. This, in turn, affects the values of tourist-related businesses, and of commercial and residential property.

The promotion of a city as a promising location for investment and an attractive place for affluent individuals to live is a different and more complex task than the selling of a tourist destination. What these two corporate-civic projects share, though, is the goal of adding to the market value of land and businesses by attracting money and people from outside; and while public investment in major sporting and cultural venues is widely seen as necessary to the success of this agenda, corporate patronage is also critical to its long-term viability. Moreover, the very example of partnership between the local public and private sectors broadcasts an image of a city with the means to build world class facilities, and a population affluent enough to support world class entertainment. Certainly the SkyDome in its early years showed that Toronto was (then at least) a city with many businesses wealthy enough to lease luxury boxes at high prices. In Winnipeg, conversely, one factor in the ultimate departure of NHL hockey was that the local private sector was unwilling to invest in the proposed new arena, and there were not enough local companies able and willing to entertain in this fashion (Silver, 1996). Indeed, an increasingly decisive measure of a "big league" city, in the new economics of professional sport, is precisely whether that city has a corporate sector large enough, wealthy enough, and in the sorts of businesses (generally financial services, law firms, and consumer goods) where this kind of corporate entertaining has become a norm.

Similarly, the successful staging of an international Games (or Exposition) is intended to signal to the world that a city has both the public resources and the political will to accomplish a major renovation of itself. World events are often catalysts for the installation or upgrading of major transportation infrastructure—the Metro in Montreal, LRT systems in Calgary and Sydney, and SkyTrain in Vancouver, as well as airport improvements in most venues. Global events also now require, as Sydney demonstrated, substantial public investment in state-of-the-art telecommunications infrastructure, an increasing necessity for any city aspiring to a place in the world of financial and intellectual services (Wilson, 1996). The more important and intangible signal, though, follows from the fact that raising money for these purposes and getting facilities built on time is a major political and organizational accomplishment. The successful staging of an international event usually demonstrates the presence of an ambitious and outward-looking local corporate sector, as well as an effective and business-oriented political leadership, both of which send positive signals to potential outside investors. However, we need to understand that this is a sign of wealth and of political support for the corporate sector, rather than a sign of any distinctive civic identity. It is intended to be read this way by "capital and people 'of the right sort' " (Harvey, 1989).

URBAN STANDARDIZATION, SOCIAL POLARIZATION

Critics like Harvey have observed that as more and more cities try to reposition themselves as centres of "world class" entertainment and shopping, and try to attract urban tourism and the investment and jobs associated with it, the downtown entertainment districts of most of our major cities have come to look substantially alike. Each successful waterfront development or historic shopping precinct, each "state-of-the-art" stadium or arena, each imaginative hotel or theatre design is promptly copied in other places. The effect is that, ironically, the leisure and consumption environments in major cities around North America have lost whatever "sense of place" their distinctive geographies and architectural histories once gave them (Harvey, 1989, 295). A further factor in the standardization of urban landscapes is the ubiquitous presence, almost everywhere in the affluent world, of the same roster of global brand names. Indeed, whether it is hotels (Hilton, Sheraton, etc.), night clubs (Hard Rock Café, Planet Hollywood), or shopping (from Gap or Benetton up to designer names like Prada and Donna Karan), for many people with money "world class" now means, in effect, brand names made familiar by global marketing. World class cities, by extension, are those that offer access to these famous brands, as well as to brand-name entertainment.

What is meant by this last point is that global media and marketing have created international brand recognition for entertainment products (to distinguish NBA basketball or the PGA Tour from the sports themselves) that once had almost exclusively American audiences. Within North America, moreover, the expansion of the four "major leagues" into regional cities like Vancouver, Edmonton, Charlotte, and Indianapolis has made major league sport almost a required feature of urban culture, and made major league franchises into highly valued "signs" of civic status. In the performing arts, of course, tours by big-name bands or musicals (U2 or *Phantom of the Opera*) are not new. Today, though, they are bigger business, with the most famous acts touring venues that can maximize returns—typically today, major league sports facilities (Renzetti, 1997, C10). The cumulative effect is a growing standardization of big-city entertainment—in all the performing arts, as well as sports—around the same set of "world class" names and events. Given a positive spin, this means that more fans can enjoy access to the same icons of "global culture."

However, the downside is that *civic* culture and identity increasingly have less to do with the vitality of local artists or the success of homegrown athletes than with access to a succession of famous stars, whose fleeting appearances in our city somehow confirm our status in the global village. All too often, unfortunately, one side effect of the globalization of entertainment and popular culture has been the slow death of civic and regional cultures, except where they survive in the nostalgic imagery of place marketing. This has led Sassen to claim that just as the economies of global cities are becoming detached from the national and regional economies they were once the "centres" of, so too are the cultures of these cities losing the connections they once had with national and regional cultures. In support of this idea, Polish sociologist Zygmunt Bauman, discussing a major study of Cultural Globalization among executives with U.S.-based transnationals, observes that what is ironic about the lifestyles of these new "extraterritorials" is their remarkable sameness. As these people live in and travel between the world's most global cities, the hotels and offices, health and golf clubs, restaurants and entertainments that these self-described "citizens of the world" choose to patronize are almost identical—"There is a sense in which they inhabit a socio-cultural bubble that is insulated from the harsher differences of national cultures" (Bauman, 2001, 55–57).

English geographer Kevin Robbins comes to the same conclusion from a different direction, noting that the downtown districts of global cities increasingly reflect the tastes of a new kind of transnational elite—educated, sophisticated, and mobile, but wanting access to the same "cappuccino lifestyle" and the same entertainment options wherever they may be. Given the pressures on cities to attract these people that were discussed in the last section, Robbins (1991) says we should not be surprised at how widely "this particular identity and lifestyle is now being mapped onto city space and landscape(s). Indeed, both Sassen and Robbins agree that much of the current talk about "world class cities," and indeed the rapid proliferation of upscale leisure and consumption sites that have transformed so many actual cities, reflects nothing so clearly as the power of a growing "symbolic analyst" class to remake cities in their own image, and according to their own interests.

What is even more important here than the standardization of urban cultures around a privileged set of tastes is the social polarization that follows when cities allocate important blocks of downtown land for "fantasy city" developments, and when they invest public resources in such developments. Social polarization is manifest most concretely in the gentrification that follows from the increases in property values that major projects in downtown districts typically produce (Ley, 1996). Rental accommodation is quickly converted to "upmarket" condominiums aimed at affluent professionals, and populations that once depended on low-rent accommodation are forced out, often to suburbs a long journey from downtown. Meanwhile, stores catering to household needs give way to gourmet shops and boutiques—all selling higher-quality, higher-margin goods and services to a new downtown population. Both dimensions of this gentrification process—the turnover of population, and of retail—are predictable; indeed they are the main object of developments designed to bring upper-middle-class consumers back downtown.

Another aspect of social polarization that may be less dramatic, but is still not insignificant, follows from the decline in public services that ensues when large sums of public money are allocated to major "fantasy city" developments. In an era of limits on public expenditures, spending on mega-projects is usually accompanied by cutbacks to public services, services that may be low-profile (e.g., municipal recreation facilities) but make tangible differences in neighbourhoods that tourists and affluent residents seldom visit. In British Columbia, for example, the same provincial government that spared no expense for Expo '86 simultaneously carried out an "austerity program" that cut back sharply on many community and social services. In Australia, likewise, the state of New South Wales imposed sweeping cutbacks in public services in order to finance Olympic construction, cutbacks which critics argued hit hardest at Australians unlikely to attend the Olympics or benefit from them in any way—the urban poor, people in country districts far from Sydney, and Aboriginal populations (Wilson, 1996). Finally, in Edmonton, in 1997–8, neighbourhood recreation facilities were closed in order to accomplish cutbacks to the Parks & Recreation budget (including, ironically, rinks where young people actually play hockey), while the city found money for a $2.4 million annual subsidy to the NHL Oilers. The general point here is that poorer citizens experience few benefits from the presence of world class events and amenities, and may often find their lives made meaner by the gentrification and urban transformations that follow predictably from such developments. Thus although the invitation to participate in the world class city is extended rhetorically to the collective "we," world class development often has the effect of polarizing the "city's population into those who consume world class entertainment and benefit in other ways from its presence, and those who cannot and do not" (Wilson, 1996, 608).

Former *Globe & Mail* editor William Thorsell has frequently made the case that Canadian cities must respond to the aspirations of our business and professional elites, and must recognize the importance of "world class" events and cultural facilities in dynamics of civic growth and decline. He suggests that many people of the sort that Reich describes as symbolic analysts were attracted to Edmonton during the 1970s oil boom, and that it was their interest and patronage, and their business and organizational skills, that transformed Edmonton from a dusty provincial capital into an urban metropolis, supporting top-quality theatre, major league hockey, and Commonwealth and Universiade Games in 1978 and 1983. However with the collapse of the boom in the early 1980s, "the city building adventure that Edmonton offered in the 1970s slipped just across the line into normalcy," and "the kind of people who had really made a difference" (including Thorsell himself) moved on to attractive opportunities elsewhere. Thorsell criticizes the opposition of groups like Bread Not Circuses to the Toronto bid for the 1996 Olympics, and the broader opposition in Toronto to "civic monuments" like the ballet/opera house and the SkyDome. For Thorsell, world events and world class facilities matter to the future of a city, and he believes that if Toronto, like Edmonton, "deliberately crosses its own line into normalcy," it will no longer be able to accommodate the ambitions of its own "best and brightest" and they too will move away, probably south of the border (Thorsell, 1991).

However, what matters more than the "brain drain" in this debate is the competition between two different kinds of claimants on civic resources. In one camp, transnational businesses and investors align themselves with local elites in making claims about the needs of central business districts for expensive capital projects, including "world class" sporting and cultural facilities. In the other, workers and other less-affluent citizens make claims about *their* needs for labour-intensive public services, often in anonymous residential neighbourhoods that are far from the city centres (Sassen, 1996). These are services that can often make real differences for populations whose routines are most of the time confined to the local, and whose quality of life depends in important ways on the quality of neighbourhood services. The growth agenda, in contrast, tends to be favoured by groups whose interests in the city are financial, often temporary, and often limited to the already affluent zones of what are much larger cities. Yet although their spokespersons routinely claim that the developments they propose will benefit the city as a whole, their knowledge of the quality of lives lived beyond their own carefully secured spaces is increasingly remote. Indeed, the "sociocultural bubble" in which many affluent business and professional people now live has increasingly insulated them from any real awareness of how people on wages (let alone on social assistance) now live, and of the impact of neoliberal social policies on those lives.

Here it is worth drawing attention to Bauman's discussion of "the secession of the successful" (drawing, in turn, on an idea first introduced in Reich's The Work of Nations). What both Reich and Bauman propose is that for many members of the new global elite, the state of the larger city—the city outside their own carefully secured "bubble"—no longer matters very much to their own well-being. "The new elites, with enough private cars not to worry about the sorry state of public transport . . . have washed their hands of the public transport issue" (Bauman, 2001, 62). Likewise, able to afford private education for their children and private healthcare, their interest in these debates is focused on reducing the demands that public education and healthcare systems make on their tax dollars. The costs of public security are generally borne without question; yet even here, withdrawal into gated communities, also known as "lifestyle enclaves," allows elites to further insulate themselves against the crime and violence that arise from growing social disparities.

Returning to the Sassen argument—that the "global" parts of global cities are becoming detached both economically and culturally from the larger communities of which they are part—it can be proposed that for business and professional elites, living in a world class city promises several kinds of benefits. Having the means to avail themselves of whatever consumer amenities the city offers, such people also benefit from developments that increase the values of their businesses and homes. The less affluent, in contrast, can rarely afford world-class prices, whether for sport, culture, or restaurants. Their leisure is more likely to revolve around neighbourhood cafés and bars, and around local parks and recreation facilities, than around the downtown entertainment district. Yet for the affluent resident—and certainly for the tourist—the decline of "community-use values" in anonymous residential neighbourhoods may well be invisible. Thus we need to challenge, following Sassen, the ways in which elites have been able to equate their own interests (their leisure as well as their economic interests) with the needs of the city as a whole, and to define what we mean by "world class."

WHAT IS A WORLD CLASS CITY? SPECTACLE AND CONSUMPTION VERSUS LIVEABILITY AND DIVERSITY

One can begin by observing that the marketing of global culture (like other global products) sets out precisely to weaken consumer loyalties to local traditions, local performers, or local teams. It does this through at least three kinds of rhetorical moves. In the most transparent of these, the notion of "world class" typically seeks to construct around the global product the connotations of excellence, more specifically the idea of being the best in the world. The global marketplace is portrayed in such discourse as a modernizing force that brings new and better choices to everyone, and we are encouraged to think that our lives are improved by access to global products and global superstars. However, we need to distinguish here between excellence and fame, and understand the effects of expensive publicity machines and corporate cross-marketing (exploiting the links between film studios and cinema chains, for example, or cable networks and sports teams) in determining the films we get to see, the songs we get to hear, and the sports we get to watch.

We also need to think about how problematic it is to determine "the best" in categories where criteria of excellence may be intangible, or may not be universally agreed upon. It is worth recalling here that the term "world class" first came into common usage in the context of athletics and swimming—sports where performances in different places could be quantitatively measured—in the 1960s, when international competition was less frequent than it is today, and the best performers from the Eastern Bloc countries and Australia (for example) might meet only in the Olympic Games. It was in this context that the "Welt Klasse" meeting in Zurich sought to attract the athletes with the best times (or distances) in their sports; and this event (and others like it that sprung up in Oslo and elsewhere) quickly became popular with fans (and athletes) as predictors of Olympic success.

Today, however, "world class" is used as a claim to superiority in so many different contexts—ranging from orchestras to universities to cities—where appropriate measures of excellence remain matters of debate that it has become a "sign without a referent" (Hartley, 1988). In all of these categories, it can be suggested that claims to "world class" status are vacuous, denoting nothing so clearly as ambition. Indeed, one rarely hears the term used in conjunction with truly global cities like New York, London, Paris, or Tokyo.

The third connotation of the term "world class" that we must examine here concerns how it works to commodify—and trade on—the idealism that was part of older discourses of internationalism. This commodification is manifest in marketers' claims that a taste for global products is somehow indicative of cultural capital or cosmopolitanism, even a marker of global citizenship (Levitt, 1983). Now, we can grant immediately that experiences or products (travel or media products, for example) that develop our knowledge of cultures beyond our own has been one of the major benefits of modern communications. However, where older models of internationalism encouraged direct encounters with other cultures on their own terms, globalism promotes a transnational or postnational culture in which difference is sanitized and made "accessible." People around the affluent world can participate in the same cultural phenomena without too much effort. "Global culture" in these circumstances has less to do with cross-cultural understanding than with the potential profits from creating global markets for trendy niche products. Not surprisingly, the result is cultural standardization around a largely Western set of practices (with the qualified exception of "cuisine") (Zukin, 1991, ch. 7).

It can be proposed that in the context of the internationalist project and the discourse (and international institutions) that promoted it, the idea of "cosmopolitanism" implied a level of detailed knowledge about cultures different from one's own as well as the kind of cultural capital that enabled people to operate knowledgeably outside the comfort zone of their home culture. In the context of "world class" culture and its associated discourse, however, cosmopolitanism is effectively de-skilled, reduced to being *au courant* with the latest sign values in global entertainment and shopping. We can see this in action, Swedish anthropologist Ulf Hannerz suggests, when connotations of sophistication are conferred on the use of commodities associated with the world's metropolitan centres, simply "by making their metropolitan derivation a significant part of their value to the consumer" (1996). This is clearest in the ways that people around the world consume brands (such as McDonald's, Planet Hollywood, or Nike) carrying associations with America. More subtly, though, it also occurs "with regard to more diffuse complexes . . . [such as] the kinds of phenomena nowadays frequently packaged as 'lifestyles'," and Hannerz suggests that the most fashionable "lifestyles" involve conspicuous consumption of cultural commodities from the "centre."

What, then, do we mean by the notion of a "world class" city? Does it mean a city big enough and wealthy enough to host world events (like the Olympics, or World's Fairs)? To have state-of-the-art cultural venues featuring regular visits by world-famous musicians and dancers, or exhibitions by renowned artists? To have famous professional sports teams, and a shopping district offering the top brand names in international fashion? All of these constitute "lifestyle" opportunities that appeal to some citizens, but they are opportunities that substantial parts of the city's population cannot afford. Alternately, the designation "world class city" can have more to do with culture that is produced within a city itself—with the diversity of neighbourhood shops and restaurants, the quality of goods made by local artisans, and the vitality of the local music scene—most of these in venues that tourists and big spenders seldom find? It may be salutary here to cite a recent claim that

"Montreal, its residents have taken an odd pride in saying, is a city where you can have no money and still have fun" (Charlton, 1997, D4). A combination of affordable housing, a genuinely cosmopolitan population, and a lively and affordable nightlife (encompassing dance, music, theatre, sports, and restaurants) make Montreal a liveable and indeed exciting city, even for those on limited budgets. And it will continue to be such even if the Expos leave.

The renowned Canadian critic Northrop Frye once proposed, "If Toronto is a world class city, it is not because it bids for the Olympics or builds follies like the SkyDome, but because of the tolerated variety of the people in its streets" (1992, 16). Frye went on to observe that Toronto is now made up of a diversity of peoples and cultural practices that would have been unimaginable 50 years ago. He maintains that it is this, rather than the presence of global consumer opportunities, that gives Toronto whatever cosmopolitan character it now enjoys. More recently, Toronto's multicultural achievements have also been lauded by Indo-American writer Pico Iyer. Iyer proposes that the challenge for truly global cities, in a world of human mobility and hybrid identities, is not only to create environments where diverse peoples can coexist peacefully and participate in public institutions. It is also to create a civic culture where, rather like a successful anthology, the whole is enriched and made more interesting by the alchemy between its component parts. Iyer recognized, "there were still many problems, inevitably, as Toronto and Vancouver raced into a polylingual future while villages only forty-five minutes away still lingered, undisturbed, in their white-bread, Protestant . . . pasts" (Iyer, 2000, 124). Yet Toronto, from Iyer's perspective at least, was in the process of becoming a genuinely cosmopolitan city (as was Vancouver), and Canada's major cities compared very favourably in this respect with Atlanta, which beat out Toronto to host the 1996 Olympics.

Atlanta, indeed, had boomed between 1970 and 2000, becoming the headquarters (or so it claimed) to more global corporations than any other U.S. city, including such giants as CNN, Delta Air Lines, Holiday Inn, UPS, and Coca-Cola. However, beyond these corporate links, Iyer was struck by how few connections Atlantans seemed to have with the world outside America. In contrast to Toronto or Los Angeles, where large segments of the populations spoke several languages, and spoke languages other than English at home, the figure for the latter in metropolitan Atlanta in 1990 was only 6 percent (Iyer, 2000, 214). Atlanta claimed to welcome diversity; indeed the city became famous in a U.S. context as a site of Black business success. However, Atlanta's diversity even today does not extend far beyond the Black and white communities that have always coexisted in the American South, and as the city prepared to host the Olympics, Iyer still observed gaping inequalities between the largely white suburbs and the largely Black central city. To Iyer, Atlanta gave the impression of an overgrown company town whose private sector was still far more visible than any public institutions, a city full of can-do slogans and harmless boasts, but a city that had a hard time understanding why wealth (and even the Olympics) had not brought it the respect it felt it deserved (2000, 198).

In their respective celebrations of urban diversity, Frye and Iyer echo an argument made by Hannerz that ethnic and cultural diversity is the defining characteristic of a global city. Describing Amsterdam and Stockholm—both cities containing substantial communities with South American, Asian, and Middle Eastern origins—Hannerz proposes that global cities (and, like Iyer, he calls them "global" rather than "world class") can be distinguished from their more provincial counterparts by the presence of at least four different categories of "transnational people." There are the business and professional elites; tourists; and expressive specialists such as actors and musicians who work in the culture industries that make these cities interesting centres of entertainment. Finally, there are significant populations of Third World migrants who provide personal services, as cooks, waiters, and nannies at very low wages to wealthier groups and service workers in public institutions. Each group reproduces aspects of the cultures of their homelands at the same time that they (and their children) make new lives in the global city. In their daily interactions with each other and with the societies which they now call home, they are *making new culture,* and the host societies are changing, as a result, in ways that make them more dynamic and more cosmopolitan (Hannerz, 1996, ch. 12, 13).

Yet Hannerz also emphasizes that this sort of positive interaction requires continuing investment in the quality of public infrastructure (schools, transit, libraries and parks, multilingual services) that can assist new migrants and their children to become fully participating—as opposed to alienated and excluded—members of the society. Without this, one gets the development of impoverished ethnic ghettos, leading to the sorts of endemic racial tensions that have divided many U.S. cities. Here, despite the success stories of immigrant adaptation and contribution to civic culture that made Toronto and Vancouver so impressive to Iyer, we need to acknowledge that tensions have grown between black youth and the police in both Toronto and Montreal in recent years, with tragic deaths occurring but no serious effort to resolve the underlying problems. It is also important to recognize the growth of Aboriginal poverty in several Western Canadian cities, a situation that several knowledgeable observers describe as a time bomb if steps are not taken to make hope realistic among Aboriginal youth (Freisen, 2000).

CONCLUSION

We need to ask ourselves, finally, whether the "world class" city is an imaged product, something to be promoted among global elites, whether as investors, tourists, and potential residents? Or is it a city whose public culture and public amenities make it a good place for most of its citizens to live? Although economic growth might be said to be a necessary condition for civic success, when the growth agenda is not balanced by concern for quality-of-life issues, and when business input into public policy is not balanced by opportunities for other voices to be heard, our vision of "the good city" is likely to be a narrow one, and ultimately unsuccessful even on its own terms (Milroy et al. 1999). In his account of Toronto's evolution over the last half of the twentieth century, Toronto writer and editor Robert Fulford (1995) proposes that the city that elected mayors like David Crombie, John Sewell, and Barbara Hall expressed a widely shared desire to build a city that was big and rich and humane—in contrast to the Toronto of Fred Gardiner's generation, that wanted simply to be big and rich. Arguably, the Toronto of that era (roughly 1969–1988) aspired to be a good city in which to live—where this meant concern with the quality of public facilities, public spaces, and public culture, rather than simply a concern with growth—the "economy first" agenda that came to characterize the city again during the Harris/Lastman years.

Global events can provide occasions for extended public parties, and (to reverse Hartley's phrase, above) for putting the global on show for the locals. They can leave legacies of good memories, wider horizons, and sometimes changes in aspirations, and the value of these intangibles should not be discounted. Similarly, professional sports teams can offer occasions for public celebrations and the re-enactment of communal identities, as the Oilers did in the late 1980s and the Blue Jays in 1992. Yet we also have to remember that hosting an Olympics or constructing a new arena or stadium complex constitute occasions for the major redevelopment of downtown districts, with subsequent effects for the city as a whole. This was clear in the debates about Toronto's bid for the 1996 Olympics and about SkyDome, as it was in the struggles in Winnipeg and Quebec over whether to build new NHL-standard arenas. Such projects require major commitments of public resources, and they inevitably involve strains on the public purse (and usually cutbacks in public services), even as they create business opportunities. There are thus major public interests at stake, as well as major corporate interests; yet public-interest groups typically have a hard time getting their concerns heard in the local media, where they are typically painted as "spoilsports" (Silver, 1996). It is precisely for these reasons that corporate claims that these developments are good for the city as a whole need to be carefully and publicly examined, and detailed outlines of the costs and benefits, as well as the "opportunity costs"—the other benefits foregone when public funds are allocated to this rather than other projects—made the subject of public debates. Whatever their outcomes, such debates should help those who take part to clarify whether a world class city is necessarily a good city to live in.

No vision of the city that widens social disparities to the point of excluding significant proportions of its people is sustainable for very long. The discourse of possessive individualism that made the Common Sense Revolution seem common sense to suburban voters wanting to insulate themselves against the costs of solving urban problems can only heighten the potential for conflicts, exacerbating "the indifference and greed of the new elites versus the hopelessness and rage of the poor" (Sassen, 1996). Again, this doesn't mean that the economy is unimportant; the left needs to acknowledge that a stagnant or declining economy makes it difficult to sustain public services. However, the kind of economic growth that produces spectacular wealth and lifestyle opportunities for some, alongside poverty and exclusion for others, is not the answer. Edmonton business leader Robert Stollery took Albertans to task last year for allowing income disparities to widen in what Alberta publicity claims to be "the best province in the best country in the world." Stollery observed that only a handful of developed countries have worse child poverty rates than Canada, and that within Canada, wealthy Alberta spends less than half per child what Quebec spends. Challenging his comfortable charity-dinner audience to reflect on this, he urged "If we can't bring ourselves for *humanitarian* reasons to fund our children, we should do it for selfish reasons, as the cost of *not* investing in kids is quickly translated into . . . crime, early school dropouts, early pregnancies, and the perpetuation of poverty" (Stollery, 2001, A17).

At a 1998 conference entitled "World Class Cities: Can Canada Play?" Caroline Andrew proposed that responding creatively to urban problems will require that we abandon metaphors like "world class" that are drawn from the world of competitive sports. For Andrew, the major challenges facing Canadian cities have to do with containing social polarization, and managing ethnocultural diversity so that cities can successfully integrate new non-European migrant populations, as well as migrants from the poorest parts of rural Canada, notably Aboriginal reservations. The two issues become one, effectively, when visible minorities—and especially their youth—find that they cannot achieve full participation in the urban economy, and that civic institutions are unwilling or unable to address their grievances. For Andrew, addressing these kinds of challenges will require new thinking, and ultimately a comprehensive strategy that includes "policies for primary and secondary schools, ways of ensuring that social institutions are open to diversity, employment strategies, housing strategies, and so on" (Andrew, 1999, 102). Finally, it will require significant reinvestment in cites whose public institutions are severely strained after more than a decade of "economy first" thinking. Like Stollery, Andrew warns that the costs of inaction are likely to be even greater.

REFERENCES

Andrew, Caroline. 2000. "The Shame of (Ignoring) the Cities." *Journal of Canadian Studies 35* (4): 100–111.

Barber, Benjamin. 1996. *Jihad vs. McWorld*. New York: Random House.

Bauman, Zygmunt. 2001. *Community*. Cambridge: Polity.

Betke, Carl. 1983. "Sports Promotion in the Western Canadian City: The Example of Early Edmonton." *Urban History Review 12*, (2): 47–56.

Bocking, Stephen. 2001. "The Games Cities Play." *Journal of Canadian Studies 36*, (2): 5–7.

Britton, Samuel. 1991. "Tourism, Capital and Place: Towards a Critical Geography of Tourism." *Society and Space 9*, 451–478.

Charlton, Jacquie. 1997. "Montreal: Ville Vivante." *Globe and Mail*. November 4, D4.

Fainstein, Susan and R. Stokes. 1998. "Spaces for Play: The Impacts of Entertainment Development on New York City." *Economic Development Quarterly 12*, (2): 150–165.

Freisen, Gerald. 2000. *The West*. Penguin Books.

Frye, Northrop. 1992. "The Cultural Development of Canada." *Australian-Canadian Studies 10*, (1): 16.

Fulford, Robert. 1995. *Accidental City: The Transformation of Toronto*. Toronto: Macfarlane Walter Ross.

Hannerz, Ulf. 1996. *Transnational Connections: Culture, People, Places*. London: Routledge.

Hannigan, John. 1998. *Fantasy City: Pleasure and Profit in the Postmodern* Metropolis. New York: Routledge.

Hartley, John. 1988. "A State of Excitement: Western Australia and the Americas Cup." *Cultural Studies 2*, (1): 117–126.

Harvey, David. 1989. *The Condition of Postmodernity*. Oxford: Blackwell.

Hiller, Harry. 1989. "Impact and Image: The Convergence of Urban Factors in Preparing for the 1988 Calgary Olympics." In G. Syme et al. (eds.), *The Planning and Evaluation of Hallmark Events*. Brookfield: Avebury Press.

Iyer, Pico. 2000. *The Global Soul*. New York: Vintage Books.

Kidd, Bruce. 1992. "The Toronto Olympic Commitment: Towards a Social Contract for the Olympic Games." *Olympika 1*, 154–167.

________. 1995. "Toronto's SkyDome: The World's Greatest Entertainment Centre." In John Bale and Olof Moen (eds.) *The Stadium and the City*. Leicester: University of Leicester Press.

Lash, Scott and John Urry. 1994. *Economies of Signs and Space*. London: Sage.

Levitt, Theodore. 1983. *The Marketing Imagination*. London: Collier Macmillan.

Ley, David. 1996. *The New Middle Class and the Remaking of the Central City*. London: Oxford University Press.

Milroy, Beth Moore, Philippa Campsie, Robyn Whittaker and Zoe Girling. 1999. "Who Says Toronto Is a 'Good' City?" In C. Andrew, P. Armstrong and A. Lapierre (eds.), *World Class Cities: Can Canada Play?* Ottawa: University of Ottawa Press.

Murray, Glen. 2002, January 11. "New Cities for a New Century." *Globe and Mail*, A11.

Reich, Robert. 1991. *The Work of Nations*. New York: Knopf.

Renzetti, Elizabeth. 1997, May 3. "Monster Musicals take to the Road." *Globe and Mail*, C10.

Robbins, Kevin. 1991. "Prisoners of the City: Whatever Could a Postmodern City Be?" *New Formations 15*, 1–22.

Sassen, Saskia. 1996. "Whose City is It? Globalization and the Formation of New Claims." *Public Culture 8* (2): 205–223.

________. 1998. *Globalization and Its Discontents.* New York: New Press.

Silver, Jim. 1996. *Thin Ice: Money, Politics, and the Demise of an NHL Franchise*. Halifax: Fernwood Books.

Stollery, Robert. 2001, September 27. "In Alberta, It's Time to Reassess Our Priorities." *Edmonton Journal*, A17.

Thorsell, William. 1990. *Globe and Mail*. November 17.

Whitson, David. 1999. "World Class Leisure and Consumption: Social Polarization and the Politics of Place." In C. Andrew, P. Armstrong, and A. Lapierre (eds.) *World Class Cities: Can Canada Play?* Ottawa: University of Ottawa Press.

Whitson, David, Jean Harvey and Marc Lavoie. 2000. "The Mills Report, the Manley Subsidy Proposals, and the Business of Major League Sport." *Canadian Public Administration 43* (2): 127–156.

Whitson, David and Donald Macintosh. 1993. "Becoming a World Class City: Hallmark Events and Sports Franchises in the Growth Strategies of Western Canadian Cities." *Sociology of Sport Journal 10* (3): 221–240.

Wilson, Helen. 1996. "What is an Olympic City? Visions of Sydney 2000." *Media, Culture, and Society 18*, 603–618.

Zukin, Sharon. 1991. *Landscapes of Power: From Detroit to Disney World*. California: University of California Press.

WEBLINKS

Culture of Cities Project
www.yorku.ca/culture_of_cities

New Urbanism
www.newurbanism.org

Olympic Bid News
www.gamesbids.com

chapter six

The Democratic Deficit

Neoliberal Governance and the Undermining of Democracy's Potential

Steve Patten

INTRODUCTION: DEMOCRATIC TRIUMPHALISM AND THE PROBLEM OF COMPLACENCY

The final decade of the twentieth century was marked by a spirit of democratic triumphalism. Particularly in the United States, but throughout the Western world, liberal democrats were emboldened by the demise of the Soviet Union and the end of the Cold War. As an increasing number of formerly authoritarian regimes moved to establish electoral democracy and protect the civil and political rights of their citizens, there was talk of a global "democratic revolution." At the end of the Gulf War in 1991, former President George Bush declared that American-led forces had done more than liberate a small country (Kuwait). They had advanced a "big idea"—a New World Order in which justice, freedom, the rule of law, and democracy would triumph. According to Francis Fukuyama, the triumph of Western liberal democracy marked the "end of history," the arrival of the final form of human government (1992). In the popular news media the message was clear—not only were democratic principles globally ascendant, but the epitome of democracy was the model of democracy found in Western liberal capitalist societies like Canada.

While liberal democracy is a significant human accomplishment, the hubris of democratic triumphalism is unwarranted. In Canada, our experience with democracy is short and incomplete and, within the context of neoliberal globalism, increasingly vulnerable. State power is concentrated within a limited number of executive institutions; new governing practices are undermining the potential of democratic citizenship; national sovereignty is being lost to supra-national governing institutions; and the goals and purposes of the state are being altered in such a way that the body politic is losing its capacity to act collectively to regulate and improve social and economic life. Not all is gloomy on the democratic front, but there is good reason to be concerned about the growing "democratic deficit."

The purpose of this chapter is to encourage students to think critically about the quality of democracy in Canada. Following some introductory comments on the meaning of democracy and a review of some enduring problems with electoral and parliamentary democracy in Canada, we will examine four trends associated with the transition to "neoliberal governance" that currently threaten the quality of Canadian democracy. These trends include: 1) the popularization of new notions of the goals and purposes of the state; 2) a neoliberal-inspired rethinking of how we understand political community, social groups, and the politics of civil society; 3) the rise of new market-oriented state governing practices; and, 4) the development of new supra-national institutions of governance. The chapter's argument is, quite simply, that the current historical era of neoliberal globalism is marked by approaches to politics and governance that are a threat to democracy. The gap between democracy's potential and the realities of twenty-first century democracy is widening. And, in light of this growing democratic deficit, strong democrats should know that now is not a time for complacency; there are reasons for concern, and for vigilance in our defence of democracy.

DEFINING OUR ASPIRATIONS: EXTENSIVE DEMOCRACY

There was a time when democracy was an idea charged with egalitarian idealism, a time when democracy was associated with curbing the power of the political elite, and establishing institutions for "rule by the common people." Prior to the early twentieth century, opinion leaders in politics, business, and the media were skeptical about democracy's radical egalitarianism. For example, Canada's first prime minister, Sir John A. Macdonald, often expressed his doubts about the wisdom of political institutions that went too far in enhancing the influence and power of the masses of ordinary working people. Indeed, it was this sort of anxiety about popular self-rule that explained and justified Canada's highly undemocratic origins. Canadians are often surprised to learn that our original electoral system excluded almost 90 percent of the population from voting. In the first election after Confederation, voters were exclusively adult male property owners. But even this limited degree of popular control concerned the mid-nineteenth-century elite, and that is why the new Dominion of Canada was established with a Senate. This "upper chamber" of Parliament, with membership restricted to well-off property owners, was to act as a chamber of "sober second thought." In effect the Senate protects the "minority interests" of wealth and property from threats from the elected House of Commons.

By the end of the First World War, however, much had changed. Voting rights were extended to most adults (women and men) and the political elite were speaking favourably about democracy. Of course, democracy's newfound legitimacy was not a result of a new commitment to egalitarianism and popular self-rule. It was, instead, a commitment to a new understanding of democracy. The popular meaning of democracy had been transformed so that twentieth-century democracy would mean little more than allowing adult citizens to participate, as individual voters, in a competitive electoral system which allowed citizens to decide which rival elite group would be granted the right to govern. This is known as "electoral democracy" or, perhaps more accurately, "competitive elite democracy." It is democracy, but it is democracy stripped of much of its egalitarian potential.

In the mid-twentieth century, the deeply conservative notion that democracy can mean little more than competition among elites was popularized in academic circles by scholars such as Joseph Schumpeter (1942). Today, many liberal democratic scholars implicitly accept a Schumpeterian definition of democracy. One popular text on Canadian politics, for example, defines democracy as a political system in which the formal "political equality" that is associated with basic civil and political citizenship rights serves to ensure "there is a realistic possibility that voters can replace the government" (Brooks, 2000, 14). The author of this text admits to social and cultural factors that influence the possibility of democratic politics; however, at bottom, democracy is politically equal citizens voting in elections. Democracy, however, means much more than this. We should never be satisfied with limited electoral democracy and the existing institutions of liberal representative government. Democracy is always a matter of degree, and competitive elite democracy should be considered no more than minimally satisfying to strong democrats who desire the type of meaningful self-rule that allows citizens to take control of their own lives and destinies.

Imagine a vertical democratic continuum. Towards the low end of the continuum is liberal electoral democracy. Near to the top is "extensive democracy." An extensively democratic social order is one in which people are free and equally capable of commanding the material and symbolic resources necessary to hold all forms of socially consequential power accountable and to determine the conditions of their own existence and self-development (Macpherson, 1973). Extensive democracy is about much more than formal political equality, holding state power accountable, or the availability of electoral mechanisms that empower voters to select and, later, replace the government of the day. Extensive democracy is about meaningful self-rule and self-determination in all spheres of life. It is a conception of democracy centred on social equality and popular empowerment. The egalitarianism of extensive democracy demands that in addition to traditional civil rights (freedom of thought, speech, assembly, etc.) and political rights (the right to vote, run for office, etc.), there must exist an extensive system of social rights (positive entitlements in terms of education, healthcare, economic well-being, etc.), a high degree of substantive social and economic equality, and a highly politicized civil society in which individuals and groups with roughly equivalent organizational and communicative competence play meaningful roles in shaping the norms and values that are dominant in civic and public affairs.

In a capitalist society structured by social and economic inequality, extensive democracy requires a commitment to equalizing the political capacities of competing interests, as well as a commitment to respecting both expert opinion and the "situated knowledge" of more marginal social interests. Moreover, extensive democracy requires that we take social differences seriously and make a normative political commitment to facilitating group self-organization, protecting the right of groups to self-define their political identities and interests, and creating space for groups to have a voice and self-representation in public policymaking (Phillips, 1996). In doing so, we must respect the collective nature of many political interests, and respond to inequalities of social economic power with a willingness to use the power of the state to equalize the organizational and deliberative capacities of disadvantaged groups and protect the rights and interests of those who are most marginalized (Young, 1989). Clearly, extensive democracy is about more than process; it is also about a substantive state of affairs.

THE ENDURING CRISIS OF ELECTORAL AND PARLIAMENTARY DEMOCRACY

Canada's experience with democracy, even minimalist electoral democracy, is short and incomplete. While property qualifications for voting in federal elections were eliminated in the nineteenth century, women did not have the vote until 1918 (1940 for Quebec women wishing to vote in provincial elections), and a variety of racial, ethnic, and religious exclusions from voting continued through to 1960 when the law was changed to grant the vote to, among others, Aboriginal persons who were "Status Indians" as defined by the *Indian Act*. Thus, contrary to Canada's popular democratic myth, it was not until the early 1960s that Canadian elections were conducted under conditions of universal adult suffrage.

Of course, granting the vote to all adults does not guarantee the democratic credentials of an electoral or political system. Canada's "single member plurality" (SMP) electoral system is based on what many consider to be a highly undemocratic method for transforming the votes of Canadians into seats in the House of Commons (Milner, 1999; Pilon, 2000). As most students are aware, the basic rules of the SMP system are as follows: votes are a simple preference (everyone has one vote for their preferred local candidate), and one member is elected per constituency based on a simple "plurality rule" (the most votes wins). This is a "winner takes all" system in that votes cast for candidates other than the winning candidate have absolutely no impact on the composition of the House of Commons.

The representational and democratic consequences of SMP are significant. First, a political party does not require the support of a majority of Canadians to win an election. In fact, in a system with three or more political parties, minority of voters can elect the governing party. Moreover, the cumulative effect of multiple local victories based on the support of a mere plurality of voters is that the party that wins the election is likely to be artificially overrepresented—that is, they are likely to control a majority of the seats in the House of Commons without the support of the majority of voters. Second, while major (particularly winning) parties are overrepresented relative to their share of the national vote, smaller parties with geographically dispersed electoral support will be underrepresented and small parties with geographically concentrated support will be overrepresented. The result is that the balance of power between the parties in the House of Commons is a system-created artifact with little grounding in the electorate's support for the various parties. In the 2000 federal election, for example, the Canadian Alliance won almost one in four (23.6 percent) Ontario votes, but the party won only 2 Ontario seats in the House of Commons. The Liberals, on the other hand, won slightly more than twice as many votes in Ontario (2.29 million Liberal votes compared to 1.05 million Alliance votes), but won 50 times the number of seats (100 Liberal seats compared to 2 Alliance seats). In that same election, the Bloc Québécois (BQ) earned just under 11 percent of Canadians' votes compared to the Conservatives who earned just over 12 percent of the total votes cast. In terms of seats, however, the Quebec-focused BQ won 38 seats, a total that was over three times higher than the 12 seats won by the nationally focused Conservatives.

The undemocratic nature of Canada's SMP electoral system has attracted academic and political criticism frequently in the past decades (for example, Irvine, 1979). Not surprisingly, however, the governing parties that tend to benefit from the system have resisted calls for change. Indeed, when appointing the Royal Commission on Electoral Reform and Party Financing in the 1980s, the Mulroney government was direct and explicit in instructing the Commission *not* to investigate or make recommendations related to alternatives to SMP. But, in the end, governments may not be able to escape the pressure for electoral system reform. Not only has political pressure been increasing in recent years, but in May, 2001, the Constitutional Test Case Centre at the Faculty of Law, University of Toronto, launched a constitutional challenge against the *Canada Elections Act* on behalf of the Green Party of Canada (Beatty, 2001). The legal experts at the University of Toronto argue that the SMP electoral system violates sections 3 and 15 (the political and equality rights sections) of the *Charter of Rights and Freedoms*. Although it could take as long as five years for this case to wind its way through the Ontario Supreme Court and Court of Appeals to the Supreme Court of Canada, we may soon be in a situation where the courts force the government to take action to correct this enduring bias in Canadian electoral democracy.

Between elections the quality of Canadian democracy depends, to a significant extent, on the workings of the Westminster model of parliamentary government. The most obvious problem with parliamentary government is the extent to which the prime minister and cabinet dominate public policymaking. It has long been a truism that parliamentary government is "cabinet government." In recent decades, however, academic observers such as Donald Savoie have argued that the problem of unchecked government power and weak parliamentary control has worsened (Savoie, 1999). State power is increasingly concentrated within a limited number of executive institutions, particularly the Prime Minister's Office (PMO) and Privy Council Office (PCO), and central agencies like the Department of Finance and Treasury Board. The power of the prime minister to control cabinet and direct key executive and central agencies has led some cynical observers to refer to the system as an "elected dictatorship." This state of affairs, it should be said, is in keeping with competitive elite democracy so long as citizens have a realistic chance of voting to circulate state power among the elite groups at the apex of the party and parliamentary system.

TRANSFORMATIONS IN THE GOALS AND PURPOSES OF THE STATE

The essential elements of liberal electoral democracy—elected, representative, and responsible government; and the guarantee of formal political equality through the extension of civil and political citizenship rights—were institutionalized during the nineteenth and early twentieth centuries. This was the era of Canada's minimalist laissez-faire state form. With the rise of the twentieth century's modern welfare state, the goals and purposes of the state were enlarged. Social welfare policies were expanded and social citizenship rights emerged in the form of positive entitlements to education, healthcare services, a minimum level of economic well-being and, in some policy fields, more opportunities for direct citizen input into policymaking. Although never as extensive as in the social democratic European welfare states, social citizenship rights in Canada ensured a greater degree of substantive equality than had existed historically. By focusing on social welfare and raising the "social minimum," the welfare state's social citizenship rights ensured that a larger proportion of the population had the social and material capacity to take fuller advantage of their basic civil and political citizenship rights. The thinking here is as follows: Since civil and political citizenship rights are of little meaning or utility to the socially and economically dispossessed, social citizenship rights are essential to fostering meaningful democratic citizenship—they provide, in other words, the "means of citizenship" (Plant, 1991).

A distinguishing feature of the welfare state was that, unlike the classically liberal laissez-faire state, which existed first and foremost to protect economic property rights, enforce contracts, and maintain market freedoms, the welfare state existed to mediate between the conflicting imperatives of capitalist free markets and the needs of citizens. The state, in the context of welfare liberalism, was larger and more interventionist. But more significant to the quality of democracy was the fact that the welfare state was more responsive to the popular democratic demands of citizens. Acting as something of a mediator between the conflicting pressures and obligations associated with capitalist democracy's economic imperatives, on the one hand, and its democratic imperatives, on the other, the welfare state strove for greater balance. Of course, the tension between economic and democratic imperatives is a tension inherent in capitalist democracy; it can never be fully resolved. But the welfare state aimed to establish an equilibrium that privileged democracy more than had been considered desirable in the era of laissez-faire liberalism (Nuefeld, 1999).

By the 1970s, however, sections of elite opinion were aggressively questioning the goals and purposes of the welfare/mediator state. At bottom, these elite concerns pertained to the impact of democracy and welfare liberalism on government's capacity to ensure social order, economic growth, and the continued competitiveness and profitability of corporate enterprises. In 1973 David Rockefeller of America's Chase Manhattan Bank founded the Trilateral Commission, a private corporate-oriented think tank headed by business, media, and academic elites from Europe, North America, and Japan. His purpose, it is often argued, was to provide a forum for the dissemination of ideas and policy advice that would safeguard Western capitalism in a volatile and globalizing world. One of the first Trilateral Commission task forces resulted in the publication of *The Crisis of Democracy*, a book which argued Western democracies were becoming ungovernable because growing democratic processes generated a breakdown in traditional means of social control and gave rise to an overload of demands on government (Crozier, Huntington, and Watanuki, 1975). These concerns about the excesses of democracy, combined with the dilemmas of economic stagflation in the 1970s and a prolonged recession in the early 1980s, laid the ground for sweeping ideological attacks on the welfare state and social citizenship.

During the 1980s elite opinion abandoned welfare liberalism in favour of a new classical liberalism (commonly labelled *neoliberalism*) that embraced the old ideas of laissez-faire governance and the minimalist state. By the 1990s, Canadian governments, both Progressive Conservative and Liberal, were championing the notion that the goals and purposes of the state must adjust in accordance with the imperatives of global competitiveness and corporate profitability. This marked the transition to "neoliberal governance." In the context of neoliberalism, the mediator role of the postwar welfare state was abandoned and democratic demands took a back seat to economic imperatives. The neoliberal state is not entirely undemocratic. The commitment to liberal electoral democracy remains. But the dominant thinking regarding the goals and purposes of the state have shifted, and this has led to the curtailing of social citizenship rights and to a new willingness on the part of governments to privilege policies that respond to economic imperatives over popular needs and the democratic demands of ordinary citizens. Neoliberalism is concerned with enhancing the competitiveness of the Canadian economy by adjusting to the perceived imperatives of global capitalism. This process of adjusting is disruptive, and sometimes difficult and painful; thus, neoliberals expect the state to be strong in its resolve to force adjustment. Rather than committing itself to the vitality of a politicized civil society, the neoliberal/forced-adjustment state shrinks the politicized public sphere of life in an effort to curtail popular democratic demands and, in essence, to protect economic markets from democratic society. This purposeful limiting of the democratic state in favour of globalizing capitalist markets is highly undemocratic; it deserves to be questioned, debated, and perhaps challenged.

RETHINKING POLITICAL COMMUNITY: DELEGITIMIZING GROUPS AND DEPOLITICIZING CIVIL SOCIETY

The way in which we understand and think about "political community" has consequences for the quality of democracy. Neoliberalism promotes a profoundly atomistic view of the social world we inhabit. Always privileging the individual as the primary unit of analysis, neoliberals assume that the political community is little more than an aggregation of individuals. Indeed, one early champion of neoliberalism, former British prime minister Margaret Thatcher, was fond of saying, "there is no such thing as society," we are, in other words, autonomous individuals whose meaningful interactions are market interactions in the economy, not social and political interactions in civil society. From this perspective, the politics of democracy do not require consideration of political community or social groupings within the broader community. Democracy, the neoliberal assumes, requires little more than formal political equality and electoral mechanisms for registering *individual* opinion.

For strong democrats, however, atomism distorts social reality. It is argued that society is more complex than the image of a collection of isolated and autonomous individuals. Society is actually a mosaic of social relations—not social relationships between individuals, but social systems of power and privilege related to gender, race, ethnicity, class, sexual orientation, ability, and so on (Bowles and Gintis, 1986). We *are* all individuals, but we exist as "individuals in relation" in the sense that our social and political identities and interests are constructed by the social relations that shape our lives (Gould, 1988). The consequences of this are complex. Nevertheless, it is clear that the ways in which different social systems of power and privilege intersect in our lives will play a role in shaping how we understand our political identities and political interests.

It is also clear that understanding society as a mosaic of social relations draws attention to the collective nature of many political interests. Social collectivities, or groups, are defined by the social relations that shape our lives. Group differences and their associated political identities and interests are a function of political agency in the context of social relations. Put differently, the political meaning and significance of being, for example, a Native woman, a working person, or a Northerner is shaped by discursive struggles (struggles about meaning) in the context of social relations of power and privilege. With this in mind, it is argued that discerning the political wishes of citizens requires a commitment to facilitating group self-organization, protecting the right to group self-definition, and providing political processes that create space for both individual and group self-representation. Moreover, while this is anathema to neoliberals, recognizing that group interests are a consequence of the structure of unequal social relations requires that democrats be willing to respond to inequalities of power by, among other things, using the power of the state to equalize the representational and deliberative capacities of disadvantaged groups.

In the latter part of the twentieth century some progress was made in terms of advancing more extensively democratic approaches to thinking about community, groups, and civil society. Between the 1960s and 1990s, a range of progressive social movements emerged to challenge oppression, politicize a wider range of social relations, and draw attention to themes such as sexism, heterosexism, and homophobia, racism, and discrimination against people with disabilities. In addition to problematizing once-accepted social relations and politicizing new themes, these social movement organizations challenged liberal electoral democracy's narrow understanding of the requisite features of political democracy. Movements associated with feminism, anti-racism, and gay and lesbian rights, among others, sought to politicize civil society in ways that embraced liberal democratic principles, and then transformed those principles by extending them to a whole new series of social relations. The result was a growing consciousness of civil society, and a new legitimacy for social group politics. Some observers have labelled this new social movement politics the "politics of cultural recognition"—an identity-based group politics advanced by ethnocultural minorities, feminists, Aboriginal peoples, and others who are seeking, to varying degrees, extensively democratic goals such as socio-economic equity, self-determination, or official recognition through state policies that actively valorize diversity (Tully, 1995).

For a time in the late 1980s and early 1990s, there was some optimism that the politics of cultural recognition was transforming how people thought about political community, group politics, and the prerequisites of democracy. But then came the backlash. Social conservatives who were uncomfortable with social change and, more importantly, neoliberals wishing to defend individualism and a narrow conception of politics and democracy, challenged the legitimacy of social movement organizations and public interest groups. Labelling feminists, environmentalists, anti-racists, and the like as "special interest groups," neoliberals who opposed the politics of cultural recognition warned that social movements would be unwilling to set aside their self-interest in favour of the general interest of the broader political community. Neoliberal antagonists managed thus to delegitimize social movements and their politics of cultural recognition.

Claiming that the special demands of interest groups and the generous social programs aimed at meeting the demands of minority special interests were at the root of the fiscal crisis of the state, the neoliberals of the 1990s also managed to push back popular conceptions of the appropriate boundaries of the political sphere and the legitimate range of state authority and intervention. This had the effect of depoliticizing civil society and narrowing the space for extending democracy. Indeed, supported by the Royal Commission on Electoral Reform and Party Financing, neoliberals popularized the idea that social movement organizations and public interest groups were *anti*-democratic forces (Dobrowolsky and Jenson, 1993). Arguing that social movements and public interest groups are incapable of acting in the national interest, neoliberalism demanded that group politics take a back seat to aggregative institutions like political parties. Strong democrats responded that there is no one single national interest and, moreover, that it is disempowering and undemocratic to expect that minority and minoritized groups would quietly accept an articulation of the general will when it is, in fact, little more than the subtle imposition of majoritarian conceptions of the national interest. But, in the context of neoliberal hegemony, such arguments fell on deaf ears. The rise of neoliberal governance has, therefore, privileged an atomistic and less-than-extensively democratic understanding of political community, an understanding that simultaneously delegitimizes the group politics of social movements and depoliticizes civil society.

NEW GOVERNING PRACTICES: THE MARKETIZATION OF THE STATE AND CITIZENSHIP

The transition from the welfare/mediator state to the neoliberal/forced-adjustment state has been accompanied by a paradigm shift in terms of the culture and governing practices inside the state. At the core of the public bureaucracy's new administrative culture and governing practices is "new public management" (NPM), a market-oriented organizational and management theory that provides the public sector with the theoretical tools for the practical implementation of neoliberal governance. Like neoliberalism in general, NPM grew out of a libertarian (or classical liberal) critique of public bureaucracy and the administrative culture of the postwar welfare state. At its core, this critique is as follows: the growth of the public bureaucracy and state interventionism is a threat to personal and economic liberty because the administrative state can only be successful if individual freedoms are unlimited; limitations on individual freedom in favour of state activity crowd out private initiative in the free market and, by doing so, undermine the dynamic potential of competition in capitalist markets; in the end, we are left with inefficient state institutions that are *inherently* ill-suited to ensuring quality, efficiency, and responsiveness in public service delivery.

In keeping with their critique of public bureaucracy, neoliberals have, since the 1970s, been pushing for the privatization of many aspects of government. Their goal is to shrink the state and enlarge the sphere of private markets. NPM is consistent with privatization, but focuses, instead, on transforming government by importing market-based theories and market mechanisms into the public sector—a process that has come to be known as the "marketization of the state" (Pierre, 1995). NPM marketizes the state by fostering a change in the administrative values, organizational culture, vocabulary, and practices of the public sector (Mitchell and Sutherland, 1997). Government is encouraged to act as a manager of public business. The marketplace values associated with efficiency, initiative, flexibility, and risk taking are championed over traditional administrative values associated with prudence, stability, and equity. A new results-oriented culture is to replace the public bureaucracy's traditional emphasis on accountability through hierarchical processes. And the market language of "efficiency and service" is to triumph over the administrative state's discourse of fairness and the public interest. In practice, NPM demands the devolution of administrative control to independent public service agencies that operate free from political and central bureaucratic control, as well as contracting service provision out to the private sector, creating new public–private partnerships, establishing public markets that allow citizens (read: consumers) to choose between competing public and private service providers, and developing business plans that put in place results-oriented performance measures for bureaucrats and state programs.

At its core, NPM's marketization is the transformation of "citizens" into "customers"—a process known as the marketization of citizenship. NPM enthusiasts contend that by championing a new emphasis on consumer satisfaction and giving customers more choice, citizens are actually empowered to exert influence upon the public services provided to them. But this type of empowerment is not in keeping with extensive democracy. First, there are issues of inequality arising from citizens' uneven capacities to act on this new freedom of choice. It should be clear that public markets that empower some citizens more than others cannot be considered extensively democratic. But more fundamental to the quality of democracy is the way that neoliberalism and NPM conceptualize empowerment. As in consumer markets, NPM offers a form of economic empowerment that allows citizens the right to take their business elsewhere. Citizens can, in other words, influence public service provision by "exit." This is quite different, and less democratic, than political empowerment, which focuses on representation and voice (Pierre, 1995). Political empowerment in an extensively democratic public bureaucracy requires meaningful dialogue between citizens and public service providers. The focus of political empowerment is on enhancing opportunities for the self-representation of citizens to the state, allowing citizens to play a role in shaping public services. NPM actually moves in the opposite direction by importing business-style management into service delivery and promoting commercialization of state services. The end result is arguably the undermining of the real potential for citizen–state dialogue and democratic citizenship.

The libertarianism at the heart of NPM reinforces the atomistic view of society that is central to neoliberal governance. The marketization of citizenship isolates and individualizes citizens, and this has an important anti-democratic consequence. It results in the depoliticization of public administration and a move away from notions of collective control of the state for public purposes. This new emphasis on the depoliticization of public administration is evidence of a newfound faith in a workable politics/administration dichotomy. The thinking behind this old dichotomy view is, first, that policymaking should be left to the realm of partisan politics and, second, because administration is meant to be policy-neutral, public administration should focus on narrow issues of efficiency and effectiveness. Throughout most of the latter part of the twentieth century, public administration scholars questioned the suggestion that administration could ever be truly apolitical and policy-neutral. However, with its emphasis on managerialism—letting managers of public service delivery manage as they see fit—NPM expounds a view of public management as being about nothing more than striving for efficiency and effectiveness. Strong democrats, on the other hand, worry that NPM governing practices, such as contracting out, establishing special service agencies, and entering into public–private partnerships, place too many policy-significant administrative decisions out of reach of democratic politics. While those searching to enhance the quality of democracy have been advocating a new "democratic administration," NPM and neoliberal governing practices are serving to create a less democratic and more business-like public bureaucracy (Shields and Evans, 1998).

SUPRA-NATIONAL GOVERNANCE: ECONOMIC RIGHTS AND THE DECLINE OF SOVEREIGNTY

Economic globalization is, without a doubt, a defining aspect of contemporary life. Trade and production are being increasingly deterritorialized as borders become less and less significant to corporate investment, production, and marketing strategies (Sholte, 2000). As corporations engage in global sourcing and nation states pursue export-led development strategies, the social space of the economy is less and less limited by the territorial boundaries of states. But globalization is not a purely economic phenomenon; culture and politics are also being globalized (Held et al., 1999). In terms of politics, globalization is taking the form of free trade agreements and institutions of supra-national governance. In the twenty-first century the North American Free Trade Agreement (NAFTA) and the World Trade Organization (WTO), among other agreements and institutions, are the sources of many policies and rules that apply, not just in one state but across a number of states.

Thinking beyond our own national borders is good, and potentially democratic. Indeed, there are even good reasons for supra-national rules of governance that limit what one country can do in light of the rights of others who reside on other parts of the globe. But supra-national governance can take many forms, and in the context of neoliberal globalization the emphasis has been placed on supra-national rules for the protection of capitalism, not democracy, empowerment, or human rights. Because the processes of globalization have been thoroughly neoliberalized, the core of supra-national governance has been the development of free trade agreements that are designed to protect economic rights and the free market. These trade agreements serve to entrench, or constitutionalize, marketization as the core governing principle of the twenty-first century. In doing so, they have encouraged the shift from the welfare/mediator state to the neoliberal/forced-adjustment state.

To be sovereign is to claim independent power, to be self-determining, and to posses supreme and final decision-making authority. The process of governing a sovereign nation-state is free from externally imposed limitations. Many nations have struggled against colonialism in the hope of attaining the degree of sovereignty that is necessary to ensure that citizens have the capacity to democratically determine the state policies that shape their destinies. Traditionally, Canadian democracy has depended on the contribution that state sovereignty makes to the democratic empowerment of citizens. When Canadian sovereignty is limited, it is likely that democratic citizenship will be less meaningful and democracy, therefore, will be constrained. Free trade agreements like NAFTA and institutions like the WTO have the effect of pooling the sovereignty of multiple nations—power and authority are devolved upward to the supra-national level. As such, the participating nation states are declaring their willingness to place limits on their own democratic policymaking authority. Most obviously, the countries involved agree to refrain from instituting tariffs (essentially border taxes) that would hinder the free flow of trade. But free trade agreements go much further. They are designed to protect the economic property rights of private sector investors and corporations. They restrict governments from putting in place policies and programs that restrict market freedoms, favour domestic over foreign economic interests or, in some other way, undermine the profit-making potential of specific private corporations. By limiting the capacity of democratic governments to regulate corporate activity, supra-national trade agreements institutionalize rules that favour the economic imperatives of capitalist democracy over the democratic imperatives of capitalist democracy. To point this out is not to identify some hidden conspiracy; it is, simply, to identify the obvious purpose of trade agreements.

To understand the anti-democratic character of supra-national trade agreements, one needs simply to contrast their decision processes with the principles of extensive democracy. Initially, these agreements were negotiated between state elites, often in closed-door meetings (the supra-national equivalent of executive federalism in Canada). Input was welcomed, if sometimes only informally, from neoliberal think tanks and business organizations. But democratic public consultations have been avoided. Hiding behind the technocratic myth that supra-national trade policy is an apolitical exercise for expert decision-makers, NAFTA and the WTO have expressed little interest in openness and transparency. There are no processes for popular democratic accountability. Once the agreements take effect, the new trade rules are enforced by supra-national tribunals that are guided by formal dispute settlement procedures laid out in the text of the relevant trade agreement. Acting like courts of trade law, these tribunals have the effect of judicializing trade policy decision making. They often meet in secret, and when they rule, they have the power to decide whether or not the actions of a government violate the economic property rights of a foreign corporation or corporate sector. Their decisions are of significant social consequence, but their decision-making power is not held democratically accountable.

Defenders of NAFTA and the WTO regularly point out that free trade agreements have been approved by our democratically elected governments. This is true. Defenders also stress that trade agreements contain exit clauses for nations wishing not to abide by the terms of the agreement. Again, this is true. But the realities of governance in the context of globalizing capitalism are such that Canada's continued participation is necessary to the maintenance of business confidence. If Canada exited NAFTA, foreign investment would dry up, our currency would drop in value, and the economy would take a significant turn for the worse. Governments of capitalist democracies *must* worry about business confidence; the rules of the game demand our continued participation in NAFTA and the WTO. This is an example of the structural power of business in capitalist democracies.

In this situation, the best option for strong democrats is to engage in efforts to influence the future course of free trade agreements, and to demand agreements that privilege democratic imperatives by better balancing economic and human rights. This is why advocates of extensive democracy, like the Council of Canadians, worked hard to derail the efforts within the Oganization for Economic Co-operation and Development (OECD to negotiate a Multilateral Agreement on Investment (MAI) (Clarke and Barlow, 1997). That is why these same progressive social movements are resisting negotiations leading toward a NAFTA-like Free Trade Area of the Americas (FTAA). But, in the anti-democratic world of trade negotiations these voices are seldom influential. The image of the massive fence keeping protestors away from the FTAA summit meeting in Quebec City in April 2001 captured very clearly the restrictions on popular participation in defining an agenda for trade and hemispheric integration. The processes for creating supra-national institutions of governance are not democratic and, moreover, the regime of trade agreements that is now so central to twenty-first century governance actively undermines the quality and potential of Canadian democracy.

CONCLUSION

In the interests of balance, it is important to remind students that liberal electoral democracy and the institutions of representative and responsible government are significant human accomplishments that required considerable struggle to achieve. The achievement of greater formal political equality through the extension of civil and political citizenship rights has done a lot to improve the lives of Canadians. All the same, competitive elite democracy is only limited democracy. As such, we should not allow ourselves to become complacent democrats; we should set our sights on extensive democracy as a primary political goal. At this moment in history, however, the dominant approaches to politics and governance are threatening, not extending, democracy. There are enduring anti-democratic features to our electoral system, state power is increasingly concentrated within a limited number of executive institutions, new governing practices are undermining the potential of democratic citizenship, national sovereignty is being lost to supra-national governing institutions, and the goals and purposes of the state are being altered in such a way that the body politic is losing its capacity to act collectively to regulate and improve social and economic life. These trends currently underpin a growing democratic deficit. They are reason for concern, and for vigilance in our struggle to defend democracy's potential.

REFERENCES

Beatty, David. 2001. "Making Democracy Constitutional." *Policy Options*. (July/August).

Bowles, Samuel and Herbert Gintis. 1986. *Democracy and Capitalism: Property, Community, and the Contradictions of Modern Social Theory.* New York: Basic Books.

Brooks, Stephen. 2000. *Canadian Democracy: An Introduction.* 3rd ed. Toronto: Oxford University Press.

Clarke, Tony and Maude Barlow. 1997. *MAI: The Multilateral Agreement on Investment and the Threat to Canadian Sovereignty*. Toronto: Stoddart.

Crozier, Michel, Samuel H. Huntington, and Joji Watanuki. 1975. *The Crisis of Democracy: Report on the Governability of Democracies to the Trilateral Commission.* New York: New York University Press.

Dobrowolsky, Alexandra and Jane Jenson. 1993. "Reforming the Parties: Prescriptions for Democracy." In Susan D. Phillips (ed.), *How Ottawa Spends 1993–1994: A More Democratic Canada...?* Ottawa: Carleton University Press.

Fukuyama, Francis. 1992. *The End of History and the Last Man*. New York: Free Press.

Gould, Carol C. 1988. *Rethinking Democracy: Freedom and Social Cooperation in Politics, Economy, and Society.* Cambridge: Cambridge University Press.

Green, Philip. 1985. *Retrieving Democracy: In Search of Civic Equality.* Totowa, New Jersey: Rowman & Allanheld Publishers.

Held, David, et al. 1999. *Global Transformations: Politics, Economics and Culture*. Stanford: Stanford University Press.

Irvine, William. 1979. *Does Canada Need a New Electoral System?* Kingston: Queen's University Institute of Intergovernmental Relations.

Macpherson, C.B. 1973. *Democratic Theory: Essays in Retrieval.* Oxford: Oxford University Press.

Milner, Henry. 1999. *Making Every Vote Count: Reassessing Canada's Electoral System.* Peterborough: Broadview Press.

Mitchell, James R. and Sharon L. Sutherland. 1997. "Relations between Politicians and Public Servants." In Mohamed Charih and Arthur Daniels (eds.), *New Public Management and Public Administration in Canada*. Toronto: The Institute of Public Administration of Canada.

Neufeld, Mark. 1999. "Globalization: Five Theses." Retrieved February 12, 2002 from www.chass.utoronto.ca/tamapp/ Neufeld.PDF.

Pillips, Susan D. 1996. "Discourse, Identity, and Voice: Feminist Contributions to Policy Studies." In Laurent Dbouzinskis, Michael Howlett & David Laycock, eds. *Policy Studies in Canada: The State of the Art*. Toronto: University of Toronto Press.

Pierre, Jon. 1995. "The Marketization of the State: Citizens, Consumers, and the Emergence of the Public Market." In B. Guy Peters and Donald J. Savoie (eds.), *Governance in a Changing Environment.* Montreal & Kingston: McGill-Queen's University Press.

Pilon, Dennis. 2000. "Canada's Democratic Deficit: Is Proportional Representation the Answer?" Toronto: The CSJ Foundation for Research and Education.

Plant, Raymond. 1991. "Social Rights and the Reconstruction of Welfare." In Geoff Andrews (ed.), *Citizenship*. London: Lawrence & Wishart.

Savoie, Donald J. 1999. *Governing From the Centre: The Concentration of Power in Canadian Politics*. Toronto: University of Toronto Press.

Scholte, Jan Aart. 2000. *Globalization: A Critical Introduction*. New York: St. Martin's Press.

Schumpeter, Joseph Alois. 1942. *Capitalism, Socialism, and Democracy.* New York: Harper & Bros.

Shields, John and B. Mitchell Evans. 1998. *Shrinking the State: Globalization and Public Administration Reform*. Halifax: Fernwood Press.

Tully, James. 1995. *Strange Multiplicity*. Cambridge: Cambridge University Press.

Young, Iris Marion. 1989. "Policy and Group Difference: A Critique of the Idea of Universal Citizenship." *Ethics, 99.2*.

__________. 1990. *Justice and the Politics of Difference.* Princeton: Princeton University Press.

WEBLINKS

Democracy Watch
www.dwatch.ca

Canadian Study of Parliament Group
www.studyparliament.ca

Fair Vote Canada
www.fairvotecanada.org

part two

Recasting Identities and Citizenship

chapter seven

"Race Matters" and "Race Manners"[1]

Malinda S. Smith

INTRODUCTION

Canada entered the twenty-first century with a national self-understanding and, arguably, a global reputation as a tolerant, multi-ethnic, and even colour-blind society. Despite the historical record that suggests otherwise, "the prevailing myth in Canada is that we are a country without a history of racism" (Aylward, 1999, 12). Likewise, Blackhouse claims, "Canada has a mythology of racelessness despite remarkable evidence to the contrary" (quoted in Landsberg, 2000, L2). Central to this Canadian myth of a raceless or colour-blind society is an enduring belief in Canada's difference from its southern neighbour (Satzewich, 1998). As Satzewich puts it, "one of our most enduring national myths is that there is less racism here than in the United States" (1998, 11). This imagined difference between Canada and the United States is an inextricable aspect of Canadian national identity in a globalized world increasingly shaped by United States hegemony and cultural industries. However, it is not a new phenomenon. What Reitz and Breton (1994) have called an "illusion of difference" between Canada and the United States has played out in political and cultural debates for several centuries. By sifting through the historical and contemporary record, this chapter attempts to make sense of this shared history in relation to processes of racialization, "race"[2] relations, and racism in Canada. Such a review is needed in light of the emergence of new contradictions within Canada's celebrated "diversity model" (Jenson, 2000) and the tensions in "race" relations evident in the late twentieth century. These tensions will pose a challenge to Canada's commitment to heterogeneity and soft tolerance for diversity.

Since the September 11, 2001, attacks on the World Trade Center and the Pentagon and the subsequent globalized "war on terrorism," some notable contradictions have appeared in the Canadian "diversity model." This globally celebrated model seemed to be giving way to a more open fear of difference (Jenson, 2000), including the popular stereotyping and the officially sanctioned racial profiling of all Arabs and Muslims simply because many of those involved in the 9/11 tragedy were of this ethnic background. Despite all the efforts "not to stigmatize," Jenson (2000, 2) writes, the fact that "everything from speeches about the 'evil' of some societies to the fears that Bill C-36, the new federal security law, will allow targeting of Arabs and Muslims" means that respect for and celebration of diversity is not a given.

There have been some public and media claims that racial profiling, which deliberately targets Arabs and Muslims, is morally and legally justifiable. In the *Globe and Mail*, columnist John Ibbitson wrote that, "racial profiling is both necessary and desirable" (June 3, 2002, A15). The example he used to justify why skin colour, facial features, and family name or heritage matter points to the challenges ahead for the diversity model. According to Ibbitson, "a middle-aged European woman who persisted in taking flying lessons despite her obvious incompetence would probably not have excited police suspicions. But Zacarias Moussaoui was dark of skin and strange of name, and so they hauled him in on a technicality." Ibbitson concludes that, "Extremism in defence of public safety is no vice." The assumptions of this column are important to note. The first wrong assumption is that xenophobia, or fear of difference, whether based on colour or family name and background, is defensible. Second, the column stereotypically assumes that an elderly white woman could not be a Muslim (and that an Arab could not be a Christian or Jew), and generally would not be seen as threatening in the eyes of law enforcement. The third contention is that although racial profiling is extreme, it is desirable to limit the personal privacy and security of all "dark of skin and strange of name" persons in order to protect those who do not have such "suspicious" physical features or ethnic and cultural heritage.

The contradiction of resorting to xenophobia and racial profiling in order to oppose the xenophobia of al Qaeda or any other group seems to have escaped Ibbitson. As the responses to Ibbitson in the *Globe and Mail* make clear, there is a contradiction in how racial profiling is applied, and against whom; it is almost always an action that a dominant ethnic group enforces against a racialized minority ethnic group. Thus, it is inherently discriminatory and always indicative of social power. In one letter to the editor, Yeung-Seu Yoon draws attention to the colour-coding (Blackhouse, 2000) of those targeted for profiling. Yeung-Seu Yoon noted that if "Mr. Ibbitson's ideas had been in use, the terrible crimes of Timothy McVeigh, Theodore Kaczynski, Paul Bernado, Marc Lepine, Clifford Olson, Ted Bundy, Jeffrey Dahmer, and the Columbine killers might all have been prevented" (*Globe and Mail*, June 4, 2002, A16). The point is a straightforward one. Despite heinous crimes committed by white men in Canada and the United States, there never has been a national law enforcement or immigration policy or global strategy to racially profile *all* white men or to violate the privacy, security, and freedoms of all white men because of the actions of a few.

Canada has experimented with racial equality only since the 1960s. The kinds of contradictions and challenges to Canada's diversity model that Ibbitson draws our attention to are not new. During World War I Ukrainian Canadians were targeted by the Canadian state, declared "enemy aliens," and interned in concentration camps. Similarly, during World War II, Japanese Canadians were interned in concentration camps and those who lived in British Columbia saw their homes and businesses appropriated by the state and sold at a fraction of their value. In the war on terrorism, it seems the new "enemy aliens" in Canada are of Arab descent and Muslims. It remains to be seen how far the Canadian state, prodded by the United States, is prepared to go in racial profiling and in curtailing the rights and privileges of its citizens and permanent residents whose only "crime" is their national origin or ethnic and cultural heritage.

The chapter shows that despite a very recent and soft commitment to being a "diversity of diversities" (Jenson and Papillon, 2000) and to the recognition and respect for "multiculturalism and multinationalism" (Eisenberg, 2000), Canadians have been shaped both by support for the principle of equality and, at the same time, by political and legal support for inequality among diversities. Since Confederation and certainly before, this tension manifested itself in social marginalization and exclusion based on "race," national origin, and civilization, even as "race manners" led to a national failure to take this "race problem" seriously. With few exceptions (Walker, 1989; Reitz, 1988), most of the cutting-edge work on "race" in Canada has been in the areas of sociology, critical legal studies, and cultural studies. Theoretical and empirical works in politics have focused primarily on multiculturalism and immigration policies, and not on race politics and policies, per se. Drawing on historical and contemporary examples, this chapter critically discusses several themes: First, it provides a working definition of key concepts such as "race," racism, and racialization; second, it examines the ideas of "race matters" (West 1994) and "race manners" (Jacobs, 1999) in Canada; third, it reviews the ways in which the racialization of public policy has been pivotal to the Canadian state's efforts to create a white settler society; and, finally, it provides contemporary examples to explain why "race" continues to matter in Canada.

"RACE" FICTIONS

"The fiction of 'race'," as Blackhouse puts it, "is never so obvious as when one looks backward in time" (2000, 274). Whatever the fiction of the idea of "race," it has had an indelible impact on Canada's social formations and institutions. "Canadian history is rooted in racial distinctions, assumptions, laws, activities" (2000, 7) and, thus, a failure, "to scrutinize the records of our past to identify the deeply implanted tenets of racist ideology and practice is to acquiesce in the popular misapprehension that depicts our country as largely innocent of systematic racial exploitation." The notion of "race" matters in Canada and it always has; to claim anything to the contrary, Blackhouse insists, would be "patently erroneous."

Theorizing about "race," racism, and race relations in Canada requires a working definition of some of the important concepts used throughout this chapter. In Canada, as elsewhere, the meaning of "race" has shifted over time. In the eighteenth century, the popular conception of race was "commonality of descent or character," and it constituted an idiom in which people developed conceptions of themselves in relation to "others" (Banton, 2000, 51–63). A century later, this idiom evolved into the association of racial identity with nation (*Volk*) and the belief in "national character." European colonial discourses, readily reproduced by white settlers in Canada, advanced the view that the status of white Europeans in the Americas derived from their racial superiority and good breeding (Berger, 1970, 1969). Where the eighteenth century's conception of "race" focused primarily on innate physical attributes, the nineteenth century witnessed a shift to privileging conceptions based on an assumption of "distinct nations," and from a focus on origins and species to one that assumed permanent racial "types." This shift to typologies was also linked with "scientific racism" and an opposition to "race" mixing or hybridity. Theorists who advanced this view felt that hybridity would lead to sterility, diminish the racial "stock," inhibit progress, and result in human decline (Banton, 1977).

Ideas of "race" difference and racial superiority were central to nation building in nineteenth and twentieth-century Canada. White settlers in Canada constructed an image of Blacks as "fun loving, imitative, and naturally obsequious" (Berger, 1966). Other references to Blacks in popular discourse linked them with "animal passions" and in popular discourse, particularly as related to white women, settlers expressed fear and loathing of the "demoniacal rage and lust" of Black and Asian men (Walker, 1997, 126). The geographical "origin" of Blacks, the so-called Dark Continent of Africa, also contributed to the belief of white settlers that Blacks were from naturally inferior stock. By the twentieth century "a once vague mythology about what the Negro could and could not do had taken on a more exact form. Language, literature, the theater, science, and even history had informed generations of Canadians of the Negro's inability to adapt to the north, of his love of pleasure, of his sexual appetites, his unreliability, laziness, and odor" (Winks, 1997, 298). Consequently, there was both political and popular support for preventing such "undesirable" immigrants from coming to Canada (Shepard, 1997, 1985).

The emergent colour line in Canada was evident in the language used to characterize immigrants from Asia, in particular the "colour coding" of Chinese as "yellow" and, in the early twentieth century, the extension of the colour "yellow" to Japanese immigrants. The association of the colour yellow with moral inferiority was also evident in the use of expressions such as "yellow belly" to connote cowardice, the "yellow dog" epithet used by trade unionists to refer to "scab labour," and "yellow press" to mean sensationalist or questionable journalism (Blackhouse, 2000, 136–9). By the early twentieth century, the vast majority of "Canadians seem to have gravitated complacently towards the concept of colour as a defining racial attribute," Blackhouse writes (136). "Race" also came to be associated with moral worthiness and almost exclusively in favour of the white settlers. In the words of John G. Shearer, a Presbyterian minister from Toronto and founder of the Moral and Social Reform Council of Canada, "most of the dens of vice are owned by Chinese and Japanese" (*Regina Daily Province*, March 16, 1911; June 21, 1912). The media of the time is replete with references to Blacks and Asians as having "demoralizing habits" and, in contrast, with associations of "white" and white people with cleanliness, purity, and godliness. The Chinese and Black immigrants to Canada came to represent "dangers of dilution and contamination of national blood, national grit, national government, national ideas," wrote popular writer Agnes C. Laut (quoted in Winks, 1997, 299).

By the late twentieth century, the dominant conception of "race" was as a social construct (Anthias and Yuval Davis, 1992) and this gave rise to reflective debates within the social sciences about the analytical value of the concept. However, the continuing significance of "race" in the Canadian context was reinforced with the release and robust discussion of the work of Western Ontario University psychologist Philippe Rushton (1994) who claimed that science does support the belief in distinct "races." Rushton's work, reproducing the already discredited claims made in works characterized as "scientific racism" (example: focusing on brain size, and genitalia), renewed the claim that there are natural differences between the "races" in Canada. Where the earlier theories of "race" tended to depict both Blacks and Asians as inferior, Rushton argued that Asians and whites are biologically superior to Blacks. He also conflated notions of biological superiority with claims of social and intellectual superiority. In effect, in the late twentieth century, "race" discourse in Canada was shaped both by social science arguments that "race" is a social construct and, by the return of arguments among scientists like Rushton, that "race" is a biological fact with moral and social implications (1994).

In an examination of both the market and social value of "race," Peter Li explains that "the process by which society attributes social significance to groups on superficial physical grounds is referred to by social scientists as *racialization*" (1998, 116). Li further explains that this significance is relational, that is, "people so marked" are in "relation to a dominant group, which has the power to set the terms and conditions of racial accommodation" (116.). Racialization, as Miles also notes, is a process that transforms by naming and by attributing meaning to persons and things, which all suggests a certain social capital that most racialilized minorities do not have in Canadian society. Thus, for Miles, racialization encompasses the "process by which meanings are attributed to particular objects, features, and processes, in such a way that the latter are given a special significance and carry or are embodied with a set of additional meanings" (1989, 70).

Among the early governing elite in Canada there was a strong, although by no means unanimous, Manichaean worldview. The word *Manichaeism* derives from the Persian word *Mani*, which as a doctrine assumes an objective material world of good and evil (Wilson 1967, 149–50). Manichaeism assumes that people are either materially good or materially evil, "not because of their actions and deeds but because of who or what they are" (italiacs original, Gordon, 1995, 35). This worldview, when extended to notions of "race" and racialism, opposes miscegenation in order to preserve the "race" (physical or genetic purity), and supports exclusionary immigration policies in order to "keep out" those "races" classified as evil, unsuitable, incompatible, and so on. Historically in Canada, Manichaeism was also manifested in the belief that some "races" are good and others are evil; white people—who were good—and racialized minorities—who were bad—could not live together in Canada; they were incompatible. "Canada built itself around "whiteness," differentiating itself through 'whiteness' and creating outsiders to the state, no matter their claims of birthright or other entitlement" (Dickson, 1998, 124). Both modern conceptions of ethnic and cultural diversity and of social exclusion were developed, in part, in relation to this idea of whiteness because, as Dickson continues, "Inclusion in or access to Canadian identity, nationality and citizenship (de facto) depended and depends on one's relationship to whiteness" (124.)

There is perhaps no better example of this Manichaean logic than the views expressed by Canada's first prime minister, Sir John A. Macdonald, in the House of Commons on May 4, 1885. According to Macdonald, "If you look around the world you will see that the Aryan races will not wholesomely amalgamate with Africans or the Asiatics." Anticipating the late–twentieth century clash of civilizations debate unleashed by Samuel Huntington (1993, 22–49), the prime minister claimed that African and Asian civilizations were incompatible with European civilizations. Macdonald went on to conclude that, "It is not desired that they come; that we should have a mongrel race; that the Aryan character of the future of British America should be destroyed" (Hansard, May 5, 1885). A sentiment similar to Macdonald's was expressed several decades later by Prime Minister Mackenzie King who thought that if "lower races" were permitted into Canada they would "debase" Anglo-Saxon civilization just as surely as "the baser metals tended to drive the finer metal out of circulation" (Hansard, May 8, 1922). Reinforcing the consensus among political elites, the leader of the

Official Opposition, Arthur Meighen, added that the temperaments, habits, and natures of Orientals made coexistence with them an, "impossibility" and, thus, it was essential "that we maintain here our racial purity" in Canada (Hansard, May 8, 1922).

Over the decades the discourse of racialism intensified and the common use of words like *Aryan*, *nigger*, and *white race* was indistinguishable from the "race" discourse in the United States. William Thoburn, the Conservative MP for Lanark North, argued in the House of Commons on April 3, 1911, for stricter immigration rules "to preserve for the sons of Canada the lands they propose to give to the niggers" (Hansard, April 3, 1911). Likewise fellow Conservative William H. Sharpe, MP for Lisgar, argued that banning Blacks was desirable in order to "preserve Canada for the white race." By the 1920s, the legalization and institutionalization of racism was uneven across Canada, but it was an integral feature of Canadian social formations and underwrote disparate policies and widespread practices of social exclusion. Well into the 1960s and in some cases the 1970s, "race was often pivotal to access to public services such as theatres, restaurants, pubs, hotels, and recreational facilities" (Blackhouse, 2000, 275). In effect, the reality for racialized minorities in Canada paralleled the "Jim Crow" South, where segregation of Black and white Americans was legally enforced in both public and private places.

There was a shared Manichaean belief among elites that the causes of the "race problem" in the United States during the American Reconstruction (1865–1877) resided with Black people; with their physical, intellectual, and moral inferiority rather than with the brutalizing legacies of slavery. In Canada, this view also was pervasive in the media, among elected officials of both the Liberal and Tory parties, and among career civil servants who implemented various pieces of legislation. In the language of Canada's own immigration policy, the problem was in the "undesirability" of racialized minorities, which Macdonald attributed to incompatible civilizations. Throughout nineteenth-century and early-twentieth-century Canada, there was a firm belief among many white settlers, at least, in the shared humanity of white folks across North America. A common assumption at the time was that if a "race"-based experience was "true for the United States [it] must be true in Canada" (Walker, 1997, 126). This position is clearly expressed in an April 1911 Toronto *Mail and Empire* story: "If Negroes and white people cannot live in accord in the South, [then] they cannot live in accord in the North . . . If we freely admit Black people from that country we shall soon have the race troubles that are the blot on the civilization of our neighbours" (April 28, 1911; Walker, 1997, 126; Boyko, 1998, 163). Several years later, W.D. Scott, Superintendent of Immigration, made a similar claim. "The Negro problem, which faces the United States and which Abraham Lincoln said could be settled only by shipping one and all back to a tract of land in Africa," Scott wrote, "is one in which Canadians have no desire to share" (quoted in Shortt and Doughty, 1914, 531).

The fiction of an Aryan "race" was the basis upon which early political leaders like Sir John A. Macdonald, Mackenzie King, and others argued for exclusion of African and Asian immigrants. In his opposition to Blacks immigrating to Canada, Macdonald used "Aryan" to refer to the white settlers. The free uses of words like *Aryan* and epithets like *nigger* in the House of Commons make clear the extent to which "race" politics, and racialized policies and relations, were fundamental to the Canadian political establishment well into the twentieth century. "Aryanism," as Tony Ballantyne (2001) explains, encompassed "the notion that certain communities shared cultural features as a result of their shared common 'Aryan stock'—as one of the most significant racializing discourses." It had a positive connotation for white folks in Canada and the United States. Further, the idea of an Aryan or superior white "race" seemed to transcend divergent national contexts within the Empire. As such, Empire was a powerful influence in shaping ethnocultural discourses from India and Nigeria to the Pacific, and to nation building in Britain's so-called white dominions that included Canada, New Zealand, and, paradoxically, South Africa (Lowe, 1989)[3]. While the British Empire's project of civilization implied an equality of outcome for subjects, whether they were in Canada, India, or Egypt, in actuality it produced a "racinated world of ethnic subjection" (Comaroff, 1998). British imperial discourse, as Adele Perry puts it, "spoke of the unity of all that was British, but produced and managed, with varying degrees of success, a set of overlapping, many-levelled hierarchies that ranked and arranged natives, settlers, nations, citizens, colonies and subjects" (2001). The imperial myth that the Empire's civilizational project transformed indigenous subjects and even the enslaved into equal citizens along with white settlers continued in post-Confederation Canada despite the empirical evidence that revealed the deepening of inequality and social polarization, often along colour lines.

Nigger, on the other hand, has been used almost exclusively as an epithet. As Lawrence Hill wrote in *Maclean's*, one of the things his father advised him of in addition to studying and achieving success in school and work was that "if anybody called me 'nigger,' I was to beat the hell out of them" (2002, 60). In the twenty-first century, we are witnessing a reversal in the word's fortunes. In his book-length genealogy, *Nigger* (2000), Randall Kennedy notes that the word's etymology is the Latin word *niger,* which simply meant the colour black. It is unclear when or how the word *niger* changed to *nigger* and an epithet, and became associated with contempt and all things derogatory. Moreover, the epithet was extended to non-Blacks who were held in social contempt. Thus, the Irish were called "the niggers of Europe" (Hill, 2002, 62) and author Pierre Vallieres (1971) argued that the experiences of the Québécois in Canada made them the "white niggers" of the Americas. Kennedy writes that beginning in the late twentieth century, "As a linguistic landmark, *nigger* is being renovated." Today, the word is used among some African-American men, for example, as a term of affection. It is pervasive in the American cultural industries, especially among hip hop and gangsta rap musicians, in films, and in comedy acts, as well as in everyday street conversation. The derivative word *nigga* is now used frequently in the lyrics of Canadian hip hop artist Choclair (Hill, 2002, 62). Evocations of the word *nigger*, Kennedy suggests, can be counted among the "innovations" of African Americans. However, the context in which this occurs, and by whom and to whom it is used (or against whom), are all cultural landmines that can explode at any time as, for example, in the emergence of the word *wigger* to refer to white youth accused of "acting black." This complicated language game speaks to the word's genealogy as among the most negative epithets used primarily against people of African descent in North America.

The meaning of racism in Canada as elsewhere has shifted over time and space. Tzvetan Todorov has distinguished two useful senses in which the term is most often employed today, namely racism as *behaviour* and racism as *ideology* (2000, 264). In the first instance, racism "is a matter of *behaviour,* usually a manifestation of hatred or contempt for individuals who have well-defined physical characteristics different from our own." In the second usage, racism can be understood as an "*ideology,* a doctrine concerning human races." To clarify the two conceptions further, Todorov distinguishes between *racism* as it relates to behaviour or action and *racialism,* which refers to ideology or doctrines. For Kwame Anthony Appiah (1992), the two meanings can be distinguished as follows: where racialism assumes there are clearly distinguishable races, racism extends this to the belief that some "races" are superior and others inferior. As well, racism accepts as legitimate not only the differential treatment of the "races," but also their unequal treatment. It is this defence of inequality, and the rationalization of direct material and psychic disadvantage to racialized minorities, that makes racism politically and economically relevant today.

PRESERVING A WHITE SETTLER SOCIETY

In January 2002, Prime Minister Jean Chrétien shuffled his cabinet, resulting in Winnipeg Liberal MP Rey Pagtakhan becoming Minister of Veteran Affairs. The veteran affairs critic for the Canadian Alliance, Saskatchewan MP Roy Bailey, was asked to comment on this appointment and his remarks highlighted the persistence of Manichaeism in Canada, a view that had enabled discrimination against Asians for two centuries. Bailey, presumably relying on physical appearance, mistakenly referred to Pagtakhan as "Chinese"—according to Bailey, "Oh, the Chinese chap. Oh, you know, this breaks my heart. Oh my God" (Southam Editorial, January 18, 2002). Bailey's heart was broken, he told the reporter in a convoluted discourse, because in his view Pagtakhan is "not Canadian. He's not next to, originally not Canadian." Bailey explained further that what he meant was that Pagtakan was not a real Canadian because "he wasn't born here." In effect, Bailey's rant against Pagtakhan exposed the problem of Canada as an immigrant society in which racialized minority immigrants are almost always seen as outsiders. First, it should be noted again that Pagtakhan is not Chinese. He was born in the Philippines and came to Canada in 1968; he is Canadian. For Bailey, place of birth inauthenticated Pagtakhan's belonging in Canada and his physical "looks" marked him as a racialized minority and therefore as suspect. Second, and more important than the question of national origin, was Bailey's view that because Pagtakhan was an immigrant, he could never be Canadian or represent Canadians, in this case the war veterans. As the editorial notes, "by what he said, Bailey is revealed as ignorant and insensitive," and, because of his subsequent denials despite the fact that his remarks were taped, "by denying it, he is revealed as cowardly, and if not dishonest, then remarkably unthinking in what he said."

Bailey's comments reminded Canadians of the expressions of racial intolerance that had come to mark the Canadian Alliance's predecessor, the Reform Party of Canada. In May 1996, Reform MP Bob Ringma was quoted in an interview as saying that Blacks and gays should be removed to "the back of the shop" if their presence in front was causing customers discomfort and the employer business (quoted in Han, 1996, 14–17). Both the story and its reporting reveal some of the dilemmas faced by racialized minorities in drawing critical attention to opinions and practices of exclusion. Sheridan Hay (1996) found that in the print media's reporting of the incident, the support for discrimination against Blacks was largely erased from the story. The propensity for racial intolerance among some Reform Party members also reared its head within the party. The competition for the Edmonton Strathcona nomination in 1996 was a case in point. There were five candidates, although some felt the party was discriminating in favour of Rahim Jaffer, an Ismaili Muslim whom party critics called a "token visible minority candidate" (Jenkinson, 1996, 9). Margaret Rutsch, the board secretary, suggested that Jaffer, an immigrant from Tanzania, should be tested for "exotic diseases" and that he should run in the riding of Edmonton Southeast where his "own people" resided (1996, 9). Rutsch went further, "It's reverse discrimination. Preston wants to get rid of the stigma of Reformers as being anti-immigrant. So, this 24-year-old boy with the off-colour skin coming from a North African country is the ideal person" (1996,9).

The political effort to craft a white Canada though immigration and other public policies was an integral component of nation building in the nineteenth century. White settlers used various policy instruments to try and create the Canadian state in their own image, as Anglo-Saxons, and this aim was not officially abandoned until 1962. The preamble to the *British North America (BNA) Act* states that Canada's constitution is "similar in principle" to Britain's. The early legal and public policy interpretations of its articles functioned to reproduce the "race" and gender inequalities of Britain, and its empire, within Canada. This is particularly true of the contradictions of slavery in Canada (see Winks, 1997; Howe, 1969), as it is with the unequal treatment of subjects across the British Empire; those from the "white dominions" were favoured relative to immigrants from India. Post-Confederation, various policy instruments were used to "preserve a white Canada"—an assumption that itself rendered the pre-existing First Nations groups invisible—by excluding non-white and, specifically, non-Anglo-Saxon immigrants. The separation of powers between federal and provincial governments resulted in some differences in policy environment across Canada but by and large there was consensus that racialized minorities would not make good citizens, in fact, they were "deemed undesirable" (Shepard, 1997).

There have already been numerous thoughtful analyses of "race" and immigration policy in Canada. What is useful to note is that both what a given piece of legislation states and how it is "understood" by those empowered to interpret it at the Canadian borders are important. The 1869 *Immigration Act* did not explicitly restrict the nationality of immigrants because white policymakers had British subjects in mind and assumed only white subjects would apply. However, when this assumption proved false, it led to the 1910 *Immigration Act* being more explicit on the grounds for exclusion. Section 38(c) of the 1910 act held that entry could be denied to:

> . . . any nationality or race of immigrants . . . because such immigrants are deemed unsuitable having regard to the climatic, industrial, social, educational, labour . . . or because such immigrants are deemed undesirable owing to their peculiar customs, habits, modes of life, methods of holding property and because of their probable inability to become readily assimilated or to assume the duties and responsibilities of Canadian citizenship . . .

The 1910 *Immigration Act* granted considerable leeway to civil servants to exercise their discretion to ensure that its normative underpinnings—the assumption of maintaining Canada's national character as British and white—would not be "diluted." One result was that the act became an instrument for preserving Canada as a "white nation" and for the colour-coding of nationality and citizenship. The act did not explicitly call for exclusion on the ground of "race," rather racialized minorities were excluded because of their difference based on civilization, national character, customs, and habits. An ostensibly "race"-neutral legislation is produced through a process of "ideological deracialization" (Jakubowski, 1997) and "sanitary coding" (Reeves, 1984). By ideological deracialization, Jakubowski meant to capture a discourse that, on the face of it, seems to be "race"-neutral because it makes no specific reference to "race," nor does it use racist language and concepts; however, in practice and by an examination of its consequences it is possible to see its racist effects. This appearance of "race"-neutrality was possible because the language of the legislation had been de-raced and sanitized. Policymakers communicated their private, racist thoughts and desired outcome—for a white Canada—using a public discourse that, on its face, can be defended as non-racist. White settlers and policymakers in Canada "understood" that this legislation was designed to exclude racialized minorities whatever its literal wording.

A prerequisite to understanding these issues is knowledge of the history of "race" relations and policies in Canada and their contemporary legacies. Knowledge of this history is important because, "Once we become totally conscious of it we have it half beaten" (Carter, 1979). If we accept for the moment that "race" is a social construct—leading some theorists to talk about "colour consciousness" (Appiah and Gutmann, 1996) because of the focus on physical appearances—what accounts for the apparent complacency among Canadians about "race matters" as West (1994) calls it? This complacency exists, in part, because of ignorance about the role that "race," racism, and rationalization have played, and continue to play, in Canadian public policies and political economy, from colonialism to post-Confederation.

Science, politics, and law have shaped how "race" was understood and experienced in Canada. A dominant narrative today depicts Canada's history in terms of its past as a refuge for fugitive slaves fleeing the United States on the Underground. As Cooper puts it, "Canada had styled itself as a haven for the oppressed, those blacks who had fled the United States because of slavery and virulent racism. But on coming to Canada, many blacks found the only difference between the new country and the old was that in the new country the law protected ex-fugitives from re-enslavement" (Bristow et al., 1994, 153). At the time, Lord James Bruce Elgin, Governor General of Canada (1847–1854), expressed his fear that Canada would become "flooded with blackies who are rushing across the frontier to escape from the bloodhounds whom the Fugitive Slave Bill has let loose on their track" (quoted in Bristow, 1994, 70). This section elaborates further the extent to which "race" politics and discourse and a corresponding racialization of policy were central to nation building in Canada (Miles, 1989, 70).

"Race" has long been the basis for exclusionary attitudes, policies, and practices in Canada and it was the basis on which British settlers, in particular, sought to construct Canada as a white, Anglo-Saxon state. Canada, like Australia and New Zealand, emerged from its "white dominion" status in the British Empire as a settler colony in which policymakers developed and implemented racialized policies aimed at maintaining a white Canada. It also shows how and why a colour-coded conception of nation, citizenship and belonging emerged in Canada. The debates in the House of Commons between 1867 and 1914 reveal the extent to which both Conservative and Liberal policymakers of the time believed that Canada should remain a white nation and therefore that non-whites should be excluded as "undesirable people." In an April 1908 House of Commons debate, Vancouver Liberal MP R.G. Macpherson claimed Canada would "never expect to maintain a high standard of nationality unless we keep the strain white." A year earlier Macpherson had argued that reconciling the chasm between "Orientals and Caucasians" was "just as impossible to do . . . as to mix oil and water" (Hansard, December 16, 1907).

Although these policymakers were mindful of the principle that all subjects of the British Empire were equal, most eschewed this principle in practice. Thus, for example, in a March 1908 debate Liberal Secretary of State R.W. Scott acknowledged the contradiction that whites could "go to India and rule there" but Indians were restricted from coming to Canada. Yet, he rationalized, "They are not the class of citizens that we want." Scott also raised the spectre of whites being overwhelmed by immigrants from India, claiming that, "they will come in like a flock of locusts and destroy the country." One month later, another Liberal, W.A. Galliher, reproduced the same paradoxical arguments, stating that

TABLE 7-1 ***Viva la "Difference:*** **"Race," Racism and Law in Canada**

1830s "Nigger Heaven" was used to describe the back of the gallery where some churches forced Black worshippers to sit.

1860s Theatres in Victoria banned Blacks from seats in dress circle area; when prominent Blacks sat in the dress circle in the Empress Theatre it led to white patrons rioting. The Palace Theatre in Windsor, Ontario called its Black section the "Crow's nest." The Loew's (Capital) restricted section was called the "Monkey's cage."

1875-1909 Voting restrictions: franchise denied to Indigenous peoples and Chinese (1875), extended to Japanese (1895, 1896), and "Hindus" (1907). Restrictions removed on Chinese (1947) and Japanese (1949) provincially and federally (1948); Indigenous peoples (1960).

1885 Chinese Immigration Act. Immigration statute explicitly identified "race" as a ground for exclusion. A new Chinese Immigration Act in 1923 lasted until 1947. (Also known as Chinese Exclusion Act).

1891-1965 *Separate Schools Act* designed to segregate Black and white students. Impact and duration varied across Canada: Chatham (until 1891), Harrow (1907), Amberstburg (1917), North Colchester and Essex (1965). Alberta had racialized schools until the 1960s.

April 1911 Edmonton City Council passed a resolution that banned Blacks from the city.

March 5, 1912 *An Act to Prevent the Employment of Female Labour in Certain Capacities*– Saskatchewan legislation designed to "protect" white women from the dangers of being employed in establishments run "by any Japanese, Chinaman or other Oriental person."

1924 Blacks excluded from public pools and parks in Edmonton.

June 11, 1936 Montreal resident, Fred Christie, Emile King, and Steven St. Jean were denied service at a tavern in the Montreal Forum where they went for a drink prior to a hockey game. Christie sued the York Tavern and lost (*Christie v. York Corporation*).

November 8, 1946 Viola Desmond thrown out of the Rosedale Theatre in New Glasgow, Nova Scotia, for sitting in seats reserved for whites, and subsequently charged and found guilty of violating Nova Scotia's *Theatres, Cinematographs and Amusement Act* (1915).

December 6, 1949 Chatham City Council referendum asked, "Do you approve the passing of legislation compelling restaurant owners to serve, regardless of race, creed or colour?" Results: 517 against, 108 in favour of desegregation.

1951 *Fair Employment Practices Act* outlawed discrimination in hiring in Ontario.

1952 *Immigration Act* (g)(i) continued restriction on entry based on "Nationality, citizenship, ethnic group, occupation, class or geographical origin."

1954 *Fair Accommodation Practices Act* banned discrimination in public establishments in Ontario.

1969 Black students and their supporters occupied the computer centre of Sir George Williams University to protest racial discrimination at the university and in Montreal.

Source: John Boyko, *Last Steps to Freedom: Evolution of Canadian Racism* (J. Gordon Shllingford, Inc., 1998), 164; "Our Secret Past: Canada's History of Race Discrimination," *Canada and the World Backgrounder,* 61-6 (April 1996), 16-17; Connie Blackhouse, *Colour-Coded: A Legal History of Racism in Canada, 1900–1950* (Toronto: The Osgood Society, 2000); and Robin W. Winks, "Negro School Segregation in Ontario and Nova Scotia," *Canadian Historical Review* 50, 2 (1969).

although "in principle" it was not fair to exclude some members of the Empire because of skin colour, in practice it was acceptable because "they are not suitable citizens."

This sentiment was repeated in numerous debates throughout 1914 that discussed prospective immigrants from India. In March 1914 Liberal MP W.E. Knowles claimed that although Indians were British subjects, "the less of the Hindus we have in Canada, the better." In May 1914, Conservative MP Cockshutt basically agreed with the Liberal position that Canada should exclude "Hindus [East Indians] and all kinds of Asiatics, and all kinds of undesirable people." Another MP, Stevens, suggested Indians should go to Tibet, Egypt or elsewhere in North Africa because "climatic, social and labour conditions . . . are peculiarly suited to their race."

Throughout this period, a number of ministers acknowledged the contradictions between principle and practice in the treatment of subjects of the Empire. Other ministers did depart from racialism and racism in politics and immigration policy. In the April 1908 debate, Conservative MP J.G. Haggart insisted this discrimination was indefensible. According to Haggart, "a good subject of the empire in one part of it" should not be denied equal privilege in another part of the empire. However, Sir Wilfrid Laurier, Canada's prime minister (1896–1911), accused Haggart of taking the "principle which is very good in itself a little too far" by extending it from whites to Indians. Laurier insisted that in matters relating to Anglo-Saxon supremacy, "logic" was not pertinent. In a May 30, 1914, House of Commons debate, MP Cockshutt summed up the views of those who tried to separate theory from practice by maintaining that not to allow "colour or skin or class or creed . . . to enter into my imperialism . . . may be good doctrine to preach but whether it is sound in practice is another question."

The early experiences of Chinese-Canadians also offer insights into the evolution of "race," law, and public policy in Canada. Efforts to exclude immigrants from China and Japan took some of the most discriminatory forms. Two consistent themes among policy-makers were the incompatibility between Eastern and Western civilizations, and racial purity. An editorial in the Winnipeg *Tribune* (March 22, 1911) aptly captured the dominant political view about the relationship between racism and public policy: Prime Minister Macdonald associated Chinese with immorality and in the House of Commons insisted that "Asiatic principles" were fundamentally "abhorrent to the Aryan race" and the "Aryan principles" upon which, he argued, the House of Commons was built (Hansard, May 4, 1885). While a number of Chinese migrant workers had entered Canada to work on the railway, once this project was completed various governments moved to restrict Chinese immigrants. This began with a head tax paid primarily by railways; by the 1900s it had increased to $100 and by 1903 to $500 (Chan, 2000/01, 145–7) or roughly the equivalent of the annual wages of a Canadian manufacturing worker.

In a 1902 Report of the Royal Commission on Chinese and Japanese Immigration, John Charlton argued it was "a prudential principle," held among Anglo-Saxons, that "foreign races" should be excluded from Canada unless they were readily assimilated into Anglo-Saxon habits (Canada, 1902). The task of immigration was "to maintain these [Anglo-Saxon] privileges and institutions; and we can maintain them best by excluding them." In particular, Charlton argued it was merely a "precaution" not to grant the franchise and citizenship to "the Chinese and Mongolian races"; he, and many of his colleagues, felt they were incompatible with Anglo-Saxons.

While Indians were part of the empire and under British common law equal subjects in their own rights, thus warranting some explanation for inequality among subjects, a different kind of argument was advanced against the Chinese. Political and popular discourses were filled with references to the Chinese as the "yellow peril" and the "Oriental menace," in part because of fear of their civilization. In a 1914 federal debate, Minister of the Interior Frank Oliver framed the exclusion of the Chinese in civilizational terms. "As the civilization of the West differs radically from the civilizations of the East, it will be agreed that if Western or European civilization is to prevail on this continent, it must be without the influence of Asiatic civilization." In other words, Oliver felt that inclusion of Chinese in Canada through immigration would mean the dilution of European civilization in Canada; the two civilizations were seen as incompatible. Oliver added the zero-sum perspective that if "Asiatic civilization is introduced . . . European civilization loses ground." The two civilizations were considered "radically different" and unable to "exist together."

While the majority of policymakers accepted racialism and were prepared to use immigration policy to maintain a racialized order, not all policymakers were so inclined. There were dissenting voices both in the House of Commons and the Senate. Senator L.G. Power argued that it was wrong for the parliament to "make any distinction of race at all; that the Chinese, Negroes, Indians and Whites should be on the same footing." Similarly, in a July 1892 House of Commons debate, MP T. Christie pointed out the contradiction of Prime Minister Macdonald's position by arguing that "if the same treatment should be extended to white men going to China, a storm of indignation would arise at their barbarous action." In the June 25, 1900, debate, MP W.E. Edwards suggested that the only foundational principle for such wrong-headed legislation was "barbarism and nothing else." Finally, drawing on the principles of liberal political economy, Christie argued during the same debate that the "poor oppressed and persecuted Chinaman [should] come in free . . . this legislation [head tax] is not in accordance with our free, liberal institutions" (Hansard, June 25, 1900).

An examination of disparate policies at the federal and provincial levels, and legal decisions, in particular, reveals a discernable pattern that can loosely be called a "white Canada policy." One source of these policies is the disciplinary practices of Empire and Canada's own colonial history, as well as regional influences from the United States. These disparate policies and practices, and the conception of an "Aryan race" embodied within them, functioned to construct racialized minorities (and some Europeans) as "undesirable." For racialized minorities already in Canada the white Canada policy helped to legitimize segregation and social exclusion across the public and private sectors.

THEORIZING "RACE MATTERS"

In the twenty-first century, "race," processes of racialization, and racism matter because they are part of the stuff of the Canadian body politic and way of life; they affect/shape the life chances and quality of life of racialized minorities. "Race matters" encompasses the ways in which we all experience, but fail to acknowledge, how racism works. Various technologies of marginalization and social exclusion maintain the centuries-old colour line within residential neighbourhoods, social relationships, workplaces, and, importantly, in life chances with regard to economic opportunities and social mobility. In *Outsider Blues* (1996), Clifton Ruggles maps what really is the normalization of racism, in the everyday experiences of suspicious looks, personal and technological surveillance, racial slights and slurs, and other acts of exclusion that are a constant reminder to racialized minorities of their "not belonging" in Canada. Similarly, Cecil Foster (1996) argues that these destabilizing experiences remain true whether one is a recent immigrant, a second-generation Black, or whether one's family can trace their lineage to centuries in Canada. Jacobs offers some other instructive examples concerning the ordinariness with which racism shapes our daily lives, from perceptions of personal security and fear of the "other" to issues of interracial love and intimacy, as well as whether and how we talk about racism in Canada. Some common misperceptions manifest themselves in, for example, "white women clutching their purses in the presence of black men; black women bristling at white women who date black men; . . . whites backing away from racial topics because blacks seem 'so sensitive'; [and] blacks blowing off racial discussion because whites will 'never understand,' " and so on (Jacobs, 1999, 9–10).

It would be a mistake to think, however, that these experiences are just about private preferences and individual tastes, and that they do not have political economy implications that play out in the areas of employment opportunities, equitable wages, and the distribution of wealth and power in Canadian society (Li, 1998, 115–30). The "social geography of racism" (Frankenberg, 1993) is also evident in the creation of what musician George Clinton calls "chocolate cities and vanilla suburbs" (quoted in West, 1994, 9). These social developments suggest the need to return to, and think seriously about, the ways in which Canada's "vertical mosaic" (Porter, 1965) and racialized social hierarchies are deepening. As a consequence, it is producing a social condition in which "not all ethnic groups have equal access to power, status, education, income, occupation, social mobility, or other cultural and material resources, as discourses of multicultural equality might lead us to believe" (Gunderson, 1999, 106–8).

A challenge to consciousness about "race" relations in Canada relates to an ongoing lament of Canadian historians: Canadians are woefully ignorant of their own history. Another challenge relates to "race manners," discussed in the next section. Suffice it to say, although Canada's national self-understanding is as a "polite" and tolerant society, a genealogy of "race" relations in Canada reveals a near hysteria among white settler priests, politicians, and civil servants about the need to bar immigrants who were racialized minorities. The records of the House of Commons, and popular magazines and print media in the late nineteenth and early twentieth century, are replete with stories suggestive of white fear, even loathing and the openly expressed desire to exclude the "niggers," "Oriental menace," "yellow peril," and East Indians who would "flock to Canada like locusts" (Smith, 1997, 1998; Walker, 1997; Blackhouse, 2000). White settlers routinely encouraged the use of public policy as a vehicle for social exclusion. They frequently invoked the idea of a shared humanity among white people as a trump card to exclude racialized minorities who were depicted as "undesirable" immigrants and "unsuitable" citizens. It was claimed that their "race" and "civilization" made them unlikely to fit into Canada's national identity as an "Aryan" or "white nation." In light of this naked racism, renowned author and filmmaker, Dionne Brand refers to the "stupefying innocence" of Canadians about this aspect of their history and the legacies for contemporary society (Landsberg, 2000).

The defence of "tolerance is a relatively new development" in Canada (Granatstein and Hillmer, 1999, 31). Although Granatstein and Hillmer suggest contemporary "attitudes are different" from those of the past, this assumption of tolerance might be no more than a kind of repressive tolerance which is built not on respect for difference—or recognition of Canada's diversity model—but rather on legendary Canadian politeness. Consider other examples from over a century and a half ago; they are emblematic of another Canadian paradox—the belief that there would be no prejudice or racism in Canada as long as racialized minorities knew and maintained their "proper place" and did not cross the colour line.

One example, from the 1840s, involves the case of a Black man who was physically ejected from the Mansion House Hotel in London, Ontario (Walker, 1997, 131). When the victim sought a warrant against the establishment to ensure access for racialized minorities in the future, the court convicted him of racial discrimination of assault; his actions caused the owners to physically eject him. Similarly, Rev. C.O. Johnson was barred from the Queen's Hotel in Toronto in 1880. Despite this, *Saturday Night* magazine ran a story that claimed, "In Canada, there is no active prejudice against the colored race." The magazine went on to clarify its point in the following terms: The "colored race" was treated without prejudice, "except when they forgot that no well-bred person will endeavour to force himself into a place where he is not wanted" (August 15, 1888). In other words, to expect equal treatment was impolite, unmannerly, and a clear sign of lack of good breeding.

In Windsor, Ontario, racially restrictive covenants were designed to exclude minorities from certain residential areas; in other areas the colour line was maintained by an "understanding" among white homeowners and real estate agents that homes were not to be sold to non-whites. The *Windsor Herald* argued this legally and conventionally enforced colour line was acceptable and should be respected by racialized minorities. According to the *Herald,* in those cases where "a certain locality is prohibited, let them avoid it, as they will experience no difficulty in finding places of settlement." However, if racialized minorities attempted "to force themselves into positions where they are not wanted, under the idea that the British constitution warrants them in doing so, they may discover in the end that the privilege which they now enjoy will become forfeited" (November 3, 1855).

The London, Toronto, and Windsor examples illustrate a longstanding paradox in Canada. On the one hand, there is a denial that racism exists or is a serious issue. On the other hand, there is a belief that to talk openly about "race matters" is an affront to good manners; this limits a serious national engagement of the issues related to racial discrimination in Canada. Claims about "race manners" or "good breeding" can preserve the colour line. Arguably, today, this same notion carries over in claims about politeness. A recent case illustrates the continuity of this paradox. On February 4, 2002, the *Globe and Mail* ran an editorial, "To raise the question of racial profiling." The case involved Dee Brown, a basketball player with the Toronto Raptors who was pulled over by the police in 1999, and subsequently charged with "impaired driving," although his attorney argued it was more a case of "driving while Black." During the trial in the Ontario Court, Dee's lawyer raised a number of troubling questions about the police actions that evening. He theorized about the police seeing a Black man in an expensive Ford Bronco, running his license plates, and, when the vehicle showed up as not stolen, deciding to proceed with a trumped-up charge. In effect, the lawyer argued, this was a case of racial profiling.

Mr. Justice David Fairgrieve, however, took exception to this and argued that the mere accusation of racial profiling was "distasteful," that it was a "nasty, malicious" accusation. Dee was found guilty and told it was he who should apologize to the police officers whom the judge described as "polite." The editorial suggested Mr. Justice Fairgrieve's "response was inexcusable. In spite of all inquiries, in spite of the common sense that tells us discrimination exists in Canada and takes many different forms, an argument that there might have been racism could not be put on the table." With some irony, the editorial asked, "After all, didn't everyone see how polite the officer was?" Politeness or the presentation of oneself in a mannerly fashion in no way precludes the simultaneous existence and practice of racism. In other words, politeness and racism are not mutually exclusive. The lower court's decision was overturned on appeal and Mr. Justice Brian Trufford expressed puzzlement over the lower court's decision to reject, out of hand, the issue of racial profiling raised and, worse, the decision to make Dee apologize to the officers. As the editorial concluded, "even polite officers might engage in it [racial profiling] unconsciously."

In the *Invisible Empire*, Margaret Cannon (1995) draws on a number of examples to challenge the view that Canadian racism should be characterized as "polite," particularly if this is meant to suggest that racism in Canada is somehow less toxic than in the United States. Cannon argues that racism dehumanizes the victims and perpetrators alike and it underwrites a polarization in social attitudes, experiences, and life chances that make complacent claims that there is no "race problem" in Canada dangerous. Politeness or "race manners" can function to inhibit serious public dialogue and debate about prickly race matters, as well as to obscure the need for sustained personal and institutional efforts to address "race"-based social exclusion. Arguably, unlike the brash, in-your-face racism often witnessed in the United States, for example, racism in Canada might be more invidious precisely because the cloak of politeness masks the fact of racism and its brutal effects on racialized minorities.

THINKING AND TALKING ABOUT "RACE" IN CANADA

One of the difficulties in discussing "race matters" and racism in Canada relates to what Bruce Jacobs has termed "race manners" and the "fear of frankness," or what others refer to as Canadian politeness. Consider the popular and media discourse after the racially motivated riots in Toronto on May 4, 1992. In a commentary on the riots, Austin Clarke analyzed the conventional view that "prejudice" in Canada is more "polite" than in the United States and, that, in "race matters" Canada is radically different from the United States. While Clarke rejected the claim of polite Canadian prejudice, he nonetheless reproduced the myth that Toronto, and Canada, "is still north of the border of America and of racism" (1992, 18). This view is really akin to an article of faith, one that is repeated frequently in Canadian life. In a July 1996 interview, for example, sprinter Donovan Bailey was reported to have said that Canada "is as blatantly racist as the United States" (Corelli, 1996, 38). Subsequently Bailey was called upon to account for this heresy, and he argued that what he had said was that, "Canada is not as blatantly racist as the U.S., but it [racism] does exist" (1996, 38). In effect, Bailey was called upon to explain what should be a truism; there is racism in Canada and, in fact, no society on earth can claim it is racism-free.

There were mixed responses to Bailey's comments and they are worth detailing here because the paradoxes of "race" knowledge and understanding that these comments reveal speak directly to some of the challenges to thinking and talking about processes of racialization and racism in Canada. Particularly noteworthy is the contradiction Bailey pointed out between the media's and the public's reaction to sprinter Ben Johnson testing positive for a banned substance (steroids) at the Olympics, and their reaction to rower Silken Laumann testing positive for a banned substance (in a cold medication) at the 1995 Pan-Am Games. According to Bailey the central issue was the wrongful use of drugs in sport. However, whereas Johnson's heritage as "Jamaican" was raised repeatedly in reports of the story, this was not true for Laumann's unnamed European heritage. The fixation on Johnson's national identity and "origin" was a challenge to his Canadianness and sense of belonging; this was not true before Johnson tested positive for steroids and it seemed a non-issue for Laumann.

Lyle Smordin, then president of the B'Nai Brith's League for Human Rights, agreed with Bailey, both about the fact of racism in Canada and how, in cases like that of Ben Johnson, "we tend to indicate how they're not 'pure' Canadians" when they do not succeed.

While Bailey attributed the problem to one of racism, Smordin argued it was one of national origin. In addition to flagging some contradictions of issues of "race" and national identity in Canada, the Bailey story is tied up with "race manners"—what we dare speak publicly about ourselves and where. Rosemary Brown, then chair of the Ontario Human Rights Commission, claimed she had "a real sense of hurt that he [Bailey] would have gone outside Canada" (quoted in Corelli, 1996, 38) to draw attention to these issues. Perhaps while not intending it, Brown's comments suggest racism in Canada is some kind of dirty little secret, about which we dare not speak outside the country's borders and certainly not in the United States. In fact, Brown went on to reject the view that the experiences of racism in Canada are in any way comparable to those in the United States, where it is "more blatant." As well, according to Brown, "The United States has a history of racism entrenched in law and that's not the experience we have had here." Perhaps the strongest response to Bailey's comments were made by Sylvia Sweeny, a former Olympian and then assistant chief of mission in Atlanta where Bailey was training. Sweeny suggested that Bailey's comments were about his "personal experience," and should not be generalized because, "In Canada, we're not living in the same reality as the Americans" (1996, 38).

The above story speaks to at least four aspects of Canada's foundational myth about "race" and particularly racism. First, there is a belief that Canadian "prejudice" is more "polite" than racism in the United States. The second myth is that whereas racism in the United States has a long history and was supported by legislation, this was not the case in Canada. This myth suggests that experiences of racism have a recent origin and were never supported by law and public policy. The third myth is that the experiences of members of racialized minorities like Bailey are "personal" and not systemic and, therefore, such experiences do not resonate throughout Canada's "national" story: they speak to isolated incidents that are not generalizable. The Bailey story also draws our attention to the conventional understanding about what is appropriate to speak about outside the country, as if despite globalization, Canada's border with the United States is impermeable to political, economic, and social influences. This imagined difference in the histories of "race" in Canada and the United States and their experiences of interracial relations is contingent, in part, on accepting a "dichotomy between a supposedly multicultural Canada and an American melting pot" which, Satzewich (1998) adds, "appears to be significantly overblown." More like the United States than not, Canadian society has never been "a race-neutral one. It is built upon centuries of racial discrimination. The legacy of such bigotry infects all of our institutions, relationships, and legal frameworks" (Blackhouse, 2000, 274).

Another aspect of this foundational myth, which depicts Canada as a kind of multicultural utopia, seems to be deeply embedded in the national psyche. Increasingly, however, a number of scholars of critical "race" theory and cultural studies (Goldberg, 1990; Back and Solomos, 2000) have challenged the stubborn "complacency" about "race" and racism embedded in Canadian society, polity, and economy. They draw attention to the history of these experiences and how they have played out across some public institutions and private enterprises (Smith, 1997; Blackhouse, 2000). These works, and others, also have revealed how what might be called "official" and "corporate" multiculturalism (Goldberg, 1994; Gunderson, 1999) can act to mask processes of racialization and everyday lived experiences. Language, after all, is not value-neutral.

Public discourse and policies can act to delimit the terrain of public debate and even to occlude our understanding of ongoing processes of racialization. Canadian multicultural discourse has largely ignored the political economy of "race", particularly as it relates to issues of wealth, power, social status, and their increasing distribution along a "colour line." Where corporate multiculturalism shows a "relative lack of concern with the redistribution of power or resources" (Goldberg, 1994, 1–4), official multiculturalism prioritizes "support for the expression and celebration of private forms of difference: in family, food, religious conventions" (Knowles, 1996, 49). In other words, the celebrations of multicultural difference can and often do elide "race" and class inequalities in Canada (Gunderson, 1999, 106–23).

CONCLUSION

The aims of this chapter were modest, however the issues addressed speak to the need for further study of "race" relations by students of Canadian politics, administration, and public policy. At its core this chapter has been about how "race" and a Manichaean world-view became iterated into popular notions of national identity despite the myth of racelessness or colour-blindness. It surveyed the ways in which "race" has always mattered, and continues to matter, for the Canadian body politic in innumerable ways. Thinking and talking about this fact can be inhibited by discourses of multiculturalism, denial, a wilful blindness that assumes experiences of racism are isolated incidents, and by a kind of "race manners" that assume polite Canadians do not tell their ugly stories of racism, particularly to strangers outside the country. The chapter also explored the early public debate about Canada as an Aryan, or white, society and how this history is too often "white-washed" or "blacked out" of contemporary discussion, research, and writings in the areas of politics, administration, and public policy. Revisiting these ideas and practices in the twenty-first century can increase our consciousness and understanding about how and why ideas of "race" became a part of the Canadian way of life, and how and why a colour-coded conception of nation, citizenship, and belonging emerged in Canada. Finally, it discussed the dominant discourse of "race" in Canada and how it continues to be shaped by centuries-old ideas, policies, and social configurations that naturalized the "colour line" in an ostensibly colour-blind society.

Canadian society, as this chapter makes clear, was never a raceless, colour-blind or "race"-neutral one. Historical and contemporary processes of racialization and racism have left an indelible mark on notions about who belongs in Canada. Active "race"-based discrimination was practised for centuries and legally permissible well into the 1960s. Racism persists today, and continues to shape our institutions, social and intimate relationships, employment opportunities, and way of life. Processes of racialization impact our intellectual and cultural imagination about what it means to be Canadian in a historical moment shaped by North America integration. And "race manners," continue to shape how we think and talk about a national identity in a country that is shaped by globalization, migration, and ethnocultural heterogeneity. Thus, "race" and racism will continue to matter in Canada in the twenty-first century.

NOTES

1. Some parts of this chapter appeared earlier in Malinda S. Smith (1997, 1998).
2. Throughout this chapter "race" is placed in brackets to emphasize its contested and problematic nature as a social science concept.
3. Canada became the first of the British colonies to receive Dominion status in 1867, followed by Australia in 1900, New Zealand in 1907, South Africa in 1910 and Southern Ireland in 1922 as the Irish Free State. In 1931 the Statute of Westminster granted these so-called "White Dominions" the status of freely associated members of the British Commonwealth. See, N. Lowe (1989).

REFERENCES

Anthias, F. and N. Yuval Davis. 1992. *Racialized Boundaries: Race, Nation, Gender, Colour and Class and the Anti-racist Struggle.* London: Routledge.

Appiah, Kwame Anthony. 1992. *In My Father's House: Africa in the Philosophy of Culture.* Oxford University Press.

Appiah, K. Anthony. 1996. *Color Conscious: The Political Morality of Race.* Princeton, NJ: Princeton University Press.

Aylward, Carol A. 1999. *Canadian Critical Race Theory: Racism and the Law.* Halifax: Fernwood.

Ballantyne, Tony. 2002. "Introduction: Debating Empire," *Journal of Colonialism and Colonial History 3*, 1.

Ballantyne, Tony. 2001. "Race and the webs of empire: Aryanism from India to the Pacific," *Journal of Colonialism and Colonial History 2*, 3.

Banton, Michael. 2000. "The Idiom of Race: A Critique of Presentism." In *Theories of Race and Racism: A Reader*, ed., Les Back and John Solomos. New York: Routledge.

Banton, Michael. 1997. *The Idea of Race.* London: Tavistock.

Berger, Carl. 1970. *The Sense of Power: Studies in the Ideas of Canadian Imperialism, 1867–1914.* Toronto: University of Toronto Press.

Berger, Carl. 1969. *Imperialism and Nationalism, 1884–1914: A Conflict in Canadian Thought.* Toronto: Copp Clark.

Bolaria, S. and P. Lee. 1998. *Racial Oppression in Canada.* Toronto: Garamond Press.

Boyko, John. 1998. "Slavery, Segregation and Evacuation," *Last Steps to Freedom: The Evolution of Canadian Racism.* J. Gordon Shillingford, Inc.

Bristow, Peggy, Dionne Brand, Linda Carty, Afua P. Cooper, and Sylvia Hamilton. 1994. "We're rooted here and they can't pull us up": *Essays in African Canadian Women's History*. Toronto: University of Toronto Press.

Canada. 1913. *Royal Commission on Chinese Frauds and Opium Smuggling on the Pacific Coast,* Report of Mr. Justice Murphy, Royal Commissioner, 1910–11. Ottawa: The Commission.

Canada. 1908. *Royal Commission Appointed to Inquire into the Methods by which Oriental Labourers have been Induced to Come to Canada,* Report of the Royal Commission appointed to inquire into the methods by which oriental labourers have been induced to come to Canada. W.L. Mackenzie King, c.m.g., Commissioner. Ottawa, Government Printing Bureau.

Canada. 1907. *Report by W. L. Mackenzie King, C.M.G. Deputy Minister of Labour commissioner* appointed to investigate into the losses sustained by the Chinese population of Vancouver, B.C. on the occasion of the riots in that city in September 1907. Ottawa: King's Printer.

Canada. 1902. *Report of the Royal Commission on Chinese and Japanese Immigration*. New York: Arno Press, 1978.

Canada. 1885. *Royal Commission on Chinese Immigration.* Report of the Royal Commission on Chinese Immigration. Ottawa: Printed by order of the Commission.

Cannon, Margaret. 1995. *Invisible Empire: Racism in Canada*. Toronto: Random House of Canada.

Carter, Gerald Emmett Cardinal. 1979. *Report to the Civil Authorities of Metropolitan Toronto and Its Citizens*. Toronto.

Chan, Ada. 2000/2001. "'Glorious and free': one young woman's hope for a racism-free Canada," *Canadian Woman Studies 21*, (1) December-February: 145–147.

Clarke, Clarke. 1992. *Public Enemies: Police Violence and Black Youth.* Toronto: HarperCollins.

Comaroff, John L. 1998. "Reflections on the Colonial State, in South Africa and Elsewhere: Factions, Fragments, Facts and Fictions," *Social Identities 4*, (3) October.

Corelli, Rae. 1996. "Resurrecting the Racism Row: Canada's (Donovan) Bailey sets off a new controversy," *Maclean's 109*, 31 (July 29): 38.

Desai, Meghnad. 1983. "Political Economy." In *A Dictionary of Marxist Thought*. Tom Bottomore et al., (eds), Cambridge, Mass.: Harvard University Press.

Dickson, Peter. 1998. "'In another place, not here': Dionne Brand's Politics of (Dis)Location." In Veronica Strong-Boag et al., (eds). *Painting the Maple: Essays on Race, Gender and the Construction of Canada*. Veronica Strong-Boag et al., Vancouver: University of British Columbia Press: 113–29.

Eisenberg, Avigail. 2000. "Citizenship and the Recognition of Cultural Diversity: The Canadian Experience: A Response to Jenson and Papillon Backgrounder," *A Structured Dialogue on Diversity: The Values and Political Structures That Support It.* Canadian Policy Research Networks, Ottawa, Canada, May 12.

Foster, Cecil. 1996. *A Place Called Heaven.* Toronto: HarperCollins.

Frankenberg, Ruth. 1993. *The Social Construction of Whiteness: White Women Race Matters*. Minneapolis: University of Minnesota Press.

Goldberg, David Theo. 1994. "Introduction: Multicultural Conditions." In D.T. Goldberg (ed.), *Multiculturalism: A Critical Reader*. Oxford, UK: Blackwell; 1–4.

Goldberg, David Theo (ed.), 1990. *Anatomy of Racism.* Minneapolis: University of Minnesota Press.

Gordon, Lewis R. 1999. "Fanon, Philosophy, and racism," *Racism and Philosophy*. Susan E. Bobbitt & Sue Campbell (eds.). Ithaca and London: Cornell University Press.

Granatstein, J. L. and Norman Hillmer. 1999. "How Canada tried to bar the 'yellow peril'," *Macleans 112*, 26 (July), 31.

Gunderson, Michele. 1999. "Managing diversity: the economies of community in Denise Chong's The Concubine's Children," *West Coast Line 33*, (2) (Fall): 106–23.

Han, Sheridan. 1996. "Blacks in Canada: the Invisible Minority," *Canadian Dimension 30*, (6) (November–December): 14–17.

Hardt, Michael and Antonio Negri. 2000. *Empire,* Harvard University Press.

Hill, Lawrence. 2002. "Don't call me that word," *Maclean's* (February 25, 2002): 61.

Hill, D. G. 1981. *The Freedom Seekers: Blacks in Early Canada.* Agincourt: Book Society of Canada.

Howe, S. G. 1969. *Report to the Freedmen's Inquiry Commission 1864: The Refugees from Slavery in Canada West*. Ayer Co. Pub.

Huntington, Samuel. 1993."A Clash of Civilization," *Foreign Affairs* (Summer).

Ibbitson, John. 2002. "Why racial profiling is a good idea," *Globe and Mail* (June 3, 2002): A15.

Jacobs, Bruce A. 1999. *Race Manners: Navigating the Minefield Between Black and White Americans.* New York: Arcade Publishing.

Jakubowski, Lisa Marie. 1997. *Immigration and the Legalization of Racism.* Halifax: Fernwood.

Jenkinson, Michael. 1996. "Dirty tricks in Strathcona: an RPC nomination fight gets ugly as racism charges fly," *Western Report 11*, (45) (December 2, 1996): 9.

Jenson, Jane. 2000. "Time to Strengthen Canada's Commitment to Diversity," *Canadian Policy Research Network–Backgrounder: Thinking about Marginalization*. Ottawa, Canada, November: 1–14.

Jenson, Jane and Martin Papillon. 2000. "Citizenship and the Recognition of Cultural Diversity: The Canadian Experience: Backgrounder," *A Structured Dialogue on Diversity: The Values and Political Structures That Support It*, Canadian Policy Research Networks, Ottawa, Canada, May 12.

Kennedy, Randall. 2002. *Nigger.* Random House of Canada.

Knowles, Caroline. 1996. "Racism, Biography, and Psychiatry." In V. Amit-Talai and Caroline Knowles (eds.), *Re-Situating Identities: The Politics of Race, Ethnicity, and Culture*. Peterborough, Ontario: Broadview, 46–67.

Landsberg, Michele. 2000 February 26. "Canada Sweeps Racism Under the Carpet," *Toronto Star*.

Li, Peter S. 1998. "The Market Value and Social Value of Race." In V. Satzewich (ed.), *Racism & Social Inequality in Canada: Concepts, Controversies & Strategies of Resistance*, Toronto: Thompson Educational Publishing, Inc.

Lowe, N. 1989. *Mastering Modern British History.* London: Macmillan Press.

Miles, Robert. 1993. *Racism after "Race Relations*." London: Routledge.

Muldoon, James. 1999. *Empire and Order: The Concept of Empire, 800–1800.* New York: St. Martin's Press.

Perry, Adele. 2001. "The State of Empire: Reproducing Colonialism in British Columbia, 1849–1871," *Journal of Colonialism and Colonial History 2*, 1.

Philip, Nourbese M. 1992. "Why Multiculturalism Can't End Racism," *Frontiers: Essays and Writing on Racism and Culture.* Stratford, Ontario: Mercury.

Porter, John. 1965. *The Vertical Mosaic: An Analysis of Social Class and Power in Canada*. Toronto: University of Toronto Press.

Reeves, Frank. 1984. *British Racial Discourse: A Study of British Political Discourse about Race and Race-Related Matters.* Cambridge University Press.

Regina Daily Province, "Dr. Shearer Gives Regina Bouquet" (March 16, 1911), 5.

Regina Daily Province, "Rev. Moore on Social Evil" (June 21, 1912), 1.

Reitz, J. 1988. "Less racial discrimination in Canada, or simply less racial conflict? Implications of comparison with Britain," *Canadian Public Policy 14,* (4), 424–441.

Reitz, J. and R. Breton. 1994. *Illusions of Difference: Realities of Ethnicity in Canada and the United States.* Toronto: CD Howe Institute.

Roy, P. 1989. *A White Man's Province: British Columbia's Politicians and the Fear of Asians.* Vancouver: University of British Columbia Press.

Ruggles, Clifton. 1996. *Outsider Blues*. Halifax: Fernwood.

Rushton, Phillipe. 1994. *Race, Evolution and Behaviour: A Lifestyle Perspective.* New Brunswick, NJ: Transaction Publishers.

Satzewich, Vic. 1998. "Introduction," *Racism and Social Inequality in Canada: Concepts, Controversies, & Strategies of Resistance*, ed. Vic Satzewich. Toronto: Thompson Educational, Inc.

Shepard, R. Bruce. 1997. *Deemed Unsuitable: Blacks From Oklahoma Move to the Canadian Prairies in Search of Equality in the Early 18th Century Only to Find Racism in their New Home.* Toronto: Umbrella Press.

Shortt, Adam and Arthur Doughty, (eds.) 1914. *Canada and Its Provinces,* vol. 7. Toronto: Publishers' Association of Canada.

Siegfried, A. 1907. *The Race Question in Canada*. London: E. Nash.

Smith, Malinda S. 1997. "Quilting Canada's 'Race' Policy," Part I: The Making of a White Settler Society, *African Link*, vol. 6, no. 4 (Fourth Quarter): 12, 29–30.

Smith, Malinda S. 1998. "Quilting Canada's 'Race' Policy," Part II: "Sons of Canada…[or the Niggers]"? *African Link*, vol. 7, no, 1 (First Quarter): 29–30.

Smith, Malinda S. 1998. "Quilting Canada's 'Race' Policy," Part III: "Gentiles Only. No Jews or . . . Allowed," *African Link*, vol. 7, no 2 (Second Quarter): 31, 40.

Smith, Malinda S. 1998. "Quilting Canada's 'Race' Policy," Part IV: "East Indians, 'Like A Flock of Locusts . . . '," *African Link*, vol. 7, no. 3 (Third Quarter): 27–28, 36.

Smith, T.W. 1899. "The Slave in Canada." *Collections of the Nova Scotia Historical Society*: 97–105.

Southam Editorial. 2002. "Why Alliance can't shed redneck stereotype," *Edmonton Journal* (January 18, 2002): A16.

Spray, W. A. 1972. *The Blacks in New Brunswick.* Fredericton, N.B.: Brunswick Press, 23–6.

Todorov, Tzvetan. 2000. "Race and Racism," trans. Catherine Porter, *Theories of Race and Racism: A Reader*. ed. Les Back and John Solomos. New York: Routledge.

Vallieres, Pierres. 1971. *Negres Blancs d'Amerique*, English trans. Joan Pinkham. *White Niggers of America*. Toronto: McClelland and Stewart.

Walker, James W. St. George. 1997. *"Race," Rights and the Law in the Supreme Court of Canada: Historical Case Studies*. The Osgoode Society for Canadian Legal History and Wilfrid Laurier University Press.

Walker, James W. St. G. 1989. "'Race' Policy in Canada: A Retrospective" in *Canada 2000: Race Relations and Public Policy*, Proceedings of the Conference held at Carleton University, Ottawa, October 30-November 1, 1987. O.P. Dwivedi, Ronald D'Costa, C. Lloyd Stanford and Elliott Tepper (eds.). Guelph: Department of Political Studies, University of Guelph, 1989.

Walker, James W. St. G. 1976. *The Black Loyalists: the Search for a Promised Land in Nova Scotia and Sierra Leone, 1783–1870*. (New York: Africana Publishing Company and Dalhousie University Press).

Wilson, R. McL. 1967. "Mani and Manichaeism" (149–150). In: *The Encyclopedia of Philosophy,* vol. 5, ed. Paul Edwards. New York: Macmillan and Free Press.

Winks, Robin W. 1997. *The Blacks in Canada, 2nd edition*. Montreal and Kingston: McGill-Queen's University Press.

Winks, Robin W. 1969. "Negro School Segregation in Ontario and Nova Scotia," *Canadian Historical Review,* 50, 2.

Yeung-Seu Yoon, 2002. "The white, male profile," letter to the editor (Toronto), *Globe and Mail* (June 4, 2002): A16.

WEBLINKS

Canadian Race Relations Foundation
www.crr.ca

Queen's University Race and Racism Resources
www.queensu.ca/idis/resource.htm

The Internment of Japanese Nationals
http://canada.justice.gc.ca/en/justice2000/44mile.html

chapter eight

Women and the Politics of Citizenship

Linda Trimble

INTRODUCTION

A newspaper article titled "Female operators OK'd to wear pants" reported a victory for women employed by a company contracted by the British Columbia government to provide toll-free telephone access to provincial departments and services—the right to wear slacks to work. Although the employees never came into contact with the public, the company had been enforcing a strict no-pants dress code for women telephone operators. After intense media coverage and numerous meetings with provincial government officials, the company finally agreed to change its controversial policy.

When do you suppose this newspaper article was written? If you think the answer is the 1950s or 1960s—after all, the so-called sexual revolution and the popularity of unisex clothing has long since challenged the idea of sex-based dress codes—you are wrong. This report appeared in the *National Post* on February 5, 2001. And the article also mentioned more restrictions on women's freedoms imposed by the employer, Robertson Telecom, which did not allow employees to keep purses and personal items near their workspaces (Beatty, 2001, A8). At a time when most Canadians believe they enjoy, and certainly would assert their right to claim, basic personal liberties, this story seems archaic and bizarre. Denying women the right to wear pants certainly appears out of line with the fact that the idea that "women are equal to men and deserve the same opportunities now dominates the way our society thinks about gender. Feminism has triumphed" (LaFramboise, 1997, D1, D3).

But has it? In 1997, a fully employed female doctor was refused a mortgage unless her husband agreed to co-sign the papers and guarantee payment (Galbraith, 1997, A22). The same year, Calgary's remaining all-male Rotary Club voted to continue excluding women (Jeffs, 1997, B7). Former Ontario premier Mike Harris decided in April 1998 to stop giving pregnant women on social assistance a $37 food allowance on the grounds that the women might spend the money on beer (Vipond, 1998, A27). Also in 1998, a B.C. man who stabbed his wife 47 times with a hunting knife only received a four-year jail term as he claimed she provoked the attack by nagging him continuously during a four-hour truck ride (Bindman, 1998, A3). A young woman who suffered a catastrophic gym class injury in 1991 that left her a quadriplegic received substantial general damages based on loss of future income. But the school board found responsible for the injuries appealed, and in 2002 these damages were reduced by over $150 000. The judge reasoned that, given the girl's pre-injury intention to marry and bear children, her actual earnings would have been affected by time taken out of the workplace (Mitchell, 2002, 8). And in 1998, an Alberta man was acquitted of sexual assault on appeal even though the victim repeatedly said no to his attempts to engage in sexual activity. The victim said no but really meant "yes," said the judge who heard the appeal; after all, she was dressed in shorts and a T-shirt (Laghi, 1998, A1, A11).[1]

Given these stories, and the many others like them not recounted here, why do the mainstream media and anti-feminist pundits declare that feminists have won the "gender war" (Crittenden, 1990, 38)? Why, at the end of the twentieth century, did Canadian journalists pronounce the "end of the women's movement" (Chwialkowska, 1998, B5)? One reason is that feminist ideas, expressed by the women's movement, have had a demonstrable impact on the status of some women in Canadian society. Women's progress is tangible, evident in our everyday lives, where most enjoy the rights and freedoms won by the first and second waves of the women's movement. Women can lawfully use birth control, keep their "maiden" names after marriage, enter the paid labour force, control their own money and property, claim custody of children after divorce, vote, run for political office, and retain Aboriginal status after marriage. However, even in 2002, women cannot expect to see themselves adequately represented in political office, rely on governments to enforce custody arrangements and child support awards, or count on the legal system to adequately punish those who physically and sexually assault them. Canadian women cannot be assured that they will be treated with dignity and respect regardless of the colour of their skin, their sexual orientation, where they were born, how much money they earn, how old they are, and whether they have mental or physical disabilities. In other words, women have not yet achieved full and substantive citizenship. Freedom, equality, and a sense of belonging within Canada are mediated, and often mitigated, by gender, ethnicity, class, ability, age, and sexual orientation.

This chapter explores the political forces that have shaped the evolution of women's citizenship in Canada. It argues that ideas about citizenship, originally formulated to expressly exclude women on the basis of their sex, have been changed to accept some of women's claims for equal rights and responsibilities. How and why citizenship came to be informed by gender in the first place is explained in the first section of the chapter. The second section shows that, despite winning the formal rights of citizenship, including the right to vote and contest political office, and being able to exercise the politics of activism and empowerment, Canadian women remain, in many respects, second-class citizens.

Using political representation as a litmus test of citizenship, this section illustrates women's continued under-representation in political office. The final part of the chapter examines three contemporary, and competing, visions of citizenship in Canada—welfare liberalism, neoliberalism, and neoconservatism—exploring the implications of each ideology for women. The chapter ends with a discussion of the prospects for women's political inclusion and citizenship in the twenty-first century.

GENDER AND THE EVOLVING MEANING OF CITIZENSHIP

Citizenship is "a way of meeting one of our deepest needs, the need to belong; it gives voice and structure to the yearning to be part of something larger than ourselves" (Kingwell, 2000, 5). This thing larger than ourselves is membership in a national community; we think of citizenship as the rights, responsibilities, values, and beliefs associated with belonging to a country. Moreover, we believe that being Canadian is meaningful; that is, substantively different than being, say, Norwegian. The meaning structures of citizenship have also been shaped by assumptions about gender roles. Until very recently belonging has been socially and politically constructed as the nearly exclusive domain of white men. Indeed, the very idea of citizenship was developed on the premise that women should be denied the basic rights of citizens because they did not have the capacity to perform its duties (Lister, 1997, 3). At Confederation, only property-owning white men held citizenship rights such as the vote. Women belonged as mothers, wives, and daughters of the (male) citizens, and their social role was defined accordingly—the provision of domestic labour and the reproduction of the citizenry through bearing and rearing children.

The exclusion of women from citizenship has a long history in Western political thought and practice and is rooted in the patriarchal assumptions once embraced by philosophers, politicians, professionals, and ordinary folks. The underlying ideas of patriarchy have been expressed differently across time, cultures, and political practices, but at heart patriarchy means rule by men. In patriarchal societies, men have more power and greater access to what is valued by the social group (Code, 1993, 19). Patriarchal thought prescribes power and authority to men, both individually, as head of the domestic household, and as the economic and political elite of the public realm where business is conducted, wages are set and earned, and rules are made (Walby, 1996, 24). Patriarchal thinking considers men to be "natural" rulers (of themselves and women) on the grounds that sex differences determine personality characteristics, individual capabilities, and social roles. Patriarchal attitudes are often grounded in biological determinism—"the belief that a woman's nature and all of her possibilities are determined by her biology" (Code, 1993, 22–23). A "biology is destiny" view sees women as bodies governed by hormones and reproductive destiny, not as bearers of minds with the capacity for intelligence, rationality, and free will. When regarded as the "natural" caregivers of children, women are characterized as emotional, sentimental, irrational, illogical, and, generally, inferior to men. On the other hand, the view of men that arises from biological determinism is of beings genetically programmed to be rational, active, objective, independent, impartial, and intelligent, thus destined to rule lesser beings like women and children. Biological determinism lays the foundation for the notion that women are naturally subservient, incapable of acting as free citizens, and appropriately subordinate to men.

The distinction between public and private (domestic) gives these assumptions a foundation for mutually exclusive gender roles. Characteristics, roles, and standards are seen to be separated, by sex, into two distinct spheres: the private sphere of family and domestic life, and the public world of business, government, official culture, sports, and organized religion. Women are regarded as passive, compliant, sentimental, dependent, and subordinate, thus as naturally suited for private sphere roles. On the other hand, men are seen to have the appropriate characteristics for engagement with public sphere activities and duties, namely assertiveness, rationality, objectivity, independence, and dominance. For instance, in an opinion piece written for the *National Post* (March 22, 2001), Tom Flanagan argued that men are better suited to the very public role of leading political parties, as they are genetically programmed to be more competitive and power-seeking than women. Flanagan pointed to the seeming inability of women party leaders to win elections and form governments as evidence that females are not well equipped for these top political jobs.

The Exclusion of Women from Canadian Citizenship

Until the twentieth century Canadian women were treated by law as dependent wives and mothers, not as independent citizens with all the rights and duties necessary for full citizenship. Before and after Confederation, political, clerical, and medical elites embraced biological determinism, promoting an idealized domestic and maternal image of a woman's role. In 1938, for example, Canada's *Chatelaine* magazine declared: "Women's instinct is to find her mate. It is not a matter of choice. It is the whole sum and substance of her existence. It is like that because life must go on, children must be born, homes must be provided for" (Fraser, 1997, 50). Thus it is not surprising that Canada's earliest electoral law explicitly excluded women, along with children and so-called mental incompetents, from exercising a fundamental democratic right—choosing representatives of the people to serve as political decision-makers.

Since patriarchal assumptions guided political decisions about citizenship rights, Canadian women were initially denied the rights associated with liberty, equality, and solidarity. Table 8.1 illustrates the understandings about citizenship rights, duties, and virtues common to Western liberal democracies. Liberty rights, including physical autonomy, the free expression of ideas, and economic independence, are essential to the practice of citizenship, and represent its first pillar. Canadian laws refused women economic liberty until at least the 1920s in most respects. Men were legally designated as the heads of households, with all the rights that status entailed, including the exclusive right to control family finances (including their wives' wages), to own and sell property, to sign contracts, and to exercise guardianship rights over children (Burt, 1993, 213–14). Women who left their marriages, or were abandoned by their husbands, had no basis in law or policy to make financial demands on their estranged spouses and were often left destitute as a result.

Canadian women, moreover, did not have physical autonomy or the right to control their own bodies. From 1892 until 1967, the *Criminal Code* banned the sale, advertisement, or distribution of birth-control information, procedures, and devices. Laws reflected the patriarchal notion that women and children were in effect the legal property of their husbands or fathers. This is clearly illustrated by rape statutes, which regarded husbands and fathers as the true victims of the crime. The only women protected by early rape laws in Canada were chaste or married women, for their value to their husbands or fathers declined if their virtue was sullied. Morally "suspect" women (e.g., prostitutes, sexually active or promiscuous women), separated and divorced women, and women in common-law relationships were not offered the support of the legal system because they were the property of no man or no

TABLE 8-1 Liberal-Democratic Conceptions of Citizenship

ASPECTS OF CITIZENSHIP	CITIZEN RIGHTS	CITIZEN OBLIGATIONS	CITIZEN VIRTUES
LIBERTY	*Rights necessary for individual freedom:* Liberty of the person; Freedom of speech, thought, and faith; Right to own and control property; Physical independence (freedom from bodily violation or threat of it).	To work, thereby contributing to the economic well-being of the community; To conduct oneself in an autonomous manner; To obey the laws and respect the liberties of others.	Independence Self-reliance Self-restraint Obedience
EQUALITY	*Rights necessary for the pursuit of equality;* Right to vote and run for office and generally to participate in the exercise of political power; equal access to and benefit of the law (justice).	To participate in the political life of the community, via voting, political discourse and participation in political institutions (parties, parliament, etc.).	Intelligence Rationality Impartiality
SOLIDARITY	*The right to be included in the community:* Recognition via right to legal citizenship status.	Allegiance to the nation-state; Willingness to die for one's country.	Patriotism Loyalty Courage

one man (Boyle, 1984, viii). As well, men had legally sanctioned sexual access to their wives, regardless of the degree of coercion used to claim this access, until 1983, when the *Criminal Code* was changed to allow the Crown to charge men with sexually assaulting their spouses.

Canadian laws and policies were not premised on women's right to independence, rather they promoted women's economic dependence on the male head of the household and their physical confinement to the domestic sphere. Because women were seen to lack the virtues of the free and independent citizen, they were regarded as incapable of carrying out most of the duties associated with liberty, especially paid work and economic autonomy.

The second pillar of citizenship in liberal democracies is based on legal, social, and political equality. Equality rights include equal rights to participate in the political sphere, as well as equal treatment before and under the law. More recently, ideas about equality have been expanded to include equal access to social entitlements provided by the state, including education and social welfare programs that take care of basic human needs for food and shelter. As well, equality in post-*Charter* Canada means protection from discrimination and equal treatment under the law regardless of sex, ethnicity, mental or physical ability, family status, and, very recently, sexual orientation.

Before the 1960s, equality claims were not a dominant element of Canadian citizenship. Even the minimalist notion of equality voiced now by conservative organizations such as the Canadian Alliance party, where equality means the same treatment for everyone, would have been greeted with surprise and disdain in the early decades after Confederation. Indeed, the idea that women should be treated the same as men by lawmakers was considered ludicrous if not dangerous. Women were seen as different, and accordingly were denied legal and political equality. For instance, the very notion of voting rights for women (and other marginalized groups, including persons with mental disabilities, Aboriginal peoples, and Black, Indo-, and Asian-Canadians) was met with shock and ridicule in early twentieth-century Canada. The vote was almost exclusively limited to white male property owners. That women's political participation and activism violated the norm of separate spheres for men and women was illustrated by the obfuscation employed by the first women's suffrage association. Formed in Toronto in 1876, the group clearly felt the need to disguise its true purpose, because it adopted the name "Toronto Women's Literary Club" (Prentice et al., 1996, 195–6).

Women were also excluded from appointments to the bar and the Senate because they were not considered qualified "persons" as defined by the *British North America Act*. Five women from Alberta challenged this interpretation of Canadian law in a constitutional reference popularly known as the Person's Case. In 1929, the British Judicial Committee of the Privy Council, which was Canada's highest court at the time, decided that women could be considered "persons" qualified to serve in public life (*see* www.famous5.org).

In addition to being barred from formal electoral politics, women were denied equal treatment by employment laws and practices. Labour and welfare rules were designed to keep women in the home where they could realize their reproductive destinies (Boychuk 1998, 30–31). Application of the criminal law to women reinforced the notion that women should achieve a higher level of morality and virtue than men. As a result, women found guilty of crimes received longer sentences and were more likely than men to be incarcerated for "moral" offences. Chastity laws also guarded the sexuality of women and girls. In general, public-sphere values "such as equality, liberty, and democracy, were treated as incompatible, indeed as threats to the very workings of the family" (Brodie, 1995, 35). The patriarchal family was considered the cornerstone of social order and women's claims of equality were sacrificed to maintain the separation of public and private spheres.

Solidarity is the third pillar of citizenship. It includes the legal right to membership in the political community, and the feelings of belonging associated with acceptance by that community. Canadian women did not have the independent right to claim membership in the Canadian nation state until 1947, when the *Citizenship Act* was passed. Before 1947 all Canadians were British subjects under law and a woman's citizenship status was determined by that of her father or husband. A woman who married a non-Canadian man lost her citizenship. In contrast, a man who married a non-Canadian woman both kept his citizenship and transferred it to his wife (Canada, 1970, 362). Similarly, until 1985, Aboriginal women holding Indian status under the *Indian Act* who married non-status or non-Aboriginal men lost their status and the rights associated with it (Weaver, 1993, 95). These included the right to live on the reserve, to be active band members, and to confer Indian status upon their children.

Although they could not legally belong in their own right, Caucasian women from Western Europe or the United States could at least strive to exemplify the virtuous "citizen mother." Biological determinism, coupled with racism, structured a hierarchy of womanhood in Canada. Middle- and upper-class Anglo-Saxon women who did not stray from the domestic fold could achieve the pinnacle of womanly superiority—the devoted, morally upright wife and mother. But Eastern European women were regarded as prolific child-bearers with loose morals, and Caucasian Canadian women were determined to undertake their social reformation through assimilation into British cultural norms (Wilton, 2000). Women of colour were considered potential dangers to the moral and familial order, so non-white women who sought entry to Canada faced racist and sexist immigration laws designed to keep the country "white" and sexually virtuous (Agnew, 1997, 19).

In sum, Canada's understandings of citizenship originated from, and developed within, the context of a patriarchal society. At the time of Confederation, and for several decades thereafter, laws and policies were designed to keep women in their place, under the social and political control of men. For many women this meant economic dependency on the male head of the household. Women, regardless of their ethnicity, were regarded as biologically destined for domestic duties, naturally subject to men, and singularly incapable of participating in the public sphere of business and government. Canadian women were denied the rights of citizens *because* they were women.

Claiming Citizenship Rights

Although women were assumed to lack the virtues of the good citizen, and were denied most of the basic rights of citizenship, they did not simply accept their lot as dependent subjects. Indeed, Canadian women exercised a key duty of citizenship—political participation—to win their fundamental rights. Freedom of expression and association, albeit accompanied by the presumption that women were properly confined to the domestic household, gave women a political voice. Women of various ethnicities, classes, languages, and regions joined political parties, protest groups, church organizations, unions, and social movement groups. They lobbied for political rights, and demanded social policies and legal reforms designed to improve the daily lives of men, women, and children. The quest for basic citizenship rights represented decades of effort by diverse women's groups and, at times, relied on support from male politicians and activists.

Women were not seen as a monolithic group in Canadian society, and different groups of women were granted citizenship rights at different times. The observation, typical of most textbooks and commentaries, that women got the federal franchise in 1918 is incorrect. The right to vote in federal elections was extended to white women who were British subjects in 1918. Earlier, in 1916, white women won the vote in the prairie provinces of Alberta, Saskatchewan, and Manitoba. But the federal franchise was not extended to male or female Asian, and Indo-Canadians until 1948, and Aboriginal peoples classified as status Indians under the *Indian Act* were barred from voting in federal elections until 1960 (Canada, 1997, 78). Male and female persons with mental disabilities were not granted the right to vote until 1991, and those with physical disabilities only gained full access to polling stations in 1992 (Valentine and Vickers, 1996, 155, 173). Finally, it was not until 2000 that Elections Canada made it possible for the homeless, and people without fixed addresses, to cast their ballot.

The first century of women's movement activity focused on the quest for legal citizenship rights. Women wanted to gain a basic or even university education, to work for pay in all professions, to control their own bodies, to vote and contest public office, and generally to be recognized as independent citizens. Early activists saw patriarchal ideas and the public/private dichotomy as firmly entrenched, but as offering a strategy for claiming citizenship. They argued that women would be better wives, mothers, protectors of the household, and advocates of social reform if they were granted basic rights (Errington, 1993, 75). Later, when the vote and other legal equality rights had been won for some, feminists argued for more rights, and more government action to improve women's lives, on the basis of fairness, justice, and equality (Burt, 1993, 231). To do so, they had to make the case that women could display the virtues and perform the obligations of the "good" citizen—as defined, of course, by the prototypical male citizen. Participation in military service, entry into the paid labour force, and increased political involvement allowed women to defy patriarchal assumptions about their potential for active citizenship.

FORMAL EQUALITY AND POLITICAL UNDER-REPRESENTATION

Contemporary citizenship is officially gender-neutral. The *Canadian Charter of Rights and Freedoms*, incorporated into the *Constitution Act* in 1982, guarantees, through section 28, a variety of democratic, legal, and equality rights and fundamental freedoms equally to men and women. Section 15 of the *Charter*, which came into effect in 1985, guarantees legal equality:

> Every individual is equal before and under the law and has the right to the equal protection and equal benefit of the law without discrimination and, in particular, without discrimination based on race, national or ethnic origin, colour, religion, sex, age or mental or physical disability.

Women now perform key citizen duties, such as active military service. And although patriarchal sentiments about a woman's character are still not uncommon, most Canadians accept that women can be independent, self-reliant, intelligent, and patriotic. So why do men and women continue to have different experiences of citizenship?

Take a look at the obligations and virtues of citizens listed in Table 8.1. When one examines the expectations of citizens, and the attributes of "good" citizenship, it becomes clear that the citizen is normatively male. The characteristics, roles, duties, and values associated with the traditionally male-dominated public territory of business and government determine what citizenship is all about. For instance, modern citizenship theorists consider the following duties to be the core obligations of citizens in liberal democracies: to work and pay taxes, to obey the law, to serve in the military in times of war, and to show an interest in political and public affairs (Kymlicka, 1992, 2). Performing "men's work" became key to women's citizenship claims, as illustrated by the extension of the franchise to white women after the First World War, during which women were central to the Canadian war effort. Similarly, working outside the home, running for office, gaining educational qualifications, and entering the professions have illustrated that women can exercise the duties of citizens. The problem was, and still is, that traditionally female duties and virtues have not been reassigned. Women remain largely responsible for childcare, domestic duties, and unpaid work in the home and community. The conception of women as nurturing, often dependent, self-sacrificing, and emotional has not been fundamentally challenged. The fact that the characteristics and duties of the good citizen were defined at a time when women were excluded from the exercise of citizenship, and when white, upper-class men epitomized the exemplary citizen, is shown by the experiences of women in formal politics.

Most, but not all, women have had the right to contest political office for several decades, yet it was not until the mid- to late 1980s that the number of women elected to the House of Commons and the provincial and territorial legislatures crossed the 10 percent mark. Only three decades ago, women were elected so rarely and so sporadically that their presence in political life was considered aberrant. Canada's first woman MP, Agnes Macphail, elected in 1921, was told, "You can't go in there, miss!" when she tried to enter the chamber to perform her parliamentary duties (Sharpe, 1994, 36). In the 1960s and 1970s, Canada's (few) women MPs were asked by journalists, "Are you a politician or a woman?" (Robinson and Saint-Jean, 1991, 136). Clearly the roles were considered mutually exclusive. Politics was a man's world, and women who entered the legislative arena were seen to be treading on male turf. The pinnacle of citizen participation, the top jobs in electoral politics, were assumed to be the exclusive purview of men. In many ways, they still are.

Even with the election of more women in the 1990s and early years of the twenty-first century, the goal of equal representation seems unlikely to be attained anytime soon. As of March 2002, women comprise 20 percent of the legislators across Canada (Trimble and Arscott, 2003). The numbers range from just under 8 percent in Nova Scotia to almost 30 percent in the Yukon Territory. In the federal parliament, women won 62 seats of 301 (20.6 percent) in the 2000 election, the same number as in 1997, suggesting that progress for women in electoral politics has stalled. While the percentage of elected women has climbed fairly steadily in most jurisdictions since the mid-1980s, recent elections have resulted in a plateau or decline in the numbers. For instance, after 2001 elections in British Columbia and Alberta the number of women declined. Very few Aboriginal and ethnic-minority women have won seats in Canada's parliament and legislatures (Abu-Laban, 2002, 272). Almost 90 years after the first woman was elected to legislative office in Canada, women continue to be under-represented in public office. And women are still largely shut out of the top jobs, as indicated by the paucity of women party leaders. In all of Canada's history only 20 women have led mainstream political parties, and presently only three women head parties.[2] One leader, Pat Duncan, is premier of the Yukon; the other two lead New Democratic parties with remote chances of winning official opposition status, let alone of forming governments.

More telling than the numbers, perhaps, is that women continue to be told they are not fit for political life, or that they cannot combine politicking with their "natural duties" as mothers. Sheila Copps, now national Minister of Heritage, wrote in her autobiography, *Nobody's Baby*, "if a young man ascends the political ladder and successfully combines that effort with a happy family life, he becomes complete. If you are a woman, there is always the question, 'How can you look after your children?' " (1986, 85). Women politicians are constantly confronted with their difference from the "norm" as defined by the male politician. For instance, journalists persist in domesticating female politicians by focusing on their looks, clothing, hair, marital status, sex lives, and domestic roles (Trimble and Arscott, 2003). In 1997, Liberal MP Mary Clancy told a filmmaker that women remain an oddity in politics, as "the old boy network and the theory that politics is the purview of men is still there" (Ralston, 1999).

One additional example illustrates the patriarchal thinking underlying women's claims for equality in political representation. In January 2002, Liberal MP Carolyn Bennett publicly criticized the newly shuffled cabinet because it featured fewer women overall and only one woman was among the 10 new members of this powerful policymaking body.

Bennett pointed out, "the image of six men lined up to become secretaries of state sent the wrong message to Canadian women because the new group was dominated by 'white male faces' " (Clark, 2002, A1). In return, Bennett was scolded by the prime minister for damaging his reputation as a politician who has advanced women's representation by appointing women to the Senate, and naming a woman Governor General and Chief Justice of the Supreme Court of Canada. Underlying the prime minister's response was the assumption that the status quo constitutes adequate representation for women. Gender parity, or equality in representation, is an important element of women's citizenship regardless of whether or not it translates into policy outcomes for women. To suggest that less than one-quarter of the top positions in public life is good enough assumes that women, who comprise more than half of the population, do not merit their fair share of political power.

When asked why she wanted to be in the House of Commons, Alexa McDonough replied, "because that's still where power gets exercised, decisions get made" (Ralston, 1999). Canada's elected politicians play a direct and significant role in setting the legal parameters and policy determinants of everyday experiences of citizenship by setting out formal rights and determining informal privileges. As we saw earlier in this chapter, provincial and federal governments decided when to accord women citizenship rights such as the right to vote, enter the professions, and hold property in their own names. The state (defined as including the various elements of government, including the executive, legislature, civil service, and judiciary) determines how citizens will be treated in law and policy. In Canada, we take for granted that our governments will uphold our freedom, equality, and sense of solidarity by offering income protection in the case of unemployment, by guaranteeing free access to education and healthcare, and by providing for those who cannot care for themselves. The state determines the practices and meaning of citizenship. Governments can promote equality, or turn a blind eye to discrimination. Governments can protect individual liberty, or avoid interfering in "private matters" (as in the case of wife battering until the 1980s). The political realm is where the appropriate role for the state in the protection and promotion of citizenship is discussed, and decisions about state action are implemented. Therefore, women's representation in federal, provincial, and territorial legislatures will continue to shape deliberations and decisions affecting their citizenship status.

THE ROLE OF THE STATE AND WOMEN'S CITIZENSHIP—CONTEMPORARY DEBATES

Debates about women's citizenship claims in the last two decades have revealed three competing sets of ideas, each with different views of the appropriate balance between liberty, equality, and solidarity. These three ideological stances—welfare liberalism, neoliberalism and neoconservatism—feature different, often conflicting, ideas about the obligations of the citizen, the state, and the private sphere in protecting and promoting citizenship. While neoliberalism is arguably the dominant ideology shaping governance in the early twenty-first century, welfare liberalism has not been fully uprooted, and neoconservatism is championed by many voices on the right. This section sketches these ideologies and discusses what they imply for the future of women's citizenship in Canada.

Welfare Liberalism

Some of women's citizenship demands were met by the welfare state, which evolved in Canada in response to the ideology of welfare liberalism. Welfare liberalism is, first and foremost, a liberal ideology, in that it assumes that individual responsibility and liberty are the cornerstones of a good society. People are best able to develop, as individuals and citizens, when left alone to provide for themselves and make rational decisions about their own life choices. However, welfare liberals believe the state has a crucial obligation to step in when people cannot provide for themselves or live independently. As Table 8.2 shows,

TABLE 8-2 Contemporary Ideologies and their Implications for Citizenship

IDEOLOGY	STATE OBLIGATIONS	CITIZEN DUTIES AND VIRTUES
Welfare Liberalism Liberty seen as the primary good, but a balance is sought between liberty, equality, and solidarity	Appropriate for governments to ensure equality and solidarity, sometimes at expense of liberty *Social rights:* fulfilment solidarity of basic human needs for food, shelter, education, health Promotion of equality before and under the law Provision of protection from discrimination on the basis of group membership	To achieve a basic education To work, pay taxes and contribute to the funding of the welfare state Responsibility, tolerance of diversity, acceptance
Neo-Liberalism Puts individual liberty before equality and solidrity; stresses economic freedom	Minimal role for the state Governements should withdraw from the welfare state and from interference in the private lives of citizens State should privatize, cut spending, de-regulate, and generally, create the conditions for the market liberty (economic freedom)	Economic Independence Self-reliance Ability and willingness to provide for self and family members
Neo-Conservatism Stresses solidarity (in he form of social order), and is willing to deny equality and liberty	Significant role for the state in enforcing law and order, social stability State should establish or re-establish traditional hierarchies and authority structures (patriarchal family; class order; organized religion and charity)	Respect for authority Willingness to occupy one's "proper" place in the social order, according to class, gender, etc.

welfare liberalism recognizes the need to balance liberty with equality and solidarity. Contemporary versions of welfare liberalism advocate *social rights*, defined as the "collective provision of a minimum level of economic security" (Brodie, 1997, 229). This vision accepts that individual liberty must occasionally be sacrificed in the interests of protecting disadvantaged groups from discrimination, providing a social safety net for all citizens, and promoting a sense of belonging regardless of ethnicity, ability, sex, language, or sexual orientation. In Canada, social rights have come to be defined as access to public education, universal healthcare, shelter, social assistance, and income security programs. These social rights imply a substantive set of obligations for the state, in order to meet the basic needs of citizens.

The *welfare state* includes the types of policies and services federal, provincial, and municipal governments implemented as welfare liberalism took root in Canadian political culture. The creation of the welfare state, which took place between the late 1940s and 1960s, brought about the introduction of public education, universal healthcare services, income security, and wage replacement programs. Later, in the 1970s and 1980s, Canadian governments began to respond to women's policy demands. Equal pay for equal work legislation, funding for women's shelters and childcare centres, parental leave policies, and (for civil servants and federally regulated employees) employment equity rules, were put into place. These policies promoted women's inclusion in the public realm of the paid workforce in two ways. They created a large number of public sector jobs in healthcare, education, and social work, as well as clerical and support positions, many of which were taken up by women. Government jobs provide part and full-time work for many women. As well, unemployment insurance, social assistance, maternity leave, and equal pay for equal work provided some measure of economic independence for women. Childcare subsidies; care of elderly, disabled persons who are or infirm; and social services designed to support families, assisted women's entry into the paid labour force by shifting some private sphere responsibilities into the public realm of state action. The welfare state, however, was no panacea for women's lack of empowerment. In reflecting the ideology of welfare liberalism, the welfare state is premised on the existence of stable, self-sufficient nuclear families wherein women continue to perform caregiving and domestic duties for free. As Linda Gordon writes, if "the state were a family, it would be assumed that welfare is a woman's affair" (1990, 9). The traditional sexual division of labour is not challenged by the ideas or practices of the welfare state because the state steps in only when the traditional family model "breaks down." Single mothers, elderly widows, and persons with mental and physical disabilities who have no employed family members to support them can receive assistance from Canadian governments, but give up considerable liberty as a result. While men claim the social rights associated with the welfare state as independent citizens, women are "cast as dependent citizens—dependent either on the family wage or social welfare" (Brodie, 1997, 233). Women on social assistance continue to endure considerable state intervention into their private lives, including scrutiny of their sexual relationships and evaluation of their mothering practices (Evans, 1996).

Some women's movement activists believe the welfare state could, with sufficient political will, be revived and reshaped to promote women's full citizenship, while others see welfare liberalism as a barrier to women's equality claims (Brodie, 1995, 21–26). This debate will not likely be resolved, as the welfare state is being whittled away by neoliberal governments; what is clear, however, is that even during its halcyon years in the 1960s and 1970s, the Canadian welfare state had not rectified women's economic, social, and political inequality. As a result, economic independence, physical autonomy, equality, and solidarity remain elusive goals for most women.

We have seen that women remain under-represented in the House of Commons and provincial legislatures, where men hold four of every five seats. A Statistics Canada report released in 2000 documented other lingering, and significant, gender inequities (Canada, 2000). On average, Canadian women working full time earn 73 percent of what full-time male wage earners make. But almost one half (41 percent) of women in the paid labour force are not working full-time, but rather are employed in part-time, casual, or temporary jobs. Women also remain concentrated in traditionally female, poorly paid occupations such as childcare, clerical, administrative, and sales and service work, and thus hold 68 percent of Canada's lowest-paying jobs. Women occupy only 22 percent of the highest-paying jobs. Over half of Canadians living in poverty, 54 percent, are women, and elderly women and single mothers are among the poorest. Immigrant, disabled, Aboriginal, and ethnic-minority women are also very vulnerable to unemployment and poverty. Women continue to do more than their fair share of unpaid domestic work, despite their increasing participation in the labour force. And, the Statistics Canada report indicates that women live in fear of sexual and physical violence, both inside and outside the home.

Since the mid-1980s, the welfare liberal emphasis on citizen rights and state obligations has increasingly come under attack from what is often called "the new right," not least because of annual government over-expenditures and burgeoning debt loads. This label—used synonymously with "right-wing" and "conservative" by the mass media—conflates neoliberalism and neoconservatism, two distinct ideologies, each of which has its own vision of citizenship. But both ideologies maintain Canadians must take more responsibility for their own lives, and for exercising the duties of citizens.

Neoliberalism

Neoliberal ideas are of particular concern to women and other historically disadvantaged groups, for they champion a minimalist view of citizenship rights and state responsibility and stress the individual citizen's responsibility to become, and remain, economically self-reliant. Neoliberals emphasize a particular brand of liberty—economic freedom—at the expense of the other pillars of citizenship—equality and solidarity. Neoliberalism's overriding goal is to promote a market-driven approach to organizing political, economic, and social affairs in the interests of achieving the freest possible market for increasingly fluid transnational capital. Indeed, the economic market is seen as the proper sphere for the distribution of economic and social goods. Neoliberals regard state interference in the economy as destructive to individual liberty and competitive economic relations.

Not surprisingly, then, neoliberals are against "big government" and wish to dismantle the welfare state. According to this perspective, the welfare state is costly and inefficient, and it promotes a culture of dependency among citizens who come to rely on the state rather than on their own fortunes. Moreover, it is argued that corporate support of the welfare state through payment of taxes, Employment Insurance premiums, worker's compensation and so on, reduces competitiveness in an era of globalization and increasing competition between nations to attract transnational capital. In sum, economic liberty is the most important political good, one which demands that the state must shrink. Neoliberals therefore want governments to privatize, deregulate, and cut spending on programs and services, especially those associated with the welfare state. Social rights are rejected because they violate market sovereignty; the economic sphere must distribute social and economic goods, not the state.

This is quite a different view of citizenship than the welfare-liberal vision. The neoliberal wants the individual to act freely in an unfettered economic marketplace, and believes this kind of freedom will produce independent, self-reliant, responsible citizens. Neoliberals believe people learn how to be good citizens through participation in the economic marketplace as property owners, employees, entrepreneurs, and the like (Mulgan, 1991, 43). When citizenship is defined by the market, rights for individuals are conflated with consumer choices; the right to choose jobs, products, services, mutual funds, healthcare providers, and so on. The state's primary obligation is to provide an arena of choice for the consumer by protecting and promoting the market and the free flow of capital. Equality, democracy, and community are downplayed by neoliberal advocates, perhaps deliberately, for free political choices can undermine market sovereignty. Citizens may, through their political action and democratic participation, promote state regulation of certain sectors of the economy in the interests of employment equity and other social goals. Equality, and democratic rights in particular, may therefore conflict with market freedom. Neoliberals obfuscate increasing restrictions on the democratic freedom of citizens and nationstates by emphasizing the liberty associated with economic choices.

Neoliberal citizenship can claim to have gender-neutral effects, for in theory all citizens can be represented as free market players and independent actors with the same rights, duties, and virtues. But feminists point out that such a view ignores the prevailing sexual division of labour and other sources of inequality. When market performance is emphasized, the only fully actualized citizens are those who are able to exercise their economic rights and perform the duty of fiscal self-reliance. Everyone else—the poor, single mothers, persons with disabilities, and others—has little recourse, for they cannot turn to the state for assistance and protection. Neoliberal good citizens demand little or nothing of the state; they are independent actors who perform their duties in the economic marketplace. The neoliberal version of the common good reflects market values such as efficiency and competitiveness. As a result the "new good citizen is one that recognizes the limits and liabilities of state provision and embraces his or her obligation to work longer and harder in order to become more self-reliant" (Brodie, 1995, 57).

The irony of neoliberal spending and program cuts for women is that they lead to economic insecurity, not economic self-reliance, as government jobs are lost and the state no longer provides the supports many women need to compete in the job market. Neoliberal restructuring in Alberta after the 1993 election of the Klein government led to massive spending cuts in key welfare state policy areas, social assistance, education and healthcare, resulting in disproportionate job loss and job degradation for women, as well as service gaps (Dacks, Green, and Trimble, 1995, 272–3). Another significant material consequence of restructuring is the redistribution of labour, in particular the re-privatization of nurturing and caring work. When the state stops providing services such as healthcare and social assistance, the labour does not disappear. It is performed by the family, the community, and charitable organizations, leading to stresses within civil society, including the overburdening of community groups and individual family members (Jenson, 1998, 7). Women, who traditionally carry out much of the voluntary and caring work, are feeling the strain of increased obligations.

Neoliberal citizenship is about pursuing one's interests in one arena of the public sphere—the marketplace. The activities of women in the unpaid domestic sphere don't even enter into the neoliberal picture of citizenship, which stresses the competitive, self-interested economic activities of individuals. Similarly, issues of equality, community, and solidarity, when voiced politically, are rejected as irrelevant to the market-focused neoliberal state. In the wake of government restructuring, downsizing, and cuts to social spending, women's policy claims are increasingly characterized as the self-interested demands of "special interest" groups (Brodie, 1995, 69–70). In short, the persistent sexual division of labour prevents many women from exercising the duties of the good neoliberal citizen, but attempts to politically voice displeasure about inequality and demand state action are ruled selfish and contrary to the neoliberal version of the public good.

Neoconservatism

Neoconservatism presents a moral and political agenda, and is sometimes referred to as moral conservatism, or social traditionalism. Neoconservatives[3] value order, stability, and continuity. They are concerned with disciplined and predictable social relations and, unlike neoliberals, believe individual behaviour must be constrained in the interests of the collectivity. The excesses of individualism worry neoconservatives, who see increased crime rates, the erosion of the traditional family model, the selfish pursuit of individual wealth, and decreased religiosity as profound threats to the well-being of society. Neoconservatives don't trust individuals, acting freely in the market, to act in an unselfish and civic-minded fashion and therefore they advocate various social and political constraints on individual liberty.

Neoconservatives recycle many of the key assumptions of patriarchal thinkers, including biological determinism and the gender-based division of labour. As such, neoconservatives believe patriarchal power relations are functional, that is, necessary to the orderly functioning of society. For instance, William Gairdner argues, in *The War Against the Family* (1990, 302), that biology is truly destiny, and therefore society as we know it will crumble if the patriarchal family is disrupted. Because men "vigorously pursue power and personal, largely material, goals, often to the detriment of children," says Gairdner, it is up to women to "protect and promote the interests of children."

In their quest for order and stability, neoconservatives support social, political, and economic hierarchies such as the patriarchal family, class distinctions, religious schooling, and a strong criminal justice system. Proponents of neoconservatism believe morality should be inculcated via the traditional family and religious instruction, including religious teaching in schools. It should be reinforced by the state by, among other things, "getting tough on crime," sanctioning the traditional family model, and criminalizing "deviant" behaviour. In many ways, neoconservatives advocate a strong, punitive, and active state in the interests of a vision of social order that puts stability above liberty. For instance, neoconservatives support the re-criminalization of abortion, the reinstatement of the death penalty as a deterrent to violent crime, and the right of parents to spank their children (Reid, 2002, A11). They oppose laws protecting gays and lesbians against discrimination, decry government support for feminist organizations, and bemoan the separation of church and state. In sum, neoconservatism sees a significant role for the state in promoting a hierarchical and authoritarian society.

According to this conception of citizenship, people belong by occupying their appropriate niche in the social order. Various social and political mechanisms, such as the traditional family, should therefore be empowered to keep people in their proper place, performing the roles assigned to them. Rights are intensely problematic for neoconservatives because they provide citizens with the tools to challenge authority relations. Neoconservatives argue that children, criminals, gays and lesbians, women, and others, do not require legal rights and protections from those who exercise authority over them, be it men or the state. The right to freedom from discrimination on the basis of sexual orientation runs up against the adamant heterosexism of neoconservative thinking, which sees same-sex couplings as deviant and a threat to both public morality and the "natural" patriarchal family. Women's demands for reproductive and sexual liberty, economic independence, and freedom from sexual violence present a particular affront to neoconservatives because they want women's sexuality, reproduction, mothering, and employment to be scrutinized and regulated by the male head of the household, and in his absence (e.g., in the case of the single mother on social assistance), the state. Proponents of neoconservatism see the *Charter of Rights and Freedoms*, which protects a range of liberty and equality rights, as a profoundly destabilizing and even destructive force in Canadian society (Morton, 1992, 294–314).

Neoconservatism is antithetical to an egalitarian vision of citizenship, and it clearly does not advocate a universal approach to citizenship rights, duties, and virtues. The neoconservative citizen is a conformist who accepts inequality and lack of freedom in the interests of an orderly and stable society. For instance, the good adult female citizen is, in the neoconservative view, responsible for marrying, producing, and caring for children, imparting morality to these children, attending to the sexual needs of her husband so he will not commit adultery, performing the duties of the household, and obeying the edicts of the male wage earner. Virtues for women flow from these duties; the good female citizen is dependent, submissive, hard-working, nurturing, and moralistic. Good fathers earn a family wage and maintain authority relations in the family by, for instance, disciplining children and regulating the extra-domestic activities of their wives. The good father is independent, decisive, and authoritarian.

This perspective, which evokes the patriarchal theories about citizenship discussed earlier in this chapter, makes a sharp distinction between good and bad citizens. The lesbian, the single mother, the mother who works outside the home for pay, the divorced woman and her children, and the same-sex family, are dangerous violations of the "natural" social order. For neoconservatives, feminists are the antithesis of virtuous citizens, because they promote "moral decay" and challenge the hetero-patriarchal family (Klatch, 1987, 119–53). The neoconservative vision of citizenship advocates women's subordination and dependence, not their liberty, equality, and authentic sense of belonging.

CONCLUSION

Neoconservatism informs influential streams of thinking about the meaning and practices of citizenship. The Canadian Alliance Party most strongly associates with neoconservative values and policy positions, though some members of other political parties embrace these ideas too. Darrel Reid, president of a conservative lobby group called Focus on the Family, recently said, "There are a lot more social conservatives around than you think," so Canadians "better get used to us" (2002, A11). However, even those governments featuring the most vocal proponents of neoconservatism, namely the Conservative regimes in Alberta and Ontario, have not implemented the ideology's key policy demands, such as re-criminalization of abortion, denial of citizenship rights to gays and lesbians, and the de-secularization of the public sphere. One reason is clear—the Canadian people don't accept these policies or their philosophical precepts. Public opinion surveys consistently show that most Canadians support individual rights guarantees such as reproductive choice, equality in the workplace, and equal access to and benefit of the law. Almost three-quarters of Canadians (74%) surveyed in 2002 agreed their rights are better protected because of the *Charter* (Makin, 2002, A1). The majority of Canadians agreed with the Supreme Court's decision, later implemented by the federal government, to extend the definition of "spouse" to include same-sex couples (Angus Reid Group, 1999). While neoconservative ideas present a clear threat to women's quest for freedom and equality, they have not yet achieved the support necessary to dominate the public policy agenda.

The contemporary discursive terrain of citizenship reflects a battle between neoliberal and welfare liberal views. Canadians are concerned about the fiscal sustainability of the welfare state at the same time as they cling to its core elements, especially universal education and healthcare. We want less government and lower taxes, but are unhappy with the consequences of neoliberal restructuring, especially when they threaten cherished social programs. Nonetheless, governments are doing less, and citizens are expected to do more, and this has clear implications for women, who have long performed domestic, voluntary, and community roles without pay. Neoliberal policies have led to job loss and job insecurity for women, rendering the goal of economic independence even more remote. But arguably the most pernicious effect of a neoliberal vision of citizenship is that of limiting democratic spaces for the articulation of policy measures designed to promote full citizenship for women. Neoliberalism adopts a language of universality which depicts the rational individual/taxpayer/market player as a universal social actor whose interests are paramount. Indeed his interests (for in the gendered social and economic order, market players are predominantly male actors) are regarded as representative of the "common good." Those who make demands on the state, especially demands based on particular needs arising from social or economic inequality, are accused of derailing the common good by acting selfishly and insisting on "special rights." Democratic debate is, therefore, limited to the narrow interests of the privileged, male, able-bodied white taxpayer, and these interests are presented as common to all, or universally good. Women's demands, be they for universal daycare, or fair immigration policies, or equitable political representation, are thus seen as antithetical to the goals of the neoliberal order.

Yet the neoliberal order is neither stable nor impermeable. It is unstable because even those governments most supportive of neoliberal principles have not fully implemented their policy consequences, not least because Canadians are unwilling to let go of cherished social programs. A commitment to democracy and key values of welfare liberalism, such as fairness, equality, and acceptance of diversity, leads Canadians to resist many aspects of neoliberalism. Neoliberalism is permeable because its discourses of autonomy and choice can be taken up by those who fundamentally disagree with its assumptions. Women's liberty claims have not been fully developed, perhaps sidetracked by the focus on equality fostered by the *Charter*. Freedom, personal autonomy, and economic independence remain key goals for Canadian women, and neoliberals are hard-pressed to argue against these values as they lie at the heart of their conception of citizenship.

As was the case in the twentieth century, political actors, ideas, and decisions will shape women's citizenship in the twenty-first. Women's active engagement in political life is crucial in the early decades of the new century, as the different visions of citizenship continue to be debated in both formal and informal political arenas. Women need to be involved in these deliberations, be it in social movement groups, civil society organizations, cultural exchanges, or the formal institutions of political deliberation. The presence of women, and the active representation of women's diversity in political life, has the potential to revitalize egalitarian ideals of citizenship, champion political freedom, and foster intercultural dialogues about national solidarity.

NOTES

1. The Alberta decision was overturned on appeal to the Supreme Court of Canada (see *R. v. Ewanchuk*, 1999). In the Supreme Court decision, Madam Justice L'Heureux-Dub argued that the Alberta court decision was based on archaic and erroneous assumptions about consent, specifically the idea that a woman may be giving consent even if she directly, definitively, and assertively says no.
2. The three women presently serving as party leaders are Pat Duncan, Liberal leader and Premier in the Yukon, Joy MacPhail, New Democratic Party leader in British Columbia, and Elizabeth Weir, NDP leader in New Brunswick.
3. This depiction of neoconservatism is based on a variety of sources, including newsmagazines like *Alberta Report* (now *Report*), the works of William Gairdner, 1990 and 1992, David Frum, 1996, Rebecca Klatch, 1987, and F.L. Morton, 1992.

REFERENCES

Abu-Laban, Yasmeen. 2002. "Challenging the Gendered Vertical Mosaic," in Joanna Everitt and Brenda O'Neill, eds., *Citizen Politics: Research and Theory in Canadian Political Behaviour.* Toronto: Oxford University Press. 268–282.

Agnew, Vijay. 1997. *Resisting Discrimination: Women from Asia, Africa and the Caribbean and the Women's Movement in Canada*. Toronto: University of Toronto Press.

Angus Reid Group. 1999. Press Release, "Majority (55%) Agree With Supreme Court Decision," (9 June, http://www.Angusreid.com/pressrel).

Beatty, Jim. 2001. "Female Operators OK'd to Wear Pants," *National Post*, Monday 5 February, A8.

Bindman, Stephen. 1998. "Provocation Defense Under Federal Review," *Edmonton Journal*, Monday 29 June, A3.

Boyle, Christine. 1984. *Sexual Assault*. Toronto: Carswell.

Boychuk, Gerard. 1998. *A Patchwork of Purpose: The Development of Provincial Social Assistance Regimes in Canada*. Kingston and Montreal: McGill-Queen's University Press.

Brodie, Janine. 1997. "Meso-Discourses, State Forms and the Gendering of Liberal-Democratic Citizenship," *Citizenship Studies* 1:2, 223–242.

Brodie, Janine. 1995. *Politics on the Margins: Restructuring and the Canadian Women's Movement.* Halifax: Fernwood.

Burt, Sandra. 1993. "The Changing Patterns of Public Policy," in Sandra Burt, Lorraine Code and Lindsay Dorney, eds., *Changing Patterns: Women in Canada*. Toronto: McClelland & Stewart, 212–242.

Canada. 2000. *Women in Canada, 2000.* Ottawa: Statistics Canada, online at http://www.statcan.ca.

Canada. 1997. *A History of the Vote in Canada*. Ottawa: Public Works and Government Services.

Canada. 1970. *Report of the Royal Commission on the Status of Women in Canada*. Ottawa: Supply and Services Canada.

Chwialkowska, Luiza. 1998. "The End of the Women's Movement," *National Post,* Saturday 28 November, B5.

Clark, Campbell and Rod Mickleburgh. 2002. "PM Scolds Liberal Dissenter," *Globe and Mail*, Monday 28 January, A1.

Code, Lorraine. 1993. "Feminist Theory," in Sandra Burt, Lorraine Code and Lindsay Dorney, eds., *Changing Patterns: Women in Canada*. Toronto: McClelland & Stewart, 19–58.

Copps, Sheila. 1986. *Nobody's Baby*. Toronto: Deneau.

Crittenden, Danielle. 1990. "Let's Junk the Feminist Slogans: The War's Over," *Chatelaine* (August), 38.

Dacks, Gurston, Joyce Green and Linda Trimble. 1995. "Road Kill: Women in Alberta's Drive Toward Deficit Elimination," in Trevor Harrison and Gordon Laxer, eds., *The Trojan Horse: Alberta and the Future of Canada.* Montreal: Black Rose, 270–285.

Errington, Jane. 1993. "Pioneers and Suffragists," in Sandra Burt, Lorraine Code and Lindsay Dorney, eds., *Changing Patterns: Women in Canada*. Toronto: McClelland & Stewart, 59–91.

Evans, Patricia. 1996. "Single Mothers and Ontario's Welfare Policy: Restructuring the Debate," in Janine Brodie, ed., *Women and Canadian Public Policy*. Toronto Harcourt, 1996, 11–171.

Famous Five Foundation website: www.famous5.org

Flanagan, Tom. 2001. "Women and Other Party Animals: MacBeth is the latest in a short line of losing female pols," *National Post* 15 March. (Accessed from the *National Post* website, www.nationalpost.com, 22 March 2001).

Fraser, Sylvia, ed. 1997. *Chatelaine - A Woman's Place: Seventy Years in the Lives of Canadian Women.* Toronto: Key Porter Books.

Frum, David. 1996. *What's Right*. Toronto: Random House.

Gairdner, William. 1992. *The Trouble With Canada*. Toronto: Stoddart.

Gairdner, William. 1990. *The War Against the Family*. Toronto: Stoddart.

Galbraith, Ruth. 1997. "Finance and the X-Factor," *Globe and Mail,* Tuesday 16 September, A22.

Gordon, Linda. 1990. *Women, the State and Welfare*. Madison: University of Wisconsin Press.

Jeffs, Allyson. 1997. "Club Stays Men-Only," *Edmonton Journal*, Thursday 6 February, B7.

Jenson, Jane. 1998. *Mapping Social Cohesion: The State of Canadian Research* (Ottawa: Renouf Publishing; Canadian Policy Research Networks Inc.)

Kingwell, Mark. 2000. *The World We Want: Virtue, Vice and the Good Citizen*. Toronto: Viking.

Klatch, Rebecca. 1987. *Women of the New Right.* Philadelphia: Temple University Press.

Kymlicka, Will. 1992. *Recent Work in Citizenship Theory*. Ottawa: report prepared for Multiculturalism and Citizenship Canada, Government of Canada.

Laframboise, Donna. 1997. "You've Come a Long Way, Baby—And For What?" *Globe and Mail,* Sunday 26 July, D1, D3.

Laghi, Brian. 1998. "Alberta Judge Stirs Outrage in Sex Case," *Globe and Mail*, Saturday 21 February, A1, A11.

Lister, Ruth. 1997. *Citizenship: Feminist Perspectives*. New York: New York University Press.

Makin, Kirk. 2002. "Most Still Firmly Believe in Charter, Poll Finds," *Globe and Mail*, Saturday 6 April, A1, A6.

Mitchell, Teresa. 2002. "The Law and Ms. McCabe," *Law Now* , February/March, 8.

Morton, F.L. 1992. *Morgentaler v. Borowski: Abortion, the Charter and the Courts.* Toronto: McClelland & Stewart.

Mulgan, Geoff. 1991. "Citizens and Responsibilities," in Geoff Andrews, ed., *Citizenship.* London: Lawrence & Wishart.

Prentice, Alison, et al. 1996. *Canadian Women: A History*, 2nd edition. Toronto: Harcourt Brace.

Ralston, Meredith. 1999. *Why Women Run.* Toronto: National Film Board.

Reid, Darrel. 2002. "You Better Get Used to Us," *Globe and Mail*, Wednesday, 23 January, A11.

Robinson, Gertrude and Armande Saint-Jean. 1991. "Women Politicians and Their Media Coverage: A Generational Analysis," in Kathy Megyery, ed., *Women in Canadian Politics: Toward Equity in Representation.* Toronto: Dundurn Press, 127–169.

Sharpe, Sydney. 1994. *The Gilded Ghetto: Women and Political Power in Canada*. Toronto: HarperCollins.

Trimble, Linda and Jane Arscott. 2003. *Still Counting: Women in Politics Across Canada*. Peterborough: Broadview.

Valentine, Fraser and Jill Vickers. 1996. "'Released From the Yoke of Paternalism and Charity': Citizenship and the Rights of Canadians with Disabilities," *International Journal of Canadian Studies* 14, 155-177.

Vipond, Robert. 1998. "The Two Mike Harrises," *Globe and Mail*, Wednesday 29 April 1998, A27.

Walby, Sylvia. 1996. "The 'Declining Significance' of the 'Changing Forms of Patriarchy,'" in Valentine Moghadam, ed., *Patriarchy and Economic Development.* Oxford: Clarendon Press.

Weaver, Sally. 1993. "First Nations Women and Government Policy, 1970-92: Discrimination and Conflict," in Sandra Burt, Lorraine Code and Lindsay Dorney, eds., *Changing Patterns: Women in Canada*, 2nd edition. Toronto: McClelland & Stewart, 92-150.

Wilton, Shauna. 2000. "Manitoba Women Nurturing the Nation: The Manitoba IODE and Maternal Nationalism, 1913-1920," *Journal of Canadian Studies* 35:2 (Summer), 149–165.

WEBLINKS

Vancouver Sun: Women in Pants Can't Answer Telephones at Enquiry B.C.
http://peter.communic-8.com/nopants/nopants1.html

National Action Committee on the Status of Women
www.nac_cca.ca/

The Famous 5 Foundation
www.famous5.org

chapter nine

Citizenship and People with Disabilities

The Invisible Frontier

Laura Bonnett

INTRODUCTION

In Canada, approximately 16 percent of the total population has a disability that affects their standard of living. In actual numbers, approximately 4.2 million Canadians have disabilities; 3.9 million live in households, and 300 000 live in institutions (Canada, 1998). Disabilities affect approximately 30 percent of the Aboriginal population in Canada—almost twice the national average. For many, their disabilities affect their ability to work, their financial status, their relationships with their families and friends, their ability to get an education, and how much they need the healthcare system and/or other government programs. In other words, disabilities can affect all aspects of one's everyday existence. Some people are born with disabilities, and some become disabled in the course of their lives. The vast majority of the global population will be affected by disability and/or health concerns *at some point in their life*. Those presently without disabilities are only temporarily able-bodied people.

In Canada inclusion as a full citizen has been elusive for many people with disabilities. A 1994 article in the *Globe and Mail* tells the story of Mohammed Mussa, a refugee from wartorn Somalia who came to Canada in 1989 with his family. The family was granted refugee status and, with his university degree in economics, Mussa had little trouble finding a full-time job as a revenue clerk for the Government of Ontario (Cherry, 1994, A4). This new Canadian clearly meets the standard obligations of citizenship; he is well educated, law-abiding, holds gainful employment, and pays taxes. But while wife and daughters were welcomed as Canadian citizens, an immigration official told Mussa he doesn't qualify for permanent resident status in Canada because he is "a cripple." Injured in a car accident in Somalia, Mussa uses a wheelchair. The *Globe* article argues that Mussa is a good citizen, even in the context of the deficit-ridden, pared-down welfare state, because he "requires almost no extra health or social services because of his paralysis" (Cherry, 1994, A4). The *Globe*'s cost–benefit analysis asserts that Mussa should be allowed to stay in Canada, because, as a taxpayer, he puts in more than he takes out.

This example highlights key issues surrounding the citizenship status of persons with disabilities. It shows that a crucial stepping stone of citizenship—the legal right to belong to a nation state, with its attendant rights, privileges, and duties—is denied to newcomers with disabilities *because of* their disabilities. Identifying disability is one way for the Canadian state to keep people out. Mussa's plight also reveals important questions about the appropriate obligations of governments towards citizens with disabilities. What should the state do to ensure political, legal, and social equality for persons with disabilities? Finally, the *Globe* article asserts that Mussa is a good citizen because, despite his disability, he is able to perform the standard duties of citizenship. This perspective suggests that persons with disabilities are considered good enough citizens only when they act as though they don't have disabilities. Where does this leave those people with disabilities who are unemployed or underemployed? Are people with disabilities only fully accepted when they "pay their own way"?

In this chapter we will examine what full citizenship means for people with disabilities. We will look at the meaning of disability as well as how the legal, political, and social citizenship rights for people with disabilities have evolved in Canada. While many improvements have been made over the last three decades in terms of the provision of programs and services, and there has been a positive change in societal attitudes towards people with disabilities, the neoliberal trend of downsizing the welfare state has meant that these services are in flux, and their permanence cannot be taken for granted. Substantive citizenship has not yet been realized for people with disabilities; rather, they are still struggling to maintain the existing hard-won rights, state support, and resources necessary to live a full life. However, before we examine the citizenship of people with disabilities, we will first look at how disability is defined, in order to understand how disability becomes a politicized citizenship factor.

DEFINING DISABILITY

Language plays a very powerful role in influencing our attitudes, ideas, and perceptions. Historically, people with disabilities have been variously termed "invalids," "insane," "handicapped," "retarded," "crazy," "idiots," "cripples," "victims," "abnormal," "wheelchair bound," or collectively "the disabled," to give but a few examples. In general the use of these terms has had a negative impact on people with disabilities, and on the way that society views and values people with disabilities. One reason for this impact is that these terms define people with disabilities solely by their impairments and/or disabilities and not by any other characteristic. A second reason for the harmful consequences of these terms is that they are imbued with negative connotations that define people with disabilities as somehow substandard, "less than," or deviant from temporarily able-bodied individuals. Thus, instead of viewing the positive contributions made to society, or other attributes of personality or roles, society often judges individuals with disabilities in terms of their impairments and finds them lacking.

The broadest attempt to define disablement in terms that were to become internationally recognized first occurred in 1980. In that year the World Health Organization WHO published the *International Classification of Impairments, Disabilities, and Handicaps* (ICIDH). This document was the first to differentiate between three distinct elements of disablement: impairment, disability, and handicap.[1] Impairments are any abnormality of body structure and appearance, or disturbances of organ or system functioning, due to any cause. The second element, disability, is the *consequence of impairment* in terms of the limits on performance and activity of an individual's functions. In other words, a disability is an inability to perform a recognized social role or occupation, or any activity considered "normal." Handicaps are any attitudinal or environmental disadvantages experienced by an individual in society as a result of their impairments and disabilities. For example, an woman who experiences paralysis in her legs (impairment) and who uses a wheelchair, is not able to perform many activities considered "normal," such as standing or walking (disability) and may not be able to enter or travel freely throughout a building which does not have a ramp or an elevator (handicap). In terms of citizenship, this handicap would be especially disadvantaging if she were searching for housing, looking for employment, or accessing government services.

Each of these three elements of disablement is associated with an ever-broader level of focus:

- impairments are associated with the level of the body function within an individual.
- disability focuses on how the whole individual with an impairment interacts (or does not) with society.
- handicap defines how the state and society responds (or does not) to an individual or a group of people with disabilities.

Impairments Disability Handicap

Medical Model Elements of Disablement

Many organizations representing people with disabilities have argued, however, that the application of the WHO definition of disability has focused too much on impairments. The medical community and healthcare practitioners have been at the forefront in diagnosing, addressing issues related to, and making decisions regarding the impairments of people with disabilities, such as who is eligible for government assistance and healthcare facilities. For many, this approach is faulty because it prioritizes the medical "problem" of disablement and focuses only on the individual (Bickenbach, 1993). Moreover, many disability theorists and activists argue that this approach ignores the vast social and political forces that define who is considered disabled and who is not, and what that citizen is entitled to from the state. For example, Lennard Davis argues that the concept of "disablement" really only came into being after the onset of industrialization, when many workers began to be injured in the workplace. It was the political organization of the workers that eventually led to the establishment of state-sponsored workers' compensation and other injury-related programs. According to Davis, then, disablement cannot be defined only by looking at the situation of an individual and diagnosing him or her; rather, disablement is socially constructed through a set of social, historical, economic, and cultural processes that regulate and control the way that we think and act about the body (1995, 12). The proponents of the social-constructionist definition of disablement, therefore, recognize that impairments are still a part of disablement, but put more emphasis on the environmental influences and barriers that need to be addressed before people with disabilities can live fully in society.

Individual with Impairments + Environmental Influences/Attitudes and External Barriers = Disablement

Social Constructionist Model of Disablement

THE EVOLVING CITIZENSHIP OF PERSONS WITH DISABILITIES

People with disabilities have started asking questions about their citizenship and looking for a lot of answers: What would Canadian society and politics be like if they thoroughly embraced people with disabilities? What are the rights of people with disabilities? What are the responsibilities? What are the government's responsibilities? In the next section, we will look at the three areas that make up full citizenship: political participation; legal and equality rights; and the responsibilities that the state must bear to ensure its citizens maintain a minimum standard of living and sense of belonging in their communities.

POLITICAL PARTICIPATION

One of the most important ways that people with disabilities have tried to establish their full citizenship is through political organizing and involvement. The earliest organizing took place right after World War II, when veteran groups were created to advocate for the establishment of government programs and facilities for those injured in the war. The majority of disability organizing in Canada, however, has taken place over the last three decades. During this time people with disabilities have mobilized in groups and as a movement to challenge governments and society to be more inclusive, and to empower people with disabilities to live full and satisfying lives.

Many people with disabilities require the use of personal support services—physicians, home-care attendants, interpreters, rehabilitation counsellors, and so on—in order to function. Before the 1970s, when the consumer advocacy movement emerged in Alberta, Manitoba, and Saskatchewan, many of the decisions concerning these services were made without consultation with the people requiring them. In protest, people with disabilities started to identify themselves not as patients or dependents, but as consumers of these services. Moreover, this new "consumer control" led to a situation where those receiving the services were also the ones providing the service, since people with disabilities (rather than able-bodied service providers) would be best able to protect their own interests. Their mobilization was influenced by both the civil rights movement and the disability movement in the United States. In 1976 advocacy organizations from across Canada came together to establish the Coalition of Provincial Organizations of the

Handicapped (COPOH). COPOH's mandate was to focus on human rights legislation, building-code, revisions, public transportation, and employment issues, as they pertained to people with disabilities. In 1980 the Canadian movement was strongly influenced by the American Independent Living philosophy, adopting the values of peer counselling, self-help, consumer control, and barrier removal (Valentine, 1994, 15).

The United Nations declared 1981 the Year of Disabled Persons. During that year, the Canadian Parliament published a lengthy report entitled *Obstacles*, after significant consultation with people with disabilities, healthcare professionals, and others. The 129 recommendations from this report have formed the basis of many of the social and legal changes achieved over the last two decades for people with disabilities. One of the main recommendations of the report was to implement community-based living—the deinstitutionalization of people with physical and mental disabilities—in order to increase their independence and to decrease government costs. Community-based or independent living has slowly been implemented across Canada since that time, with varying degrees of success. A second major recommendation in Obstacles was to require that the services to assist people with disabilities be provided by people with disabilities, and that they be funded by the federal government. Ever since the release of this report, disability organizations have been lobbying and working with government institutions to implement these recommendations.

Three main types of disability organizations have formed in Canada: 1) those focused on political advocacy and legislative change; 2) those providing support advocacy for people with disabilities; and 3) those working towards independent living. Each of these organizations has worked in its own way to improve the quality of life for people with disabilities.

The Coalition of Provincial Organizations of the Handicapped (COPOH) became the primary organization to lobby for individual rights and political equality. In particular, COPOH has worked to change or expand legislation concerning people with disabilities, especially at the federal level. Recently, the organization's name was changed to the Canadian Disability Rights Council, but its mandate—political lobbying and the promotion of rights—has remained the same. When the federal government decided to entrench a bill of rights into the Canadian Constitution in 1980, COPOH, among other disability organizations, became involved in the discussions. The *Charter of Rights and Freedoms* was created to protect the rights of individuals in Canada—including the rights of some groups of people who had historically faced discrimination. COPOH wanted to ensure that the proposed Canadian *Charter* included protection from discrimination for people with disabilities. In the end, disability organizations were successful in ensuring that their rights were included. Today, section 15 of the Constitution reads:

> Every individual is equal before and under the law and has the right to equal protection and equal benefit of the law without discrimination and, in particular, without discrimination based on race, national or ethnic origin, colour, religion, sex, age, or *mental or physical disability*. (italics added for emphasis)

In response to lobbying efforts, the federal government also amended the *Canadian Human Rights Act (CHRA)* in 1983 to include protections for people with mental and physical disabilities. *CHRA* protects individuals from discrimination in employment and service provision when dealing with federal departments, agencies, and Crown corporations, or other federally regulated industries.

Support Advocacy groups are also very active in Canada. These groups are established by people acting on behalf of people with disabilities, such as parents, caregivers, or healthcare practitioners. One of the earliest support advocacy groups was the Canadian Rehabilitation Council for the Disabled (CR), founded in Toronto in the 1970s. CR was a national coalition of charitable organizations that employed rehabilitation professionals to lobby government on behalf of people with disabilities. Today, CR is known as the Easter Seals/March of Dimes. Other organizations, such as those for parents of children with intellectual disabilities, have successfully organized to influence legislation and improve standards regarding group homes and education in British Columbia and Manitoba, among other provinces (Crichton and Jongbloed, 1998, 189).

A third type of disability organization in Canada has focused on securing independent living for people with disabilities. In the 1980s the Independent Living Movement emerged in Canada with the goal of assisting and empowering people with disabilities with skills, knowledge, and advocacy support. Independent Living Resource Centres were created across Canada, and in 1986 the Canadian Association of Independent Living Centres (CAILC) was established. Today CAILC represents 23 centres from across Canada located in every province except Prince Edward Island. Member organizations are operated *by* people with disabilities, not "for them," and are intended to act as enablers, not "experts," for people with disabilities. This mandate reflects the challenge that the Independent Living philosophy makes to the traditional medical model of disablement, which many people with disabilities considered too paternalistic.

While the original organizers of the disability movement were men, in the last 15 years women with disabilities have become very politically active. In 1985 women formed the DisAbled Women's Network of Canada (DAWN). DAWN provides support, information, and research for and by women with disabilities, and also provides a voice for women within the larger disability movement. DAWN Canada is a national, cross-disability organization with member organizations in most provinces. Representatives of DAWN work with the women's movement to introduce the knowledge and issues of disablement, and with "mainstream" disability organizations to ensure that their concerns as women are addressed.

Each of the various types of disability organizations has had a significant impact on the political process in Canada. Not only have they influenced legislation in various parts of the country, they have also empowered and enabled many people with disabilities to re-envision what full citizenship looks like.

EQUALITY AND LEGAL CHALLENGES

> Diane Satre is a student with a full-time job, a family, and a dog. Unlike most Albertans, she's called taxis only to have them show up an hour late or not at all. Restaurant owners have refused her access to their restaurants and one health club denied her a membership. Why? She thinks it's because she is a blind woman with a guide dog. "It's humiliating and embarrassing," Satre said. "You're treated like a second-class citizen." (Brieger, 2000, B11).

People with disabilities often face discrimination on a daily basis. In some instances, people with disabilities are using political lobbying to make change; many others, however, are using the legal system to challenge their "second-class" status.

After the *Charter of Rights and Freedoms* came into effect in the early 1980s, people with disabilities started to use the "equality clause" to contest the laws that were having a discriminatory impact. The Supreme Court of Canada adjudicated many of these cases. For example, in 1986, the Supreme Court of Canada ruled it unconstitutional to force intellectually disabled people to undergo sterilization for non-medical reasons. Previously, in the 1920s and 1930s, the provincial governments of British Columbia and Alberta had enacted laws that permitted the sterilization of people with disabilities, among others, against their will. People with emotional problems or physical handicaps were sterilized to prevent them from procreating. Alberta had this law in place from 1928 until 1971, during which time approximately 3000 boys and girls were sterilized (Jeffs and Thomson, 1998, A5). After the Supreme Court ruling, Leilani Muir, a woman who was sterilized because she had been placed in an institution (despite an average level of intelligence) sued the Alberta government and received compensation of $750 000. In response, the Alberta government tried to limit the compensation of people who had been affected by the sterilization laws, and threatened to invoke the notwithstanding clause—a rarely used clause that allows governments to "override" individual rights protection in the *Charter*. The outcry from people with disabilities and the rest of the public was swift and angry; many people considered the government's actions an "abuse of power" (*Editorial, Edmonton Journal*, 1998, A12). As a result, the Alberta government backed down from using the notwithstanding clause and from trying to limit the amount of compensation that victims could be granted.

Another case, in 1988, furthered the citizenship rights of people with disabilities. In this instance, in response to a legal challenge brought by the Canadian Disability Rights Council, the Supreme Court ruled that it was unconstitutional for people with intellectual disabilities in institutions to be denied the federal vote. The franchise, or the ability to vote, has long been considered one of the most important aspects of citizenship. In 1991, the *Canada Elections Act* was amended to enable Canadians with a psychiatric or mental disability to vote. Full access to the federal franchise for people with mobility and sensory limitations, however, was not secured until 1992 when it became mandatory that all polling stations be made accessible. As well, voting materials must now be made available in large print and in Braille.

In the 1990s three other cases in Canada captured significant attention and raised controversial questions about citizenship rights for people with disabilities—especially questions about the right to control one's life, and the right to equality of treatment. The first was the *Rodriguez* case.

In 1993 the Supreme Court of Canada decided on the fate of British Columbia resident Sue Rodriguez, who was seeking to end her own life with the aid of a physician. Rodriguez was a 42-year-old woman, married, and the mother of an eight-year-old son. She suffered from amyotrophic lateral sclerosis (ALS), which is more widely known as Lou Gehrig's disease. At the time her case was heard by the Supreme Court her life expectancy was between two and fourteen months, and her condition was rapidly deteriorating. Her lawyers argued that Rodriguez did not wish to die while she could still enjoy life; however, by the time she could no longer enjoy life, she would be physically unable to terminate her own life without assistance. As a result, she was asking the Court for an order which would allow a qualified medical practitioner to set up the technological means by which she could, by her own hand and at the time of her choosing, end her life. In particular, she argued that the federal law prohibiting physician-assisted suicide was unconstitutional and discriminated against her on the basis of her disability. However, the Supreme Court ruled against Rodriguez's application and refused to legalize physician-assisted suicide, arguing that it would contravene the "government's objective in protecting the vulnerable" (*Rodriguez,* 1993, 3).

A second controversial case concerning the quality of life for persons with disabilities began in 1994. That year a jury in Saskatchewan convicted farmer Robert Latimer of second-degree murder for gassing his severely disabled daughter, Tracy, to death with carbon monoxide in his truck. Tracy Latimer, age 13, had extreme cerebral palsy and was quadriplegic. As a result of her physical condition, Tracy often experienced a great deal of pain, was largely immobile, and required her family to provide her with constant care. During the legal case, Robert Latimer indicated that he had taken Tracy's life in an attempt to deliver her from her pain. He challenged the court's conviction of his case, and appealed the decision to the Supreme Court of Canada.

Six organizations of people with disabilities, including the Council of Canadians with Disabilities (CCD), Saskatchewan Voice of People with Disabilities, Canadian Association for Community Living, People First Canada, the DisAbled Women's Network of Canada, and People in Equal Participation were granted intervenor status in the case, to request that the Court deny Latimer's appeal. In their view, the citizenship rights of people with disabilities were at issue; granting leniency for Latimer's crime would diminish the value placed on the lives of people with disabilities, and would condone "mercy killings." They also argued that the implications of not penalizing Latimer were frightening for the people with disabilities who relied upon caretakers for daily needs, and could put their lives in danger.

A long series of events followed the appeal. Latimer's conviction was overturned by the Supreme Court of Canada in 1997, due to irregularities in the jury selection process, and a new trial was ordered. That same year a second jury found Latimer guilty of second-degree murder, but the judge limited his sentence to less than two years. That decision was later dismissed by the Saskatchewan Court of Appeal and the mandatory sentence of second-degree murder was reinstated. On January 18, 2001, the Supreme Court of Canada refused to grant Latimer's second appeal, and upheld the mandatory sentence, stating that "[Latimer's] care of his daughter for many years was admirable. His decision to end his daughter's life was an error in judgment. The taking of another life represents the most serious crime in our criminal law" (*Latimer*, 2001, 6). Latimer is currently serving a 10-year sentence at the Bowden Institution in Alberta.

A third significant legal precedent was set in 1997, when the issue of equality of treatment came to the forefront for people with disabilities. At that time, the Supreme Court of Canada ruled that British Columbia was contravening the equality clause (section 15) of the *Charter of Rights and Freedoms* by not providing sign-language interpreters for deaf users of the healthcare system. In this case, B.C. residents Robin Eldridge, John Warren, and Linda Warren argued that the failure of the government to provide sign-language interpretation resulted in misdiagnosis and ineffective treatment. In many instances prior to this case, deaf citizens had obtained and paid for sign-language interpreters with their own funds in order to ensure proper treatment.

John and Linda Warren were expecting the birth of their first children and had planned to hire an interpreter during the birthing process. The babies were born prematurely, however, and they were not able to secure an interpreter in time. During the births the Warrens were unable to communicate with their physician or the nurses, and found the process confusing, frustrating, and frightening. When one of the infants experienced an elevated heart rate and was whisked away, no one was able to communicate the problem to the parents.

In court, the physician for the Warrens testified that proper communication is essential for childbirth. In light of this and other evidence, the Supreme Court found that the quality of care that was being provided to deaf citizens was below that provided to hearing citizens. In response, the Court ordered the government of British Columbia to provide sign-language interpreters where necessary in the provision of healthcare. According to Supreme Court Justice La Forest:

> It is an unfortunate truth that the history of disabled persons in Canada is largely one of exclusion and marginalization. Persons with disabilities have too often been excluded from the labour force, denied access to opportunities for social interaction and advancement, subjected to invidious stereotypes and relegated to institutions . . . they have been subjected to paternalistic attitudes of pity and charity, and their entrance into the social mainstream has been conditional upon their emulation of able-bodied norms (*Eldridge*, 1997, 24).

The cases discussed above demonstrate the wide variety of issues that people with disabilities have sought to redress through the legal system. In many ways, the courts have been instrumental in ensuring that people with disabilities secure their full citizenship in terms of the right to equal treatment of services provided by the state, as well as in challenging stereotypes concerning "value of life," which in the past have typically deemed people with disabilities to be worth "less than" able-bodied citizens.

These, and other legal decisions, have required the state to re-evaluate its responsibilities to people with disabilities, and in many cases, to expand those responsibilities to ensure that they are assured of equality. However, legal rights are not sufficient to guarantee full citizenship; the state must also ensure that people with disabilities maintain a minimum standard of living that will provide them with a sense of belonging in their communities. In this next section we explore how the state in Canada has responded to these citizenship requirements.

MAINTAINING AN EQUITABLE STANDARD OF LIVING

Neoliberalism has influenced the way in which we value people—especially in terms of economic self-sufficiency and/or labour force participation. One of the first questions we ask when we meet someone is "What do you do?" While at one time being a good citizen meant going to war for your country, today the liberal individualist definition of a good citizen is one who works for a living, pays taxes, and contributes to the economy. The economic well-being of people with disabilities, however, challenges these traditional understandings of citizenship. While for many people with disabilities independence is considered valuable, the reality is that many people with disabilities also require ongoing assistance to be/feel fully integrated into our society. In other words, people with disabilities have challenged our ideal of citizenship to become relational and interdependent, contesting the ideal of the "liberal individual" who does not need anyone.

Citizenship that is relational and interdependent also requires the participation of the state in order for full citizenship to be realized. With the expansion of the welfare state in the 1970s and part of the 1980s, the needs of people with disabilities began to be met—through the establishment of employability programs, income support, and legislation intended to accommodate disability needs in the workplace. However, the growing dominance of neoliberalism in the last few decades has meant that these supports have not been ensured for people with disabilities.

In the first instance, some government policies have been geared towards the introduction (or reintroduction) of people with disabilities into the workforce. In general, these policies seek to make people "employable" through medical intervention or rehabilitation.

These programs are most often provided through the Canadian healthcare system, or through the Employability Assistance for People with Disabilities (EAPD) program administered jointly by the federal and provincial governments. The EAPD program offers a range of programs and services such as employment counselling, wage subsidies, and assistive aids and devices (Canada, 1998, 4).

In some cases rehabilitation may appear too costly, and/or people may not be "employable" for other reasons. In many instances people with disabilities have not had equal access to education, training, and employment opportunities. As well, people with disabilities have struggled to address the stereotypes that they are "passive," "dependent," and "unemployable." In Canada, only 56 percent of men and 40 percent of women with disabilities are in the labour force. (Canada, 1998, Appendix B).

In response to the needs of people with disabilities who are not in the workforce, the Canadian state has established a second approach—income replacement programs. These programs can be grouped into three different categories: workers' compensation, social insurance, and social assistance. *Workers' compensation* is funded by mandatory contributions made by employers, and is used to support workers injured on the job (if they are found by the government to be suitably disabled). In Canada these programs are administered by the provinces. *Social insurance* is a plan in which employees, while working, pay into a fund that will support them when they retire, or if they become disabled in the course of their employment. In Canada, employees who pay into the plan are eligible for the Canada Pension Plan when they retire, and if their disability becomes too severe for them to continue working prior to retirement, they are eligible for a disability pension. *Social assistance,* or welfare, programs are available to people regardless of whether they have been employed or not. Applicants to these programs must demonstrate that they do not have other means of financial assistance (e.g., savings or employment income) above a predetermined level. Moreover, people on social assistance must often prove repeatedly that they are disabled, and their lives can be monitored quite closely by the state.

Governments in Canada have also developed a third approach to addressing the economic needs of people with disabilities—accommodation. In this approach, instead of changing the person to meet the needs of the workplace, ideally the workplace and surrounding environment is changed to meet the needs of the person with a disability.

The reasons that people with disabilities have cited for not finding employment include lack of accessible workplaces, lack of accessible transportation, lack of appropriate training, unwillingness of employers to modify work hours, discrimination, and not wanting to lose their existing government supports (such as healthcare benefits) when they do find work (Canada, 1998). In order to improve the employment situation for people with disabilities, the *Canadian Human Rights Act* was changed in 1998 to make it law that employers have a "duty to accommodate" the needs of certain groups, including people with disabilities. Within reason, employers that fall under the act's jurisdiction must now provide for any technical aids, equipment, attendants, or other specialized services identified by employees with disabilities so that the employees can perform their tasks and functions more easily, and without significant risk. In other words, employers are required to make the necessary accommodations to eliminate the barriers that would otherwise impede the employment of people with disabilities. A major drawback to this piece of legislation is that the majority of employers in Canada do not fall under the jurisdiction of the act.

Over the last two decades, however, the downsizing of the welfare state in Canada has meant that programs and service-delivery for people with disabilities have been substantially reduced. In many instances this has been manifested in drastic financial cutbacks to services or tightening of the eligibility requirements for programs. For example, the federal government has restricted eligibility for the Canada Pension Plan and the Disability Tax Credit. Under the Canada Pension Plan and similar plans, applicants or recipients are often ineligible for support because they have participated in training, education, or rehabilitation, or because they return to work (Council of Canadians with Disabilities, 1999, 14). Similarly, people with disabilities have identified that the current income tax system provides only partial recognition of the costs of disability. In recent years, eligibility for the Disability Tax Credit has been made much more restrictive, and many people who used to claim the credit have been reassessed and determined ineligible. As well, other income tax provisions for medical expenses have been determined to be ineffective in recognizing disability costs (CCD, 1999, 13).

The neoliberal restructuring of the welfare state has also significantly affected provincial programs. In the 1990s the federal government reduced transfer payments to the provinces, and changed the organization of federal–provincial shared-cost programs. Now, provincial governments have substantially more control in deciding how to fund health, welfare, and education programs. As a result, provincial and territorial governments have slashed basic income support programs for people with disabilities, or made them significantly harder to access. As well, provinces have limited access to services such as personal care, drugs, transportation, and education (CCD, 1999, 4). The shift has also meant that the supports for people with disabilities can vary dramatically from province to province, and in some cases, within provinces.

These changes do not bode well for people with disabilities in Canada. In many cases they have meant growing difficulties for people with disabilities, as the welfare state shrinks and the provision of services declines. Many others face increased poverty as they are removed from, or determined to be ineligible for, federal or provincial income support programs. The early gains that people with disabilities had made are being compromised by the neoliberal focus on independent citizenship rather than interdependent citizenship. As a result, the responsibilities of the state for ensuring the full equality and participation of people with disabilities in Canadian society are not being met.

CONCLUSION

The lives and perspectives of people with disabilities have altered the way that citizenship is constructed in Canada. In many cases, the state has recognized that creating full and equal citizenship means embracing the differences that people with disabilities bring to the table—without considering their needs to be "less than" those of able-bodied people. The challenge that lies ahead is to rethink the neoliberal assumptions about citizenship in ways that will ensure a political, legal, and social sense of belonging for people with disabilities in Canada.

NOTES

1. The term *disablement* will be employed here to encapsulate three of the elements that are commonly used to define disability: impairment, disability, and handicap.

REFERENCES

Bickenbach, Jerome. 1993. *Physical Disability and Social Policy.* Toronto: University of Toronto Press.

Brieger, Peter. 2000. "Advocates for Blind Want Tougher Laws to Counter Discrimination." *Edmonton Journal*, June 17, B11.

Brodie, Janine. 1995. *Politics on the Margins: Restructuring and the Canadian Women's Movement.* Halifax: Fernwood Publishing.

Canada. 1998. In Unison: A Canadian Approach to Disability Issues. A Vision Paper of Federal/Provincial /Territorial Ministers Responsible for Social Services. Ottawa: Human Resources Development Canada. Retrieved from www.socialunion.gc.ca

Canada. Human Resources and Development, Office for Disability Issues. (1998). *A Way With Words: Guidelines and Appropriate Terminology for the Portrayal of Persons With Disabilities.* Ottawa: Minister of Public Works.

Canada. Parliament. (1999). Reflecting Interdependence: Disability, Parliament, Government and the Community. Report of the House of Commons Subcommittee on the Status of Persons With Disabilities. Retrieved March 3, 2002 from http://parl.gc.ca/infoComDoc/36/1/HRPD/Studies/Reports/sspdrp06.e-html

Cherry, Lisa. 1994. "Disabled Refugee Denied Citizenship," *Globe and Mail*, 2 September, p.A4.

Council of Canadians with Disabilities (CCD). 2000. Retrieved June 5, 2002 from www.pcs.mb.ca/~ccd.html

Council of Canadians with Disabilities. 1999. *A National Strategy for Persons With Disabilities: The Community Definition.* Retrieved March 10, 2002 from www.pcs.mb.ca/~ccd/nation~4.html

Crichton, Anne and Lyn Jongbloed. 1998. *Disability and Social Policy in Canada.* North York: Captus Press Inc.

Davis, Lennard. 1995. *Enforcing Normalcy: Disability, Deafness and the Body*. London:Verso.

Disabled Women's Network of Canada. Retrieved June 6, 200 from http://indie.ca/dawn/index.html

Driedger, Diane. 2000. *Speaking For Ourselves: A History of COPOH on Its 10th Anniversary.* Retrieved June 4, 2000 from www.pcs.mb.ca/~ccd/ahistory.html

Editorial. 1998. "An Outrage and an Abuse of Power," *Edmonton Journal.* March 11, A12.

Eldridge and Warren v. British Columbia. 1997 Supreme Court Reporter.

Jeffs, Allyson and Graham Thomson. 1998. "Victim's Anger Moved Klein." *Edmonton Journal,* March 12, p. A5.

Latimer v. The Queen. 2001. Supreme Court Reporter.

Rodriguez v. British Columbia. 1998 Supreme Court Reporter.

Valentine, Fraser. 2001. Enabling Citizenship: Full Inclusion of Children with Disabilities and their Parents. Canadian Policy Research Networks Discussion Paper, No. F13. Retrieved March 19, 2002 from www.cprn.org/docs/family/ecf_e.pdf. Accessed March 19, 2002

________. 1994. *The Canadian Independent Living Movement: An Historical Overview*. Ottawa: The Canadian Association of Independent Living Centres.

———. and Jill Vickers. 1996. "Released From the Yoke of Paternalism and 'Charity': Citizenship and the Rights of People With Disabilities.", *International Journal of Canadian Studies 14*, 155–177.

WEBLINKS

International Classification of Functioning, Disability, and Health
www.who.int/icidh

International Day of Disabled
www.unac.org/en/link_learn/monitoring/rights_disabled.asp

Active Living Alliance
www.ala.ca

chapter ten

Sexual Minorities in Canada

Gloria Filax

Debra Shogan

INTRODUCTION

At the dawn of the twenty-first century, sexual minorities have achieved a status in Canadian law that would have been unthinkable even 10 years ago. Many Canadian provinces, for example, now include sexual orientation in their human rights codes. Quebec was the first, in 1977, to provide a legal mechanism for members of sexual minorities to seek redress for discrimination from private actors such as landlords, employers, and businesses. In the late 1980s and throughout the 1990s, sexual orientation was included as grounds for protection in human rights legislation in all the other provinces. Moreover, only Alberta undertook this change reluctantly, having been forced to do so by a Supreme Court decision. The federal government incorporated sexual orientation into its *Human Rights Act* in 1996 but, more important, it has been challenged to change numerous pieces of federal legislation that discriminate against members of sexual minorities because the Supreme Court has progressively read sexual orientation as a grounds for protection under the equality guarantees of the *Canadian Charter of Rights and Freedoms* (1982). In a partial response, the federal government introduced Bill C-23 which sought changes to the terms of more than 60 federal statutes that include same-sex and common-law couples in federal legislation from income tax provisions and pensions to immigration. The bill passed third reading in the House of Commons on April 11, 2000. To many, Bill C-23 signals that sexual minorities have finally been recognized in law as full and legitimate participants in Canadian communities. In this chapter we will explore this assumption, examining how legal discourses have produced sexual minority status in this country and how they function to maintain notions of "normal" and "abnormal" citizenship, even as possibilities have been opened up for sexual minorities.

In order to address these issues, we conduct what French intellectual Michel Foucault referred to as a "history of the present" (1979). In this history, we will outline the conditions that made it possible for sexual minorities to achieve legal status in Canada, while pointing out that this status nevertheless has been established and maintained in relation to a heterosexual norm. The conditions that we identify in our discussion include discourses about crime, sin, and illness, public and private sex, and equality and freedom. There are, of course, many other conditions that have produced sexual minority identity in Canada. The ones we discuss here, however, are an important place to start. In the sections that follow, we will outline how the emergence of sexual minority identity in Canadian legal discourse is an effect of various conditions, some legal, some not. In the last section of the chapter, we will question the stability of current notions of sexual minority identity by introducing the notion of "queer" politics and theory.

Before we proceed with this, it is important to say something about "discourse." By discourse we mean a regulated system of knowledge, supported by social institutions that shape what can be spoken and who can speak it. In legal discourse, for example, legislators, judges, and lawyers have particular positions from which they can speak and act that are different from and have more status than what clients or citizens can say or do. Moreover, what legislators, judges, and lawyers talk about and do creates social positions for others in a society to occupy. Law helps to define the distinction between, among other things, police officer and lawbreaker, citizen and non-citizen, married and never married, and public and private sexual activity. In this chapter, we are interested in the conditions that make it possible to talk about and act in relation to sexual minorities.

DISCOURSES OF SIN, CRIME, AND ILLNESS

In white settler societies such as Canada, Europeans took on an early and formative role as agents of successful nation building in the interest of the colonial state (McClintock, 1995). Indigenous peoples were considered by Europeans to be more primitive, closer to nature, and without culture (Bleys, 1995). Entailed in this view about Indigenous people was a belief that they engaged in sexually sinful practices that were to be vanquished by Christian missionaries. Before Confederation, Indigenous people were subjugated to "the marginalization and destruction of their diverse forms of erotic, gender and social life and their subordination to white, European derived social and sexual organizations" (Kinsman, 1996, 92).

Non-reproductive sex practised by Indigenous people was generally considered by the settler hierarchy to be not only sinful but a "crime against nature," even though this claim contradicted other talk about Native people that linked them with nature. Within New France and Upper Canada, the legal charge of a "crime against nature" could result in death (Kinsman, 1996, 98). Non-Natives engaging in these activities were thought to have been contaminated by primitive practices as a consequence of being too long away from European culture. The effect of nation building was "to expel from reality the forms of sexuality that were not amenable to the strict economy of reproduction: to say no to unproductive activities, to banish casual pleasures, to reduce or exclude practices whose object was not procreation" (Foucault, 1980, 36).

European societies as well as those of the New World often punished homosexual activity, but it was not until the latter part of the nineteenth century and early twentieth that the "homosexual" was identified as a specific type of individual and as a member of a particular social group. The identity—a homosexual identity, most often thought of as male, emerged out of a number of quarters, for example, from the social-purity movement and from developing legal discourse. Most important, however, were the newly formed sexual sciences, including forensic psychiatry, sex psychology, and later sexology, which began to classify all forms of sexual behaviour (Kinsman, 1996, 58). Not only did the sexual sciences actually produce the group identity of homosexual when such a group had not before been recognized, those who were seen to belong to this group were considered to be mentally ill. A group identity was also established for heterosexuality. The "heterosexual" was part of the normal group against which the homosexual group could be compared and, of course, evaluated as deviating from the normal.

Homosexuality, as a group identity, was strengthened by a shift in the nineteenth century in Europe and North America from agricultural, trading societies to urban, industrial societies. Capitalism became the dominant form of economic organization. Capitalist productive relations were premised on the reproductive relations of the heterosexual family (Sayer, 1991). Consequently, capitalism reinforced the importance of the reproductive family unit. It was supported by a universal prohibition against incest (Levi-Strauss, 1969) and a taboo against homosexuality (Butler, 1990, 64). However, the rise of urban industrialized centres in Canada and elsewhere created public spaces and concentrations of people not necessarily bound by family and community norms in the same way as in agricultural, rural communities (Kinsman, 1996; Adam, 1995). Urban centres created the possibility for anonymity and places for those who wished to engage in non-reproductive sex to meet and socialize (Adam, 1995). Once recognized only as isolated, individual acts, homosexuality became identified as a characteristic of certain persons and then a specific group—those who engaged in same-sex sexual activity. Once named, they were seen in public in ever-larger numbers as threats to community values.

The Canadian legal system predictably responded to these dangerous deviations from the normal. In 1869, "buggery" was classified in criminal legislation as an unnatural offence, and from 1892 until the 1950s, it was classified as an offence against morality (Kinsman, 1996, 129). "Gross indecency" was introduced into Canadian statute law in 1890 and entered into the first *Criminal Code* when it was adopted in 1892 (Kinsman, 1996, 129). Gross indecency referred to all sexual acts between males not considered to be "buggery." In the latter part of the nineteenth century and the early part of the twentieth century, social-purity movements advocated for increased regulation of sexuality in response to prostitution and to the utilization of public space by men seeking sex with other men. *Criminal Code* classifications were used to direct the police against men engaged in this illicit activity (Kinsman, 1996, 127). In effect, people were grouped and identified as criminals by virtue of sex acts, such as "buggery."

Canadian history is replete with examples, many quite recent, of arrest and incarceration as a result of being convicted of engaging in prohibited sexual acts. For example, in 1965, a man confessed to the police during the course of another investigation that he was gay and had engaged in sex with men. He was charged and convicted on four counts of gross indecency and sentenced to three years for each charge. A court later determined that the man was a "dangerous sexual offender" and was thus sentenced to indefinite detention in a federal penitentiary. It was also a regular practice, especially in the 1970s, for police to raid men's bathhouses and to subject those arrested to publicity and humiliation.

The *Vriend* case provides a more recent example of how an individual life can be caught up in the discourses of homosexuality as sin as well as in long and expensive litigation to secure what most others simply take for granted. In 1991, Delwin Vriend, a laboratory coordinator employed at King's College, Edmonton, was fired from his job for the sole reason that he was gay, even though it was acknowledged by college officials that he was a competent instructor. Vriend turned for redress to the Alberta Human Rights Commission but was turned away because the province's *Individual Rights Protection Act* (IRPA) did not prohibit discrimination on the grounds of sexual orientation. Vriend thus challenged the constitutional validity of IRPA under section 15 of the *Charter of Rights and Freedoms.* The Supreme Court eventually ruled in Vriend's favour in 1998, arguing that the Alberta legislation denied gays and lesbians the equal benefit and protection of the law.

The Supreme Court decision established that employer pronouncements of sin would not take precedence over fundamental human rights. The *Vriend* decision was thus an important advance for gays and lesbians in Canada. The reaction in Alberta, however, was less than celebratory. The editorial pages of the *Edmonton Journal* and the *Calgary Herald* soon filled with letters, some verging on hate-speech, accusing the Supreme Court of granting homosexuals "special rights" and of fomenting, among other things, sin, bestiality, pedophilia, and the destruction of the family. The Klein government, in turn, considered invoking the notwithstanding clause of the *Charter* so as to avoid complying with the Supreme Court's decision. In the end, however, Premier Klein rejected this constitutional option. The episode, however, cast in stark relief the continuing political force of discourses of homosexuality as sin in Canada.

DISCOURSES OF PUBLIC AND PRIVATE SEX

For most of the past 50 years, the legal identity of those who engaged in homosexual acts was profoundly affected by British jurisprudence and public policy. Issued in 1957, the *Wolfenden Report* was a policy document that was concerned with homosexuality as a "large-scale deviation" that needed to be managed. The report made a distinction between public and private homosexual acts. This distinction created classifications that made it possible to officially police and regulate homosexuality (Kinsman, 1996, 215). The public/private distinction also linked *crimes* with the public sphere and established the need to protect the public from homosexual acts. *Sins* were characterized as those homosexual acts which occurred in private (1996, 215). The public–private dichotomy produced by the *Wolfenden Report* officially created subgroups of homosexuals—the appropriate/private homosexual and the inappropriate/public homosexual. The report created a safe yet sinful space for consensual acts between adults within the private sphere but criminalized consensual acts between adults if these acts occurred in what legislators determined to be public places.

The *Wolfenden Report* implied that heterosexuality is a "fragile and tenuous identity that is easily displaced by any positive image of homosexuality" (Stychin, 1995, 41). The report promoted monogamous, heterosexual family relations as a way to prevent homosexuality. Distinctions between adult and youth identities also were emphasized by the report. Fears of homosexuals recruiting the young or having sexual activity with children were extended to concerns about teachers and other adults who had contact with the young. Specifically, the report warned that homosexuals ought not to have contact with youth. Youth were characterized as easily seduced and therefore readily recruited into "sin" and "crime."

Canadian legislators relied heavily on the *Wolfenden Report* in the preparation of the *Criminal Law Amendment Act*. This act included abortion and prostitution reforms and removed from the *Criminal Code* the prohibition of sexual activity between two consenting adults of the same sex in private. In supporting this amendment to the *Criminal Code*, then–Justice Minister Pierre Trudeau made his now famous statement that "the state has no place in the bedrooms of the nation." While the *Wolfenden Report* eased state regulation of homosexuality and the Canadian amendment to the *Criminal Code* decriminalized homosexuality, the effect was an intensification of legal discourse about homosexuality. As a consequence of this increased legal interest in homosexuality, there was a 160 percent increase in the conviction rate for homosexual offences in England and a similar increase in conviction rates in Canada (Kinsman, 1996). Increased prosecution of public homosexual acts and the creation of the appropriate, private homosexual and the inappropriate, public homosexual forced sexual minorities into the private realm or "into the closet." The overriding effect was to silence and stigmatize all those identified and identifying as homosexuals.

The Klippert case provides a revealing example of the legal struggle about what was to count as public and private and what constituted criminal or deviant activity. Everett George Klippert was convicted on four counts of gross indecency for having consensual homosexual sex in what was considered to be public space. Based on the emerging psychiatric discourse that produced the notion of the "sick homosexual," Klippert was designated as a dangerous sexual offender in 1965 (Kinsman, 1996). Klippert's "crime" was having consensual sex in a car. This case underscores the ways in which legal distinctions, in this case the distinction between public and private spheres, were interpreted to criminalize homosexuality. Because heterosexuality was state-sanctioned and homosexual sex was to remain hidden, heavier state regulations were imposed on the few places that many practising homosexuals engaged in sexual activity. In this case, a car was designated as a public place, even though cars were often sites of sex between consenting heterosexuals.

The *Wolfenden Report* and the *Criminal Law Amendment Act* also further entrenched the notion of "the homosexual" as a group identity. Having a group identity was not necessarily an improvement over being labelled a criminal or sinner as an individual. Individuals still experienced silence, fear, and punishment, at the same time as being considered as part of a group that had been established by legal discourse. Establishing a homosexual group identity in legal discourse was, however, beneficial for those who wished to control and regulate the lives of "sexual deviants." At the very least, a group identity provided legal mechanisms to force homosexuals into privacy.

DISCOURSES OF EQUALITY AND FREEDOM

While Canadian law is based on a British parliamentary system, the adoption of the *Charter of Rights and Freedoms* in 1982, with its American-style, constitutionally entrenched bill of rights, made Canada into a more complex legal culture. While sexual orientation is not listed as a protected category in the *Charter of Rights and Freedoms*, the *Charter* has been very significant in designating sexual minority identity in Canada. Subject to certain limitations, the *Charter* guarantees a series of individual and group rights from interference by governments. Of particular importance to the rights of lesbians and gay men are section 2(b), which ensures freedom of expression, and section 15(1), which ensures rights of equality before and under the law. Section 15(1) does not include "sexual orientation" in its list of protected categories, but sexual orientation has recently come to be read in by judges in some cases of discrimination against lesbians or gay men.

As a consequence of legal decisions based on the *Charter,* lesbian and gay group identity and same-sex couples have been legally recognized. Other sexual minorities such as bisexuals, transsexuals, and transgendered people have not benefited in the same way from the *Charter*. As well, sexual minority categories recognized in ethnic and Native cultures have not been legally recognized. Native Two-Spirited people, for example, can only be legally recognized if they abandon their own identification and take on the labels "gay" or "lesbian." It remains the case, however, that "sexual orientation" is used to refer to lesbians and gay men and not heterosexuals. This erases the ways in which heterosexuality as a sexual orientation permeates Canadian law. By reading sexual orientation into sections 2(b) and 15(1) of the *Charter*, heterosexuality is reinforced as the norm and lesbians and gay men have become "special" others who require legal interventions to arrest discriminatory behaviours. Legal discourse based on the *Charter* constructs homosexuality and heterosexuality as dichotomous and essentially different.

The *Charter of Rights and Freedoms* has improved the legal rights of lesbians and gay men in certain respects but they continue to be denied things that heterosexuals take for granted, among them, benefits and freedom from harassment. The cases we cite below demonstrate that Canadian law valorizes heterosexually as the norm, to the exclusion of other sexual orientations. Moreover, these cases suggest that the full inclusion of gays and lesbians into the Canadian community will involve contesting the law on a variety of fronts.

The *Egan* Case

Egan and Nesbit v. *Canada* (1995) is an example of how the *Charter* has not always worked to protect lesbians and gays because of the assumption that people are heterosexual. James Egan and John Nesbit had lived together for more than 40 years and, when Egan turned 65 in 1986, he applied twice to the federal government for a spousal allowance for Nesbit under the *Old Age Security Act* (1985). Nesbit was turned down both times because "spouse" was defined in the *Old Age Security Act* as a person of the opposite sex. Egan and Nesbit took the federal government to court and their application was dismissed, as was their appeal to the federal court of appeals (Greer, Barbaree, and Brown, 1997, 174). They then appealed to the Supreme Court of Canada where they argued that the definition of spouse in the *Old Age Security Act* discriminated against them on the basis of sexual orientation and thus denied them equal protection under section 15(1) of the *Charter*. The majority decision of the Supreme Court ruled "that although there may have been discrimination in violation of section 15(1) of the *Charter*, because the *Old Age Security Act* defined "spouse" to include only opposite-sex couples, such discrimination could be reasonably justified" (Yogis, Duplak, and Trainor, 1996, 21).

Justice La Forest, in support of the majority decision, based his comments on the primacy of the "traditional family," in which procreating is the primary function. According to La Forest, " marriage is by nature heterosexual." He continued to argue that it "would be possible to legally define marriage to include homosexual couples, but this would not change the biological and social realities that underlie the traditional marriage."

(*Egan and Nesbit* v. *Canada,* 1995, 625). In effect, his point was that the equality rights under the *Charter* that might have been expected to acknowledge same-sex relationships could not be reconciled with the definition of spouse used in acts and laws covering families at that time. In the words of Justice Cory, who disagreed with the majority decision, the distinction made between same-sex and opposite-sex couples reinforces "the stereotype that homosexuals cannot and do not form lasting, caring, mutually supportive relationships with economic interdependence in the same manner as heterosexual couples" (*Egan*, 1995, 677).

While the Supreme Court decided in the *Egan* case that sexual orientation was an analogous ground of discrimination for purposes of Section 15 of the *Charter*, the Supreme Court nevertheless decided that this discrimination was justified, thus denying same-sex benefits under the *Old Age Security Act*. This case is an example of how the *Charter* made it possible for lesbians and gay men to claim some legitimacy in Canadian communities while being excluded from provisions of family law which would have entitled them to spousal benefits.

The *Little Sisters* Case

Little Sisters Book and Art Emporium in Vancouver is a significant distribution point for cultural materials for the gay and lesbian communities in Western Canada. For many years, Canada Customs has consistently seized or detained publications that Customs officers ruled to be obscene in content. While Little Sisters had often successfully contested the seizure and detention of materials through the appeals processes provided by the *Customs Act*, the actions by Customs officials did not stop. The seizures were a constant harassment and a financial hardship for the store.

In order to remedy this situation, Little Sisters filed suit and charged that, "the relevant customs regulations violated freedom of expression under Section 2(b) and equality rights under Section 15 of the *Charter of Rights and Freedoms.*" The bookstore also sought a declaration that the customs regulations had been applied in a manner that violated Sections 2(b) and 15 of the *Charter*" (Greer, Barbaree, and Brown, 1997, 171). While the Supreme Court declared that custom officials frequently contravened the *Charter* when they seized Little Sisters' materials, it also found that the *Customs Act* itself did not violate the *Charter*. Instead, the Supreme Court ruled that disadvantage to lesbians and gay men arose from Section 163(8) of the *Criminal Code*. The court ruled that, "homosexual obscenity is proscribed because it is obscene (under s. 163 (8) of the *Criminal Code*) not because it is homosexual" (Greer, Barbaree, and Brown, 1997, 173).

This case is another example of the contradiction between *Charter* rights and other laws, such as laws governing freedom of expression and the *Criminal Code* that limit homosexual erotica by labelling it obscene. Commentators have pointed out that this case reflects an inability to distinguish between homosexuality and pornography (Bull & Gallagher, 1996, 163). Others suggest that gay pornography should be treated differently from heterosexual pornography because there are so few images of gay and lesbian sexuality available to gay and lesbian people (Stychin, 1995, 56). Stychin argues that the freedom to create and have access to explicit sexual images is essential if homosexuality is to be regarded as a legitimate way in which to live one's life. As Stychin writes,

> [t]he offensiveness of such attempts at discursive control through law is that they deny to some a right of citizenship; that is, a right to articulate a sexual identity within a shared communal space. Finally the material reality of these laws should not be ignored. Individuals have been lost unnecessarily, young people who are confused and miserable have been denied access to information that might instil a positive image, and prejudice and bigotry have been given an official outlet and *promoted* (1995, 54, emphasis in original).

The *Anglican Priest* Case

On June 22, 1993, Daniel Webb was arrested by a police officer who had enticed him into the bushes by offering Webb sex. Shortly after Webb's arrest, the local newspaper printed a short piece stating that Webb had been charged with sexual assault while police worked to "clean up homosexual behaviour" in the park where the incident occurred. A day after the news item appeared Webb was asked to resign from his position as Anglican priest in Cambridge, Ontario. On December 7, 1999, Webb announced that he was "suing the Waterloo Region Police Service for close to $4 million and [was] seeking compensation for the turmoil that the 1993 arrest and media release caused him" (*National Post,* 1999, A3).

It is clear from this example that police entrapment of men suspected of trying to have homosexual sex in a public place contradicts, 2(b) of the *Charter,* which ensures freedom of expression, and section 15(1) of the *Charter,* which ensures equality before and under the law. In the case of Webb, while sexual touching occurred between two consenting adults, no sex took place in this public place. This case makes clear that, despite the *Charter*, homosexual consensual contact is not treated in the same way under the law as heterosexual consensual contact. Except in the case of prostitution, people looking for heterosexual sex is a common, public activity that interests neither the police nor the courts, nor do people lose their livelihoods for engaging in this kind of behaviour. To the contrary, the image of young heterosexual lovers embracing in the park is idealized both in advertising and in the movies.

QUEER SEXUALITY AS POST-GROUP IDENTITY

We started this chapter by saying that we are interested in a history of the present status of sexual minorities in Canada. In legal terms, the status of sexual minorities in the early part of the twenty-first century is largely defined by the provisions of Bill C-23. The legislative changes that it enacted have provided some newfound legitimation for lesbians and gay men. Same-sex domestic partners, common-law partners, and, of course, married couples can have similar legal relationships with the federal state, especially with respect to taxation. While these represent important legal gains for some, others are not so certain. There has also been resistance to legal recognition of same-sex partner status. Some argue that this limited recognition isolates those who are not in long-term same-sex relationships as abnormal in relation to both legally recognized same-sex partners and to the "normal" heterosexual couple. Others point out that the federal government's willingness to expand the definition of family has come precisely at the moment when governments everywhere are downloading the costs of care and security onto the family unit.

There are sexual identities, however, that remain unrecognized by Canadian law. These "outlaw" identities have been created in popular culture including movies, television, the

Internet, music videos, alternative presses, bookstores and theatres, clubs, and activist discourse. Among these are the television shows *Ellen*, *Will and Grace*, and *Queer as Folk*; movies such as *All About My Mother* and *Ma Vie en Rose*; publications such as *The Advocate*, *Out*, and *Curve*; gay pride marches and the Gay Games, and queer figures such as Rupaul, Dennis Rodman, and Patrick Rice Califia, former leather dyke, now transitioning to a male body and contemplating marriage to a gay man. Identities are also produced from resistance to such things as police raids, court decisions, and AIDS policy. Popular cultural representations and performances of a range of sexualities disrupt the notion that the only sexual minorities in this country are same-sex couples all of whom have the resources to take advantage of benefit packages and tax and immigration provisions.

Central to the emergence of "queer" sexuality in the 1990s and the early part of this century is resistance to attempts to make everyone the same. To identify as queer is a strategy that opposes group sexual identity and resists regimes of normalcy (Warner, 1994). Queer strategy exposes and resists the way in which "the heterosexual" is constructed as "the norm" but it also exposes and resists attempts to make sexual minorities more like this norm. The very idea of queer challenges how legal discourse has managed and minimized sexual difference by only recognizing gay men and lesbians. Queer strategy also opposes the control of sexual difference within sexual minority communities through judging and punishing those who, while not heterosexual, are also not gay or lesbian. Queer identity is hybrid, partial, not fixed, and stresses "the fractious, the disruptive, the irritable, the impatient, the unapologetic, the bitchy, the camp" (Dinshaw and Halperin, 1993, iii–iv).

As we have indicated, when reading "sexual orientation" into the *Charter*, judges and legislators have understood sexual orientation to mean same-sex sexual activity. Sexual orientation, as it has been read into the *Charter of Rights and Freedoms* and subsequent legal decisions and legislation, refers to the gender of a person's sexual object choice, that is, to whether the person is male or female. On queer terms, fixing sexual orientation in this way is rigid and significantly reduces the opportunity to recognize other differences in sexual practice. Queer theorist Eve Sedgwick further develops this point:

> [I]t is a rather amazing fact that, of the very many dimensions along which the genital activity of one person can be differentiated from that of another (dimensions that include preference for certain acts, certain zones or sensations, certain physical types, a certain frequency, certain symbolic investments, certain relations of age or power, a certain species, a certain number of participants, etc. etc. etc.), precisely one, the gender of object choice, emerged from the turn of the century, and has remained *the* dimension denoted by the now ubiquitous category of "sexual orientation" (1990, 8).

By questioning how sexual minority status has been produced by legal discourse, queer politics and theory also reveal that heterosexuality is limited by legal discourse. Not only does legal discourse confine sexual minority status to same-sex activity, heterosexual status is also limited to include only those practices that can be understood when they occur in long-term relationships. It is, however, no more possible for the law to fully contain or describe the various forms of heterosexuality than it is possible to contain or describe "queer."

CONCLUSION

This chapter has identified some of the conditions that have made it possible for legal discourse at the beginning of the twenty-first century in Canada to produce a particular type of sexual minority status. It has discussed how the *Criminal Law Amendment Act*, the *Charter of Rights and Freedoms*, and Bill C-23 each assume a heterosexual norm. Opening legal discourse to include sexual minorities has not diminished the force of heteronormativity in legal discourse. The *Criminal Law Amendment Act* privatized homosexual affection and sex while heterosexual affection and some sexual activity retained its status as public sex. Court interpretations of the *Charter of Rights and Freedoms* established sexual orientation as something that lesbians and gay men have while heterosexuals retained their status as the unnamed norm. Bill C-23 has made it possible for same-sex couples to take up many of the benefits previously only afforded heterosexual couples but it protects marriage for those who are "normal." Moreover, Bill C-23 recognizes same-sex relations only when they mirror heterosexual partnerships. Those who identify with other sexual arrangements remain outside the legal discourse.

The chapter has also introduced the notion of queer sexuality as fluid, partial, and opposed to sameness to underline how legal discourse fixes sexual identity and presumes that there is a "normal" sexuality. "The homosexual" was produced as an identity category in Canada through social conditions that made it possible for people to congregate in urban centres and engage in sexual behaviours outside the purview of marriage and the heterosexual family. This category was reinforced by social-purity movements, sexology, and legal discourse that cast homosexuals as sinners, mentally ill, or criminals. The category *homosexual* also created positions from which individuals could resist these ascriptions and from which countermovements advocating for rights could be fought. Without the creation of a group identity for same-sex sexual activity, the decriminalization of same-sex sexual activity in the *Criminal Law Amendment Act*, reading in sexual orientation into the *Charter of Rights and Freedoms*, and Bill C-23 could not have emerged. The latter, in particular, has created opportunities for inclusion in Canadian communities for people who, for more than half of the twentieth century, were subject to punishment for same-sex sexual activity. It is worth emphasizing, however, that since legal discourse in Canada assumes that people are heterosexual, it is not possible for sexual minorities to be fully protected or acknowledged by the law. It is also important to underline that recognizing sexual minorities in legal discourse only when they appear to act in the same way as legally recognized heterosexuals continues to deny full inclusion in Canadian communities to those with sexual practices that refuse to be fixed by dominant norms and discourses.

REFERENCES

Adam, B. 1995. *The Rise of a Gay and Lesbian Movement.* (Rev. Ed.) London: Prentice Hall.

Bleys, R. 1995. *The Geography of Perversion: Male-to-Male Sexual Behaviour Outside the West and the Ethnographic Imagination, 1750–1918.* New York: New York University Press.

Butler, J. 1990. *Gender Trouble: Feminism and the Subversion of Identity*. New York & London: Routledge.

Criminal Law Amendment Act. (SC 1968–69, Chap. 38, s.7).

Dinshaw, C. and D. Halperin. 1993. "From the Editors". *GLQ*, 1,1: iii–iv.

Egan and Nesbit v. Canada (1995), 124 DLR (4th) 609 (SCC).

Foucault, M. 1970. *The Order of Things: An Archaeology of the Human Sciences*. (A. Sheridan, Trans.) New York: Pantheon.

Foucault, M. 1979. *Discipline and Punish: The Birth of the Prison*. (A. Sheridan, Trans.) New York: Vintage Books.

Foucault, M. 1980. *The History of Sexuality Volume I: An Introduction*. New York: Vintage Books.

Greer, A., H. Barbaree, & C. Brown. 1997. "Canada." In D. West and R. Green (eds.), *Sociolegal Control of Homosexuality: A Multi-Nation Comparison*. New York & London: Plenum Press.

Humphreys, A. 1999, December 8. "Gay Former Pastor Sues Police Force for Outing Him." *National Post*, A1.

Kinsman, G. 1996. *The Regulation of Desire: Homo and Hetero Sexualities*. Montreal: Black Rose Books.

Levi-Strauss, C. 1969. *The Elementary Structures of Kinship*. (J. H. Bell, J. R. von Sturmer, and R. Needom, eds.) Boston: Beacon Press.

Little Sisters Book and Art Emporium v. Canada (1996), 131, DLR (4th) 486 (SCC).

McClintock, A. 1995. *Imperial Leather: Race, Gender and Sexuality in the Colonial Context*. New York & London: Routledge.

Sayer, D. 1991. *Capitalism & Modernity: An Excursus on Marx and Weber.* New York & London: Routledge.

Sedgwick, E. Kosofsky. 1990. *Epistemology of the Closet*. Berkeley, Los Angeles: University of California Press.

Stychin, C. 1995. *Law's Desire: Sexuality and the Limits of Justice*. London & New York: Routledge.

Warner, M. 1994. "Introduction." In M. Warner (ed.), *Fear of a Queer Planet: Queer Politics and Social Theory*. Minneapolis & London: University of Minnesota Press.

Wolfenden, J. 1957. *Report of the Committee on Homosexual Offences and Prostitution*. London: Her Majesty's Stationary Office.

Yogis, J., R. Duplak, J.R. Trainor. 1996. *Sexual Orientation and Canadian Law: An Assessment of the Law Affecting Lesbian and Gay Persons*. Toronto: Emond Montgomery Publications Limited.

WEBLINKS

GayCanada.com
www.gaycanada.com

Canadian Lesbian and Gay Archives
www.clga.ca

Gay Seniors, Canada
http://gayseniors.tripod.ca

chapter eleven

Whither the Social Citizen

Lois Harder

INTRODUCTION

State-provided social services, or social entitlements, and the political struggles surrounding them are central features of Canadian citizenship. Together with hockey and cold winters, social programs have helped to define the Canadian national identity. Social citizenship, however, is a precarious achievement. In part this is because social rights, the "right to a modicum of economic welfare and security, the right to share in the social heritage and to live the life of a civilized being according to the standards prevailing in the society," are relatively new and hence less entrenched than civil and political rights in the lexicon of citizenship entitlements (Marshall, 1964, 71–72). But more importantly, the tenuous legitimacy of social rights in Canada results from their challenge to the established constitutional and economic order. The provinces, for example, have long argued about the federal government's practice of using its superior financial resources to advance social programs that individual provinces did not necessarily view as policy priorities. More recently the provinces have criticized the federal government for refusing to use its financial resources to maintain those programs. Business interests have asserted that social policies contribute to prohibitive income tax rates and that income-replacement policies, such as unemployment insurance and social assistance, undermine productivity and diminish the competitiveness of the Canadian economy in the new global economy. Even groups that support social rights have been critical of their operation, pointing to the sexist and racist assumptions and the class bias implicit in many social programs. Rather than viewing Canadian social rights as overly disruptive, however, these groups assert that social rights have not been disruptive enough.

Currently, social policy and the content of the citizenship it confers are undergoing a profound shift. The reconfiguration of the Canadian state from a welfare to a neoliberal state form, and the related project of recasting citizenship to meet the demands of a globalizing economy, have framed the social policy debate in new terms. Rather than using social policy as a tool for the creation and solidification of a Canadian national identity, linking the country's dispersed population through access to common services, contemporary visions of social policy have abandoned the national project. Social policies are being redesigned to diminish their impact on provincial and federal budgets, to reinforce the importance of employment as the primary source of individual security, and to promote private sector services as offering citizens, now consumers, the greatest choice in addressing their social needs. The objective of increasing the program choices available to citizens is certainly worthy. Moreover, to the extent that the nationalist vision created a false sense of commonality by excluding important groups within Canadian society, a new social policy regime is also a welcome development. Nevertheless, the emphasis on the individual and their capacity to make the market work are concerning. The reliance on the market as the primary agent for the delivery of social services undermines our relationships with and responsibilities to each other and individualizes responsibility for social and economic forces that are beyond the control of particular citizens. The consequences for democratic governance are profound.

This chapter examines social policy as a component of Canadian citizenship and identity. It provides an overview of the primary forces shaping Canadian social policy and social citizenship, the trajectory of social policy reform from welfare to neoliberal governance, the generation of citizen compliance with the new policy direction, and the consequences of neoliberal social policy implementation for the well-being of citizens. Underscoring this discussion is the contention that the current reforms are motivated by the desire to address the "crisis of ungovernability" alleged to have resulted from the failure of democratic governments to make good on the welfare state's promise of equality (Offe, 1984). Because of this promise and the asserted impossibility of its realization, neoliberals argue that the welfare state encouraged citizens and "special interest groups" to demand an ever more inclusive social safety net. These demands led to the expansion of the state's powers over individuals and the market and embroiled the state in political struggles that it could not resolve. According to proponents of the "ungovernability" thesis, the expansion of the state's role unduly hampered the operation of the market and involved the state in matters more appropriately addressed in the private sphere. Thus, the neoliberal state has attempted to achieve a new governing consensus that emphasizes the state's role in providing the basic conditions required for economic growth and social policies that "empower" individuals to seize the opportunities that a strong economy is sure to produce. For proponents of globalization, the apparently uncomplicated and single-minded pursuit of a growing economy works as a shield against the acrimony generated by the more complex ambitions of the Keynesian welfare state.

CANADIAN SOCIAL POLICY IN BRIEF

For most industrialized countries, including Canada, welfare state programs emerged under a common set of circumstances. These included the unemployment crisis that was a central feature of the Great Depression of the 1930s, the need to reward soldiers for their enormous sacrifices during the Second World War, the fear of creeping communism, and the success of workers in asserting their political legitimacy. However, relative to most of its industrialized cousins, the Canadian welfare state and the social citizenship rights it conferred were a long time in coming and not particularly generous when they did arrive. Indeed, the consolidation of Canada's social programs into a form that might be recognized as a national welfare state did not occur until the late 1960s, the moment at which the crisis of the welfare state is often said to have begun. Among the key programs of the Canadian welfare state were:

- Unemployment Insurance 1940 and greatly expanded in 1971
- Family Allowance 1949
- Canada Pension Plan/Quebec Pension Plan 1966
- *Medical Care Act* 1966
- Canada Assistance Plan (CAP) 1966

The delay in establishing the Canadian welfare state is generally explained by the obstacle of the Canadian constitutional division of powers. The *Constitution Act*, 1867 places responsibility for social programs squarely in the purview of provincial governments, though their capacity to finance these programs was severely constrained by their limited revenues. The federal government, by contrast, had the revenue-generating capacity and a growing sense that its legitimacy would require the implementation of national social programs, but no constitutional authority to do so. In the case of unemployment insurance, this impasse was breached through constitutional amendment. In virtually every other situation, however, national social policy was achieved through federal–provincial negotiations and the implementation of the federal spending power.

Another important factor contributing to the laggardly establishment of the Canadian welfare state is related to the British colonial heritage of liberalism. Suspicion of the state and the belief that the unregulated market would deliver the greatest good to the greatest number of people were deeply ingrained within the policies of the Canadian government. Certainly the Great Depression had given cause to question this faith in the market and to recommend the state as the only institution suitably powerful to deliver adequate relief for market failures. But the older ideas lingered. Indeed, the echo of laissez-faire liberalism has contributed to Canada's designation as a residual, or liberal, welfare state (Esping-Andersen, 1990) in which few social programs are universally available, citizens with adequate resources are expected to purchase required social services in the market, and those who lack adequate financial resources must prove their need in order to benefit from the public system. As the Australian sociologist Anna Yeatman has argued, this residualism contributes to a situation in which market-provided services are accredited a kind of moral superiority while publicly provided services are deemed inferior, catering to those who have failed to make the market work for them (1994, 77).

The peculiar shape of the Canadian economy also contributed to the unique pace of development of the national welfare state. In terms of economic management, the purpose of welfare state policies was to counterbalance the boom and bust cycles of a capitalist economy by ensuring a relatively consistent level of demand. Following the logic of Keynesian economic management, national governments implemented policies that maintained full employment and ensured that, in times of recession, citizens would continue to have the resources necessary to fuel the economy. Public coffers drained during hard times would be replenished through economic growth and subsequent taxation in good times. In Canada, however, the theory came up against some significant obstacles. Keynesianism was developed for relatively closed national economies. The Canadian economy, however, relied on the export of natural resources to fuel its growth. As a result, the Canadian government's capacity to manipulate demand through employment and taxation policies was circumscribed, since demand was largely a function of the international market rather than the domestic one.

Further, the relative weakness and geographical concentration of Canada's manufacturing sector also limited the efficacy of Keynesianism, which was designed around a mass production and mass consumption industrial model in which the buying power of industrial workers was central to the continued growth of the economy. This gave workers considerable political power, since the withholding of their labour would stifle both production and consumption. In Canada, however, the manufacturing sector did not stand on its own but was intimately tied to the products necessary for the extraction of natural resources and for natural resource processing (Watkins, 1997, 28). As a result, workers in the manufacturing sector were not viewed as integral and independent contributors to the country's economic growth, but rather, as one more economic interest whose political legitimacy was subjected to regular contestation. The Canadian economy's dependence on resources and the distribution of resources through geographic lottery meant that regional, rather than class affiliations, were the defining cleavages of Canadian society (Jenson, 1989, 81). As a consequence, the political power of workers and the generosity of the welfare state were much less significant in Canada than in Western Europe.

Despite all of the obstacles to its creation, a welfare state did eventually emerge in Canada. In no small measure, its development can be tied to the Quiet Revolution and Quebec's desire to use the provincial state to secure and maintain a distinctive Québécois culture. As a means to quell Quebec's disenchantment with its historic treatment by English Canada and integrate the province into the broader Canadian community, the Liberal governments of Lester Pearson undertook a series of social policy initiatives in the 1960s that attempted to establish relatively uniform services across the country while also acknowledging Quebec's desire to administer these programs in its own jurisdiction and the constitutional authority of the provinces. Perhaps the most familiar example of this policy thrust can be seen in Canada's old age pension plan. With the exception of Quebec, the federal government administers the Canada Pension Plan in all of the provinces. In Quebec, the program is provincially administered, run with federal funds, and known as the Quebec Pension Plan.

In other cases, such as the *Medical Care Act* and the Canada Assistance Plan, the federal government provided funding to the provinces, which then administered programs designed to address local circumstances. In order to obtain the federal funding, however, the provinces had to abide by unilaterally imposed, federally mandated national standards. Through the use of its spending power and the age-old principle of "he who pays the piper calls the tune," the federal government was able to circumvent the constitutional division of powers and establish a national welfare state. As the programs were implemented, however, both the federal and provincial governments expressed growing concern. The federal government was particularly vexed by its lack of control over the total budget for programs, since the funding formula under both CAP and the *Medical Care Act* involved a 50/50 split with the provinces but without an upper limit on spending. Provinces felt little obligation to maintain fiscal prudence since they were assured that the federal government would contribute 50 percent of the funding as long as the basic standards were maintained (Silver, 1996, 71). The provinces, and especially Quebec, argued that the federally concocted initiatives had little relevance to specific local situations and sensitivities, although such views were not always uniformly shared by provincial residents. Feminist groups, in particular, used these differences of opinion to lobby for services such as childcare in situations in which the provincial government was unlikely to provide the service on its own but might be persuaded with the help of federal dollars.

As this brief discussion of the federal spending power suggests, the understanding of equality operative in Canadian social policies was also infused with the nation-building objective. Equality, in as disparate a federation as Canada, was not a term that implied sameness, except at the most general level of funding formulas and basic standards. Provinces insisted that both their constitutional authority and their proximity to citizens gave them an important level of decision-making autonomy. Given Canada's constitutional realpolitik, it is not surprising that the federal government targeted its equality initiatives at the level of regions as well as at individuals. Flattening income gaps between rich and poor areas of the country through transfer payments and strategic spending initiatives, and between rich and poorer citizens through taxation and income replacement programs, ensured that the federal government would continue to be relevant. Perhaps the most familiar and oft-cited example of such a policy purpose is offered by the regionally specific provisions of the Unemployment Insurance (UI) program. In areas of the country in which unemployment rates were high, especially in Atlantic Canada, the number of weeks of work required for insurance eligibility was fewer than in areas of lower unemployment. As a result, unemployment insurance functioned as a support to the seasonal employment of the fisheries and sustained the social structure of Atlantic Canada despite the tenuous economic viability of the region.

Of course, individuals and citizen groups did not necessarily accept the limits of the nation-building purpose and, particularly outside Quebec, used the federal government's thirst for legitimacy to advance political projects that addressed non-regional social cleavages. In this way, feminists were able to demonstrate that many Canadian social policies displayed a bias towards the nuclear family unit supported by a sole, white, male breadwinner. As a result of this presumption, the social policies accessed by women, such as Family Allowance, were much less generous than those available to men, since the policy design presumed that women would be able to rely on their spouses to support them. Women who participated in waged work were presumed to do so to acquire pocket money and not because their wages were essential to maintaining the family income. Hence, women's low wages and concentration in particular job categories were claimed to be justifiable. However, once women succeeded in persuading decision-makers that some families depended on two incomes, or on the income of women alone, and that the opportunities for women and racial minorities in the workplace were circumscribed by policies and attitudes that were unrelated to the abilities of specific individuals, new social policies emerged, including maternity-leave, employment equity, and pay equity.

Social citizenship under the Canadian welfare state, then, can be characterized by its integration into the project of nation building, by its regional focus, and by a steady challenge to its shortcomings by groups who did not feel that their aspirations for equality were being met through the nation-building initiative. Of course, not all of these initiatives undertaken by citizens groups were successful, while those that did find their way into public policy bore the marks of the political purposes of elected representatives and the limits of available resources. Nonetheless, a key feature of Canadian citizenship was the expectation that the state had an obligation to listen to and address the demands of its citizens concerning their social well-being. In the current moment, the state's social obligation to the equality of both citizens and regions is rapidly diminishing. Citizens are being encouraged to make use of the market and their familial resources to address their needs in good times and in crisis. Provinces and regions are expected to rely on their own economies to sustain social programs.

CONTEMPORARY SOCIAL POLICY

Among the primary elements contributing to the reform of social citizenship in Canada are the increased globalization and continental integration of the Canadian economy; a subsequent desire, on the part of decision-makers, to remove the state from the sightlines of political controversy; and a new approach to national unity issues that focuses on decentralization rather than nation building. Some commentators have also pointed to various alterations in Canadian social structure, including the increased participation of women in the labour force, more single mothers, and higher rates of divorce as precipitating the need for new social policies. However, when we examine the social policy reforms that have been undertaken, this latter set of motivations is almost undetectable. Instead, social policy is increasingly geared towards enhancing Canada's attractiveness to global investment. At its most basic, this policy objective is achieved by reductions to social spending, but it is also detected in weaker protections for the unemployed and the emergence of more punitive social assistance regimes at the provincial level, as national standards have been abandoned. In a more positive, but largely rhetorical policy direction, the federal government has emphasized the importance of advanced training and education, has promised increased funding for research and development, and established the Millennium Scholarship Fund.

The link between reduced social spending and Canada's attractiveness to international investors lies in the state of the country's finances. Although Canada has recently attained a budget surplus, a 20-year history of budget deficits and indebtedness to foreign lenders decreased the country's capacity to undertake an autonomous policy agenda. Developments in the international political economy that increasingly entwined national and provincial governments as well as individual citizens in the whimsy of stock and

TABLE 11-1 Types of Social Programs

Universal Programs Services provided to all citizens within a particular category, regardless of income. Canadian examples include healthcare, and primary and secondary education.

Means Tested Programs Services provided to citizens who are able to prove that they do not have sufficient financial resources to acquire basic necessities. That is, they lack the means to purchase services in the market. Childcare subsidies and eligibility for public housing are examples.

Needs Tested Programs Services provided to citizens on the basis of the source of their need, or whether their need is considered worthy. For example, people with disabilities are entitled to a federal tax credit and provincial income support and assistance if they can prove that their physical or mental limitations prevent them from earning a living.

currency trading further constrained the range of options available to governments. The need to ensure investor confidence in order to prevent a sell-off of the national currency and to encourage investment in Canadian enterprises meant that governments felt obliged to pursue policies that would elicit positive response from international markets. Moreover, many of Canada's elected officials, state bureaucrats, and extra governmental power brokers supported the constraint of Canadian political decision making by the discipline of the globalizing market. In the minds of some of these people, welfare state policies had created a dependent citizenry with an unquenchable thirst for public resources. The means to break this dependency, and hence reduce the strain on the public accounts, was tied to a series of initiatives that reduced the overall level of government spending and attempted to persuade Canadians that their personal well-being was a matter of individual responsibility. Citizens had to be convinced that the best thing that governments could do to protect the interests of citizens was to safeguard the market. A strong economy would equip citizens with the tools to make their lives better.

As noted earlier, this emphasis on the importance of the market and employment was not, in fact, a radical departure from the foundations of the welfare state. What has altered, however, is the commitment to equality of both regions and individuals, and the integrity of the safety net that was to protect Canadian citizens when markets weakened and employment prospects dwindled. This weakening of the equality principle and the safety net is manifested in a number of policy reforms including the abolishment of CAP and the creation of the Canada Health and Social Transfer (CHST); the conversion of Unemployment Insurance into Employment Insurance; and the creation of a series of tax measures, some of which have served to replace universal benefits with means-tested benefits, such as old age security and family allowance (now the Canada Child Benefit) and others which may abolish public services and replace them with tax credits to individuals.

In broad terms, there have been two approaches to policy reform—incremental, technical changes that have been dubbed "the politics of stealth" or "death by a thousand cuts" and more dramatic overhauls of social provision. As Battle and Torjman have persuasively argued, stealth is the preferred technique since it draws the government into the least amount of controversy (Battle and Torjman, 1996, 53). In those cases in which more overt initiatives have been undertaken, other political motivations, such as creating distance from the policies of previous governments and courting the favour of particular sectors of Canadian society, have recommended a bolder approach. As an example of the politics of stealth, the Mulroney government ended the universality of old age security payments by continuing to provide senior citizens with regular payments, but increasing the rate of taxation such that higher-income seniors effectively had their cheques "clawed back." Hence, the program continued to appear universal on the surface, but was, in fact, means-tested at tax time. The CHST, by contrast, represents a much more significant alteration in the federal government's commitment to the social welfare of Canadian citizens. Under the CHST, the federal government provides the provinces with a combination of cash and tax points (the federal government reduces its level of taxation in order for the provinces to take it up, but with no alteration to the overall level of taxation for Canadians) in order to fund provincial social programs. The amount of money available is unilaterally fixed by the federal government, and, at least as it was initially proposed, decreases over time such that federal transfers would be almost insignificant to provincial social assistance budgets.

The consequences of this new funding mechanism are serious. Since the federal government has greatly reduced its financial contribution to social programs, it has lost the authority to impose national standards on the provinces. Indeed, the only standard of CAP that remains under the CHST is that provinces cannot impose a residency requirement on recipients. Provinces can now exclude assistance applicants on the basis of the source of their need and require them to work in exchange for their cheques. Moreover, applicants and recipients are not guaranteed a right of appeal if they feel they have been treated unfairly. Because the CHST comes in the form of a block grant and is transferred to the general revenues of the provinces, there is little oversight available to citizens or to the federal government regarding the programs in which the money is actually invested. Fewer federal guidelines and less money also mean that the provinces have been forced to reduce or eliminate social programs, among the most notable being public housing. Money available to social assistance programs has been substantially reduced, a policy decision made all the more strategically compelling due to public anxiety concerning funding for the poor. Social assistance payments, historically pegged below the poverty line, have now fallen even further. As social transfers decrease and income tax breaks for the highest income earners come into effect, the polarization of income between the poorest and wealthiest Canadians is increasing. Finally, because the CHST is a fixed sum, the amount of money transferred to the provinces does not alter in accordance with fluctuations in the strength of the economy. When citizens face economic crisis due to market downturns, the provinces will have to bear the burden of increased demand for social services on their own (Prince, 1999, 179).

Although the federal government recognized that its diminished contribution to social services undermined its claim to impose national standards on social welfare programs, it has not made a similar concession in the area of healthcare. The five principles of the *Canada Health Act* (CHA), listed in Table 11.2, have been maintained, largely because of overwhelming public support for a publicly funded health system. Yet despite this support and official commitment to national standards, erosion of the healthcare system is also evident. Many provinces have excluded particular treatments and diagnostic services from their lists of insured services, thus undermining the principle of comprehensiveness. In turn, private sector providers have stepped in to address the demand, but require patients to pay a fee. Although the payment of fees contravenes the accessibility clause of the CHA and private facilities appear to contravene the notion of public administration, the fact that the services being offered are no longer found on the list of insured services means that the work of these private clinics inhabits an ambiguous realm in the legislation.

Because healthcare is an issue of such political importance to voters, both federal and provincial politicians wish to have the actions of their respective levels of government appreciated by their constituents. At the same time, however, fiscal austerity is a paramount objective. Tensions have increased as the federal government has decreased its level of funding and provinces have scrambled to cope, with both levels of government insisting that they respect the desire of Canadians for a universal, public healthcare system. Given the tensions in the system, it is not surprising that some gaps in the universality principle are beginning to emerge. Despite the political rhetoric, then, the question remains open as to whether governments will see the solution to the fiscal challenges posed by healthcare as lying in the reinforcement of the public system, or in the emergence of a private tier of provision. Given the centrality of universal, public healthcare to the Canadian identity, the resolution of this funding crisis will have an impact that extends well beyond the health of Canadians.

Reforms to the Unemployment Insurance program (UI) implemented in 1996 also indicate a remaking of the Canadian social citizenship regime in response to the pressures

TABLE 11-2 National Standards

Medical Care Act 1966 (revised as *Canada Health Act* 1984)

1. *Universality:* all provincial residents must be covered under uniform terms and conditions.
2. *Accessibility:* services should be provided in a manner that does not impede or preclude, whether by fees or other means, reasonable access to insured services.
3. *Portability:* all Canadians can receive healthcare services across Canada regardless of their province of residence.
4. *Comprehensiveness:* all approved hospital services and physician services are to be covered.
5. *Public Administration:* each provincial plan must be publicly administered on a non-profit basis without the involvement of the private sector.

Canada Assistance Plan 1966

Residency: provinces cannot impose a minimum residency requirement on Canadian citizens seeking assistance.

Eligibility: Canadians who lack financial resources can qualify for assistance regardless of the cause of that need.

Right of Appeal: assistance recipients are entitled to challenge decisions made with respect to their cases.

Source: Compiled from Silver, 1996, 69.

of globalization. The original funding model for UI included contributions from the federal government, employers, and employees. As an insurance program, UI was designed to allow workers to draw a percentage of their earnings from the insurance pool, to which they had previously contributed, in times of temporary unemployment. In this way, workers and their families were kept from destitution and money continued to flow in the economy. In the early 1970s, the program was reformed to include maternity benefits, and, as noted earlier, measures to offset regional disparities emerging from the seasonal character of employment in some areas of the resource sector. More recently, and under more dire economic circumstances, changes to the program undertaken by the Mulroney government resulted in the elimination of federal financial contributions to its key components, a reduction in benefits, and more arduous conditions for eligibility (Prince, 1999, 180). The subsequent Liberal government undertook even more far-reaching reforms, further reducing benefits and increasing the amount of time required in order to qualify. As a result of the changes undertaken throughout the 1990s, the number of workers who qualified to receive benefits fell from 83 percent of unemployed Canadians in 1989 to 42 percent in 1997 (Prince, 1999, 181).

As the Minister of Finance recently acknowledged, these changes to the unemployment insurance system have exerted a disproportionate disadvantage on women. More hours of work were required in order to qualify for maternity benefits, and because women with young children are more likely to be employed part-time rather than full-time in order to accommodate the demands of their families, the program changes mean that many women found themselves ineligible for maternity-leave benefits. Others were obliged to delay childbearing in order to ensure that they would qualify. Although the federal government has subsequently improved the maternity-leave provisions, allowing leave for a period of 50 weeks, and reducing the number of hours one is required to have worked in order to qualify from 700 to 600, the level of benefits remains at 55 percent of wages. Not surprisingly, single mothers have been particularly hard hit and are now the poorest of the poor in Canada.

Yet the level of social control exerted by alterations to unemployment insurance have not been limited to maternity benefits or to women. At a more general level, these changes can be read as a means of ensuring that Canadian workers are willing to accept lower paying jobs and to tolerate unsatisfying, if not unsafe, work. According to the new rules, workers are only eligible to claim EI if they have been laid off from their positions. Hence, workers who are harassed by their employers or fellow workers (often due to gender, race, or sexuality), who find that their skills are inadequately utilized, or who are regularly expected to perform tasks that are outside of the terms of their job descriptions have their options severely constrained. Resignation means an absence of income. Moreover, in a competitive labour market, the possibility of finding alternative employment quickly also may be limited. Additional changes to the program, including the reduction in benefits from 60 to 55 percent of earnings and the reduction in the duration of benefits from 50 to 45 weeks also ensure that workers will be more willing to comply with the demands of their employers (Prince, 1999, 181).

In addition to program changes, the transformation of social citizenship has also been undertaken through tax reform measures. The income tax system is not a new player in the realm of social policy. Indeed, a progressive income tax has been the grease of welfare state programs since their inception. Moreover, like social programs, the design of tax systems has reflected contemporary thinking regarding appropriate familial relations and gender roles. What is different about current uses of the tax system, however, is the degree to which tax returns increasingly represent the actual delivery of social policy. In the context of the CHST and the federal government's diminished contribution to the public delivery of social programs, income tax initiatives such as the Child Care Expense Deduction can be viewed as a means to support the purchase of services in the market. Such tax measures represent a form of rebate for services deemed to have a social benefit, but that are provided by private interests rather than the state. Rather than the state directly incurring the expense of a national daycare program, for example, the market receives an indirect stimulus to provide increased childcare services. The success of such provisions relies on the capacity of the market to receive the signal. If the supplement is insufficient to stimulate supply or if other, more deeply rooted market imperfections come into play, such as sexism, the success of such measures may be limited. Certainly the inadequacy of childcare in many Canadian centres and the shortcomings of the federal government in addressing child poverty points to existing limitations in the general realm of child benefits. Indeed, in 1998, 18.8 percent of Canadian children lived in poverty (National Council on Welfare, 1998).

Perhaps the strongest examples of this new approach to social policy delivery through the tax system are the Registered Retirement Savings Plan (RRSP) and the Registered Education Savings Plan (RESP). Underlying these plans is the presumption that publicly supported pension plans and post-secondary institutions will continue to be undermined by reduced funding. In part, this lack of funds results from the demographics of an aging population, but as Gosta Esping-Andersen has argued, the advancing years of the baby boomers do not necessarily imply crisis. Rather, the cost of an aging population depends on long-run economic growth and political management (Epsing-Andersen, 1996, 7). In the contemporary Canadian context, however, political decision-makers assert that the market offers citizens a wider range of options, that the needs of increasingly diverse populations cannot be addressed through standard social service delivery methods, and that increased taxation is a political non-starter. In this context, a citizen-directed approach to social policy recommends itself. Of course, providing citizens with the opportunity to manage their own retirement and education savings does allow them to seek out the greatest return on investment that their tolerance for risk can withstand. Additionally, however, it places the blame for the failure of those investments, whether because of market downturns or unfortunate investment decisions, squarely on the shoulders of individuals. If retirees, for example, discover that they have not adequately provided for their non-working years, public pensions will provide little comfort.

In the case of RRSPs, this policy shift towards increased personal responsibility for financial well-being in retirement is indicative of the abandonment of collective responsibility that underscored welfare state policies in favour of the individualism of neoliberal social policy. While many welfare state policies fell short of their objectives, Canada's efforts to raise its elderly population out of poverty was, by most accounts, its greatest social policy success. Moreover, it was an initiative that rested on the collective responsibility of Canadians to provide for their elderly, in return for similar support upon reaching retirement age. RRSPs, by contrast, have no foundation in collective responsibility. One earns, saves, and, given the popularity of mutual funds as the RRSP investment vehicle of choice, rests one's future on optimistic prospects for the performance of financial and equity markets. Whether this shift towards individual responsibility will be successfully entrenched, however, is not yet clear. It remains to be seen whether it will be politically feasible to insist that the elderly fend for themselves, particularly when one considers the electoral clout of as large a group of elderly as the baby boomers will represent.

In terms of improving the well-being of citizens, the use of the tax system as a delivery vehicle for social policy does offer some advantages. Under the welfare state, the granting of benefits was subject to the whims of individual social workers, allowing for considerable inconsistency in the determination of who qualified for benefits (Myles, 1996, 123). Relying on a tax return rather than a highly subjective application process is thus a real improvement in terms of the personal experience of accessing the system. Additionally, it allows low- as well as middle- and high-income citizens to determine their needs and to address them in the, purportedly, option-filled marketplace. On the other hand, the disciplining of citizens through the use of the tax system may be as intense as its welfare state precursor, and all the more menacing because of the lack of opportunity to confront it. For example, the fact that poor parents in the workforce receive a supplement to the Child Benefit that is not available to unemployed poor parents sends the clear message that employment is what the government expects of its citizens, even when there are children to attend to. The fact that a tax return offers no opportunity for unemployed parents to explain the cause of their lack of work (which might relate to inadequate childcare) underscores the shortcomings of this impersonal approach to social provision and the potentially incorrect assumptions upon which specific measures are based.

THE CONSEQUENCES FOR CITIZENSHIP

The social policy reforms undertaken in the last decade represent an attempt to address, in a radically new way, the particularities of life in a resource-based, export-led economy dominated by competitive federalism, a lurking national unity crisis, and increasing social cleavages. Rather than continuing with the fractious and seemingly thankless task of seeking to forge a collective identity and a relatively uniform national citizenship through the construction of national social programs, recent Canadian governments have sought to navigate this rocky political terrain through a strategy of individualization, decentralization, and privatization. As might be expected, the outcomes have varied widely depending upon one's location within Canadian society.

Recent media reports indicate that Canadians are feeling optimistic about their future prospects but are also experiencing high levels of stress (Edwards and Mazzuca, 2000). Canada's impressive levels of economic growth, decreasing rate of unemployment, and budget surpluses in the national accounts are important contributors to this optimism. As for the stress, stagnant wages, increased time demands on families as a result of decreased funding, and the elimination of many social programs are contributing factors. Canadians must work longer hours in order to ensure adequate savings to meet their long-term needs and those of their family members. Schools, hospitals, shelters, and other service agencies are in need of volunteer labour. Further, these increased time pressures, in conjunction with government hostility towards advocacy organizations and a fostering of public mistrust towards "special interest groups," have meant fewer opportunities for people to participate in political action and in the democratic life of their communities. As Jane Jenson and Susan Phillips have observed, the role of organized interests in the current era is to represent the state in civil society rather than the other way around. Advocates for social change are no longer viewed as legitimate, but groups that provide services formerly viewed as the responsibility of the state enjoy enhanced relevance (Jenson and Phillips, 1996, 129).

The adoption of neoliberal principles of governance in Canada has meant that citizens must now prove their worthiness to receive social entitlements, rather than obtaining the benefits of social citizenship as a function of the state's need to demonstrate its relevancy to the lives of the citizens it governs. Worthiness is determined on the basis of one's economic contribution (Brodie, 1997, 239) and hence the benefits of citizenship are increasingly individualized. The more money one makes, for example, the more one is entitled to enjoy the tax deductions that derive from RRSP contributions and later, a more prosperous retirement. Such benefits are seen as incentives designed to encourage Canadians to work harder, invest more, and subsequently fuel the economy. But such incentives rest on the presumption that all Canadians enjoy the same opportunities and that talent is evenly distributed among the population. A condition of equal opportunity, however, is not a natural state. Without a national commitment to ensuring these opportunities, the capacity of Canadians as a society to meet the demands of globalization will be weakened.

CONCLUSION

The reduction of federal funding and the diminishment of national standards have meant that the content of social citizenship in Canada is much less uniform across the country than it once was. It would appear that the nation-building objective of previous federal governments has been largely relinquished. In the late 1990s, Canada's first ministers signed the Social Union Framework Agreement (SUFA), which was designed to breathe coherence back into Canada's social policy regime. While the Social Union Framework Agreement might be viewed as an attempt to rethink decentralization and reinvigorate a national social project, its focus is on the process of policy making rather than the content. SUFA does not articulate a substantive commitment to social citizenship. Its concern is that the various parties receive adequate notification when alterations to social policy rights are undertaken and that all provinces receive the same treatment. Nonetheless, Canada is becoming increasingly regionalized and the only hope of addressing the social exclusion of poorer areas and poorer citizens in the long term is said to lie in enhanced economic competitiveness. It is in this formulation of the decreased power of the federal government that one might be tempted to proclaim the death of the Canadian nation state, just as globalization proclaims the death of the nation state more broadly.

And what of citizenship? On this score, perhaps, some argue there is a new form emerging—a global citizen whose primary allegiance is to hospitable investment climates, or, alternately, to the protection of the environment and human rights through international coalitions. On the other hand, the continued need for, reform to, and surveillance over social services suggest some kick remains in the Canadian state. Indeed, recent social policy reforms have enhanced the state's discretion in determining who may take advantage of the opportunities it provides and who may not, who is worthy of care, education, and a helping hand and who is not. Hence, the state continues to exert ongoing and significant power over the life chances of the individuals who reside within its boundaries.

Recent budget surpluses and improving economic indicators have created an opening for the discussion of social policy and social citizenship in Canada. The terms of the debate are decidedly constricted by the form of Canada's integration into the global economy, but there are, nonetheless, emerging opportunities to debate some new content and direction for the shape of Canadian citizenship. This debate will require us to think seriously about the meaning of our citizenship and our relationships and responsibilities to each other. Most importantly, it will involve reminding our governments that the economy should be designed to operate for the best interests of people and that it is through democratic processes that those interests are to be determined.

REFERENCES

Battle, Ken and Sherri Torjman. 1996. "Desperately Seeking Substance: A Commentary on the Social Security Review." In Jane Pulkingham and Gordon Ternowetsky (eds.), *Remaking Canadian Social Policy: Social Security in the Late 1990s.* Halifax: Fernwood.

Brodie, Janine. 1997. "Meso-Discourses, State Forms and the Gendering of Liberal Democratic Citizenship," In *Citizenship Studies 1* (2).

Canada. Human Resources Development Canada. 2001. "Maternity, Parental and Sickness Benefits." Retrieved from www.hrdc-drhc.gc.ca/ae-ei/pubs/in201_e.shtml#new

Edwards, Gary and Josephine Mazzuca. 2000. "Optimism over Future Standard of Living Continues to Climb." *Gallup Poll* 60(7): 1–2.

Esping-Andersen, Gosta. 1996. "After the Golden Age? Welfare State Dilemmas in a Global Economy." In Gosta Esping-Andersen (ed.), *Welfare States in Transition: National Adaptations in Global Economies.* London: Sage.

———. 1990. *The Three Worlds of Welfare State Capitalism.* Cambridge, Polity Press.

Jenson, Jane and Susan Phillips. 1996. "Regime Shift: New Citizenship Practices in Canada," *International Journal of Canadian Studies 14* (Fall).

Jenson, Jane. 1989. "'Different but not 'exceptional': Canada's permeable fordism," *Canadian Review of Sociology and Anthropology 26* (1).

The picture is but one example of evocations of the innocent and victimized child, often a baby and sometimes even a fetus, taking a central position in people's awareness and imagination of the nation and citizenship. Today children provide images of national vulnerability, victimization, hope, or degeneracy, as in the case of school shootings by teenagers (Scobey, 2001). Social problems such as sexual abuse of children and missing children serve as platforms for adults to constitute themselves as civic actors (Ivy, 1993).

In public policy processes, rhetoric about children can usually generate impressive justification for claims on collective resources (Best, 1990). For example, Child Poverty Action Groups in Britain and Canada have achieved some success when they deliberately choose a child-centred argument for government support for the poor. The symbol of suffering children has worked as a way of keeping unpopular issues like poverty on the public agenda in the midst of the New Right backlash against the welfare state (McGrath, 1997). At the same time, neoliberal restructuring of the child protection system in the province of Ontario has also deployed a child-centred approach, producing a dichotomy in which children are construed as the deserving clients, and parents the undeserving villains. In a similar vein, the federal Department of Justice is considering creating child-specific offences such as child homicide, which would make the murder of a child worthy of harsher punishment than that of an adult.

In effect, what has emerged in recent years is the notion of the child-citizen. The newborn child-citizen is embedded in the public policy rhetoric of both left-wing advocacy groups and right-wing governments. In citizenship studies much has been written on the constitution of the active, self-reliant, and responsible worker citizen, in relation to the diminishing sovereign state. It would be incorrect, however, to think that there are no neoliberal citizens who can expect provisions from the state. The state is not dead and neither is the citizen who can lay claim on the state. This citizen, however, is different. Certain citizen identities, such as the soldier-citizen, the worker-citizen, and the parent- (more accurately, mother-) citizen have seen their postwar entitlements eroded (Turner, 2000). At the turn of the twenty-first century, a new citizen identity for making "legitimate" claim on the state—the child-citizen—has been constituted through discursive practices. Innocence and victimization constitute the ethical and political foundation of the child-citizen's claim on the public agenda and entitlement to collective resources. Like the baby-victim of the terrorist attacks, children are blameless victims of, to name a few things, poverty, abuse and neglect, drunken driving, and smoking in restaurants. Children's victimization often presupposes losing the much-fetishized quality of innocence. The innocent, victimized child is a rare subject who can pass neoliberal scrutiny and be recognized as the citizen with legitimate entitlements.

Prior to the ascendance of neoliberalism, substantive aspects of citizenship, particularly the rights connected with being a citizen, were defined from the standpoint of adults, hence the aforementioned soldier-citizen, worker-citizen, and mother-citizen. In that sense modern citizenship in Western liberal states was a universal adult model (Ignatieff, 1995). Social and political theorists writing on citizenship and its transformation often do not feel the need to make the adult standpoint of modern citizenship explicit or to examine the possible shift of the adult standpoint. The debates on citizenship are mainly preoccupied with the erosion of social citizenship rights (for adults), claims to differentiated citizenship by women and other marginalized groups, and the implications of globalization processes for national citizenship. The birth of the child-citizen raises several theoretical issues that should be taken seriously in citizenship studies. Principal among these are the ways that the identity of the child-citizen is constituted; the effects of the child-citizen identity on the identity of adults in the configuration of relationship between individual citizens and the state; and the implications of the paradox that child-citizens cannot yet act as citizens and thus their entitlements have to be defined and asserted by adults and the state. Exploring these issues will extend the now familiar analyses of neoliberal disentitlement to a critique of neoliberal criteria of entitlement (for example innocence and victimization), examine the inclusive and exclusive consequences of such criteria, and reveal the neoliberal imagination of the entitled but infantile, passive, and helpless citizen. Discussions along these lines are important not only for students of citizenship theory, but also for social activists whose child-centred advocacy may play directly into neoliberal citizenship politics.

This chapter develops a critical analysis of the child-victim citizen, drawing upon child protection ideas and practices in Ontario in particular and in Canada more generally. The objective is to make a case for scholars who are engaged in debates about the transformation of citizenship to take an interest in both the history and current practices of child protection, given the way in which protecting innocent children from various forms of violence and ensuring their personal safety has become crucial to citizenship today. As Kymlicka and Norman note recently (2000), citizenship can be used to refer to a wide variety of ideas, concepts, and values. Here there is an emphasis on three interlinked aspects of citizenship that have been noticeably redefined through the discourse of the innocent child-victim at the turn of the twenty-first century—the ideal citizen identity; the distribution of citizenship rights and obligations along the adult/child line of division; and political participation of adults as civic actors in the name of children. However, before discussing those issues in detail, the chapter provides a sketch of an earlier discourse of children as "future citizens" framed within the adult model of citizenship and the nation-building project at the turn of the twentieth century. This format follows the Foucaultian "history of the present" approach (Foucault, 1977), in that it uses selective historical analyses to develop a critical understanding of the transformation of today's citizenship ideas and practices and the crucial position of the innocent child-victim. The main value of that exercise is to put in place some historical distance for us to see our present conception of children as citizens in a more skeptical light. Then, the second section focuses on the constitution of the innocent child-victim as the ideal citizen during the last decade of the twentieth century and the beginning of the twenty-first century, a route which seems to be the most, if not the only, legitimate one for making ethical and political claims on the state and the collective. Drawing on the case of Ontario's Child Welfare Reform (1997–2000), the chapter will discuss how in the same area of child protection the child is reconceptualized as the child-citizen bearing rights to "personal safety," as opposed to the "citizen in the making" who did not have individual rights. The effects of children's identity as proper citizens with rights will be assessed in contrast to children's identity as "future citizens" without independent status in the earlier period. The main argument of this chapter is that there is a historical quality to the identity of the innocent child-victim citizen at the turn of the twenty-first century. The crucial position of children in contemporary citizenship politics in Canada as well as other Western liberal states signifies profound transformation of citizen identities, ownership of rights and obligations, and modes of power for governing individuals at large in the "post-social" era. It also argues that people on the political Left who are struggling to fight the New Right erosion of citizenship rights should be more reflective about mobilizing behind the rhetoric of children's rights.

CHILDREN AS "FUTURE CITIZENS"

Throughout the history of Western political history, children have been excluded from citizenship. Much historical work has documented campaigns for citizenship waged by various groups of adult non-citizens, among them slaves, women, and resident aliens, and the consequent expansion in the twentieth century of citizenship rights to virtually all natural-born adults and naturalized residents (Turner, 1986). Although children remained non-citizens in the midst of nation building at the turn of the twentieth century, they were recognized as future citizens, or citizens in the making. This identity shaped the political rationality of child-saving and provided a discursive site for fostering good citizenship among adults.

Building a nation with a useful, strong, and Christian citizenry was the overall objective of social and moral reform in urban English Canada at the turn of the twentieth century. The reform sought to purify and reshape individual ethics so as to raise the moral tone of Canadian society in general and working-class communities in particular (Valverde, 1991). Unlike the influential Marshallian understanding of citizenship in terms of rights that was typical of the second half of the twentieth century, the discourse of citizenship during the nation-building and reform eras was about the virtues of citizens. Since this earlier discourse about citizenship virtues was situated in the context of overarching concern with the collective, it is also different from today's New Right discourse on citizenship virtues which downplays the collective and emphasizes individual economic liberty and responsibility.

As part and parcel of the broader reform, the child-saving movement was conceptualized within the framework of building national citizenship. Its aim was to ensure that children would grow up to be good citizens, as opposed to worthless and harmful citizens. Child saving activities, undertaken by organizations such as the Children's Aid Society of Toronto, had two main components, each of which targeted a type of parenting deemed problematic. One was the protection of children from cruel treatment by parents (a predecessor of today's category of child abuse). The other, much larger part of child-saving activities concerned child neglect.

These concerns reflected a particular understanding of childhood in Europe at the time. This understanding assumed that the character was most responsive to external influences during childhood. How parents reared their children would thus have a direct and obvious impact on their adult lives (Schultz, 1995). Concerns with parenting were initially raised by clergymen and scholars who promoted the instruction and discipline of children, but condemned both excessive use of force on children and negligent parenting (which usually was regarded as a greater sin) (Ozment, 1983). The eighteenth-century notion of childhood as a moulding stage of life was adapted to the idea of children as future citizens, or citizens in the making in the nation-building project of the late nineteenth century. John Joseph Kelso, one of the most enthusiastic and compelling advocates for the child-saving movement in Canada, and broadly considered the architect of Canadian child welfare, enlightened the public and authorities in 1891 by arguing that "in the child we see the future citizen, and carrying the same principle farther we see typified in his expanding intellect the future State and nation" (Kelso Papers, 1891). How children were parented would largely determine what kind of citizens they would become.

In the child-saving discourse, gardening metaphors with English middle-class overtones were widely used to explain and promote the ideal mode of parenting. As Kelso advised, "grow your children as you grow your flowers, and you will push evil out of the world, and make a generation which will make this world a wonderful, beautiful place" (Kelso Papers, n.d.). In contrast to this ideal mode of parental power, which was intimate, gentle, intelligent, and incessant, cruel parenting erred on the side of using too much force. Neglect erred on the side of too little guidance and discipline. Both were ineffective parenting, which produced wayward children destined to become criminals, paupers, or prostitutes. In that sense, the identity of "future citizens" simultaneously signified hope and potential danger to society. While other reformers were focused on treating the criminal, the pauper, the fallen, and the drunkard, people like Kelso believed that future social problems could be prevented through saving children from bad parents and corrupting family environments. Although treatment and prevention were not contradictory, the child savers, sense of superiority about the prevention approach was obvious in Kelso's claim that "child-saving [was] universally recognized as the best philanthropic work of the age because [it was] most effective and far reaching in its results [*sic*]" (Kelso Papers, c.1910).

The child-saving movement framed its project within the context of collective interests. Children were defined as "future citizens" who represented to collectivity either "Hope of the Future" or "danger and curse" (Kelso Paper, n.d.). The reform movement's concern with bad parenting was less about the actual suffering of children caught in unfortunate circumstances than the threat that such parenting posed to the future interests of society. The primary concern for the collective was evident in the statements of the objective of the child-saving movement. These frequently and explicitly described child-saving as a means of building a better citizenry. For example, the Children's Aid Society of Toronto, first of its kind in Canada and the prototype for many across the country, chose as its motto "It is wiser and less expensive to save children than to punish criminals" (Children's Aid Society of Toronto, n.d.) to express its core belief and purpose. This core assumption contrasts greatly with the ethos of contemporary child protection which starts and stops with individual children. Furthermore, unlike today, in the early history of child protection, it was uncommon to use the language of children's rights because children were not citizens. There were occasions when children's rights were invoked, expressed as children's rights to a proper environment, appropriate parenting, and rights to moral training. As such, children's interests were, as a rule, not recognized independently, but instead were conflated with society's interests with respect to morality, order, and productivity. Children were sometimes described as victims of cruelty or neglect, but individual victimization was not the ultimate concern or the justification for intervention. Kelso, the father of the child protection system in Canada, put in unambiguous terms that the objective of child-saving was "not so much to rescue the victims of poverty, vice, and crime but rather to reach the children before they have become altogether corrupt, remove them from dwarfing, degrading influences, and train them to a useful, intelligent maturity" (*Kelso Papers,* c 1906,).

It was clear that the identity of "future citizens" accorded to children generated society's interest in their circumstances, particularly how they were treated by their parents. The motivation for societal attention, resources, and action was primarily the moral well-being of the society. Such society-oriented thinking was characteristic of the "social" era, which advocated state intervention in the "private sphere" of the family. Kelso stated in 1891 that it was "reasonable and natural to suppose that no effort will be spared by the municipality or State to see that every child, no matter what his or her misfortune of birth or environment, shall have opportunity and assistance to develop into an honest, useful and industrious citizen." In the name of the society, child-saving activities, ranging from pastoral acts such as giving advice on parenting, to discipline such as inspecting homes and issuing warnings, to the use of sovereign power in removing children from homes, were gradually put in place and spread across the country. As well, interventions with mixed purposes and effects of normalizing and providing resource support for parents, such as the Mother's Allowance program established in 1920 in Ontario, were also gradually introduced in the twentieth century. In most cases, parents were conceived of as indispensable gardeners tending to the development of children's character.

Child-saving not only worked on the "moulding" of future citizens, it was also an avenue for child savers to constitute themselves as good and civilized citizens. For one thing, the ability to see cruelty and neglect was assumed to be an indicator of child savers' civility. Cruelty and neglect both had moral connotations. Cruelty was defined as a problem with "the heart," usually of a working-class man. By the same token, cruelty was to be discerned by a civilized heart, not by a trained eye or medical evidence of bruises and fractured bones as is the case with today's child abuse cases. Neglect was almost always an accusation against a mother who was guilty of either omission of children's moral training, or active corruption of children through her own immorality. Neglectful mothers failed in taking the responsibility for building children's character and thus caused social and moral problems such as crime, dependency, and immorality. In that context, the accusation of being a bad mother in effect made the statement that the accuser identified with the proper way of parenting and was aware of the connection between parenting and societal problems. Those who cared about issues of cruelty and neglect were already good citizens in that they were concerned with the fate of the nation.

The child savers' engagement in child-saving activities and devotion of time and energy to the child-saving movement were "noble" ways to fulfill their own citizenship duties and to constitute their own identity as good Christian citizens. George Macdonald, President of a Children's Aid Society, stated in 1916 in an article titled "Real Civic Patriotism" that "before the war [World War I] perhaps there was no other work so truly and completely patriotic as the work of the Children's Aid Society. Good citizenship is admittedly the foundation of true greatness, so efforts for the making and moulding of better citizens is assuredly the highest type of noblest patriotism." When Macdonald praised Kelso, head of the child-saving movement, as the "Prince of Patriots" in the same article, he had no doubt that all child savers were model citizens because of their contribution to "building up a better citizenship and the patriotic work of the making of a greater nation." He asked rhetorically, "If this is not truly [civic] patriotic work, then what service more far-reaching in its benefits can we give for King and Country?".

To sum up, children were considered by child savers mainly as "future citizens" in contrast to proper citizens, who were, at the time, white male adults. This had specific implications for the logic of child-saving. The primary objective of child-saving was to ensure that these "future citizens" grew up to be good adults, and as such it can be argued that child-saving was undertaken from the standpoint of adulthood. Consequently, both cruelty and neglect were defined as problems from the stance of society, rather than from the lives of children. The "social" mode of thinking, which connected the conduct of individual parents and children in the private sphere with issues of society and national importance, encouraged organized collective intervention, and even allowed a consideration of resource issues in related areas. Through child-saving practices, child savers were engaged as in much in making "future citizens" as making themselves good citizens, which was, again, defined in terms of nation, the moral tone of the society, and collective greatness.

THE NEW CHILD-VICTIM CITIZEN OF THE TWENTY-FIRST CENTURY

In contrast to children's identity as "future citizens" a century ago, today's children tend to be construed as proper citizens, particularly in discussions about children's claims on the state. When children were thought of as "future citizens," children's interests were defined from the adult standpoint and were conflated with those of the society. In contrast, contemporary children are construed as citizens with rights, which are defined from the standpoint of childhood, albeit still by adults.

Since the 1980s there have been concerted efforts to promote the idea of children's citizenship rights. At the international level, the notion of the child-citizen is exemplified by the UN Convention on the Rights of the Child. Hillary Rodham Clinton's book *It Takes a Village* (1996), which includes chapters such as "Children are Citizens Too" is one of the best-known works associated with the increasing prominence of the child-citizen. As mentioned at the opening of this chapter, child poverty advocates ranging from organizations such as the Child Poverty Action Group to several parliamentary committees studying child poverty, to journalists, have argued that poor children should be entitled to public provisions. Experts on early childhood development have produced additional influential knowledge, usually of a neuroscientific kind, which calls for government programs to stimulate child development.

While all these have managed to keep problems like poverty on the public agenda, the child-centred approach has had mixed consequences. The contemporary focus on the child is by and large a political decision, seeking to "avoid the dichotomy of the 'deserving' and 'under serving' poor which has been part of social policy debates" (McGrath, 1997, 179). As Maureen Baker observes, "After all, if the focus is on children, no one can blame their poverty on laziness, lack of job skills, or defrauding the unemployment [insurance] system" (1997, 166). The notion of child poverty, while very marketable, misdirects the search for solution, as *Edmonton Journal* columnist Paula Simons shrewdly pointed out in an article on December 3, 2001. Critically responding to an *Edmonton Journal* special Sunday report on the crisis of child poverty in the city, Simons declared that, "We don't have a child poverty problem. We have a poverty problem—We can't solve the problem of 'child poverty' here at home, until we acknowledge the basic truth that poor children, universally, live in homes with poor adults [who are mostly single mothers with a lack of education and job skills]." Furthermore, the focus on children, with its emphasis on children's status as innocent victims and advocacy for their citizenship rights, has inadvertently lent support to the New Right construction of a new dichotomy which juxtaposes children as the deserving victims against parents as undeserving villains. This is played out in the recasting of child poverty as child neglect and the failures of bad mothers (McGrath, 1997).

Like child poverty advocacy, the restructuring of child protection also prided itself on its child-centred approach. If in the area of child poverty, a child-focused advocacy strategy has been co-opted by the New Right agenda, in child protection we observe an original New Right initiative of constituting the child-citizen. Ours is an era in which governments and the general public tend to think of children's rights in personal and private terms; for example in the case of child protection, children's rights specifically refer to personal safety. The society-oriented rationality in the early history of child protection can be criticized, and rightly so, as not really being about children. Nevertheless, such social rationality also allowed the gradual introduction of social services and benefits beyond child protection. Today's view of children as citizens seems progressive in that it appears to be about children. However, the conception of children as individuals bearing rights is not translated to the conception of children as autonomous individuals. Children are certainly not granted the autonomy to define their interests. In child protection procedures a child's wish is often overruled by social workers who have the ultimate authority in deciding what is in the child's best interests. The failed court fight launched by two Edmonton high school students in August 2001 to lower the voting age in municipal elections to 16, which was covered in *Edmonton Journal*, also attests to the limits of the surging notion of the child-citizen.

The discourse of the child-citizen has specific parameters. The entitlement of the child-citizen hinges on innocence and victimization. Second, it is still "expert" adults who act on behalf of children, define what counts as victimization, assess risks of harm, and decide how to prevent victimization. The difference from the earlier period is that at present this is done in the name of children's personal human rights. Third, the notion of the child-citizen operates in a neoliberal framework that enshrines individual and private goods such as personal safety. As such the neoliberal notion of children's citizenship rights tends to severely limit the scope of claims. No less importantly, it also results in positioning children's interests independently of and even in opposition to those of their parents. Parents are thus perceived as potential criminals to be risk-managed or punished, as opposed to being helped and supported through collective means.

The increasingly influential discourse of innocent children as proper citizens in their own right organizes ideas and practices involved in the restructuring of Ontario's child protection system as well as other aspects of the welfare state such as social assistance programs. This chapter will show that in the case of Ontario's Child Welfare Reform (1997-2000) the child-citizen is constituted through the innocent victim discourse. Children's citizenship rights and parents' obligations are formulated mainly in terms of the personal safety of the child. Furthermore, children are considered the most, if not the only, legitimate citizens with rights to safety and to state actions to deliver safety primarily through risk-managing parents.

THE CASE OF ONTARIO'S CHILD WELFARE REFORM

On September 18, 1996, in the midst of events leading to the Child Welfare Reform in Ontario, the headline pictures of two murdered babies hit readers of the *Toronto Star*. There were two absolutely innocent and defenceless children—one's eyes were not even open and the other was shown sucking his thumb. The caption provided their names and explained that Sara Podniewicz was six months old when she was murdered by her parents, and Johnny James died from a severe blow to the lower abdomen when he was sixteen months old. Sparked by several similar high-profile child deaths, the Ontario government launched the Child Welfare Reform, which resulted in a restructuring of the child protection system. Unlike restructuring in some other policy fields, Child Welfare Reform was characterized by the assertion of state regulatory authority and financial responsibility (Chen, 2000).

The Reform was overwhelmingly supported by the public, political parties of all stripes, the media, and the mainstream of child welfare professionals, who were united by the outrage engendered by the images and stories of murdered babies and the seemingly unassailable mission of guaranteeing children's safety. The Reform put in place a standardized risk assessment system, set up a new information database for tracking high-risk families, and amended the *Child and Family Services Act.* The major changes brought about by the amendment included a shift in emphasis from the interests of the family as a whole to the privileging of the child's best interests, recognizing "patterns of neglect" as a ground for mandatory protection services, stricter regulation of professionals' duty to report suspicions of child abuse and neglect, permanent severance of parent–child relations within a shorter time frame, and more restrictive access of family relatives or friends to children who have been made Crown wards. Together these changes will likely result in more reports of child abuse and neglect, more intervention, more children in care, and earlier permanency planning for the long-term care of children who will not return to their families.

At the provincial level similar reforms have been implemented in British Columbia. At the federal level, the Department of Justice is also taking part in the rethinking and retooling of the child protection system through its jurisdiction over criminal law. Specifically, it is conducting a "Child Victims and the Criminal Justice System" consultation which started in November 1999 and is still ongoing at the time of this writing. The consultation paper identifies three areas of possible reform of the *Criminal Code*: creation of more child-specific offences; tougher sentencing for child-specific crimes; and facilitation of child victims' testimony and assistance to child witnesses (Canada, Department of Justice, 1999).

Critics point out that the federal government's focus on creating child-specific criminal offences as well as designing punishment and deterrence mechanisms indicates a preoccupation with regulating individualized obligations owed by adults, particularly mothers, to children (Chen, forthcoming 2002). At the provincial level, the Reform will achieve little in preventing most child deaths or in improving the child protection system as was claimed to be the objective. A close look at patterns of child deaths shows that in Ontario, as in other provinces, there are many more deaths in the general population of children who have never been abused or neglected, with for example vehicle accidents being a leading cause (Chen, forthcoming 2002). As for the question of whether the Reform improves the child protection system, it is important to note that the Reform was driven by a few extreme cases which were quite isolated from the broader context. The Reform steers child protection services further in the direction of investigation, assessment, analysis, and documenting of parental inadequacy, rather than meeting the needs of the family in providing up-to-standard care for children through direct access to supplementary resources (Baines, 2000). This is particularly a problem given that "murdered babies" hardly represent the reality of the vast majority of cases in the child protection system. Data accumulated by the Ontario Child Mortality Task Force on child deaths in 1995 suggests that out of 150 000 children and youth who received child protection services only 57 died (0.038 percent). The death rate for children receiving services from the Children's Aid Society was lower than the death rate in the general population of children. As scholars have pointed out child protection cases are primarily the results of chronic poverty and the effects of associated disadvantage such as single motherhood, lack of education, substance use, mental health problems, low-standard housing, or no housing (Armitage, 1993).

If a century ago abused and neglected children were often represented by the image of a dirty-looking, ill-clothed, wayward boy posing potential harm to the society, today in the minds of Canadians the typical image of children needing protection is a baby or a young child threatened by harm, usually committed by adults but particularly by their parents. Since the 1980s, sexually abused children and missing children are two enduring images of child-victims (Best, 1990; Ivy, 1993). The image of murdered babies, the icon of the child protection restructuring, is a more recent one. In Canada, British Columbia's well-publicized Gove Inquiry on Child Protection (1995) was the first example of effecting policy and service system restructuring through a massive inquiry into the tragic death of a child involved with the child protection system. In Ontario, the same year marked the shifting attention to the issue of child deaths. Through official knowledge produced by the coroners and the Child Mortality Task Force, and no less importantly through media accounts of how children are victimized by their parents and failed by the system of child protection, Canadians conceptualize abused and neglected children in the image of murdered babies. They are ultimate innocent victims and thus the most entitled citizens.

Victimization of course is not limited to children. The rights of victims have become an effective argument in generating numerous claims on government in recent years. At a recent conference (1999) on child victimization, Anne McLellan, then Minister of Justice Canada, made her commentary on child victims in the context of the general victims' rights discourse:

> These children [when they become victims, need care and support, but they] also need a justice system that works for them. They need our commitment to continue to work for improvement and innovation in this area. Certainly, the voice of victims, including child victims, has been given greater resonance as a result of recent legislative changes.

Among various groups, however, children have become the icon of victims. Innocence is probably one of the most important ideas in the making of this icon. As Ivy observes, "[T]he child can take on the full weight of victimhood in total purity" (1993, 235). Berlant also points to the paradoxical fact that the child who is made the icon of citizen-victims happens to be incapable of acting as a citizen yet; this legitimates adults to articulate children's interests and to wage struggles on their behalf (1997). In addition to these observations, remnants of "children as future citizens" thinking from the social era also may be a factor in the iconicity of the current model citizen-victim. The value of children to the continuation of the society is still recognized to some extent. For example, Janet Ecker, the former Ontario Minister of Community and Social Services, who presided over the recent Child Welfare Reform, pleaded with her fellow members of the legislative assembly: "I know that all members will agree with me that children are Ontario's most precious asset. They deserve the best our society can provide—a loving, nurturing environment, and above all, safety and security" (Ontario Ministry of Community and Social Services, April 26, 1999). Similarly, in Justice Canada's Child Victims Consultation, references have been made to societal interests. For example, the consultation document stated that "[t]he victimization of children and young people has significant Canada, costs both for the victims and their families and for the future of our society as a whole" (Canada, Department of Justice, 1999, 26).

Children's status as innocent victims makes them the only legitimate "consumer" of the child protection system and the only ones who were failed by the system. Parents are no longer recognized as consumers of child protection services. Certainly the consumer status is fraught with neoliberal limitations (Mueltzelfelt, 2000). However, losing the consumer status is to fall into the category of the excluded. Since the late 1960s and 1970s, the rights of individual consumers have proved to be a useful conceptual and political tool in critiquing systems and programs established for the sake of society, particularly their arbitrary, repressive, and intrusive aspects. In earlier times, parents and family units considered themselves consumers and demanded rights on their own. The "due-process" and "least restrictive or disruptive" principles adopted in Ontario's *Child and Family Services Act* proclaimed in 1985 resulted from such criticisms. However, these same principles were done away with in the 1990s in the name of protecting the rights of child-consumers, whose special status as the exclusive customer is in tandem with their status as the model victim.

Children's identities as consumers of the child protection system and victims menaced by deviant parents have consequences for the distribution of entitlements and obligations. Not only are parents not recognized as consumers of the child protection system, they are represented as perpetrators of harmful acts upon child-victims. Considering problems such as child abuse and neglect in terms of child victims versus parent perpetrators individualizes the analysis of problems to the level of parents' personal pathologies and criminal acts. Thus, the individual rights of children as victims have been invoked by authorities, the media, and the public to portray parents as perpetrators "getting away with murder of children" and to justify subjecting them to harsher regulation and punishment (*Toronto Star,* 18, May, 1997).

It is also worth pointing out that the performance of service providers appears to be measured by degrees of the child's personal safety, ranging from minimum risk to death. A staff person (Karstulovich, 1999) at the Toronto Children's Aid Society noted that a child protection worker's worst fear was the death of a child. This has not always been the case. Certainly in the past some children involved with the child protection system died. It was undoubtedly considered a tragedy, but not the result of the system's or individual worker's failure. Instead, in the early period what were most likely to be considered failures on the part of the system and individual workers would be a child's "criminal career" and damage to the society despite intervention. In other words, the child protection system has not throughout its history subscribed to or been judged against the objective of delivering individual safety to children. Its current mission of "keeping children safe" is defined not from the perspective of the society or with adult-citizens in mind; instead it is formulated, albeit by adults, from the imagined perspective of individual children.

Currently, citizenship is increasingly constructed through identification with innocent children (and even innocent fetuses) (Berlant, 1997). In the earlier period, people like Kelso created themselves as proper national subjects through child-saving activities. Today's discourse about children draws upon the New Right assumption that victimization of the innocent is a result of personal criminal acts and not poverty or other structural conditions. This discourse then allows the public who read stories about murdered babies, sexually abused children, kidnapped children, or exploited children in other countries to constitute themselves as civic actors, particularly under the banner of protecting innocent child-victims. The icon of child-victim is very effective in conveying tragic feelings of loss, polarizing the dichotomy of innocence and guilt, and demanding action. Thus, child victims have become important symbols in many movements. The most familiar examples include movements against drunk driving which are organized by describing killer drunks and their child victims, and pro-life attacks on abortion in terms of millions of murdered babies (Best, 1990). Civic acts such as organizing the neighbourhood to push out the pedophile, public discussion characterized by outrage provoked by tragic stories concerning children, demands for state measures to protect children, a national agenda on children, charities in the name of children, all these have increasingly become technologies of citizenship in the sense that they generate identification with a broader, national, or even global issue—the child-victim—and supply venues for operating agency and criticism.

CONCLUSION

The birth of the innocent child-victim citizen signifies a shift in the position of children in the modern framework of citizenship. Instead of being considered "future citizens" as in the adult model of citizenship, today children are constituted as the ideal citizen, with the most legitimate entitlements. The child-citizen, first, is an innocent victim. The New Right rendition further restricts victimization to that resulting from interpersonal and criminal acts. For example, the child-citizen discourse as it operates in the site of child protection accentuates children's rights to personal safety. Children are described as citizens whose rights to personal safety are violated by their abusive and neglectful parents. Similarly, poor children are perceived as victims of lazy, irresponsible, neglectful mothers, as opposed to a result of the structural problem of poverty which mothers also suffer.

The notion of the child-citizen needs to be critically understood not just in terms of the current dominance of a particular political right-wing ideology, but also in terms of broader shifts in citizenship. If the earlier notion of children as future citizens and its associated political rationality of child-saving were representative of the "social" era, the current notion of child-victims as citizens illustrates the post-social aspects of the citizenship model at the turn of the twenty-first century. One can argue that innocence and victimization have long been two criteria for determining citizenship entitlements. A case in point is the postwar perception that the unemployed worker was a victim of economic turbulence through no fault of his own. His entitlement to public unemployment insurance benefits was part of a social rationality typical of the welfare state era. However, today's representation of victimization through the image of the child points to several changes in the citizenship model. First, the category of entitled citizens has shrunken drastically. Today's criteria of innocence and victimization have been contracted so much that only children, often young children, babies, and fetuses, can be considered innocent victims and thus entitled morally, politically, and economically. For adults to be considered entitled citizens, they have to emulate the defining features of the child-citizen—innocence and victimization. Unless adults can demonstrate childish, passive, helpless innocence and victimization, their claims on the state will have less force.

Second, citizenship is being privatized in the sense that public discussions about rights, power, ethics, and actions by the state or communities are organized by questions of personal significance at the expense of excluding questions of poverty, capitalism, racism, and so on (Berlant, 1997). This is manifested in the New Right discourse of the child-victim citizen, with its emphasis on victimization as a result of parents' personal pathology and criminality. Victimization by societal conditions such as the social-oriented understanding of the unemployed worker's misfortune is no longer regarded as valid.

Third, the conception of children as citizens with rights, anchored in innocence and victimization, operates to position individuals in a dichotomy of victims and perpetrators—children victims with rights vs. parent perpetrators. The conceptual division between victims and perpetrators produces new differentiated relationships between the state and individuals: innocent young children as the icon of victims, hence the model citizens with rights; potential perpetrators to be risk-managed; and perpetrators to be punished in the criminal justice system.

Fourth, the objective of governance, as manifested through public policy, is to deter and punish individuals who supposedly victimize children or child-like and innocent adults. Thus, in the case of child protection, risk management and criminal punishment policies are directed at detecting risk factors of abuse and neglect and punishing offences without actually addressing problems of poverty, inadequate housing, isolation, and substance use. They also render invisible the fact that resources for meeting the needs of poor parents, mostly women unable to earn a decent wage, and their children have been drastically diminished in recent years. Structural questions of capitalism, poverty, patriarchy, and racism must be brought to the fore in discussions of what ought to constitute citizenship entitlements and obligations.

REFERENCES

Berlant, Lauren. 1997. *The Queen of America Goes to Washington City: Essays on Sex and Citizenship.* Durham and London: Duke University Press.

Best, Joel. 1990. *Threatened Children: Rhetoric and Concern about Child-Victims.* Chicago and London: University of Chicago Press.

Chen, Xiaobei. 2000 "Is It All Neo-liberal? Some Reflections on Child Protection Policy and Neoconservatism in Ontario." *Canadian Review of Social Policy,* 45–46: 237–246.

Chen, Xiaobei. Forthcoming in 2002. "Constituting Dangerous Parents through the Spectre of Child Death: A Critique of Child Protection Restructuring in Ontario." In Deborah Brock (ed.) *Making Normal: Social Regulations in Canada.* Toronto: Harcourt Canada.

Children's Aid Society of Toronto Fonds, Toronto: City of Toronto Archives.

Clinton, Hilary Rodham. 1996. *It Takes a Village: And Other Lessons Children Teach Us.* New York: Simon.

Canada, Department of Justice. 1999. *Child Victims and the Criminal Justice System: A Consultation Paper.*

Foucault, Michel. 1977. "Nietzsche, Genealogy, History." In Donald F. Bouchard (ed.) *Language, Counter-memory, Practice: Selected Essays and Interviews.* (Donald F. Bouchard and Sherry Simon, Trans.) Ithaca, New York: Cornell University Press.

Ignatieff, Michael. 1995. "The Myth of Citizenship." In Ronald Beiner (ed.) *Theorizing Citizenship.* Albany, N. Y.: State University of New York Press.

Ivy, Marilyn. 1993. *Have You Seen Me? Recovering the Inner Child in Late Twentieth-Century America.* Social Text 37: 227–252.

Kelso, John Joseph Papers. Ottawa: National Archives of Canada.

Kymlicka, Will and Wayne Norman. 2000. *Citizenship in Diverse Societies.* Oxford: Oxford University Press.

McGrath, Susan. 1997. "Child Poverty Advocacy and the Politics of Influence." In Jane Pulkingham and Gordon Ternowetsky (eds.). *Child and Family Policies.* Halifax: Fernwood Publishing.

McLellan, Anne. 1999, September 27. "Working Together for Children: Protection and Prevention," notes for an address at the Conference on Child Victimization and Child Offending. Hull, Quebec. Retrieved February 21, 2000 from http://canada.justice.gc.ca/en/news/sp/1999/sp270999.html

Ozment, Steven. 1983. *When Fathers Ruled: Family Life in Reformation Europe.* Cambridge, Mass.: Harvard University Press.

Scobey, David. 2001. "The Specter of Citizenship." *Citizenship Studies* 5(1): 11–26.

Turner, Bryan. 1986. *Citizenship and Capitalism: The Debate Over Reformism.* London: Allen & Unwin.

_____. 2000. "Cosmopolitan Virtues." In Engin Isin (ed.). *Democracy, Citizenship, and the Global City.* London and New York: Routledge.

Valverde, Mariana. 1991. *The Age of Light, Soap, and Water: Moral Reform in English Canada, 1885–1925.* Toronto: McClelland & Stewart.

WEBLINKS

Children's Aid Society of Toronto
www.torontocas.ca

Child Welfare Resource Centre
www.childwelfare.ca

The Gove Inquiry
www.qp.gov.bc.ca/gove

part three

Reinventing Governance

chapter thirteen

Canadian Federalism

The Myth of the Status Quo

Garth Stevenson

INTRODUCTION

Few myths about Canadian federalism are as persistent, and as questionable, as the myth of "the status quo." Public opinion polls, particularly in Quebec, repeatedly show that "the status quo" ranks low in popularity when included among a list of possible constitutional options. Taken at face value, these findings suggest massive dissatisfaction with Canadian federalism and an overwhelming desire for constitutional change. Paradoxically, three referenda in Quebec, and one in the rest of Canada, since 1980 have all supported "the status quo," or at least preferred it to the proposed alternative. Perhaps Canadians, despite what they hear from their political, journalistic, and academic elites, recognize that Canadian federalism is a remarkably flexible system of government that can accommodate considerable change.

If so, Canadians are right. The formal constitutional framework of Canadian federalism changed remarkably little between 1867 and 1982, apart from three amendments (in 1940, 1951, and 1964) that gave Parliament authority to legislate some portions of the modern welfare state. Further changes followed in 1982, including the introduction of a *Charter of Rights and Freedoms* that shifted some power from legislatures to courts, a clarification of provincial authority over natural resources, and an amending formula that essentially made explicit what was already the usual practice of requiring provincial consent. Two attempts to make formal changes of major significance, the

Meech Lake and Charlottetown accords, have failed since then for lack of public support, as has another attempt by the government of Quebec to secede from the federation. All in all, the formal framework for federal-provincial relations provided by sections 90 through 101, 109, 121, and 125 of the *Constitution Act* (1982) remains largely intact. Yet Canadian federalism in practice has changed almost beyond recognition since 1867. It is continuing to change and evolve at the present time, as will be discussed below.

The acceptance of the myth of the status quo in the face of fundamental change is a paradox. Another related paradox is that the few formal changes, and the far more significant informal changes to Canadian federalism, have tended to pull it in opposite directions. The few formal changes to the constitutional framework have tended to increase the authority of federal institutions over the provinces. In this respect they resemble the formal changes that have been made in other federations such as Australia and the United States. However the informal trends, especially in recent years, have tended to give the provinces, or at least the four largest ones, more autonomy. This suggests that ideological, social, and economic developments, many of them originating outside Canada, have more influence on the evolution of Canadian federalism than does the formal constitution. This is not a new observation. It was the major theme of J.R. Mallory's classic work, *Social Credit and the Federal Power in Canada,* which was first published in 1954. However, as we discover below, it is still true.

A CHRONOLOGY OF CANADIAN FEDERALISM

At the risk of some oversimplification, the history of Canadian federalism can usefully be divided into five periods of time. In the first and shortest period, from 1867 to about 1880, the reality closely resembled John A. Macdonald's dream of a powerful "General Government" with weak and subordinate provinces. J.R. Mallory has referred to this as "quasi-federalism" (1965, 3–15). Federal and provincial parties and governments were closely associated, with some politicians simultaneously occupying seats at both levels, the provincial governments collecting more from federal subsidies than from their own taxes, and the federally appointed lieutenant-governors helping to keep the provinces under tight control.

In the second period, roughly from 1880 to 1940, Canada had what Mallory and others have called "classical federalism." This means that two levels of government, equal in status, independently exercise power over their respective spheres of jurisdiction while the judiciary (in Canada's case the Judicial Committee of the Privy Council) interprets the constitution in such a way as to protect the authority and independence of each level of government against any threatened expansion of jurisdiction by the other level. The Judicial Committee described and formally endorsed this concept of federalism in two of its early decisions, *Hodge* v. *The Queen* (1883) and *Liquidators of the Maritime Bank* v. *Receiver General of New Brunswick* (1892). By the 1930s the concept, and the Judicial Committee itself, had lost popularity, and the federal government began the process of prohibiting appeals from Canada to that institution.

In the third period, from 1940 to the mid-1960s, Canada enjoyed "co-operative federalism." (Both the term and the practice were derived from the United States, which made the transition from classical to co-operative federalism in the 1930s.) Although the provinces continued to operate independently in certain areas, the federal government took the lead in managing the economy through its fiscal policy and in building the welfare state. It also assumed the dominant role in imposing direct taxes on personal and corporate incomes. Conditional grants, with which the federal government offered financial incentives for the provinces to establish programs that fell under provincial jurisdiction but contributed to national objectives, were particularly characteristic of this kind of federalism. Judicial interpretation of the constitution was not very important or influential.

The fourth period, from the mid-1960s to the mid-1980s, can best be described as "confrontational federalism." Throughout this period the federal government was engaged in a bitter struggle against separatist or quasi-separatist Quebec nationalism even though, or perhaps because, the same federal government depended on electoral support from Quebec to stay in office. For much of the time, it waged war on a second front against resource-rich western provinces whose governments at times made common cause with the Quebec nationalists. This period was marked by dramatic initiatives at both levels of government, high levels of conflict and animosity, often accompanied by rhetorical excess, diminished co-operation, and a revival of judicial influence (now exercised by the Supreme Court of Canada) over the shape of Canadian federalism. Conferences between the prime minister and the provincial premiers were held frequently and became an accepted, although not strikingly successful, way of doing business.

Since the era of confrontational federalism as defined above ended in the mid-1980s, we are now in the fifth, or possibly the sixth, of the phases through which Canadian federalism has passed. This somewhat oversimplified, but still useful, categorization of the chronological phases of Canadian federalism conceals the fact that the operation of Canadian federalism did not always have a uniform impact across the country. The western provinces, whose political and social institutions were immature and whose lands and resources (with the partial exception of British Columbia's) remained in federal hands until 1930, did not benefit fully from dual federalism until that phase had nearly ended. Quebec, especially under the rule of Maurice Duplessis and his Union Nationale, tried with some success to minimize the impact of co-operative federalism on its way of life. The Ontario government was the federal government's ally and supporter during most of the federal-provincial disputes that marked the period of confrontational federalism.

All the transitions from one phase to another were brought about by a combination of new circumstances and events, some originating within Canada and some external to it. Quasi-federalism ended with the re-emergence of competitive party politics in Ontario under Oliver Mowat, and the regional stresses created by Macdonald's National Policy, itself a response to the global depression that began in 1873. Classical federalism ended with the Second World War and the subsequent development of the Keynesian welfare state. Co-operative federalism ended with Quebec's Quiet Revolution and the subsequent energy crisis and stagflation of the 1970s. Confrontational federalism ended with the temporary exhaustion of the Quebec sovereignty movement in the mid-1980s, the sudden collapse of energy prices, and the shift by both levels of government to more market-oriented neoliberal economic policies.

The transition from each kind of federalism to its successor was probably not evident to observers at the precise time it occurred. Only in retrospect, one suspects, could each period of transition be identified for what it was. At the beginning of the twenty-first century it is not clear whether the phase that followed the end of confrontational federalism in the mid-1980s is still continuing or whether we have again moved into a new period which would be the sixth in the history of Canadian federalism. The evolution of Canadian federalism is a continuous process, and it is probably too early to assess the significance of the present situation or even to identify its most important features. What is attempted in this chapter is only a preliminary sketch, followed by some even more tentative indications of future trends.

THREE INFLUENCES ON FEDERALISM TODAY

Before examining the specific changes that have taken place in the operation of Canadian federalism, mention should be made of three ongoing circumstances that have shaped the Canadian political system since the mid-1980s and that seem almost certain to continue for the foreseeable future. These three circumstances are increasing economic integration with the United States, the almost hegemonic status of market-oriented, neoliberal, economic policies, and the unresolved problem of Quebec nationalism.

A close economic association between Canada and the United States is probably inevitable, given their geographical situation and cultural similarity, and the process of integrating the two economies has been proceeding since at least the end of the Second World War. However, until 1989 the process was gradual and the federal government of Canada took at least occasional steps to ensure that it would remain so. The Canada–United States Free Trade Agreement (CUFTA) that came into effect that year, followed by the trilateral treaty involving Mexico that replaced it a few years later (NAFTA), marked the beginning of a new phase in which the Canadian government essentially surrendered control over the speed and direction of change in this area.

The treaty prohibits many of the policies of economic nationalism by which Canadian governments historically tried to control, impede, or even reverse the process of integration. NAFTA has also had the predictable effect of producing massive increases in the flow of commodities across the border. These flows for the most part link Canadian provinces with the neighbouring states and have produced a relative and in some cases absolute decline in the importance of the east–west commodity movements that historically linked the provinces with one another in relations of interdependence. The events of September 11, 2001, and the subsequent tightening of the Canada–U.S. border underlined just how critical relatively open borders have become to the economies of both Canada and the United States. Although Canada, for the moment, has rejected the idea of a common North American border, the coordination of border security is an increasingly inescapable reality. A final impact of NAFTA is to promote further stages of integration, which appear to result logically from it, such as a customs union or a common currency, referred to as dollarization, now that the psychological barriers to formal integration with the United States have apparently been removed. These notions have already appeared on the agenda and although the initial response is to dismiss them as unthinkable (in the same way that free trade was dismissed less than two decades ago), their implementation is probably only a matter of time.

This prospect is both a cause and a consequence of the second circumstance that will shape the further evolution of Canadian federalism—the hegemony of neoliberal ideology and of the public policies that result from it. This governing philosophy originated simultaneously in the United Kingdom and the United States in the late 1970s and spread to Canada soon afterwards. It facilitated both CUFTA and NAFTA, since Canadian political elites had already lost interest in pursuing the types of policies prohibited by those treaties, but also has been reinforced by them, since a reversion to many of the earlier interventionist policies is now impossible. Both federal and provincial governments are now less inclined to intervene in the economy, and more inclined to rely on the operation of the market, than they were in the past. This in turn has largely shifted the political agenda towards a preoccupation with non-economic issues.

The neoliberal trend is in one sense desirable for Canadian federalism since it removes from the agenda many of the issues, initiatives, and projects that led to disputes between federal and provincial governments, or between neighbouring provinces. Province-building and nation-building projects frequently clashed with one another because they redistributed wealth, income, and economic power between provinces or between levels of government. One only needs to think of the many disputes in the Trudeau era about mineral resources, hydroelectricity, Crown corporations, agricultural marketing boards, railway and airline transportation, or regional economic development. Neoliberal governance is undesirable in that interventionist economic policies at the federal level were traditionally a large part of what held Canada together and created (artificially, as neoliberals would argue) interdependence between the regions and provinces. Whether Canada can be held together in their absence, given its vast geographical extent and scattered population, the proximity of the United States, and the deep cultural and psychological divide between Quebec and the rest of the country, remains to be seen.

This brings us to our third factor, the unresolved question of Quebec nationalism and the sovereignty movement. This issue has dominated Canadian politics for the past four decades. For most of that time, however, there was a general expectation that it could and would be brought to an end, either by the independence of Quebec or by some mutually acceptable arrangement within the framework of Canadian federalism. At the present time, and for the foreseeable future, neither seems likely. The Supreme Court's decision of August 1998 in the *Reference re. Secession of Quebec*, and the so-called *Clarity Act* which Parliament adopted more than a year later, have placed significant obstacles in the way of Quebec's independence that are probably insurmountable in the foreseeable future, given that Quebec's support of the independence option has declined at the same time as sovereigntists hold to this goal with less intensity.

The project of an independent Quebec, however, is not likely to disappear, since Quebec has most of the attributes of a nation state and since the economic risks of sovereignty have probably declined in recent years. As the federal government retreats from the regional development and social policy fields, the most obvious costs of separation diminish. Neither is the Parti Québécois likely to disappear. It remains the party most deeply rooted in the society of francophone Quebec, and the only obvious alternative to the provincial Liberals. The prospect is therefore one of an indefinite period of stalemate, during which avowed sovereigntists will govern Quebec about half the time, while all significant parties and political forces in the province will resist any hint of centralization that would lessen the power of the province or its National Assembly.

Having established these basic underlying features of the current scene, it remains to examine and explain some recent changes in the operation of Canadian federalism that do not seem likely to be reversed in at least the near future, and to explore their implications for Canadian federalism in the twenty-first century. Central among these are the changing role of Ontario in Confederation, the erosion of postwar social programs, ongoing fiscal controversies, the decline of executive federalism, and the future role of the Supreme Court.

THE CHANGING ROLE OF ONTARIO

The first change to be noted concerns the role of Ontario in Canadian federalism. With almost two-fifths of Canada's population and almost half of its economic activity, Ontario's dominant position within Confederation is unusual among the subnational units in federations. By way of contrast, California has less than one-eighth of the population of the United States. In part for this reason, and in part because of Ontario's large immigrant population—about one-quarter of its total population—Ontarians have a low sense of provincial identity and a tendency to give overwhelming priority to their Canadian identity. Traditionally this sentiment was reinforced by self-interest because Ontario's economy, based on the supply of manufactured goods and of services to other parts of Canada, gave it the largest stake in Canadian economic interdependence and in national unity.

For several decades after the Second World War, Ontario governments and premiers responded to these facts by trying to play a unique role in the politics of Canadian federalism. They viewed themselves as sharing with the federal government the responsibility for keeping the country united and promoting harmony among its parts. This might take the form of trying to bridge the gap between the positions of the federal government and Quebec on contentious issues. Premier John Robarts, for example, summoned the Confederation of Tomorrow conference in 1967 to pressure the federal government into considering Quebec's proposals for constitutional change. Two decades later, Premier David Peterson risked the survival of his government by supporting the unpopular Meech Lake Accord, which he viewed as a necessary compromise with Quebec. Less typically, but consistent with the same preoccupation, Premier William Davis in the 1970s and early 1980s was a firm ally of the federal government against decentralizing initiatives from Quebec and the western provinces.

In the early 1990s, however, Ontario began to discard this traditional pattern of behaviour in favour of a narrower focus on its own self-interest, and a diminishing concern with the rest of the country. In part this was a response to what were viewed as anti-Ontario initiatives by the Mulroney government, whose political base was largely in Quebec and Alberta. More fundamentally, as Thomas Courchene and Colin Telmer have argued, the change reflected the fact that, since CUFTA and NAFTA were adopted, Ontario's economy has become more interdependent with that of the United States than with other parts of Canada (Courchene and Telmer, 1998). Thus Ontario no longer has its traditional interest in a strong and relatively centralized Canadian state, still less in policies of interventionism and economic nationalism undertaken by the federal government. Although the government and the voters of Ontario opposed CUFTA and NAFTA at the time they were under consideration, Ontario has quickly adapted its behaviour in the federal–provincial arena to its new circumstances. No longer preoccupied with national unity, it now appears to define its interest as a rich province with a right-of-centre government, and thus its positions tend to have more in common with those of Alberta, traditionally the most anti-centralist of the predominantly anglophone provinces, than with those of the federal government.

THE EROSION OF CENTRALLY FUNDED SOCIAL PROGRAMS

A second recent change in Canadian federalism is the decline of the federal role in shaping and extending the Canadian welfare state. Although Canada's welfare state tradition has been somewhat romanticized of late, particularly for the purpose of making invidious comparisons with the United States, Canada was in fact relatively late in developing social welfare programs. The lack of a strong left-wing political party, the social conservatism of Catholic Quebec, and the interpretation of the constitution by the Judicial Committee of the Privy Council all contributed to this delayed development. When it came, however, the welfare state was mainly an achievement of the federal government, not the provinces, even though health and welfare appeared to fall mainly under provincial jurisdiction. As noted earlier in this chapter, three constitutional amendments were needed to establish federal authority over universal pensions and unemployment insurance. Other federal programs were established through the use of the spending power implied in the constitution, either to make grants to individuals, such as family allowances, or the Child Tax Benefit, which replaced them in 1993, or to make conditional grants to provincial governments, such as hospital insurance, medical insurance, and the Canada Assistance Plan (CAP). It has been rightly observed that the spending power "has proved to be the single most dynamic element of Canadian federalism" (Cameron and Dupre, 1983, 333–9, 340).

In recent years, however, this spending power has been the target of much criticism. Some critics argue that conditional grants and shared-cost programs reduce the accountability of both levels of government and the efficiency of public administration. Others, particularly in Quebec, view them as illegitimate federal intrusions into provincial fields of jurisdiction. The federal government itself has come to view conditional grants as open-ended commitments to uncontrollable spending, whose long-term costs outweigh the short-term popularity that results from their introduction. Thus it has ceased to introduce new social programs, and the three major, central ones—post-secondary education, health insurance, and the Canada Assistance Plan—were replaced in 1996 with a single grant, smaller in total than its predecessors, known as the Canada Health and Social Transfer (CHST). Although the CHST has gradually increased in size since 1996, provincial governments argue with some justification that it covers a small and diminishing share of the cost of the programs. Some Canadians, moreover, regret that the CHST provides no guarantee that the funds will actually be used for those programs to which it is ostensibly dedicated.

The federal tendency to abdicate leadership in social programs has been a mixed blessing for the provinces, since federal involvement in that field mainly took the form of spending, which has now been reduced. In other fields of activity the provinces to a greater extent have welcomed the erosion of federal leadership. For example, an agreement in November 1996 shifted much of the enforcement of environmental standards to the provinces and involved them in the process of setting national standards in this area (*Globe and Mail*, November 20, 1996). Soon afterwards responsibility for labour training was shifted to the provinces through a series of bilateral agreements. The federal government had traditionally claimed that this subject fell under its constitutional responsibility for unemployment insurance, while Quebec in particular had argued that it was part of the provincial field of education. A promise by Prime Minister Jean Chrétien during the Quebec referendum campaign of 1995 led to agreements over the next few years with every province except Ontario, whereby the provinces took over responsibility for training and received financial compensation from the federal government to cover the costs. Quebec voters were apparently not impressed. A poll in the summer of 1998 showed that only one-third of them were even aware of the change, a lower proportion than in any other region of the country (*Globe and Mail*, August 19, 1998).

FISCAL ARRANGEMENTS IN QUESTION

Closely associated with the erosion of federal leadership in social programs has been the increasing fragility of the system of fiscal federalism, known as tax sharing. This system has been in place since 1962, when it replaced the more centralized tax rental system established during the Second World War. Under tax sharing the federal government offers to collect income and corporation taxes on behalf of the provinces. The provinces are free to set their own rates, provided their tax regimes are broadly compatible with the federal one. The federal government also makes equalization payments, which began in 1957, to most of the provinces, so that even the poorest can have per capita revenues and, by implication, public services comparable to the national average. It also makes stabilization payments to any province that suffers a major short-term decline in its economy. Initially nine provinces (all except Quebec) accepted the federal offer to collect personal income tax on their behalf, while eight provinces (all except Quebec and Ontario) agreed to have the federal government collect their corporation tax. Alberta began to collect its own corporation tax in 1982. To prevent further defections, the federal government has allowed the provinces, for whom it collects taxes, increasing leeway in introducing exemptions, tax credits, and other modifications.

Tax sharing, with frequent incremental adjustments, appeared to be generally acceptable for many years. In recent years it has become more controversial, particularly in the larger provinces, which might follow Quebec's example by opting out of the system. Partly this is because it has become increasingly entangled with the arrangements for funding the welfare state, discussed above, even though tax sharing and conditional grants were originally separate and largely unrelated. This trend began as far back as 1977, when the federal government began to make part of its contribution to social programs in the form of "tax points" rather than cash. In other words, the federal government allows the provinces to increase their own taxes without additional cost to the taxpayer. After 25 years it is perhaps understandable that the provinces no longer regard this part of their revenue as a federal "contribution," but the federal government continues to insist that it be considered as one. Provinces, increasingly caught in a global competition for investment, are also increasingly reluctant to raise taxes for any purpose, let alone for social programs.

A more fundamental problem with fiscal federalism, as Harvey Lazar has argued, is the erosion of the postwar consensus about the role of the state (2000, 3–39). This can be attributed to a neoliberal rhetoric imported from south of the border, whereby politicians seek popularity not by promising new programs and expenditures, as they did in the past, but by promising to reduce taxes. If this means waiting lists at hospitals, underfunded universities, homeless people living on the streets, and military personnel risking their lives in helicopters that should have been replaced 20 years ago, that is presumably a problem to be solved by someone else. To say the least, this attitude is not conducive to a responsible sharing of costs and responsibilities between levels of government. Nonetheless, it seems destined to continue for the foreseeable future.

Although the rhetoric of provincial governments still suggests at times that provinces are weak and helpless vassals of an all-powerful central government, the reality is quite different. Canadians pay more in taxes to their provincial and local governments combined than to the federal government, a situation found in no other federal country apart from

Switzerland, and unknown in Canada itself as recently as the 1970s. Federal program spending (including such things as foreign policy and defence) is less than provincial program spending. Federal cash grants to the provinces as a percentage of all provincial revenue have declined from about 50 percent in the nineteenth century to 22 percent in 1961, 18 percent in 1981, and 13 percent in 1999 (Lazar, 2000, 11, 12, 14). This trend does not seem likely to be reversed in the near future.

THE DECLINE OF EXECUTIVE FEDERALISM

A more positive development in the recent history of the federation is the declining importance of what Donald Smiley called "executive federalism" (Smiley, 1980, 91–119). This uniquely Canadian practice reached its peak during the confrontational period from the mid-1960s to the mid-1980s. It was based on the belief that a conference of the prime minister and the 10 provincial premiers could be used to make major decisions about public policy. Such conferences had been held occasionally before 1963, usually to consider proposed amendments to the constitution, but they were relatively rare before Prime Minister Lester Pearson took office. During the two decades of Liberal government from 1963 to 1984 "first ministers' conferences," as they began to be called, were held almost every year, and sometimes more often. The Meech Lake Accord of 1987 would even have created a constitutional obligation to hold two such conferences each year, one on the economy "and other matters" and one on the constitution. Ottawa's downtown railway station was converted in 1966 into a conference centre, primarily to serve as a setting for these events. Some conferences were televised, a practice that began in 1968, nine years before TV cameras entered the House of Commons. All were conducted with pomp and ceremony worthy of an international summit conference, which in some ways they resembled.

Subjects discussed at first ministers' conferences after 1963 included the constitution as well as fiscal arrangements, major innovations in social policy and, between 1975 and 1989, the economy. Conferences on the economy began when Prime Minister Pierre Trudeau sought provincial support for his wage and price controls. They were successful in this immediate purpose but in the longer run proved particularly disastrous, as they gave the premiers a platform on which to sound off about matters that fell under federal jurisdiction, and for which they had no responsibility. The practice of executive federalism, however, also worked to the advantage of the federal government. Prime Minister Trudeau used multilateral conferences to demonstrate that Alberta's views on energy policy, and Quebec's views on the constitution, were not shared by other provincial governments.

The practice of executive federalism began to decline in the late 1980s, partly because of its mediocre record in arriving at meaningful decisions and partly because Prime Minister Brian Mulroney preferred bilateral negotiations with individual provinces rather than confronting all of them simultaneously. Executive federalism was further discredited by the rejection of the Meech Lake and Charlottetown constitutional accords, amid arguments that a private or semi-private meeting of "11 white men in suits" was not a proper way to conduct public business of national concern in a democracy. Another argument against executive federalism is that it fosters the illusion that the federal government is only one of 11 "senior governments" that are equal in importance. The artificiality of a decision-making institution that appears to give Prince Edward Island equal power with Ontario or Quebec should be even more obvious.

Bilateral discussions between the federal government and a single province are a more effective way than multilateral conferences to deal with many kinds of problems. The decline of executive federalism, however, does not mean that multilateral discussions between Canadian governments are extinct. They continue mainly at the ministerial level, sometimes in institutionalized bodies like the Canadian Council of Forest Ministers, the Canadian Council of Ministers of the Environment, or the Provincial/Territorial Council on Social Policy Renewal. These specialized councils can discuss particular issues in a fruitful manner, free of the political grandstanding and ballyhoo that often accompanies a first ministers' conference. Agreements such as that of November 1996 on environmental standards have resulted from these meetings. At the same time, the councils allow some access for interest groups with a legitimate concern about the issue under discussion.

Another set of multilateral negotiations led to the Agreement on Internal Trade (AIT), signed in July 1994. The origins of this document go back to the 1970s, when concerns began to be expressed that the interventionist economic policies of the provinces were leading to trade barriers between them. In 1980 and again in 1991 federal governments proposed constitutional changes to deal with this problem but the provinces, apart from Ontario on the first occasion, were unsympathetic to formal constitutional change. A non-binding agreement posed fewer risks to provincial interests. The advent of NAFTA, and the general trend towards neoliberal economic policies at both levels of government, led to negotiations that began shortly before the federal election of 1993. In contrast to negotiations over the constitution, they attracted little interest from the public or the media. The first ministers played a very limited role which has been described as "more philosophical than practical" (Doern and MacDonald, 1999, 53). Most of the work was done by ministers of industry or trade and by the officials in their departments.

The agreement, on paper at least, is a fairly impressive document. It provides a code of conduct to limit the incentives provinces can use to lure investment; encourages harmonization of regulations that govern consumer, capital, and labour markets; prohibits discrimination in favour of local suppliers when governments or their agencies purchase goods and services; and provides procedures for resolving disputes between governments or dealing with complaints from the private sector. Even the politically sensitive areas of agricultural marketing and the retailing of alcoholic beverages in provincial liquor stores are included. It has been suggested, however, that the practical consequences of the agreement fall far short of what was promised, and presumably intended, at the outset (*Gazette,* May 24, 2001). The harmonization of provincial regulations in areas of consumer regulations, labour, and professional certification has been, to say the least, slow.

Still another multilateral agreement, from which Quebec significantly excluded itself, was the Social Union Framework Agreement of February 1999. This agreement followed several months of meetings among ministers of health and welfare, in most of which Quebec participated. The nine provinces that signed it agreed to respect the principles of universal, portable, and publicly administered medicare, to create no new barriers to mobility of persons between provinces, and to eliminate by February 2002 any residence requirements that limit access to social programs. They also admitted the legitimacy of the federal spending power, a sore point in Quebec. In return the federal government agreed to consult with the provincial governments at least a year before significant changes in funding of social programs, to introduce no new conditional grants without the consent of a majority of provinces, and to give three months notice of new spending programs involving grants to individuals (Gagnon and Segal, 2000, 243–9).

THE SUPREME COURT: A RETURN TO NORMALITY?

Before leaving the subject of recent changes in the operation of Canadian federalism, one additional development should be noted. In contrast to the 1970s and 1980s, the contemporary Supreme Court of Canada has played a much less prominent role in recent years in federal-provincial relations. In the decade 1991–2000 the Supreme Court issued only six major decisions on the federal-provincial distribution of powers (*Canada Assistance Plan* [1991]; *Goods and Services Tax* [1992]; *R.J.R. Macdonald* [1995]; Hydro-Quebec [1997]; *Westcoast Energy* [1998]; *Firearms Act* [2000]). All six involved federal legislation: reduced funding for CAP, the GST, restrictions on tobacco advertising, environmental standards, pipeline regulation, and gun control. In each case federal powers were upheld, despite various provinces intervening to argue the contrary, and in no case were constitutional lawyers surprised by the outcome. For the first time in many decades there were no really important decisions involving provincial powers or activities. In a sense this modest role for the Court in federal–provincial relations is a return to the situation before 1970, with the significant difference that the Court now has the additional and very important responsibility of interpreting the *Charter of Rights and Freedoms*. Less activist government at both levels, and a lower level of intergovernmental conflict as compared with the era of confrontational federalism, probably explain the change, rather than any change in the personnel or judicial philosophy of the Supreme Court itself.

CONCLUSION

This chapter has highlighted a number of significant changes in Canadian federalism that have taken place recently, despite various failures to change the formal constitution. Given the rigidity of the constitutional amending formula adopted in 1982, the repeated frustrations of efforts to use it, and the lack of any Canada-wide consensus on constitutional change, it seems unlikely that significant formal changes will be attempted again in the near future. The only likely exceptions will be amendments to constitutional provisions referring to only one province, which are relatively easy under the bilateral amending procedure in section 43 of the *Constitution Act* (1982). A number have been made in recent years at the request of various provinces, including changes to guarantees of denominational education in Newfoundland and Quebec, removal of the federal obligation to provide ferry service to Prince Edward Island which now has a bridge to the mainland, and recognition of the collective rights of the Acadian community in New Brunswick.

Informal change, however, will continue in the twenty-first century, just as it did in the nineteenth and the twentieth. For the foreseeable future it will be affected by the three underlying circumstances referred to earlier—continental economic integration, neoliberal free market governing practices, and the stalemate in Quebec. All three of these circumstances make it unlikely that major shifts of power towards the federal government will take place in the near future. This conclusion does not necessarily imply shifts of power to the provincial level. Both levels of government might lose power to the United States government and to the private sector, or, if one prefers less-provocative terminology, the market. In any event, there may be some informal trading of powers and responsibilities in both directions, as each level of government seeks the fields of influence that correspond best with its interests and capabilities, as well as the demands of its constituents.

Another possibility, of which the Social Union Framework Agreement may be an early indication, might be a gradual and incremental shift towards de facto special status for Quebec, although without formal constitutional amendment. Formally Quebec has the same constitutional status as other provinces, with the minor exception that it is exempted from section 23.1(a) of the *Charter of Rights and Freedoms.* In fact, Quebec already exercises more power than other Canadian provinces in a number of ways. For example, it has its own pension plan, collects its own personal income tax, and selects its own immigrants. Further moves in this direction might harmonize the aspirations of moderate Quebec nationalists with the desire of many Canadians for Canada-wide social programs and a central government that exercises meaningful powers. There are precedents elsewhere, such as Scotland in the United Kingdom, Catalonia in Spain, and Corsica in France, for parts of a country having levels of autonomy which other parts do not have. Prediction is always a hazardous exercise, but it can be stated with certainty that Canadian federalism will continue to evolve and change. Whatever imperfections the Canadian constitution may have, and it has many, the myth of a rigid and inflexible "status quo" is not supported by the evidence.

REFERENCES

Cameron, David M. and J. Stefan Dupre. 1983. "The Financial Framework of Income Distribution and Social Services." In Stanley M. Beck and Ivan Bernier (eds.) *Canada and the New Constitution: The Unfinished Agenda, Volume 1.* Montreal: Institute for Research on Public Policy.

Courchene, Thomas and Colin Telmer. 1998. *From Heartland to North American Region State: The Social, Fiscal, and Federal Evolution of Ontario: an Interpretive Essay.* Toronto: Center for Public Management, University of Toronto.

Doern, G. Bruce and Mark MacDonald. 1999. *Free Trade Federalism: Negotiating the Canadian Agreement on Internal Trade*. Toronto: University of Toronto Press.

Gagnon, Alain G. and Hugh Segal (eds.). 2000. The Canadian Social Union without Quebec: 8 *Critical Analyses.* Montreal: Institute for Research on Public Policy.

"Free Trade Begins at Home." 2000, May 24. *The Gazette.*

"Pollution Foes Attack Federal Plan." 1996, November 20. *The Globe and Mail.*

"Quebecers Unaware of Power Transfer." 1998, August 19. *The Globe and Mail.*

Lazar, Harvey. 2000. "In Search of a New Mission Statement for Canadian Fiscal Federalism." In Harvey Lazar (ed.). *Canada: The State of the Federation 1999/2000.* Kingston: Institute of Intergovernmental Relations.

Mallory, J. R.. 1965. "The Five Faces of Federalism." In P.A. Crepeau and C.B. Macpherson (eds.) *The Future of Canadian Federalism*. Toronto: University of Toronto Press.

———. 1954. *Social Credit and the Federal Power in Canada*. Toronto: University of Toronto Press.

The Queen v. *Hydro-Quebec*, [1997] 3 Supreme Court Reports 213.

R.J.R. Macdonald v. *Canada*, [1995] 3 Supreme Court Reports 199.

Reference re. Canada Assistance Plan, [1991] 2 Supreme Court Reports 525.

Reference re. Firearms Act, [2000] 1 Supreme Court Reports 783.

Reference re. Goods and Services Tax, [1992] 2 Supreme Court Reports 445.

Smiley, Donald V. 1980. *Canada in Question,* 3rd ed. Toronto: McGraw-Hill Ryerson.

Westcoast Energy v. *Canada*, [1998] 1 Supreme Court Reports 322.

WEBLINKS

Transfers: An Investment in Canadians
www.fin.gc.ca/activty/transfers_e.html

The Supreme Court of Canada
www.scc-csc.gc.ca

The Clarity Act
http://laws.justice.gc.ca/en/C-31.8/32182.html

chapter fourteen

The Evolution of Environmental Governance

Kathryn Harrison

INTRODUCTION

Canadian governments have enjoyed mixed results in their efforts to protect the environment. Ambient levels of some air contaminants have declined, acid rain has been reduced, and sewage treatment has been extended to an increasing fraction of the population. At the same time, the list of threatened and endangered species continues to grow, average levels of ground-level ozone have increased, and emissions of greenhouse gases have continued to grow even as scientists have reached consensus that human activities have had a discernable impact on global climate. Hundreds of Canadian communities face advisories to boil their drinking water. Canadian governments confront these persistent challenges in a new context. Patterns of governance concerning the environment have undergone significant changes in Canada over the last 10 to 15 years, which have witnessed the entry of new players into the policy community and changing relationships among both new and old actors. This chapter will examine four important trends in environmental governance and raise questions about the implications of each for protection of the environment and democratic accountability.

The first of these trends has been an expansion of the environmental policy community to include environmental groups, First Nations, organized labour, and other non-governmental actors. While Canadian environmental policymaking in the 1970s and early 1980s was characterized by closed negotiations between governments and industry, a much broader range of "stakeholders" now routinely has a place at the table in advising government decisions. The second change in environmental governance concerns the evolving relationship between the federal and provincial governments. Although federal–provincial conflict was provoked by assertions of federal environmental authority in the late 1980s, during the late 1990s the federal government adopted a more deferential, and devolutionary, posture with respect to the provinces. Federal–provincial harmony has thus largely been restored. Third, new approaches to environmental policy are transforming the relationship between the state and non-state actors. Canadian federal and provincial governments are increasingly rejecting coercive regulatory approaches in favour of "partnerships" with non-governmental actors via co-operative, voluntary programs. The role of the state in environmental policy is thus evolving from that of police officer to teacher and even, in some cases, cheerleader.

Finally, the fourth and perhaps most fundamental trend has been the emergence in recent years of various forms of private environmental governance—in effect, governance without government. Environmental groups have bypassed the state altogether in mounting market campaigns to influence the behaviour of private companies. Non-governmental certification bodies, such as the Forest Stewardship Council and the International Organisation for Standardisation (ISO), invite firms to voluntarily commit to their private standards. In still other cases, individual firms and trade associations have adopted their own systems of self-regulation. The next section of this chapter will consider several background forces that have prompted these changes in environmental governance. Thereafter, each of the four trends will be examined in greater detail before speculation about the future of Canadian environmental governance is offered in the conclusion.

BACKGROUND FORCES

Patterns of environmental governance in Canada are the product of changes in the political environment and the broader policy agenda. An understanding of why environmental governance has changed, as well as whether current trends are likely to continue, thus demands a brief review of some of these background forces. Perhaps most important to note is that public and thus governmental concern for the environment has been cyclical (Harrison, 1996). Interest in the environment first peaked in the late 1960s, followed by a rapid decline as public attention was diverted to the economy in the early 1970s. A second surge in public interest emerged in the late 1980s, but this second "green wave" also subsided quickly in response to the recession of the early 1990s. Although public opinion polls continue to reveal strong public concern when Canadians are prompted by questions about the environment, the environment barely registers when they are asked to identify their policy priorities.

It is also significant that some of the issues that supplanted the environment at the top of the political agenda in the 1990s did not bode well for environmental policy. The first of these was the deficit. As the federal government and most provincial governments opted for budgetary restraint in the mid-1990s, environment ministries in many Canadian jurisdictions experienced budget cuts of up to two-thirds, fundamentally limiting their capacity to develop and implement environmental policies. Although the last two federal budgets have emphasized a number of environmental spending initiatives, and may thus signal a turnaround for Environment Canada, they have not yet come close to reversing the cuts made in previous years.

Another issue that replaced the environment on the political agenda in the early 1990s was national unity. In the wake of the election of a Parti Québécois government in Quebec in 1994 and the narrow victory for federalist forces in the Quebec referendum of 1995, the federal government was understandably less inclined to antagonize Quebec, which like many other provinces tends to closely guard its ownership of natural resources, by asserting strong federal environmental jurisdiction. Indeed, in the face of waning public attention to the environment, the environment was a particularly attractive candidate for demonstrating the Liberal government's commitment to "renewing the federation" through federal–provincial co-operation.

The 1990s was also a period of global economic integration. The implications of free trade for the environment are hotly contested (Vogel, 1999). Environmentalists fear that trade-induced economic growth will increase unsustainable demands on the earth's resources, that governments seeking to defend the competitiveness of domestic producers will be more reluctant to regulate industry's environmental impacts and may even engage in a "race to the bottom" with other jurisdictions, and that international trade agreements will constrain individual jurisdictions' ability to protect the environment unilaterally. Their concerns have been heightened by World Trade Organization (WTO) decisions that ruled some domestic environmental standards to be barriers to trade (Vogel, 1999) and by the chilling effect of the investment chapter of the North American Free Trade Agreement (NAFTA) (Juillet, forthcoming). Environmentalists have thus been prominent participants in the anti-globalization movement and the associated demonstrations in Seattle and Quebec.

Sometimes, however, trade indices are races to the top, in which smaller jurisdictions have been pressured by trading partners to raise their standards to those of larger and wealthier jurisdictions. Similarly, it is noteworthy that Canadian environmentalists themselves have successfully relied on global trade to foster improved environmental practices within Canada. Some of the most effective environmental campaigns in Canada in recent years, including Greenpeace's campaign against clearcut logging and the James Bay Cree's campaign against the Great Whale hydroelectric project, have taken advantage of the greater environmental sensitivity of foreign consumers to place pressure on domestic industries.

A final background factor worth noting is the increasing internationalization of environmental policy (Toner and Conway, 1996). The United Nations Conference on Environment and Development in Rio de Janeiro in 1992 yielded Agenda 21, the Framework Convention on Climate Change, and the Convention on Biological Diversity. In signing each of these agreements, Canada committed itself to an ambitious international environmental policy agenda that is sometimes at odds with the domestic forces for devolution and deregulation. International commitments have thus prompted the federal government to launch a third attempt to pass national endangered species legislation, despite strong opposition from all sides to its previous attempt (Amos, Harrison, and Hoberg, 2001) and to pursue ambitious greenhouse gas reductions, despite the risk of federal–provincial conflict (*Globe and Mail*, March 29, 2000). However, Canada's failure to fulfill its obligations under the Biodiversity Convention to pass national endangered species legislation, as well as its failure to meet its climate change commitments under the Montreal Protocol, or to even ratify the subsequent Kyoto Protocol, suggest that domestic forces for deregulation may prevail over international pressures for regulation.

In summary, several background forces point in the direction of deregulation. Environmental groups' claims to represent the public interest have been undermined by the relatively low level of public attention to the environment in the 1990s. At the same time, industry's opposition to environmental regulation has been strengthened by the growing emphasis on economic competitiveness in the global economy. It is thus not surprising that federal and provincial governments would both favour voluntary "partnerships" as an alternative to imposing costly regulatory burdens on industry. This is reinforced by the fact that, in light of deep budget cuts, many environment departments have scarce resources with which to develop and enforce regulations. In the Canadian context, deregulation has been accompanied by a trend toward decentralization. In the current climate of public opinion, no Canadian governments have strong incentives to test the limits of their environmental jurisdiction, but this is particularly true for the federal government, which risks running afoul of Quebec's and other provinces' sensitivities concerning their jurisdiction over natural resources. The following section will consider how these forces have been played out in terms of changing patterns of environmental governance.

It should be noted, however, that there are competing forces for regulation and centralization in the form of trade pressures for upward harmonization of national environmental standards, pressures from the international environmental agenda, which tend to counter devolutionary trends by focusing attention on *federal* government policy, and occasional bursts of public attention, such as those prompted by the contaminated drinking water in Walkerton and North Battleford, which also tend to prompt calls for national environmental standards. The concluding section will return to this tension in speculating about the future of Canadian environmental governance.

EXPANSION OF THE POLICY COMMUNITY

The most obvious change in environmental governance in recent years has been an expansion of the policy community to include environmentalists, Aboriginal groups, and, to varying degrees, other non-governmental actors. Prior to the mid-1980s, Canadian environmental standards were typically developed and enforced through private negotiations between industry and federal and provincial governments (Schrecker, 1984). Although this model of "bipartite bargaining" (Hoberg, 1993) between the state and industry was uncontroversial when it was introduced in the 1970s, it could not survive calls for greater openness and public participation in the 1980s, not only in the environmental field, but in government more generally.

The result was the emergence in the mid-1980s of an alternative "multi-partite bargaining" model (Hoberg, 1993), in which a broad range of "stakeholders" are invited to participate in policy deliberations. Prominent examples include the federal and provincial roundtables on sustainable development (Howlett, 1990), the British Columbia government's Commission on Resources and the Environment (CORE) (Owen, 1980), and the climate change "issue tables" convened more recently by the federal government. These and dozens of other "multi-stakeholder consultations" in recent years share two characteristics. First, in a departure from the bipartite bargaining model of the 1970s, an effort is made by the state to identify and include a broad range of stakeholders. Both industry and environmental groups now routinely have a place at the table and, depending on the process, may be joined by an array of other actors, from well-defined and organized groups such as First Nations and trade unions, to representatives of more amorphous interests such as "youth" and "local communities." The second defining characteristic is the degree of emphasis placed on bargaining and compromise. In contrast to public input via public hearings and "notice and comment rule-making" that typify U.S. environmental policymaking, Canadian policymakers encourage participants in multi-stakeholder consultations to develop consensual recommendations.

While few would question efforts to open up the policymaking process to a broader range of interests, the multi-partite model does raise important questions about democratic legitimacy. A decision rule of consensus has intuitive appeal, offering as it does the promise of making everybody happy. However, the equitable *procedure* of granting all participants an opportunity to veto any decision may not always yield equitable *outcomes*. A critical issue is what will happen in the event of a failure by stakeholders to achieve consensus. If, as is often the case, the status quo will prevail, then those who are privileged by the current state of affairs will continue to be advantaged by a consensual decision-making process (Hoberg, 1993). The opportunity to exercise a veto is simply more valuable for them than for those who have nothing to lose. This might be expected to privilege the interests of business if the objective of a consultation is to strengthen environmental protection, but could on occasion advantage environmentalists when a consultation process has been convened with an eye to relaxing current standards.

The move from bilateral to multilateral consultations also raises questions about the role of government vis-à-vis societal interests. Different visions of the state are implied by each model (Beierle, 1999). Implicit in the bilateral model is an assumption that it is the government's role to defend the public interest. In contrast, multi-partite bargaining offers a pluralist vision in which the state serves as a broker among competing interests. Both models have characteristic strengths and weaknesses.

Although one can certainly challenge the privileged position afforded business in bipartite bargaining, the more general idea of the state being responsible for representing the public interest is quite consistent with traditional notions of representative democracy, in which elected representatives are chosen by and held accountable to the electorate at large, rather than to any "special interests." This model can be criticized from two quite different directions, however. Some would argue that some interests really are "special," and that those most affected by a decision should thus be afforded a greater say. While this argument might be used to justify special consultations with business, it would also support consultations with, for instance, local communities that suffer from a facility's pollution or from consumers most affected by a hazardous product. The second critique is that it is a myth that the state can be impervious to interest group pressures; it is thus essential to open up the decision-making process to diverse interests to avoid "capture" of the state by dominant societal actors. Both of these critiques suggest a move towards greater pluralism.

However, closer examination of the pluralist model reveals that it is not a panacea. In turning responsibility for policymaking to varying degrees over to "stakeholders," the state is transferring authority to private actors who not only were not chosen by the Canadian electorate, but who may have little or no accountability to the groups they purport to represent. There is also the question of who should count as a stakeholder. First Nations and other orders of government in particular resent being treated just like other stakeholders, and typically demand parallel consultation processes. Even with respect to non-governmental actors, obvious questions arise about how to limit participation to a manageable number, while striking a balance between big business and small, local versus national environmental groups, and clearly identified versus diffuse and unorganized interests. At the limit, one can ask who should represent the public at large, since there is a risk that invited stakeholders will achieve a mutually beneficial compromise by shifting the costs to those not at the table. Finally, there is a practical risk of "consultation fatigue," as multi-stakeholder processes place heavy demands on groups with limited staff and resources to provide representatives to a plethora of concurrent consultations.

Who ultimately makes the decision is a critical issue for either model. A more pluralist approach to interest group consultations might be reconciled with representative democracy if one views consultations as merely advisory to an elected government. However, if that is the case, it is not clear why it is so important for the relevant stakeholders to achieve consensus. An alternative melding of the two models was offered by the B.C. Commission on Resources and the Environment, which offered a vision of "shared decision making" in which "those with authority to make a decision and those affected by that decision are empowered jointly to seek an outcome that accommodates, rather than compromises, the interests of all concerned." However, it is at best an uneasy compromise to depict the government as just another stakeholder. It is also a compromise that seems unlikely to satisfy either the electorate or stakeholders around the table should the parties to a "shared decision" fail to agree.

Although multi-stakeholder processes have been the most dominant mechanism for expansion of the policy community in recent years, it should be noted that it is not the only one. Litigation emerged in the late 1980s as an alternative to multi-partite bargaining in Canadian environmental policy (Hoberg, 1993). Although litigation also provides opportunities for a broader range of interests to participate in policymaking, it does so via an adversarial, "winner takes all" process, in contrast to the negotiation and compromise that characterize multi-stakeholder processes. The use of litigation in Canadian environmental policy emerged when environmental groups realized in 1987 that they were in a position to sue the federal government to demand that it perform environmental impact assessments of various projects.

Environmental groups successfully sued the federal government to force it to perform environmental assessments of the Rafferty and Alameda dams in Saskatchewan and the Oldman River Dam in Alberta, thus prompting a rash of subsequent lawsuits concerning other proposed developments. However, environmentalists' access to the courts was conditional upon the relatively unusual appearance of non-discretionary language in the federal environmental assessment regulation in place at the time. In contrast, it is extremely difficult to sue the government if the relevant statute only states that the Minister "may" take actions he or she considers appropriate. Non-discretionary language is unusual in legislation produced by a parliamentary system such as ours, in which the executive responsible for implementing laws also proposes them in the first place, and thus has few incentives to tie its own hands. For that reason, Hoberg (1993) has argued that legalism is unlikely to make the kind of inroads in Canadian environmental governance that it has in the United States. However, litigation concerning Aboriginal land claims may prove an important exception.

RATIONALIZING FEDERAL AND PROVINCIAL ROLES

Constitutional authority, with respect to the environment, is shared by the Canadian federal and provincial governments. As owners of Crown resources, the provinces have clear and extensive environmental jurisdiction. Historically, the scope of federal environmental authority has been less clear. However, since the late 1980s, the Supreme Court has interpreted federal environmental jurisdiction quite generously in a series of landmark cases, including Hydro-Québec (1997) (Harrison, 1996).

As noted above, the federal and provincial governments managed their overlapping jurisdiction quite harmoniously prior to the late 1980s. The provinces typically took the lead in developing and implementing environmental standards, while the federal government played a supporting role of conducting research, monitoring ambient environmental quality, and facilitating consensus on a small number of national standards (Thompson, 1980). Federal–provincial discussion took place behind closed doors under the auspices of the Canadian Council of Resource and Environment Ministers, later renamed the Canadian Council of Ministers of the Environment (CCME).

This harmonious relationship gave way to conflict, however, in the late 1980s as both orders of government scrambled to respond to growing public demand for environmental protection. The first challenge to federal–provincial co-operation was the federal government's introduction of its *Canadian Environmental Protection Act*, a law that some provinces considered an infringement on their constitutional authority. However, more serious conflicts emerged in the wake of the aforementioned litigation concerning environmental assessment. Not only did environmentalists force the federal government to second-guess projects that had in many cases already been approved by provincial governments, but some of the highest profile cases concerned the provinces' own resource development projects. Environmentalists' lawsuits thus prompted a direct federal challenge to provincial authority with respect to natural resources. Moreover, in the face of inflexible Court orders, the federal government and the provinces could no longer retreat behind closed doors to resolve their differences. When the federal government proposed its *Canadian Environmental Assessment Act* to replace the regulation that had been vulnerable to legal challenge, the provinces were unanimous in their opposition to the new statute.

By the early 1990s, however, environmental issues had faded from the spotlight. The federal government not only had less electoral incentive to test the limits of its jurisdiction, but in the face of budgetary retrenchment also had scarce resources with which to implement its ambitious new statutes. At the federal government's initiative, CCME renewed efforts to restore intergovernmental harmony in the environmental field (Harrison, 1994). After producing various interim projects and suffering at least one false start, the ultimate result was the Canada-wide Accord on Environmental Harmonization, which was signed by the federal government, the territories, and all provinces other than Quebec in 1998.

In the accord, federal, provincial, and territorial governments commit to work together to achieve consistent environmental objectives. In so doing, they propose to enhance their efficiency by rationalizing federal and provincial roles and responsibilities to avoid overlap and duplication, while at the same time identifying and addressing gaps in environmental protection. The language of the accord is quite broad, with most of the details remaining to be worked out in a series of anticipated sub-agreements and implementation agreements. Since these laudatory goals seem relatively uncontroversial, how can one explain the almost unanimous opposition to the accord from Canadian environmental groups, as well as from the government's own Standing Committee on Environment and Sustainable Development?

Critics of the accord raised several concerns (Fafard, 2000). First, they argued that the accord would inevitably lead to a reduction of the federal government's role in environmental policy, since the accord strongly implied that the level of government that would normally take the lead to avoid overlap would be the provinces'. The accord's critics remained unconvinced that overlap and duplication were even a problem, particularly in light of deep budget cuts in the 1990s at both the federal and provincial levels. And if such a problem did exist, environmental groups were particularly distrustful of relying on provincial governments to take the lead given their historical emphasis on economic development through exploitation of Crown resources. The apparent hostility to environmental regulation of the neoconservative governments in Ontario and Alberta did little to assuage environmentalists' concerns. Finally, many argued that the rationalization of federal and provincial roles proposed by the Canada-wide accord was merely a replay of a similar series of federal–provincial environmental accords in the 1970s, which failed abysmally both when provincial governments declined to fulfil their commitments to implement national standards and when the federal government declined to step in (Harrison, 1998a).

A second set of objections concerned a subtle redefinition of national standards. Rather than focusing on harmonizing product and discharge standards, the standards subagreement calls for a focus on consistent standards for ambient environmental quality. The intention is that "lead governments," normally the provinces, will have considerable flexibility in deciding how to achieve those objectives. While agreement on environmental quality standards is certainly not objectionable, critics of the accord fear that in the absence of uniform *discharge* standards, individual provinces will be reluctant to regulate unilaterally, lest they hinder the competitiveness of local industries relative to competitors in other provinces. Finally, concerns were raised by about the accord's emphasis on consensual decision making, similar to those raised concerning consensual stakeholder processes. If all of the federal, provincial, and territorial governments have to agree to Canada-wide standards, the concern is that the least environmentally sensitive jurisdiction will be in a position to veto any standards more stringent than it considers acceptable.

FROM REGULATION TO VOLUNTARISM

Governments can employ a variety of alternative means to pursue their policy goals. These "policy instruments" include regulation, spending, public enterprise, and exhortation. A common analogy concerns the various ways to get a donkey to pull a cart. The driver can encourage the donkey to move with carrots (spending programs, such as subsidies and tax breaks), compel the donkey to move using a stick (laws and regulations that mandate behavioural changes using threats of fines or jail terms), or pull the cart him or herself (public enterprise). The driver can also befriend the donkey by stroking its ears, and gently requesting that it move (exhortation).

This last option has been increasingly popular in the environmental field in the last decade (Gibson, 1999). In the late 1980s, in the face of unprecedented public concern for the environment, politicians promised to "get tough" by passing and strictly enforcing new laws and regulations. It was significant at the time that the federal government rejected the informal, negotiated approach to compliance that had evolved since the 1970s in its enforcement and compliance policy for the new *Canadian Environmental Protection Act*. However, during the 1990s, that tough rhetoric gave way to calls for cooperative "partnerships."

While the particular choice of policy instrument is a product of the system of environmental governance, it in turn conditions relationships among the actors within that system. The proposed partnerships have different implications for different players in the environmental policy community. Policymakers have broadened their focus to include environmental groups, consumers, and the public at large. Environmental education and stewardship programs to promote more environmentally sensitive behaviour are thus more prominent. However, the shift away from coercion to cooperation is arguably most significant in the relationship between government and business. In devising new control strategies in recent years Canadian federal and provincial governments have shown a distinct preference for voluntary programs that encourage and facilitate, rather than demand, changes in industry behaviour. Prominent examples include the Accelerated Reduction/Elimination of Toxics (ARET) program, the Voluntary Challenge and Registry for greenhouse gases, and various government–industry memoranda of understanding.

How can we explain the growing popularity of voluntary approaches? An optimistic view is that policymakers have embraced them because they are more effective. Business managers who face pressures from green consumers or opportunities to cut costs by reducing waste already have incentives to reduce their environmental impacts. When that is the case, encouragement and technical assistance from the state may suffice to achieve policy objectives. Alternatively, even a recalcitrant donkey may be motivated by a gentle request if it perceives that the driver still has the stick hidden behind his or her back. Voluntary programs backed by an implied threat of regulation may be preferred by government and business alike because they offer potential cost savings both to the government, which can shift monitoring and compliance costs to business, and to firms, which gain greater flexibility to devise their control strategies.

A less-hopeful analysis, however, suggests that the retreat from regulation is a response to a changing political environment, in which public pressure concerning the environment has declined, environment departments have reduced budgets with which to develop and enforce regulations, and governments are loathe to impose costs of regulatory compliance on domestic producers competing in global markets. Not surprisingly, donkeys prefer ear stroking to being hit with sticks. This alternative explanation suggests several concerns with respect to the effectiveness of voluntary programs.

First, one can question whether the appeal of voluntarism from businesses' perspective lies merely in greater flexibility relative to regulation (the optimistic view) or rather in relaxed expectations. Voluntary agreements between government and industry often require that firms only "commit to achieve," rather than actually achieve, objectives. Indeed, in many of the earliest voluntary programs, performance objectives and deadlines were unclear at best. It has not helped that proponents of voluntary approaches, including those in government, have tended to overstate the benefits of voluntary programs, for instance by attributing to the programs progress achieved by non-participants or before the program was even launched (Harrison, 1998b). Indeed, there is a risk that in rushing to embrace voluntary programs, governments will undermine the credibility of the threat of regulation necessary for their effectiveness.

A second set of concerns emerges with respect to public participation and democratic accountability. Some of the most prominent Canadian and European voluntary programs have been developed through bilateral government–industry negotiations, reminiscent of the regulatory approach of the 1970s. Third parties and the public at large typically have no guarantee of access to compliance monitoring (if it exists), nor the legal basis to demand compliance in court in the case of informal voluntary agreements. Yet as Gunningham and Grabosky (1998) have argued, when the state opts to "govern at a distance" via voluntary initiatives, it is all the more important that environmentalists and other third parties be in a position to step in as "surrogate regulators," to defend the interests of a sympathetic but often distracted public.

THE EMERGENCE OF PRIVATE GOVERNANCE

It can be a short step from "governing at a distance" to "governance without government." The shift in instrument choice from regulation to voluntary programs is, in many respects, consistent with the emergence of private systems of governance. Just as there has been a great deal of activity in terms of government-sponsored voluntary programs in recent years, there has also been a plethora of privately led voluntary initiatives.

Without waiting for government, some industry sectors have developed systems of private regulation of varying scope and specificity. The flagship example of self-regulation is the Responsible Care program that was launched by the Canadian Chemical Producers Association (CCPA) and has since been copied by the chemical industry in dozens of other countries as well as by other trade associations (Moffett and Bregha, 1999). As a condition of membership in CCPA, firms are required to comply with six codes of environmental practice comprising more than 150 requirements. CCPA members thus commit to continuous improvement of their environmental performance subject to a minimum baseline of compliance with all applicable laws, public reporting of their discharges, and periodic external verification of their compliance with the elements of Responsible Care. It is noteworthy, however, that other national Responsible Care programs and the codes of practice adopted by other industrial sectors tend to be less far-reaching. Moreover, even CCPA's version of Responsible Care focuses on a firm's management practices, such as record-keeping, reporting, and community relations, rather than actual environmental discharges, and it is compliance with these management practices rather than environmental performance criteria, that is evaluated by the independent audit team.

Environmental groups have also increasingly bypassed the state in recent years. The most visible examples are Greenpeace's international "market campaigns." In the late 1980s, Greenpeace was instrumental in prompting European consumer demand for "chlorine-free" paper, which in turn placed considerable pressure on the paper industries in both Europe and North America to transform their processes. Greenpeace is now using a similar market strategy to pressure British Columbia forestry companies to forgo clear-cut logging of old growth forests. And Greenpeace and other groups have also drawn the public's attention to commercial food products that contain genetically modified organisms, to create consumer pressure on manufacturers in Europe and North America. A similar market strategy was used by the James Bay Cree, who took their opposition to Hydro-Québec's Great Whale project to the corporation's customers in the United States. Other environmental groups, including the U.S. Environmental Defence Fund and Pollution Probe in Canada, have chosen to work directly and co-operatively with private industry.

Finally, there are a variety of independent organizations that offer to certify that a firm's environmental practices adhere to various private codes of practice. Examples include the ISO 14001 environmental management standard (Nash and Ehrenfeld, 1996), and the Forest Stewardship Council's labelling scheme for environmentally sensitive forestry. As with the other private initiatives discussed above, it is noteworthy that some firms submit to these standards voluntarily, while others simply decline to participate.

As with government-sponsored voluntary programs, a critical question concerning the efficacy of these programs is what motivates firms to change their behaviour voluntarily. Although government may not be directly involved in private voluntary codes, the shadow of the state may loom large in motivating industry via the threat of regulation. Many of the same concerns as raised above with respect to government-sponsored voluntary programs apply to voluntary groups. These include clarity of commitments, credibility of claims, and mechanisms for public accountability.

Voluntary initiatives motivated by market incentives seem less problematic. If consumers care enough about the environment to demand that firms reduce their environmental impacts, there is no need for the state to get involved. However, there is ample reason to question whether consumers have the depth and scope of commitment needed to sustain such initiatives. Although environmental groups have been able to buck the trend of declining green consumerism since the early 1990s by mobilizing latent public concern in discrete campaigns, for example, for chlorine-free paper and against genetically modified foods, they have been successful by focusing on only one or two issues at a time. Moreover, they arguably have had the greatest impact with respect to products from which consumers perceive personal health risks, rather than those that cause diffuse environmental impacts across a larger population. One can question whether even the most conscientious consumers will take the time to evaluate the environmental impacts of each and every product they purchase, particularly if that requires deciphering a series of competing labels and claims from industry, environmentalists, and other organizations. It is worth remembering that it was the failure of unfettered markets to protect the environment that prompted the emergence of state involvement in environmental policy in the first place (Andrews, 1998).

CONCLUSION

Environmental governance in Canada has undergone a period of tremendous change in the last decade. Environmentalists are now accepted players in an expanded policy community, but they nonetheless have been fighting an uphill battle. Governments with limited resources and priorities other than the environment have been inclined to repair their relationships with each other via rationalization of federal and provincial roles, as well as with industry through voluntary partnerships and self-regulation as alternatives to regulation, both of which are opposed by Canadian environmental groups. While some environmentalists have opted to bypass government and attempt to influence industry behaviour directly via highly focused market campaigns, their efforts to mobilize a distracted public on a broader range of issues are likely to have limited success.

What are the prospects for Canadian environmental governance in the twenty-first century? Several background forces suggest a continuation of current trends towards decentralization and voluntarism. Public opinion polls continue to indicate that the environment is a relatively low priority for voters, federal and provincial environment departments have yet to recover from the budget cuts of the 1990s, national unity is likely to remain a sensitive issue for the foreseeable future, and the global trade agenda is likely to increase concerns about the competitiveness of Canadian business. The election of the deregulation-oriented Bush administration in the United States is also likely to discourage regulatory initiative by Canadian governments fearful of being "out of step" with the United States. In the coming decade, however, high-profile international issues such as climate change can be expected to continue to place considerable pressures on Canadian governments as well as to provoke tensions between federal and provincial governments. In addition, budgetary purse strings are starting to loosen. However, the direction of environmental governance ultimately will turn on how much pressure Canadians put on their governments to protect the environment. The success of environmentalists' recent market campaigns has hinted at the depth of latent public concern available to be mobilized. Should a third "green wave" of public attention to the environment emerge, it could easily transform the patterns of governance that have evolved in recent years.

REFERENCES

Amos, William, Kathryn Harrison, and George Hoberg. 2001. "In Search of a Minimum Winning Coalition: The Politics of Species at Risk Legislation in Canada." In Karen Beazley and Robert Boardman (eds.), *The Politics of the Wild*. Toronto: Oxford University Press.

Andrews, Richard N.L. 1998. "Environmental regulation and business 'self-regulation'," *Policy Sciences 31*: 177–97.

Beierle, Thomas. 1999. *Public Participation in Environmental Decisions: An Evaluative Framework Using Social Goals*. [Discussion Paper 99-06.] Washington, DC: Resources for the Future.

Canadian Institute for Environmental Law and Policy. 1999. *Ontario's Environment and the "Common Sense Revolution": A Four Year Report*. Toronto: CIELAP.

Clark, K. 1995. *The Use of Voluntary Pollution Prevention Agreements in Canada: An Analysis and Commentary*. Toronto: Canadian Institute for Environmental Law and Policy.

Dorcey, Anthony H.J., and Timothy McDaniels. Forthcoming. "Great Expectations, Mixed Results: Trends in Citizen Involvement in Canadian Environmental Governance." In E. A. Parson, (ed.), *Governing the Environment*. Toronto: University of Toronto Press.

Environment Canada. 1987. *Canadian Environmental Protection Act: Enforcement and Compliance Policy*. Ottawa: Environment Canada.

Fafard, Patrick. 2000. "Groups, Governments, and the Environment: Some Evidence from the Harmonization Initiative." In Patrick Fafard and Kathryn Harrison (eds.), *Managing the Environmental Union*. Kingston: Queen's University School of Policy Studies.

Gibson, Robert. Ed. 1999. *Voluntary Initiatives: The New Politics of Corporate Greening*. Peterborough, ON: Broadview.

Gunningham, Neil, and Peter Grabosky. 1998. *Smart Regulation: Designing Environmental Policy*. New York: Oxford.

Harrison. Kathryn. 1994. "Prospects for Harmonization in Environmental Policy." In Douglas Brown and Janet Hiebert (eds.), *The State of the Federation 1994*. Kingston: Institute for Intergovernmental Relations.

———. 1996. *Passing the Buck: Federalism and Canadian Environmental Pol*icy. Vancouver: UBC Press.

———. 1998a. "The Canada-Wide Accord: A Threat to National Standards," *Canada Watch* 6: 13–14.

———. 1998b. "Talking with the Donkey: Cooperative Approaches to Environmental Protection," *Journal of Industrial Ecology 2*. 51–72.

———. 1999. "Retreat from Regulation: The Evolution of the Canadian Environmental Regulatory Regime." In G. Bruce Doern, Margaret M. Hill, Michael J. Prince, and Richard J. Schulz (eds.), *Changing the Rules: Canadian Regulatory Regimes and Institutions*. Toronto: University of Toronto Press.

Hartman, Cathy L, and Edwin R. Stafford. 1997. "Green Alliances: Building New Business with Environmental Groups." *Long Range Planning 30*, 184–96.

Hoberg, George. 1993. "Environmental Policy: Alternative Styles." In Michael M. Atkinson (ed.), *Governing Canada: Institutions and Public Policy*. Toronto: Harcourt Brace Jovanovich Canada.

Hornung, Robert. 1999. "The VCR is Broken." In Robert Gibson (ed.), *Voluntary Initiatives: The New Politics of Corporate Greening*. Peterborough, ON: Broadview.

Howlett, Michael. 1990. "The Round Table Experience: Representation and Legitimacy in Canadian Environmental Policy-Making." *Queen's Quarterly 97*. 580–601.

House of Commons Standing Committee on Environment and Sustainable Development. 1998. *Enforcing Canada's Pollution Laws: The Public Interest Must Come First!* Ottawa: Parliament of Canada.

Juillet, Luc. Forthcoming. "Regional Models of Environmental Governance in the Context of Market Integration." In E. A. Parson (ed.), *Governing the Environment*. Toronto: University of Toronto Press.

Kennett, Steven A. 2000. "Meeting the Intergovernmental Challenge of Environmental Assessment and Intergovernmental Relations." In Patrick Fafard and Kathryn Harrison (eds.), *Managing the Environmental Union*. Kingston: Queen's University School of Policy Studies.

Krajnc, Anita. 2001 "Wither Ontario's Environment? Neo-Conservatism and the Decline of the Environment Ministry," *Canadian Public Policy XXVI*, 112.

Lucas, Alastair R. and Cheryl Sharvit. 2000. "Underlying Constraints on Intergovernmental Cooperation in Setting and Enforcing Environmental Standards." In Patrick Fafard and Kathryn Harrison (eds.), *Managing the Environmental Union*. Kingston: Queen's University School of Policy Studies.

Lukasik, Lynda. 1999. "The Dofasco Deal." In Robert Gibson (ed.), *Voluntary Initiatives: The New Politics of Corporate Greening*. Peterborough, ON: Broadview.

McCloskey, Michael. 1996, November. "The limits of collaboration," *Harper's Magazine*, 34–6.

Moffet, John, and François Bregha. 1999. In Robert Gibson (ed.) *Voluntary Initiatives: The New Politics of Corporate Greening*. Peterborough, ON: Broadview.

Nash, Jennifer and John Ehrenfeld. 1996. "Code Green: Business Adopts Voluntary Environmental Standards," *Environment 38*, 16–20, 36–45.

National Round Table on the Environment and Economy. 1996. *Building Consensus for a Sustainable Future*. Ottawa: National Round Table on the Environment and Economy.

Organisation for Economic Co-operation and Development. 1999. *Voluntary Approaches for Environmental Policy: An Assessment*. Paris: OECD.

Owen, S. 1998. "Land use planning in the nineties: CORE lessons." *Environment 25*, 14–26.

R v. Hydro Quebec, [1997] 3 Supreme Court Reports 213.

Schrecker, Ted. 1984. *The Political Economy of Environmental Hazards*. Ottawa: Law Reform Commission of Canada.

Thompson, Andrew. 1980. *Environmental Regulation in Canada*. Vancouver: Westwawer Research Centre.

Toner, G., and T. Conway. 1996. "Environment." In G. Bruce Doern, Leslie A. Pal, and Brian W. Tomlin (eds.), *Border Crossings: The Internationalization of Canadian Public Policy*. Toronto: Oxford University Press.

Van Nijnatten, Debora L. 1998. "The day the NGOS walked out," *Alternatives 24*, 10–15.

Vogel, David. 1995. *Trading Up: Consumer and Environmental Regulation in a Global Economy*. Cambridge: Harvard University Press.

Vogel, David. 1999. "International Trade and Environmental Regulation." In Norman Vig and Michael Kraft (eds.), *Environmental Policy: New Directions for the Twenty-First Century*. 4th ed. Washington, DC: CQ Press.

WEBLINKS

Environment Canada
www.ec.gc.ca

Hydro-Quebec
www.hydro.qc.ca/visit/virtual_visit

CCPA Responsible Care
www.ccpa.ca/english/position/enviro/index.html

chapter fifteen

New Public Management and Canadian Politics

Allan Tupper

INTRODUCTION

In early twenty-first century Canada, public management is unusually controversial. The size of the public sector has been reduced and Canadian governments have been revolutionized by "new public management"—an amalgam of ideas, structural changes, and administrative processes. New public management demands that governments be more businesslike and cost-conscious, that government bureaucracies be radically changed, and that better service to citizens become the primary aim of government. This chapter portrays new public management as a complex political phenomenon that is subject to multiple interpretations. A major mistake is to conceive it as the handmaiden of neoliberalism or as a rhetorical smokescreen that allows government to be rolled back under the guise of management reform. Such views, while appealing and convincing in some ways, ignore that new public management is also interpreted as a major improvement to governance, as a politically progressive way of decentralizing power and as an antidote to perennial problems of bureaucracy.

New public management is deeply controversial in Canada although the term itself is seldom used in public debate. Its emphasis on "alternative service delivery" through privatization engenders intense debates about the role of government. So too does its weight on "partnerships" between governments, businesses, and not-for-profit organizations. Such undertakings are complex, politically contentious and difficult to evaluate. Finally, new public management has not entirely replaced the "traditional" administrative state in Canada. To the contrary, various administrative systems co exist, each with distinct controversies, structures, and values. Since as early as the mid-1980s, the federal government, provinces, and urban governments have proceeded with differing emphases, speed, and commitment. New public management has been pursued vigorously especially in Alberta and Ontario, and most recently in British Columbia.

This chapter also analyzes the "traditional" Canadian administrative state. This is necessary because new public management aims to change assumed deficiencies of "conventional" public management as it had developed since the end of World War II. The chapter then outlines the core principles of new public management and differences, both operationally and conceptually, with the Canadian civil service as it operated from through the 1950s until the mid-1980s. It pays particular attention to new public management's emphasis on alternative service delivery and partnerships with corporations and not-for-profit agencies. The chapter traces the rise of new public management ideas to prominence in modern democracies. In this vein, it argues that new public management gained leverage in the mid-1980s when it became intertwined with arguments about the need to balance budgets, to restrain government's growth, and to weaken the democratic state as an economic and social force in society. The chapter then examines major controversies about new public management, especially the claim that it debases democracy by importing market principles into government decision making, by glorifying efficiency as a value, and by portraying citizens as customers. The chapter concludes with an examination of the future of public administration in Canada. It speculates about continuing controversy over public administration as citizens cope with the full brunt of public management reforms that have been implemented piecemeal since the mid-1980s.

NEW PUBLIC MANAGEMENT

New public management is difficult to study and evaluate both because it embraces a tremendous range of administrative practices and because it has been applied differently in different Canadian jurisdictions. Such diversity of practice is frustrating for many citizens. Governments are in flux. Many public organizations now operate according to new principles that attract some citizens and repel others. Moreover, new public management practices are widely applied in the public sector, including hospitals whose practices are being transformed and even universities that now embrace the rhetoric of partnerships and "customer service." New public management, while omnipresent, is also elusive. Its advent has been subtle, its tenets are nowhere enshrined in law, and its principles are seldom explicitly debated. As a result, citizens sense major changes that they neither fully understand nor fully approve of. In an uneven manner, valued public institutions and programs are being transformed and dismantled. On the other hand, who could oppose more efficient and responsive government?

New public management is changing government in Canada. It is also changing political science, which must now grasp a "not-for-profit" sector lying between government and the private sector, and that delivers government services. Political scientists struggling with health and social policy reform in Ontario, for example, must understand such organizations as the Victorian Order of Nurses and the Children Aid's Society. New public management's emphasis on citizens as recipients of government services compels political scientists to examine "street level" civil servants not simply powerful senior officials. Such an expansion of political science is salutary. New public management connects public administration with basic questions about the role of government. Its emphasis on "empowered" communities and citizens links it with contemporary thinking about citizenship and political identities.

THE CANADIAN ADMINISTRATIVE STATE

In the twentieth century the civil service grew substantially in both size and power in Western democracies. Canada was no exception to this trend. A strong civil service was required to administer public policy as government assumed new roles. The simultaneous growth of government and a powerful civil service is not surprising. Two basic roles of democratic government—controlling industrial capitalism and developing a welfare state—demanded a strong civil service. The regulation of industries, the control of monopolies, and the development of industrial strategies required knowledge of the modern economy and of the international order. A potent civil service was the vehicle for housing such knowledge. New ideals of citizenship and political demands also led to a major expansion of social assistance programs in Canada after the Second World War. Federal and provincial governments launched programs in such areas as health and hospital insurance and social security. These programs required a civil service to develop them and to administer them fairly. Two basic elements of Canadian politics since the end of World War II—Keynesian economic management and the welfare state—were in large measure products of the civil service. As remarkable as it may now seem, the administrative state was seen as a benign development in the 1950s. An active state was thought able to tame the business cycle, to sustain the economy, and to provide a welfare state that symbolized a prosperous and fair democracy.

The administrative state had several cardinal characteristics. First, it was staffed on the basis of merit. Merit can be defined differently, but its essence is that technical skills, not political connections, are essential qualifications for holding a civil service position. Second, the civil service was housed in large bureaucracies. As described by Max Weber, a bureaucracy is an organization built around a complex division of labour, a hierarchy of offices, impersonal rules, and permanence of tenure for its office-holders. Bureaucracies are powerful because they harness expertise and focus it on policy and administrative questions.

Although modern corporations also have large bureaucracies, public organizations have fundamentally different purposes. In particular, public organizations must also be responsive, alert to democratic pressures, and accountable. Until the mid-1980s, public administration generally argued that public organizations could not be easily evaluated because of the complexity of their tasks and because, in a democracy, citizens often disagreed about the objectives being pursued. Governments labour under many constraints, so the argument went, and face multiple centres of accountability, conflicting demands, and pressures to be transparent.

The administrative state assumed a clear separation between politics and administration. This division of labour is referred to as the "politics–administration dichotomy." The dichotomy asserts that politics is about making controversial choices. Such choices often involve compromises between conflicting ideas and values. In a democracy, politicians must make basic political choices. Administration, on the other hand, was seen as a "scientific" process concerned with how best to implement the political will. It was an activity to be undertaken by expert civil servants.

A clear division between politics and administration has proven hard to achieve. In Canada, the senior federal civil service became an influential elite that was committed to a mixed economy and closely allied to the Liberal Party. Far from being neutral servants of the state, they were deeply involved with pressure groups, provincial governments, and foreign governments. Moreover, civil servants sometimes implemented political decisions lethargically. In policymaking and implementation, civil servants wielded discretion when interpreting the political will and in applying laws on a day-to-day basis.

In Canada and other advanced democracies, administrative power raised three paramount concerns. First, could the civil service be controlled by democratic politics? Or was its size, expertise, and continuity in office so great that it had transformed democracy into government by unelected officials? Second, the administrative state gave rise to deep concerns about pathological and inefficient behaviours of government bureaucracies. Government organizations were often rule-bound, inflexible, and unable to see the merits of individual cases. Finally, the administrative state was eventually seen as an impediment to national economic performance. Its great size, its alleged slowness to adapt, and its commitment to active government, it was argued, stifled initiative, creativity, and entrepreneurship. These latter ideas in particular assumed unprecedented credibility and wide purchase in the 1980s.

NEW PUBLIC MANAGEMENT: ESSENTIAL ELEMENTS

New public management has many dimensions, eclectic roots, and diverse supporters and critics. It arguably has six essential elements, all of which stand in contrast to the principles and ideals of the administrative state described in the preceding section. New public management asserts that government administration must be focused on the achievement of results, in contrast to public management as it evolved in postwar Canada, which allegedly was preoccupied with processes and rules. New public management argues that effective organizations must know where they want to go and how to get there. A focus on results leads to new public management's stress on strategic plans that are tied to budgets. Through the 1990s, government agencies have tried to determine their core priorities and to shed peripheral activities. New public management's emphasis on results leads to the complaint that it causes government agencies to imitate corporations.

New public management demands the rigorous, formal measurement of organizational performance. The new idea is that public organizations, to be effective and accountable, must constantly examine their performance in relation to clear goals and benchmarks. This explicit focus on performance measurement is in stark contrast to traditional thinking that assumed that government programs, especially in social policy spheres, could not be meaningfully evaluated by quantitative techniques. Here lies a major difference between public management as traditionally and presently practiced in Canada. For example, Alberta's complex system of "performance indicators" which are used to evaluate the "success" of public programs are a highly developed expression of the new emphasis on quantification. So too is the increasing use of student test results and international comparisons and benchmarks in the evaluation of Canadian students, teachers, and school systems.

New public management emphasizes enhanced managerial freedom that should be aggressively exercised. The idea is that government managers need freedom to allocate resources, to hire personnel, and to make decisions. They must not be slowed by bureaucratic rules that stifle managerial initiative and frustrate citizens. The slogan "let the managers manage" is a revered one in public administration. New public management combines the traditional idea with two other dimensions. It advocates considerable autonomy for those at the front lines of government service. The police officer on the beat, the front-line social worker, and the emergency ward nurse must be "empowered" to make decisions. And while advocating managerial freedom, new public management also demands increased political direction over the entire administrative apparatus (Aucoin, 1997). Indeed, a famous new public management slogan is "Governments must steer not row" (Osborne and Gaebler, 1992). New public management tries to fuse centralized policy authority with decentralized service delivery.

New public management asserts that government bureaucracies are generally ineffective instruments for delivering public services. Governments thus must explore "alternative" mechanisms for service delivery. This tenet has complex roots and represents one of the fundamental changes in thinking about Canadian government since the 1980s. It asserts that government bureaucracies are by their very nature inflexible and inefficient. Corporations, not-for-profits, or "reinvented" government organizations, on the other hand, are free of dead weight. It is assumed that public management suffers because competition is absent and thus public managers must introduce competitive practices wherever possible.

New public management's emphasis on "alternative service delivery" has spawned new administrative practices. Public programs are now delivered by "partnerships" with non-profit agencies; government buildings are sometimes built and run as "profit centres"; and many government agencies, such as Revenue Canada, have been converted into semi-autonomous organizations with day-to-day freedom from direct political control and centralized personnel and financial supervision. Public universities have struck many arrangements with corporations in the support of their research or the delivery of services. This aspect of new public management is the most visible to citizens and the most controversial. Among critics, it evokes two negative images—a fragmented public sector with weak accountability and an emasculated government where private sector norms, not the public interest, dominate.

New public management sees the citizen as the primary object of civil service attention. This idea shares close intellectual links with the customer-service revolution in the retail and service sectors. Governments now devote great effort to "customer" satisfaction. An example is "one-stop shopping" for government services where programs previously operated by several agencies and governments are grouped together in a single facility. The premise of such activity is that government administration has been preoccupied with procedures that, while well-intentioned, have lost sight of citizen needs for efficient and courteous service. Hierarchy compounds the problem by causing civil servants to manage "upwards" with undue emphasis on the whims of politicians and administrative superiors.

New public management has a distinctive rhetoric. Its language of downsizing, rightsizing, business plans, performance indicators, and networking is taken from the private sector. For citizens, the vocabulary is either uplifting or offensive. Regardless, it is replete with images of government as business. Like all significant changes in thinking, new public management reflects several intellectual currents, political changes, and economic trends. It certainly embraces new ideas about management that have revolutionized corporations in the 1980s and 1990s (Hood, 1991). The notion is that large firms underwent a management revolution that made them aggressive competitors in the new economy. The logic is that if corporations can be reinvented, so too can governments, if correct reform principles are applied.

New public management is closely related to prevailing wisdom that governments must limit their roles, that government deficits and debts are intolerable, and that markets must have more sway. Its slogan "doing more with less" captured the spirit of the 1990s. So too does its concern with responsive and citizen-focused government. New public management's anti-bureaucratic stance is part of a long search for alternatives to bureaucracy. In contrast to faceless bureaucracy, new public management promises flexible, decentralized, and customer-friendly public organizations.

The links between new public management and political ideologies are complex (Cohn, 1997). In Britain, Prime Minister Thatcher's Conservatives, and in the United States, the Republican presidency of Ronald Reagan, sought to radically reduce the role of government. But their plans for a massive reduction of the state's size proved politically impossible. Both leaders reduced their ambitions. New public management then became an ally. If a large role for government was inescapable, government could be run like a business, by people with entrepreneurial zeal and with an eye to the bottom line. New public management thus made virtue of necessity.

New public management was also an accessory of more centrist governments like the Clinton Democrats in the United States and the Jean Chrétien Liberals in Canada. For them, new public management held out a magnificent prospect. If properly implemented, it would allow citizens to enjoy the benefits of active government without a menacing bureaucracy or the economic perils of deficits. In Canada, failed efforts at "mega-constitutional" reform also aided new public management. In the 1990s, governments argued that federalism must be shown to work and that citizens' needs must not be lost sight of in intergovernmental negotiations. Such ideas were fertile ground for new public management ideas, although their application has been condemned for masking Ottawa's lust for power, for demeaning the provinces, and for ignoring Quebec's distinctiveness (Noel, 2000).

Many social democrats also saw merit in new public management. It offered escape from age-old links between socialism and oppressive bureaucracy. It also offered a vision of a politically progressive decentralization of power.

ALTERNATIVE SERVICE DELIVERY: WHITHER THE ADMINISTRATIVE STATE?

New public management's emphasis on alternative service delivery leads to new links between business and governments, between citizens and the state, and between the not-for-profit sector and governments. The face of Canadian government has been altered. Alternative service delivery is a complex phenomenon. It means the delivery of public services by a range of non-governmental organizations and/or government organizations operating according to commercial criteria. It embraces privatization, contracting out, and partnerships between governments, firms, and not-for-profit organizations. It can be very visible through devices like toll roads run by private firms or by public high schools in Nova Scotia that involve private funding and management. Another controversial manifestation is the enhanced use of "user fees" by government agencies whose self-image is that of profit centres.

Advocates of alternative service delivery approach their task with almost religious devotion (Langford, 1997). They want a public sector that creatively devises new partnerships notwithstanding a possible loss of policy coherence and accountability. Alternative service delivery has supporters across the ideological spectrum. Fiscal conservatives lust after its cost-saving potential. Social democrats like the idea of power sharing that devolves decision making to communities. And hard-nosed neoliberals see alternative service delivery as a halfway house before governments abandon certain activities altogether.

In the 1990s, Canadian governments also rediscovered the not-for-profit sector as a vehicle for program delivery (Hall and Reed, 1998). Not-for-profits were portrayed as expressions of community spirit. They were also seen as organizations that were immune from the assumed deficiencies of government bureaucracies and profit-seeking firms. As such, not-for-profits assumed a heavy burden in an era of financial restraint.

Such optimism seems ill-founded. The Canadian not-for-profit sector is diverse, embracing modest organizations such as local "Meals on Wheels," as well as substantial national organizations such as the Salvation Army. The sector's capacity varies considerably across the country. Moreover, not-for-profits, like governments and businesses, are themselves in turmoil. Government cutbacks have pressured them to provide more services as they become a "second safety net." Yet as demand grows, their resources dwindle and they face greater competition in fundraising. They depend on volunteers as volunteers are becoming fewer and more demanding of experiences that are relevant to paid employment. Not-for-profits, some of which are themselves substantial bureaucracies, are not exempt from societal suspicion of established power. Organizations like the once-revered Canadian Red Cross have been condemned. Not-for-profits like Uncles at Large have been implicated in sexual abuse scandals. Women's and immigrants' organizations are sometimes scorned as pleaders for "special interests."

"Homecare" is an excellent example of new public management in practice. It is now an important element of healthcare policy in Canada and refers to a range of policies united by the idea that healthcare is often better provided in the home of the person who is sick than in a hospital or other institutions. Homecare can be a welcome alternative especially for elderly people and others who require continuing healthcare. For governments it offers the prospect of reduced healthcare costs. A recent comparison of policy in Ontario and Quebec shows homecare to be a bewildering tangle of government agencies, community organizations, not-for-profits, and private firms linked through partnerships, overarching government organizations, and contracts (Jenson and Phillips, 2000). Distinctions between government, firms, and not-for-profits are extremely unclear. Strong accountability is certainly not the system's hallmark. Second, Ontario and Quebec pursue quite different policies. Quebec favours an active role for the provincial government while Ontario, especially under the Conservatives' Common Sense Revolution, plays a steering role and is more partial to "for profit" delivery. In both provinces, serious issues arise about the capacity of the homecare sector. As healthcare reform proceeds, hospital care is both less frequent and generally of shorter duration than in the past. As a result, homecare service providers face increased demand for services within limited budgets. Homecare patients require more sophisticated treatment that often involves complex equipment and expertise for which volunteers are ill-prepared.

New public management recommends "partnerships" for the delivery of public services. Once heralded as efficient ways to provide public services and to save money, partnerships are under fire (Phillips and Graham, 2000). They are complex undertakings that bring government organizations, not-for-profits, and corporations into collaborations even though such organizations have radically different rationales. Some partnerships work well, while others do not. Definitive conclusions are difficult to arrive at.

Partnerships in social policy areas are especially complex. The AIDS Network of Toronto is a working partnership between governments, corporations, and community organizations that has successfully mounted public awareness campaigns. Careful planning, detailed administrative agreements, and clear, shared objectives form the foundations of the partnership (Phillips and Graham, 1999). Other partnerships are less successful, especially when governments become overbearing. Efforts to employ the Immigrant Services Society of Vancouver as a federal government vehicle for service delivery to refugees floundered over questions of program control. Moreover, public concern is mounting about partnerships between universities and corporations. Critics argue that universities are sacrificing their independence for short-term financial gain. Contracts between universities and major soft-drink companies that confer campus-wide monopolies to the companies in exchange for scholarship funds and services are particularly controversial.

Not-for-profits are romantically portrayed as alternatives to markets and bureaucracy and as feasible vehicles for the delivery of public services (Drucker, 1993). Under new public management logic, Canadian governments are creating new relationships with civil society without any sense of overall priorities, long-term objectives, or desired outcomes (Langford, 1997). The complexities of partnerships and the resources required by not-for-profits are seldom thoroughly assessed. Partnerships and other mechanisms of alternative service delivery may avoid rigorous government accounting, privacy legislation, and equity laws. A checkerboard administrative structure arises that, without compelling rationale or public debate, treats Canadians differently (Bennett, 1999; Langford, 1997).

EVALUATING NEW PUBLIC MANAGEMENT

New public management has evoked a major debate about public administration, the role of government, and democratic principles. The charges against it are complex, serious, and difficult to evaluate. Nevertheless, they should evoke reflection by political scientists and citizens. A basic indictment is simple—new public management is unnecessary. Since the mid-1980s, the civil service has been incessantly and wrongfully vilified as politically menacing and economically wasteful. The critique of bureaucracy has been deliberately one-sided, rooted in stereotypes and old prejudices and indifferent to the substantial contribution of public service to citizen well-being, social justice, and equity. The view of new public management as an unnecessary revolution highlights modern politics' unrelenting criticism of the civil service. It is also an academic critique in the real sense of the word. New public management is a day-to-day reality for Canadians that will not go away simply because its principles are thought to be erroneous.

A related, but different, analysis sees new public management as an instrument of government restraint. Christopher Hood (1991) warns against conflating debates about the role of government and debates about new public management. In his view, they involve different issues and politics. But whatever the intellectual merits of Hood's view, public debate links new public management and government restraint. With few exceptions, Canadians worried about the weakening of government, the excessive power of business, and the "Americanization" of Canada oppose privatization and other new public management methods. By the same token, advocates of reduced government support new public management. Ideology and management philosophy thus combine to create opposing views about what government should do and how it should do it. This situation makes evaluation of competing claims very difficult. On some major matters, notably the financial savings achieved by public management, evidence is lacking. Ideological differences mean that the criteria for evaluation are themselves in dispute.

Another basic critique is that new public management debases Canadian democracy in deep but subtle ways. It denigrates democratic citizenship by portraying citizens as customers of government. New public management's stress on private sector management theories, market tests, and partnerships transforms government from a unique institution into a commonplace fixture that can be managed by the same principles as a grocery store. Over time, government organizations become ordinary in our eyes.

A single-minded emphasis on results and efficiency may have the same consequence. Performance indicators may devalue such crucial things as accountability, responsiveness, and equity because they are hard to quantify. And performance measures may be biased against government activity per se. It is sometimes argued that, if government expenditures cannot be shown to contribute directly to societal well-being in intended ways, they should not be undertaken at all. New public management also transforms the administrative state, once driven by high ideals of public service and unity of purpose, into a jungle of partnerships in which citizens have little confidence and where accountability is weak.

Such important ideas must not be accepted at face value. For one thing, wholesale rejection of new public management leaves critics in the impossible position of defending bureaucracy with its massive accumulation of weaknesses. Second, new public management is arguably less radical than its critics maintain. As Hood notes, management philosophies shift over time and emphasize different values. New public management simply elevates efficiency as a value and downplays accountability and process (1991). Moreover, is a focus on results, efficiency, and performance always antithetical to good government? Should we ignore government performance simply because its measurement is complex or because we disagree about the standards? Might clear standards and transparent government objectives not enhance democracy by exposing implicit priorities, by exposing disagreements about values, and by prompting citizen scrutiny of neglected administrative and policy matters?

Peter Aucoin, a leading Canadian student of governance, makes a compelling contribution to this debate. He writes:

> [T]here can be no absolute standards of clarity, performance and objectivity in any of these regards. The absence of such standards is not a justification for diminishing a commitment to pursuing good government. To deny the possibility of progress in these respects is to accept that responsible government can only be partisan; that half-truths, even falsehoods, must be accepted as the norm and that parliamentarians and citizens must simply trust ministers and officials because public management is too complex and seamless to accommodate contractual distinctions in relation to authorities and responsibilities in the area of policy and operations (1997, 235).

Another line of attack stresses the impact of new public management rather than its deeper democratic merits. This critique, unlike the previous one, sees virtue in new public management, especially its quest for citizen-centred administration and reduced bureaucracy. It concludes, however, that new public management's drawbacks and unintended consequences generally outweigh its merits. First, it is argued that new public management's emphasis on alternative service delivery is flawed. Governments have wrongly assumed that not-for-profits can easily deliver public services. They presupposed that not-for-profits had the capacity and the commitment to be an alternate safety net. Moreover, alternative service delivery lacks an overarching democratic philosophy or plan. It is defined differently and implemented differently in different jurisdictions and evaluated by competing standards. As a result, the public sector is being transformed into a maze. Accountability suffers and citizens are bombarded by conflicting claims about deregulation, privatization, and partnerships. A related concern is that laws and administration will be unevenly applied when government services are delivered by corporations and not-for-profits.

A further complaint is that new public management has reduced neither government's size nor the power of bureaucracy. Over-managed government organizations are still commonplace. New public management has transformed government managers from service deliverers into program evaluators, performance measurers, and contract supervisors. A policy-making and policy-delivery bureaucracy becomes an evaluation bureaucracy. Business planning, results management, and performance measures can inflict their own rigidities. Such processes have their own rhythms, their own biases, and their own indifference to alternative viewpoints. Performance indicators, for example, can easily become ends in themselves. Schoolteachers, administrators, and politicians often boast that higher scores on tests—the performance indicator—mean that students are being "better educated." Or are the teachers simply "teaching the test"? Do test results measure "learning" or better memorization?

LOOKING TOWARDS THE FUTURE

In the early 2000s, Canadian public management is in turmoil. A pessimistic view is that deficit-inspired new public management has led Canadian governments to manifest the worst of two administrative traditions. On the one hand, the traditional administrative state has been transformed into an instrument of prime ministerial power. As Donald Savoie argues, the senior federal civil service is highly politicized, closely linked to the needs of an imperial prime ministership and driven by the view that it must be responsive to political leadership (1999). It lacks the capacity to develop robust public policies. It is demoralized after two decades of anti-government rhetoric.

At the same time, new public management is under fire. It is no panacea and it has not been fully implemented in Canada especially when compared with the United Kingdom and Australia. A number of reasons account for this situation including lack of political will, the indifference of a stodgy bureaucratic elite, and growing public opposition to alternative service delivery (Aucoin, 1997). Moreover, new public management in the federal government has proceeded on the principle that administrative reform is principally achieved through attitudinal change. What is required is the inculcation of entrepreneurial ideas into the minds of civil servants. Other governments have proceeded on the view that administrative reform is driven by budget cuts.

The future does not look much brighter. The administrative state and new public management are both badly tarnished. The administrative state bears the heavy legacy of alleged inefficiency, rule-bound behaviour, and power-hungry conduct. And the bloom is off the new public management rose. Canadians are growing weary of the incessant worship of business culture, practices, and rhetoric. Privatization, once a panacea, now conjures up images of sieve-like prisons, dirty hospitals, and unsafe schools where, under the guise of maintaining public education, firms advertise their wares to children. In this vein, the tragedy at Walkerton, Ontario, in 2000, where 11 citizens died as a result of contaminated municipal water, may mark a watershed in public opinion. Much of the debate has focused on new public management principles and practices. Was water quality management unwisely "downloaded" from Queen's Park to local governments? Were there too many unclear reporting relationships? Should water quality testing be done by private laboratories?

The new public management revolution is stalled, unable to move ahead or backward. It cannot move ahead because there is no strong public support for it. New public management loses its core logic as fears of government deficits subside in the public consciousness. Why should we even try to do more with less? In this sense, new public management is firmly linked to government restraint. Canadians won't have one without the other. By the same token, administrative reforms cannot be reversed easily even if there is a will to do so. For example, new public management practices have transformed the operations of public hospitals in Canada. Many services such as laundry, food preparation, and laboratory work are contracted out; some nurses have been replaced by lesser qualified and lesser-paid nursing assistants; and surgical practices presume that most patients will recover at home instead of in the hospital. Examples abound across the federal, provincial, and municipal sectors in Canada. Such major changes cannot be easily reversed. Witness the confused and confusing spectacle of Canadian student loans whose administration bounces around between direct federal government provision and provision under contract by the chartered banks.

Democratic politics are unlikely to break the logjam. As public finance issues fade from the agenda, no Canadian political party has a public philosophy that will sort out the administrative malaise. The situation is further complicated by different levels of commitment by governments to new public management. In Alberta, the "Klein Revolution" elevated new public management to the status of a secular religion. The provincial government is driven by a business planning process, results management, and a strong performance indicator system. Alberta mocks the federal government as timid, wasteful, and indifferent to serious management reform.

CONCLUSION

This chapter demonstrates that new public management has created new tensions in Canadian society and exacerbated existing ones. Its focus on results, performance measurement, and client service are new ways of thinking about public administration. Its emphasis on alternative service delivery, a concept rooted in the view that government programs can often be better delivered by corporations or not-for-profits, is particularly controversial. Alternative service delivery has both supporters and critics. It is seen as an attack on democratic government as well as a creative solution to the problem of bureaucracy, and a way to save money. The argument here is that alternative service delivery, especially through partnerships and not-for-profits, is a multi-faceted phenomenon. Governments have romantically portrayed not-for-profits as a source of volunteer initiative and as a symbol of vibrant community spirit. Little serious thought has been given to the dynamics of not-for-profits or to their troubled environment.

New public management challenges political scientists to evaluate carefully its deeper logic and practical consequences. Interesting arguments can be made for and against it. Several of these have been presented. At the end of the day, Canadian politics will have to establish a working synthesis of new public management ideals within the administrative state. Each paradigm poses challenges for democratic government in Canada.

REFERENCES

Aucoin, Peter. 1997. *The New Public Management: Canada in Comparative Perspective*. Montreal: Institute for Research on Public Policy.

Banting, K.G. 1987. *The Welfare State and Canadian Federalism*, 2nd ed. Montreal and Kingston: McGill-Queen's University Press.

Bennett, Colin J. 1999. "Where the Regulators are Regulated: Privacy Protection within the Contemporary Canadian State." In G.B. Doern, Margaret M. Hill, Michael J. Prince and Richard J. Schultz (eds.), *Changing the Rules: Canadian Regulatory Regimes and Institutions*. Toronto: University of Toronto Press.

Boychuk, Gerard William. 1998. *Patchworks of Purpose: The Development of Provincial Social Assistance Regimes in Canada*. Montreal and Kingston: McGill-Queen's University Press.

Cohn, Daniel. 1997. "Creating Crises and Avoiding Blame: The Politics of Public Service Reform and the New Public Management in Great Britain and the United States." *Administration and Society 29*, 584–616.

Drucker, Peter F. 1993. *Post-Capitalist Society*. New York: HarperCollins.

Hall, M.H. and Reed, P.B. 1998. "Shifting the burden: How much can government download to the non-profit sector?" *Canadian Public Administration 41*, 1–20.

Hood, Christopher. 1991. "A Public Management for all Seasons?" *Public Administration 69*, 3–19.

Jenson, Jane and Phillips, Susan. 2000. "Distinctive Trajectories: Homecare and the Voluntary Sector in Quebec and Ontario." In K. Banting (ed.), *The Nonprofit Sector in Canada: Roles and Relationships*. Kingston, Ont.: School of Policy Studies, Queen's University.

Langford, John L. 1997. "Power Sharing in the Alternative Service Delivery World." In Robin Ford and David Zussman (eds.), *Alternative Service Delivery: Sharing Governance in Canada*. Toronto: Institute of Public Administration of Canada.

Noel, Alain. 2000. "Without Quebec: Collaborative Federalism with a Footnote?" *Policy Matters*, 1 (2) Montreal: Institute for Research on Public Policy.

Osborne, David, and Gaebler, Ted. 1992. *Reinventing Government*. Reading, Mass.: Addison-Wesley.

Phillips, Susan and Graham, Katherine. 2000 "Hand in Hand: When Accountability meets Collaboration in the Voluntary Sector." In K. Banting (ed.), *The Nonprofit Sector in Canada*. Kingston, Ont.: School of Policy Studies, Queen's University.

Savoie, Donald. 1999. "The Rise of Court Government in Canada." *Canadian Journal of Political Science 32*, 635–664.

Tupper, Allan 1999. "The Civil Service." In Janine Brodie (ed.), *Critical Concepts: An Introduction to Politics*. Scarborough, Ont.: Prentice-Hall Canada.

Whitaker, Reg. 2000. "Politics versus Administration: Politicians and Bureaucrats". In M.S. Whittington and Glen Williams (eds.), *Canadian Politics in the 21st Century*. 5th ed. Toronto: Nelson.

WEBLINKS

Institute of Public Administration of Canada
www.ipaciapc.ca

Canadian Red Cross: Homecare
www.redcross.ca/english/homecare

Public Management in Canada
www1.oecd.org/puma/country/canada.htm

chapter sixteen

The Old and the New Constitutionalism

David Schneiderman

INTRODUCTION

After numerous rounds of constitutional reform and intermittent constitutional crises, it could be said that Canadians appreciate the difficulties of living with each other in a single constitutional space. Canadian familiarity with constitutional conflict turns on Canada–Quebec axes, but that familiarity is being challenged by other constitutional developments from within. Following the entrenchment of the *Charter of Rights and Freedoms,* it is said, Canada confronts another constitutional challenge heralded by the arrival of the *Charter* "revolution."

This fundamental restructuring of Canada's constitution, as the argument goes, follows as a result of the new powers accorded to particularistic interests to reshape Canada's general political landscape. These interests—termed the "Court Party" by Morton and Knopff (2000)—employ *Charter* rights and constitutional litigation in order to achieve social and political change otherwise unattainable in ordinary legislative arenas. An emphasis on the "post-material"—on claims concerning equal rights for women, racial and ethnic minorities, gays and lesbians, or Aboriginal peoples—marks a striking and new departure, it is claimed, from the constitutionalism of times past.

What is underscored in this narrative is the newness—revolutionary in its impact—of rights-based constitutional litigation in Canada. This narrative distances Canadians from their constitutional past, fought on the terrain of equality rights. Not only is this constitutional past forgotten but such an approach fails to take heed of other aspects of our constitutional present. An emphasis on contemporary rights litigation ignores developments occurring both within and without the boundaries of national states. Within, constitutional constraints are being employed to help shape domestic policy so that it conforms to the perceived demands of globalized patterns of production and distribution. From without, there is emerging a constitution-like regime of rules and structures intended to tame domestic politics.

This chapter examines claims to constitutional "newness" being made on a number of these fronts. The argument will proceed in the following way: The first part outlines the "Court Party" thesis, articulated by Morton and Knopff (2000). The next part contrasts this present with the past, drawing on earlier Canadian experiences of constitutional litigation in the pursuit of equality rights, experiences that often are overlooked in contemporary critiques of rights litigation. The third part outlines a version of the "new constitutionalism" that may have more of a legitimate claim to authenticity. This legal regime for trade promotion and investment, though, also exhibits elements of the old constitutionalism which are explored in the final section.

POST-MATERIALISM WITHIN

The legitimacy of the Canadian Supreme Court has long been questioned by academic commentators from Quebec, who have argued that the Court's decision making in federalism disputes exhibits a bias in favour of the federal government (Lajoie, Mulazzi, and Gamache, 1986). This contention was followed by an early and vigorous assault on the *Charter* from the academic left (Mandel, 1989; Bakan, 1997). Their critique concerned the use of rights to attack state regulation and simultaneously to shield private power from public scrutiny. The most recent academic assault, coming from the academic right, concerns other matters. This critique expresses anxiety and resistance to such matters as the equality rights of women in matters of abortion, equal treatment of gays and lesbians in the public realm, and the recognition of the constitutional rights of Aboriginal peoples.

In an influential 1990 essay, Alan Cairns identified a fresh phenomenon in Canadian constitutional discourse. New political actors had landed on the constitutional stage as a direct result of the 1982 *Constitution* and *Charter* for they had "received some kind of recognition" (1995, 120). They included women, the disabled, Aboriginal peoples, official language minorities, and "third force" ethnic Canadians, all of whom "now see themselves as part of the constitution" (120). According to Cairns, these groups "occupy niches in the constitution, possess constitutional clauses, carry constitutional identities, own stakes in their constitution, and in their own eyes have constitutional standing" (127). Cairns's objective in this and related work, was to measure the impact of these new constitutional identities on the older and previously dominant discourse of Canadian federalism. Cairns admitted, however, that the old constitutional discourse was not entirely dissimilar from the new. Other constitutional actors previously had coalesced around particular constitutional provisions. The business community, for instance, "have fought, as self-interest dictated, for generous or restrictive interpretations of clauses impinging directly on their pursuits" (1995, 128). The relevant difference was that these older actors did not cling to particular constitutional texts, as occurs now, which then generates particularistic "constitutional identities."

Similar arguments about newness have spawned claims of a *Charter* "revolution" (Morton and Knopff, 2000). These critics express dismay at "special interests" that, armed with new constitutional rights, have captured the national political agenda. Transforming the judicial arena into a legislative one, with the acquiescence of Canada's Supreme Court, these groups have sought not to restrict government policy but to expand it. Morton and Knopff (2000) dub these interests the "Court Party," they are those who seek to transform failed policy initiatives into legal victories.

The revolution precipitated by the *Charter of Rights and Freedoms* entitles special interests to litigate new claims having to do with rights of recognition. These issues are characterized as "post-material," as they concern claims to status and equal respect for groups. This is contrasted with traditional claims concerning the "material," organized around occupational interests like the labour movement (Morton and Knopff, 2000, 78). Though group claims often have to do with interests that are "material" in nature (Fraser, 1997, 15)—such as, in the *Vriend* case, keeping one's job—Morton and Knopff hold fast to this distinction. It is another way of bolstering their argument about newness.

Disputes concerning the post-material, these critics claim, move the judiciary outside their traditional realms of expertise and into the unfamiliar terrain of public policy. As there is nothing in the text of Canada's constitution that compels these results, the Canadian judiciary are simply putting into effect the preferences of well-organized cadres of professional litigants and academics (drawn mostly from Canadian law schools) (Morton and Knopff 2000, 113). Rather than displace ordinary politics, judges should restrain themselves and leave such matters for elected officials in Parliament and provincial legislatures.

The language of liberal rights—those familiar terms *freedom, liberty,* and *equality*—has been seized upon by groups without privileged access to the corridors of power. As the experience of the National Association for the Advancement of Coloured People (NAACP) in the United States suggests, rights can be a resource for the articulation of claims by groups made subordinate by society's social and political relations (*Brown* v. *Board of Education*; Tushnet, 1987). In Canada, the women's movement, anti-poverty and labour activists, and gays and lesbians, among others, have viewed the *Charter of Rights and Freedoms* as a vehicle for promoting and advancing claims informed by their participation in a larger political struggle for dignity and equality. But not every case is expected to be won—quite the opposite (Herman, 1997). Rather, it is claimed that the discourse of rights can improve political dialogue by enabling voices, otherwise silenced, to participate in Canadian political life (Jackman, 1996). Charter litigation, according to this view, emerges as a viable strategy through which to pursue legal reform.

It also is true that these social movements often look to government as a vehicle for realizing their policy objectives. The anti-poverty movement, for example, expects government to provide adequate means by which the poor can sustain themselves. The redistribution of wealth via the personal and corporate income tax system remains a key government function with which to combat poverty. Similarly, the women's movement looks to government to guarantee protection from domestic and sexual violence, to prohibit pornography, and to regulate reproductive technologies.

While these groups may be seeking to maintain levels of state action, it is misleading to suggest that the *Charter* will be the vehicle by which these groups can secure it. The catalogue of *Charter* cases, both in trial and appellate courts, demonstrates that the *Charter* has worked primarily to the benefit of the accused in the criminal trial process.

Even in these cases, the practical result has been changes in police and prosecutorial practices rather than wholesale acquittals (Stuart, 1994).

Moreover, many of the cases heralded as "victories" by social movements—and losses by critics on the right—have been defensive ones, that is, laws sought to be struck down by reason of the *Charter* are "saved" by the Supreme Court. Consider that in the cases of *Edwards Books* (concerning a secular Sunday-closing law), *Keegstra* (concerning criminal prohibitions on the promotion of racial hatred), and *Butler* (concerning obscenity law), the state's ability to regulate in each area was assailed using the *Charter*. Significantly, in each case, laws were attacked using the *Charter's* protections of individual rights. By virtue of the Court's "contextual" approach, which takes into account the larger social, political, and historical context and which then saves a greater range of government activity from judicial invalidity, these laws withstood *Charter* scrutiny.

Some gay and lesbian equality rights litigation has achieved limited success and so, in this area, it could be said that litigious activists have used the *Charter* to achieve social change otherwise difficult to secure. Among the notable cases in this regard is the one concerning Delwyn Vriend. Vriend wanted to contest his discharge from employment on the ground that he was discriminated against by reason of his sexual orientation. Alberta human rights law prohibited discrimination on a variety of grounds, like "race" and "sex," but not "sexual orientation." The Court's ruling required that Alberta also protect gays and lesbians from discrimination. Yet the Court's decision in *Vriend* merely elevated to national constitutional status a legislative reality recognized in every provincial legislature, with the exception of Alberta. Few provinces permitted discrimination in the provision of public services, in employment practices, in the rental of accommodation, and in the access to services ordinarily available to the public. The result in this case was that the rogue province of Alberta was asked to comply with this national standard. In the case of *M.* v. *H.* (1999), the Court required that same-sex couples be entitled to claim the same spousal support under Ontario law that heterosexual couples can. The Court could not even find that the exclusion of gay couples from the statutory scheme was rationally connected to the legislative objective of providing for "the equitable resolution of economic disputes that arise when intimate relationships between individuals who have been financially interdependent break down" (para. 85). It should be emphasized that the claim in *M.* v. *H.* concerned private obligations owing to financially dependent spouses—not those owed by the state. Public opinion across Canada, Fletcher and Howe suggest, is inclined to arrive at similar conclusions. Legislatures "that had refused to protect gay rights through human rights legislation," they write, "were clearly out of line with public attitudes" (Fletcher and Howe, 2001, 275).

THE PRESENCE OF THE PAST

Is this stream of constitutional litigation "new," in any real sense? A simple focus on the fact that Canada, prior to 1982, had no entrenched constitutional regime for the general protection of rights and freedoms signals that this phenomenon is new—after all, this was a country historically without a constitutional bill of rights. But this approach may be overly formalistic. The late Chief Justice Dickson (1994) suggested that there is a long tradition in Canada of judges reviewing laws for their conformity to constitutional text under the division of legislative powers. Even in this context, he added, the Supreme Court of Canada had been developing a "rights-oriented jurisprudence" (Dickson, 1994, 4–6). What is new is the expanded grounds for judicial review, he argued, not the judicial review function itself. Critics are right to reply, however, that the volume of rights litigation really has been turned up in the *Charter* era.

What about the "Court party" thesis—that a well-organized cadre of post-materialist groups have turned to constitutional litigation as the principal tactic for achieving recognition of certain elite interests? As Dobrowolsky argues, it simply is not the case that social movements were "born out of the *Charter*." This is an approach that "denies years of activism on the part of these groups" (Dobrowolsky, 1997, 312). A turn to the historical record, then, may unsettle claims about the new nature of *Charter* litigation. Cairns, for one, admits that "an unbiased re-examination of the past . . . may discover traditions we have lost" (1995, 128). But this is unlikely, he states. These kinds of "copious pursuits" are efforts at "historical revisionism," he maintains, or the "invention of tradition" (128). Hein adds that "few organizations entered the courtroom to affect public policy [prior to the *Charter*] . . . few imagined that litigation could be turned into an instrument of reform" (2001, 222).

The historical record, however, reveals that minorities in Canada have resorted to litigation to promote the idea of equality rights. Though they may have been defensive measures or tactical mistakes (Roach, 1993, 161), this record confirms that the phenomenon of groups using rights in order to advance conceptions of equality is not new. Walker (1997) reveals that, in a series of key Canadian cases concerning race, well-organized minority communities turned to rights litigation in order to advance the cause of equality. We need only take up a few of the cases Walker discusses. In *Quong Wing* (1914), a Saskatchewan law prohibiting the employment of "white girls or females by Orientals in restaurants, laundries, etc." was challenged by Moose Jaw restauranteur Quong Wing. The Chinese community of Moose Jaw had decided at an earlier mass meeting that they would resist the law and "fight a test case" (Walker, 1997, 90). Quong Wing's unsuccessful appeal of his conviction to the Supreme Court of Canada was, according to Walker, a "deliberate test of the law" for which Quong Wing "had the support of the Chinese community" (1997, 100).

In *Christie* v. *York Corporation* (1940), Fred Christie was denied service at York Tavern (in the old Montreal Forum) on the grounds that the tavern did not serve "coloured people" (1997, 123). Christie launched a suit for damages against the tavern, and the "Fred Christie Defence Committee" was born, headed by a distinguished list of Montrealers. Most every Black family in Montreal made some small contribution to the fund. According to Walker, "Christie . . . sparked a mass community crusade to confront the humiliations of racial discrimination" (1997, 143). When, in 1951, a group of property owners sought to enforce a restrictive covenant restraining the sale of resort property to Jews (*Noble Wolfe* v. *Alley*), the Canadian Jewish Congress stepped in to help finance the case all the way to the Supreme Court of Canada (1997, 220–1).

These are hardly instances of organizations supporting "some challenges at a distance" (Hein, 2001, 221) or when the broad "policy consequences of a judicial opinion are unimportant" (Morton and Knopff, 2000, 26). Rather, local and national organizations were involved directly in mobilizing their communities in support of rights litigation. These groups often were critical to the success of the case, as in *Noble Wolfe*. Moreover, the object of the litigation was not merely to defend individual liberty but to shift public policy in an equality-enhancing direction.

Morton and Knopff do acknowledge historical parallels to the contemporary scene. They take up the wrong cases, however. Rather than drawing on these earlier struggles in equality rights litigation, they liken the contemporary period to the one in the 1930s when the U.S. Supreme Court blocked the implementation of President Roosevelt's New Deal plan. The Court there held that the legislation putting the plan into effect denied the right of individuals to liberty of contract. In other cases, the Court held that the law did not concern matters within the federal government's commerce power. A much weakened Canadian plan, introduced by Prime Minister R.B. Bennett, similarly failed to survive constitutional scrutiny for the reason that it concerned matters more properly enacted by provincial governments. "The current debate about judicial power," Morton and Knopff argue, "is largely a reprise of the similar debate that occurred in the 1930s, with only the partisan positions reversed" (2000, 31). Their complaint is that the judiciary, then as now, should act in a more restrained fashion.

The Courts of the 1930s, however, were concerned with prohibiting new state initiatives that could enhance the impoverished position of people wrought by the Depression. The opinions of the U.S. Supreme Court reflected constitutional values of an earlier time, the *Lochner* era. The structure of interpretation in the *Lochner* era was to halt uses of state power that unsettled the status quo in order to advance what were called "partial" (or class) interests (Gillman, 1993). The judicial decisions that are the subject of complaint today are not, in the main, about limiting government conduct as much as shaping that conduct so that it conforms with principles associated with equal respect and concern. These decisions are not about putting a halt to new legislative initiatives, nor are they very often about instituting new state initiatives. Rather, they are modest modifications of the law that ensure existing initiatives conform to values that reasonably derive from the text of the Constitution.

Yet there are other parallels that Morton and Knopff and other critics on the right have missed. These concern new intergovernmental initiatives and judicial decisions that reinforce the values we associate with the idea of "economic globalization." In the face of pressures generated by the seemingly globalized economy, states have made it a priority item to promote trade and the movement of goods, services, and people across national borders. The Canadian Supreme Court has not been immune to these tendencies. Paralleling these developments is the construction of a regime of rules and structures that is constitution-like in form, but operating outside the boundaries of traditional state structures. We shall examine each of these developments, in turn, below.

THE MATERIAL IN AND OUT OF COURT

It is curious that critics like Morton and Knopff would dismiss the role that economic interests play in shaping not only constitutional law, but also what arguably is now the dominant discourse in Canadian political culture. As Hein shows, "corporate interests" are actively engaging in *Charter* litigation—they represent nearly 40 percent of the cases that target the decisions of elected officials (2001, 231). At a general level, business firms have had some success in using *Charter* litigation to resist government regulation. According to Bauman, constitutional challenges "have become an important strategic device for businesses as they have made political gains through the process of *Charter* review" (1997, 66). In their zeal to expel the Court from the realms of abortion rights, family law, and Aboriginal rights, critics like Morton and Knopff have failed to notice this trend.

What is missing from the account so far, then, is the turn to economic rights—to the movement, both intergovernmental and juridical, to deepen and strengthen the hold of economic and consumer citizenship in the Canadian constitution. That analysis could begin by taking into consideration intergovernmental arrangements like the Agreement on Internal Trade (AIT). This 1994 agreement between the provinces and the federal government was borne out of a failed attempt to reform the text of the Canadian constitution in the direction of enhanced economic rights.

The AIT is designed to remove non-tariff restrictions on the movement of goods, services, and persons across provincial boundaries (Schneiderman, 1995). The AIT is modelled on other trade agreements, like the North American Free Trade Agreement (NAFTA) and the Uruguay Round General Agreement on Tariffs and Trade, policed by the World Trade Organization (WTO). AIT's central organizing principle is that of "non-discrimination." Provinces are prohibited from enacting laws that discriminate against another province's goods, persons, services, and investments; that restrict or prohibit their movement; or that create obstacles to internal trade. The provinces are entitled to seek resolution of complaints before dispute-resolution panels. There is even a qualified right of business firms to file complaints. Operating at the level of an intergovernmental agreement, the scheme appears innocuous enough. An AIT panel decision that thwarted the federal government's plans to ban the manganese-based fuel additive MMT, however, should have brought the AIT to greater prominence (Schneiderman, 1999b).

MMT has been blended in gasoline fuel sold in Canada for almost 20 years. Invoking environmental, health, and consumer protection grounds, the federal government moved to prohibit the importation of and interprovincial trade in MMT in June 1997. The Ethyl Corporation of Richmond, Virginia, the sole producer of MMT, answered by invoking the investment-protection provisions of the North American Free Trade Agreement (NAFTA), claiming $250 million (USD) in damages as compensation for the alleged expropriation of the company's investment interests (we turn to a more detailed discussion of NAFTA in the next part).

The government of Alberta (supported by three provinces) also filed an AIT complaint against the federal government for prohibiting interprovincial movement of MMT. The decision by an AIT dispute panel ultimately preempted Ethyl's NAFTA claim. AIT was armed with enough ammunition to force the federal government to back down. By a vote of four to one the dispute panel held that the federal ban on MMT was inconsistent with the AIT. According to the panel, the scientific evidence concerning the effects of MMT on vehicle emission systems and on the environment was "inconclusive." The panel did concede that there was a "reasonable basis" for the federal government to limit access to MMT in the interests of promoting environmental objectives. But the panel was not willing to give the benefit of the doubt to the federal government in any other respect. The panel, instead, adopted a strict approach to interpretation of the AIT—an approach most favourable to the complaining provinces, oil refiners, and to "free trade." By blocking the movement of MMT across provincial borders, the AIT panel concluded, the federal initiative ran afoul of the agreement. One year later, the government of Canada paid Ethyl the sum of $13 million (USD), representing legal fees and lost profits, rescinded the legislation, and admitted publicly that the use of MMT poses no environmental or health risks.

Though the scientific evidence of health risks associated with MMT may be ambiguous, Canada remains one of the few countries in the world where MMT is blended into automotive fuel. MMT was banned for 17 years in the United States by the Environmental Protection Agency (EPA). It was not until a court ruled in 1995 that the EPA had no legal authority to consider health issues under the *Clean Air Act* that MMT was legally available in the States (though it is still banned in California, the state with the toughest emission standards). Three years later, the Environmental Defence Fund reports that over 75 percent of U.S. oil refining capacity remains MMT free.

Judicial review under the Canadian constitution, under both the division of powers and under the *Charter of Rights and Freedoms*, also has enhanced the objective of promoting market relations. In the realm of federal–provincial constitutional litigation, the decision of the Supreme Court of Canada in *Hunt* (1993) deserves special mention. There, the Court struck down a Quebec "blocking statute" which prohibited the removal of documents from within Quebec required for legal proceedings taking place outside the province. Justice La Forest wrote an opinion on behalf of the Court without reference to any textual foundation, relying entirely on a structural reading of the Canadian constitution. He found the Quebec law was constitutionally beyond the capacity of the provincial legislature. Justice La Forest here built on his earlier decision in *Morguard* (1990, 1098) where he invoked the same neoliberal themes: "Accommodating the flow of wealth, skills and people across state lines," he declared, "has now become imperative." However desirable it may be to remove these kinds of impediments to civil proceedings, it is startling how far the Court was willing to bend constitutional law in order to satisfy these economic imperatives without grounding the analysis in the actual law of the constitution.

The Supreme Court of Canada has also enhanced the capacity of business enterprises to promote commercial products in a series of *Charter* decisions concerning freedom of expression. By endowing commercial speech with constitutional protection, the Court has helped to promote what Leslie Sklair calls the "culture-ideology of consumerism"—a "set of practices, attitudes and values, based on advertising . . . that encourages ever-expanding consumption of consumer goods" (1994, 260). In the *Rocket* case (1990), the Court declared constitutionally invalid a prohibition on professional advertising by dentists. This mode of expression—commercial speech— is typically accorded "low value" in the hierarchy of constitutional rights. Courts will often be deferential to government schemes that aim to regulate low-value speech. While the Court in *Rocket* acknowledged this, the judges characterized the speech in this case as having a significant "consumer component which required stricter scrutiny" (1990, 248). In a subsequent case, the Court vindicated the claims of the tobacco companies that federal legislation restricting the promotional activities of the tobacco industry and mandating health warnings on cigarette packages unjustifiably infringed freedom of expression (*RJR MacDonald* [1995]). According to the majority of the Court, consumers would have been "deprived" by this ban on advertising "of an important means of learning about product availability to suit their preferences and to compare brand content with an aim to reducing their risk to their health" (1995, para. 162). Despite the fact that the claim concerned low-value speech, it should not be "undervalued" as this speech imparted important information to consumers regarding "price, quality, and even health risks" (1995, para. 170). More recently, the Court has admitted that the need to constitutionally protect commercial speech "derives from the very nature of our economic system, which is based on the existence of a free market" (Guignard, 2002, para. 21). The Court has brazenly constitutionalized market relations between consumer and producer. One might fairly conclude that, in these cases, the Court has tilted constitutional interpretation in the direction of promoting the values and objectives we associate with economic globalization.

THE PRESENCE OF THE FUTURE

The Court party critique also elides the presence of an emergent regime to protect and promote trade and foreign investment that has many features of national constitutions. Stephen Gill characterizes this regime as giving effect to the "new constitutionalism" (1995, 412). The new constitutionalism refers to the quasi-legal restructuring of the state and the institutionalization of international political forms that emphasize market credibility and efficiency. These institutions place rigid limitations on processes of democratic decision making within national states. Key aspects of the economy are insulated from the influence of politicians or the mass of citizens "by imposing, internally and externally, 'binding constraints' on the conduct of fiscal, monetary, trade and investment policies" (412). By limiting state action with regard to these aspects of economic life, the new constitutionalism confers privileged rights of citizenship and representation on corporate capital, while at the same time constraining democratic processes (413).

Representative of the "new constitutionalism" is the proliferation of rule-making and rule-enforcement mechanisms designed to constrain state regulation of the market. The World Trade Organization, for instance, monitors the movement of goods and services across state borders and ensures state compliance with the Uruguay Round General Agreement on Tariffs and Trade (GATT) principle of "non-discrimination." The North American Free Trade Agreement and over 1700 Bilateral Investment Treaties (BITs) protect and promote foreign investment and generate an interlocking network of rules and rule-making structures so as to place further limits on state action (Schneiderman, 2000).

This new legal regime can be likened, as Gill suggests, to a new form of constitutionalism. This is a constitutionalism concerned with placing limits on the state—of inhibiting the possibilities for political action—by enacting binding constraints, in the form of general legal principles, on the ability of the state to intervene in the market. These rules operate both externally to the state—as independent legal regimes that discipline state action—and, as suggested above, internally, through the agency of constitutional reform and oftentimes judicial review. These rules are like constitutions in that they bind future generations of citizens to certain predetermined institutional forms through which politics are practised (Elster, 1984, 1992). In addition, they, like constitutions, are difficult to amend, include binding enforcement mechanisms together with judicial review, and, are sometimes even drawn from the language of domestic constitutions (Schneiderman, 1999a).

It is instructive to focus on Chapter 11 of NAFTA, which sets high levels of protection for foreign investors resident within the three party states—Canada, the United States, and Mexico. Many of the obligations undertaken in NAFTA, as in AIT, are organized around the idea of "non-discrimination." States may not distinguish, for the purposes of legal regulation, between domestic and foreign investors. Also connected to the principle of non-discrimination are prohibitions on "performance requirements," such as rules that mandate the use of local labour, goods, and services—these too are forbidden.

The rule prohibiting expropriations mandates not just equality of treatment, but places substantive limits on the law-making capacity of national states. This rule (the "takings rule") prohibits measures that "directly or indirectly" expropriate or nationalize investment interests or measures that are "tantamount to" expropriation. The classic candidates caught by this prohibition are outright takings of property by the state—the nationalization of the forces of production under socialism, for instance. Outright expropriations have greatly diminished in number, however, and are of little concern to contemporary investors (Powers, 1998, 128). Rather, what is of concern here are not express takings but what are called "creeping" expropriations (measures that cumulatively amount to expropriation), "regulatory" expropriations (measures that so impact on an investment interest that they are equivalent to a taking), and "partial" expropriations (measures that take only part of an investment interest), all of which are prohibited (Vandevelde, 1992, 121). Regulatory changes that "go too far," in other words, are intended to be caught by this rule (*Pennsylvania Coal*, 1922). The underlying premise is that governments can be expected to perform only minimal regulatory functions, all of which are subordinated to the market.

Regulatory measures of an uncertain magnitude are prohibited entirely unless they are for a "public purpose" (as opposed to a "private" interest), are "non-discriminatory" (that is, are general and do not target foreign investors), and are in accordance with the "due process of law" (drawn from the language of the Fourteenth Amendment to the U.S. Constitution and likely necessitating access to courts). If a taking meets these preliminary criteria, the expropriating state must then provide compensation according to the strictest available criteria—compensation equivalent to fair market value, paid without delay, and fully realizable and transferable. These disciplines are enforceable not just by states party to these agreements but by foreign investors themselves.

Given the variety of measures caught by this rule, it comes as no surprise that businesses have invoked the expropriations rule in NAFTA (or an earlier incarnation in the Canada-U.S. Free Trade Agreement) to challenge market regulations that impair their investment interests. A public auto-insurance plan, proposals for the plain packaging of cigarettes, and the cancellation of contracts to transfer public property into private hands (at Toronto's Pearson Airport) all triggered threats of litigation under NAFTA (Schneiderman, 1996). While threats alone do not trigger NAFTA's dispute settlement procedure, they played a role in limiting the range of social policy options available to these governments.

Of the arbitral proceedings launched under NAFTA, the Ethyl Corporation challenge of the Canadian ban on the import and export of the toxic gasoline additive MMT is instructive. The classification of MMT as a "dangerous toxin," Ethyl claimed, amounted to an expropriation under NAFTA. As mentioned earlier, the Canadian federal government settled the Ethyl claim for $13 (USD) million subsequent to losing an interprovincial trade dispute under the non-binding AIT. In another dispute, United Parcel Service is claiming $230 million in lost profits as a result of Canada Post cross-subsidizing courier services with profits generated from its publicly funded regular delivery service. Not all disputes emanate from U.S. firms. In a reverse-Ethyl case, Vancouver-based Methanex is suing for losses suffered by the phasing out of the gasoline additive MTBE in the state of California. Arbitration panels are constituted under the auspices of international arbitration facilities (like the International Centre for the Settlement of Investment Disputes [ICSID] located at the World Bank in Washington) at the behest of complaining states or investors. Panel decisions are binding on state actors and are enforceable like any other order issuing from a domestic court of law.

Only a handful of dispute-panel decisions under NAFTA's Chapter 11 have been rendered so far. We have learned, to date, that non-discriminatory regulations (measures that do not target foreign investors but that are neutral between domestic and foreign economic actors) are caught by the expropriations rule. Only those measures, however, that are "substantial enough" (*Pope and Talbot*, para. 96) or are "sufficiently restrictive" (*Pope and Talbot*, para. 102) will give rise to a claim of expropriation. We also have learned, in another case, that NAFTA's rule will catch not only instances of outright seizure of property (the easiest case) but also "incidental interference" with an investment that has the effect of depriving owners of a "significant part" of the "use or reasonably-to-be-expected economic benefit of property" (*Metalclad*, para. 103). Governments may be obliged to compensate owners for "lasting deprivation" of their economic rights, even if "the deprivation may be partial or temporary" (*S.D. Myers*, para. 283).

The characterization of NAFTA as "constitutional" should no longer be viewed as controversial. The recent decision of the NAFTA panel in the *S.D. Myers* case lays to rest any further doubt in this regard. One panellist describes trade agreements like NAFTA as having "an enormous impact on public affairs in many countries" (*S.D. Myers,* supplementary opinion, para. 34). He goes so far as to liken these agreements to "a country's constitution" for they "restrict the ways in which governments can act and they are very hard to change." While governments usually have the right to withdraw from these agreements with proper notice, this "is often practically impossible to do." "Pulling out of a trade agreement may create too much risk of reverting to trade wars, and may upset the settled expectations of many participants in the economy," the panellist admits. Amendment is made no easier, he writes, "just as it is usually very hard to change a provision of a domestic constitution" (*ibid.*, para. 34). The decision in *S.D. Myers,* in addition to a number of other recent NAFTA dispute panels, confirms that the investment-protection provisions of NAFTA have the effect of prohibiting state behaviour that substantially impairs even only a part of an investment interest. Neither the federal nor the provincial governments are likely to come out of these processes with enhanced regulatory authority.

Is this new constitutionalism all that "new"? We might resist this conclusion by drawing on a number of insights made by Karl Polanyi in *The Great Transformation* (1957). Polanyi maintains that there is a connection between constitutionalism and the maintenance of national markets. Accompanying the spread of markets was the principle of constitutionalism as a means of inhibiting the power of government. Constitutionalism demanded binding legal limitations on the authority of government, isolating economic from political power, and shielding the institution of private property with the highest conceivable legal protections. Polanyi also helps us to understand that the state was deeply implicated in the processes and institutions that gave rise to the market system.

Though the U.K. was without a written constitution, a similar pattern is identified by T.H. Marshall (1965). The emergence in the eighteenth century of what Marshall calls "civil rights" gave expression to the idea of economic freedom—of the right to work and to contract. Up until the mid–eighteenth century, both labourers and manufacturers could rely on the state to mediate social relations by ensuring, through appropriate legislation, the "getting of a competent livelihood" (Webb and Webb, 1920, 49). This consensus broke down in the latter half of the century as the state abandoned the legal regulation of trades in the interests of promoting industrial "efficiency." By the end of the eighteenth century, Parliament had seized on the idea of freedom of contract with "unflinching determination" (1920, 55). By 1806, a select committee of Parliament would report that economic liberty "is one of those privileges which the free and happy constitution of this country has long accustomed every Briton to consider as his birthright" (Webb and Webb, 1920, 62; Marshall, 1965, 83–84).

In the United States, James Madison gave expression to the need to check "factions" organized for the purpose of taking property away from the propertied. The Fifth Amendment to the U.S. Constitution made concrete this constitutional objective by providing that private property shall not be "taken for public use without just compensation." Enforcement of this constitutional requirement has been relaxed for much of the twentieth century, though the U.S. Supreme Court has been expanding the class of measures that now require compensation. This has been accomplished, in part, by advancing the idea that there are "regulatory" takings—the regulation of property that "reaches a certain magnitude" but rises short of an outright expropriation of property (*Pennsylvania Coal,* 1922, 1659). As the category of regulatory takings expands, measures that control property, such as municipal zoning bylaws, land-use regulations, or environmental laws, may more likely be caught by the rule (McUsic, 1996). Mirroring these developments at the domestic level is an emergent international law discourse requiring the payment of compensation for constructive, indirect, or partial takings of property (Vandevelde 1992). It is only a short step from here to the NAFTA rule prohibiting measures that are "tantamount" to expropriation.

The objectives and institutional forms of the new constitutionalism, then, resemble those of old. What is significantly different, however, is that decision-making structures reside outside the traditional state form. Once the process has run its course, however, the mechanism of enforcement returns to the traditional locale of the state where these decisions may be lodged and then enforced as if they had been issued from local courts.

CONCLUSION

In this chapter we have reviewed arguments concerning recent constitutional developments. We first examined arguments that the *Canadian Charter of Rights and Freedoms* has generated a new set of constituent actors who have organized themselves around the various rights and freedoms catalogued in the *Charter.* These groups, it is argued, have relocated public policy discussions from Parliament to the courts and the courts have, for the most part, willingly acceded to the arguments made by these various constituencies. We questioned the claim to newness that these arguments make and suggested, instead, that there is a long history in Canada of social-movement litigation in the pursuit of equality rights. This is not to say that the magnitude of the judicial function under the *Charter* has not expanded considerably, it is only to say that groups and associations have long organized themselves in the pursuit of social and political equality through the vehicle of the courts. This emphasis on new constitutional actors distracts us from other developments occurring through constitutional and quasi-constitutional forms. These developments, such as the Agreement on Internal Trade and judicial interpretation of *Charter* rights, have significantly advanced the values we associate with economic globalization.

We next examined another argument about constitutional change, this time emanating from without, though authored by states themselves. This argument concerned the construction of a regime of rights that has parallels to traditional constitutional law and which has features common to ordinary constitutional regimes. This "new constitutionalism" endows transnational economic actors with extraordinary rights of protection, particularly in those instances where regulatory measures substantially impair protected investment interests. We also learned that constitutional rights have traditionally been instrumental in the development of national economies, and that the idea of constitutionalism was developed to shield economic subjects from majoritarian tendencies.

In both instances, new constitutional formations have relationships with old ones. Neither "new" version takes adequate account of the old; nor do they take adequate account of each other. Might there not be a relationship between diminishing state regulatory capacity over the economy and the swelling number of affirmations of national sovereignty via constitutional bills of rights? In a world where the market rules transnationally and where states are under pressure to adopt constitutional regimes that replicate the model upon which economic success is more likely secured, there might be more to this relationship than meets the eye.

REFERENCES

Bakan, Joel. 1997. *Just Words: Constitutional Rights and Social Wrongs*. Toronto: University of Toronto Press.

Bauman, Richard W. 1997. "Business, Economic Rights, and the Charter." In David Schneiderman and Kate Sutherland (eds.), *Charting the Consequences: The Impact of the Charter of Rights on Canadian Law and Politics*. Toronto: University of Toronto Press.

Cairns, Alan C. 1990. "Constitutional Minoritarianism in Canada." In Cairns, *Reconfigurations: Canadian Citizenship and Constitutional Change*. (Douglas E. Williams, ed.) Toronto: McClelland & Stewart.

———. 1992. *Charter versus Federalism: The Dilemmas of Constitutional Reform*. Montreal & Kingston: McGill-Queen's University Press.

Dickson, Chief Justice Brian. 1994. "The Canadian Charter of Rights and Freedoms: Dawn of a New Era?" *Review of Constitutional Studies 2*, 1–19.

Dobrowolsky, Alexandra. 1997. "The Charter and Mainstream Political Science: Waves of Practical Contestation and Changing Theoretical Currents." In David Schneiderman and Kate Sutherland (eds.), *Charting the Consequences: The Impact of the Charter of Rights on Canadian Law and Politics*. Toronto: University of Toronto Press.

Elster, Jon. 1984. *Ulysses and the Sirens: Studies in Rationality and Irrationality*. Cambridge: Cambridge University Press.

———. 2000. *Ulysses Unbound*. Cambridge: Cambridge University Press.

Fletcher, Joseph F. and Paul Howe. 2001. "Public Opinion and Canada's Courts." In Paul Howe and Peter Russell, (eds.), *Judicial Power and Canadian Democracy*. Montreal & Kingston: McGill-Queen's University Press.

Fraser, Nancy. 1997. *Justice Interruptus: Critical Reflections on the "Postsocialist" Condition*. New York: Routledge.

Gibson, James L., Gregory A. Caldeira, and Vanessa A. Baird. (1998). "On the Legitimacy of National High Courts." *American Political Science Review 92*. (2): 343–358.

Gill, Stephen. 1995. "Globalisation, Market Civilisation, and Disciplinary Neoliberalism" *Millennium: Journal of International Studies 24*, 399–423.

Gillman, Hoard. 1993. *The Constitution Beseiged: The Rise and Demise of Lochner Era Police Powers Jurisprudence*. Durham: Duke University Press.

Hein, Gregory. 2001. "Interest Group Litigation and Canadian Democracy." In Paul Howe and Peter Russell (eds.), *Judicial Power and Canadian Democracy*. Montreal & Kingston: McGill-Queen's University Press.

Herman, Didi. 1997. "The Good, the Bad, and the Smugly: Sexual Orientation and Perspectives on the Charter." In David Schneiderman and Kate Sutherland (eds.), *Charting the Consequences: The Impact of the Charter of Rights on Canadian Law and Politics*. Toronto: University of Toronto Press.

Howe, Paul and Peter Russell, (eds.), 2001. *Judicial Power and Canadian Democracy*. Montreal & Kingston: McGill-Queen's University Press.

Jackman, Martha. 1996. Protecting Rights and Promoting Democracy: Judicial Review Under Section 1 of the Charter," *Osgoode Hall Law Journal 34*, 661–680.

Jackson, John H. 1997. *The World Trading System: Law and Policy of International Economic Relations*, 2nd ed. Cambridge: The MIT Press.

Lajoie, Andrée, Pierrette Mulazzi and Michéle Gamache. 1986. "Political Ideas in Quebec and the Evolution of Canadian Constitutional Law," In Ivan Bernier and Andrée Lajoiec (eds.), *The Supreme Court of Canada as an Instrument of Political Change*. Toronto: University of Toronto Press.

Mandel, Michael. 1989 *The Charter of Rights and the Legalization of Politics in Canada*. Toronto: Wall & Thompson.

Marshall, T.H. 1965. "Citizenship and Social Class," In T.H. Marshall, *Class, Citizenship, and Social Development*. Garden City, NY: Anchor Books.

McUsic, Molly. 1996. "The Ghost of *Lochner*: Modern Takings Doctrine and its Impact on Economic Legislation." *Boston University Law Review 76*, 605–667.

Morton, F.L. and Rainer Knopff. 2000. *The Charter Revolution and the Court Party*. Peterborough: Broadview Press.

Polanyi, Karl. 1957. *The Great Transformation*. Boston: Beacon Press.

Powers, Linda F. 1998. "New Forms of Protection for International Infrastructure Investors." In Theodore H. Moran (ed.), *Managing International Political Risk*. Oxford, UK: Blackwell.

Roach, Kent. 1993. "The Role of Litigation and the Charter in Interest Advocacy." In F. Leslie Seidle (ed.), *Equity and Community: The Charter, Interest Advocacy and Representation*. Montreal: Institute for Research on Public Policy.

———. 1999. *Due Process and Victim's Rights: The New Law and Politics of Criminal Justice*. Toronto: University of Toronto Press.

Schneiderman, David. 1995. "Economic Citizenship and Deliberative Democracy: An Inquiry Into Constitutional Limitations on Economic Regulation" *Queen's Law Journal 21*, 125–170.

———. 1998. Constitutionalizing the Culture-Ideology of Consumerism. *Social & Legal Studies 7*, 213–238.

———. 1999a. The Constitutional Strictures of the Multilateral Agreement on Investment. *The Good Society 9*(2): 90–95.

———. 1999b. MMT Promises: How the Ethyl Corporation Beat the Federal Ban. *Encompass Magazine 3*(3) February: 12–13.

———. 2000. Investment Rules and the New Constitutionalism. *Law & Social Inquiry 25*(3): 757–87.

Schneiderman, David and Kate Sutherland (eds.), 1997. *Charting the Consequences: The Impact of Charter Rights on Canadian Law and Politics.* Toronto: University of Toronto Press.

Sklair, Leslie. 1994. "The Culture-Ideology of Consumerism in Urban China: Some Findings From a Survey in Shanghai." In Clifford J. Schultz II, Russell W. Belk, and Güliz Ger (eds.), *Research in Consumer Behavior, Volume 7: Consumption in Marketizing Economies*. Greenwich: Jai Press.

Stuart, Don. 1994. "Policing Under the Charter." In R.C. Macleod and David Schneiderman (eds.), *Police Powers in Canada: The Evolution and Practice of Authority*. Toronto: University of Toronto Press.

Tushnet, Mark V. 1987. *The NAACP's Legal Strategy Against Segregated Education, 1925–1950.* Chapel Hill: University of North Carolina Press.

Vandevelde, Kenneth J. 1992. *United States Investment Treaties: Policy and Practice*. Deventer: Kluwer.

Walker, James W. St.G. 1997. *"Race," Rights and the Law in the Supreme Court of Canada.* Waterloo: Osgoode Society and Wilfred Laurier University Press.

Webb, Sidney and Beatrice Webb. 1920. *The History of Trade Unionism*, Revised Edition. London: Longmans, Green and Co.

CASES

Brown v. *Board of Education*, 347 US 483 (1954).

Christie v. *York Corporation* [1940] SCR 139.

Hunt v. *T&N* PLC [1993] 4 SCR 289.

Irwin Toy v. *Quebec (Attorney-General)* [1989] 1 SCR 927.

M. v. *H.* [1990] 2 SCR 3.

Metalclad Corporation and the United Mexican States, (24 August 2000) World Trade and Arbitration Materials (2001) 13: 47–80.

Morguard Investments Ltd. v. *De Savoye* [1990] 3 SCR 1077.

Pennsylvania Coal v. *Mahon*, 438 U.S. 393 (1922)

Pope & Talbot Inc. and the Government of Canada, Interim Award (26 June 2000) World Trade and Arbitration Materials (2001) 13: 19–55.

Noble Wolfe v. *Alley* [1951] SCR 64.

Pennsylvania Coal v. *Mahon,* 260 US 393 (1922).

Quong Wing v. *The King* (1914) 49 SCR 440.

R. v. *Askov* [1990] 2 SCR 1199.

R. v. *Edwards Books and Art Ltd.* [1986] 2 SCR 713

RJR-MacDonald Inc. v. *Canada* (1995) 127 D.L.R (4th) 1.

Rocket v. *Royal College of Dental Surgeons of Ontario* [1990] 2 SCR 232.

S.D. Myers, Inc. and Government of Canada, In a NAFTA Arbitration Under UNCITRAL Rules, Partial Award, November 13, 2000.

Vriend v. *Alberta* [1998] 1 SCR 493.

WEBLINKS

GATT-guide
www.ciesin.org/TG/PI/TRADE/gatt.html

Canadian Charter of Rights and Freedoms Decisions Digest
http://canada.justice.gc.ca/en/dept/pub/ccrdd/cdtoc.htm

The *Charter* at 20
http://cbc.ca/news/features/constitution/national.html

chapter seventeen

Canadian Parties in the New Century

David Stewart

Miriam Koene

INTRODUCTION

In one of the most famous statements made by a Canadian prime minister, Wilfred Laurier proclaimed that the twentieth century would belong to Canada. It is possible to debate the accuracy of his prophecy, but it is indisputable that Canada's twentieth century belonged to the Liberal Party that Laurier once led. At both the beginning and the end of the twentieth century, and for most of the time in between, the Liberals held a majority in the House of Commons. The twentieth century saw 28 general elections and the Liberals formed a government after 19 of these. Indeed, the party governed Canada for 67 years of the century, an incredible pattern of dominance. The Conservative Party, which has tinkered with its name from time to time, held power for the remaining one-third of the century.

While the Liberals appear unchallenged in their position as Canada's dominant political party, the role of the Conservative Party is ambiguous. In 2000, for the third successive federal election, they trailed another "right wing" competitor in the popular vote and barely held on to official party status in Parliament. While election results hint that the official opposition, the Canadian Alliance party, has displaced the Conservative Party as Canada's major opposition party, infighting over the party's leadership and debate over the nature of the party provide the Conservatives with hopes of survival and recovery. To place current party politics in context, this chapter will briefly review some of the major changes in party fortunes in the twentieth century and discuss the parties currently represented in the House of Commons and the challenges each faces in the early twenty-first century.

THE EVOLVING CANADIAN PARTY SYSTEM

Although the Liberal Party dominated the twentieth century electorally, it faced a number of different competitive environments during these years. Essentially there were three different party systems as well as transitional periods between them. In what Carty (1992) has termed the first party system, the Liberals faced the Conservative Party in a classic two-party battle with no other electorally relevant rivals. Both parties were largely pragmatic entitities that differed from each other only by degree (Seigfried, 1907). This system ended with the emergence of another party. The Progressive Party, a western-based agrarian populist group, challenged the two-party model in the 1921 federal election and, although it proved to be only a transitional party, its rise and demise helped create a second party system in which the Liberals were dominant, but faced electoral challenges not only from the Conservatives, but also from the Social Credit and the Co-operative Commonwealth Federation (CCF).

These new parties received their first parliamentary representation during the Great Depression and consistently elected members to the Commons thereafter. The second party system, then, saw the emergence of a divided opposition as well as limited success for parties that approached politics from a more ideological perspective. During this period the Liberals rarely faced the prospect of an electoral defeat, although their overall levels of support were not as high as in the first party system. Table 17.1 shows the average percentage of the federal vote for each party.

The dominance of the Liberal Party, for most of the past century, was based in part on support from the province of Quebec, where other parties found it extremely difficult to secure seats. Between 1930 and 1957 the Liberals failed to win a majority of Quebec's seats only once. The Conservatives had no regional fiefdom of their own during these years, although Ontario often served as a stronghold. The CCF and Social Credit parties were successful only in the western provinces and, even there, faced challenges from the Liberals.

The third party system emerged after the Conservatives under John Diefenbaker surprised the Liberals by winning a minority government in 1957 and then took a huge majority in 1958. This ushered in another transitional period that saw the Liberals reduce the Conservatives to minority government status in 1962, and saw Social Credit support

TABLE 17-1 Federal Party Support, 1870s to 1950s

	First Party System (1878-1911)	Second Party System (1930-1957)	Third Party System (1963-1980)
Liberal	43.7%	45.9%	41.7%
Conservative	49.7	33.9	33.2
Other	6.6	20.2	25.1

Source: Compiled from data supplied by Chief Electoral Officer of Canada

move from Alberta to Quebec. In 1963 the Liberal Party replaced the Conservatives in office and, with the exception of six months in 1979–80 ruled for the next 21 years. This third era saw the gradual demise of the Social Credit party in the western provinces and in Quebec and the transformation of the CCF into the New Democratic Party. It was an era in which the Liberals both increased their dominance in Quebec and became more dependent on that province to gain a majority of the seats in the House of Commons. Under Diefenbaker, the Conservatives became the most popular party outside Quebec, a status they held until 1993. Without their overwhelming support in Quebec, the Liberals would have won only a minority of seats in every election as the Conservatives consistently won more seats in the other provinces save 1968 when the Canadian electorate fell under the spell of Trudeaumania. Thereafter, the Liberal Party support base narrowed more and more to Quebec. This base however, combined with their competitive status in Atlantic Canada and Ontario, kept them in power. The Conservative Party won most of the seats in western Canada and the New Democrats generally won more seats in that region than the Liberals. This period was marked by occasional minority governments, situations in which the Liberals were generally dependent on the NDP to stay in office.

Like the second party system, the third ended with a Conservative victory of unprecedented proportions, in 1984, which ushered in another transitional period. The Conservative Party, under the leadership of Brian Mulroney, accomplished a remarkable feat and won the majority of seats in Quebec and in every other region as well. The party formed a truly national majority, albeit one that would not and could not last. Although the Conservatives retained office in 1988 in an election that focused on free trade with the United States, their support subsequently underwent a consistent decline as they negotiated unpopular constitutional accords, instituted a dreaded goods and services tax, and presided over an economic decline that was only surpassed by the Great Depression of the 1930s. In 1993, in what Carty, Cross, and Young describe as "the first step in the establishment of the fourth Canadian party system" (2000, 3), the Conservative government was repudiated in dramatic fashion, falling from majority government status to only two seats in the House of Commons.

To understand the Tory collapse and the current state of Canadian party politics, one must look at the results of the 1988 election. In that election the Conservative Party was successful because it combined support from Quebec and western Canada. This, however, was a fundamentally incoherent base of support (Johnston et al., 1992). The votes from Quebec came largely from more nationalist voters while many of the party's western Canadian supporters were convinced that governments were biased in favour of central Canada and that too much time was devoted to issues surrounding the place of Quebec in Canada. The difficulty in keeping these pillars together soon became obvious.

The difficult became the impossible as the Conservative government faced challenges for both portions of its support base. The 1988 election saw a new party, Reform, in the federal field. Reform campaigned on the slogan of "The West Wants In" and criticized the Conservative government for being insufficiently attentive to western needs. However, the main Conservative theme in 1988 was free trade, and this theme was popular in much of the west. The ability to mount an effective challenge against the Conservatives was therefore somewhat constrained.

By 1993, Reform was ready to launch a stronger campaign. Their populist emphasis, which included opposition to the Charlottetown Accord negotiated by the federal government and rejected by the majority of Canadians and a demand for reform of Parliament, as well as their staunch opposition to the Goods and Services Tax left them well placed. Moreover, efforts in 1990 to salvage the ill-fated 1987 Meech Lake Accord resulted in the defection of a Conservative Cabinet minister from Quebec, as well as a number of other nationalist MPs. These members joined together in creating another new political party, the Bloc Québécois, which campaigned on a separatist platform.

In 1993 the Liberals won a majority government while the Bloc Québécois formed the official opposition. Reform secured more votes than any party other than the Liberals (and 52 seats). The Liberal majority in the House of Commons was based on strong electoral support in Ontario, instead of Quebec. The Liberals won all but one of Ontario's seats in the 1993 election, a dominance they essentially maintained in the 1997 and 2000 federal elections.

The 1997 results confirmed both the Liberal majority (albeit with only 38 percent of the federal vote) and the regional nature of party politics in Canada. The Liberals won almost every seat in Ontario, but were unable to secure majority support in the rest of the country. The Bloc continued to be the most popular party in Quebec, while Reform dominated western Canada, particularly B.C. and Alberta. The Conservatives recovered from their near oblivion to win 20 seats, mainly in Atlantic Canada, while the New Democrats elected 21 members (8 from Atlantic Canada and 13 in the west).

The electoral dominance of the Liberal Party was partially attributable to the fact that there was a division in the vote among conservatives. Reform in particular believed that the Liberals were not sufficiently conservative and thus launched an initiative to unite the right. With this initiative they hoped to integrate Reform and Conservative activists and voters and prevent the Liberals from winning seats. The Conservatives declined to participate, however, arguing that only the Conservative Party could appeal to moderate voters throughout Canada and mount a serious challenge to Liberal hegemony. Reform nonetheless transformed itself into the Canadian Alliance and proved somewhat successful in reaching out to provincial Conservatives and convincing them to support the Alliance rather than the federal Conservatives.

Regardless of the manoeuvres on the right, the 2000 election altered the federal election terrain only marginally. The Liberals increased their majority and their share of the popular vote (41 percent), but still received majority support only in Ontario. Support for the Bloc in Quebec dropped slightly, but it still held a slight majority of provincial seats. Under its new title the party formerly known as Reform did in fact increase its share of seats and the popular vote. The Alliance, however, proved unable to break out of its western base. Both the Conservatives and the New Democrats suffered setbacks and barely hung on to official party status.

THE CANADIAN PARTY SYSTEM IN THE TWENTY-FIRST CENTURY

As the twenty-first century begins, Canadian party politics is marked by two important characteristics—the overwhelming electoral dominance of the Liberal Party and a highly regionalized party system. The dominance of the Liberal Party can be seen in two ways. First, the party has more than twice as many Members of Parliament as any other party in the House of Commons. Second, in the last three elections the Liberal Party has won levels of electoral support that are greater than those of its two closest competitors combined. The regionalized party system is one in which different parties dominate elections in different parts of the country. In Ontario, as discussed above, the Liberals are now virtually unchallenged. In Quebec, the Bloc wins the majority of francophone seats while the Liberals enjoy support from areas with significant anglophone populations. This leaves the Bloc as the party to beat in Quebec. In the Atlantic region there is now a three-way competition among the Liberals, Conservatives, and, to a lesser extent, the NDP. Finally, in western Canada the Canadian Alliance holds a majority of the region's Commons seats. As a consequence, Parliament has a large number of parties, each with its support based in different regions.

As Table 17.2 reveals, creating a unified party on the right to challenge the Liberals is no easy task. First, the Liberal government itself appears to be part of the right. It forced dramatic budgetary cuts in social programs in order to balance the budget for the first time in more than two decades, and it is cutting taxes, although perhaps not as quickly as some "conservatives" would like. Second, it is not clear that Conservative voters prefer the Alliance to the Liberals. Indeed, voter surveys in 1997 indicate that the second preference of a majority of Conservative voters was the Liberal Party, not Reform. As Nevitte et al. point out, "Outside Quebec, the Liberals were the most frequent second choice of PC, Reform and NDP voters alike" (2000, 15). Thus the disappearance of the Conservatives might well strengthen the Liberals more than the Alliance. Third, the policies of the Alliance appear to have little resonance with voters in Quebec or Atlantic Canada. The more socially conservative views of many of its activists may limit the party's growth outside its western base. For it to grow, it must win seats in Ontario, but in order for that to happen the Liberals must become more unpopular than they are, thus draining voters away from the Liberals and convincing erstwhile Conservative voters that the Liberals are not preferable to the Alliance. This will prove difficult. For the Conservatives to displace the Alliance as the leading opposition party, they also need a breakthrough in Ontario, and such a breakthrough is very unlikely.

Ontario now dominates federal politics in an unprecedented fashion. The Liberals need to win the vast majority of Ontario's seats in order to remain in government, the Alliance must win seats in the province if it wishes to be perceived as a credible contender for government, and the Conservatives must win seats in the province in order to survive. The Alliance has a solid base in western Canada, but this is not sufficient to win national elections. The Bloc has a solid base of support in Quebec, but for obvious reasons, it does not contest seats outside the province and has no hope of forming a government. No party

TABLE 17-2 2000 Popular Vote by Province

	NF	PE	NS	NB	QC	ON	MB	SK	AB	BC
Liberal	45%	47%	37%	42%	44%	52%	33%	21%	21%	28%
PC	35	38	29	31	6	14	15	5	14	7
NDP	13	9	24	12	2	8	21	26	5	11
BQ	–	–	–	–	40	–	–	–	–	–
Alliance	4	5	10	16	6	24	30	48	59	49

Source: Compiled from data supplied by Chief Electoral Officer of Canada

controls Atlantic Canada, but the fact that the Conservatives and the NDP, parties without a strong base of support elsewhere in Canada, are competitive, suggests the growing irrelevance of this small region for national politics. The Liberal Party however needs a measure of support in the region in order to win majorities, so the region cannot be totally excluded from campaign strategies.

The New Democratic Party, despite winning more seats than the Conservatives in 1993, 1997, and 2000, appears to be in the weakest competitive position in the federal party system. It owes its official party status to its breakthrough in Atlantic Canada—a breakthrough that saw the party win eight seats in the region in 1997 and hold onto four of them in 2000. It is unclear, however, that the Atlantic breakthrough will continue, particularly when the party is no longer led by a Maritimer. Its remaining seats are distributed throughout western Canada, but very few of those seats are clearly safe. The party is also undergoing some debate about its future. Some social democratic parties (for example the Labour party in the U.K. and the Social Democrats in Germany) have abandoned a good deal of their traditional ideological arsenal and appear to have become more moderate.

This is also the path followed by two of the three provincial NDP governments in Canada. The Saskatchewan NDP instituted serious cuts in program spending in order to balance its budget and is actually in a coalition with the Liberal Party. Manitoba's NDP won a 1999 election in part by presenting themselves as "Today's NDP" and indicating that the policies they pursued as a government would differ from those the party has championed in the past. The federal NDP has less incentive to compromise since its chances of forming a government are miniscule. Indeed, discussions at the party's 2001 convention focused on reforms that would actually move the party farther to the left. Demands for a new politics and a redesigned NDP, however, were rejected on the convention floor.

THE CHANGING ROLE OF PARTIES

As support patterns for parties have varied over time so has their role and the way they are perceived. Many observers see a decline in the role of political parties in Canada, as they are "now sharing with others in the discharge of functions that were once their exclusive purview" (Meisel and Mendelsohn, 1995, 178). The rise of the bureaucratic state has seen a transfer of power from politicians to civil servants while interest groups and social movements are performing representational functions that were previously the almost exclusive domain of political parties. This point is made dramatically by former Conservative Party president Dalton Camp. In his words, "There remains some primordial ambition that lurks in the heart of a few citizens to participate in the formulation of policy through the party apparatus. I would advise them that if they insist on doing so, not to join a political party. The very least they should do is join a parapolitical pressure group. The very best thing they could do is join the civil service" (as quoted in Lyon, 1996, 536).

Interest groups and social movements engage in direct lobbying and pay little attention to party structures. Citizens seem to prefer engaging in political activities through these more focused entities rather than engaging in the kind of political compromises that parties produce as they attempt to aggregate different interests. As Amyot explains, new social movements seem unable "to stomach the fact that established parties which have recognized their concerns have had to compromise them because of conflicting demands from other segments" (1996, 522). Moreover, changes in technology have enhanced the role of the media in the political process and decreased the role parties play in political education.

For these and other reasons, parties are no longer as able to count on a strong base of permanent supporters. In recent decades there has been evidence of a decline in stable partisan allegiance, a decline in the turnout of voters during elections, and increased levels of electoral volatility. Finally, globalization, with its attendant emphasis on international agreements which limit the autonomy of national governments, clearly inhibits the ability of parties to institute dramatic economic reforms.

Not surprisingly, the public appears to have lost confidence in parties and, more generally, in the institutions of representative government. Research for the 1991 Royal Commission on Political Parties and Electoral Financing revealed the depths of this dissatisfaction. A survey of Canadian voters, conducted as part of the research for the Royal Commission, revealed that two-thirds of Canadians value the down-to-earth thinking of ordinary people over the theories of experts and intellectuals while three-quarters endorse bringing decisions on big national problems closer to the people. Canadians are often cynical about our political processes and feel that public policy decisions should be closer to the grassroots.

Political parties are unpopular with the Canadian population who generally feel that the parties do not represent their views, that there is too much squabbling among parties, that parties confuse the issues, and that parties are the same. As Blais and Gidengil (1993) summarize, "Canadians just do not have much confidence in those whom they elect. One source of this dissatisfaction appeared to be the feeling that they simply do not have enough of a choice. Political parties are perceived to engage in too much unproductive squabbling and to confuse issues rather than provide a clear choice on them."

Parties have been rather slow and ineffective in responding to these negative evaluations. There have been virtually no reforms in the operation of Parliament. Parliament continues to be dominated by parties, and votes in which individual MPs are free to vote against the party line with impunity are extremely rare. Perhaps a result of this, in the 2000 election only 63 percent of registered voters bothered to cast a ballot. Also troubling for parties is the level of participation of young Canadians in their activities. In a recent study for the IRPP, O'Neill showed that Canadians between 18 and 27 were four and a half times more likely to have been a member of an interest group than they were to have been a party member (2001, 13).

PARTY LEADERSHIP

One area in which Canadian party politics has remained constant is in leadership. Writing in the middle of the twentieth century, Maurice Duverger noted that "two essential facts seem to have dominated the evolution of political parties since the beginning of the century: the increase in the authority of the leaders and the tendency towards personal forms of authority" (1978, 168). Actually, Canadian leaders have dominated their parties and electoral politics since Confederation. As Andre Seigfried pointed out in his analysis of Canadian politics at the turn of the twentieth century, "it is of the first importance to the success of a party that it should be led by someone whose mere name is a program in itself" (as quoted in Carty, Erickson, and Blake, 1992, 2). Almost half a century later Hugh Clokie reinforced this point, noting that:

> The dominant position of the party leader in Canadian politics has often been commented on by foreign observers. It is far greater than in Great Britain, where the allegiance to party principles or programmes competes with loyalty as a bond of partisanship. It is also far greater than in the U.S., where party candidates are nominated locally without any obligation to support the national

> leader of the party. In Canada more than anywhere else it is possible to define a party as being a body of supporters following a given leader (1945, 91).

In recent years, leaders have become, if possible, even more dominant. Indeed, leadership selection represents one of the few responses of political parties to citizen dissatisfaction. This change has increased the role of ordinary members and strengthened the leader's position of dominance and has almost certainly further weakened the role of party organizations (Courntney, 1995). All of the parties represented in the federal House of Commons now have to some degree placed the choice of the party leader in the hands of ordinary members. For rather nominal fees, citizens can purchase memberships in the federal parties and, when leadership vacancies occur, cast a vote for the person they wish to see become leader. Indeed, for the Bloc, Conservatives, and Canadian Alliance, such votes were used to elect their current leaders. Nonetheless, Canadians are not rushing to avail themselves of these opportunities. The 1998 Conservative leadership election resulted in only a tiny proportion of those who voted for the party in the 1997 election actually voting for the party's leader. Similarly, although more than 120 000 people voted in the 2000 Canadian Alliance leadership election, this represents less than 5 percent of the total who voted for the Reform party in the 1997 election.

A change of leaders is seen as a way to dramatically improve a party's electoral chances. For example, Stockwell Day's defeat of Preston Manning for the leadership of the Canadian Alliance in 2000 was interpreted by many pundits as essential in demonstrating that the new party was more than just a renamed Reform Party. Following a disappointing electoral performance by Day in 2001, a number of MPs who had served under Manning declared that the party could never win under Day and formed a parliamentary coalition with the Conservatives. The Alliance eventually decided to hold another leadership election in 2002 in the hopes that this would reinvigorate the party and restore unity.

Even the Liberal Party is not immune from leadership discussions. Some pundits have suggested that the Liberal Party would prove even more popular if it replaced Prime Minister Chrétien with Paul Martin, the former finance minister. Such changes of leadership, even without wider changes in either personnel or policy, are expected to influence the way Canadians vote and perceive the parties. When this is combined with the new method of leadership selection, it appears that Canadian parties can be seen as "a loose coalition of supporters of the leader" (Stewart and Archer, 2000).

This tendency was exemplified in the 2000 Canadian Alliance leadership election. A number of former supporters of the federal Conservative Party took out membership in the Alliance to vote for a particular candidate (Tom Long). Some of them made clear that their support of the new party was contingent on the victory of the candidate they preferred and that the victory of another candidate might lead them to rethink their particular conversion.

CONCLUSION

Parties remain important in Canadian politics. As Blais and Gidengil note:

> [O]ur whole system is predicated on the view that parties are central players on the political stage. After an election, it is the leader of the party with the most votes who becomes Prime Minister. The parliamentary system supposes that legislators form teams with strong internal discipline. By reimbursing expenditures incurred by parties during an election, the state indicates that parties perform a public service (1991).

Moreover, the majority of Canadians believe that without parties, democracy is impossible. The functions that parties perform well, such as organizing government and structuring the vote, simply cannot be performed as well by other political actors. Perhaps most importantly, parties set the rules by which leaders are chosen, while party members actually choose the leaders.

The Liberal Party remains the leading Canadian party in the federal party system. No other party possesses the ability to compete for seats across the entire country and no other party is the second choice of as many voters. The Liberals provide continuity in Canada's political system and although their current levels of support are below their mean share in any of the previous party systems, they appear to be unchallenged in this role.

Many observers believe that an important function of Canadian parties is nation building. Indeed, historically the Liberal and Conservative Parties were described as "brokerage" parties. This type of political party deliberately eschews divisive appeals to the electorate to play down divisions in society. Brokerage parties are inclusive, act to moderate fissiparous tendencies, and aim for the integration of all segments of society. Under Joe Clark the Conservatives are attempting to resurrect their fortunes by making clear that the party retains this focus. Clark attacks the Canadian Alliance for espousing a narrower ideological viewpoint that cannot appeal to all Canadians. Although the Conservatives very much wish to assert themselves as a brokerage party, it is no longer clear that Canada has room for two such entities, as it did for most of the last century. The Liberal Party has had the strongest brokerage claim. In the last three elections it is only the Liberal Party that has been able to elect people in every region.

The other parties do not fit the brokerage mould. Because of their emphasis on a particular ideology or region, the Canadian Alliance, Bloc Québécois, and NDP refuse to describe or present themselves as carriers of the brokerage-party tradition. These parties focus more on distinguishing themselves from other parties and emphasising issues on which they have clear and distinctive positions. As Carty, Cross, and Young note: "Not only do they [voters] have more parties to choose from, but the parties are also increasingly staking out distinctive policy positions. Gone are the days when all the major parties agreed on the essence of all the major issues" (2000, 8). Throughout the last century, support for such third parties has grown. Since 1993 more than 40 percent of the electorate has chosen to vote for non-brokerage parties.

The other side of the coin is, of course, that in 2000 over one-half of the voters selected a brokerage party and most of them voted Liberal. Currently, as well as throughout most of the last century, the Liberal Party has demonstrated a willingness to adopt popular measures advocated by other parties. The Liberal Party possesses a philosophical flexibility that bodes well for its ability to remain in office. The party seems well on its way to being the lone pragmatic (or catch-all) party in the Canadian system. Pragmatic parties have huge advantages as they engage in electoral competition with more ideologically distinct competitors. The willingness to compromise allows them to borrow policies from whatever party seems most threatening at a particular point in time. Throughout the third party system, the Liberal Party borrowed heavily from the NDP. More recently Reform and the Canadian Alliance have been the source of new policy ideas.

The success of the Liberal Party is somewhat ironic given the views Canadians express about their political system. Canadians readily criticize parties for confusing issues and for enforcing party discipline in Parliament. It seems however that the actions of voters belie their words. The Liberal Party regularly enforces party discipline and has resisted calls for more free votes in the House of Commons. The Liberal Party actually promised in the 1993 election campaign to negotiate significant changes to the North American Free Trade Agreement, to change the Goods and Services Tax, and to allow more free votes in the House of Commons, but reneged on these commitments without suffering severe electoral consequences in the 1997 federal election. Moreover, the party that roundly condemned the 1984–1993 Conservative government for its attempts to cut spending in order to balance the budget, itself instituted a series of dramatic program cuts, which enabled it to accomplish that goal. The Liberal Party has developed the fine art of borrowing some policies and reneging on others without, for the most part, suffering at the cost of the polls. This is unlikely to change in the near future. The twenty-first century, like the 20th, may well belong to the Liberal Party.

REFERENCES

Amyot, G. Grant. 1996. "Democracy without Parties? A New Politics?" In Brian Tanguay and Alain G. Gagnon (eds.), *Canadian Parties in Transition,* 2nd ed. Toronto: Nelson Canada.

Blais, Andre and Elizabeth Gidengil. 1991. *Making Representative Democracy Work: The Views of Canadians.* Toronto: Dundurn.

Carty, R.K. 1992. "Three Canadian Party Systems." In R.K. Carty (ed.), *Canadian Political Party Systems.* Peterborough: Broadview.

Carty, R.K, William Cross, and Lisa Young. 2000. *Rebuilding Canadian Party Politics.* Vancouver: UBC Press.

Carty, R.K, Lynda Erickson, and Donald E. Blake. 1992. "Parties and Leaders: The Experiences of the Provinces." In R.K. Carty, Lynda Erickson, and Donald E. Blake (eds.), *Leaders and Parties in Canadian Politics.* Toronto: Harcourt Brace Jovanovich.

Clokie, Hugh. 1945. *Canadian Government and Politics.* Toronto: Longman.

Courtney, John C. 1995. *Do Conventions Matter.* Montreal: McGill-Queen's University Press.

Duverger, Maurice. 1978 [1954]. *Political Parties.* London: Methuen.

Johnston, Richard et al. 1992. *Letting the people decide: Dynamics of a Canadian election.* Montreal: McGill-Queen's University Press.

Lyon, Vaughn. 1996. "Parties and Democracy: A Critical View". In Brian Tanguay and Alain G. Gagnon (eds.), *Canadian Parties in Transition,* 2nd ed. Toronto: Nelson Canada.

Meisel, John and Matthew Mendelsohn. 1995. In Hugh Thorburn (ed.), *Party Politics in Canada* Seventh Edition. Scarborough: Prentice-Hall.

Nevitte, Neil et al. (2000). *Unsteady state: The 1997 Canadian federal election.* Don Mills, Ont.: Oxford University Press.

O'Neill, Brenda. 2001. "Generational Patterns in the Political Opinions and Behaviour of Canadians: Separating the Wheat from the Chaff." *Policy Matters IRPP Enjeux Publics* Volume 2, No.5.

Royal Commission on Electoral Reform and Party Financing. 1991. *Reforming Electoral Democracy*, Volume 1, Ottawa.

Siegfried, Andre. 1970 [1907]. *The Race Question in Canada.* Toronto: McClelland & Stewart.

Smith, David E. 1992. "Party Government in Canada." In R. K. Carty (ed.), *Canadian Political Party Systems.* Peterborough: Broadview.

Stewart, David K. and R.K. Carty. 1993. "Does Changing the Party Leader Provide an Electoral Boost?" *Canadian Journal of Political Science 25*, 3.

WEBLINKS

Canadian Political Parties
http://home.ican.net/~alexng/can.html

Political Thought
www.psr.keele.ac.uk/thought.htm

Canadian Political Parties, Elections and Politics
www.library.ubc.ca/poli/cpwebpr.html

chapter eighteen

Reinventing Governance in the North

Gurston Dacks

INTRODUCTION

At the dawn of the twenty-first century, the residents of Canada's North are significantly reshaping their political and institutional landscape. The creation of the new territory of Nunavut, for example, appears to be a radical departure from past practice. However, the processes by which governance is being reinvented in the territories are less a matter of swift transformation than of evolutionary change in response to developments that have been underway for a considerable period of time. The most important of these has been the settlement and implementation of the land claims of the Aboriginal peoples of the territories. The federal government's recognition of the inherent right of Aboriginal self-government in 1995 may strengthen the hand of Aboriginal negotiators. In the future it may give constitutional protection to the agreements they achieve. However, the reality of practical politics in the North is that the processes of reinventing government, now actively underway, originated in the terms of the various claims settlements and owe relatively little to the affirmation of the inherent right. Moreover, consistent with the theme of evolution rather than transformation, these processes are unfolding very much within the conventional constitutional context of Canada. The reinvention of governance in the North is a matter of shaping institutions that provide opportunities for Aboriginal self-determination within this context. It is also about expanding the capacity of northern Native people to operate these institutions effectively in pursuit of their common goals. This slow and steady work of capacity building will be one of the most important determinants of Aboriginal self-determination as the new governance of the North unfolds.

Since the earliest days of contact between the Aboriginal inhabitants of Canada and the newcomers from Europe, inter-ethnic relations have presented a great challenge to effective governance in Canada. Inter-cultural politics also dominate the task of shaping governance in Canada's three northern territories, but in a different way than in southern Canada. During the last two-and-a-half centuries, effective governance in Canada has required, first and foremost, integrating its anglophone and francophone communities. In the North, building common purpose primarily involves adequately representing Canada's Aboriginal and non-Aboriginal communities and responding to their partly shared and partly divergent cultural, social, economic, and political needs.

Each of the three territories has taken a different approach to this task, although the approaches of the Yukon and Northwest Territories (NWT) now appear to be converging. This chapter will first describe the contexts within which institutions of governance are evolving in the three territories. It will then describe the institutions that are taking shape and close with a discussion of how these new institutions are likely to fit in the overall pattern of territorial governance.

CONTEXT

In many ways the governments of the three territories closely resemble their provincial counterparts. They began very much as colonial institutions—administrative agencies of the federal government. However, over a number of decades legislators elected by northerners replaced decision-makers appointed by Ottawa, and cabinets led by premiers became the focus of decision making (Cameron and White, 1995, 15–20, 47–53). In 1979 in the Yukon, and gradually during the 1980s in the Northwest Territories (NWT), the commissioner of each territory (the senior administrator, appointed by and responsible to the Minister of Indian and Northern Affairs Canada) lost the authority to veto legislation passed by the territorial legislature. With this step, responsible government arrived in the North.

The territories also resemble provincial governments in that they exercise jurisdiction over almost the full range of areas in which provinces have authority. The major provincial powers they lack are authority over Crown prosecutions in criminal cases, labour law and relations, and, as was the case for Alberta and Saskatchewan before 1930, control of Crown lands and resources. This last power is the most important exception because natural resources figure so centrally in the economy of the North. Unlike the provinces, the Northwest Territories and Nunavut do not own the Crown lands and resources within their boundaries. These are owned by the Government of Canada, which therefore has the authority to pass laws regarding their use and to receive any royalties that resource extraction generates. It should be noted that it shares a portion of these royalties with the Aboriginal group from whose lands a resource has been extracted, if the group has signed a land claims agreement (Canada, 1992, 26). This generalization applies in the Yukon as well, except that in 1998 the federal government in effect transferred ownership of oil and gas deposits on Crown land and authority over them to the Yukon government. The federal government has also transferred ownership of oil and gas resources on First Nations' land and legislative authority over these resources to the Yukon First Nations that have signed self-government agreements. As a result of this devolution of authority, the Yukon territorial government enjoys the advantages of using energy policy to promote economic development and of receiving income from energy resources not available to the other two territories. The Yukon has made great progress in negotiating for control over, and the resource revenues from, about 90 percent of its land, including its water, forest, and mineral resources. Not surprisingly, gaining ownership and control over all Crown lands and resources is a major policy goal of the Government of the Northwest Territories (GNWT) in its relations with the federal government (GNWT, 1999, 9, 15).

In the realm of federal–provincial relations, the territories are "semi-provinces." Territorial ministers and premiers regularly participate in consultations and negotiations with their federal and provincial counterparts. For example, the two then-existing territories participated in the negotiations that led to the creation of the Charlottetown Accord package of constitutional amendments in 1992. However, the territories fall short of provincial status in that they play no role in the formula for amending the Constitution of Canada. Moreover, to the great dismay of the territorial governments, the provisions of the *Constitution Act* (1982) governing amendments give the provinces power over the creation of new provinces and the extension of existing provinces into the territories. These provisions reflect the lower status of the territories in Confederation compared to that of the provinces. However, these powers are unlikely to be of much practical importance because the territories are very far from being candidates for provincial status, and it is unlikely that any province will seek to annex part of a territory. More significant indicators of the status of the territories in Confederation are the wide span of territorial government authority and the active participation of the territories in the intergovernmental discussions that are so important in shaping public policy.

Finally, governance in the territories generally (with some significant exceptions) resembles that in the provinces. In the Yukon, candidates contest elections to the legislative assembly on the basis of party affiliation. The relations between the assembly and the cabinet are shaped by the convention of party discipline that enables cabinets in the provinces and Ottawa to dominate the policy processes of their governments. In contrast, party politics are absent from the politics of the territorial governments of the NWT and Nunavut. The NWT government has operated on the basis of what has been termed "consensus government." The assembly, at its first meeting after an election, chooses from among its members the premier and the MLAs who will be cabinet ministers. The new premier then assigns departmental responsibilities to his or her ministers. This is a form of responsible government in that the premier and cabinet must retain the confidence of a majority of the members of the assembly in order to stay in office. While the premier and cabinet do not have the benefit of party discipline in helping them to maintain the support they require, they have been so effective in organizing coalitions of support and avoiding the coalescing of opposition that no cabinet has been voted out of office in the two decades that the system has been in operation. One source of this success is that the territorial MLAs can hold the executive accountable by dismissing individual cabinet ministers, a power that they have exercised. Also, the cabinet–MLA relationship differs from the usual pattern in that MLAs enjoy a much more active and influential role in the making of policy than is the case in the provinces.

These features depart significantly from the Westminster model of government that is found in Ottawa and the provinces. Still, a visitor from southern Canada observing the operation of the Government of the Northwest Territories would note more similarities with provincial governments than differences. The visitor would note that in the NWT, as elsewhere in Canada, a cabinet develops and presents to the assembly a legislative program, including a budget, and that the bulk of this legislation is passed into law. The visitor would also observe that the members of the cabinet are responsible for the operation of departments that contain a considerable amount of technical and administrative expertise. In these important aspects of governance, the NWT resembles the provinces to a considerable extent.

While the governance of the territories resembles that of the provinces in many ways, it also contrasts in very significant respects. One important contrast is in the realm of public finance. Particularly in the NWT and Nunavut, the per capita costs of providing public services are very high because their governments must service small numbers of people spread out over a huge span of territory. The result is that the territorial budgets depend much more on funding transfers from Ottawa than do the provincial budgets.

A second contrast is that the governments of the NWT and Nunavut are less formalized than are the governments of the Yukon and the provinces. The government structures of the Yukon are almost as fully institutionalized as those of the provinces. The Yukon structures have operated successfully and unchanged for more than two decades. Indeed, Parliament is expected to pass a new *Yukon Act* in 2002, which is anticipated to confirm the institutions of the Yukon government in the Westminster form in which they have matured, as well as to greatly expand the Yukon's control over its land and resources. The people of the territory see their public government institutions as legitimate and expect them to endure in roughly their current configuration, particularly as this configuration matches federal and provincial practice throughout Canada. Adding to this legitimacy has been the Yukon government's practice of consulting very actively with Yukon First Nation governments and fully respecting their authority and their views on policy questions. In contrast, many Native people in the NWT view its territorial government as not fully legitimate (Cameron and White, 1995, 44). They note that it was imposed upon them without their consent and that it operates on the basis of principles that conflict with the values of their political cultures. Also, it does not embody the inherent right of Aboriginal self-government and does not interact with First Nations governments in the way the Yukon government does, in part because these governments are not nearly as well established as are the Yukon's Aboriginal governments. This alienation has influenced the evolution of Aboriginal thinking about how best to arrange the governance of the NWT. The government of Nunavut is fully legitimate, reflecting as it does the intense efforts of the Inuit to become self-governing. At the same time, it cannot be considered highly institutionalized as its structures are very new and its operations are still in a fledgling state. There is considerable room to adjust them in the face of experience.

Another important contrast with the provinces is that Aboriginal people constitute a much larger proportion of the territorial populations than of the provincial populations. Aboriginal people comprised 2.7 percent of Canada's population in 1996. In contrast, they accounted for about 20.1 percent of the population of the Yukon and about 62.4 percent of the population of the former NWT. These figures include all individuals who identified themselves as Aboriginal people, that is, registered status First Nations people, non-status Indians, Métis, and Inuit (Canada, 1996, Vol. 1, 22). Aboriginal people represent 50 percent of the population of the NWT after division and 85 percent of the people of Nunavut. As a result, northern Native people have considerably more political power than other Native people enjoy in provincial politics, including a greater ability to pursue the forms of self-determination that they desire.

THE PURSUIT OF ABORIGINAL SELF-DETERMINATION

As in the rest of Canada, the Native peoples of the territories generally want to be able to make for themselves the political decisions that affect their fundamental interests, in particular decisions relating to their cultures. They want to enjoy their legal right to self-determination and to put behind them their history of unhappy experiences with the policies of the public governments of Canada. To explain this term, which will recur in this chapter, a "public government" governs all of the people in the territory over which it has jurisdiction. In this way it is different from, for example, a school board that serves a particular religious group and thus has authority over only a fraction of the people living in the area in which it has authority. Native people in the North prefer to make decisions in an environment that emphasizes their cultural approach of building consensus around communal goals and values (Alfred, 1999, 59–60). They tend to be uncomfortable with the processes of public government in Canada, which are oriented towards individualism and adversarial politics.

In the last two decades, northern Aboriginal peoples have enjoyed an advantage in pursuing self-determination that has not been available to most Aboriginal peoples in Canada. This is because, as recently as 20 years ago, the Aboriginal rights of the Native peoples of the Yukon and NWT had not been extinguished by their having entered into treaties with the Crown. The Government of Canada and the territorial governments have been anxious to end this situation by settling the claims of the Aboriginal peoples of the territories. The federal government wants to settle claims in order to discharge its obligation to give fair recognition to the principle of Aboriginal rights. Probably more significant to the governments, settlement of claims removes the legal uncertainty that unsettled claims cast over the lands where Aboriginal peoples claim these rights. Until these uncertainties are removed, resources developers are anxious about the returns they might gain on investments they make on these lands. Their hesitation to invest thwarts the governments' attempts to encourage resource development, which would contribute to economic growth for Canada and enhance governmental revenues.

Moved by these considerations, the federal and territorial governments began in the 1970s to negotiate with northern Aboriginal peoples in order to settle the claims these peoples had advanced on the basis of their Aboriginal rights. These claims sought affirmation of Aboriginal ownership of a portion of their traditional territories, wildlife harvesting rights, a role in managing wildlife harvesting and the environment in these territories, cash compensation for giving up aspects of their rights, and self-government. The federal government was willing to negotiate all but the last of these issues as part of Aboriginal claims and to guarantee the settlements reached under section 35 of the *Constitution Act* (1982). It was not willing to negotiate self-government in the claims processes or to constitutionally entrench any arrangements that might be made concerning Aboriginal self-government (Canada, Indian and Northern Affairs, 1987, 18). The best that the Aboriginal peoples could negotiate were commitments from Ottawa and the territorial governments that they would negotiate self-government, or in the case of the Inuit, the division of the Northwest Territories, in processes separate from the land claims processes.

These commitments have enabled the Aboriginal peoples of the territories to negotiate the governance arrangements that will be described in detail below. Thus, it was through the land claims processes that Aboriginal self-determination has made the advances that have taken place in the North. In considering these advances it should be kept in mind that, to date, the Aboriginal peoples of the Yukon and NWT have only been able to achieve self-government on a contingent basis. This means that their governments have been created by the authority of the government of Canada with powers that the federal government has been willing to transfer to them. Most of these First Nations governments, indeed, all of them in the NWT, have been established on the basis of the federal *Indian Act*. This means that these governments are "contingent," that is, they draw their authority from a law passed by the federal government, rather than from any basic right that Aboriginal peoples possess, and they can be altered without the approval of the Aboriginal peoples they govern.

The *Indian Act* gives certain powers to a First Nations government, but limits its authority in several ways. For example, the Minister of Indian Affairs and Northern Development can veto any decision of a First Nation's council. Moreover, the federal government can make decisions relating to the First Nations' reserve land without the agreement of the First Nation. Provincial laws generally apply to reserves and, while First Nations administer many programs, the principles that underlie these programs are established by either the federal or provincial government. This much-criticized arrangement has often been attacked as being more a matter of self-administration than of self-government (Frideres and Gadacz, 2001, 253). As will be seen below, the situation of the seven (of fourteen) Yukon First Nations that have signed self-government agreements is considerably better, although these agreements also exist only on a contingent basis.

The alternative to the contingent basis of Aboriginal self-government is to conceive of the authority of Aboriginal governments as being based on an inherent right to self-government that Aboriginal peoples enjoy. This right is "inherent" in part because Aboriginal peoples are the original inhabitants of Canada. The right is inherent rather than contingent in that it was not conferred upon First Nations by European imperial governments or by the Government of Canada. The First Nations enjoyed this right long before the arrival of the first explorers and settlers. Also, if it is an inherent right, the government of Canada cannot deny self-government to First Nations, nor can it set conditions that must be met before First Nations can enjoy it (Canada, 1996, Vol. 2, Part 1, 184–93). While this is the meaning of the inherent right, successive governments of Canada have denied that First Nations are entitled to this right. These governments argued that it was not explicitly provided for in constitutional documents and ignored the Aboriginal systems of law on which the right is based. While section 35 of the *Constitution Act* (1982) protects Aboriginal and treaty rights, Canadian governments rejected the idea that these included the inherent right of self-government. In 1992, the Government of Canada reversed this policy and supported the recognition of the inherent right to self-government in the Charlottetown Accord of 1992. However, this proposed constitutional recognition died when the people of Canada rejected the accord in a national referendum. The concept of recognizing the inherent right was revived when the Liberal Party included it in its "Red Book" of policy commitments that it produced for the 1993 general election campaign. In 1995, the minister of Indian Affairs and Northern Development announced that it was now the policy of the government of Canada to recognize the inherent right as an existing right under section 35. However, as this policy statement did not constitutionally entrench the inherent right, but rather only interpreted section 35, a future federal government could rescind this policy by asserting a different interpretation. A more pressing drawback to the 1995 policy announcement was that First Nations would not be able to enjoy the inherent right immediately because, while the right existed, its implementation would have to be negotiated within conditions set by Ottawa (Canada, 1995, 3).

NEGOTIATING GOVERNANCE

The recognition of the inherent right has strengthened the ability of the Aboriginal peoples of the North to pursue self-determination. However, it has had relatively little effect on the structures of public government in either the Yukon or the NWT. Why would this be the case? The answer is that, while the inherent right certainly implies the prospect of free-standing Aboriginal governments, considerations of efficiency would encourage the development of public governments to embody the inherent right, at least to some extent. These considerations include the huge cost of operating within a single territory, numerous governments with very small population bases, and large, overlapping responsibilities. Money spent operating a large number of governments is money not available for actually delivering services. It would be better from an efficiency point of view to have a single institution governing some of these issues, provided that Aboriginal northerners are adequately represented in it. Moreover, in the NWT, Natives and non-Natives live intermingled in many communities, a pattern that would greatly complicate the task that separate Aboriginal and non-Aboriginal governments would face in effectively serving their constituents. For this reason, the *Federal Policy Guide: Aboriginal Self-Government* asserts that "In the western NWT, the Government would prefer that the inherent right find expression primarily, although not exclusively, through public government. . . . In the federal government's view, the self-government aspirations of Aboriginal peoples in the NWT can be addressed by providing specific guarantees within public government institutions" (Canada, 1995, 20–21).

However, the vision of public governments expressing the inherent right has not been realized, primarily because for this to occur to a degree that would be meaningful to Aboriginal people would require revisions to the territorial governments that would be incompatible with the basic liberal-democratic values of Canada. The majority of non-Aboriginal northerners have considerable sympathy for the wish of northern Native peoples to be self-determining and to build into their institutions of governance particular aspects of Aboriginal political culture. These include the high values Native political culture places on decision-making by consensus, and, should conflict arise, on the needs of the community as contrasted with the priorities of the individuals who comprise these communities. However, non-Aboriginal northerners cherish their own political values, and place a premium on such principles as majority rule and individualism that lie at the heart of liberal democracy. The fact that these values form the basis of the parliamentary system of government practised throughout Canada reinforces the conviction of non-Native northerners in the correctness of these values. It also strengthens their expectation that, as time passes, these beliefs will be confirmed as the basis of northern public governments.

The following discussion shows that the evolution of governance and Aboriginal self-determination in the territories can be understood in terms of three factors. The first is the liberal-democratic convictions of non-Native northerners. The second is the proportion they represent of the population of each territory. The third is the practical challenges that limited financial and personnel resources pose to the implementation of Aboriginal self-government.

THE YUKON

The population of the Yukon is about 80 percent non-Aboriginal. The territorial legislature represents an almost century-old tradition of governance based on liberal-democratic values. For these reasons, Aboriginal as well as non-Aboriginal Yukoners have never pursued the notion of transforming the territorial government to embody Aboriginal self-government. The idea is simply a non-starter. Instead, Yukon Indians vote for both their own governments and the territorial legislative assembly. This makes sense because, even should First Nations governments become fully empowered, the territorial government will continue to have jurisdiction over a great many issues that affect the daily lives of First Nations people.

Given the legitimacy of the territorial government, the 14 Yukon First Nations sought to negotiate their own institutions of self-government in a process linked to the settlement of their land claims. Seven of the First Nations have completed self-government agreements with the governments of the Yukon and Canada. These agreements give the First Nations the authority not just to administer, but to actually legislate regarding almost as wide a span of authority as the territorial government enjoys. First Nations laws will apply both to their own lands and to their people living anywhere in the Yukon. Moreover, the laws that they pass will possess considerable legal force. Territorial legislation does still apply to First Nations people and reserves. However, if a First Nation passes a law within its jurisdiction that conflicts with a territorial law, the First Nation's law will prevail. This is a considerable improvement over First Nations governments based on the *Indian Act*, with two important exceptions. First, the future of these governments is not protected from erosion by the federal or territorial government because the agreements that created them explicitly state that these governments are not protected by section 35 of the *Constitution Act* (1982). While it is most unlikely that either government would attack the governments of the Yukon First Nations, the fact that the Constitution does not close off this option means that their enjoyment of these governments remains contingent on the honour and self-interest of others. In addition, these governments do not have even the protection of being deemed to be based on the inherent right, because they were negotiated before the federal government recognized this right. Negotiations have been proceeding to determine whether there are aspects of the Yukon First Nations governments that might be considered to be based on the inherent right.

The second limitation to the power of the new Yukon First Nations governments is that they do not possess the trained personnel to exercise in practice the jurisdiction they possess in theory. Yukon First Nations governments gained authority over the entire span of their jurisdiction on the day that each of them was created. However, they have chosen to exercise that authority very gradually. It is a complex, costly, and difficult task to create the governing structures to develop and implement policy and to deliver government services. Also, Yukon First Nations do not yet possess enough people trained in the diverse types of expertise necessary to operate modern governments to be able to take on an extensive range of jurisdiction. It is difficult to recruit skilled Native people because they face competition from the federal and territorial governments, which are committed to increasing the proportion of Aboriginal people among their employees. Particularly in view of their very small size, it will take many years for Yukon First Nations governments to assume the full span of authority available to them. Initially, they have chosen to concentrate on passing legislation implementing their right to levy taxes, and on developing the capability to manage the lands and resources that were identified as theirs by claims settlements. They are generally allowing the territorial government to continue to provide health, education, and social services programs to their people. In some instances they have negotiated program service transfer arrangements by which they deliver specific territorial or, more usually, federal programs to their people. This creates the opportunity for a more culturally sensitive system of administration than may have existed before. However, it does not change the policies that are being administered, as the territorial or federal government retains authority over them.

In the future, Yukon First Nations may expand their authority without straining their capacity by using the provision of their self-government agreements that allows them to legislate regarding certain matters, and then to delegate the implementation of their legislation to the territorial government. This would combine the advantages of their controlling the broad outlines of policy with the efficiencies of having a single government delivering particular services in the territory. First Nations would lose some control over aspects of the programs and services delivered because the territorial government would probably insist on some uniformity among the programs it administers in order to make its task more coherent and easy to manage. However, the efficiencies to be gained could outweigh the costs. If they did not, presumably, the First Nations would not agree to this type of delegation. Alternatively several neighbouring First Nations might co-operate to deliver certain programs, or First Nations might delegate certain powers to the territory-wide Council of Yukon First Nations.

Clearly, the Yukon is set on a path of developing First Nations governments that are completely separate from the public government. What is new and important about this path is the much higher status and potential jurisdiction that Yukon First Nations governments enjoy as contrasted to First Nations governments established under the *Indian Act*. These include almost all First Nations governments in Canada. As a result governance in the Yukon will focus as never before on the processes by which the public and Aboriginal governments negotiate how they will share jurisdiction and service delivery in a manner that is both efficient and culturally sensitive.

THE NORTHWEST TERRITORIES

With every passing year, it appears increasingly likely that governance in the NWT will follow the trail blazed by the Yukon, at least regarding the institutions of the territorial government. It was not always this way. For almost two decades, residents of the territories struggled to accomplish the vision of building a public government that would satisfy the aspirations of their Aboriginal peoples for self-determination. This seemed a plausible goal for several reasons. The first was that the institutions of the territorial government were relatively new. Indeed the administration of the territories was only transferred to Yellowknife from Ottawa in 1967. Being so new, these institutions did not enjoy the authority of long experience and tradition. They seemed reasonable candidates for alteration if a consensus could be reached on the types of changes that would make them better "fit" the society that they governed. Second, while Native people are accustomed to receiving services from the territorial government, many view it as illegitimate and have expected that it would change to accommodate their particular needs for collective representation as Aboriginal peoples. Third, and very important, before the division of the NWT in 1999, Aboriginal people accounted for about 60 percent of the population of the former territory. The ballot box thus gave them the power to place their desires for a transformed public government on the territorial agenda and to compel non-Natives to consider them seriously.

To incorporate Aboriginal governance into public institutions it is necessary first to understand how Aboriginal peoples conceive of themselves politically. As is the case generally with traditional ethnic groups, Aboriginal political culture places considerable emphasis on the well-being of the Nation or people as a whole and the maintenance of its culture and collective identity. Aboriginal peoples in the NWT attach such importance to these collective goals and their right to govern themselves in pursuit of them that they are reluctant to exercise this right in public institutions that operate on the liberal–democratic premise of "one person, one vote." This formula does not provide for the representation of each Aboriginal nation on the basis on which they conceive of themselves, as collective groups, as peoples. Moreover, this formula has only modestly protected their culture and values, even when the NWT has had an Aboriginal majority. It would afford them even less protection if non-Aboriginal people come to form a larger proportion of the territorial population. As the individualist principle does not adequately safeguard their cultural and other communal interests, the Aboriginal peoples of the NWT have only been interested in public governance arrangements that would give them significant power as cultural collectivities.

There are several ways of accomplishing this goal. One would be a federal arrangement that would divide the NWT into areas that are populated predominantly by Aboriginal people and others in which non-Native people predominate. In effect and on a very large scale, this is the logic underlying the creation of Nunavut, whose population is overwhelmingly Inuit. However the federal principle does not fit the NWT because Aboriginal and non-Aboriginal people live in such an intermingled pattern that it is not possible to subdivide it into areas each of which would be relatively ethnically homogeneous.

In view of this problem, the NWT, with the blessing of the federal government, attempted to apply the principle of consociation. Consociation, often termed "partnership" in the territories, is an approach to designing institutions of governance that will integrate ethnically divided societies. It has been employed in a number of such societies around the world. Its basic elements include representation of each "cultural community" as such in the legislature and executive of the government. Consociation also gives each major cultural community a veto or at least a great deal of power over the passage and implementation of laws that are deemed to affect the basic interests of the cultural community. An example of an attempt to establish a consociational practice in the larger Canadian context is the proposal in the Charlottetown Accord of 1992 that francophone members of a revised Senate of Canada could veto a bill affecting the French language, even if a majority of Senators, all told, supported the bill. In addition to this principle, known as "mutual veto," consociation arrangements can involve "segmental autonomy." This principle protects the fundamental interests of groups by giving exclusive jurisdiction over these issues to the governments of the respective groups. This, of course, is the practice of federalism, except applied to groups of people rather than to separate regions. A general principle of consociation is that there is a reciprocal relationship between the principles of mutual veto and segmental autonomy. The stronger the veto that cultural groups can exercise in the institutions they share with one another and the larger the span of subjects concerning which they exercise this veto, the less will be the need for them to develop their own institutions of government and to seek wide powers for them. Conversely, to the extent that cultural communities control the most important questions in their own governments, there will be less need to suspend the liberal-democratic principles of political equality and majority rule in the public government. It will be the community governments, not the common government, that will represent and protect their interests.

The major benefits of consociationalism are the responsiveness to the fundamental interests of the cultural communities that it builds into structures of government, and the confidence that members of the cultural communities feel in these structures. This leads them to view these institutions as legitimate and to give them the support they need. Consociation's major drawback is the way in which it can complicate the process of decision making and limit the ability of government to respond promptly and vigorously to problems that arise. Skeptics of consociation in the territories emphasize this lack of decisional efficiency (as well as the practice of basing representation on groups rather than individuals) as a major drawback to the approach. They argue that giving vetoes to groups, particularly groups with fundamentally different assumptions, would immobilize the legislature. Supporters of the idea have replied that, so long as there exists an underlying commitment to make the system work, consociational governance can operate successfully on the basis of a great deal of negotiation and compromise. While this may delay decisions, it is better to have policies that respect the interests of all of the major cultural communities than it is to quickly reach decisions that shortchange the needs of some of the groups. The Aboriginal peoples of the territories have experienced this subordination in the past and will not welcome constitutional reforms that make it likely in the future.

Because it would be very costly to operate multiple governments each governing very small populations, the Northwest Territories has concentrated its efforts on designing consociational institutions that emphasize mutual veto rather than segmental autonomy. Four major proposals appeared between 1981 and 1996 (Dene Nation and Métis Association of the NWT, Western Constitutional Forum of the NWT, Commission for Constitutional Development, Constitutional Working Group of the Western Caucus of the Legislative Assembly and the Aboriginal Summit), each attempting to strike a balance between Aboriginal self-government and the principles of liberal democracy that both the Aboriginal and non-Aboriginal people of the territories would accept. The last of these is "Partners in a New Beginning," made public in 1996 by the Constitutional Working Group, which was composed of members of the legislative assembly and representatives of the Aboriginal Summit of the Northwest Territories. A summary of its provisions will suggest what consociational principles might look like in the context of the NWT.

"Partners in a New Beginning" proposed a dual system of MLAs. All residents of the territories would elect 14 MLAs. These MLAs would comprise the "General Assembly" in the legislature. In addition, each of the eight existing regional or tribal Aboriginal political bodies would select an individual to be an MLA representing it. These eight MLAs would compose the "Aboriginal Peoples Assembly." Approval of legislation would require the support of a majority of the members of each of the two assemblies. If a bill did not receive this double majority, it could only pass if it received the votes of two-thirds of all of the MLAs voting as a single group. Thus, the Aboriginal groups would not enjoy the absolute power to veto legislation, but they would have more power as cultural communities than they do at present, when MLAs represent all the people of their geographically defined constituencies rather than specific Aboriginal peoples. "Partners in a New Beginning" also proposed that the cabinet would be organized on a consociational basis; the cabinet would have no fewer than six members, of whom at least four would come from the General Assembly and two from the Aboriginal Peoples Assembly. At the same time, "Partners in a New Beginning" proposed to apply the principle of segmental autonomy by suggesting that Aboriginal governments at the regional and local levels would exercise some authority.

The reception that territorial residents gave to "Partners in a New Beginning" demonstrates the great difficulty of attempting to integrate Aboriginal governance within public governance. Non-Aboriginal northerners rejected the proposal vigorously, arguing that the idea of them voting for a single MLA and their Aboriginal neighbours selecting two MLAs violated the basic principle of political equality and the provisions of the *Canadian Charter of Rights and Freedoms*. They also worried about the uncertainty surrounding the operations of the proposed institutions, and whether it would lead to indecisive government. At a time of shrinking government budgets, and in anticipating the additional costs of the 1999 division of the NWT, they were concerned about the expense of the proposed institutions and the policy compromises they might produce. Aboriginal northerners have not been as absolute in their rejection of "Partners in a New Beginning," but they have been quite unenthusiastic. Many feel that the proposal will create institutions that do not reflect their traditional political cultures. Also significant is their expectation that future years will see the inherent right interpreted to give Aboriginal peoples more political power than the concept currently appears to provide. They do not want to permanently sign away their right in order to receive what might be much less than they could negotiate a number of years in the future. For all of these reasons, Aboriginal leaders have not fought for the proposal.

The conclusion that the cultural communities of the NWT will not find the will to build Aboriginal governance into their public government was reinforced by a court case concerning electoral boundaries that was decided in 1999. Historically, more MLAs have represented the rural areas of the NWT than their population has warranted. This has violated the democratic principle of relative equality among all voters. However, it has been accepted, not only because of the physical difficulty of representing the scattered populations of the rural ridings, but because changing this situation would be seen as prejudicing the process of planning for the new institutions of government for the NWT. Rural overrepresentation means more MLAs for the Native people who make up the bulk of the population in rural constituencies. To reduce their representation in the middle of negotiations concerning integrating their inherent right within the public government territories would signal a lack of will to make this accommodation and possibly harm the negotiating process (NWT Electoral Boundaries Commission, 1998, 4). Nonetheless, a group of territorial residents challenged the electoral boundaries in court, arguing for more urban seats. Their victory very strongly suggests that the courts will apply the *Charter* in a fashion that would emphasize the equal representation of individuals so rigorously as to leave no room for the kind of consociational arrangements that are the only conceivable way of integrating Aboriginal self-government within public governance.

It is now apparent that the vision of the federal government's self-government policy will not come to pass. There are at present no discussions or other processes considering how to accommodate the inherent right within the institutions of government at the territorial level. For its part, the territorial government is much more interested in negotiating with Aboriginal peoples concerning questions of economic development. Two considerations lead most of the Aboriginal peoples of the territories to welcome the opportunity to pursue economic development together with the territorial government. The first consideration is the urgent need to create jobs for the growing number of young Native workers who are entering the labour force. The second is that, for the groups that have settled their land claims, collaborating on economic development will not be interpreted as a sign of weakness and lack of conviction in claims negotiations, as it formerly might have. Indeed, the convergence of interest between most Aboriginal groups and the territorial and federal governments on the desirability of economic development is probably the biggest change in territorial politics in the last two decades.

With economic development the dominant issue in pan-territorial politics, attention has focused on implementing the inherent right at the regional and local level. This is unfortunate in the sense that the territorial government makes a great many decisions that touch the heart of Aboriginal cultural and other interests but in which the Aboriginal peoples will not be able to participate as peoples—as integral social, cultural, and political communities. This surely flies in the face of the principle of their inherent right. At the same time, the political culture of Aboriginal peoples emphasizes politics at the local and regional level, in small-enough groups to facilitate the sense of community and mutual responsibility that infuses Aboriginal political tradition. Focusing on the inherent right at this level is therefore culturally authentic, provided that the governments that are created exercise sufficient power and will not just implement policies and deliver services designed by others.

As of the middle of 2002, a number of self-government negotiations are actively under way. The Inuvialuit and the Gwich'in and the federal and territorial governments are working towards a Beaufort Delta Regional Government, which would be a public government, to be accompanied by public governments in the communities of the Beaufort Sea and Mackenzie Delta. At the same time, the Gwich'in and the Inuvialuit would each have their own regional governments and local governments. One possibility would be that the various regional governments would be composed of members of the respective local governments. Such an arrangement would provide for segmental autonomy, but because the division of powers among these governments has not yet been decided or made public, it is not possible to assess how much segmental autonomy, which is to say self-government at the regional level, the approximately 3000 Inuvialuit and 2500 Gwich'in will enjoy. Moreover, because the structural details of the public governments are not known, it is also impossible to assess the extent of power sharing that they will embody.

The Dogribs, who live to the north and east of Great Slave Lake, are negotiating a Dogrib First Nation government. For at least the first 10 years of the creation of this government, it will participate in a "partnership institution" with the Government of the NWT. This will enable the Dogribs and GNWT to jointly deliver programs and services in such important areas as health, education, and social services to all residents of the Dogrib area. Local governments also will be public governments, with the provision that their leader must be a Dogrib chief and that, should the ethnic balance of the population become significantly more non-Aboriginal, the Dogrib would retain not less than 50 percent of the seats on local councils. The third active negotiating table, for the community of Deline, is proceeding according to a similar logic. The community will be governed by an "inclusive Aboriginal government," inclusive in that all residents, regardless of ethnicity, will be able to vote, stand for election, and appeal administrative decisions of the Deline government. However, the Chief, who will lead the government, must be a member of the Deline First Nation and there will be a guaranteed minimum below which the proportion of Aboriginal councillors will not fall, regardless of shifts in the ethnic balance of the town's population.

What can be said of these unfolding arrangements? It is hard to avoid the conclusion that the apparent promise of the inherent right to reshape northern governance will not be realized. There is clearly no place for the inherent right in the institutions of the territorial government. Moreover, the Aboriginal peoples of the NWT have not responded to this realization by attempting to create a territory-wide Aboriginal government. This is understandable in view of the differences of interest that divide them. At the same time, the absence of such a government by default gives the territorial government authority over many questions that ought to be decided by the Aboriginal peoples on the basis of their inherent right. This possibility seems especially likely because the negotiations to date about the implementation of the inherent right have involved the creation of public institutions at the local and regional levels. Because these are public institutions, the territorial government can be expected to assert very forcefully that the democratic principle of treating citizens uniformly requires that non-Aboriginals governed by these institutions not be disadvantaged. This means that they should not be subject to laws different from those that apply to residents governed by public governments that do not embody the inherent right.

Moreover, the territorial government is likely to argue that it will be asked to deliver services for these public governments or to certify that they meet appropriate standards in such areas as education. It will also note that people should not be hindered in their desire to move from the jurisdiction of an Aboriginal government to that of a public government and vice versa by incompatible policies on such questions as vaccinations, education levels, or family arrangements. On the basis of these concerns, the territorial government is likely to argue, indeed to require, that the Aboriginal/public governments work within uniform policies and standards set by the territorial government. The most pessimistic interpretation of such an outcome is that the Aboriginal peoples of the NWT will not experience their inherent right as enabling them to make fundamental decisions. Indeed, what may happen might be worse than if they had not implemented the inherent right, in that it will leave them doing little more than implementing the policies of the territorial government. The big winner will be the territorial government, for two reasons. First, it will have reduced to insignificance the threat to its authority that the inherent right poses. Second, it will have downloaded onto the local and regional governments the headaches of meeting citizens' expectations and dealing with their complaints about the quality of services they receive.

This cannot be said to be the fate of all of the Aboriginal groups of the NWT, because a number of them have not yet opted to pursue their rights within public government institutions. However, to the extent that they may wish, for reasons of efficiency, to collaborate in the future with the territorial government, they are likely to find themselves compelled to accept its policies and standards.

NUNAVUT

Nunavut presents a unique situation in North America. It comprises a large area in which the Aboriginal population outnumbers the non-Aboriginal population by such a wide margin that Aboriginal people can achieve fully effective self-determination through their participation in the public government. Moreover, because it is very unlikely that the population balance will shift fundamentally, the Inuit can anticipate with a very high level of confidence that they will continue to dominate the governance of Nunavut for a great many years. This expectation has made the Inuit confident about seeking institutions that do not embody the inherent right of Aboriginal self-government. This means that Nunavut rests on a base of ordinary legislation, the *Nunavut Act*, rather than having the protection of a constitutional foundation. As a result the federal government has the authority, which it is most unlikely actually to use, to reunite Nunavut with the Northwest Territories or to divide up Nunavut and to attach the various portions of it to several of the existing provinces. In addition, the government of Nunavut is clearly a public government, for which all adult citizens, not just Inuit, resident in Nunavut can vote and seek office. The Nunavut government contains no consociational arrangements such as were contemplated for the Northwest Territories. Finally, should the unexpected come to pass and large numbers of non-Aboriginals settle in Nunavut or Ottawa does away with Nunavut, the Inuit will be able to take up their inherent right and create institutions of Inuit self-government, which would exist alongside the institutions of public government.

A number of powerful reasons led the Inuit to pursue Nunavut, and its formula of self-determination through the public government of their own territory. Of course, Nunavut expresses the identity of the Inuit as a people; it is a source of pride and hope. Nunavut also enables the Inuit to control their territorial government without resorting to the expensive and cumbersome pattern of dual systems, Aboriginal and non-Aboriginal, of governance found in the other two territories. Also, the creation of Nunavut has enabled the Inuit to build a government that will be less physically remote than was the Government of the Northwest Territories. The Nunavut government intends to make itself even more readily accessible to Nunavut residents by decentralizing its operations. Services will be delivered in all of the communities, as they were before division, and a number of government departmental headquarters will be located outside of the territorial capital of Iqaluit. This will improve access to government. The Inuit also hope that administrative decentralization will enable more Inuit to obtain government employment without having to leave their home. The Inuit are working to create a government whose policies and internal processes will be more culturally responsive to them. Finally, Nunavut is crucial to protecting important benefits that the Inuit received in their land claim settlement. This settlement created several government agencies on which both Inuit and representatives of the territorial and federal governments sit. These boards rule on such questions as water use, wildlife management and harvesting, and the exploration plans of mining and energy companies. These are questions that are particularly important for the Inuit, many of whom rely on the land and waters for hunting, fishing, and gathering plants. While the boards generally have equal numbers of Inuit and governmental members, their decisions are reviewed by governmental ministers. Thus the only way to ensure that decisions in these "co-managed" areas are sensitive to Inuit needs is to ensure that the minister is an Inuk or is responsive to the needs of the Inuit by being electorally dependent on them. The means of accomplishing this has been realized by the creation of a territory where the Inuit dominate the ballot box.

The territory of Nunavut, the product of these hopes, came into being on April 1, 1999. Its government is taking shape gradually because it is a huge task to develop the organizational structure of a modern government from scratch. The organization of government and, based on it, a staffing plan must be designed, employees hired and trained for their particular responsibilities, policies developed and service delivery systems created and implemented. With such a huge task still very much in progress, it is not possible yet to offer a report card on the success of the government of Nunavut.

However, it is possible to offer some impressions of issues that are likely to prove perennial challenges for Nunavut. One of these will be the challenge of public finance. As noted above, the Government of Nunavut has relatively little control over its finances, as it is dependent on funding from Ottawa, which is determined to keep its spending levels from growing. It is a reasonable assumption that developing new policies that respond to the particular needs of the Inuit will be more expensive than simply adopting existing policies. However, every extra dollar spent developing new programs is a dollar not available for the delivery of badly needed programs. Moreover, to the extent that meaningful government decentralization in order to spread out employment opportunities and increase access to government will cost more than the former centralized model, funding for service delivery will be affected. The same is true of the costs of training Inuit for specialized forms of government employment. The tight finances of the Nunavut government are certain to challenge its leaders as they attempt to reinvent governance in ways that will realize the dreams that animated its creation.

As is the case for the fledgling Yukon First Nations governments, another serious challenge to the practical realization of self-determination for the Inuit of Nunavut is teaching Inuit workers the specialized and technical skills needed to gain employment in the middle and senior ranks of the Nunavut government. It is important that Inuit hold as many of these jobs as possible for several reasons. The first is to provide good, stable employment for the expanding Inuit work force. In addition to reducing the Inuit unemployment rate, employing Inuit in the public service provides role models that encourage young Inuit to stay in school and to avoid the despair that seems more prevalent than in non-Aboriginal communities in southern Canada. Inuit public service employment also increases the likelihood that public administration will operate in a manner sensitive to Inuit cultural needs. Finally, the more Inuit public servants, the more the Inuit people will come to see the Nunavut government as theirs.

The anecdotal evidence that exists suggests that the Inuit identify with the organizations that have been created to administer the lands and funding that the claims settlement provided to the Inuit. However, they do not yet have the same sense of ownership of the territorial government. Populating the Nunavut public service with as high a proportion of Inuit staff as possible will encourage the Inuit to recognize the government as theirs. While an Inuit staffing policy will provide these benefits, it will not be easy to accomplish. Because Inuit educational attainment trails the Canadian average, it will be necessary to provide academic upgrading for many workers before they can begin more specialized preparation. Moreover, the territorial government will have to compete for trained Inuit workers with the organizations established by their land claim settlement to administer Inuit lands and finances. Various training programs are now preparing Inuit for government employment. Still, it will take considerable amounts of time and money to train a significant proportion of Inuit for employment in the territorial government above the current level of approximately 47 percent.

A third issue confronting the Nunavut government will be managing its relations with the resource management boards created by the Inuit land claim settlement. These bodies, described above, represented a major victory for the Inuit in that they are quite powerful. While the similar bodies created by the Yukon land claims settlement are merely advisory, the Nunavut agencies actually make decisions. The federal minister can overturn decisions of the Nunavut co-management boards, but it is expected that this will happen rarely. This power will limit the ability of the territorial government to develop and implement its own policies for the economic development of Nunavut. In reality what is evolving is a mixed form of public government. All of the agencies that will be making policies critical to economic development will be public government bodies. However, the co-management boards will not be part of the territorial government—they will contain representatives of the Inuit claims settlement organizations, and if they have the funds they need to do their jobs effectively, they will become quite powerful. This novel form of governance will make it very important for the Government of Nunavut to maintain close communication with these boards and to develop a consensus with them on the needs and priorities of the new territory and on the impacts of board decisions on these priorities (Legare, 1997, 417–18).

It should be noted that the claims settlements in the NWT provide for similar co-management agencies. These also represent a significant departure from previous institutions in which Aboriginal peoples had no collective representation as cultural communities.

The Government of Nunavut will confront two additional governance-related issues. The first, already suggested, is the challenge of developing culturally responsive policies and practices of governance. Financial limitations will reduce the government's ability to innovate. Also, the government will have to rely on non-Inuit staff for a considerable period of time until substantial numbers of Inuit staff can be trained and gain the experience in government that they need before assuming senior roles. Non-Inuit staff employed by the government of Nunavut will undoubtedly be sympathetic to Inuit aspirations, but may well find it difficult to accommodate these aspirations within their professional norms and administrative experiences. Moreover, the Government of Nunavut may find its ability to innovate somewhat cramped by the need for its policies to conform to national standards, or at least practices. For example, the government will feel some pressure to ensure that educational curricula sufficiently conform to national standards that they will be recognized for admission to post-secondary institutions or enable students to move into and out of the territory with as little disruption to their educational progress as possible. Similarly, any co-operative arrangements on such matters as medical care may require the territorial government to operate in a manner that conforms more with provincial practices than it might wish.

The second challenge will be to realize the promise that Nunavut holds for representing Inuit interests at intergovernmental bodies and meetings. With the creation of Nunavut, the Inuit become the only Aboriginal people in Canada to be represented automatically at federal/provincial/territorial meetings. Also, the Inuit will be able to participate through their territorial government in international circumpolar meetings that give them additional opportunities to impress their views on their Arctic neighbours, and also on the Government of Canada. Representation of course does not guarantee policy success. In addition to "growing into" its mandate and addressing the very pressing social needs of its people, the Government of Nunavut will have to develop the capacity to make effective use of the opportunities that these intergovernmental encounters afford.

In summary, Nunavut is not a form of Inuit self-government, but it represents a potentially powerful approach to self-determination. Part of its potential flows from the fact that it rests so completely within Canadian constitutional tradition; it is a parliamentary government, but one that an Aboriginal people control. For this reason, it does not raise the conceptual problems of integrating the divergent principles of the inherent right and liberal democracy in a single set of institutions. It faces many difficult problems of developing the human and financial capacity to govern effectively; however, these are more problems of good governance than of intercultural governance.

CONCLUSION

The people of Canada's northern territories are reinventing governance, but they are not reinventing the basic institutions of their public governments. The liberal-democratic values that these institutions embody simply represent too powerful a principle to modify to express the political rights of Aboriginal northerners, however much other northerners might sympathize with Aboriginal political goals. Given this hierarchy of values, residents of the Yukon and the NWT and the federal government are working towards new patterns of governance that will accommodate separate Aboriginal and public institutions. Where the Aboriginal institutions fit in the pattern will depend on several factors. They will be able to grow only as much as financial and human resources available to them permit. For the foreseeable future in the North, the issue of "capacity" will be more important than any question of rights in deciding the actual degree of self-determination Aboriginal peoples enjoy. Also, to the extent that the territorial governments act in a manner responsive to Aboriginal interests, the Aboriginal peoples will feel less need to assume a wide range of responsibilities. It seems that this is the calculation that has led some Aboriginal peoples in the NWT to accept public forms of regional government that will limit their ability to actually make policy in a number of culturally important areas. However, if the territorial governments behave unresponsively, and to the extent that the Aboriginal peoples can overcome their resource and capacity problems, they will be motivated to take on more of the jurisdiction that is potentially theirs, gaining responsiveness at the cost of efficiency. Finally, the willingness of the territorial and federal governments to share powers with Aboriginal governments will have an important effect on the overall pattern of governance in the North. As noted above, these problems of intercultural relations among institutions will figure much less importantly in the governance of Nunavut.

What can be said of all three territories is that institutions of Aboriginal self-determination are appearing and that most of the Aboriginal peoples of the North are gaining strength from their recently settled claims. They can be expected to grow stronger as a result of their experiences with their new institutions and their success in capacity building. The farther they travel down this road, the more real and meaningful institutional choices they will enjoy. They will be able to judge how fully to employ the opportunities they are now constructing, how much they will exercise their inherent right of self-government, and how their own institutions will relate to the public governments of the territories. It is the answers to these questions that will reinvent the overall patterns of governance in Canada's North.

REFERENCES

Alfred, Taiaiake. 1999. *Peace Power Righteousness: An Indigenous Manifesto.* Toronto: Oxford University Press.

Canada. 1992. Gwich'in *Comprehensive Land Claim Agreement.* Vol. 1. Ottawa: Indian and Northern Affairs Canada.

Canada, Minister of Indian Affairs and Northern Development. 1995. *Federal Policy Guide: Aboriginal Self-Government.* Ottawa: Public Works and Government Services Canada.

Canada, Royal Commission on Aboriginal Peoples. 1996. *Report.* Ottawa: Minister of Supply and Services Canada.

Cameron, Kirk and Graham White. 1995. *Northern Governments in Transition.* Montreal: Institute for Research on Public Policy.

Cardinal, Harold. 1999. *The Unjust Society.* Rev. ed. Vancouver: Douglas and McIntyre.

Commission for Constitutional Development. 1992. *Working Toward a Common Future.* Yellowknife: Publisher to come 1st pass) __ not supplied

Constitutional Working Group of the Western Caucus of the Legislative Assembly and the Aboriginal Summit. 1996. *Partners in a New Beginning.* Yellowknife.

Dene Nation and Metis Association of the NWT. 1981. *Public Government for the People of the North.* Yellowknife: Dene Nation and Metis Association of the NWT.

Frideres, James and Rene R. Gadacz. 2001. *Aboriginal Peoples in Canada: Contemporary Conflicts.* 6th ed. Scarborough: Prentice Hall Canada.

Government of the Northwest Territories (GNWT) (see p. 256). 1999. *Agenda for the New North: Achieving Our Potential in the 21st Century.* Yellowknife: Government of the Northwest Terriories.

Hicks, Jack and Graham White. 2000. "Nunavut: Inuit Self-Determination Through a Land Claim and Public Government?" In Jens Dahl, Jack Hicks, and Peter Jull (eds.), *Inuit Regain Control of their Lands and Lives.* Copenhagen: International Working Group for Indigenous Affairs.

Canada Indian and Northern Affairs. 1987. *Comprehensive Land Claims Policy.* Ottawa: Minister of Supply and Services Canada.

Legare, Andre. 1999. "The Government of Nunavut (1999): A Prospective Analysis." In Rick Ponting (ed.), *First Nations in Canada.* Toronto: McGraw-Hill Ryerson.

McRae, Kenneth (ed.). 1974. *Consociational Democracy: Political Accommodation in Segmented Societies.* Toronto: McClelland & Stewart.

Morse, Brad. 1999. "The Inherent Right of Aboriginal Governance." In John H. Hylton (ed.), *Aboriginal Self-Government in Canada.* 2nd ed. Saskatoon: Purich Publishing.

Statistics Canada. 1996. *National Census.*

NWT Electoral Boundaries Commission. 1998. Yellowknife: Office of the Clerk, Legislative Assembly of the NWT.

Western Constitutional Forum of the NWT. 1985. *Partners for the Future.* Yellowknife: Western Constitutional Forum.

WEBLINKS

Government of the Northwest Territories
www.gov.nt.ca

Government of Nunavut
www.gov.nu.ca

Government of the Yukon
www.gov.yk.ca

part four

Redrawing Boundaries

chapter nineteen

Security, Immigration, and Post-September 11 Canada

Yasmeen Abu-Laban

Christina Gabriel

INTRODUCTION

The September 11, 2001, attacks on the World Trade Center in New York and the Pentagon in Washington have ushered in a new era of concern over security in Canada. In the weeks following what is now commonly referred to as "9/11," the Canadian government responded rapidly on a number of fronts. Prime Minister Jean Chrétien established the Ad Hoc Cabinet Committee on Public Security and Anti-Terrorism. The Liberal government also introduced, in quick succession, an *Anti-Terrorism Act* which is designed to identify, prosecute, and convict terrorists; a *Public Safety Act* that includes immigration amendments designed to protect Canadian citizens; and an amended *Aeronautics Act* to ensure the effectiveness of the aviation security system. At the same time, the Government committed $7.7 billion to fight terrorism and strengthen public security (Canada, Department of Foreign Affairs and International Trade, 2002, 1–4).

A key concern in this effort, emanating from Canadian business groups and political leaders in both the United States and Canada, was to ensure the security of the Canada–U.S. border in order to maintain the continental flow of goods and services (Gabriel and Macdonald, 2002). This led to a renewed focus on the idea of a "North American Security Perimeter," which would involve some measure of Canadian and American co-operation in the area of immigration and refugee policies. This idea has not been popular with all Canadian leaders. In his capacity as Minister of Foreign

Affairs, and as chair of the Ad Hoc Cabinet Committee on Public Security and Anti-Terrorism, John Manley raised concerns about a North American perimeter on grounds of both Canadian sovereignty and human rights. Although he noted that the movement of goods across the Canada–U.S. border was an obvious priority for his government, he also cautioned that "Working closely with the United States does not mean turning over to them the keys of sovereignty in the areas of immigration, border control or foreign policy." He also suggested that Canada might be more responsive to the human rights claims of refugees than would the United States (Migration News, 2001, 6).

Such a position's emphasis on Canadian sovereignty may prove difficult to sustain in the face of American concern, however unwarranted, about the security of the Canadian border. In April 2002, the American television show *60 Minutes* aired a documentary entitled "North of the Border" in which Canada was portrayed as a "launching pad for terrorists." Such representations do not square with the facts. None of the September 11 hijackers came through Canada, and there are few cases of law breaking among the 20 percent of Canadians who are immigrants (including Arab-Canadian and Muslim-Canadian immigrants). Yet, once again, questions of immigration and security were debated in the House of Commons (McCarthy, 2002, A1, A8).

Although post–9/11 political debates and policy concerns about security, immigration and particular ethnocultural groups, and the economy may appear new, this chapter challenges this perspective. The contemporary focus on these issues is in keeping with Canada's historical record. Additionally, while some social theorists of globalization have suggested that state power is declining or eroding (Strange, 1996) we concur with those who have pointed out that state sovereignty still finds considerable expression in attempts to control territory, police borders, and regulate population. However, as the Canadian case illustrates, this exercise of sovereignty needs to be explored further. The aftermath of September 11 indicated very clearly Canada's continuing and deepening economic dependence on the United States but has also served to link questions of security and border control to Canadian sovereignty. Continental integration and issues of economic sovereignty have been a longstanding preoccupation of Canadian nationalists (see McBride and Sheilds, 1997, 141–88). But calls for a common perimeter for the continent, as a means of addressing security and border control, raise other types of sovereignty-related questions that need to be considered.

In advancing these arguments, this chapter is divided into three parts. First examined are the ways in which conceptions of sovereignty are connected to immigration, security, and border control. Second, the Canadian state and immigration policy are examined from a historical perspective, with special attention to developments in the twentieth century, to show how security concerns have always been woven through Canadian political discourse and public policy. Finally, both the ways in which the Canadian state has moved to craft a response to September 11 and related questions about sovereignty in a globalizing era are addressed.

SOVEREIGNTY

All national states claim sovereignty on the basis that they "have supreme authority to make and enforce laws" within a given territorial space (Baylis and Smith, 2001, 150). This particular understanding of sovereignty carries specific assumptions about the state's internal and external powers. It is assumed that, internally, states are the final and supreme political authority within a national territory. For example, they have the ability to make laws, raise taxes, implement public policies, and so on. The external dimension of sovereignty encompasses the state's right to pursue such actions free of interference by other states because state sovereignty is *recognized* by other members of the international community (Biersteker and Weber, 1996, 2–3).

This conceptualization of state sovereignty has been criticized on the basis that state power is far from absolute and indivisible. Critical interpretations highlight how sovereignty has been socially constructed (and reconstructed) over time and place. Working from this starting point, Biersteker and Weber illustrate how territory, population, and authority are the constitutive elements of sovereignty. They argue that sovereign recognition assumes a "territorial state as a geographically contained structure whose agents claim ultimate political authority within their domain" (1996, 13). But population is also an important aspect of sovereignty insofar as a state's identity is premised on a series of exclusionary practices, such as the criteria for formal citizenship, that establishes the national community. Lastly, authority claims centre on the state's ability to exercise control over its affairs (1996, 13–15). Yet this aspect of sovereignty is also qualified because, as has been pointed out, the state's authority is checked by a number of international commitments (Overbeek, 2000, 61).

Processes of globalization have challenged the capacity and autonomy of the nation state in a number of ways. In the Canadian case, trade agreements such as the Free Trade Agreement (1988) and North America Free Trade Agreement (NAFTA) are often seen as neoliberal responses to changes in the global political economy. NAFTA contributed to the further integration of the Canadian and U.S. economies. U.S. officials estimate that total trade between the two countries has increased by 50 percent since the agreement was signed in 1993. Currently, it is estimated that over $1 billion in goods and services crosses the Canada–U.S. border daily. Indeed, "Canada is the number one trading partner of the United States, with $365 billion in two-way merchandise trade in 1999. This is more than U.S. trade with either the rest of the western hemisphere or the entire European Union" (Meyers, 2000, 256). The deepening economic integration created pressure for both countries to lift border controls as they were seen as a barrier to cross-border trade. Such pressures underscore the shifting nature of territoriality and sovereignty within an increasingly globalized environment.

Trade agreements such as NAFTA have also had an impact on state power and authority. While these agreements were negotiated by sovereign states, their provisions include measures that prevent governments (and future governments) from using or adopting certain policy options and instruments. Stephen Gill refers to such measures as a form of "new constitutionalism." They influence politicians or the mass of citizens by imposing, internally and externally "binding constraints on the conduct of fiscal, monetary, trade and investment policies" (1995, 412).

Chapter 11 of NAFTA offers a telling example. Under its provisions, foreign investors can challenge and sue governments directly by arguing that policies and programs constitute expropriation. In the interests of public health, the Canadian government attempted to impose a ban on the gasoline additive MMT. The government was sued by the Ethyl Corporation whose lawyers argued that such an action was expropriation because it would adversely impact future sales of the product in Canada. The Canadian government paid Ethyl an out-of-court settlement of $13 million in damages plus costs. It also had to repeal the ban on the additive and announce publicly that MMT is safe (McBride, 2000, 112). NAFTA-related provisions have had an impact on the ability of the state to use certain policy instruments or to pursue certain actions, especially in relation to the economy and market.

Processes of globalization have challenged the capacity and autonomy of the nation state in a number of uneven and contradictory ways. While economic globalization might suggest a decline in state capacity vis-à-vis the market, state power is not restrained across the board. This is especially true in the areas of immigration policy and attendant security concerns. The response by industrialized states to the flow of people across international borders and within regions, which has increased with globalization, is to attempt to reassert sovereignty and exercise territorial closure. Consequently, NAFTA has facilitated the flow of goods and capital between the three member countries but this free flow of goods has been accompanied by concerted efforts to police the borders and to limit the flow of people within the region (see, for example, Andreas, 1998–1999). NAFTA has very limited labour mobility provisions as Stephen Clarkson has pointed out; free trade and continental integration have also meant that, "each federal state has to build higher, more impermeable barriers to immigration" (1998, 16).

The post–September 11 response by the Canadian government needs to be framed against the paradox of the simultaneously open and closed borders that NAFTA created and the broader processes of globalization involving the movement of people. Contemporary patterns of international migration have led scholars to a number of conclusions. First, the flow of illegal and undocumented migrants (economic and non-economic) demonstrates the limited capacity of many nation states to secure independently their own borders. Second, the growth of international attempts to control or coordinate national policies with respect to migration demonstrates a recognition of the changing nature of state autonomy and sovereignty and the necessity to increase transborder co-operation in this domain (Held et. al., 1999, 321–2). Consequently, the increasing attempts to police borders against the undocumented have yielded only limited results. With respect to the Mexico–U.S. border, Peter Andreas has argued that "enhanced border policing has less to do with actual deterrence" and "more to do with managing the image of the border and coping with deepening contradiction of economic integration" (1998–1999, 592). The outcome of these campaigns had immediate negative economic consequences and "almost zero effect on illegal immigration" (Bigo, 1998).

These observations underscore the difficulty that nation states, such as Canada, encounter in addressing questions of immigration control, and they also raise the question of whether immigration policy and border control are any longer the exclusive domain of sovereign states. Certainly these questions have taken on greater salience in recent years. Indeed, it has been suggested that in terms of policy, "international migration has moved from the realm of 'low politics' (i.e., problems of domestic governance, especially labour market and demographic policies) to the realm of 'high politics' (i.e., problems affecting relations of states)." In particular, "attempts have been made by governments to recast international migration as a problem of national security" (Cornelius, Martin, and Hollifield, 1994, 7).

THE CANADIAN STATE AND IMMIGRATION: THE HISTORICAL RECORD

A starting point for understanding Canada's immigration policy historically is Canada's origin as a European settler colony built on the expropriation of land from Aboriginal peoples. Groups of both British and French origin asserted dominance over the indigenous population, but with the conquest of New France in 1760, Britain was able to impose control over most of North America. The intention of British settlers was to develop a "white settler colony" (Stasiulis and Jhappan, 1995, 96–99). Not surprisingly then, when Canada became a self-governing dominion in 1867, the Canadian state continued to reflect ethnic and racial hierarchies, and Canada explicitly favoured white, British-origin Protestants as "model citizens" (Abu-Laban and Gabriel, 2002). Indeed, it was not until 1967 that overt racial and ethnic criteria were removed from Canada's immigration legislation (Abu-Laban, 1998).

By beginning with this understanding of the foundation of Canada as a white settler colony, and of its historic preference for immigrants of specific ethnic, racial, and religious backgrounds, the other ways in which the Canadian state exercised discretion (and therefore its sovereignty) over the selection of immigrants become clearer. Three other factors that have influenced this selection process relate to 1) the demands of business on policymakers and the perceived needs of the economy; 2) gendered assumptions and understandings about the roles immigrants would or could play in Canadian society; and 3) perceived threats to public security. By the latter part of the nineteenth century and in the early twentieth century there was a more explicit legislative focus to all of these factors. In this way, ethnic and racial hierarchies interacted in a complex, and malleable, way with other considerations.

One clear example of how ethnic and racial considerations were malleable, gendered, and responsive to business interests is seen in Prime Minister John A. Macdonald's national policy, which involved the construction of a national railway to link the new country from sea to sea. Between 1880 and 1884, the Canadian state responded to the demands of the Canadian Pacific Railway Company for cheap labour, by recruiting Chinese male labourers to work on the most dangerous jobs in constructing the CPR. As Prime Minister Macdonald argued in 1883, "it will be all very well to exclude Chinese labour, when we can replace it with white labour, but until that is done, it is better to have Chinese labour than no labour at all" (as cited in Bolaria and Li, 1985, 86). Following the completion of the railway, the federal government passed the 1885 *Chinese Immigration Act*, which introduced a "head tax"—an exorbitant fee for Chinese immigrants wishing to enter Canada. The head tax also had gender-specific consequences because it specifically served to prevent the entry of Chinese women who might otherwise be able to come to Canada on the basis of their marriage to a male Chinese labourer (Das Gupta, 1995, 153). Along with the Chinese, other groups, including South Asians and Japanese, historically encountered an array of policies enacted by the state which were designed to discourage permanent settlement by preventing the entry of wives and offspring (Das Gupta, 1995, 141–74).

Another example of the complexity of immigrant selection policies emerged during the tenure of Clifford Sifton (the federal Minister of the Interior from 1896 to 1905). Sifton has been called the "founder of the concept of selective immigration" (Canada, Manpower and Immigration, 1974, 6). As the 1885 *Chinese Immigration Act* suggests, immigration policy was "selective" in a racist way prior to the leadership of Sifton. But immigration policy became even more explicitly designed to achieve certain goals at the turn of the twentieth century. Specifically, in an effort to "settle" western Canada, under Sifton, immigration policy was used to attract immigrants who would till the land, and add to the population. For the first time southern and eastern Europe became important sources of immigrants. Equating the presence of women and children with permanent settlement, Sifton argued that a good-quality immigrant would be a male "stalwart peasant in a sheepskin coat, born on the soil, whose forbearers have been farmers for ten generations, with a stout wife and a half-a-dozen children" (as cited in Vipond, 1982, 82). Between 1896 and

1914 about one million immigrant farmers entered Canada (Avery, 1995, 24). The fact that some of those who entered Canada as agriculturalists went on to become part-time or full-time industrial workers aided in meeting the demand of business for workers (Avery, 1979, 9).

The outbreak of World War I led to a new security focus on some of the immigrants that were admitted at the turn of the century. Specifically, those born in countries that were fighting the British Empire came to be defined by the state as "enemy aliens." The *War Measures Act* of August 1914 allowed the Governor in Council to authorize any acts, orders, or regulations "he may deem necessary or advisable for the security, defence, order and welfare of Canada" including the arrest, detention and deportation of so-called enemy aliens; some 80 000 people were required to register in a system overseen by the police and military, and some 8500 were actually interned (including Germans, Austro-Hungarians, Turks, and Bulgarians) (1995, 71).

Concerns over security became more elaborate and politicized after World War I, a period which saw widespread labour unrest with the return of combat soldiers and with the Russian Revolution. This security focus had implications for specific groups. As Reg Whitaker explains, "the Bolshevik Revolution in 1917 and the Winnipeg General Strike and sympathy strikes in other Canadian cities in 1918 together provided a new source of alarm to the Canadian state and to Canadians with property: the 'dangerous foreigner,' the alien as Red revolutionary, anarchist, or labour agitator" (1987, 13). By the 1920s, the federal government attempted to prevent both the entry of entire groups (such as Finns, Ukrainians, and Russians) for their perceived Communist views and the naturalization of those immigrants in Canada was deemed undesirable. Some of the latter group, often involved in trade unionism, were deported (1987, 14).

During the Depression in the 1930s and World War II, immigration was effectively halted, and the Department of Immigration was actually disbanded (Abu-Laban, 1998, 72). During World War II, concerns over security were manifested towards Japanese Canadians. On December 7, 1941, Japan attacked Pearl Harbor and Hong Kong. An immediate response came from the Canadian government—fishing boats owned by Japanese Canadians were impounded; Japanese language schools were closed; and many Japanese-language newspapers were closed (Ujimoto, 1985, 120). Once again the *War Measures Act* was invoked in the name of national security, but this time internment was sweeping, effectively confining over 20 000 men, women, and children of Japanese origin to detention in British Columbia and other project areas (including sugar beet farms in Alberta, Manitoba, and Ontario) (1985, 127). Between 1943 and 1946, all property owned by Japanese Canadians was sold, with any costs associated with the owner's living in confinement deducted from the proceeds (Sunahara, 2000, 1207).

Immigration again picked up after World War II, with Prime Minister Mackenzie King announcing that it was clearly a matter of domestic policy, and that immigration from "the orient" was not wanted (Abu-Laban and Gabriel, 2002). In addition, in the context of the Cold War, concern about Communism led to the emergence of even more refined security controls within the Canadian state directed at differentiating potential immigrants on the basis of their ideological leanings. South of the border, in the United States, overt barriers to immigrants and even visitors who might have Communist sympathies were erected, while in Canada the RCMP and senior bureaucrats established similar screening mechanisms to bar immigrants and refugees on grounds of national security, but in a less open manner (Whitaker, 1987, 21–54). Whitaker suggests that this came about not so much because of direct pressure from American officials on Canada to preserve the world's longest unprotected border by having similar immigration criteria, but rather because many Canadian officials held the same views as American officials (1987, 21). As a result, there was a decided bias against potential immigrants perceived to be "left wing" and critical of capitalism.

It has often been suggested that the period after 1945 is qualitatively different concerning immigration, in part because of the growing internationalization of a discourse on human rights (that is, rights that are to be given to everyone, irrespective of citizenship, ethnicity, gender, and so on) (see Soysal, 1994). Within Canada, growing attention to human rights, including the development of a policy of official multiculturalism in 1971, paved the way for a very different climate for minorities. But despite this, it is notable that it took until 1988, after considerable lobbying, for the Canadian state to issue a formal apology for the gross violation of rights experienced by Japanese-Canadians during World War II, and to extend a redress package (one component of which was the creation of the Toronto-based Canadian Race Relations Foundation in 1997). In the case of other groups who have experienced human rights violations, the response of the state has been at best uneven, and at worst, hostile (such as towards living Chinese-Canadians who had to pay the head tax) (Abu-Laban, 2001).

When it comes to immigration selection criteria, in 1967 the Canadian state removed the overt ethnic and racial preferences that had marked its policy historically and in the immediate postwar period, in part because of a changing international climate in which discrimination based on race/ethnicity became increasingly "embarrassing" (Hawkins, 1988, 30). But it should be noted that the Canadian state retained a highly selective immigration policy, one which employs an elaborate grading system (known as the "point system"). The point system, designed to meet the needs of business for skilled workers, works by numerically assessing the worth of potential immigrants on a number of criteria (including education, training, occupational demand in Canada, knowledge of official languages, etc.). This system clearly demonstrates the continued power of the state in deciding "who gets in." Indeed, the point system criteria favour class-advantaged male applicants from countries with extensive opportunities for an education based on the Western scientific model. Women who enter Canada frequently come in as the "dependent spouse" of a male immigrant (or part of the family-class), resulting in a host of issues relating to their rights in Canada, and their status within families.

A major international norm pertaining to human rights and immigration relates to refugees. In 1951, the United Nations developed a convention on Refugees which requires states that are party to the Convention to protect refugees against expulsion (known as *non-refoulement*). Notably, Canada did not sign the convention until 1969 because there was concern on the part of Canadian officials that it might interfere with the ability of the state to deport (Canada, Manpower and Immigration, 1974, 115). While this lends credence to the idea that asylum for refugees fundamentally clashes with state sovereignty, in many ways the Canadian state has maintained control over the selection of refugees. For instance, Canada is selective of refugees from camps abroad, employing a kind of informal point system that judges their skills and training (Abu-Laban, 1998, 76).

The question of security also enters into the refugee arena. For example, during the Cold War, refugees who were perceived as fleeing oppression from Left governments tended to find a more responsive welcome from Canada than those fleeing persecution from Right governments (Dirks, 1977, 247–58; Whitaker, 1987, 264), although by the 1980s the threat of "international terrorism" began to even supercede the threat of communism as a Canadian national security concern (Whitaker, 1987, 6). Not least, during the 1980s and 1990s, in the name of both efficiency and security, the Canadian state enacted a variety of legislative measures to manage and control the process of refugees making asylum claims on Canada's shores (Basok, 1996). It may be true that relying on the security information of other countries, a process increasingly common among countries in Europe and North America attempting to deal with refugees, may lead to the diminution of state sovereignty (Whitaker, 1998), but in the end, the Canadian state still determines who is entitled to enter and stay.

In examining the historical record, it becomes clear that immigration has long transcended Canadian domestic policy because the movement of peoples across state borders for purposes of settlement is a process that by definition involves more than one state. In addition, Canada's historical roots as a settler colony and its patterns of migration were interwoven with Europe (France and particularly Britain). Thus the policies of Britain in the context of Empire were important in shaping Canada as a "white settler colony" and worked in conjunction with meeting the concerns of business to result in ever-shifting definitions of the "acceptable immigrant" and "immigrant threat." Clearly though, throughout the twentieth century issues of national security have been directly implicated by factors both inside and outside Canada's borders. Thus, determining who could be legitimately included or excluded from entry into Canada, and the nature of their rights if admitted, has also been tied to historically specific definitions of security in which the state exercised both internal and external sovereignty.

THE CANADIAN STATE AND IMMIGRATION POLICY SINCE SEPTEMBER 11, 2001

One of the outcomes of the events of September 11, 2001, was to focus public attention in Canada more squarely on the issues of security, border control, and immigration policy. By extension, the broader questions of state sovereignty and Canada–U.S. relations also came to the fore. In this section we briefly outline some of the relevant policy developments that have taken place in the post–September 11 environment.

The immediate response of Jean Chrétien's Liberal government to the September 11 attacks has been described as "business-as-usual" (Greenspon, 2001, A23) insofar as the government maintained that it would make some changes to immigration and other policies but would not harmonize them with those of the United States. Chrétien stressed the need for a "balanced approach" and emphasized the importance of Canadian sovereignty by telling the House of Commons that "the laws of Canada will be passed by the Parliament of Canada." Liberal MPs, such as Carolyn Parrish, went on the record, stating, "People in the States want to build a wall around North America and that's not realistic," and adding "We need to protect our sovereignty—we need to make sure we're still going to be Canadians at the end" (McCarthy and Clark, 2001, A1). Additionally, the Minister of Citizenship and Immigration, Elinor Caplan, emphatically maintained that the Liberals' new immigration legislation, Bill C-11. the *Immigration and Refugee Protection Act*—then before the House of Commons—contained sufficient provisions to address terrorism and other security concerns.

The Liberal government had embarked on a process to review and overhaul Canada's immigration legislation during its second mandate. Bill C-11, introduced in Spring 2001, charted the key directions the government would pursue in relation to the management of Canadian immigration and refugee policy in the twenty-first century. These directions were explicitly framed against a globalizing environment and economic imperatives. Thus Minister of Citizenship and Immigration Elinor Caplan noted in a speech that Canada had "to confront a vexing international problem, which threatens to disrupt the free flow of skills and expertise among nations [and that is] the growing international problem of criminally organized smuggling, trafficking, and forced labour of human beings" (Canada, Citizenship and Immigration, 2000, 2).

The dual mandate that underscored the legislation attempted to address the dichotomy of opening the country's borders to those construed as "desirable" while simultaneously exerting strong border control to keep "undesirables" out. This was captured in the metaphorical phrases "opening the front door wider" and "closing the back door" (2001a). In short, the government claimed that its new legislation would improve the family-class provisions through measures such as raising the age of dependent children, expanding the definition of spouse by recognizing common-law and same-sex couples, and making changes to sponsorship obligations. There was also an increasing emphasis on developing a selection model to attract highly skilled workers, both permanent and temporary. The intent, according to the government, was "to attract and keep high skilled, adaptable immigrants that Canada needs to succeed in the future" (2001b, 3). But more significant for the purposes of this section are the measures that would tighten up immigration and "close the back door." These measures explicitly addressed security concerns that pre-dated September 11.

In Bill C-11 were provisions that focused on trafficking and people smuggling, security concerns, and refugee determination. Provisions in the bill outlined strong penalties for people engaged in people smuggling, including life in prison and/or $1 million penalties (2001d, 4). While this measure addressed the need for the state to preserve the integrity of its territorial borders, other measures in the bill centred on its ability to deny people entry to the country or deport permanent residents. Under Bill C-11, categories of inadmissibility included "security, human and international rights violations, criminality, organized crime, health, financial reasons, misrepresentation and noncompliance, inadmissible family members." It added organized criminality and misrepresentation as new categories of inadmissibility (2001c, 6). It should be noted in terms of security that the bill retained previously existing—but undefined—clauses that indicated that terrorism and membership in a terrorist organization also constituted grounds for inadmissibility. A number of groups appearing before the government expressed strong reservations about this measure. For example, it has been pointed out that:

> The absence of legislative definition in Bill C-11 for the terms "terrorism," "membership in a terrorist organization" and "security of Canada" leaves refugees and immigrants impermissibly susceptible to unprincipled, arbitrary and even unconstitutional decision making with wholly inadequate opportunities for meaningful review or recourse. (Aiken, 2001a, 3)

Provisions in the bill removed appeal rights in those cases where people were found inadmissible on the grounds of security or human or international rights violations. In short, as the Canadian Bar Association noted:

> There is no requirement or process for considering whether deportation is appropriate or justified in the public interest, for distinguishing between long-term residents and short-term residents, for considering family interests, or considering the real possibility for rehabilitation (National Citizenship and Immigration Law Section, CBA, 2001, 2).

In sum, the control and security measures within Bill C-11 have been characterized as increasing penalties and reducing individual rights and protections for refugees and immigrants (Canadian Council for Refugees, 2001, 1).

In the aftermath of September 11, the government repeatedly emphasized that its proposed immigration legislation would "contribute to the security of Canada's borders" (2001e, 1). In October 2001, it announced that it would spend an additional $49 million to accelerate security and control measures already within the proposed legislation. Initiatives included fast-tracking the permanent resident card for new immigrants by June 2002, front-end security screening of refugee claimants, increased detention and deportation capacity, and the hiring of up to one hundred new staff to enforce upgraded security at Ports of Entry (2001e, 1). These security provisions of Bill C-11 were presented as an integral part of Canada's response to terrorism. However, by late Fall 2001, the government pursued additional measures to address fears regarding security concerns. The centrepiece of the government strategy was its anti-terrorism legislation.

Justice Minister Anne McLellan introduced Bill C-36, the "Anti-Terrorism Bill," in October 2001. It was the cornerstone of the Liberal government's anti-terrorism plan, which aimed to protect Canada and the Canada–U.S. border against terrorism, contribute to international efforts against terrorism, and address roots causes of such acts (2001e, 1). Bill C-36 omnibus provisions attempted to provide a definition of terrorist activity through the creation of a list of suspected terrorist groups and activities as well as significantly expanded police powers through measures such as investigative hearings, preventive arrests, and enhanced electronic surveillance. In the ensuing debate, critics charged that many of Bill C-36's provisions compromised fundamental rights of Canadians (Borovoy, 2001, A17; Roach, 2001) and the bill was subsequently amended. Controversial clauses respecting investigative hearings and preventive arrests would be subject to a review by Parliament every five years and if not renewed these clauses would lapse. Additionally, the broad definition of a terrorist act was revised to address concerns that actions such as illegal strikes or environmental protests could be wrongly construed as terrorist activities under original provisions (LeBlanc, 2001, A1).

The new *Immigration Act* and the provisions of Bill C-36 can be read as compelling evidence of the exercise of state sovereignty within a globalizing environment. While a distinction may be made between the state's ability to enact legislation and the efficacy of such legislation, recent developments, far from signalling a diminution of power, suggest that the Canadian state continues to wield significant powers over citizens and non-citizens alike in areas of migration and security. Provisions within both offer examples of the way in which the state attempts to control and regulate population. The new immigration legislation, for example, underscores a construction of the type of person Canada wishes to attract, notably one who is highly skilled, experienced, well-educated, and fluent in French or English. At the same time, the security measures within both the new *Immigration Act* and Bill C-36 speak to the idea that the threat of terrorism may be contained in immigration and even within the Canadian population. Because Canada is constitutionally committed to non-discrimination and equality (Choudhry, 2001, 375), and, indeed, these are major emphases in the tenets surrounding international rights, neither of these pieces of legislation suggest that specific ethnic, racial, or cultural groups are to be targeted. Nonetheless, there is little question that the spectre of ethnic profiling haunts this legislation, as seen in the concerns raised by many Canadian legal scholars, ethnocultural groups, and politicians (Abu-Laban, 2002). "Ethnic profiling" in the post–September 11 environment refers to the differential targeting, by law enforcement and immigration officials, of those of Arab origin or Middle Eastern "appearance," or of Muslims (Choudhry, 2001, 368).

The events of September 11 also created renewed interest in the vision of a common North American security perimeter. While the arrangement remains undefined and ambiguous, proponents of current versions seem to recommend that Canada and the United States co-operate around certain aspects of public policy including immigration and refugee policy and border security. The idea of common perimeter control had already been floated by the federal government in January 2000 (Duffy, 2000, A1), in part to address U.S. security concerns.[1] It subsequently gained momentum among business groups, some elements of the media, and the new American ambassador to Canada, Paul Cellucci (Bliss, 2001, A7). The latter saw harmonization as a way in which the "border effect"—traffic congestion, bureaucratic delays, and lengthy waits at crossing—could be addressed (Chwialkowska, 2001). The common perimeter vision predates the events of September 11. However, what was new in the wake of 9/11 was the more explicit emphasis on security concerns and the linking of these concerns to cross-border commercial trade.

The tightening of border security by the American government in the immediate aftermath of September 11 led to major economic repercussions in Canada. Subsequent ill-founded American perceptions, fuelled by such American media icons as *West Wing* and *60 Minutes*, that Canada is "terrorist friendly," prompted renewed calls for a security perimeter. The business position, which had previously emphasized trade concerns and economic ties, now linked these concerns more explicitly to so-called security threats. Immigration, refugee determination, entry and exit control, and air safety all came up as issues that had to be addressed, within the terms of a perimeter concept, to keep the border open to commerce (Toulin, 2001; Coalition for Secure and Trade Efficient Borders, 2001). Indeed, British Columbia Premier Gordon Campbell went on the record stating that Canada needed a "secure perimeter for the continent" because one of the country's "biggest assets—whether you want to accept that or not—is the free flow of goods into the United States" (McCarthy, 2001, A10).

Canada and the United States began negotiations towards a "smart border" in December 2001. The "Smart Border Declaration" included a 30-point "Action Plan for Creating a Secure and Smart Border." The two countries pledged to review, and in some cases change, a number of policies and procedures, including refugee processes, visa policies, common security features on travel identification cards, the sharing of information about airline passengers, joint immigration databases, and common border policing teams. Additionally, a number of points in the plan address ways in which the flow of goods could be enhanced through the use of measures such as truck pre-clearance away from the border (Canada, Department of Foreign Affairs and International Trade, 2002b). The declaration was immediately hailed by business groups as "a major step towards the creation of a North American security and trade perimeter" (Alberts, 2001).

The conception of a common security perimeter—underwritten by increasing continental economic integration—challenges conventional understandings of sovereignty. However, it is difficult to determine the degree to which state power and autonomy have shifted or become transnationalized (Clarkson, 2002, 11). As Canada and the United States pursue discussions about the Smart Border, the exact nature and scope of harmonization is less than certain. For example, Canada and the United States (and Mexico if it is included in the arrangement) can choose between several conceptions of a common security perimeter that emphasize stronger or weaker variants of harmonization. It has been pointed out, for example, that there are models of harmonization that merely involve better coordination between states in terms of information sharing and intelligence gathering between agencies.

Other conceptualizations of harmonization go much further than this and envision a model that is much closer to that of the European Union. In this model, member countries would harmonize entry requirements for all third-country nationals and implement a single external border. Once a person crosses the external border there would be no internal border controls—between member countries—for purposes of travel. This idea of the common perimeter finds expression in calls for a "Fortress North America." Still other—and stronger—versions of harmonization emphasize a model in which current methods of selection, admission, and control are replaced by a joint program managed by Canada and the United States (Macklin, 2001, 386–87). It should be emphasized that there are considerable differences in immigration policy and the treatment of refugees between Canada and the United States. There will be significant consequences in these domains if a common perimeter approach embraces strong variants of harmonization of policy and practice because, given our asymmetrical economic relationship with the United States, harmonization may well be to an American standard.

The common security perimeter—whatever its form—has generated considerable debate. Much of this has revolved around issues of sovereignty. For some, the Smart Border accord compromises Canada's control over territory and population. For others, the accord and the concept of a security perimeter are seen as a way to address security concerns on both sides of the border while still keeping the border open to cross-border trade. Proponents suggest that addressing security concerns "might require pooling some sovereignty with the United States but only in the greater interest of protecting Canadians" (Greenspon, 2001, A15). While the Liberal government has sought to negotiate this security/sovereignty tension by using phrases such as the "seamless but sovereign border" (Chwialkowska, 2001), the Smart Border may signal a shift in the way in which the state controls territory, while still allowing it to do what it has long done—scrutinize the entry and residence of nationals and foreigners in the name of security.

Indeed, the common security perimeter image invoked in the shadow of September 11, it is argued, "speaks to a different vision" of territory, one which cedes "primacy to the unfettered movement of goods and investment capital but where the border intrudes into the everyday life for all non-citizens and the periphery is mapped by high fences in the name of safeguarding those on the inside from dangerous foreigners" (Aiken, 2001b, A7). The security and control aspects emphasized in the post 9/11 common perimeter debates are premised on the misleading assumption that immigrants and refugees are the source of the problem (A7).

CONCLUSION

The events of September 11 have placed security and border control issues at the centre of the public agenda, and raised to the fore concerns about specific ethnocultural groups. While these concerns may appear to be new, we have demonstrated through an examination of Canada's record of immigration policy that such concerns about security, territorial control, population, and specific groups have always been present, albeit in shifting ways. From its foundations as a "white settler colony," Canada gave preference to the entry of white, British-origin Protestants. Specific events of global significance (World War I, World War II, and the Cold War) served to focus attention on both foreign and citizen "others" who were construed as posing a security threat to the national community. The new "War on Terrorism" may prove to do the same thing, despite the formal commitments to human rights, equality, and non-discrimination.

The continued concern about security, territorial control, and population reflects on issues relating to state sovereignty. In Canada, sovereignty issues have dominated our relationship with the United States. Frequently, this was cast in terms of economic sovereignty, and, indeed, as economic integration continues to deepen within a continental framework, sovereignty questions are increasingly linked to issues of border control and security. While Canada continues to exercise considerable powers in the area of immigration and security, recent discussions about a Smart Border and a common security perimeter may give rise to a different conception of sovereignty.

NOTES

1. In December 1999, U.S. Immigration stopped a 32-year-old Algerian, Ahmed Ressam, who was entering the United States from Canada. Subsequent searches of his car revealed bomb-making equipment. This case is frequently cited—on both sides of the border—as an example of Canada's lax immigration and refugee regime and has raised concerns in the United States about the integrity of the northern border.

REFERENCES

Abu-Laban, Yasmeen. 2002. "Multiculturalism and Essentialism: Canadian and International Developments." Paper prepared for the Workshop on Immigration and Integration. Annual Meetings of the Canadian Political Science Association. Toronto.

Abu-Laban, Yasmeen. 2001. "The Future and the Legacy: Globalization and the Canadian Settler State." *Journal of Canadian Studies 35*, 262–276.

Abu-Laban, Yasmeen. 1998. "Keeping 'em out: Gender, Race and Class Biases in Canadian Immigration Policy." In Veronica Strong-Boag, Sherrill Grace, Avigail Eisenberg, and Joan Anderson (eds.), *Painting the Maple: Essays on Race, Gender and the Construction of Canada.* Vancouver: University of British Columbia Press, 69–82.

Abu-Laban, Yasmeen and Christina Gabriel. 2002. *Selling Diversity: Immigration, Multiculturalism, Employment Equity and Globalization.* Peterborough: Broadview Press. (In Press).

Aiken, Sharryn. 2001a. "Centre for Refugee Studies, York University 'Comments on Bill C-11' Submission to the House of Commons Standing Committee on Citizenship and Immigration" Retrieved from www.web.net/-ccr/crsbrief.htm

Aiken, Sharryn. 2001b. "Comment: The Enemy Within," *Globe and Mail*, 24 October, A17.

Alberts, Sheldon. 2001. "Accord called step toward North American Perimeter," *National Post*, 13 December.

Andreas, Peter. 1998–1999. "The Escalation of U.S. Immigration Control in the Post-NAFTA Era," *Political Science Quarterly* 113.4.

Avery, Donald H. 1979. *"Dangerous Foreigners: European Immigrant Workers and Labour Radicalism in Canada 1896–1932.* Toronto: McClelland & Stewart.

———. 1995. *Reluctant Host: Canada's Response to Immigrant Workers, 1896–1994.* Toronto: McClelland & Stewart.

Basok, Tanya. 1996. "Refugee Policy: Globalization, Radical Challenge or State Control?" *Studies in Political Economy 50* (Summer), 133–166.

Baylis, John and Steve Smith (2001). *The Globalization of World Politics.* 2nd ed. Oxford: Oxford Press.

Biersteker, Thomas and Cynthia Weber. 1996. "The Social Construction of State Sovereignty." In Thomas Biersteker and Cynthia Weber (eds.), *State Sovereignty as Social Construct.* Cambridge: Cambridge University Press.

Bigo, Didier. 1998. "Frontier and Security in the European Union: The Illusion of Migration Control," In M. Anderson and E. Bort (eds.), *The Frontiers of Europe.* London: Pinter Press.

Bliss, Michael. 2001, September 29. "Attacks hasten the end of our border" *National Post.*

Bolaria, B. Singh and Peter S. Li. 1985. *Racial Oppression in Canada* Toronto: Garamond Press.

Borovoy, A. Alan. 2001, November 20. "Bill C-36 undermines the very rights on which our society is based" *Globe and Mail.*

Canada, Citizenship and Immigration (CIC). 2000. "Notes for an Address by the Honourable Elinor Caplan, Minister of Citizenship and Immigration to the Canada China Business Council—Statement." Retrieved from www.cic.gc.ca/english/press/speech/china-e.html

———. 2001a. "Notes for an address by the Honourable Elinor Caplan, Minister of Citizenship and Immigration to the Standing Committee on Citizenship and Immigration on Bill C-11 The Immigration and Protection Act—Statement." Retrieved March 23, 2001 from www.cic.gc.ca/english/press/speech/c11.html

———. 2001b. "Making the System Work Better—Backgrounder #2." Retrieved from www.cic.gc.ca/english/press/01/0103-bg2.html

———. 2001c. "Bill-C-11 Immigration and Refugee Protection Act: What is New in the proposed Immigration and Refugee Protection Act" March. Retrieved from www.cic.gc.ca/English/aboutpolicy/c11-new.html

———. 2001d. "Bill C-11 Immigration and Refugee Protection Act: Overview" Retrieved from www.cic.gc.ca/English/about/policy/c11-overview.html

———. 2001e. "Strengthened Immigration Measures to Counter Terrorism—news release" Retrieved from www.cic.gc.ca/english/press/01/0119-pre.html

Canada, Department of Foreign Affairs and International Trade. 2002a. "Canada's Actions Against Terrorism Since September 11—Backgrounder." Retrieved January 30, 2002 from www.can-am.gc.ca/menu-e.asp?print=1&act=v&mid=1&cat=1&did=1250.

———. 2002b. "Action Plan for Creating a Secure and Smart Border" Retrieved from www.can-am.gc.ca/menu-e.asp?

Canada, Manpower and Immigration. 1974. *A Report of the Canadian Immigration and Population Study, Volume Two: The Immigration Program.* Ottawa: Information Canada.

Canadian Council for Refugees. 2001. "Bill C-11: What it Means"

Clarkson, Stephen. 1998. "Fearful Asymmetries: The Challenge of Analyzing Continental Systems in a Globalizing World." *Canadian American Public Policy 35* (September).

Clarkson, Stephen. 2002. *Lockstep in the Continental Ranks: Redrawing the American Perimeter After September 11th.* Ottawa: Centre for Policy Alternatives.

Chwialkowska, Luiza.2001. "Impossible became possible on September 11," *National Post.*

Choudhry, Sujit. 2001, December 11. "Protecting Equality in the Face of Terror: Ethnic and Racial Profiling and s. 15 of the Charter." In Ronald J. Daniels, Patrick Macklem, and Kent Roach (eds.), *The Security of Freedom: Essays on Canada's Anti-Terrorism Bill.* Toronto: University of Toronto Press: 367–381.

Coalition for Secure and Trade Efficient Borders. 2001. Retrieved from www.cme-mec.ca/coalition/english/home.html

Cornelius, Wayne, Phillip Martin, and James Hollifield. 1994. "Introduction: The Ambivalent Quest for Immigration Control. In Wayne Cornelius, Philip Martin and James Hollifield (eds.), Controlling Immigration. *A Global Perspective.* Stanford: Stanford University Press.

Das Gupta, Tania. 1995. "Families of Native Peoples, Immigrants and People of Colour." In Nancy Mandell and Ann Duffy, (eds.), *Canadian Families: Diversity, Conflict and Change.* Toronto: Harcourt Brace, 141–74.

Dirks, Gerald. 1977. *Canada's Refugee Policy: Indifference or Opportunism?* Montreal and Kingston: McGill-Queen's University Press.

Duffy, Andrew. 2000, January 12. "Ottawa urges US to adopt continental security ring," *National Post.*

Gabriel, Christina and Laura Macdonald. 2002. "From 'Undefended Border' to 'Zone of Confidence': The Politics of a North American Security Perimeter." Paper delivered at the "Challenges to Governance in North America and the European Union" conference. Ottawa: Carleton University, February.

Gill, Stephen. 1995. "Globalisation, Market Civilisation, and Disciplinary NeoLiberalism," *Millennium 24*, 3.

Greenspon, Edward. 2001, November 15. "Comment: Seizing the day on Canada–US border flows," *Globe and Mail.*

Hawkins, Freda. 1988. Canada and Immigration: *Public Policy and Public Concern* 2nd ed. Kingston and Montreal: McGill-Queen's University Press.

Held, David, Anthony McGrew, David Goldblatt, and Jonathan Perraton. 1999. *Global Transformations.* Stanford: Stanford University Press.

Hollifield, James. 2000. "The Politics of International Migration: How Can We 'Bring the State Back In'?" In Caroline Brettell and James F. Hollifield (eds.), *Migration Theory: Talking Across Disciplines.* New York: Routledge.

LeBlanc, Daniel. 2001, September 21. "Ottawa softens terror bill" *Globe and Mail.*

Macklin, Audrey. 2001. "Borderline Security." In Ronald J. Daniels, Patrick Macklem, and Kent Roach (eds.), *The Security of Freedom.* Toronto: University of Toronto Press.

McBride, Stephen. 2000. *Paradigm Shift.* Halifax: Fernwood.

McBride, Stephen and John Shields. 1997. *"Dismantling a Nation: The Transition to Corporate Rule in Canada."* Halifax: Fernwood.

McCarthy, Shawn. 2002, April 30. "Liberal likens Alliance to Le Pen," *Globe and Mail*, A8.

McCarthy, Shawn. 2001, October 17. "Tighten immigration laws, Ottawa told." *Globe and Mail,* A10.

McCarthy, Shawn and Campbell Clark. 2001, September 20. "Canada will make its own laws, PM vows" *Globe and Mail.*

Meyers, Deborah Waller. 2000. "Border Management at the Millennium," *The American Review of Canadian Studies 30*, (2) (Summer): 255–268.

Migration News. 2001. "Preventing Terrorism." November. Vol. 8. No. 11. Retrieved October 31, 2001 from http://migration.ucdavis.edu

National Citizenship and Immigration Law Section, Canadian Bar Association. 2001. "Submission of the National Citizenship and Immigration Law Section, Bill C-11 to the Senate Standing Committee on Social Affairs, Science, and Technology." Retrieved from www.cba.org/News/Archives/2001-10-02_submission.as

Overbeek, Henk. 2000. "Globalization, Sovereignty and Transnational Regulation: Reshaping the Governance of International Migration." In Bimal Ghosh (ed.), *Managing Migration.* Oxford: Oxford University Press.

Roach, Kent. 2001. "The Dangers of a Charter-Proof and Crime-Based Response to Terrorism." In Ronald J. Daniels, Patrick Macklem, and Kent Roach (eds.), *The Freedom of Security*. Toronto: University of Toronto Press.

Soysal, Yasmin. 1994. *Limits of Citizenship: Migrants and Postnational Membership in Europe.* Chicago: University of Chicago Press.

Stasiulis, Daiva and Radha Jhappan. 1995. "The Fractious Politics of a Settler Society: Canada." In Daiva Stasiulis and Nira Yuval Davis (eds.), *Unsettling Settler Societies: Articulations of Gender, Race, Ethnicity and Class.* London: Sage.

Strange, Susan. 1996. *The Retreat of the State.* Cambridge: Cambridge University Press.

Sunahara, Ann. 2000. "Japanese Canadians," In James H. Marsh (ed.), *The Canadian Encyclopedia.* Toronto: McClelland & Stewart, 1207.

Toulin, Alan. 2001, December 3. "Business group wants police at all crossings," *National Post.*

Troper, Harold Martin. 1972. *Only Farmers Need Apply: Official Canadian Government Encouragement of Immigration from the United States, 1896–1911.* Toronto: Griffin House.

Ujimoto, R. Victor. 1985. "Japanese." In B. Singh Bolaria and Peter S. Li, *Racial Oppression in Canada.* Toronto: Garamond Press, 105–135.

Vipond, Mary. 1982. "Nationalism and Nativism: The Native Sons of Canada in the 1920s." *Canadian Review of Studies in Nationalism 9* Spring: 81–95.

Whitaker, Reg. 1987. *Double Standard: The Secret History of Immigration.* Toronto: Lester and Orpen Dennys.

Whitaker, Reg. 1998. "Refugees: The Security Dimension." *Citizenship Studies 2*, 3.

WEBLINKS

Canada's Actions Against Terrorism Since September 11
www.dfait-maeci.gc.ca/anti-terrorism/canadaactions-en.asp

Smart Border
www.canadianembassy.org/border/index-e.asp

Strengthened Immigrations Measures to Counter Terrorism
www.cic.gc.ca/english/press/01/0119-pre.html

chapter twenty

Canada and the Hemisphere

The Summit of the Americas Process and the Free Trade Area of the Americas (FTAA)

Terry Kading

INTRODUCTION

As negotiations on the Free Trade Area of the Americas (FTAA) progressed at the Summit of the Americas held in Quebec City in April of 2001, it was apparent that numerous people vehemently disagreed with the claim made by our Minister for International Trade that the FTAA would be democratic. News images beamed around the world of well-equipped security forces confronting protestors amongst an intricate system of barricades and clouds of tear gas captured the animus between the supporters and detractors of the FTAA and *free trade* generally. The Summit of the Americas process is distinct from other trade forums, as the FTAA is but one of many themes under discussion. But the Quebec Summit highlighted the fact that the prominent role of the Canadian government in the summit process is focused on the FTAA over all other hemispheric issues.

The FTAA has become the cornerstone of the Summit of the Americas process, forging the largest "free trade" zone in the world, and referred to as the "Mother of all Regional Trade Agreements" (Johnstone, 1998, 22–26). Comprising 34 nations (all but Cuba) of vastly different levels of economic and social development, the agenda proposed would culminate in the integration of some of the poorest regions of the world with the two wealthiest under a uniform set of procedures and rules, equally applicable to all.

The justification by our government for promoting a hemispheric free trade agreement is based on the view that other issues in the summit process will be largely addressed in terms of the benefits of free trade alone. This is a questionable premise on which to risk substantive change across the Americas, when direct action by issue (for instance, health, education, and infrastructure) would be both more effective and immediate. Left unexplained is why Canada did not advocate "free trade" decades earlier to "solve" the problems of the Americas, and why Canada (particularly our trade minister) should develop a sudden concern with broader social and political issues. Even from a national interest perspective, the government's position on the FTAA is varied and confusing.

The purpose of this chapter is to provide an overview of what is being proposed, and to critically evaluate Canada's high-profile role in this process. The chapter begins with a review of the multiple and contradictory explanations given by the Canadian government for promoting free trade in the Americas, and then examines the series of events that led to the disputes between governments and protesters at the Quebec Summit. This is followed by an overview and analysis of the Summit of the Americas process and the proposals in the FTAA. The chapter concludes with a critical evaluation of our government's engagement with the Americas to date. What becomes evident, this chapter argues, is a Canadian role in the Summit of the Americas process that we should neither be proud of nor condone, as the negotiating position of the Canadian government is hampering, rather than advancing, the possibilities for more democratic and prosperous Americas.

WHY IS CANADA PROMOTING FREE TRADE IN THE AMERICAS?

An oft-repeated refrain is that "Obviously, Canada stands to gain a great deal from a future Free Trade Area of the Americas (FTAA). The FTAA will be the largest free trade zone in the world. With a population of 800 million and a combined GDP of $17 trillion a year, its potential defies the imagination. So do the opportunities it promises" (Pettigrew, 17 April 2001). With the exception of the GDP figure, which varies by commentator, this has been the standard line of the Department of Foreign Affairs and International Trade (DFAIT). However, as astute observers have noted, over 80 percent of any GDP figure cited is covered by our participation in the North American Free Trade Agreement (NAFTA). Thus, the FTAA appears to be a time-consuming and expensive effort to bring on side 31 other nations for the sake of less than 20 percent of hemispheric economic activity created largely by one country, Brazil (which a bilateral agreement would address).

Another justification iterated on occasion is that the FTAA will reduce our reliance on the United States by opening other secure markets for Canadian goods and investment (5, March 2001, B1). Again, the FTAA is a clumsy and precarious means to achieve such ends, as the majority of nations offer no opportunity for meaningful diversification, and cumulatively, would not offset the primacy of markets in the United States. This position also fails to observe that Europe and Japan represent our next most important trade and investment links, after the United States, and flies in the face of obvious trends showing that the United States accounts for over 85 percent of our exports, due to past agreements. Trade analysts often note the need for clarification and resolution with the United States and other First World countries on a variety of trade-related issues, suggesting our efforts in the FTAA are misdirected

A more promising explanation for our lead in the creation of the FTAA lies not in a concern with the fate of the Americas or specific Canadian opportunities, but with larger global strategic goals, on which we act in concert with the United States. Mentioned on occasion in the press, and as stated by the former minister for International Trade, "Canada is well positioned and well regarded. It is seen by many countries as a balance to the United States and the hemisphere" (Marchi, 3 March 1999). Offering *balance*, Canada assumed a role the United States could not, due to a long history of U.S. military intervention, support for military dictatorships, and questionable economic practices likely to arouse nationalistic sentiments in the rest of the Americas.

Canada's lead role, then, may be interpreted to obscure a congruence of Canadian and United States interests versus the rest of the Americas. The end result is to establish a preferential trade bloc providing Canada and the United States with numerous trade and investment advantages not available to other First World businesses (Cook, 2001, B7). A finalized FTAA would then serve as decisive leverage to force upon Asia and Europe a new and expanded round of WTO negotiations in light of the failed attempt at Seattle in 1999, and explains the desire for a rapid conclusion to the FTAA. As our minister for International Trade has stated, "Now that we have our hemisphere on our side, when we present ourselves at the WTO, we will have a lot more weight" (Greenspon, 2001, A11). What gets lost in this grand strategy are the special development concerns of the rest of the Americas to which a number of organizations and governments have committed time and resources out of a faith in the principles of the Summit of the Americas process. Thus, the negotiating position of the Canadian government to date hampers the possibilities for a more democratic and prosperous Americas.

ARRIVING AT THE QUEBEC SUMMIT

To understand how Canada has been able to assume a lead role on free trade for the Americas, several events prior to the 1990s need to be taken into account. Twenty years ago, the negotiation of a free trade agreement across the Americas would have been unimaginable. Since the 1940s the reigning development paradigm for the nations of Latin America and the Caribbean called for regulated investment and trade and government planning as the measures necessary to create domestic industries and foster economic growth. The idea of unrestricted access to foreign goods, investment, and services, particularly from the United States and Canada, was considered antithetical to these goals. These protectionist measures served a variety of ends, from generating government revenues, creating value-added activities using the resource base, enhancing the purchasing power of a larger percentage of the population, and diversifying economies away from an export reliance on a few minerals or agricultural exports. Trade and investment within the region and from First World countries remained an important component of these economies, but it was a complex system. Each nation had its own set of rules concerning the access and treatment of foreign goods and investment, further subject to a variety of restrictions or even expropriation depending on the government of the day. From the 1940s to the early 1980s, most Latin American nations made significant economic advances under this economic model. New infrastructure was installed, utilities and services were created, the domestic economy expanded, and the standard of living improved for a large proportion of the population. Although this strategy never resolved the problems of poverty or disparities in wealth characteristic of the region, the functions of states were increased, fostering the growth of a diverse middle class.

The reduction in global economic growth by the late 1960s—compounded by problems of rising inflation, unemployment, and then sharp increases in world oil prices—ignited the debate in the North about the virtues of state intervention and regulation. Confronted by similar problems in Latin America, the economic expansion was maintained into the early 1980s by borrowing more heavily from First World sources. Such heavy borrowing was predicated on an unprecedented period of generosity by First World sources and the strong world demand for certain exports, including agricultural goods, minerals, and oil. These conditions came to an end in the early 1980s. The dramatic increase in First World interest rates and low world prices for important mineral and agricultural exports left nation after nation in Latin America in arrears on their debt-servicing obligations. This *debt crisis*, in combination with shrinking economies, negative growth, and declining government revenues, set the stage for a major economic restructuring throughout the 1980s and 1990s.

Fearing the ramifications of a substantial default on outstanding global debt, the major financial institutions of the First World endorsed an imposing strategy to resume interest payments in exchange for renegotiated terms, renewed financing, and continued participation in the global economy. Designated as Structural Adjustment Policies (SAPs), the new terms of global engagement forced open the economies of Latin America to foreign investment and trade, encouraged the privatization of government assets, reduced government spending, realigned producer subsidies towards export promotion, and ended consumer price controls and subsidies. The SAPs were meant to induce export "competitiveness," reduce "inefficiencies," and earn foreign exchange to resume payments. While compliance varied from one nation to another, by the late 1980s the majority of Latin American nations had conceded to the terms of the SAPs and become members of the General Agreement on Tariffs and Trade (GATT).

The effect of GATT membership was to prevent any possibility of returning to the interventionist policies of the past. With the nascent features of liberal-democratic structures in place by the early 1990s, the return of foreign and domestic investment to the region, and positive economic growth figures beginning to emerge, a new confidence about the potential benefits of global free trade set in among Latin American leaders. With the largest nations in the region (Chile, Argentina, Brazil, Mexico) having acquired the shibboleth of *emerging markets*, efforts were directed towards advancing policies to further attract foreign investment. Of these, the most dramatic drive towards adopting "free market" principles was under President Carlos Salinas of Mexico (1988–94). Following a rapid and extensive privatization and deregulation of the Mexican economy, President Salinas's ability to negotiate a free trade agreement with Canada and the United States (NAFTA) broke new ground in developed–developing nations interactions. Having made Mexico a preferred site for First World investment, with preferential access to the most important market in the world, the incentive was established for other regions in the hemisphere to adopt NAFTA-like terms to equal the Mexican advantage. This situation set the context for discussions at the Miami Summit in December 1994, encouraged by the prospects for the means to address a variety of social and economic needs. Thus, in a brief time period, the governments of Latin America became participants in the creation of a free trade agreement for the Americas.

In contrast to the Latin American experience, Canada in the postwar period has been an active participant in several institutions promoting the liberalization and deregulation of trade and investment across borders. The primary forum for this agenda has been multilateral trade negotiations. Canada is an original member of the 23 nations that signed the

GATT in 1947, the express purpose of which was to reduce tariffs between GATT members. The central principle of the GATT has been the recognition of Most Favoured Nation (MFN) treatment, where imports and exports among member nations on agreed-upon product areas are guaranteed non-discriminatory treatment. For Canada, with a small economic base and a long history of exporting primary and semi-finished resource goods, the GATT was viewed as a means to secure access to the important markets of the United States in agreed-upon product areas. The GATT enhanced Canada's trade position by offering a larger forum for negotiations and the potential support of other nations against violators of the MFN principle. Though not a perfect means to advance Canada's export interests, as member nations often ignored GATT rulings, the consensus by officials until the early 1980s was that this forum had benefited Canadian export growth by reducing tariff restrictions and opening new markets.

A series of events altered the position of Canadian officials and led to an emphasis on bilateral trade agreements. This new direction began with Canada's waning faith in the GATT at the conclusion of the GATT–Tokyo Round (1973–1979). In the Tokyo Round "a major exercise was undertaken to strengthen disciplines on non-tariff measures, on counter-action against unfair trade and on the prevention of disguised obstructions to trade," (Lal Das, 1999, 5), addressing issues that Canada hoped would expand access to U.S. markets. In the end, GATT members were not obliged to accept the Tokyo Round Codes, suggesting a weakening of the principle of MFN treatment, and for Canada, no significant breakthrough on access to the United States through the GATT. This impasse was considered critical at the time, as Canada was growing as an exporter of investment capital, and despite efforts to the contrary, trade liberalization had increased rather than diminished our trade dependence on the United States (Smythe, 1996). Concerned over rising U.S. protectionist measures against the backdrop of a weakened GATT with a poor dispute settlement mechanism, Canadian officials sought a more secure agreement through direct negotiations with the United States.

By 1987, the government of Prime Minister Brian Mulroney had concluded a comprehensive bilateral trade agreement, the Canada–U.S. Free Trade Agreement (CUSFTA), which expanded trade and investment liberalization into new areas. Canada delayed joining the bilateral "free trade" negotiations between the United States and Mexico, but then trilateral talks began in 1991 and were concluded with the CUSFTA being superseded by NAFTA in 1994. Over the same time period, the Uruguay Round of the GATT (1986–1994), in which Canada had a prominent role in proposing an international trade forum to better enforce Uruguay Round agreements and what became the World Trade Organization (WTO), had concluded. With the formation of the WTO by 1995, a considerably more binding dispute-settlement mechanism applied to the GATT. From the perspective of Canadian officials, Canadian exporters had secured important advances through both bilateral and multilateral forums, NAFTA and the WTO, confirming renewed trade and investment security, perceived as in peril only a decade earlier.

Having achieved its main objectives of broader and more secure access to U.S. markets, and in light of Canada's overwhelming dependence on the United States, the question remains as to why Canadian officials are adamant promoters of economic integration with the Americas. This is only more puzzling in light of a House of Commons standing committee observation that "Canada's relations with Latin America are not so extensive (both in breadth and depth) and can at best be described as having been a low priority—at worst as much neglected—until the 1990s" (Canada, 1999). It is also a region confronted by financial instability and high rates of poverty, complicating the notion of "unimaginable opportunities" available to Canadian exporters and investors. Nevertheless, Canada assumed the lead negotiating position on the FTAA for the first 18-month term, chaired the Summit Implementation Review Group, and hosted a Trade Ministerial meeting, a meeting of the General Assembly of the Organization of American States, and numerous other summit-related meetings.

In addition to this hemispheric forum, the Canadian government has been engaged in a variety of bilateral trade initiatives with the Americas. For instance, outside the summit process, Canada has signed bilateral trade agreements with Chile (1997) and Costa Rica (2001). Canada has also signed or negotiated Foreign Investment Protection Agreements (FIPAs) with a majority of the countries in the Americas. Canada was then chosen to host the all-important Third Summit of the Americas in Quebec City in April of 2001. In short, Canada is more than an active participant. Indeed, Canada assumed a lead role matched by few other nations of the Americas. Still, it is unclear what motivated Canadian officials to engage in a costly, time-consuming, and unprecedented agreement with a region that has not interested officials in the past, unless one includes the extra-hemispheric goals that may result from the creation of the FTAA. These extra-hemispheric goals, though, serve to complicate our relations with the rest of the Americas, and undermine the ideals of the Summit of the Americas process.

Despite the fact that negotiations had been under way for years, it was only in the lead-up to the Quebec Summit that a belated public debate revealed problems with the summit process and raised serious questions about Canada's deeper engagement with the Americas. The Canadian government not only affirmed in the January Throne Speech its intention to play a leading role in negotiating the FTAA by 2005, but shortly thereafter sought support for a Chilean proposal to move forward the completion date of the FTAA to 2003 (McCarthy and Koring, 2001, A1). The editorial staff of the *Globe and Mail* fully endorsed the FTAA, stating that "[f]reer trade will boost investment flows to Mexico and other Latin American and Caribbean nations, raising living standards across the board, creating millions of new jobs and reducing pressures on illegal immigration" (17 February 2001, A14).

Through March, the upbeat mood changed. The security measures being adopted were creating a "Fortress Quebec," and raising questions about *Charter* violations and our own respect for democratic practices. The larger context of hemispheric relations did not foretell a harmonious summit. The Canadian government broadened its dispute with Brazil over aerospace subsidies to include suspect allegations of "mad-cow" disease, invoking a ban on Brazilian beef products that, due to NAFTA, included bans in Mexico and the United States, sparking the ire of the average Brazilian. In addition, Canada–U.S. relations were on a downward slide, as Canada was snubbed on a "tradition" of first official visit with the new U.S. president, along with a continuing U.S. ban on P.E.I. potatoes, and a looming softwood lumber dispute (MacKinnon, March 5, 2001). It was then revealed that the Canadian government had sold access to the summit, circulating a price list for corporate sponsorship a year in advance (March 20, 2001, B1). As the government claimed the corporate sponsorship was a benefit to Canadian taxpayers, the federal ethics counsellor considered launching an investigation, and the *Globe and Mail*, while denying any quid pro quo between corporate monies and political influence, condemned the practice, asking "Why arm your critics?" (March 22).

A meeting of finance ministers from across the hemisphere in early April restored an upbeat tempo leading to the Quebec Summit, with participants expressing optimism about current economic events and their support for the FTAA (Scoffield, 5 April 2001, B4). Such enthusiasm was brief, as at a subsequent meeting of trade ministers, Brazil and Venezuela rejected conclusion of the FTAA by 2003, pushing the date back to 2005 and revealing the United States as the instigator of rapid finality on the negotiations for the FTAA (Hester, 10 April 2001, A 13). Such tactics raised suspicion among some countries that the United States and Canada, the only developed nations, held little interest in any mandate save the FTAA.

Then, with the summit in Quebec City, it was not Canadian ministers, but the President of Mexico who garnered kudos. While critical of the demonstrators, President Vicente Fox articulated the spirit that had been advanced in Miami: the summit process was about multilateral action on all topics ranging from drugs to poverty; financial resources needed to be made available to fulfil the mandates, and there should be "preferential treatment for the region's poor" (Knox, 19 April 2001, A4). Brazil echoed these sentiments with the statement "the north has to pay for free trade" (21 April). Conflicting comments in the *Globe and Mail*, ranging from "FTAA is no revolution, just a logical first step" and "FTAA offers chance to address NAFTA's worst excesses" (April 21) to "FTAA matters little to Canada" (April 20) left ambiguous the purpose of Canada's lead role in negotiating the agreement. In a final irony, while summiteers patched together a last-minute "democracy clause" as a condition for future hemispheric participation, commentaries on the security measures adopted during the Quebec Summit proclaimed our own "*Democracy demolished*" (April 21) and suggested "*A police state in the making*" (April 24). In the end there were mixed reviews as to what had been accomplished for Canada and the other nations of the Americas, but it was evident that there had been a betrayal of the original vision for the summit process.

CANADA AND THE SUMMIT OF THE AMERICAS PROCESS

When President Bill Clinton convoked the first Summit of the Americas, in Miami in 1994, he established a broad agenda for the future. Going beyond just "free trade," the Miami Summit set the task of creating an economic, social, cultural, and political agenda that in depth and breadth had not been contemplated before. In an effort to portray a significant departure in U.S.–Latin American relations, for the first time there was to be an equal partnership advancing a common vision of democracy and prosperity. Captured in the expression "words to deeds," the summit process was to exceed the rhetoric of the past by determining and implementing concrete measures. The summit process is understood as "an institutionalized set of meetings at the highest level of government decision-making in the Western Hemisphere" with the purpose to "seek solutions to problems shared by all countries of the Americas, be they economic, social, military, or political in nature" (Summit of the Americas Information Network, 21 March 2000).

First established were broad mandates based on Preserving and Strengthening the Democracies of the Americas, Expanding Prosperity Through Economic Integration and Free Trade, Eradicating Poverty and Discrimination in the Hemisphere, and Guaranteeing Sustainable Development While Protecting the Environment for Future Generations. To these ends, 23 initiatives, ranging from broad themes such as strengthening democracy, human rights, and civil society, to more specific concerns of corruption, terrorism, drug trafficking, education, health, women, telecommunications, and tourism, were divided up among member teams as the Miami Plan of Action. A Summit Implementation Review Group (SIRG) was created, with a rotating national chair, to oversee progress on the various initiatives. Coordinated though the Organization of American States (OAS), with support from the Inter-American Development Bank (IDB) and the United Nations Economic Commission on Latin America and the Caribbean (UNECLAC), the summit process has enhanced the profile of the OAS, reviving the status of a largely moribund forum. The Santiago Summit in 1998 and the Quebec Summit in 2001 followed the Miami Summit, the purpose of each being to review the progress accomplished through numerous rounds of meetings between summits, and to ratify further measures on respective initiatives. By the conclusion of the Quebec Summit, the mandates shown in Table 20.1 had been adopted. As Table 20.1 represents a summary of thousands of pages of reports from numerous rounds of meetings involving input from government representatives, multilateral organizations, and a variety of non-governmental organizations (NGOs), it is not possible to convey all the specific projects undertaken and proposed to date. Nevertheless, this summary provides the basis from which to make observations concerning the evolution of the summit process since 1994 and evaluations of the priorities and resolutions.

The most positive aspect is the priority of *Strengthening Democracy*, and here the debate has transcended the singular emphasis on just "holding elections" to examining the context of the electoral process, the role of the media, transparency on government actions, and facilitating citizen participation. A move away from highly centralized forms of national authority is apparent in the ideal to strengthen the effectiveness and responsiveness of local government. In addition, it is evident that there is a concerted effort to address issues of human rights and individual freedoms in a substantive manner. Measures to strengthen and broaden the scope of the inter-American human rights systems, ratify and accede to international and hemispheric charters, promote rights education, introduce legal equality for women, and enhance the functioning of judicial systems are significant advancements in the debates on political development.

Of note is the effort to address the plight of migrant workers and their families as both a human rights issue and an economic institution that requires recognition and reform. It is also one of the few mandates that may have implications for Canada and the United States, and not the just the developing nations of the Americas. The definitive debates on legal equality for women across the hemisphere, advancing the rights of children and youth, and the special recognition of Indigenous peoples, represent important gains within the hemisphere. The overall structure offers the potential for a stronger hemispheric system that will be able to more effectively investigate and act on behalf of individuals and groups on charges of systemic discrimination and other rights violations by national governments. The considerable involvement of numerous NGOs in the formulation of certain mandates and action plans, the cross-border interaction, and increased awareness of extra-national bodies of appeal provide the basis for forms of hemispheric action and pressure unknown to date. Thus, the possibilities for a variety of groups within *civil society* to be more assertive and confident in their claims is promising, and a notable endeavour is the attempt to reverse the "culture of fear" ingrained by decades of elite rule and military impunity.

Where there is an apparent weakening of resolve concerns the action plans for *Creating Prosperity* and *Realizing Human Potential* across the Americas. After the first summit in 1994, the mandates contained decisive language, such as *Eradicating Poverty*

TABLE 20-1 Mandates from the Third Summit of the Americas (2001)

I) STRENGTHENING DEMOCRACY
1) Making Democracy Work Better: Electoral Processes and Procedures; Transparency and Good Governance; Media and Communications; Fight Against Corruption; Empowering Local Governments
2) Human Rights and Fundamental Freedoms: Implementation of International Obligations & Respect for International Standards; Strengthening Human Rights Systems; Migration; Human Rights of Women; Human Rights of Children and Adolescents; Freedom of Opinion and Expression
3) Justice, Rule of Law, and Security of the Individual: Access to Justice; Independence of the Judiciary; Hemispheric Meetings of Ministers of Justice; Combating the Drug Problem; Transnational Organized Crime; Prevention of Violence
4) Hemispheric Security: Strengthening Mutual Confidence; Fight Against Terrorism.
5) Civil Society: Strengthening Participation in Hemispheric and National Processes
II) CREATING PROSPERITY
6) Trade, Investment, and Financial Stability: Trade and Investment; Economic and Financial Stability; Corporate Social Responsibility
7) Infrastructure and Regulatory Environment: Telecommunications; Transport; Energy
8) Disaster Management
9) Environmental Foundation for Sustainable Development: Environment and Natural Resources Management
10) Agriculture Management and Rural Development
11) Labour and Employment
III) REALIZING HUMAN POTENTIAL
12) Growth and Equity: Development Financing; Enabling Economic Environment; Migration; Enhancing Social Stability and Mobility
13) Education: Science and Technology
14) Health: Health Sector Reform; Communicable Diseases; Non-communicable Diseases; Connectivity
15) Gender Equality
16) Indigenous Peoples
17) Cultural Diversity
18) Children and Youth
Follow Up to the Plan of Action: Summit Management; Implementation and Financing
Source: Compiled from documents from the Third Summit of the Americas (2001)

and Discrimination in Our Hemisphere, and *Guaranteeing Sustainable Development*, the latter openly affirming the desire to advance sustainable-energy use, biodiversity, and pollution prevention. By the second summit in 1998, the sustainable development initiatives had become subtexts within other mandates, and by the third summit the *Eradication of Poverty and Discrimination* had been replaced by *Realizing Human Potential*. Only three mandates have definitive dates for completion: legal equality for women by 2002; access to education by 2010; and the conclusion and adoption of the FTAA by 2005. All other mandates contain vague language such as *to seek*, *to recognize*, *to promote*, *to strengthen* and *to support*, and remain ill-defined as to when, and particularly how, compliance is to be achieved on important subject matters.

In early 2001, the Leadership Council for Inter-American Summitry listed a number of flaws in the summit process, stating, "in short, Summits have successfully focused leaders' attention on policy initiation, but governments have paid insufficient attention to policy implementation" (Summit of the Americas Information Network). The Council recommended that "summit initiatives should be responsibly crafted to contain practical goals, quantifiable targets, and realistic timetables" and that "[i]nitiatives should be assigned to follow-up mechanisms with adequate technical and financial resources." While the requirement to establish such ends would serve to "significantly bolster the realism and credibility of Summits in the Americas," it was evident from the Quebec Summit that a major impediment to policy implementation is the issue of resources.

On this topic there is a clear North–Sourth (Canada and the United States–rest of the Americas) divide. Where Canada and the United States have the means and resources to address shortfalls in mandate compliance, the rest of the Americas do not. However, in the critical category of *Development Financing* there is but an *acknowledgement* of *need*. In one of the great understatements of the summit process, there is only *recognition* that debt servicing *constitutes a major constraint on investment*. Without addressing the reasons for the unequal availability of and access to resources across the Americas, the mandates insinuate that the reason for the problems outside of the North derive simply from a lack of *political will* and/or a knowledge and technology gap between North and South. This ahistorical evaluation carries pejorative overtones, and suggests that problems may be easily rectified by compulsory deadlines, adopting the North's "best practices," and purchasing the right technology. Canada's Minister of Finance expressed such sentiments prior to the Quebec Summit, lecturing officials from the rest of the Americas on the need to spend more on health and education if their nations were to prosper (as if this *idea* had not already crossed their minds). In urging health and education spending as a priority along with balancing budgets and debt servicing, our minister neglected to mention where the necessary financial resources would appear from. (Scoffield, 4 April 2001, A6).

The issue of the resources needed to comply with mandates has been complicated by the moralistic and rigid ideological stance of Canada and the United States. In the Americas, only the governments of Canada and the United States, acting in unison, have the ability to finance a new development fund or compel existing multilateral lending agencies to dispense the necessary monies. Instead of enthusiastic support for these measures, these governments have adhered to a position that the solution lies in the creation of the FTAA, arguing that from this will flow the wealth and "sustainable growth" to fulfil other social and economic mandates. In statements by trade ministers at the Quebec Summit, Canada and the United States openly affirmed a strict negotiating position. "U.S. Trade Representative Robert Zoellick and Canadian Trade Minister Pierre Pettigrew rejected the suggestion that special measures are needed to reduce the growing, potentially destabilizing gap between rich and poor. Mr. Zoellick said trade alone can reduce poverty; Mr. Pettigrew said it would be wrong to tell countries how to distribute wealth" (Knox, 23 April 2001, A17).

Where the U.S. position is at least forthright, our minister's sudden concern for *national sovereignty* openly contradicted the position of the Minister of Finance and was hypocritical (if not incredible) in view of what the whole Summit of the Americas process is proposing. The FTAA is the sole mandate that these two governments have expressed an interest in and which offers them immediate and tangible benefits both within the hemisphere and at the international level. With this negotiating position, the other mandates, at first a gesture of a new hemispheric collaboration, appear increasingly to be a means to leverage acceptance of the FTAA by the only two developed nations as the rest of the Americas await tangible evidence of monetary support for other mandates. Further proof of our limited concern for the South was later highlighted by a report that Canada's levels of development aid, as a percentage of GDP, were "ranked among the least generous in the world," but remained ahead of those of our negotiating partner, the United States (McCarthy, 27 April 2001, A5). Little wonder that at the Quebec Summit we were admonished by the Mexican president for failing to live up to our commitments to the poorer nations of the Americas. In this emerging context, the traditional power politics of the Americas are replacing an earlier emphasis on multilateral co-operation. It also suggests that what limited negotiating strength the Developing Nations of the Americas have within the summit process could disappear once the FTAA is accepted. Having derived what they desire from the summit process, only *good will* would remain as a reason for Canada and the United States to continue being engaged with the larger agenda (surely one of the least-effective incentives in international relations).

CANADA AND THE FREE TRADE AREA OF THE AMERICAS (FTAA)

Given the interest of our government in the FTAA, it is worth examining the subject areas under negotiation and the larger claim of the FTAA to be a means for creating "sustainable growth." Between the conclusion of the Miami Summit and the Second Summit that was scheduled for 1998 in Santiago, Chile, trade ministers from the 34 countries met on four occasions (called Trade Ministerials). After the fourth Trade Ministerial in Costa Rica in 1998, the San José Declaration, recommending to the Heads of State at the Santiago Summit that formal negotiations be launched to create the FTAA, was released. (Free Trade Area of the Americas, 16 February 2000). The San José Declaration established nine negotiating groups whose objectives are listed in Table 20.2 (see also www.ftaa-alca.org).

In addition to these subject areas, three other FTAA entities were endorsed, leading to a Consultative Group on Smaller Economies, a joint Government–Private Sector Committee of Experts on Electronic Trade, and a Committee of Government Representatives on the Participation of Civil Society. The last, advanced by Canada, was intended to increase the participation of representatives from civil society in the FTAA negotiations, under the principle of fostering a more *inclusive* and *transparent* process, and a further motion called for "concrete progress" on specific *business facilitation measures*. Canada then assumed the lead role as chair of negotiations for the first 18-month period, followed by Argentina, then Ecuador, and jointly the United States and Brazil for the final 18 months leading up to the 2005 deadline.

The San José Declaration proposed the principle that, where possible, negotiations would exceed existing levels of trade liberalization and encompass areas not previously agreed to under any multilateral agreement. The declaration represents the largest regional integration initiative ever proposed between developed and developing countries and sets

TABLE 20-2 Principle Goals of the San José Declaration
1. **Market Access:** progressive elimination of tariffs and non-tariff barriers
2. **Investment:** create a transparent framework to protect and promote investment throughout the hemisphere
3. **Services:** progressive liberalization of trade in services
4. **Government Procurement:** expansion of access to government procurement markets
5. **Dispute Settlement:** implementation of fair, transparent, and effective mechanism for dispute settlement
6. **Agriculture:** progressive elimination of arbitrary or unjustifiable discrimination between countries and of agricultural export subsidies affecting trade in the hemisphere
7. **Intellectual Property Rights:** creation of ensure adequate and effective protection to intellectual property rights
8. **Subsidies, Antidumping and Countervailing Duties:** enhance and deepen provisions already established by WTO
9. **Competition Policy:** curtail anti-competitive business practices at the national, sub-regional or regional levels

Source: Free Trade Area of the Americas (FTAA 2000), "The San José Ministerial Declaration, Summit of the Americas – Fourth Trade Ministerial," and "FTAA Working Groups" (www.ftaa-alca.org [16/02/00]).

in motion an unprecedented scope of negotiations even by the standards of the Uruguay Round. These negotiations will encompass areas that fall under the auspices of the World Trade Organization, but will also "include areas not presently under the WTO such as a common investment regime, government procurement, and competition policy, which are not yet subject to commonly agreed disciplines among a large number of trading nations" (www.ftaa-alca.org).

As may be discerned from the above quotation, the FTAA is an effort to strike a novel agreement that breaks new ground and expands on and deepens the terms NAFTA and WTO agreements to date. With reference to the San José Declaration (Table 20.2), it is possible to discern several features that are unique. What stands out at first, in the *Market Access* category, is the negotiating principle that there will be no exceptions in the final agreement; all parties are equally subject to the same agreed terms with only "different trade liberalization timetables" for the "integration of smaller economies." This in itself is a major departure from negotiations within the WTO, the latter forum still very cognizant of the fact that there are not just "larger" and "smaller" economies, but real differences in the types of economies and levels of economic development between developed and developing nations. What the WTO recognizes as a difference "in kind," the FTAA negotiations accept as only a difference "of degree." This acceptance of only a relative difference between the 34 national economies of the Americas leads to the incorporation of six major areas of negotiation to which the majority of nations of the Americas have, to date, been either weakly subject or wholly exempt. In this respect the FTAA is a major departure from the generally accepted terms of debate on poor versus wealthy countries. The FTAA would subject the former to far greater levels of integration, limiting their latitude on domestic decision making, and restricting trade and investment prerogatives in several new areas—*Services*, *Government Procurement*, *Agriculture*, *Investment*, and *Competition Policy*.

Prominent in the FTAA negotiations is the objective of Most Favoured Nation (MFN) treatment and liberalized trade in *Services*, an area that has failed to receive broad acceptance in WTO agreements. Involving a subject area covering a multitude of firms and occupations, including financial, commercial, transport, and construction services, the *Services* category is the fastest-growing sector of the developing and developed countries' economies. It is evident that both Canada and the United States see a decisive advantage in liberalizing trade in this area, due to technological and labour skills advantages, and recognize that an agreement would act as leverage in future WTO negotiations, having secured preferential access for the Americas versus other First World nations. Supplementary to the *Services* category, in going beyond the WTO agreements, is the area of *Government Procurement*. *Government Procurement* is seen as a lucrative and as yet untouched area of economic activity not subject to the rules of competition and foreign participation, and used by developed and developing countries alike to serve specific national ends (support domestic producers and service suppliers, create jobs, etc.). In the new *global-speak* of the Canadian government, such restrictive terms and objectives mean "taxpayers must bear the higher costs associated with procurement transacted in a non-competitive market," supposedly denying them the "best value for money" (Canada, October 1999). Nevertheless, developing nations have been loath to abandon this prerogative. Only a small number of countries under the WTO agreements allow foreign competition into select areas of procurement. Under NAFTA, this only applies to goods, services, and construction over fixed-dollar amounts and is limited to select branches at the federal level, while excluding procurements by other levels of government. The simple extension to 34 countries from 3 of NAFTA–like terms on *Government Procurement* would make available substantial amounts of money and opportunities to multinational firms, and pave the way for possible expansion of these terms to include presently restricted areas of government spending on goods and services.

The most controversial and complicated negotiations involve *Agriculture*. The effort to apply the broad *Market Access* objectives to *Agriculture*, limiting the use of health standards and eliminating export subsidies and other "trade-distorting practices" in this area, opens up a variety of complex issues. On the one hand there is little doubt that there would be advantages for a number of developing nations of the Americas. Many rely heavily on agro-exports as a basis of national wealth, and a longstanding grievance would be addressed should they achieve less-restricted access to the food markets of Canada and the United States. However, both Canada and the United States see unrestricted access to the domestic food markets of the Americas as an area in which they have a decisive advantage in terms of distribution, production costs, and quantities. In light of ongoing disputes with the protected markets of Japan and the European Union, Canada and the United States view secure access to these markets as a means to address domestic problems with little regard for the implications elsewhere in the Americas. From this may be discerned the difficult calculations for developing nations, particularly "smaller economies." The negotiating forum of the WTO provides the possibility of access to First World food markets without ceding the same degree of national control as the FTAA, but it does not offer the opportunities for additional financing in this and other areas, and may take decades to achieve.

It is the objectives under the categories of *Competition Policy* and *Investment* that could establish the most radical departure in trade negotiations to date. The extent to which sub-regions (state or provincial/municipal governments) have to comply with or are subject to NAFTA and WTO agreements is extremely unclear. With the specific objective in the category of *Competition Policy* "to advance towards the establishment of juridical and institutional coverage at the national, sub-regional or regional level, that proscribes the carrying out of anti-competitive business practices," there is a determination to clarify and deepen compliance in this vast area. It also has the potential to be the most politically charged subject area under discussion, as *regions* and *sub-regions* are considered the levels of government most responsive to local needs, and enjoy weak supervision or exemptions from NAFTA and WTO agreements at present. Subjecting the plethora of differing rules, regulations, procedures, and procurement practices at these levels to extra-national standards could open up innumerable potential conflicts, exacerbated by the objectives in the *Investment* category.

It was with the category of *Investment* that, for the year prior to the Quebec Summit, the Canadian government had maintained an independent position versus the United States by opposing the inclusion in the FTAA of the unprecedented investor–government dispute mechanism in NAFTA, known as Chapter 11. Providing foreign investors with the right to sue governments and receive monetary compensation for perceived lost profits or business opportunities, Chapter 11 amounts to a second and powerful level of surveillance on "agreement compliance" that is not in the WTO. In Canada there has been growing resentment towards this mechanism, expressed even by the Minister for International Trade, who claims that Chapter 11 has "led to numerous multimillion-dollar lawsuits against Ottawa" (Scoffield, 6 April 2000, B5). The minister had been on record as stating that Canada was not going to accept a trade agreement that included such an investor–government dispute mechanism, and, in addition, wanted its removal from NAFTA. In a separate meeting of NAFTA partners at the Quebec Summit, the issue was "resolved." The prime minister announced his support for Chapter 11, stating that it had "worked well" for Canada, and the minister for International Trade then argued that the government's position had not changed, always being "to clarify, not reopen, not renegotiate Chapter 11" (Pettigrew, 23 April 2001). In return for "clarification" on the NAFTA text, Canada dropped its official opposition to its inclusion in the FTAA, maintaining at this point a reserved position. With the likelihood of the investor–government dispute mechanism contained in NAFTA, a more comprehensive application of agreed-upon rules, and a dispute-settlement mechanism modelled on the more binding and expedient WTO agreements, the FTAA would be unique. It would encompass more areas subject to binding rules and include the mechanisms with the highest levels of surveillance and compliance of any agreement to date.

It is with an overview of what is under negotiation in the creation of the FTAA that one may discern the strategic global advantages that would accrue to Canadian and U.S. investors and exporters versus other First World countries. While the FTAA would not exclude trade and investment from outside the Americas (as this would be a violation of WTO agreements), cumulatively the categories in the FTAA would establish decisive advantages and privileged access for Canadian and U.S. corporations and investors versus non-American competitors. A combination of lower or non-existent tariffs, more secure investment guarantees, and the ability to compete in economic areas prohibited to Asian or European competitors has the potential to threaten existing trade and investment patterns.

Should the FTAA be adopted, there would be considerable pressure on European and Asian governments, by their corporations and investors, to begin, via the WTO, new rounds of negotiations expanding into *Services*, *Agriculture*, and *Government Procurement*. A finalized FTAA would ensure that progress on liberalized trade and investment is attained, and for the United States, the opportunity to introduce at a global level the unprecedented investor–government dispute mechanism from NAFTA. This is but one scenario, as the FTAA could provoke the strengthening of other regional trade blocs by governments and competitors, increasing global trade and investment disputes. Either way, there is little here that speaks to the specific development problems of the rest of the Americas if the FTAA is but a means to *pry open* more significant markets and opportunities elsewhere.

CONCLUSION: CANADA AND THE AMERICAS

That the subject areas under discussion in the FTAA are both broader and deeper in scope than NAFTA and WTO agreements is without question. For the majority of countries in the Americas, the FTAA would be a new level of compliance in subject areas to which they have had more flexible terms or outright exemptions. Were the FTAA being negotiated on its own, there is a low probability that it would be accepted by the nations of the Americas as the benefits are skewed to the advantage of Canada, the United States, and their respective corporations. What stands out is that despite all the meetings on numerous issues, the very real reasons lie elsewhere as to why these developing nations may feel compelled to accept a free trade agreement with few tangible benefits.

Not under discussion are two issues of critical importance, neither of which have found an effective multilateral forum for debate—the continuing problems related to servicing debts accrued in the 1960s and 1970s, and the high levels of currency instability related to larger global capital flows beyond the control of the region. Both factors contribute to the region having to sell itself to First World investors in an ever more extreme effort to instill *investor confidence* and encourage private capital flows as a means to service both old and new debts. Latin America has seen is popularity as an "emerging market" wane; fraught with recurring currency crises and debt-servicing problems, the "signal" that the Americas are "onboard" for a novel "free trade/free-market" experiment surely figures into the negotiations to maintain and enhance investment flows. The irony of this situation is that without addressing the long-standing *debt crisis* and the volatility of national currencies in the region, the possibilities for tangible benefits in the other mandates (beyond the FTAA) appear, at best, short-term. As the respected Peruvian economist Oscar Ugarteche has observed, the free-market measures adopted to date by the nations of the region have not resolved any problems. During the 1990s (versus the 1950s to 1970s), on average the region has experienced low economic growth, great financial volatility, greater and rising income inequality, and a loss of national autonomy for defining economic policy (Ugarteche, 2000, 201–15). At the Quebec Summit a "disillusioned" World Bank economist, Augusto de la Torre, reported that the economic reforms to date had led to only a marginal improvement in growth, while "[u]nemployment rose and incomes fell," and "180 million people—more than a third of the population of Latin America—live on incomes of less than $2 (USD) a day" (McCarthy, 20 April 2001, B8). Given the results so far, it is unclear how even less national autonomy over economic policy can address the problems of the region.

The Summit of the Americas began as an effort to address the problems of the Americas, but it had been undermined by the rigid position of Canada and the United States, and their utilization of the forum to achieve other strategic ends. Such tactics in the past had brought the OAS into disrepute, and there is the possibility that this could occur again. However, it is not hard to imagine the summit process serving all of the Americas. As Ugarteche and others have argued, by cancelling the debts of the poorest countries, reducing the debts of the middle-income countries, and placing severe limits on the amounts devoted to debt servicing, substantial and sustainable development would be initiated. This gesture, as opposed to new loans, would immediately free up billions of dollars a year that could be spent on infrastructure, services, and education, guaranteeing employment and higher incomes, and strengthening the credibility of the "fragile democracies" across the Americas. It would also create the "unimagined opportunities" for Canadian exporters. Paul Martin, former Minister of Finance, has often made this case in other international forums and called for debt cancellation for the poorest countries in the world, but this proposal has yet to be advanced by Canada in the summit process and, in light of Canada's negotiating position to date, it appears unlikely that it will be in the near future, despite the fact that these measures serve the very goals established at the first Summit of the Americas.

Canada's relationship with the developing nations of the Americas has gone from quiet observer to leader of the most important initiative, the FTAA, in a short span of time. From this initiative, though, there is little regard for the specific problems of development found within the Americas, amounting to a rejection of the initial spirit of the Summit of the Americas process. Where Canadians may believe their nation acts at a global level on values superior to our superpower neighbour, our deeds with respect to the rest of the hemisphere belie this view. This is not to say that the Summit of the Americas process could never be a meaningful forum for significant gains across the Americas, only that the intentions and actions of Canada and the United States to date betray this vision. The *balance* we have offered to the United States in the hemisphere does not include novel and alternative measures for addressing the immediate economic and social needs of the Americas. It also reveals a congruence of Canadian and United States thinking and interests of which Canadian citizens should be wary, as it is not evident that our own national interests, let alone those of the developing nations of the Americas, are best served by this partnership.

As observed, the Summit of the Americas process and the FTAA are significant negotiations, advancing into areas of economic, social, and political integration that had never before been considered for the Americas. Of this process, the FTAA is regarded as the pivotal means to achieve prosperity and strengthen democracy. It is important to point out that the term "free trade" is a misnomer, as it implies a sense of government inactivity. What is being proposed is a new regulatory environment requiring considerable government activity, both before, and after, to ensure compliance against the almost natural inclinations of another government to respond in a decisive manner to national concerns, invariably of an economic nature. That numerous developing nations in the Americas may, at the behest of the Canadian government, lose the ability to act decisively on behalf of their citizens, should concern us all. As Canada's *good reputation abroad* appears to be used to achieve *more important* strategic trade goals, it is perhaps worth reflecting on precisely which values we are exporting.

REFERENCES

Canada. October 1999. "The Free Trade Area of the Americas: Towards a Hemispheric Agreement in the Canadian Interest." In First Report of the Standing Committee on Foreign Affairs and International Trade/First Report of the Sub-Committee onmInternational Trade, Trade Disputes and Investment. www.parl.gc.ca/infocomdoc/36/2/fait/studies/reports/faitrp01-3.htm(11/03/00).

Cook, Peter. 2001, March 5 "A World Divided by So-Called Free Trade Deals." *Globe and Mail*, B7.

Daudelin, Jean. 2001, April 20. "One Big Happy Hemisphere? The FTAA Matters Little to Canada." *Globe and Mail*, A15.

Free Trade Area of the Americas. FTAA. 2000. "The San José Ministerial Declaration, Summit of the Americas—Fourth Trade Ministerial" and FTAA Working Groups." Retrieved February 16, 2000 from www.ftaa-alca.org.

———. FTAA. "FTAA Draft Agreement." Retrieved from www.ftaa-alca.org

———. FTAA. "Overview." *In Free Trade Area of the Americas*. Retrieved February 16, 2000 from www.ftaa-alca.org

Globe and Mail. 2001, March 22. Editorial: "Why Arm Your Critics?" A14.

Globe and Mail. 2001, April 21. Editorial: "FTAA Is No Revolution, Just a Logical Next Step." A16.

Greenspon, Edward. 2001, March 5. "The Talented Mr. Pettigrew." *Globe and Mail,* B7.

Hester, Annette. 2001, April 10. "Together to Face the Big Kid." *Globe and Mail,* A13.

Johnstone, Robert. 1998, December 1. "Free Trade in the Americas and a Great Deal More." *Behind the Headlines 56.*

Knox, Paul. 2001, April 12. "Fox Says Americas Pact Pointless Unless It Includes Help for the Poor." *Globe and Mail,* A9.

———. 2001, April 23. "North Has to Pay for Free Trade, Brazilian President Says." *Globe and Mail,* A4.

———. 2001, April 23. "Locking in Democracy." *Globe and Mail,* A17.

Lal Das, Bhagirath. 1999. *The World Trade Organization*. Penang: Third World Network.

MacKinnon, Mark. 2001, March 20. "Americas Trade Pact in Doubt." *Globe and Mail,* B1.

———. 2001, March 20. "Access for Sale." *Globe and Mail*, A1.

Marchi, Sergio. 1999, March 3. Presentation before the Sub-Committee on International Trade, Trade Disputes and Investment of the Standing Committee on Foreign Affairs and International Trade. Retrieved from www.dfait-maeci.gc.ca/english/statement/99_state/99_sintev24-e.htm

McCarthy, Shawn. 2001, April 20. "Attacking Poverty Key to Fixing Economic Woes of Latin America." *Globe and Mail*, B8.

———. 2001, April 27. "Canada's Development Aid Ranked Among Least Generous in World." *Globe and Mail,* A5.

McCarthy, Shawn and Paul Koring. 2001, February 6. "PM, Bush 'Break the Ice.'" *Globe and Mail*, A1.

McFarland, Janet. 2001, April 21. "FTAA Offers Chance to Address NAFTA's Worst Excesses." *Globe and Mail*, B8.

Pettigrew, Pierre. 2001, April 17. "Notes for an Address by the Honourable Pierre Pettigrew, Minister for International Trade, To the Hemispheric Trade and Sustainability Forum." Retrieved from www.dfait-maeci.gc.ca

———. 2001, April 23. Official Report*1435*Number 046 (Official Version). Retrieved from www.parl.gc.ca/37/1/parlbus/chambus/house/debates/046_2001-04-23/han046_1435-e.htm

Scoffield, Heather. 2000, April 6. "Pettigrew Rejects NAFTA Dispute Model." *Globe and Mail*, B5.

———. 2001, April 2. "Americas Officials Prepare for Summit." *Globe and Mail*, B4.

———. 2001 April 5. "Ministers End Meeting Upbeat." *Globe and Mail*, B4.

Smythe, Elizabeth. 1996. "Investment Policy." In G. Bruce Doern, Leslie Pal and Brian Tomlin, (eds.), *Border Crossings: The Internationalization of Canadian Public Policy.* Toronto: Oxford University Press.

Stevens, Sinclair. 2001, April 24. "A Police State In the Making." *Globe and Mail*, A15.

Summit of the Americas Information Network. 2000. "The Summit Process." In Summit of the Americas Information Network. www.summit-americas.org/Summit-Papers.

Ugarteche, Oscar. 2000. *The False Dilemma, Globalization: Opportunity or Threat?* New York: Zed Books.

Valpy, Michael. 2001, April 21. "Democracy Demolished." *Globe and Mail*, F1.

WEBLINKS

FTAA Official Website
www.ftaa-alca.org

Summit of the Americas
www.summit-americas.org

Indepth: Summit of the Americas 2001
http://cbc.ca/news/indepth/summit

chapter twenty-one

Canadian Sovereignty and Global Trade and Investment Rules

Elizabeth Smythe

INTRODUCTION

This chapter analyzes the impact of globalization on Canadian sovereignty and democracy through an examination of the re-emergence of a political debate over further trade and investment liberalization. This chapter examines three cases—the failed negotiations on a Multilateral Agreement on Investment (MAI), the World Trade Organization's (WTO's) Ministerial Meeting in Seattle, and the Free Trade Area of the Americas (FTAA) Summit held in Quebec City. These cases illustrate the contradictory aspects of globalization, which has both increased economic integration and generated new transnational movements opposing it. These movements have deep roots in Canada, a country that has always been a trading nation and therefore vulnerable to the vagaries of external markets.

The campaigns of opposition to the MAI, the Seattle Ministerial, and the FTAA are part of a growing questioning of the trade-off between global economic liberalization and other values. These movements have emerged in a new way; they are linked transnationally, facilitated by new technology, and nurtured by a public that has lost trust and confidence in political institutions and is uneasy with the growing uncertainty of an intensely globalized world. The result is a politics of trade policy that is messy, complicated, and uncertain, and that occurs outside the corridors of established bureaucratic and political institutions in Canada, reflecting the new politics of the twenty-first century. The chapter begins with an examination of the concept of globalization and its implications for Canadian sovereignty and democracy.

GLOBALIZATION, SOVEREIGNTY, AND DEMOCRACY

Globalization refers to a set of processes—many economic, others political and cultural—that involves the rapid increase of cross-border movements of goods, capital, ideas, and people that has characterized the late twentieth century. This increased intensity of trade has raised concerns here in Canada and elsewhere about the implications of globalization for sovereignty, policy autonomy of governments, and thus democracy. Economic globalization has been facilitated by three trends. First, the declining costs and rising speed of transportation have allowed larger and lower-cost movements of goods, capital, and services. Second, communications technology has lowered costs and increased the speed of the movement of ever larger amounts of information, data, and ideas. Third, states have lowered, either unilaterally or through bilateral and multilateral agreement, barriers to the movement of goods, capital, and, more recently, services. The size, scope, speed, and intensity of these movements are seen to have major implications for states and thus, ultimately, citizens (Held, 1999).

Analysts usually point to several measures as indicators of increased globalization. These include the increased dependence of national economies on external trade and the large and growing movements of short- and longer-term capital flows, a result of integration of financial markets and corporate investment in offshore production facilities. On the cultural side, globalization is evident in the intensified spread of ideas, values, and norms, either in themselves or as embedded in the products, brands, and images exported globally through transnationally linked networks of communication.

There is considerable debate about the impact of globalization on states. Increased national economic dependence on external trade, capital, and investment has created major constraints on states, and power has shifted to multinational firms, financial markets, and speculators. State and labour must adapt and adjust to the ability of firms and individuals to move large pools of capital and exit any economy should governments seek to manage economic activity in any way inimical to their short-term interests. Thus capital becomes privileged over labour and states run the risk of becoming hollowed-out shells. Moreover, as the interests of states become redefined to incorporate liberalized trade and investment rules and states seek to compete for capital, agreements have been made and institutions created which seek to embed binding rules at the global level. These rules make any changes to national laws increasing regulations or managing these flows prohibitively costly to states (Gill, 1995). Many claim these developments have limited state sovereignty and democracy. The voices and preferences of citizens become lost or meaningless by the need for governments to adjust to the exigencies of a globalized world. The authority derived from the consent of citizens becomes an empty one.

The process of globalization has been highly uneven and has produced many winners and losers in the global economy. The extraordinary growth in global trade and investment, which has outstripped national economic growth, masks the increasing inequality between the poorest and the richest countries. Even the International Monetary Fund (IMF), a champion of further liberalization, has had to acknowledge this aspect of globalization. In the April 2000 World Economic Outlook it admitted:

> Per capita incomes have regressed in absolute terms for a large number of countries in the past 25–30 years. As a result, the world is entering the twenty-first century with the largest divergence ever recorded between rich and poor (IMF, 2000, 32).

According to the IMF this situation is "morally outrageous, economically wasteful and potentially socially explosive." This phenomenon of growing income inequality and rising poverty in the midst of economic growth also describes Canada in much of the last decade (Canada. Statistics Canada, 1997).

This growth in inequality has resulted, in part, from the domestic policies, which have included the dismantling or shrinking of state regulation and social programs that were designed to redistribute wealth and income. This process was usually justified in the name of debt reduction, the unsustainability of supposedly high taxes given capital mobility, and the need to create a positive economic climate designed to lure or retain new private investment in the absence of state regulation. Thus domestic policy changes and the pain they have inflicted on certain sectors of society have been linked to globalization in an effort to justify decisions and defuse or discredit political opposition to them. The result for many actors, including ordinary workers, has been a rising level of economic uncertainty and instability in their lives, some of it supposedly necessitated by globalization.

If the process of globalization is really part of a broader historical struggle in which capital, at this point in history, has the upper hand, then politics has not disappeared. Even if the policy autonomy of governments is more limited, there may still be space for democratic struggle although it may take a rather different form than it has in the past. Canada's experience of globalization and the cases of the failed MAI in December 1998, the unsuccessful attempt to launch a broader round of trade negotiations in Seattle in December 1999, and the recent campaign of opposition to the FTAA provide some evidence that the space for political contestation remains. That space however, has been redefined in a way that no longer accords with traditional policy processes or territorial boundaries. The following section outlines Canada's particular experience of economic globalization.

GLOBALIZATION CANADIAN-STYLE

In many ways Canada has been ahead of its time. For much of our history the issue of integration with the dominant United States economy has been a focus of political struggle and contestation as we debated just how much policy autonomy our dependence on and integration into North American systems of production would afford various Canadian governments. Over the last decade the Canadian economy has become even more dependent on and oriented to international trade, which has risen from 25.7 percent of our GDP in 1989 to over 43 percent in 1999—the vast majority of it with the United States (Canada. Department of Foreign Affairs and International Trade, May 2000).

For Canada, globalization has really meant ever-closer integration with the United States, both as a market for Canadian goods and a source of and destination for foreign direct investment. This reality drove the desire to secure access to the U.S. market in the 1980s and is reflected in the increased integration that both the Canada–U.S. Free Trade Agreement (CUFTA) and the North American Free Trade Agreement (NAFTA) facilitated.

As Table 21.1 indicates, Canada has an enormous stake in export trade to the United States market. The Department of Foreign Affairs and International Trade annual trade update also points out that even as our dependence on the U.S. market increases (no surprise

TABLE 21-1 Export to the United States as Percent of Total Exports

Year	Percent of Export to U.S.
1950	65.1
1975	65.1
1980	63.3
1985	77.9
1991	73.6
1993	78.4
1995	77.7
1997	80.8
1999	85.9

Source: Calculated from Department of Foreign Affairs and International Trade, Trade Update 2000 (May 2000) and Statistics Canada, Canada's Merchandise Trade, January 2000

given CUFTA and NAFTA) the domestic spin-off of new jobs from exports is actually diminishing over time as the domestic content of goods exported shrinks with the globalized nature of sourcing and integrated production. In other words, to create as many jobs as we have in the past, we must export more and more with the result that a growing proportion of our economic fortunes rests on a narrow base of economic activity in the United States beyond the control of Canadian citizens and their government.

Canada, as Table 21.2 indicates, has also been a major destination for U.S. long-term capital investment for much of the postwar period. In fact, in the 1960–1980 period, a prolonged national debate took place over whether and how Canada should manage the large inflows of U.S. capital and the many acquisitions of major Canadian firms that had resulted in a rising level of foreign ownership and control of the Canadian economy. The decision in the early 1970s to establish a screening agency that made foreign investors' access to Canada conditional on showing a net benefit to the Canadian economy was fraught with political conflict. It included a leaked government report, splits in the federal cabinet and within two political parties (the Liberals and the NDP), and a prolonged public debate over the creation and operation of the Foreign Investment Review Agency in 1973. This policy was accompanied by a series of regulations and the establishment of a number of Crown corporations all designed to preserve sectors of the Canadian economy while continuing to permit the conditional access of foreign capital.

In the mid-1980s policy shifted to reduce regulation and limit screening with the passage in 1985 of the *Investment Canada Act*. At that point the issue largely disappeared from the public agenda. While levels of foreign ownership decreased in the 1980s and U.S. investment was a declining source of FDI in the mid-1990s, the pattern at the end of the

TABLE 21-2 Stocks of Inward and Outward FDI and Percent Share from/to U.S.				
Year	Stock of Inward FDI Billions $	U.S. Share % of total	Stock of Outward CND FDI Billions	U.S. Share % of total
1950	4.1	87%	1	78%
1965	17.9	81	3.7	59
1970	27.4	81	6.5	54
1975	38.7	79	11.1	54
1980	64.7	78	28.4	63
1985	90.4	75	60.3	69
1990	130.9	64	98.4	66
1995	168.4	67	164.2	53
1996	179.5	67	180.4	52
1997	196.7	67	205.7	50
1998	219.2	69	239.8	53
1999	240	72	257	52

Source: Calculated from Statistics Canada 1997 Canada's International Investment Position 1926-96 and Canada's International Investment Position, 1999.

1990s had, as a reflection of CUFTA and NAFTA, begun to revert to an earlier one as the U.S. share of inward FDI and levels of foreign ownership began to climb again. In fact, in 1999, U.S. FDI flows into Canada increased 82 percent to over $38 billion. These inflows were part of a wave of mergers and acquisitions of Canadian firms that began to raise alarms both among the long-time nationalist critics of continental integration (such as Mel Hurtig) and, surprisingly, among the same business groups that had championed investment liberalization, such as the Business Council on National Issues (BCNI). For business the issue of the fire sale of Canadian assets in the late 1990s served largely to justify even larger tax cuts than those provided for in recent federal budgets (BCNI 1999).

Overall the recent policy response to rising levels of foreign ownership and control stands in sharp contrast to the earlier debate of the 1960s partly because of a shifting view of continental integration (itself a reflection of the rising influence of international business in the political process) and the nature of Canada's commitments and obligations under various agreements. Thus at the end of the 1990s the policy debate among government and business elites over how to preserve and ensure a Canadian economic base had been reduced to an argument about the size of the tax cuts that should be offered to large corporations and the wealthy to entice them to remain in Canada. Table 21.2 also indicates the other change the mid-1980s brought a rapid increase in the amount of investment abroad by firms based in Canada. Canadian investors, too, have a stake in liberalizing investment regulations abroad.

Canada Negotiates Rules: Here, There, and Everywhere

The change in government in 1984 was followed rapidly by reforms of the policy of screening FDI and a decision to approach the United States to negotiate a free trade agreement. The Canada–U.S. Free Trade Agreement (CUFTA) and the North American Free Trade Agreement (NAFTA) reflected the negotiating demands of the United States, which included trading Canadian investment screening off against U.S. market access, and a growing conviction on the part of Canadian policymakers that competitive pressures meant that Canada could no longer afford to screen investment (Smythe, 1996). By the time of the NAFTA negotiations, a process driven more by fear of the loss of CUFTA benefits as Mexico negotiated its own access to the U.S. market, Canadian investors had also defined their interests to include stronger protection for Canadian investment abroad. The shift in favour of facilitating and guiding rules-based continental integration marked a major change in Canadian policy and was especially controversial in the case of CUFTA, where it aroused a broad national debate and became the focal point of a national election campaign.

Thus Canada was actively involved in one of the longest rounds of negotiations of the General Agreement on Tariffs and Trade (GATT), launched in Uruguay in 1986 and concluded in 1993. The Uruguay Round broke new ground as a trade agreement because for the first time it addressed services, agriculture, trade-related intellectual property, and trade-related investment measures. It also established the new World Trade Organization with a strengthened capacity to deal with the growing number of trade disputes and a more effective method of enforcing judgments through sanctioned trade retaliation or compensation.

DEMOCRACY AND INTERNATIONAL TRADE NEGOTIATIONS

To the extent that globalization constrains states or renders their policies ineffective it has the effect, many would argue, of undermining democracy. The liberal, representative notion of democracy, for example, is based on the ideas of contract, sovereignty, and territory. If sovereignty becomes limited then the authority the state derives from the consent of citizens shrinks in scope, as does the public space in which citizens can contest and challenge policies. However, this perspective, which sees globalization as shrinking public space, ignores the extent to which it has at the same time fostered the growth of transnational coalitions and movements. New information and communication technologies have further facilitated this growth by enhancing the capacity of groups to coordinate, move, and use information, shrinking both time and distance in the process. Canadian opponents of further trade and investment liberalization were able to use the transnational campaign of opposition to help reconfigure the domestic trade policy process and re-politicize the debate in Canada. That Canadian non-governmental organizations (NGOs) have been quick to play a major role at the global level is no surprise given their access to information and communications technology and the deep roots of many groups and individuals in the battle over continental integration. To understand the link between transnational and domestic processes, however, we need to begin with an overview of how trade and investment negotiations have been conducted in the past.

Negotiations have historically been conducted in a way that reflects Canada's parliamentary and federal constitution—one that is executive-dominated but also incorporates some voice for the provinces. Trade policymaking also reflected the fact that much trade negotiation in the postwar period involved tariffs and issues related to market access for goods. The policy process centred on consulting the provinces and sectoral industry or producer representatives most directly impacted by tariff changes. By 1986 this process had evolved into a set of committees including an overarching international trade advisory committee (ITAC) and a series of sectoral industry advisory (SAGIT) committees with representatives invited to sit on the committee by the trade minister. Provincial input was also sought during periodic meetings of trade officials and their provincial counterparts and occasionally ministerial meetings. This process was in play for the GATT, CUFTA, and NAFTA negotiations. It had, however, several limitations which became increasingly apparent and ultimately contributed to some discrediting of the process in the late 1990s.

First, the initial model was predicated on the assumption that negotiations centred on traditional trade issues involving tariffs on goods and the impact on producers of changes to levels of protection. Even by the time of CUFTA and the Uruguay Round in 1986 this was clearly no longer the case. Rules regarding state regulation of foreign investors and the issue of regulations to protect Canadian culture had both figured in CUFTA negotiations. The issue of access for goods produced in low-wage economies where workers did not enjoy minimum standards of protection (labour standards) and concerns about the downward pressure on environmental protection posed by footloose investment emerged as part of the NAFTA debate. There was, in fact, no committee responsible for overall investment policy within the existing consultation process, nor any process to address these other concerns. In the case of culture, a SAGIT was added. The refusal of the Canadian Labour Congress to join the ITAC because of their opposition to CUFTA also made for a lopsided and unrepresentative process as the trade agenda expanded.

Second, this model also assumed that any national debate on these issues, if it occurred at all, would come through the partisan electoral process that gives governments a broad mandate. The cabinet would authorize officials to negotiate a deal and ultimately approve it. Governments would presumably be held accountable for a bad deal in ensuing elections.

No real role exists for Parliament in debating negotiating mandates or ratifying trade and investment agreements beyond passing implementing laws or amending national legislation once a deal has been made. Many of the newer concerns about the impact of globalization were not taken up within the partisan process and the case of CUFTA, with its national debate and central role in the 1988 elections, stands out largely for its uniqueness. Even more problematic from the perspective of voters was the tendency for opposition parties, if they did address trade issues, to attack or criticize trade policies only to turn around and implement them once in office. This was justified by the necessity of keeping Canada competitive, facing the realities of globalization and the need for a rules-based system, and avoiding the massively disruptive process of reversing such a major economic change. Our electoral process and the strong majorities it often produces based on a minority of public support, coupled with very tight party discipline imposed on elected representatives and the marginal role of backbenchers in trade policy, means that any real ongoing public voice for the majority of citizens is very muted. Nor were there any other means by which citizens or groups could have a direct voice. This feeling of having no real voice in governing is part of a broader overall decline in public confidence in government as reflected in many long-term cross-national studies and declining voter turnout in national elections (Inglehart, 1999). As the agenda of trade and investment negotiations expanded to include services, the partisan political process and the limited existing consultation process proved inadequate.

A third problem with the earlier model of trade policymaking is that consultation was also geared towards discrete and episodic periods of interstate negotiation; however, trade and investment rules were increasingly being interpreted and reinterpreted. Thus trade rules are remade on an ongoing basis in a way that has had a major impact on public policies and the lives of many Canadians. These dispute processes and procedures are deliberately designed to distance and isolate those interpreting the rules from outside national "political interference." While heralded as creating a rules-based system, which ensures that the strong do not dominate, the process raises real concerns about accountability in a democracy.

THE RISE OF NGOS AND INFORMATION TECHNOLOGY

Along with the growing impact of globalization, scholars have also noted the proliferation of non-governmental organizations (NGOs) within Canada as well as globally. While some NGOs, including business, labour, and humanitarian organizations, have long histories, there was a major increase in the 1980s and 1990s in the number of environmental, development, human rights, and feminist organizations. Even though many are based in the industrialized countries and have a largely middle-class membership, there is nonetheless a growing presence of these types of organizations in developing countries as well. Estimates are that the number of international NGOs in the 1990s increased from 6000 to 26 000 (Keohane and Nye, 2000, 116). Canadian studies indicate that thousands of nonprofit organizations are active on a range of issues and account for over 21 percent of total Canadian development assistance (North-South Institute, 1999).

Two factors have facilitated this growth. First, many organizations were stimulated and financed by governments seeking to legitimize policies or find alternate means to deliver services, at both the national and the international level. The growing international concerns and international agreements, conventions, and laws gave many of these groups standing in organizations like the United Nations and contributed to the expectation that such groups would be consulted and heard on a range of issues. Second, just as the evolution of transportation and communication technology has facilitated economic globalization so, many argue, has it facilitated the creation of what some have called global civil society. The phone, the fax, satellite news, cheaper transportation, and, most recently, the development of e-mail, the Internet, and the World Wide Web have facilitated the rapid movement of ideas and information and the ability of groups to share information and coordinate action even more cheaply and quickly.

It is the presence of these non-governmental organizations and the concerns they have articulated about the impact of globalization on the environment, labour standards, and human rights and the incapacity of the existing policy trade process to respond, that have contributed to a growing critique of globalization and have challenged the legitimacy of the trade negotiation process in Canada.

Large coalitions of NGOs in Canada have their roots in the battle over free trade. Subsequent campaigns against NAFTA and Asia-Pacific Economic Cooperation (APEC) have broadened these networks to include the rest of North America, Asia, and Latin America. These campaigns also brought labour and environmental groups (not traditional allies) in both the North and the South together, and, despite divisions on tactics and specific issues, these groups have been able to unite around the articulation of a range of concerns about the impact of globalization. In contrast to previous producer-based opposition to free trade, these movements are not solely about protecting the domestic market but centre much more on issues such as damage to the environment; the exploitation of workers; the uneven spread of the gains and losses of economic adjustment; the threats to cultural diversity; and the suffering that debt and economic reform, imposed by international financial institutions, have inflicted on the world's poor. Many of these criticisms are value-based.

The concern on the part of many of these groups that all other human values appear to be subverted to the market imperative does not necessarily lead to a rejection of international agreements (which hold states accountable and thus limit some sovereignty). In the case of environmental NGOs, there is a desire to see the growing number of Multilateral Environmental Agreements become binding on states. In the absence of binding international standards to protect the environment, however, they seek to ensure that existing domestic regulations are not undermined or weakened by international trade and investment agreements. Many groups argue that the problem is not the international rules per se, but rather the balance of interests those rules serve and who has a voice in the making of the rules.

THE CASE OF THE MULTILATERAL AGREEMENT ON INVESTMENT

The case of MAI marks both a transition away from the traditional Canadian model of trade negotiations and a major effort on the part of NGOs to re-politicize the issues connected to globalization in Canada—an effort which, unlike previous trade debates in Canada, involved a broad international coalition of groups and the use of new technology. The experience of MAI is thus critical both to understanding the political conflict over WTO in Seattle and the attempts of the Canadian government, throughout the spring and summer of 1999, to manage the process.

The MAI negotiations involved a three-and-a-half-year process that ultimately resulted in the cessation of negotiations on December 3, 1998 (Smythe, 1998a). The negotiations had been formally launched in May 1995, largely as a result of a U.S.-led and business-supported initiative, and were intended to create a binding, free-standing agreement, thought to be easier to achieve within a smaller group of "like-minded" states. The Organization for Economic Co-operation and Development (OECD) membership at the time consisted of 29 countries including much of Europe, North America, Australia, New Zealand, Japan, and Korea. The resulting high standard of investment liberalization would then serve as the benchmark to which larger developing countries in Latin America and Asia, the favoured destination of much foreign investment, would need to rise in order to join the agreement. Thus it would discipline investment regulations of these states and facilitate and protect foreign investment. While Canada strongly supported the overall objective it, like the European Union, would have much preferred to pursue the negotiations at the WTO, an organization with a more universal membership and a capacity to enforce trade rules and resolve disputes (Smythe, 1998).

While the decision to launch negotiations in May 1995 was not a secret, it received almost no press attention at the time in Canada. Negotiations began in earnest in the fall of 1995 and appeared, at first, to reach agreement on the main principles. These included national treatment (that is, no discrimination against foreign investors and foreign-based firms) and strong investor protection against uncompensated state expropriation including the right for investors to lodge complaints against states and seek compensation, a provision similar to Chapter 11 of NAFTA. The contentious issues among members revolved around which economic sectors or state policies (such as culture) would be exempted from these general obligations and these were not addressed until the winter of 1997. By that time there was already some discontent with the process, especially with the role of the OECD secretariat and the chair of the negotiating group. This discontent and the real political divisions began to emerge in March and April 1997 as member states expressed their reservations about the obligations contained in the draft text.

Around the same time a copy of the February 1997 draft text was leaked and quickly ended up on the Web sites of two public policy advocacy groups in North America. In Canada, the Polaris Institute and the Council of Canadians pointed to the leaked text as proof of a secretive process underway in Paris, which threatened Canadian sovereignty and had major implications for citizens—given that the agreement would be binding and had been undertaken with virtually no public consultations (Barlow and Clarke, 1997). A few SAGITs, in fact, had been initially contacted and were, not surprisingly, benignly supportive of the project. However, a coalition of groups including the Council of Canadians, the Canadian Labour Congress, and environmental groups such as the Sierra Club began a campaign of opposition to the agreement. With the leaking of the draft text and the dramatic pronouncements of critics came an increase in media coverage in Canada and in other countries, just when the process was becoming bogged down and more political.

Domestic attention to the negotiations increased in a number of countries along with pressures on negotiators, resulting in more states lodging complaints against the obligations of the agreement. In Canada the issue figured little in the June 1997 election campaign although the anti-MAI coalition had placed a full-page advertisement in national newspapers and the NDP raised the issue. Many Liberal backbenchers and other opposition members were completely unaware of the negotiations. Stung by the secrecy charge, the Minister of International Trade asked the House of Commons Committee on Foreign Affairs and International Trade to hold hearings in the fall of 1997 and ensure that an ad hoc process of consultation and more information on the negotiations be made available to the public. Negotiators also sought to allay fears by pointing out that the intent of the agreement was merely to extend to more countries the commitments that already existed in Chapter 11 of NAFTA. Rather than reassuring, this claim alarmed many groups, especially environmental organizations, which saw the prospect of an expanded investor–state dispute process as a repetition of a serious mistake already evident in a dangerously flawed part of NAFTA (CELA, 1997). Following Canada's legislative committee hearings, legislative hearings were also held in 1998 by Australia, France, the U.K., and the European Parliament, among others. A fractious meeting between an international coalition of NGOs and the OECD negotiating group held in October 1997, and followed closely by CBC television, marked a turning point in the opposition to the agreement. At that meeting, groups asked for a suspension of negotiations, and when it was not forthcoming began to mobilize an all-out campaign in various countries to stop the agreement.

Recognizing that the likelihood of an agreement that would bring real gains in liberalizing investment regulation was slipping away, OECD negotiators attempted a high-level political meeting in February 1998 designed to break the logjam. When it failed, it became clear to a number of key players, especially the United States, that whatever limited agreement might ultimately emerge from the process was unlikely to be worth the political costs.

As enthusiasm for the agreement waned, a number of states under the most pressure, including France, pressed for a hiatus in the negotiations, which was agreed to in April

1998. Opposition continued to mount and when the negotiations were due to resume in mid-October the French government, under pressure from the Green and Communist parties within its coalition, withdrew from the negotiations (Riche, 1998), thereby ending any real hope of agreement, a fact acknowledged by the rest of the negotiators in December 1998. For Canadian officials the end of negotiations was met with a sigh of relief since the talks had been bogged down in disagreement and were rapidly becoming a political football. The impact of the MAI failure, however, was felt far beyond the walls of the Department and the OECD's chateau in Paris.

The anti-MAI campaign, built around a transnational coalition of NGOs using both traditional methods of mobilization including town hall meetings and demonstrations, as well as new technology such as the Internet and e-mail to distribute leaked documents and detailed critiques of the agreement, had its roots in a number of earlier efforts. In fact the anti-globalization movement, which opposed further liberalization of trade and investment rules at the expense, in their view, of the environment, human rights, and real development, began to emerge in the anti-NAFTA coalition (Blair, 2000), the 50 Years Is Enough campaign against the World Bank, and the anti-APEC protests (particularly in Vancouver) and counter-conferences which had accompanied each leader's summit. Canadian organizations, as research on the anti-MAI Internet campaign has shown, played a very prominent role providing a large number of the key sites for information. Those outlining the dangers of incorporating NAFTA's Chapter 11 provisions into the MAI were especially effective in arousing opposition in a number of countries and negotiators have acknowledged the role, they played (Smith and Smythe, 2000). By the time the MAI negotiations had ceased, over 600 organizations worldwide had signed on to the declaration condemning the negotiations.

What is notable is the extent to which the Canadian partisan electoral and representative processes played a limited role during and after the 1997 election. After the NGO campaign had raised awareness of the issue, the House of Commons Standing Committee on Foreign Affairs and International Trade did a thorough job of assessing the draft MAI agreement and Canada's role and was critical of the wording of the expropriation provisions and their implications. However, the committee (with its Liberal majority) ultimately endorsed Canada's involvement in the negotiations. For many NGOs this reflected the limits of the legislative process which, while allowing them a forum to address their concerns, ultimately was probably less effective than their protests, meetings, lobbying, and the Internet and media campaign. The experience of the MAI also had a direct link to the events in Seattle. It was clear to all of the major organizations active in the anti-MAI campaign that the drive to create a binding set of international investment rules would continue and the venue would merely change. Moreover, they were aware that Canada's real preference was to negotiate such rules at the WTO.

THE BATTLE OF SEATTLE AND TRADE POLICY DEVELOPMENT

As a result of the Uruguay Round, the WTO members had two key issues with built-in mandates for further negotiating—services and agriculture, the latter clearly a key priority for the Canadian government. At the same time, a number of other Uruguay Round agreements, including those on trade-related investment and intellectual property, had mandated five-year reviews. The big decisions to be made by the trade ministers' Seattle meeting was how and when these mandated negotiations and reviews would go forward and whether and what additional issues should be added to the negotiating agenda. In essence the European and Japanese position held that a broad millennium round of negotiations involving a range of new issues including investment and competition policy was the only way in which to reach a deal that would satisfy all and make the prospect of agreement on the most contentious issues, such as agriculture, most likely. In contrast, the United States was more skeptical of a broad agenda, fearing both its own protectionist Congress and the drawn-out and fractious negotiations that such a round would entail. Canada was somewhere in the middle, talking about clusters of issues. In the case of investment, however, it was clearly on the side of the European Union (EU) and had been active, along with the EU and Japan, in a working group to address the relationship between trade and investment established in 1996 as part of a compromise at the WTO Ministerial meeting in Singapore. The three groups had been trying to forge a consensus on the need to negotiate investment rules at the WTO over the determined opposition of a number of countries including India and Malaysia. Two other issues had arisen at the Singapore Ministerial—labour standards and the environment—and these were also going to be addressed, once again in Seattle.

The likelihood of severe conflict among WTO members in Seattle was already very high, given the presence of agriculture—the issue which had almost killed the Uruguay Round—on the agenda and the evidence of real discontent on the part of many developing countries, whose membership in the WTO had greatly expanded. Many of these countries had in their view, taken on onerous obligations, in areas such as intellectual property, in return for few real results in improved market access for their goods in developed economies. Many were in no mood to contemplate a broader round of negotiations until these issues of implementation were addressed.

The signs of trouble had already been evident in the protracted battle over the selection of a new WTO Director-General to replace the retiring Ruggiero, which pitted a majority of members—mostly developing countries—against a U.S.-led minority. While the WTO has supposedly been run on a principle of consensus, the reality is that the largest economies, the United States, the European Union, and Japan, have usually dominated and the U.S. political agenda has often determined the timing and cycle of trade negotiations. However, a large and growing contingent of developing countries has begun to insist that the organization serve their interests. The bitter fight over the selection of the Director-General resulted in a compromise—the U.S.-favoured Michael Moore only one term be followed by Panitchpakdi of Thailand—and left a legacy of anger and mistrust. In terms of the agenda for a new round, ministers came to Seattle with few areas of agreement mapped out in advance.

The issue of the environment had also become more controversial as a result of several WTO dispute resolution decisions that raised fears that WTO obligations, despite the exemption of Article XX for environmental regulations, would lead to further undermining of domestic environmental regulations, even as Multilateral Environmental Agreements remained largely unenforceable. The exemption states that "nothing in the agreement shall be construed to prevent the adoption or enforcement of measures to protect human, plant life or health or relating to the conservation of exhaustible natural resources." However, the application of any measure must not discriminate. Critics claim that the exemption has been interpreted too narrowly and always in favour of trade over the environment and point to two cases, one involving U.S. restrictions on the import of shrimp and the failure to protect sea turtles in shrimp harvesting and a second dealing with the export of tuna caught without the use of equipment to exclude dolphins from nets. In the case of labour standards, the lack of progress in Singapore on the issue, the growing concerns of U.S. labour as a result of NAFTA, the possibility of China's admission to the WTO, and the U.S. election ensured that any ministerial held in the United States would likely address environmental issues.

As a result of the MAI, NGOs were already organized, vigilant, and prepared for a campaign to voice their concerns about globalization at the WTO meeting. The proximity of the Seattle location facilitated the involvement of Canadian organizations, again relying on technology such as the Internet, in protests at the venue. But there were also many activities organized within Canada to raise public awareness and concern including numerous teach-ins and workshops. A number of Canadian organizations had formed a Common Front and a cross-Canada caravan to Seattle was organized. Members included the Council of Canadians, the Canadian Labour Congress, the Canadian Environmental Law Association, the Polaris Institute, the Sierra Club, and the West Coast Environmental Law Association, all of whom had been part of the anti-MAI campaign. Many of the other key groups involved in the MAI campaign, led by U.S. groups such as Public Citizen, had begun organizing for Seattle over a year before the meetings were held. They enjoyed the support of big U.S. labour and an army of volunteers drawn from a range of other groups and concerned citizens. Canadian NGOs were very much a part of this process and, with the networks already established as a result of the MAI and the APEC protests in Vancouver, were able to make their presence felt. Prominent activists such as Maude Barlow and David Suzuki were part of the International Forum on Globalization Teach-In prior to the official meeting. In addition, thousands of Canadian activists were on the street protesting while others lobbied inside the Convention Centre.

The MAI had also provided a cautionary tale of how not to develop policy, and thus it was decided in early 1999 that the Department of Foreign Affairs and International Trade (DFAIT) would consult widely pre-Seattle and go beyond the earlier ITAC–SAGIT model. The resulting process was multi-faceted but rather ad hoc. In the spring and summer of 1999, DFAIT organized a series of cross-Canada roundtables dealing with various issues, meeting with a range of business, labour, environmental, human rights, and development organizations. Two major multi-stakeholder meetings were also held in May and November. In the case of the public at large, in May 1999 DFAIT launched a new Web site dedicated to trade negotiations and agreements; the site included a number of issue papers and called for public comment and response. In addition, the Minister of Trade had once again in September 1998, called on the House Standing Committee to hold hearings on Canada's priorities in any future Millennium Round. The committee travelled across Canada in the winter and spring of 1999, heard from over 400 groups and individuals, and was able to submit its report well in advance of the November Seattle meeting.

At the WTO itself, Canada had been pushing for more transparency via the faster release of documents to the public. Canada also included members of various business, labour, and environmental organizations as advisors to the delegation—a practice which the United States, the EU, and other countries have also used—along with provincial ministers and officials and members of parliament. These delegates had access to extra briefings and contact with the negotiators but were not at the table. During the Seattle meetings Canadian officials also held nightly briefings for NGO representatives.

While the results of the Seattle Ministerial, especially the protests of November 30 and December 1 and the failure of WTO members to agree on a new round of trade negotiations, are well known, the longer-term significance is less clear. Immediately after the ministerial ended, the NGO coalition claimed credit for its failure. However, many government ministers and WTO officials, including Director-General Michael Moore, pointed to the deep disagreement between the European Union and the United States on agriculture, the discontent of many developing countries with the implementation of the Uruguay Round, and ineffective procedures and decision-making structures at the WTO. Some observers also blamed the United States trade representative and chief negotiator Charlene Barshevsky's handling of the meeting and imprudent remarks by President Clinton regarding trade sanctions and labour standards, which alarmed many developing countries.

In disrupting the meetings, the protests certainly had an impact. Streets would suddenly be closed, hotels locked down, and meetings cancelled, rescheduled, and sometimes truncated. Athough the mainstream press coverage was shallow and heavily focused on the protests, the protests also raised public awareness about the WTO. The actions of groups also brought home to negotiators the extent of public concern about globalization. Often ignored, however, is the fact that the campaign against the WTO in the streets of Seattle was accompanied by extensive activities around the world, including here in Canada, and that in Seattle itself, the ministerial was paralleled by literally hundreds of lectures, workshops, teach-ins, seminars, and debates about the WTO. A brief scan of the Internet also revealed a huge increase in the number of related Web pages and sites, in comparison to during the MAI campaign. Over 4000 sites around the world, of groups, individuals, and organizations, provided information and analysis, much of it hostile to the WTO and highly critical of globalization. In addition, numerous Web-based broadcasting systems contained thousands of audio and video files and news stories from the perspective of protestors and critics of the WTO.

What difference did all this activity make? While the protests disrupted the meetings, they did not cause their failure; but the process of raising public awareness and making negotiators more conscious of the growing concerns about trade liberalization did have an impact on further trade negotiations, as the case of the FTAA indicates. The impact, however, was not all in the direction of opening up the trade policy process further.

QUEBEC CITY: DEMOCRACY AND TRADE OPENNESS BEHIND WALLS AND TEAR GAS

The case of FTAA negotiations and the Summit of the Americas held in Quebec City in April 2001 is a continuation of the story of both the MAI and the WTO in several ways. But it also reflects a shift in the broader politics surrounding trade negotiations. Like previous trade negotiations, the FTAA was at the outset a process largely undertaken at the executive level, with the support of the business community, only to be challenged later by a coalition of transnational groups, many of which had their roots in the campaigns discussed above. The zeal of the Canadian government for the FTAA, given our limited trade links with South America (less than 2 percent of total exports in 1998); the failure of President Clinton to fast-track approval from Congress for negotiations; and the hostility of major players such as Brazil have been a puzzle to Canadian analysts (Daudelin and Molot, 2000). One source of the desire to conclude an agreement may be found in the rapid growth of Canadian foreign direct investment in the region, which had reached $45 billion by 1998 and represented 18 percent of Canadian FDI, up from 9 percent in 1990 (Canada. Industry Canada, 2001). More likely for business it was the prospect of liberalized access to the economies of the region which would facilitate integrated production and allow them, with full capital mobility, to take advantage of lower wage rates. In addition there was undoubtedly a wish on the part of the Canadian government to become a major player in a region traditionally dominated by the United States.

Like the other two cases, the FTAA illustrates the extent to which networks of opposition to trade liberalization have developed by building on previous campaigns. In this case, however, we see the growing development of a bifurcated government response. On the one hand there are efforts to further open up the process of policy consultation and render it more transparent. At the same time more and more state resources are devoted to the harsh repression of opposition and, according to some critics, the virtual criminalization of dissent within Canada.

The negotiation of the Free Trade Area originated with the Miami declaration of the leaders of the Organization of American States (OAS) in 1994, which called for the negotiation of a Free Trade Area in the Americas by 2005. Negotiations did not formally begin, however, until 1998 and proceeded slowly, with Canada chairing for the first 18 months. Nine working groups were established, covering the main areas and issues addressed in the NAFTA including services, investment, and intellectual property, along with traditional trade issues such as market access. A parallel Americas Business forum was also established. As with the MAI, the early period of negotiations was very secretive; although the Canadian government pointed to a parallel process involving civil society groups that had been established at the outset, this was largely denounced by NGOs as ineffective and meaningless.

Opposition to an agreement began to grow as critics saw the real possibility that it would contain the most egregious aspects of NAFTA, especially Chapter 11 and investor–state dispute resolution. By the fall of 2000 this provision of NAFTA had become widely discredited because of the alarming number of costly cases of foreign investors claiming exorbitant amounts of compensation for expropriation from the Canadian government because of changes to regulations. Even Canadian officials finally had to acknowledge that the provisions were flawed.

The impact of both the MAI and the Seattle protests was also evident in the way in which Canadian officials approached the meetings of the Organization of American States (OAS) in Windsor in June 2000 and the Summit of the Americas in Quebec City in April 2001. Efforts were made to provide groups with more access to officials in a process very similar to that undertaken for Seattle. This included meetings to exchange information with so-called stakeholder groups as well as a series of hearings held by the House of Commons Standing Committee on Foreign Affairs and International Trade, which reported in October 1999 (SCFAIT, 1999). As in both the MAI and Seattle reports, parliamentarians urged more engagement of civil society in the negotiation process.

However, another lesson had also been learned from the Seattle experience, about the vulnerability of major international meetings dealing with globalization to the disruptive capacity of well-organized transnational groups and movements. Many groups were increasingly oriented towards direct action at any venue, no matter how peripheral to economic globalization. Direct action and protests were seen as a means of raising awareness and mobilizing citizens, especially the young, who had little faith or interest in traditional partisan political processes. Governments, be they national or local, faced with the obligations of hosting such meetings, increasingly opted for repressive measures to limit the impact of protests and direct action. The meetings of the IMF and World Bank in

Washington in April 2000 and in Prague in September were reflective of this trend, as was the OAS meeting in Windsor where fences and tear gas were the police response. With the meeting of the FTAA trade ministers in Toronto in March 2001 this response had come to include sharpshooters on the tops of buildings. Canada's Security and Intelligence Service (CSIS) (2000) had gone so far as to issue a report on globalization protestors portraying them as a potential security threat. Part of this escalation in confrontational and contentious politics also reflects the changing attitude of mainstream media. While pre-MAI and Seattle the media had largely ignored the issue of globalization, post-Seattle the media were clearly seeking sensational images and stories of confrontation at these meetings. Protestors also recognized the access to the mainstream media that such protests provide even if the focus on the confrontation and "violence" the media crave obscures the overall message they are trying communicate (Smith et al., 2001).

At the same time, the standards by which trade negotiations were being judged had also clearly evolved to the point where the Canadian government was increasingly defensive about the secretive nature of the FTAA negotiations. Clearly, in the minds of many citizens, *secret* had become equivalent to *sinister*. Sensing the vulnerability of the government, a number of the key groups organizing for the Summit in Quebec City focused on the release of the draft text (which was to be available to negotiators by April) in their tactics of opposition. The Quebec-based group "sal AMI " (dirty MAI) released a manifesto calling for the liberation of the FTAA text and set a deadline of April 1. When the text was not forthcoming, a blockade of the DFAIT building in Ottawa was organized. Recognizing the difficulty of defending a secretive process, the Minister of International Trade began to press the other 33 countries to agree to the release of the text. Meeting with trade ministers in Buenos Aires in early April, he successfully argued his case. However, the release was delayed until well after the summit, which left many cynics viewing the minister's effort as an elaborate public relations exercise rather than real transparency. The Canadian government also released a general summary of its negotiating position for each of the nine groups and the names and contact numbers for negotiators. Reflecting the caution which both the MAI and Chapter 11 of NAFTA had engendered, no negotiating position or text had been proposed by Canada on investment. The investment chapter of the draft FTAA text was leaked, however, prior to the summit.

The activities of NGOs up to and during the Quebec Summit were similar in many ways to those in Seattle, including a large education and networking component with numerous teach-ins and workshops and the organization of the Second People's Summit of the Americas held at the same time as the official meetings. A huge range of organizations were involved, including unions and faith, feminist, environmental, anti-poverty, and Indigenous groups from across the Americas.

For protestors, the decision of police to surround the venue with a fence (the so-called security perimeter, quickly dubbed "the wall of shame") meant that they would not be able to disrupt the meeting without serious risk of violence. Thus most focused on raising awareness by challenging the premises underlying the establishment of a fence, the legitimacy of the meetings, and the dangers inherent in an agreement. Protests proved to be a magnet for a broad array of activists including thousands of students from Ontario and Quebec but also from across Canada, joined by unions, which had begun since the MAI and Seattle to embrace the movement and the tactics of protest. In an effort to maintain a broad-based movement, organizers encouraged an array of tactics and approaches that permitted groups to define for themselves what their level of engagement would be in challenging the process, although the police response did not differentiate among these groups. Like the protests in Seattle, these actions were in addition to, and did not replace, the extensive educational and traditional lobbying efforts of groups. Quebec also saw a tentative effort to bring the politics of protest into the mainstream partisan process as the leader and federal NDP members of parliament joined the largest protest march in an attempt to reach out to the youthful activists who have abandoned partisan politics. To their chagrin, the largest and most peaceful protest march, well away from the fence, was largely ignored by the media.

At the end of the meetings, with the stench of tear gas in the air and the financial losses to local business mounting, Prime Minister Chrétien pointed to the Final Declaration and Plan of Action as proof of the success of the meeting. He dismissed the protests as meaningless "blah, blah, blah" as he had done with APEC protestors in 1997. As the Declaration indicates, the summit was not intended as an FTAA negotiating session but was rather meant to endorse progress to date (as it succeeded in doing) and reaffirm the 2005 deadline (despite efforts of the United States and Canada to move it forward). It also, however, acknowledged the concerns of smaller economies, committed to promoting "compliance with core labour standards" and a host of other laudable goals including cultural diversity and respect for human rights. For the Canadian government, the centrepiece of the declaration was the commitment on democracy which stated that:

> Any constitutional alteration or interruption of the democratic order in a state of the Hemisphere constitutes an insurmountable obstacle to participation in the of that state's government in the Summit of the Americas process.

The irony of championing democracy from behind a fence in a cloud of tear gas was not lost on many activists. Many also questioned the toothless nature of the commitment and the long record of laudable commitments coupled with inaction that characterizes the history of the OAS. What difference in the end did all the protests and consultations make to the outcome?

CONCLUSION

The campaigns of opposition to the MAI, the Seattle Ministerial, and the FTAA have been part of a growing questioning of the trade-off between trade and investment liberalization and other values. The scope, intensity, speed, and volatility of movements of goods, services, and capital now known as globalization has engendered a growing uncertainty and social tension. With the shrinking of the state safety net it has left many citizens vulnerable to, and defenceless against, the vagaries of the market. Citizens (especially the young) along the way have lost faith in authoritative institutions including governments. They are distrustful of mainstream media and big business (Graves, 1999) but remain strongly committed to democracy (Inglehart, 1999). But it is a democracy in which they feel more confident of their capacity to represent their own interests and more willing to see nongovernmental organizations have a greater role.

There is a growing citizen awareness of international trade and investment issues. An Angus Reid poll indicated shortly after the Seattle meeting that 79 percent of Canadians had heard about the protests in Seattle. Other surveys, including one commissioned by DFAIT, indicate that while Canadians remain marginally supportive of international trade negotiations they are uneasy, fearing the impact on social programs and the environment and believing the primary beneficiaries of such agreements to be big business.

The events in Seattle spawned numerous large-scale protests in the following year. One response on the part of authorities, including those in Canada, has been increased repression, the criminalization of peaceful protest, and the increased monitoring of anti-globalization groups—reaching its culmination in Quebec City. However, as the APEC protests in Vancouver and the July 2001 death of a protestor in Genoa demonstrated, this can be a high-risk response which, while securing the venue from the disruption of direct action, can also discredit a government. It also burdens locales with horrendous costs so that the prestige of hosting such events quickly evaporates in clouds of tear gas. Most important, responding with repression increasingly suggests to the public in a democracy that meetings ringed by high fences, riot police, and clouds of tear gas must involve something rather sinister despite the best assurances of governments.

Despite the protests in Seattle and Quebec, trade negotiations are going forward. Efforts continue on the part of the European Union and others to push the launch of a new round at the ministerial meeting in Doha, Qatar (the only WTO member willing to host a meeting), despite the opposition of many developing countries. Business, which had maintained a fairly low profile on trade issues since Seattle, is continuing to support trade and investment negotiations and has resources available in its control of investment capital to perhaps achieve its goals behind the scenes. Moreover, the need for capital, the pressures of globalization, and the conditions of liberalization imposed by international financial institutions on developing countries may move the liberalization agenda forward. However, the slowing global economy, growing uncertainty, and the NGO transnational campaign have had an impact. Business and government are finding it difficult to control information and thus shape the public debate, making it hard to dismiss, discredit, or ignore critics who appear to have made an impression on the public. Moreover, now that the process of consultations has been opened up as a result of the MAI, Seattle, and FTAA precedents (as ad hoc and imperfect as they have been), Canadian governments will not be able to return to the old and exclusive model of trade policymaking.

On some level, even government ministers have had to acknowledge that the campaign of opposition and the protests are, at the very least, a sign of a serious and growing unease with globalization and a desire to redirect the discourse. In August 2001, the Minister of International Trade, Pierre Pettigrew, said:

> As citizens in established democracies lose faith in their political leaders and institutions, many are becoming specialized activists, supporting organizations fighting for the environment, or against GMOs, or for fair wages in the developing world, or for some other worthwhile issue. When we consider these twin phenomena—a declining engagement in politics and a growing involvement in civil society—one can conclude that political passions are being superseded by ethical passions.

Pettigrew also acknowledges the activists' far more adept use of technology. At the same time he bemoans the disorder that has arisen, he claims, out of their protests and accuses them of a nostalgia for the past. The solution he poses to their challenge is in many ways reflective of the current response of government. He argues, in essence, for greater accessibility and transparency in the policy process, in order to "demystify globalization" and promote greater acceptance of it on the part of citizens. His speech is reflective of a Canadian government that seems on the one hand to at least acknowledge the merit of some part of the critique of globalization, yet is unclear how to respond to it beyond managing, disarming, and co-opting some opponents to its agenda and where necessary using force on those who threaten disruption. The evidence suggests that this will probably not suffice. Difficult issues of accountability and representativeness will have to be addressed. Consensus will be difficult to find. One thing that will not characterize trade and investment negotiations in the twenty-first century is business as usual.

REFERENCES

Blair, David. 2000. "North American ENGOs and Resistance to Neo-Liberal Globalization: From NAFTA to the MAI." Paper presented at the Annual Meeting of the International Studies Association. Los Angeles. March.

Business Council on National Issues (BCNI). 1999. "Time is Running Short for Canada to Prevent Drain of Key People, Jobs and Assets." *Communique.* September.

Canadian Security and Intelligence Service (CSIS). 2000. "Anti-Globalization: A Spreading Phenomenon." *Perspectives.* August.

Daudelin, Jean and Maureen Molot. 2000. "Canada and the FTAA: The Hemispheric Bloc Temptation." *Policy Options.* March: 48–51.

Canada. Department of Foreign Affairs and International Trade (DFAIT). 2000. *Trade Update 2000: First Annual Report of Canada's State of Trade.* May.

Dymond, William. 1999. "The MAI: A Sad and Melancholy Tale." In Fen Osler Hampson, Michael Hart and Martin Rudner (eds.), *Canada Among Nations 1999: A Big League Player?* Toronto: Oxford University Press.

Ekos Research Associates. 2001. "Canadian Attitudes Towards International Trade." *Presentation to the Department of Foreign Affairs and International Trade.* Retrieved June 1, 2001 from www.dfait-maeci.gc.ca

Gill, Stephen. 1995. "Globalization, Market Civilization and Disciplinary Neo-liberalism." *Millennium 24* (3): 399–423.

Graves, Frank. 1999. "Re-thinking Government as if People Mattered: From *Reagonomics to Humanomics*. In Leslie Pal (ed.), *How Ottawa Spends.* Toronto: Oxford University Press.

Hart, Michael. 2000. "Canadian Business and Canadian Trade Policy." *Policy Options.* September: 50–54.

Held, David. 1999. "The Transformation of Political Community: Rethinking Democracy in the Context of Globalization." In Ian Shapiro and Casiano Hacker-Cordon (eds.), *Democracy's Edges.* Cambridge: Cambridge University Press.

International Monetary Fund (IMF). 2000. *World Economic Outlook.* Washington: IMF.

Keohane, Robert and Joseph Nye. 2000. "Globalization: What's New? What's Not (and So What?)" *Foreign Policy.* Spring: 104–119.

North-South Institute. 1999. *Canadian Development Report: Civil Society and Global Change.*

Pettigrew, Pierre. 2001. *In the Name of Canada.* Notes for an Address to the Couchiching Institute on Public Affairs, Summer Conference, August 12th.

Riche, Pascal. 1998. "Jospin: Adieu l'AMI, Salut les copains." *Liberation.* October 15th.

Smith, Jackie, John D. McCarthy, Clark McPhail and Boguslaw Augustyn. 2001. "From Protest to Agenda Building: Description Bias in Media Coverage of Protest Events in Washington, DC" *Social Forces 79*, 1397–1424.

Smith, Peter J. and Elizabeth Smythe. 2000. "Globalization, Citizenship and Technology: The MAI Meets the Internet." *Canadian Foreign Policy.* May 2000: 83–106.

Smythe, Elizabeth. 1996. "Investment Policy." In G. Bruce Doern, Leslie Pal, and Brian W. Tomlin (eds.), *Border Crossings.* Toronto: Oxford University Press.

———. 1998. "The Multilateral Agreement on Investment: A Charter of Rights for Global Investors or Just Another Agreement." In Fen Osler Hampson and Maurren Appel Molot (eds.), *Canada Among Nations 1998: Leadership and Dialogue.* Toronto: Oxford University Press.

———. 1998. "Your Place or Mine? States, Organizations and the Negotiation of International Investment Rules." *Transnational Corporations.* December: 85–120.

Canada. Statistics Canada. 1997. *Trickle Down or Fizzling Out: Economic Performance, Transfers, Inequality and Low Income.* Ottawa: Statistics Canada.

———. 2000. *Canada's Merchandise Trade.* Ottawa: Statistics Canada.

WEBLINKS

Global Issues: Multilateral Agreement on Investment
www.globalissues.org/TradeRelated/MAI.asp

International Monetary Fund
www.imf.org

Battle of Seattle
www.workers.org/ww/1999/wtoact1209.html

chapter twenty-two

Canadian Foreign Policy

Human Security with a Neoliberal Face[1]

Paul Gecelovsky

Tom Keating

INTRODUCTION

Canadian foreign policy has for a number of years attempted to balance the pursuit of two substantive areas of concern. One is an interest in promoting a policy of human security variously defined as an interest in promoting good governance, democracy, human rights, and related concerns. The second has been an attempt to promote free trade through participation in a variety of international and regional trade liberalization programs, and in support of financial liberalization in areas such as foreign investment and capital flows. For some, these two policy priorities reflect an underlying tension between economic and humanitarian interests within not only the foreign policy community, but also the wider arena of Canadian politics. One aspect of this underlying tension is an apparent contradiction in Canadian foreign policy, a contradiction between, on the one hand, emphasizing the security and political needs of individuals by promoting international bans on land mines or international criminal tribunals and, on the other hand, assuming that market forces alone will address their social and economic needs, as suggested by the declining commitments to foreign aid and the increased emphasis on market liberalization in Canada's development assistance program (Pratt, 1999).

A second feature of Canadian foreign policy is the process by which foreign policy objectives are being pursued. In both of these substantive areas Canadian officials have relied on a number of techniques, most notably, multilateral institutions, to protect

Canadian interests and promote Canadian policy objectives. Much of Canadian foreign policy over the past decade has been devoted to establishing and entrenching a rules-based international order to support policy objectives in the areas of human security and economic liberalization. One of the critical features of Canadian foreign policy, reflected in the government's approach to economic liberalization and human security, is a diminished concern for (and adherence to) principles of state sovereignty and territorial integrity. Geopolitical boundaries are expected to yield to the principles of free markets and human rights as enshrined in rules-based institutions.

The effect of such practices has been to redefine the spatial boundaries of economic policy and human security away from state-centred, territorially based approaches to transnational (regional and/or global) approaches negotiated in and administered by regional and/or international institutions. This process has been extensively encouraged by Canadian officials and has been very much at the centre of the Canadian government's approach to foreign policy in Latin America, Africa, and around the world. It is particularly evident in the two substantive pillars of Canadian foreign policy—human security and economic liberalization. It has also encouraged a new approach to policymaking, one where civil society actors are engaged both domestically and transnationally. As the policymaking process has shifted to these multilateral institutions, so too have Canadian officials encouraged transnational forums involving civil society organizations. While this can be viewed from many different vantage points, one of the effects is to reinforce and legitimate transnational policymaking processes and structures. In this way it lends support to an apparent effort to strengthen the authority of these institutions.

This chapter examines the development and significance of human security and free trade as core principles in Canadian foreign policy, reviews the processes by which these principles have been pursued, and analyzes the tension between these principles in the conduct of foreign policy. Most significantly, it calls attention to the inconsistencies and contradictions in a Canadian foreign policy that emphasizes a concern for human security and yet supports economic measures that frequently increase the insecurity of individuals and groups in poorer regions of the world.

HUMAN SECURITY

Human security emerged as a core principle in Canadian foreign policy with the election of the Liberal government in the early 1990s. This focus however, had been developing for a number of years. Some have traced its roots to the negotiations of the Conference on Security and Cooperation in Europe held during the early 1970s that concluded with the signing of the Helsinki Accords in 1975. Beginning in the 1980s, Canadian foreign policymakers had demonstrated a growing concern with matters of human rights, individual security, and democratic practices. This was in part a reflection of the changes that were underway domestically in wake of the adoption of the *Canadian Charter of Rights and Freedmoms* in 1982. Under the Conservative government that took Canada into the North American Free Trade Agreement (NAFTA) and the Organization of American States (OAS), these concerns were expressed in a commitment to good governance, defined initially as including a combination of human rights, democratic procedures, accountable public administration, and liberal economic practices.

Good governance exerted a strong influence on Canadian policy towards the relatively poorer regions of the world in the early 1990s, supporting such initiatives as the Unit for the Promotion of Democracy and securing Canada's support for the Santiago Commitment in the OAS and the 1991 Harare Declaration in the Commonwealth. Good governance also shaped Canada's response to the coup in Haiti in 1991, the constitutional crisis in Peru in the same year, and the execution of Ken Sara Wiwo and eight other Ogoni activists in Nigeria in 1995. Under the Liberal government, good governance gave way to human security and an expanded agenda of concerns. As described by the Department of Foreign Affairs and International Trade (DFAIT): "Human Security is a people-centered approach to foreign policy which recognizes that lasting stability cannot be achieved until people are protected from violent threats to their rights, safety or lives" (Canada, 2002).

Human security has become a popular phrase in recent years. It has evolved from, but seemingly taken precedence over, notions of collective, co-operative, and common security. This has been especially true in Canada, where the foreign ministry has identified human security as one of the core principles of Canada's foreign policy. Former Canadian Foreign Minister Lloyd Axworthy repeatedly invoked the phrase in his public speeches and pressed the term and substantive issues related to it on governments and institutions around the globe. Human security dominated the Canadian government's interventions during its tenure on the UN Security Council in 1999–2000, especially when it presided as president of the council.

Reviewing the speeches of the Canadian foreign minister, alongside statements from others, such as Vaclav Havel or Kofi Annan, the Lysoen Declaration, and other documents, reveals a number of key characteristics of the human security agenda. Most important, the emphnasis on the principle of human security is a rejection of the primacy that has been given to national security in the discourse of international politics. Instead, it is an attempt to give priority to the individual and to recognize and respond to the multiplicity of threats that exist to the security of individual citizens. "Human security is much more than the absence of military threat. It includes security against economic privation, an acceptable quality of life, and a guarantee of fundamental human rights" (Axworthy, 1997, 184). It thus entails an implicit, and at times explicit, challenge to the concept of national security, suggesting that national security is both more assured in the post–Cold War era and insufficient to meet the needs of individuals' security. In their application by most governments and institutions, human security initiatives have tended to focus on security from violence, specifically violence directed at individuals by states or parties to civil conflicts; security from political oppression and violations of political rights; and security from the trade in and effects of illicit drugs. For example, the Canadian–Norwegian agreement to work co operatively in pursuit of human security highlights the following areas of activity: land mines; International Criminal Court; human rights; international humanitarian law; women and children in armed conflict; small-arms proliferation; child soldiers; and child labour.

As the various statements and policy initiatives demonstrate, references to economic security, the reduction of poverty, and the provision of basic needs are less common. These matters were, however, central to the Human Development Report that highlighted human security in 1994 (United Nations Development Program (UNDP), 1994). The Human Development Report listed seven elements of human security: economic security (security of income and of work); food security (an adequate distribution of food and the necessary purchasing power); protection against threats to public health; protection against environmental degradation, pollution, and disasters; protection against violence and abuse directed against the individual; protection against community oppression and promotion of community security; and political security. While there is some overlap between the

UNDP's priorities and those that have received attention in Canadian foreign-policymaking circles, there are also clear differences. There would thus appear to be no clear consensus on the meaning of human security or on the priorities of such a policy, beyond its rejection of national security and its attempt to give greater prominence to the principles and practices that threaten the security of individual human beings.

Canada's human security initiatives have generated fairly strong popular support. Many non-governmental organizations (NGOs), especially those involved in human rights and development work, were among the early advocates for a more assertive approach to such issues. During the mid-1980s many of these groups took the conflict in Central America as their main point of concern and pressed the government to become more actively involved in protecting citizens affected by civil conflict and repressive regimes. Many of these groups have taken an active role in Canadian foreign policymaking with considerable encouragement by the minister and officials alike. The most prominent example of such involvement was seen during the negotiations on the Ottawa Treaty to ban anti-personnel landmines. Canadian foreign policy officials' support for consultation with NGOs and civil society organizations has been rather extensive, both at home and in international settings such as at the UN and, more recently, the OAS. The active participation of NGOs in the human security agenda has been an important source of support for the government and especially for those officials within DFAIT and Canadian Interational Development Agency (CIDA) who have supported such policies.

ECONOMIC LIBERALIZATION

Liberalization emerged as another major theme in the Liberal government's white paper on Canadian foreign policy released in 1994, yet its origins can also be traced to the 1970s. While Canada's support for free trade is frequently linked to Brian Mulroney and his government's pursuit of a free trade agreement with the United States, an equally significant policy shift occurred under the Trudeau government in the 1970s through Canada's participation in the Tokyo Round of the General Agreement on Tariffs and Trade (GATT) negotiations. At that time Canada was more or less forced to abandon its National Policy (which featured high tariff barriers on imports to support domestic producers, in part by protecting them from foreign competition) in order to secure what were viewed as the larger benefits to be derived through trade liberalization under the GATT. This policy change was also in response to a shift in the attitudes of Canada's business community, which lent greater support to free trade. The shift was by no means complete, nor was it wholeheartedly supported by the population at large, as evidenced by the tumultuous debate surrounding the Canada–U.S. Free Trade Agreement during the 1988 federal election. The more diffuse opposition to the North American Free Trade Agreement was as much a result of the exhaustion of opponents as it was of a consolidation of support around trade liberalization. Indeed, there remains a strong undercurrent of skepticism, if not opposition, to the policies of trade liberalization. This was made apparent during parliamentary hearings on the World Trade Organization (WTO) in 1999, during discussions on the Free Trade Agreement of the Americas (FTAA), and in a more dramatic way by extensive Canadian participation in the demonstrations at the WTO meetings in Seattle in November 1999 and in the streets of Quebec City during the Summit of Americas in April 2001.

The government's support of trade liberalization was designed in large measure to facilitate the restructuring of the Canadian economy. In this respect the policy has had rather dramatic results. As the trade minister reported in June 2000, "Exports increased by more than 11 percent in 1999—reaching $410 billion. To put it into perspective, that's 43 percent of our entire GDP. And this growth has been taking place for some time. Ten years ago, our exports represented 25 percent of our GDP, so we've increased exports from 25 percent to 43 percent in one decade" (Pettigrew, 2000). This rather significant growth strongly reinforces the country's reliance on foreign trade. Gaining and maintaining access to foreign markets is even more critically important for the Canadian economy than it was a decade ago. While the overwhelming majority of this trade is still directed at the single market of the United States, other regions, including the rest of the Americas, have seen substantial growth. Perhaps more important, however, is the increased significance of multilateral rules for protecting this heavily dependent export-oriented economy. Not only does Canada rely on strong economic performance in the United States and other countries, it also relies on a well-established and authoritative system of rules. This led former Prime Minister and Foreign Minister Joe Clark to remark that, "GATT rules are more important than the Constitution."

The growing significance of international trade rules and the organizations that administer them has certainly been a concern among many domestic groups. Despite the opposition, the government remains strongly committed to its agenda of economic liberalization. This is very much evident in Canadian policy towards the Americas as Canada continues to be at the forefront in promoting the FTAA: "The FTAA is a central element to the promotion of economic integration and free trade, but the Government strongly believes that the increased economic growth, integration and development that will be realized under a free trade agreement will reinforce the other Summit objectives. The Government supports the Summit of the Americas process as a means by which Canadian ideals and values can be furthered throughout the Americas" (Canada, 2000).

RECONCILING HUMAN SECURITY AND LIBERALIZATION

As discussed earlier, the idea of human security gained renewed prominence in the 1990s initially through the work of the UN Development Program's (UNDP's) 1994 Report on Human Development. The UNDP highlighted the concept in preparation for the Copenhagen Conference on Social Development. It has subsequently reappeared regularly as an important component of the UNDP's annual report. As employed by the UNDP, the concept of human security includes many of the basic necessities of life such as food, shelter, health, and education. Issues such as human rights, democratic development, drug interdiction, landmines, and other threats to civilians from violent conflict or criminal activity do not receive as much attention. As adopted by governments and other institutions, however, the human security discourse has seemingly reversed these priorities. Much of the attention has been focused on the political/human rights dimensions of human security. Such initiatives as the landmine ban, the International Criminal Court, and action to limit the use of child soldiers and restrict trade in small arms are all focused on matters that are, at least on the surface level, political. They are reactions to violations of human and political rights and to acts of violence committed during armed conflicts and criminal activities. Little attention has been given to what Galtung once described as *structural violence*—the violence against individuals that occurs through economic structures and practices (1969).

The violation of human security caused by economic structures and practices rivals that committed by states and other political actors, yet these structures and practices are protected, even rewarded, and are becoming more firmly entrenched in international law. There are also significant and often adverse consequences when the power of states to act in support of society is circumscribed in deference to the market, free trade, and private investors. It may be true that the private sector is better at producing wealth, but it is woefully inadequate at distributing it in a manner that protects the health, welfare, and hence the security of the impoverished and dispossessed members of society. The failure to address the threats to human security posed by the market renders it of questionable utility in meeting the needs of those in gravest danger—the victims of poverty and disease, along with those lacking adequate healthcare, education, and employment.

Thus while officials and advocates of human security might mention economic suffering and the inequalities experienced in most countries throughout the world at the beginning of the twenty-first century, there is, with a few notable exceptions, considerably less emphasis devoted to such issues. More likely, economic considerations are downplayed or ignored in much of the official discourse on human security, a point that has been noted by observers from the South. For example, in a response to Canada's human security discussion paper at the 2000 OAS General Assembly, the foreign minister of Saint Lucia argued that the Canadian approach failed "to recognize that there must be a tremendous sacrifice and a political *volte-face* which involves a return to plain living if the personal safety of the peoples of the world is to be secured." He continued in a pointed way, "in order to protect the world's people and make them secure *we must feed them, we must educate them and we must make them healthy*" (Odlum, 2000). Such criticisms challenge the prominent view that human security is compatible with the dominant economic orthodoxy of global capitalism.

For many proponents of human security, liberal economic practices and regional and global trade and monetary policies are at worst inconsequential and at best supportive of human security. Market strategies have been invoked as a remedy for the insecurities that plague individuals. This is illustrated by the Norwegian government's approach to human security, which advocates a strengthening of the private sector and development of a free market as a solution to poverty. Yet many observers have challenged such an approach. The empirical record not only questions the wisdom of applying capitalist economic principles to cure the ills of human security, it very much suggests that the "cure" has been part of the problem. While the relationship may indeed be spurious, the fact that the growth in inequality both within nations and around the globe has expanded so dramatically alongside the spread and expansion of markets is surely troubling. The failings of the global economic order and its purveyors to address threats to human security emanating from poverty and deprivation are apparent in places such as Haiti, the Philippines, and sub-Saharan Africa.

The global economic order as administered by international financial institutions has also contributed to these insecurities through, for example, structural adjustment programs that encourage a significant decline in government support in areas such as public health and education. The rush to privatize what had previously been delivered as public goods in various parts of the world has effectively prevented large sectors of the population from accessing needed health, education, and other services. The spread of preventable and treatable diseases has killed more people in the 1990s than the more politicized and publicized acts of violence. The persistence of poverty has also taken many lives, yet the hundreds who have died as a result of disease and poverty are more readily ignored, even when they die in large numbers, than those who die from acts of political violence. More of the same kinds of practices seem likely to only exacerbate the insecurities currently being experienced by billions of people throughout the globe.

There are many explanations that could be offered for emphasizing the more political and individual aspects of human security and downplaying or neglecting the economic and structural aspects of this issue. This approach does reflect the historical pattern of Western approaches to human rights. It also suggests the powerful influence that liberal economic ideology holds in the global community, and especially among Western governments, at the present time. At a more practical level, such an approach not only limits the domestic costs of providing for human security (thus making it more palatable to domestic audiences), but it also reinforces the status quo. As a result, it reinforces the view that human security is a hegemonic project designed to reinforce the position of Western states and interests in the global community. Perhaps this is, as Bull suggested, important in sustaining public and governmental support for human security: "We assume that if the division of the world into separate states were to come to an end, and a global economy, society, and polity were allowed to grow up, it would be our economies, our way of doing things, our social customs and ideas and conceptions of human rights, and the forces of modernization that we represent that would prevail" (1979, 122). And while proponents of human security justifiably challenge such defences as protecting "Asian values" as a ruse for more nefarious actions, one must question the extent to which the package of Western values can be unpacked so that the right to assembly or religious freedom can coexist with the right to deny a McDonald's franchise or devise one's own investment code.

MULTILATERALISM AND REGIONALISM IN CANADIAN FOREIGN POLICY

Regionalism has emerged as one of the more significant features of the post–Cold War international system. Its prevalence has forced many governments, including Canada's, to reassess their foreign policy orientation. The convergence of these developments in the late 1980s and early 1990s led officials in Ottawa to reassess the value of postwar multilateral associations and to consider other options, including regionalism. Regionalism has been described in many different ways. Most descriptions highlight geographical proximity and economic flows. Mansfield and Milner describe regionalism as "the disproportionate concentration of economic flows or the coordination of foreign economic policies among a group of countries in close geographic proximity to one another" (1997). A variation on this is provided by Hurrell who defines regionalism as "a set of policies by one or more states designed to promote the emergence of a cohesive regional unit, which dominates the pattern of relations between the states of that region and the rest of the world, and which forms the organizing basis for policy within the region across a range of issues" (1992, 123). The emphasis here is on policy; policy designed from and for a cohesive regional unit. An assessment of policy and the considerations that have shaped policy provides a useful approach for answering questions about the influence of regionalism on Canadian foreign policy.

The attraction of regionalism over the past decade can be explained by various factors. For some, regionalism provided a means to advance more quickly favoured policy objectives and demonstrate their viability to other states. For others it was a way of securing a firmer foundation amidst the greater turbulence of political and economic change at the global level or, alternatively, a defensive response to perceived exclusivity on the part of other regions. To some extent regional schemes reflected growing interdependencies both in terms of trade and investment flows and in terms of political and social developments such as the spread of democratic institutions and migration. It is within this context that Canadian policymakers have made the shift to regionalism.

The shift to greater regional involvement raises questions about whether this marks a departure from Canada's multilateralist practices of the past. Multilateralism, in this context, "refers both to the practice of multilateral diplomacy and to the policies supporting the establishment and maintenance of institutions and associations that facilitate and support the practice of multilateral diplomacy" (Keating, 2003, 4). It has been suggested that the turn to regionalism has been taken at the expense of other commitments. The late Arthur Andrew, for example, worried that in signing on to the NAFTA, the Canadian government would abandon its more traditional middle-power activities (1993). Neack has also identified as problematic the turn to regionalism in the aftermath of the Cold War. The effects are particularly felt by middle powers who assumed more significant roles during the Cold War that left them isolated from their respective "regions" (Neack, 1992). As the world turns towards more regionalist responses to international security and commercial problems, middle powers—such as Canada—will find it difficult to participate as regularly and constructively as they might have done, and their role might now be assumed by regional powers such as Brazil, Nigeria, or South Africa.

The Canadian government's embrace of regionalism reflects not so much a hedge against a further weakening of the global system as a deliberate attempt to employ regional initiatives and regional co-operation as a way of extending the base of support for the global system. In other words, in response to the transformations that are taking place in the international system, Canadian officials have looked to regional associations in an effort to develop new coalitions in support of Canadian foreign policy objectives. Additionally, it will be argued that these objectives include support for a global system of rules-based interaction among states. The Canadian government's response to the proliferation of regionalist tendencies suggests that the primary consideration has been to embrace regionalism while attempting to link these regions within a wider web of multilateral institutions. Thus, rather than indicating a shift away from past governments' multilateralist orientation throughout much of the postwar period, recent initiatives in regional settings reflect an effort to maintain a link between regionalism and multilateralism.

One of the principal motivating factors was the adoption of neoliberal economic policies and the interest in advancing these rapidly and widely. Years of resisting a free trade arrangement with the Americans in pursuit of the multilateral alternative through the GATT yielded to concerns about the state of the Canadian economy and the tortoise-paced progress of GATT reforms. The Canada–U.S. Free Trade Agreement (CUSFTA) of 1988 marked the first formal step into regionalism. This was soon followed by Canada's application for formal membership in the OAS, Canadian support for and involvement in the Australian-initiated Asia Pacific Economic Cooperation, the launching of the North-Pacific Security Dialogue, and the conclusion of the North American Free Trade Agreement. In the view of some observers this became a significant turning point in postwar Canadian foreign policy. CUSFTA, in Hurrell's view, "together with Canada's decision to join the OAS from 1990, marked a definite regionalist turn in Canadian foreign policy, which had previously been based on building up extra-regional relations and active multilateralism as a means of balancing the power of the United States" (Hurrell, 1992, 123).

The subsequent conclusion of the North American Free Trade Agreement (NAFTA) among Canada, Mexico, and the United States in 1993 confirmed Canada's regional credentials and emphasized its economic characteristics while overshadowing its not insignificant political dimensions. The election of the Liberal government in October 1993 brought an indication that regionalism would remain prominent in Canada's foreign policy. As but one illustration of this, the government appointed two regional secretaries of state—Raymond Chan for the Pacific and Christine Stewart for Latin America and Africa (the latter has been replaced by David Kilgour). This move, along with high-level visits by the prime minister to Latin America and the Pacific confirmed a determined shift in the geographical focus of Canadian foreign policy.

The embrace of regionalism, especially in the Western hemisphere, has been cited by some observers as the major reorientation of Canadian foreign policy since the end of the Second World War. It has been argued that the decision to join the OAS was taken by political, academic, and economic elites and that it was in large measure a response to external pressures. It is, however, also evident that there had been growing interest in the region on the part of many Canadians.

In the early 1980s intellectuals, trade unions, members of progressive churches, and representatives from non-governmental organizations strongly urged the government to place greater emphasis on peaceful change and human rights in Canada's foreign policy in the region. Along with these demands came calls for greater involvement in the region. Additionally, it also appeared that the government saw in Latin America an opportunity to develop coalitions and work for institutional reforms that would support Canadian foreign policy priorities. Among these was an interest in extending the web of multilateralism that had been limited primarily to the North Atlantic and associations such as the North Atlantic Treaty Organization (NATO), the Organization for Economic Co-operation and Development (OECD), and the Commission on Security and Cooperation in Europe (CSCE). The political changes underway in the region, including a softer line by the American government, the improved prospects for peaceful change in Central America, and the appearance of more democratic regimes in the region made Latin American governments a more desirable set of partners.

Much of Canadian policy within the OAS has been driven by the two foreign policy priorities of human security and free trade. Foreign Minister Axworthy's presentation at the 30th General Assembly raised many of the same themes that had been addressed 10 years earlier by his predecessor Barbara McDougall. These themes were also not unique to the region as they very much converged with some of the major themes then developing within the foreign policy community in Canada. As Peter Boehm and Christopher Hernandez-Roy write, "It is apparent that Canada's priorities have . . . become the hemisphere's priorities. This is not merely an accident or the result of effective Canadian diplomacy. This represents a true winnowing of real regional interests and genuine convergence of views about what needs to be done in this hemisphere" (1999, 32). What is perhaps most significant in the regional context is the importance of the OAS itself as a forum in which these Canadian policy objectives have been advanced.

In the economic arena and in the government's move to support free trade in the region, NAFTA can be identified as the critical point of departure for the Canadian government. Unlike the decision to join the OAS, the decision to join NAFTA was originally more of a defensive action—"[I]n economic terms, a regional strategy was well down the list of priorities for the Mulroney government. Canada was at the outset a 'reluctant' participant in the NAFTA project" (Cooper, 1997, 264). The government did not initiate it and at first the government was not predisposed to sharing its exclusive access to the American market. In the face of Mexican and American proposals, however, the Canadian government concluded that it would be best to join in. Among the issues that most concerned Canadian negotiators in the NAFTA was the inclusion of an accession clause that would make it easier for new members to join the agreement. This would serve the twin objectives of limiting the possibility that the entire agreement would be renegotiated every time a new member joined and of facilitating a more rapid expansion of the membership. It has been this more-rapid expansion that has motivated Canadian policymakers since. Prime ministerial visits to the region and the conclusion of a bilateral free trade agreement with Chile, Costa Rica, and the countries of Central America can be seen as an attempt to promote expansion. "Canada, by calling for wider membership and in promoting the accession of Chile to the hemispheric free trade system, was acting in a manner consistent with this definition of the country's long-term interests. It was seeking to regain control over its involvement in a process it had not initially anticipated" (Daudelin, 1995, 272). One could go on to add that it was also trying to link regional initiatives with broader policy goals in the form of an expanded system of global trade rules.

Regionalism has obviously had an influence on Canadian foreign policy practices since the beginning of the 1990s. The government has been engaged with a variety of states and institutions that had previously been ignored or downgraded in importance. Resources are being committed to institutional relationships that had previously been avoided. This has inevitably led to the emergence of new issues such as the drug trade which have a primary, but not exclusive, regional focus. It is also evident that the demographics of the Canadian population have changed and that there now exists within the Canadian community a vibrant and active group of individuals whose heritage is non-European, who trace their origins to Latin America and Asia, and who have come to have an important political influence on policymakers. Finally, important opportunities have arisen within regional contexts that any government would be negligent to ignore or avoid.

Yet after nearly a decade of more extensive regional involvement, it is in some respects surprising that the geographic orientation of Canadian foreign policy has not changed in more fundamental ways. Indeed, in spite of the greater attention which has been given to regional involvement, policy initiatives have been pursued in multiple settings, using a combination of bilateral, multilateral, and regional mechanisms, with the ultimate objective being one of establishing or reinforcing a consistent set of principles and practices around the globe. Rather than representing a differentiated approach, the most distinguishable aspect of Canada's embrace of regionalism has been the degree to which policy initiatives in different arenas have complemented one another. This is true in areas as diverse as democratic development, investment, peacekeeping, and trade. The evidence supports Nossal's view that "the strands of regionalism evident in Canada's foreign policy in the mid-1990s are interwoven with a broader multilateralism" and, further, that "if we see the emergence of regionalism as a dominant idea in the twenty-first century, it will likely be a regionalism with a heavy multilateral flavour" (Nossal, 1997, 162). There is no question that the substantive focus of policy has shifted, with more prominence being given to commercial issues and interventionist practices, but this, it could be argued, has neither caused nor been strengthened by the greater attention given to regionalism in Canadian foreign policy.

Not only have Canadian initiatives in the various regions reflected wider concerns and objectives, but is also clear that the government, in pursuit of critical foreign policy objectives in areas as diverse as human rights, investment rules, and landmines, has turned to regional associations in an effort to build support for global reform while at the same time resisting regional approaches that might impede more inclusive reforms. It would appear that the government has looked upon regionalism as an opportunity to concentrate resources in a strategic manner to win support for wider foreign policy objectives. In building regional coalitions in support of objectives such as liberalized trade and support for human security and good governance measures, the government has taken advantage of the opportunities provided by these regional connections. The underlying objectives of policy, however, have been inherently global rather than regional.

CONCLUSION

Canadian foreign policy has actively promoted the redefinition of interstate relations. This has been done to facilitate the emergence of new issues such as those encompassed as part of its human security and neoliberal economic agendas. As well, new governance structures have been encouraged by expanding the scope and authority of regional and international institutions, and by challenging the barriers of state sovereignty and expanding opportunities for NGOs to interact with these emerging transnational processes. Canadian foreign policy officials have also taken an interest in expanding the scope and power of authoritative international norms through international law. The contemporary state, and especially (though not exclusively) non-Western states, have experienced, as a result, a sustained challenge—through IMF programs; through challenges to sovereignty in the name of human rights and human security; through neoliberal ideas and economic practices; through advances in international institutions; and through the greater involvement of NGOs in international policy-making forums. There has been an attempt to design and develop a rules-based system that has at its core an expanded and more intrusive international legal regime.

The contemporary state has also promoted "civil society" strategies for enhancing human rights and human security that also serve to encourage the view that states are ill-suited to provide for their citizens. This fits neatly with neoliberal attitudes that privilege market-based solutions to a variety of social concerns including healthcare and education. One effect of this, as Kennedy has noted, has been to remove much of the politics from debates about global governance—"Real government is about the political contestation of distribution and justice. Governing an international order means making choices among groups. . . . Development policy means preferring these investors to those, these public officials to those, not the technocratic extension of a neutral 'best practice' " (1999).

As argued in this chapter, much of Canadian foreign policy has actively encouraged the development of this international legal regime. While this regime has considerable merit, the political choices that shape this regime are of even greater significance. This fact suggests a need to reflect on the directions that Canadian foreign policy might pursue. It is eminently laudable that the government should be supporting a human security regime that seeks to protect individuals from threats emanating from oppressive governments and violent conflicts. Yet, if human security is the objective, what should be done to alleviate the human insecurities that result from inadequate food, housing, and healthcare? Moreover, the Canadian government's support of a more intrusive international regime may indeed enable the international community to circumvent illegal and corrupt governments. This also raises the question of what measures are being undertaken to ensure that all parties have both the right and the full opportunity to effectively participate in determining the rules that will govern such interventions? Finally, while there is considerable evidence of Canadian support for such initiatives, there remain significant questions about the degree of the government's commitment and the willingness of the government and Canadians to commit the resources required to support such initiatives over the long term.

NOTES

1. Research for this chapter has been supported, in part, through a grant from the Social Sciences and Humanities Research Council of Canada, Grant No. 410—1197—1628.

REFERENCES

Andrew, Arthur. 1993. *The Rise and Fall of a Middle Power: Canadian Diplomacy from King to Mulroney.* Toronto: James Lorimer.

Axworthy, Lloyd. 1997. "Canada and human security the need for leadership." *International Journal 52*, 183–196.

Boehm, Peter and Christopher Hernandez-Roy. 1999. "Multilateralism in the Americas." C*anadian Foreign Policy, 7*(2): 23–33.

Bull, Hedley. 1979. "The State's Positive Role in World Affairs." *Daedalus 108*, 111–123.

Canada. 2000. Government Response to the Report of the Standing Committee on Foreign Affairs and International Trade—"The Free Trade Area of the Americas: Towards a Hemispheric Agreement in the Canadian Interest." March 15th.

Cooper, Andrew F. 1997. *Canadian Foreign Policy Old Habits and New Directions*. Scarborough: Prentice Hall/Allyn and Bacon.

Cooper, Andrew F., Richard A. Higgott, and Kim Richard Nossal. 1993. *Relocating Middle Powers.* Vancouver: University of British Columbia.

Daudelin, Jean. 1995. "The Politics of Oligarchy: 'Democracy' and Canada's Recent Conversion to Latin America." In Maxwell Cameron and Maureen Appel Molot (eds.), *Democracy and Foreign Policy.* Ottawa: Carleton University Press, pp. 145–162.

Canada. Department of Foreign Affairs and International Trade (DFAIT). 2002. "Canada's Human Security Web Site." Retrieved from www.humansecurity.gc.ca/menu-e.asp

Dosman, Edgar J. 1992. "Canada and Latin America: The New Look." *International Journal 47*, 529–554.

Fawcett, Louise and Andrew Hurrell (eds.), 1995. *Regionalism in World Politics.* Oxford University Press.

Galtung, Johan. 1969. "Violence, Peace and Peace Research." *Journal of Peace Research 3*, 167–192.

Haar, Jerry and Dosman, Edgar J. 1993. A *Dynamic Partnership: Canada's Changing Role in the Hemisphere.* New Brunswick: Transaction.

Hart, Michael. 1990. *A North American Free Trade Agreement.* Ottawa: Centre for Trade Policy Law.

Hurrell, Andrew. 1992. "Latin America in the New World Order: A Regional Bloc of the Americas?" *International Affairs 68*, 121–139.

Keating, Tom. 2002. *Canada and World Order,* 2nd ed. Toronto: McClelland & Stewart.

Kennedy, David. 1999. "Background Noise?" *Harvard International Review 21*, (3) (52–58).

MacKenzie, David. 1994. "Canada in the Organization of American States: The First Five Years." *Behind the Headlines 52.*

Mansfield, Edward D. and Helen V. Milner. 1997. "The Political economy of Regionalism: An Overview." In Edward E. Mansfield and Helen V. Milner (eds.), *The Political Economy of Regionalism.* Columbia University Press. 1–19.

Neack, Laura. 1992. "Empirical Observations on 'Middle State' Behaviour at the Start of a New International System." *Pacific Focus 7*, (1) 5–21.

Nossal, Kim Richard. 1997. *The Politics of Canadian Foreign Policy.* Scarborough: Prentice Hall.

Odlum, George. 2000. Address by the Minister of Foreign Affairs and International Trade of Saint Lucia on Human Security OAS 30th General Assembly. Windsor, Canada. Retrieved June 5, 2000 from www.oas.org/assembly/speeches/address

Pettigrew, Pierre. 2000. Notes for an address by the Honourable Pierre Pettigrew, Minister for International Trade, to the Standing Committee on Foreign Affairs and International Trade on the Free Trade Area of the Americas, Ottawa, Ontario June 14, 2000.

Pratt, Cranford. 1999. "Competing Rationales for Development Assistance," *International Journal* Spring: 306–323.

Rochlin, James. 1995. "Markets, Democracy and Security in Latin America." In Maxwell Cameron and Maureen Appel Molot, (eds.), *Democracy and Foreign Policy*. Ottawa: Carleton University Press, 257–279.

United Nations Development Program. 1994. Human Development Report 1994. Retrieved from www.undp.org/hdro/hdrs/1994/english/94.htm

WEBLINKS

Canadian Department of Foreign Affairs and International Trade
www.dfait-maeci.gc.ca

Human Security Canada
www.humansecurity.gc.ca

United Nations Development Programme
www.undp.org

chapter twenty-three

Canadian Security for a New Era

Principles and Pragmatics

Senator Douglas Roche[1]

INTRODUCTION

Canada has traditionally had an interest in being, and being viewed as, a "good international citizen" (Keal, 1992, 12). This concept suggests that a country can realize its national interests while, at the same time, working towards more principled concerns such as promoting world order, encouraging global reform, and realizing its duties to humanity (Linklater, 1992, 21). Simply put, good international citizenship entails having a strong ethical foundation for one's policies. Although this does not necessarily preclude the "national interest," it does suggest that practical concerns can be achieved through a moral lens.

Canada has demonstrated its international citizenship countless times, especially since the end of the Cold War, and most recently as a leader in the campaign to ban anti-personnel landmines and as a proponent of an International Criminal Court. As well, Canada took a principled stance on South African apartheid and has been a consistent supporter of the United Nations system. However, on certain security matters, Canada's response has been largely overshadowed by that of the United States, often precipitating tension between Canada's ethical outlook and its actions. The United States' largely militaristic response to the terror attacks of September 11, 2001, is the latest such security issue to frustrate Canadian policymakers. Although Canada's initial stance urged a calm and forward-thinking response, within weeks it committed its largest military force since the Korean War to the U.S.-led war effort and endangered its reputation as a good international citizen.

Of course, the problem is much deeper than simply laying Canada's dilemmas on the U.S. doorstep. It is not the United States' fault that Canada's Official Development Assistance budget is a third of what it is committed to be. Rather, the underlying factor appears to be a weakening of the Canadian will to play a leading role in advancing solutions to contemporary security problems. To be sure, Canada began to chart a security policy course following the end of the Cold War that sought to define and respond to the complexities of globalization and provided strong ethical underpinnings for its security policy. However, the Canadian government's participation in the Gulf War of 1991, the Kosovo bombing of 1999, and the bombing campaign in Afghanistan in 2001 all threaten to compromise Canada's ethical stance in its overall quest for peace.

The very nature of contemporary security in the post–Cold War period and its implications for "global society" mean that ethics will increasingly determine a country's reputation. If it is to remain true to its values and maintain its international status as a good international citizen, Canada must overcome the contradictions in its security policies and develop a forward-thinking approach more in tune with a globalized world. The reality of contemporary security, shockingly demonstrated on September 11, also means that a country's well-being will depend on how effectively it responds to the new environment.

In some ways, September 11 has "changed the world." Western nations now feel much more vulnerable and are adopting unprecedented security measures. However, in many ways the world remains unchanged. The terrorists served to underline the fact that, parallel with changes brought about by increased globalization, the notion of security has undergone an evolution over the past decade. No longer defined solely in terms of the power of states, security now encompasses a vast array of transnational actors and issues that affect a state's security calculus. The question then, is whether the tragic events of September 11 have finally signalled a change in how we approach security.

SEPTEMBER 11—HAS THE WORLD CHANGED?

In the immediate aftermath of September 11, Canada offered a tempered response congruent with its traditionally thoughtful and ethical character. Prime Minister Jean Chrétien stated in Parliament on September 17, 2001:

> We must be guided by a commitment to do what works in the long run, not by what makes us feel better in the short run. We will remain vigilant but will not give in to the temptation in a rush to increase security to undermine the values that we cherish. We allow no one to force us to sacrifice our values or traditions under the pressure of urgent circumstances (2001, 79).

This statement seemed to be very much in line with the Department of Foreign Affairs and International Trade's broader policy statement on security, which emphasized "new approaches" and the use of "new instruments" to respond to security threats (Canada, 1995). It was also congruent with Canada's "human security" policy, which values peace and forward thinking over war and rashness.

Canada was at the forefront in supporting two United Nations Security Council resolutions on the terror attacks. Although resolutions 1368 and 1373, passed on September 12 and 28, 2001, respectively, confirmed UN members' right to self-defence, they also obliged states to work together in a joint international effort to address terrorism (United Nations Security Council, 2001, Resolution 1368). Speaking at a General Assembly conference, Canada's ambassador to the United Nations, Paul Heinbecker, stressed that although national action was necessary—a veiled reference to the U.S. response—it would not be sufficient to ensure national security. Supporting the Secretary General's comments, he drew attention to the urgent need to strengthen international regimes against the proliferation and use of weapons of mass destruction and seize the opportunity to do "genuine and enduring good" (Heinbecker, October 4, 2001).

Canada's statements and early actions suggest that it was acting as a good international citizen and working within the innovative and principled security policy framework it had fashioned over the previous decade. However, in the following weeks, criticism began to mount suggesting that Canada, not unlike in previous crises, had surrendered its legitimacy and much of its policymaking power to the United States (Klepak, 2001, A12; Green, 2001).

The U.S. response was typical in that it represented a coalition of convenience based on old Cold War "hub and spoke" alliance models. Strategy and decisions emanated from Washington without much regard for the United Nations' ability to respond to what was defined as a "threat to international peace and security." An aerial bombing campaign ensued and reports of civilian casualties began to increase, just as they had during the Gulf and Kosovo wars. The United States chose allies of convenience, including Pakistan, a country long considered a sponsor of terror in Kashmir, and began shipping more arms into the area in an effort to build up non-state actors, namely the Northern Alliance—a group with its own dubious history.

For its part, Canada's ensuing actions seemed to increasingly mirror those of its southern neighbour. In joining NATO's invocation of Article Five of its charter and committing six warships and personnel at the request of President George W. Bush, Canada signalled that it was in agreement with the largely U.S. military campaign against Afghanistan ("Notes for an Address by Prime Minister Jean Chrétien to the 47th Annual NATO Parliamentary Assembly," 2001). Like other donor countries, Canada was quick to remove most of the sanctions imposed on Pakistan after its 1998 nuclear tests. In freezing the assets of terrorists, Canada used the list of 27 individuals and organizations provided by the United States. Canada also set up a Homeland Security special committee, mirroring the one created in the U.S., and seemed to warm to suggestions that a North American perimeter was needed to ensure U.S. security.

Lost in its eventual response were Canada's initial sentiments that the international community should adopt an internationally oriented and thoughtful approach to the terrorist dilemma. In acquiescing to the American-managed campaign instead of insisting on a UN-led response, Canada entered a process over which it had little, if any, influence. Canada also undercut the legitimacy of the UN, an institution that has traditionally been a cornerstone of its security policy, much as it had in 1999 during the Kosovo campaign. It was what was originally seen as a major test of its foreign and security policy, Canada did not capitalize on its good reputation and seek the moral high ground. As such, critics suggested that Canada had—once again—surrendered its sovereignty to the United States and, in so doing, further diluted its credentials as a good international citizen.

Canada's response to September 11 represented the third time in 10 years that the government of Canada went to war as part of a U.S.-controlled coalition. In January 1991, Washington and its coalition partners, including Canada, used force to eject Iraq from Kuwait after it had absorbed its small neighbour into its own territory. And in March 1999, Canada was part of the NATO campaign against the Federal Republic of Yugoslavia after Slobodan Milosevic's government refused to sign an international agreement intended to eliminate human rights abuses in the Yugoslav province of Kosovo.

In all cases, Canada's contribution was more symbolic than substantial. Its participation was largely a gesture in that it lent a degree of legitimacy to the American campaigns that came from Canada's foreign policy record. Canada has a very high level of acceptance in the international community for several reasons. It typically understands the hardships of the poorer and disadvantaged countries, it was not a colonial power bent on exploitation, and, when it joins a coalition, Canada generally aligns its interests with those of the international community as a whole. However, in participating in these campaigns, this reputation was arguably undercut.

Although the Persian Gulf War was an inter state war in the classical sense, it provides an insight into the dilemma Canada has had between ethics and pragmatics on certain security issues. In this instance, the ethical impulses came from the then–Liberal opposition leader, Jean Chrétien. While supporting the sanctions in place, he criticized the Progressive Conservative government of Brian Mulroney for giving its full support to the United States and not making more use of the United Nations' ability to manage the situation and strongly rejected the use of force, which he considered premature. Chrétien condemned the U.S. use of an ultimatum to compel Iraqi compliance, since it reduced the room for diplomatic manoeuvre, and went so far as to suggest that, by submitting to the U.S., Canada would be undercutting its own independence to act in accordance with its values. According to Chrétien:

> Our national interests have been peacekeeping, a voice for stability, and a voice for independence in war, peace, and stability. We have always said that embargoes, sanctions, and diplomacy are preferable to bullets. Canada and the United Nations must be agents of peace.
>
> I ask the Prime Minister, before committing Canada to a war, to remember that our country's role has always been to pick up the pieces whenever warring nations chose war over peace (1991).

However, despite this call for Canada to remain true to its values, the government of the day felt compelled to declare that diplomacy had failed and that there was no option but to resort to militarism. It is interesting to note that Canada's uncritical support of the United States was offered at a time when Canada was experiencing an increased flow of foreign direct investment, approximately two-thirds of which originated from the United States (Knight, 1999, 23). The recently signed free trade agreement with the U.S. further served to limit Canada's policy independence (Rourke, 1993, 469).

Through its unqualified support of the U.S.-led Gulf War, Canada undermined its image as a responsible international actor. As reports of civilian casualties mounted, including the deaths of approximately 1500 when the Amariyah bomb shelter in Baghdad was hit with two U.S. bombs, Canada found its actions increasingly at odds with its traditional humanitarian stance. Its subsequent support of the sanction regime, which according to various UN agencies has contributed to hundreds of thousands of deaths, and the 1998 Desert Fox campaign has done little to revitalize Canada's image in this part of the world (Mueller and Mueller, 1999).

Canada's involvement in the Kosovo campaign was somewhat different, since the campaign was defined as a humanitarian operation and thus deemed congruent with Canada's national interest in "human security." As the then–minister of foreign affairs, Lloyd Axworthy, put it, the alliance's actions in support of ethnic Albanians showed "the extent to which NATO's new roles are, in fact, all about protecting human security and promoting stability" (Axworthy, 1999, 8–11). Canada was more than willing to be involved in the Kosovo campaign, since it was portrayed as a humanitarian mission, and was convinced of the righteousness of using force despite the lack of a Security Council mandate. However, like the Persian Gulf War, the situation sat uneasily with observers of Canadian security policy.

The NATO campaign in Kosovo put Canada in an ethical dilemma. Although its fundamental values lay with the United Nations as the guarantor of international peace and security, by choosing to not only support but aslo participate in NATO's bombing of Serbia and Kosovo, Canada—for the moment—deferred to NATO rather than the UN and subverted international law. Canada has long linked its claims to morality to its support of the core principles of international law. One of those principles is that the United Nations Security Council is the sole authority able to wage war. In joining the American-led Kosovo coalition through NATO, Canada arguably weakened this link.

Also, as with the Persian Gulf War, civilian casualties often overshadowed any claims that the conflict had an ethical underpinning. Using 700 aircraft and 20 ships, NATO flew nearly 35 000 sorties, dropping 20 000 bombs on 600 cities, towns, and villages, resulting in close to 13 000 civilian casualties, including 2500 dead. Utilities, roads, bridges, hospitals, clinics, schools, and other infrastructure vital to the civilian population were destroyed as well as military targets. Any claims to moral righteousness or protecting human security were therefore drastically muted.

THE U.S. CONNECTION

Canada's entanglement with the United States is an important and unavoidable reality. There is hardly an aspect of Canadian national life that is not touched politically, economically, or culturally by its closest neighbour. Hundreds of billions of dollars worth of goods and over 200 million people cross the Canada–U.S. border every year. Approximately 85 percent of Canadian exports go to the United States and about 76 percent of what it imports comes from its southern neighbour (Hampson et al., 2001, 7). All told, about one-third of Canada's total economic activity is connected to, or dependent on, its relationship with the U.S. The relationship goes both ways in that Canada is also the most important trading partner of the U.S., which sells more to Canada than it does to either Japan or to the whole European Union. Canada and the United States are also party to 200 bilateral agreements on subjects ranging from common defence to the regulation of radio and television. Resisting American influence in its policies while at the same time reaping the benefits of the relationship has been the traditional challenge for Canadian foreign and security policy.

Throughout the Cold War, for example, the U.S. administration reminded Canada that it could not tolerate a neutral country on its long northern border. During this period, Canada recognized U.S. leadership, as shown, for example, by Prime Minister Pierre Trudeau's consent to test nuclear cruise missile delivery systems in Canadian airspace even though Trudeau personally disapproved. Likewise, Canada's security policy was based mainly upon partnerships, largely under American control, for collective defence including

NATO and the North American Aerospace Defence Command (NORAD). Although Trudeau made an attempt to guide Canada towards a more independent foreign and security policy, the exercise only ended up reaffirming the importance of the U.S. relationship.

In the post–Cold War period, the United States has maintained its influence over Canada's security policies. Canada's alliance with the U.S. is so complex that a strong body of opinion in Ottawa holds that it is not in Canada's economic interest to tangle with its powerful southern neighbour. This viewpoint has prevailed many times since the end of the Cold War, including during both the Persian Gulf and Kosovo wars, but also in accepting the expansion of NATO over development of the Organization for Security and Cooperation in Europe, acquiescence in the ongoing U.S. bombing campaign over Iraq and its bombing of Afghanistan and Sudan in 1998 and, most recently, in joining the U.S. "war on terrorism." However, in following the U.S. lead on security issues, Canada's post–Cold War security policy, based largely on a principled understanding of international relations, is likely to become increasingly untenable.

A NEW SECURITY ENVIRONMENT

During the Cold War, security and defence issues were interchangeable—security meant state security. The end of the Cold War has brought with it a redefinition of security, but this did not happen in isolation. Coinciding with the collapse of the Soviet Union was an acceleration of changes in transportation, information, finance, and international organization. This new period of increased "globalization" has brought many tremendous opportunities and benefits with it. People around the globe are more connected to each other than ever before. Information and money flow, and goods and services produced in one part of the world are increasingly available around the globe. International travel is more frequent and international communication and the exchange of ideas is commonplace.

Perhaps most important, these changes have meant that the new global society is one in which states are neither the only nor necessarily the most critical players on the international scene. Although states still exercise "sovereignty" in that they are largely in charge of their own foreign and security policies, the security of states is not purely "geopolitical," consisting of territory, resources, protection from rivals, and prestige. Globalization has empowered a global civil society made up of people and groups that operate across borders and whose preferences can drastically reduce the freedom to manoeuvre that states previously enjoyed. Consequently, states have increasingly had to take into account the demands and wishes of many national and international interests. The process of globalization, in other words, is redefining traditional conceptions of sovereignty.

This erosion of traditional state sovereignty, combined with the post–Cold War vacuum created by the absence of competing superpower interests, has led to an exponential rise in intrastate conflicts. Although unlikely to escalate into a calamitous nuclear war, these conflicts have become especially brutal, and have seen the deaths of millions of civilians and created tens of millions of refugees and displaced persons. In addition, globalization has suddenly amplified old conflicts and created many new security threats. Although globalization has increased the ability of multinational corporations and investors to move their money at lightening speed, it has also enabled drug cartels, mafias, and terrorists to go global. The suddenly many more powerful private actors has created a world of virtually unlimited vulnerability. The terrorist attacks of September 11 were tragic examples of globalization's dark underbelly. The fact that such attacks could be successful against the world's most powerful state with the most extensive intelligence system and sophisticated military underlines the fact that the international community operates in a much-changed security framework.

Another dark side of globalization is the expanding gap between the rich and the poor, both within and between countries. Although the new financial dynamic has helped reduce poverty in some of the largest and strongest economies, including China and India, the present era of globalization has had an overall marginalizing effect. National governments are increasingly unable to cope with the financial vulnerabilities and security risks inherent in globalization, often to the detriment of their populations. In fact, research on recent humanitarian emergencies has concluded that growing social polarization, intensified by globalization, is the major cause of the current wave of civil conflicts. Accordingly, any attempt to understand contemporary security also requires addressing inequality in incomes, political participation, economic assets, and social conditions (United Nations Development Program, 1999, 36).

WHERE PRAGMATICS AND ETHICS INTERSECT

More than ever, people have common interests and destinies due to the increased integration and interaction of globalization. Like global society, security is now becoming community, oriented. For wealthier industrialized countries in particular, the lifting of the constraints imposed by the superpower rivalry has meant that other issues can receive much-needed attention. As such, the concept of security has widened to include human rights, the environment, and economic and social well-being. Increasingly, these issues have forced the redefinition of security away from one based on the state to one that encompasses individuals and communities. It follows that, in responding to the new security challenges included in the post–Cold War security calculus, moral principles have become a more important variable in the security policies of wealthy industrialized countries. Although the degree to which states' declared principles are congruent with their actions varies, in using ethics in security policy, a country is better placed to tame the elements of militarism and to concentrate on achieving social justice and, ultimately, security in international society. Of course, it would be overly simplistic to suggest that a country's morality exists separate from the complex and contingent world of interests and political power. Moral principles and the actions countries take to give them substance do not exist in a vacuum. Accordingly, when discussing a moral foreign and security policy, the goal is "good international citizenship," which suggests a balance between ethics and pragmatics in a country's foreign and security policies (Franceschet and Knight, 2001, 55–61).

In their study of Canada and the International Criminal Court, Franceschet and Knight argue that good international citizenship consists of four main interrelated elements. First, good international citizenship does not necessarily mean abandoning more narrowly defined "national interests" in security. However, it does suggest that pragmatic concerns be achieved through an ethical orientation to the world. In this way, a country is able to overcome militaristic impulses and focus instead on the reconciliation of social justice in the world. Such thinking has been behind the efforts of several countries to place their foreign and security policies within a morally based framework. Such has been the case with Britain, which has used the concept of a "third way." Although originally meant to strike a balance between capitalism and socialism in the domestic sphere, it has since been extended to foreign and security policies in an effort to "tame the elements of brute power" and work towards the "reconciliation of justice and order in world politics" (Wheeler and Dunne, 1998, 856).

Second, it follows that a country that is focused on working towards social justice has an obligation to global society. Just as citizenship in a state means yielding one's self-interest to the benefit of the common good, citizenship in the context of an international community made up of a myriad of actors also entails forgoing egotistical interest in favour of the common good. Accordingly, if a country is to be a good international citizen, it is obligated to work towards goals that transcend the immediate national interest. The achievement of a secure international human rights regime is an obvious example.

Third, for an ethically based security policy to work, it necessarily requires a commitment to multilateralism. Multilateral institutions are vital to developing and communicating shared values beyond the state level and to global society as a whole. They are also necessary considering the trans-boundary nature of today's security dilemmas. At the same time, in promoting values through multilateral institutions, individual countries avoid the charge of being on a moral crusade. However, since international organizations do not exist separately from their constituent states, they cannot be wholly relied upon to provide the moral impetus for security policy. As York University's Robert Cox argues, there are essentially two forms of multilateralism—"top-down" and "bottom-up" (Cox, 1986, 161). The former simply seeks to manage interstate problems without questioning the traditional fabric of world order. However, the latter is more of a challenge in that it seeks to question the assumptions and interests of the existing framework. As such, there is an imperative for principled states to involve themselves in the bottom-up multilateral activity in order to balance the heavy influence of top-down forces. In an increasingly globalized international system, this often means working with civil society.

Fourth, although a balance between pragmatics and ethics is a key element of good international citizenship, the label also includes the notion that governments must use their moral legitimacy to influence the actors of other states. In other words, good international citizenship entails both maintaining an ethical ethos, and also taking a proactive role in leading others to the common good. Typically, this implies the use of "moral suasion," which involves appealing to existing international moral norms to rally the international community to effect change. Of course, a state can only be truly effective if it follows through consistently and sacrifices vital interests when necessary. Indeed, if states are not consistent, there is a strong possibility that they will undermine the effectiveness of such norms and be seen as hypocritical.

A major limit to practising an ethical foreign and security policy is imposed by powerful states, the prime example being the U.S.-dominated coalition arrayed against the Soviet Union during the Cold War. In this instance, policy was largely dictated from Washington and accepted by other members of the alliance, since their very security depended on doing so. However, as mentioned above, the post–Cold War period has lifted many of the old constraints and enabled countries to assume a much more active role in their own foreign and security policies. As Canada has demonstrated in leading a campaign to ban anti-personnel mines and to establish an International Criminal Court, states can indeed exercise moral authority within the context of the hegemony of one superpower.

CANADA: A GOOD INTERNATIONAL CITIZEN

In a sense, Canada's contribution to international peace and security has always been guided by certain ethical impulses. In the aftermath of World War II, during the so-called golden age of its foreign policy, Canada made a conscious choice not to follow the superpowers' lead and develop nuclear and other weapons of mass destruction. Canada chose instead to focus on creating a peacekeeping role for the United Nations. Through its scientific and diplomatic work, Canada has promoted verification techniques as an essential prerequisite to meaningful and effective disarmament. Canada was also quick to remove its armed forces personnel from Europe soon after the end of the Cold War, despite NATO's displeasure. Later Canada was a leading strategist in securing the indefinite extension of the Nuclear Non-Proliferation Treaty in 1995 and in having the NATO alliance re-evaluate its own nuclear weapons doctrine. In the field of human rights, Canada was a key player during the 1980s in using moral norms against racism to rally international condemnation of South African apartheid.

Canada's stance has often put it at odds with the United States. Historically, Canada has been a thorn in Washington's side on such issues as NATO and NORAD. During the Vietnam War, for example, Canada welcomed thousands of American draft dodgers and its universities held "teach-ins" to denounce the war. Canada was keen to opt out of the Reagan-era Strategic Defence Initiative and, more recently, was so quick to conclude an international treaty banning anti-personnel landmines that some in Washington considered their northern neighbour insensitive to the United States' security situation.

However, towards the end of the twentieth century, there was a dramatic change in Canada's security and economic environment congruent with the concurrent global changes mentioned above. Although Canada made an innovative effort to respond to the new environment, these changes had the effect of creating turbulence in Canada's foreign and security policy actions, which often seemed to alternate between pragmatism and moralism. Though Canada spearheaded several moralistic initiatives in the mid-1990s, there was a sense as the millennium drew to a close that utilitarian objectives were souring the reputation Canada had built for itself. The replacement of its humanitarian foreign minister Lloyd Axworthy with John Manley, who began focusing largely on political objectives—especially bettering the Canada–U.S. relationship—seems to have signalled a significant shift away from ethical pursuits. The message being sent is that, in trying to win Nobel Peace prizes, Canada has neglected its national interest and, specifically, its vital relationship with the United States (Baxter, 2000, A1–A2).

The events of September 11 appear to have swung the pendulum further away still. The terrorist attacks served to reinvigorate the debate surrounding Canada's commitment to continental defence. In particular, the questions of whether to participate in National Missile Defence or to be included in a North American security "perimeter" are looming choices now facing Canadian policy planners. Canadian policymakers, in a sense, face a turning point. If it intends to retain its reputation as a good international citizen, and maintain the influence it has on the many issues coming out of the globalization process, Canada will have to respond to its new security predicament while at the same time striking a balance with its ethical traditions.

In direct response to the changed security environment of the past decade, Foreign Minister Lloyd Axworthy inaugurated Canada's "human security" agenda in 1996. As historian Robert Bothwell argues, the ideas that Axworthy brought to Canada's foreign and security policy appealed to Canada's reputation of having an "international conscience" and "a standard of international morality" (Bothwell, 2000, A18). The concept of human security was first presented by the United Nations in its 1994 Human Development Report. It was an attempt to broaden the notion of state security to include the safety and dignity of individuals and to respond to the changes and problems associated with advancing globalization and the decreased ability of states to protect their own citizens (United Nations Development Program, 1994). Human security is an approach that includes safety from such chronic threats as hunger, disease, poverty, and environmental degradation, but also protection from more sudden threats, such as human rights abuses and those associated with armed conflict. Although there is a strong moral foundation for framing security in such a way, addressing such challenges also goes to the "root causes" of global insecurity.

However, for Canada, the issue was largely one of ethics. The emphasis on human security was an attempt to humanize some of the rough edges of globalization and served as a cue to other rich industrialized nations that the conduct of their affairs should always take into account the problems faced by those not so well off. For Canada, Axworthy began with the foundation that such humanitarian issues were central to the thoughts of Canadians and framed Canada's security policy so as to mirror the ethical concerns of its own citizens. Although its crowning achievement was the Anti-Personnel Mines Convention, signed on to by 122 countries in December 1997, Canada's good international citizenship can be found in other aspects of the human security agenda. The landmines treaty had the effect of renewing efforts to address the small-arms problem. Canada has since been key in elaborating an international mechanism to combat the illicit manufacture of and traffic in firearms. Other efforts revolved around putting a spotlight on the plight of children and child soldiers in situations of armed conflict, which led to an international conference in 2000. Canada also was at the forefront of the successful effort to create an Optional Protocol to the UN Convention on the Rights of the Child designed to raise the age of recruitment and participation in hostilities to eighteen.

The human security agenda also included a number of initiatives designed to strengthen international law and promote human rights. The one that received the most attention was the statute establishing a framework for the International Criminal Court, which was signed in 1998. Canada also partnered with Norway in creating a draft declaration on the rights and responsibilities of individuals, groups, and institutions to promote and protect universally agreed-upon human rights and freedoms. Approved at the 54th session of the UN Human Rights Commission in 1998, the Declaration on Human Rights Defenders, added further to the ethical framework of Canada's approach to security.

Another track of the human security framework included a series of "innovative partnerships" that Canada fashioned with a number of countries. Under the Lysoen Declaration signed in 1998, Canada and Norway, along with Switzerland, Austria, Chile, Thailand, South Africa, and Sweden, pledged to advance various aspects of the human security agenda. Not limiting the discussion to state actors, Canada initiated a series of public consultations with members of civil society. Canada also used its position as a non-permanent member of the UN Security Council between 1999 and 2000 to give prominence to the troubles of Africa, a continent that had long been excluded from countries' calculations of their national interest. In advancing ideas about the protection of civilians, peace support operations, conflict prevention, governance and accountability, and public safety, Canada was key in raising the profile of a region that had previously been ignored.

In pursuing its human security priorities, Canada's motives often crossed paths with more practical American objectives. As mentioned, Canada often appeared to act insensitively to the Americans on the issue of landmines, but also in its move to an International Criminal Court and through its embrace of Cuba on the trade front. Canada has also been criticized for taking these initiatives at a time when important demographic and political shifts were taking place in the United States that saw a generation of American policymakers who understood Canada well replaced with a younger generation of politicians who did not. At the same time, it must be noted that such tensions were not new, nor were they a result of Canada's perseverance with its moralistic pursuits. As mentioned above, there have been tensions over several issues throughout the history of the bilateral relationship.

In using human security as a guiding framework, Canada's foreign and security policy after the Cold War appears to be a match for Franceschet and Knight's criteria for a "good international citizen." Canada's interests were framed in ethical terms, it felt an obligation to honour its membership in international society and to work multilaterally, and it often achieved its morally defined objectives by leading others. Further, Canada was able to overcome potential hegemonic limits—posed by the United States—in realizing its objectives. However, although Canada was able to maintain a respectable balance between pragmatism and ethics, there were certain inconsistencies that detracted from its good image. Now, with the ascendancy of a new foreign minister and a new U.S. administration focused on terrorism, there is an urgent need for Canada to make the next instalment of its security strategy in the post–Cold War security environment.

Along with the Kosovo debate, which raised serious questions as to the moral foundation of Canada's human security policy, there are several other ambiguities that have eroded its good reputation. Critics of Axworthy's human security agenda charged that it focused too much on the humanitarian dimensions of security and did not address the broader, developmental aspects of human security as defined by the United Nations, such as poverty alleviation and income assistance to poorer countries. This appeared to be a constant source of friction between officials at the Department of Foreign Affairs and those in the Canadian International Development Agency who were nervous that too much of Canada's foreign aid was going into humanitarian assistance and emergency relief, to the detriment of basic income assistance to the world's neediest (Hampson, 2000). Canada's Official Development Assistance budget, which suddenly dropped in 1995, would appear to support this claim (Draimin and Tomlinson, 1998, 145). Likewise, Canada failed to enforce an end to the Calgary-based Talisman Energy's investments in Sudan, despite a government report confirming that the company's activities were helping the Sudanese government in its ongoing civil war. In terms of the environment, which was also figured into the human security calculus, some have suggested that Canada dragged its feet on the problems of global warming, the Arctic, and the Kyoto process (Smith, 2001).

CONCLUSION

The consequences of September 11 present an opportunity to reinvigorate the work Canada has undertaken through its human security agenda. Although the terrorist attacks were surely the work of fanatics, it is true that terrorism thrives on perceived injustice. Only in removing these perceived injustices can true peace be achieved. As Kosovo demonstrated, there might indeed be a role for the military to play in such circumstances, but there is also a corresponding duty for responsible countries to fill the void that militarism creates. Canada, through its human security precedent, is well placed to provide a "third pillar" that seeks to address the more systemic causes that provide ripe conditions for terrorism, as well as other heightened problems in this era of globalization.

Such an approach would not be incompatible with the "war on terrorism," nor would it necessarily be incompatible with the new foreign minister's focus on the Canada–U.S. partnership. The first world leader to call for a global landmines treaty was not Lloyd Axworthy, but U.S. President Bill Clinton. It was the United States, not Canada, that was the initial driving force behind the landmines treaty until the Pentagon made its voice heard. The American "ethical pulse" is especially evident in the financial support it has committed to removing landmines and assisting mine victims. In fact, the United States has been the largest single contributor to related efforts; but, due to the United States' fragmented political system, Canada has been better poised to actually deliver on the human security agenda (Fry, 2001). The Canadian and American outlooks on certain human security issues are thus not necessarily incompatible.

The horrific events of September 11 served as a stark reminder that the proliferation and existence of nuclear weapons constitute the single largest threat to human security. As confirmed in the 1996 International Court of Justice's Advisory Opinion on the legality of nuclear weapons, these devices contravene the cardinal principle of humanitarian law that prohibits states from using weapons that are incapable of distinguishing between civilian and military targets. Until now, the nuclear powers have avoided entering into a process of comprehensive negotiations to reduce—and eliminate—their stockpiles as required under the terms of the Non-Proliferation Treaty (NPT) and as reconfirmed in the 2000 NPT review. However, the terrorist attacks of September 11 have served to catalyze a new sense of urgency that was absent before. As UN Secretary General Kofi Annan stated in an address to a special General Assembly session on terrorism:

> It is hard to imagine how the tragedy of 11 September could have been worse. Yet the truth is that a single attack involving a nuclear or biological weapon could have killed millions. While the world was unable to prevent the 11 September attacks, there is much we can do to help prevent *future* terrorist acts carried out with weapons of mass destruction. The greatest immediate danger arises from a non-state group—or even an individual—acquiring and using a nuclear, biological, or chemical weapon (2001).

Of course, Annan's warning is simply the latest in a long procession of warnings that has been building steadily since the end of the Cold War (Falkenrath, 1998, 50; Ross, 1998/1999, 123–4). Common to all such warnings is a reconception of nuclear proliferation corresponding to changes coming out of the globalization process. Before, the major concern was horizontal proliferation between states and vertical proliferation in terms of the size of arsenals—the fear being that, if nuclear weapons were allowed to proliferate, "pariah" or "rogue" states might get their hands on them. However, due largely to changes related to the new security environment, a new dimension has been added to traditional fears of nuclear proliferation.

Non-state actors are now more capable than ever of acquiring the prerequisites to pose a nuclear threat. Like the many other by-products of globalization, this change is a result of economic, educational, and technological progress. The basic science behind these weapons is now being learned by more people than ever before. The new concepts of physics that the best scientists in the world had to master during the Manhattan Project are now standard curriculum in modern universities. Likewise, the requisite knowledge to pose a nuclear threat, including information relevant to planning and executing violent acts, is widely available through new information mediums. Terrorists now have access to such technologies as facsimile transmission, cellular and satellite telephones, and the Internet, and have a wide choice of efficient courier and shipping companies to move money and weapons around the globe very quickly. Not only are potential nuclear terrorists able to start much higher on the learning and organizational curve, but the ability of the state to monitor and counter contemporary security threats is being outpaced by the efficiency, sophistication, and geographic reach of non-state actors. Due to the more traditional constraints of law, human and, financial resources, and technology, states have been unable to contain the nuclear threat at the same rate non-state actors are able to pose it. With the democratization of the former Soviet Union and the decentralization of control over its nuclear arsenal, nuclear terrorism has evolved into a realistic—and rapidly growing—threat.

The unique quality of this threat means that the international community must go beyond traditional responses that tend to be passive and reactive in nature. Specifically, a determined multilateral effort that focuses on general disarmament and high-confidence verification will be the only way the nuclear threat can be put to rest. Canada, precisely because of its good record, is well placed to help guide the international community, not unlike it did during the landmine campaign, to this goal. Canada does not possess nuclear weapons, has a respected history of working to prevent their proliferation, and wants to see their political significance devalued. Although Canada's membership in NATO has been the source of some ambiguity between this reputation and its actual actions, with the end of the Cold War, Canada is better placed to advance more ambitious non-proliferation initiatives. In fact, Canada demonstrated such a willingness in 1999 when it formally requested that NATO review its nuclear weapons policy, which is considered by many to contradict its members' non-proliferation and disarmament efforts in such venues as the NPT and the Conference on Disarmament. Although the alliance ended up reaffirming the "essential" nature of nuclear weapons to maintain "credible deterrence," Canada demonstrated its morality in challenging the longstanding U.S. determination that NATO maintain nuclear weapons (NATO, 2000).

At the same time, only through a multilateral coalition will Canada be able to affect meaningfully the nuclear status quo and prevent the weapons' use by terrorists. The events of September 11 may have created an opportunity for Canada, like-minded states, and civil society to further their work on nuclear disarmament. Although the U.S. Senate rejected the Comprehensive Test Ban Treaty in 1999, and the new administration vowed not to reintroduce it, the terrorist attacks may serve to foster a mood in the United States more responsive to non-proliferation efforts. The events have served to reorder the priorities of both the United States and Russia, and have focused both countries' attention on their shared goals and co-operation rather than their disputes. This new atmosphere corresponded with the United States carrying through on previous suggestions that it would unilaterally cut its nuclear arsenal by two-thirds over the next 10 years, from the current level of more than 6000 (Gordon, November 14, 2001).

However, it is not unilateral acts that will secure international peace and security—rather it is negotiations to build a body of law that cannot be changed by political caprice. The International Court of Justice has said that the legal provisions of the Non-Proliferation Treaty must be concluded. That means that there is a legal obligation to negotiate the elimination of all nuclear weapons. That obligation cannot be papered over by a unilateral declaration to cut unneeded weapons while insisting on the retention of a base number as "essential."

As stated above, being a good international citizen does not mean giving up one's national interest. As the case of nuclear disarmament illustrates, the two are often congruent. Even if the United States decides not to join Canada in nuclear disarmament efforts, Canada must continue its principled and innovative approach to address the nuclear dilemma if it is to remain a responsible international citizen. If not, much of its previous effort may be lost in the hardening of attitudes between nuclear powers and the non-nuclear countries at precisely the time when an international threat has brought them together to address the new security environment. Canada seems to recognize this rare opportunity. Responding to the secretary general's warning, Canada affirmed that it is the "duty" of the international community to "strengthen the global norms against the proliferation and use of weapons of mass destruction" and that "à la carte multilateralism" will no longer be effective in confronting today's security challenges (Heinbecker, October 4, 2001). Of course, the question is whether Canada can find the political will to realize this objective through meaningful progress.

As good international citizenship implies, being ethical in one's security policy does not mean having to break with national interest. However, it does require a balance. For Canada, this means paying more than lip service to human security. Confirmed by the UN, through Secretary General Kofi Annan's Millennium Report, human security will continue to define how the world approaches its new security environment. The report serves as a guide for countries to help promote human security and emphasizes strengthening the rule of law, peace building, conflict prevention, international coordination, and disarmament as key objectives (Report of the Secretary General, 2001). Accordingly, the need for human-centred security has been acknowledged as the lens through which states must approach security in the era of globalization. Issues such as weapons non-proliferation, nation building, the environment, human rights, and poverty alleviation can only become increasingly important in this new period. Of course, responding responsibly to these global security threats will not come cheap and will require a strategic investment of resources. Canada's credibility and its very security in the twenty-first century will depend on making these crucial efforts.

REFERENCES

Annan, Kofi. 2001, October 1. "Address to the General Assembly on Terrorism." Retrieved from www.un.org/terrorism/statements/sg.html

Axworthy, Lloyd. 2001, October 17. "An Encounter With Emma: Rethinking Security and State Sovereignty," speech presented at the S. D Clark Lecture, University of Toronto. Retrievd from www.liucentre.ubc.ca/media_release/sdclark.htm

Baxter, James. 2000, September 19. "Advice to PM: Cut the Grandstanding," *The Ottawa Citizen,* A1–A2.

Bothwell, Robert. 2000, September 19. "Lloyd Axworthy: Man of Principle." *National Post,* A18.

Chrétien, Jean. 2001, September 17. *Edited Hansard,* No. 79, Retrieved from www.parl.gc.ca.

Chrétien, Jean. 1991, January 15. *House of Commons Debates: Official Report,* 13.

Copeland, Daryl. 1998. "Armageddon Revisited: Nuclear Weapons, Canadian Policy and the Disarmament Prospect." *Behind the Headlines 56.*

Daudelin, Jean, 2000. "Kosovo, Claymore Mines and Talisman: Is Reality Catching Up With Canada's Rhetoric?" *The North-South Institute.* Retrieveed from www.nsi-ins.ca/ensi/news_views/oped11.html

Canada. Department of Foreign Affairs and International Trade (DFAIT). 1995. *Canada in the World. Ottawa:* Government Communications Group. Retrieved from www.dfait-maeci.gc.ca.

Draimin, Tim and Brian Tomlinson, 1998. "Is There a Future for Canadian Aid in the Twenty-First Century?" In Fen Osler Hampson and Maureen Appel Molot (eds.), *Canada Among Nations 1998: Leadership and Dialogue.* Toronto: Oxford University Press.

Falkenrath, Richard A. Autumn 1998. "Confronting Nuclear, Biological and Chemical Terrorism." *Survival 40.*

Franceschet, Antonio and W. Andy Knight. Winter 2001. "International(ist) Citizenship: Canada and the International Criminal Court." *Canadian Foreign Policy 8.*

Fry, Earl. 2001. "An Assessment of the U.S. Contribution to Global Human Security." In Fen Osler Hampson et al., (eds.), *Canada Among Nations 2001: The Axworthy Legacy.* Toronto: Oxford University Press.

Gordon, Michael R. 2001, November 14. "U.S. Arsenal: Treaties vs. Nontreaties." *New York Times.* Retrieved from www.nytimes.com/2001/11/14/international/14NUKE.html

Green, Graham N. 2001, October 2. "Banalities That Aren't Legalities Do This Country No Good." *The Ottawa Citizen,* A16.

Hampson, Fen Osler. 2000, October 31. 'The Axworthy Years: An Assessment,' Presentation to the Group of 78 at the National Press Club in Ottawa, www.hri.ca/partners/G78/English/Peace/hampson-axworthy.htm

———. et al, 2001. "The Return to Continentalism in Canadian Foreign Policy." In Fen Osler Hampson et al. (eds.), *Canada Among Nations 2001: The Axworthy Legacy.* Toronto: Oxford University Press.

Heinbecker, Paul. 2001, October 4. "Canadian Statement on Measures to Eliminate International Terrorism." Retrieved from www.un.org/terrorism/statements/canadaE.html

Heinbecker, Paul. Spring 2000. "Human Security: The Hard Edge." *Canadian Military Journal 1.* Retrieved from www.journal.dnd.ca/vol1/no1_e/policy_e/pol1_e.pdf

Hoffman, Stanley. 2001, November 1. "On the War." *The New York Review of Books.* Retrieved from www.nybooks.com/articles/14660

Jockel, Joe and Joel Sokolsky. Winter 2000/2001. "Lloyd Axworthy's Legacy: Human Security and the Rescue of Canadian Defence Policy." *International Journal 56.*

Keohane Robert O. (ed.). 1986. *Neorealism and its Critics.* New York: Columbia University Press.

Klepak, Hal. 2001, October 13. "Canada Should Be More Than U.S. 'lapdog': Experts Weigh in on Role in War on Terrorism." *The Toronto Star,* A12.

Knight, Andy. Winter 1999. "Coping With a Post-Cold War Environment," *Canadian Foreign Policy 2.*

Linklater, Andrew. 1992. "What is a Good International Citizen?" In Paul Keal (ed.), *Ethics and Foreign Policy*. Canberra: Allen & Unwin.

Mueller, John and Karl Mueller. May/June 1999. "Sanctions of Mass Destruction." *Foreign Affairs 3.*

The North Atlantic Treaty Organization (NATO), "Report on Options for Confidence and Security Building Measures, Verification, Non-Proliferation, Arms Control and Disarmament." Retrieved from www.nato.int/docu/pr/2000/p00-121e/home.htm

Norton, Roy. Winter 1998. "Posture and Policymaking in Canada-US Relations: The First Two Mulroney and Chrétien Years." *Canadian Foreign Policy 5.*

'Notes for an Address by Prime Minister Jean Chrétien to the 47th Annual NATO Parliamentary Assembly.' 2001, October 9. Ottawa.

Report of the Secretary General. 2001, September 6. "Roadmap Towards the Implementation of the United Nations Millennium Declaration." United Nations General Assembly. Retrieved from www.un.org/documents/ga/docs/56/a56326.pdf

Ross, Douglas Alan. Winter 1998/1999. "Canada's Functional Isolationism." *International Journal 54.*

Rourke, John T. 1993. *International Politics on the World Stage,* 4th ed. Connecticut: The Dushkin Publishing Group Inc.

Roussel, Stéphane and Kim R. Nossal. 2001. "Canada and the Kosovo War: The Happy Follower." In Pierre Martin and Mark Brawley (eds.), Alliance Politics, *Kosovo, and NATO's War: Allied Force or Forced Allies?* New York: Palgrave.

Smith, Heather A. 2001. "Chicken Defence Lines Needed: Canadian Foreign Policy and Global Environmental Issues." In Fen Osler Hampson et al. (eds.), *Canada Among Nations 2001: The Axworthy Legacy.* Toronto: Oxford University Press.

United Nations Development Program, *Human Development Report 1994: New Dimensions of Human Security.* Retrieved from www.undp.org/hdro/1994/94.htm

United Nations Development Program, *Human Development Report 1999: Globalisation with a Human Face,* (www.undp.org/hdro/99.htm)

United Nations Security Council. Resolution 1368. 2001. September 12. Retrieved from www.un.org/Docs/scres/2001/res1368e.pdf

United Nations Security Council, Resolution 1373. 2001, September 28. Retrieved from www.un.org/Docs/scres/2001/res1373e.pdf

Wheeler, Nicholas and Tim Dunne. 1998. "Good International Citizenship: A Third Way for British Foreign Policy." *International Affairs 74.*

WEBLINKS

Lloyd Axworthy on Humanitarian Intervention
wwics.si.edu/NEWS/speeches/axworthy.htm

NATO
www.nato.int

Human Rights Watch: International Criminal Court
www.hrw.org/campaigns/icc

Index